T5-DHH-125

FOUR RESTORATION PLAYWRIGHTS

---

a reference guide to
Thomas Shadwell, Aphra Behn,
Nathaniel Lee, *and* Thomas Otway

A
Reference
Guide
to
Literature

Arthur Weitzman
Editor

FOUR RESTORATION PLAYWRIGHTS

a reference guide to Thomas Shadwell, Aphra Behn, Nathaniel Lee, *and* Thomas Otway

J.M. ARMISTEAD
with annotations of German works by
Werner Bies

G.K.HALL &CO.
70 LINCOLN STREET, BOSTON, MASS.

Library of Congress Cataloging in Publication Data

Armistead, J. M.
Four Restoration playwrights.

Includes index.
1. English drama—Restoration, 1660-1700—Bibliography.
2. Shadwell, Thomas, 1642?-1692—Bibliography. 3. Behn, Aphra, 1640-1689—Bibliography. 4. Lee, Nathaniel, 1653?-1692—Bibliography. 5. Otway, Thomas, 1652-1685—Bibliography.
I. Title.
Z2014.D7A68 1984 016.822'4 83-18384
[PR691]
ISBN 0-8161-8289-2

This publication is printed on permanent/durable acid-free paper
MANUFACTURED IN THE UNITED STATES OF AMERICA

For Jane Theresa Armistead (*née* Barber)

Contents

The Author

Former Woodrow Wilson and Danforth fellow, Jack M. Armistead took his graduate degrees at Duke University and, after two years of active duty as an Army officer, began teaching at Rider College in Lawrenceville, New Jersey. In 1975 he moved to the University of Tennessee and founded the journal, _Restoration: Studies in English Literary Culture, 1660-1700_. His publications include many articles on English and American authors and a book, _Nathaniel Lee_, which appeared as a volume of the Twayne series in 1979. At the moment, he is working on a study of occult traditions in Restoration tragedy and on a series of facsimile reprints of later seventeenth-century scientific works. A dedicated classroom instructor, Professor Armistead was awarded in 1977 the John C. Hodges Prize for Excellence in Teaching. In Fall 1983 he was appointed director of undergraduate studies in the Department of English at the University of Tennessee.

Preface

"A man who is oblig'd to write for his Bread, is forc'd to be very hasty to prevent starving; And every Man's Genius is not so sharp as his Appetite." When an anonymous author wrote this in 1698 (OT.1698.1), he had in mind playwrights whose achievements were already being forgotten. He was not thinking about men like Dryden, Etherege, Wycherley, or even Buckingham, who were coming to stand for Restoration drama at its best or most typical, for these, except Dryden, were the amateurs of the period. Each derived most of his income from sources other than the performance or publication of his few plays. Lately, through the efforts of dedicated scholars, we have become aware that the amateurs do not fully represent Restoration drama, even though some of their works can still be read as the best of the age in terms of literary artistry and intellectual profundity. In terms of generic variety and overall popularity, not to mention sheer quantity of output, the truly representative dramatists were the professionals, those who wrote for bread. They were the successors not of Heywood, Massinger, or Ford, men of means all, but of Robert Greene, William Shakespeare, Thomas Dekker, Thomas Middleton, and William Rowley, men whose livelihood depended almost entirely on the theater world. In the generation before Southerne and Farquhar, perhaps the most accomplished of these professionals, certainly the ones most frequently mentioned in the criticism published since their deaths, were Thomas Shadwell (1642?-92), Aphra Behn (1640-89), Nathaniel Lee (1649?-92), and Thomas Otway (1652-85). In chronicling more than three hundred years of critical response to their dramatic works, this book shows widespread agreement not only that their genius was often less sharp than their appetite, but also that their genius was sometimes very sharp indeed.

The term criticism is, of course, notoriously difficult to define in a limiting way. Here it will be presumed to mean any commentaries that analyze or evaluate a dramatist's artistry or plays. Supporting materials such as editions, biographies, stage histories, bibliographies, and studies of texts, contexts, dates, attribution, and performance, are listed only when they clearly lead to such analysis or evaluation. Deliberately excluded are commentaries that are confined to nondramatic works or that focus entirely on specific performances without substantial reference to a published text.

As an annotated survey of Restoration, eighteenth- and nineteenth-century criticism, this bibliography overlaps with no other reference work that I am aware of. It should, however, be distinguished from the valuable listings by Carl Stratman (et al.) and Frederick Link (see p. xxxvii below), both of whom concentrate on criticism and scholarship of the twentieth century (Stratman up to 1968, Link to about 1975). Neither of these compilers provides full annotations and neither includes specific criticism published between the Restoration and the twentieth century, though Link, in his opening sections, does list sources from the eighteenth and nineteenth centuries if they are general and if they concern the drama or its actors and actresses. He does not extract from these general works the discussions of individual dramatists. While silently correcting some of the errors in Stratman and Link, the present bibliography updates their modern listings, adds many titles that neither of them includes, omits (according to the above criteria) some that they do include, and more generously annotates titles that we have in common.

The fullness of annotation is meant to give these less familiar dramatists the sort of visibility that major authors have gained through accounts of critical reputation and "critical heritage." Each listing attempts not only to encapsule the critic's main points but also to hint at his argument and mention the key pieces of evidence upon which the argument is based. Moreover, many of the listings include quotations that convey something of the critic's general attitude toward his subject. The quotations may also compensate to some extent for the inevitable distortions and misunderstandings which, despite my best efforts to be objective, will have emerged. For these failings I ask forebearance, especially from those readers who are authors of works that have been unwittingly misrepresented. Perhaps it will help to insist that no bibliography, however richly annotated, can substitute for a firsthand reading of the sources it covers.

BIBLIOGRAPHICAL CONVENTIONS

Dating: The date given on the title page of a source is considered authoritative unless proven otherwise by a reliable scholar. Works whose title pages bear no date are dated according to information contained in prefaces and dedications or provided by scholarly research. If all else fails, the dates used in the British Museum General Catalogue of Printed Books and The National Union Catalogue are taken to be accurate. English translations are dated according to the first English edition, not the first edition in the original language. If a letter, anecdote, or passage from a diary was published relatively soon after it was written, it is dated by the first edition; otherwise, it is given the date of composition although the first published edition is cited as the primary source. In a few cases, as in that of Pepys's diary, very recent, major advances in scholarship or editing have dictated that the most modern, rather than the earliest published, edition be cited. In every instance, the new year is presumed to begin on January 1.

Attribution of Authorship: Whenever the British Museum General Catalogue and The National Union Catalogue agree in attributing authorship to unsigned works, I have accepted their attributions as authoritative, unless subsequent scholarship has shown them to be inaccurate. Occasionally I have been able to establish authorship by consulting The Wellesley Index to Victorian Periodicals (London: Routledge & Kegan Paul; Toronto: University of Toronto Press) or by finding an unsigned article reprinted in a given author's collected works. Indeed, I discovered the existence of a few of the unsigned sources by first coming upon them in a signed collection which referred me to the earlier publication. If an attribution seems controversial or derives from a source other than those just mentioned, I provide documentation.

Citation of Periodical Publications: Following the recommendations of the Modern Language Association, I list the issue number of a given periodical when the volumes of that periodical are not continuously paginated. I also list issue numbers of those pre-twentieth century journals and magazines that have tended to confuse library catalogers by their inconsistencies or changes in format, pagination, or numbering. Wherever possible, I abbreviate the titles of serials that are included in the "Master List of Periodicals" prefixing annual volumes of the MLA International Bibliography.

Manuscripts, Dissertations, Clippings, Reprints, and Foreign-Language Sources: Unpublished manuscripts are not listed. Unpublished doctoral dissertations are listed if they contain substantial discussion of one or more of the four dramatists. Most are annotated from the summaries in Dissertation Abstracts International, some are annotated from firsthand readings, and a few are listed without annotations. Each is dated to represent award of the degree, which does not necessarily coincide with the date of the summary in DAI. As a general rule, master's theses are not listed. In a few instances, I have listed and annotated important criticism appearing in unidentified or partially identified clippings seen in the Harvard Theatre Collection. I do not list reprints unless they involve significant revisions of the relevant criticism in first editions or unless failing to list them would perpetuate confusion or error. Foreign-language sources are listed when appropriate, and most are annotated. German works are annotated by Dr. Werner Bies of the University of Trier.

Asterisks: An asterisk indicates that I have not seen the publication firsthand but have found it listed in a reliable source, for example, in the National Union Catalogue or in some other publication which I cite.

ACKNOWLEDGMENTS

The research behind this book was generously supported by grants from the Graduate School and the Better English Fund at the University of Tennessee. The finding and annotating of sources was greatly facilitated by the unflagging cooperation of the staff in the Main Library of the University of Tennessee, especially Mrs. Flossie Wise in Interlibrary Services and the reference librarians working under Mr. Robert J. Basset. I wish also to acknowledge the professionalism of librarians and staff members in the Cambridge University Library, British Library, Harvard Theatre Collection, Houghton Library (Harvard), Boston Public Library, Boston Athenaeum, Firestone Library (Princeton), Perkins Library (Duke University), and Wilson Library (University of North Carolina--Chapel Hill). Additionally, a number of my students, colleagues, and former mentors have helped in various ways. As advanced graduate students, Stephen J. Stedman, William C. Spencer, and Ernest D. Lee performed for inadequate compensation a few of the more tedious parts of the job. Professor Paul Barrette (French, University of Tennessee) interpreted several difficult articles written in French. And Professors Laura Brown (Cornell) and Robert Root (Central Michigan) provided guidance in annotating their books. Without the dedicated indexing and unstinting encouragement of my wife, Jane, I could never have met my contractual deadline; and without the experienced and informed advice of Arthur Scouten (professor emeritus, University of Pennsylvania), who read the typescript as a professional courtesy, I could never have gained the confidence to publish the book at all. Welcome encouragement came also from Professors Percy Adams, John Fisher, and Joseph Trahern (English, University of Tennessee), Benjamin Boyce and Oliver Ferguson (English, Duke University), Judith Milhous (Speech and Theatre, University of Iowa), Susan Staves (Brandeis University), and James W. Clark (English, North Carolina State University). Finally, I could not have asked for more obliging and perceptive editors than Arthur J. Weitzman (English, Northeastern University) and Janice Meagher (G.K. Hall). My gratitude for the work of Dr. Werner Bies is recorded on the title page.

Introduction

TRENDS IN SHADWELL CRITICISM

Thomas Shadwell's plays have not been neglected, albeit they may not have received the kind of thorough, scholarly study they deserve. From the middle of the Restoration period on, they have been regularly damned, praised, and analyzed, the dominant themes of critical judgment showing up very early. On the negative side, it was held in the 1670s and 1680s that they are clumsy, formless, or unfinished; dull and lacking in wit; unoriginal; and shallow or unimaginative. These points continue to be made by such twentieth-century critics as Elwin (S.1928.3), Julian Symons (S.1945.1), Louis Kronenberger (S.1952.4), and Kenneth Muir (S.1970.2). From the later eighteenth century until about 1950, some critics also condemned Shadwell for coarseness and vulgarity in style, character, and subject matter, and for a briefer period, starting in the 1740s and perhaps ending with Krutch's analysis (S.1924.2), some considered him downright lewd. But to a great many commentators without political or moral axes to grind, and with less reverence for Dryden's debilitating attack in _MacFlecknoe_ (S.1682.1), Shadwell was the best comic writer of his day, one who united mirth and instruction while avoiding the worst excesses of romantic nonsense and bawdy intrigue practiced in contemporary comedy.

Gerard Langbaine (S.1691.3) first made public most of the critical observations that sympathetic commentators have elaborated upon over the years: that Shadwell wrote comedy better than Dryden did; that he was an excellent and original creator of humors characters; and that he excelled in social realism, in drawing materials "from the Life." The comparison with Dryden continues to be reiterated in recent times, as in Ronald Pearsall's "Case for Shadwell" (S.1963.3), and the interest in humor characterization has received particularly revealing analyses during the 1960s and 1970s (see S.1960.1; S.1970.1; S.1973.4; S.1975.4). Most critics who have devoted much space to Shadwell have observed that his plays often mirror the social surfaces of his day (see the recent example in S.1976.2), and in 1950 John Freehafer added that this realism is innovatively combined with a presentation of social problems. See also M.F. McBride's "Topical Index" to Shadwell's references to social history (S.1976.3). That Shadwell went against the fashionable grain in creating morally instructive plays was first noticed in the heat of the Collier controversy (S.1707.1-2), but it was not made much of by disinterested critics until Nicoll and William Archer called attention to it (S.1923.1-2). Taking up Nicoll's observation that Shadwell was important in the late-seventeenth-century trend toward sentimental and moralizing comedy, John Harrington Smith strongly argued (S.1948.5) that his growing opposition, both in theory and in practice, to "gay-couple" comedy, and his increasing substitution of "men and women of sense" for the fops, coquettes, and rakes of manners comedy, made him the forerunner of Steele. Smith's distinctions have been refined upon and more rigorously applied by Stephen D. Cox and Robert Hume (S.1977.1-2).

Of the more specialized research topics, only Shadwell's use of music and scenery continues to have a life of its own, probably because it is still too new to have been incorporated with more comprehensive approaches (see S.1919.2-3). On the other hand, his use of sources and his response to various influences (Epicurean thought, Hobbes, Shakespeare, Molière, Jonson), his own influence on later writers and movements (sentimentalism, Steele, Cumberland, Lessing, Scott, Smollett), his role as satirist and political thinker, and his attitudes toward women--all these subjects of close study have gradually become subsumed in treatments of his overall achievement. These general treatments seem to have stemmed from the key investigations of his debts to Molière, Jonson, Beaumont, and Fletcher (S.1900.1; S.1910.2; S.1912.4; S.1928.6; S.1938.4) and of ways in which his theories and art relate to those of contemporaries (S.1923.2; S.1926.2; S.1928.1; S.1948.5-6). Additional impetus came from increasing awareness of the Epicurean background (S.1934.1). Beginning in the mid-1960s, these ground-breaking studies and others became bases for increasingly comprehensive views of Shadwell's own development as dramatist and his contribution to the larger developments in the drama of his time and after, especially his movement from "knockabout content" to enlarged discussions of social problems, from hero as "man of mode" to hero as "man of honour," from "the courtly ideal of the early Restoration towards the religious based idea of the eighteenth century," from "hard" cuckolding comedy to "soft" reform or exemplary comedy, and from wit, humor, and satire to earnestness and moralizing. These shifts, qualified by Alan S. Fisher's delineation of Shadwell's Whiggism (S.1974.3), have been defined and redefined in recent criticism by Alssid (S.1967.1), Kunz (S.1972.5), Bruce (S.1974.2), Hume (S.1976.1; S.1977.2), Staves (S.1979.5), Scouten and Hume (S.1980.3), and Brown (S.1981.1).

According to these critics and their predecessors, what are Shadwell's "major" or "best" works? In this bibliography, twenty-three out of forty-one commentators who attempted to rank the plays included Epsom-Wells in the highest group, and twenty-two placed The Squire of Alsatia there. The latter piece did not begin appearing in the merit lists until the Retrospective Review critique

(S.1828.1), where it took second place to The Woman-Captain, a play whose brief period of critical acclaim lasted only from about 1764 to about 1838. From 1828 to the present, however, Squire and Bury-Fair have dominated the rankings. Only three others are praised frequently enough to deserve a place in this critical pantheon: The Virtuoso (eleven listings, fairly evenly scattered through the three centuries), A True Widow (ten listings, and progressively more interesting to critics since Dobrée, S.1924.1, named it as "possibly his best play"), and Sullen Lovers (increasingly noticed since Nicoll ranked it among the best, S.1925.2). Curiously, these "major" plays have not always been the ones commented upon most often. Epsom-Wells, Bury-Fair, Sullen Lovers, and A True Widow, for example, are among the eight or nine plays least often dealt with critically. Moreover, The Virtuoso has received less attention than The Libertine, while Squire, less frequently noticed than either The Libertine or Timon, has attracted little more attention than the 1674 Tempest, Psyche, or The Lancashire-Witches.

Ever since Robert Hooke called it an "Atheistical wicked play" (S.1675.2), The Libertine has inspired critical fascination. In the late Restoration and in the next century, this fascination took the form of a debate between those who wished to see it as an instructive drama, teaching by example the wages of sin (see S.1698.1-2, 4; S.1724.1), and those who recoiled from the brutal and horrible sacrilege practiced by Don John (for example, S.1708.1; S.1764.1). The debate ended after a rather interesting defense of the play's artistry and moral philosophy by Samuel Taylor Coleridge (S.1817.1), followed two years later by Hazlitt's condemnation of its licentiousness and impiety (S.1819.1). Thereafter, The Libertine was frequently damned for lewdness and horror, though a few isolated voices, such as those of Genest (S.1832.1) and August Steiger (S.1904.6), carried forward Coleridge's interest in its craftsmanship and underlying moral aims. Except for a few observations about its music, genuine critical interest lagged until Oscar Mandell celebrated it as a dramatization of "man living in his person the metaphysics of universal inanity" (S.1963.2). Since then, perhaps the most revealing discussions have been those of John Loftis (S.1972.7; S.1973.5) and Don R. Kunz (S.1972.5), both of whom see the play as a critique of courtly libertinism, freethinking, and the conventions of witty sex comedy and Restoration tragedy.

The Libertine interested Robert Hooke considerably less than The Virtuoso did, however, because he immediately sensed that Sir Nicholas Gimcrack in the latter play was a caricature of himself (S.1676.1). From Hooke's time on, characterization has dominated critical comment on The Virtuoso, though the focal point has moved from the humors method in the eighteenth and nineteenth centuries, to sources and models in the earlier twentieth, to behavior and philosophical attitudes more recently, the latest topics being the Epicureanism of Longvil and Bruce (S.1934.1; S.1978.1) and their kind of rakishness (S.1972.3). The longer discussions in the present century have dwelt upon the sources, nature, and targets of Shadwell's satire on science. Was he ridiculing the Royal Society, the New Science, only the more pedantic activities of scientists, or the pursuit of impractical knowledge generally? Maybe he was using the New Science as a standard against which to measure various other types of folly. These interrelated issues have grown out of Samuel Astley Dunham's observation (S.1838.2) that the play aims its barbs not at the pursuit of knowledge, but at "the bye-roads men took to find it, and the trifling objects which they seized by the way." For an overview of the various approaches, see S.1913.2; S.1929.2; and S.1970.1.

During the first two thirds of its critical history, Timon was unrelentingly attacked for its author's presumptuous surgery on Shakespeare's original play. Only a few commentators quietly insisted that, in Shadwell's hands, at least it had become a morally instructive drama (S.1698.3; S.1735.1). Then, in 1920, George C.D. Odell put an end to thoughtless condemnation of such adaptations in his Shakespeare from Betterton to Irving (S.1920.2), where he argued that Shadwell had, in fact, made Timon into "an excellent acting-medium." A number of sympathetic commentaries followed, the most thorough and enlightening being those by Hazelton Spencer (S.1927.5) and P.F. Vernon (S.1963.7). Nevertheless, at least one recent long treatment, that by Rolf Soellner, reverts in its conclusion to the eighteenth- and nineteenth-century notion that Shadwell has spoiled the ethos and argument of the original.

The Squire of Alsatia has always attracted attention to its social realism, and through most of the eighteenth century, this attention was reinforced by feelings that the play is morally exemplary (see S.1747.1). By 1800, however, its documentary quality had begun to seem the one redeeming feature in an otherwise common and shapeless terrain (see S.1800.1; S.1910.2). Twentieth-century opinion remains divided, some critics concentrating on artistic defects and conceptual inconsistencies (S.1912.4; S.1969.4), others taking up Montague Summers's challenge (S.1927.6) and finding the play worthy of close, often perceptive analysis. See the essays by Whitehall (S.1933.3), Berman (S.1972.1), Kropf (S.1972.4), and Hume (S.1976.1). Additionally, Paul Parnell has some interesting things to say about Belfond Jr. as repentant rake (S.1978.5), and Hume and Arthur H. Scouten instructively place the play in the context of trends in audience taste (S.1980.3).

The Tempest (1674) and Psyche have often been linked together, and at least one critic (S.1930.2) has classed them with The Royal Shepherdess as representing different stages in the development of an English opera. Although Matthew Lock had noted the hybrid form of both plays as early as 1675 in his preface to The English Opera, all criticism until the present century has been confined to impressionistic statements that The Tempest mutilates Shakespeare or that both works are nonsensical spectacles. Revaluation began when Gray noted Shadwell's musical skills (S.1914.2), Squire reconstructed the musical contributions to The Tempest (S.1921.3), and Nicoll asserted that after The Tempest helped drive tragedy from the stage, Psyche became "the first real non-Shakespearean opera" (S.1923.2). Since the 1920s, the two works have been fairly frequently discussed by literary critics and musical historians, the more thorough and interesting treatments being those by Dent (S.1928.2), Holland (S.1932.1), Merchant (S.1959.2; S.1965.3), Moore (S.1961.2), and Langhans (S.1980.1). The authorship of the 1674 Tempest has been a special issue of high interest in this century, beginning with an article by W.J. Lawrence (S.1904.2) and continuing to Maximillian Novak's argument in support of a collaborative authorship involving Shadwell and others (S.1968.5). For an overview of the problem, see the essays by Milton (S.1947.2) and McManaway (S.1953.3). The prevailing opinions about The Tempest and Psyche seem to be that the musicians redeem and unify the one, whereas Shadwell himself, with his rare sensitivity to the blending of music and drama, was responsible for making Psyche an effective whole.

For almost two hundred years after it was first produced, The Lancashire-Witches received only the most cursory examination by critics. Following The Spectator, no. 141 (S.1711.2), they carped at its irreverence, indecency, and apparently ambivalent stance on supernaturalism. Since Henry Morley's First Sketch (S.1873.2), however, there has been sporadic interest in its presentation of Tegue as an early instance of the stage Irishman (S.1911.2; S.1937.1; S.1954.1), and in 1926 Montague Summers called renewed attention to spectacle as one of its key formal elements. Yet only five real efforts have been made to learn how well Shadwell integrates such elements into an artistically unified drama, and these efforts (S.1873.1; S.1905.1; S.1967.2; S.1972.5; S.1979.1) leave much to be desired in scholarly thoroughness. They do at least show growing sentiment that the witches themselves should be seen as part of a larger intention which involves them with the religious, political, and romantic dimensions of the plot.

The rest of Shadwell's plays are rarely analyzed outside of the general surveys (see S.1923.2; S.1928.1; S.1948.5; S.1967.2; S.1974.2; S.1976.1, 8). Epsom-Wells keeps coming up as a peculiar example of the author's turn to witty sex comedy, but even Walmsley's introduction (S.1930.2) has failed to ignite more profound interest. Sullen Lovers has been regarded as a satire on the unexamined life (S.1975.4), and Richard Perkins's recent interpretation of The Humorists (S.1975.3) makes it seem an interesting black comedy, worthy of further study. Equally provocative is Arthur Scouten's remark (S.1976.8) that The Woman-Captain is "strange . . . unlike anything else currently being done." But for the most part the other plays are mentioned only for particular qualities or contributions to dramatic history: Bury-Fair for its lack of bawdy and its part in the growth of morally exemplary comedy, A True Widow for its play-within-the-play, The Scowrers for its originality, Sullen Lovers for its personal satire, The Volunteers for its balanced political views and mercantile interests, and The Miser for its relation to plays by Molière and Cumberland.

TRENDS IN BEHN CRITICISM

Mrs. Behn was in good repute, both as artist and as person, with most of the contemporaries who cared to comment on her in print. They saw her as a pioneer female professional, courageous, strong-minded, and witty, who wrote lively, natural, romantic comedies (see B.1675.1; B.1689.1; B.1691.1-2; B.1696.1-4; B.1698.1-2). Very soon after her death, however, she began to be seen as a purveyor of the worst sort of lewd, unprincipled entertainment, and this picture of her, perhaps initiated by Prior's savage attack in "A Satyr on the modern Translators" (B.1697.1), almost overwhelmed unbiased critics during the eighteenth, nineteenth, and early twentieth centuries. Dozens of important writers, men like Steele (B.1711.1), Pope (B.1737.1), Johnson (B.1747.3), Walpole (B.1786.1), Chambers (B.1843.1), Doran (B.1864.1), Garnett (B.1895.1), Schelling (B.1912.1), and Krutch (B.1924.1), helped perpetuate the image. Happily, there emerged independent spirits in almost every decade who tried to carry forward a more balanced view. Some, like Cibber (B.1753.1), Baker (B.1764.1), Southey (B.1807.1), Hunt (B.1828.1), Pearson (B.1872.7), and Gertrude Andrews (B.1901.1), suggested that her plays were no more indecent than those of other writers who catered to corrupt tastes in order to survive.

Many more simply emphasized her strengths and allowed the reader to judge whether these overbalanced the much-touted lewdness. Her early reputation for wit, liveliness, and excellence in depicting romantic love was reinforced in the eighteenth century by Defoe (B.1700.1), Jacob (B.1719.1), Oldys (B.1735.1), Cibber (B.1753.1), and others; and her courage and virtue as a pioneer woman professional was stressed in the Gentleman's Magazine (B.1738.1), in the Dublin University Magazine (B.1856.1), and frequently in the twentieth century, by writers such as Nicoll (B.1923.2), Elwin (B.1928.2), Hobman (B.1946.2), Duffey (B.1977.1), Cotton (B.1980.2), and Goreau (B.1980.5). In the later nineteenth century began a trend of praising Mrs. Behn as an ingenious contriver of plots (see B.1863.1; B.1872.1; B.1907.1), and in the twentieth century, this vein of criticism grew into the still-prevailing assertion that she was the best writer of intrigue comedy in her day, the point being made perhaps most influentially by Blashfield (B.1917.1) and Nicoll (B.1923.2-3) and followed up by virtually every important critic since then. Most recently, critical attention has concentrated on her handling of key social problems, particularly that of arranged or forced marriage (see B.1923.2; B.1977.6), and on her adeptness in employing the resources of the Restoration stage (see B.1952.3; B.1966.2; B.1979.2).

Her overall achievement as dramatist was first fully analyzed in an anonymous article published by Temple Bar (B.1884.1), which stressed "subjective" inspiration, social realism, and control over rapid and complex action. Since then, the give and take between specialized and general studies has resulted in an increasingly subtle understanding of her mind and art. The specialists have examined her debts to Middleton (B.1909.2), French romance (B.1911.1), Beaumont and Fletcher (B.1928.6), Molière (B.1938.3), Jonson (B.1938.1), Montfleury (B.1939.2), and Spanish drama (B.1973.3), and one critic has recently interpreted the use of sources in five plays together (B.1976.3). That she in turn influenced later writers and movements has also been noted, though not very fully (see B.1923.1; B.1926.2; B.1931.2-3). Other topics of specialized interest have been her political ideas, her use of music, her understanding of Scots dialect and folkways, and the canon and dating of her plays.

Often depending heavily on these narrowly focused studies, the more general treatments of Mrs. Behn's drama have become progressively more sensitive to the range of her ideas, the patterns in her artistic development, and the cultural contexts within which she worked. John Harrington Smith and George Woodcock (B.1948.7-8) provided the first lengthy and informed readings of most of her plays, but they could draw upon two important predecessors. Nicoll had already emphasized that Mrs. Behn used the theater to protest against fashionable vices, "to preach a return to more natural modes of life, and to present a genuine problem" (B.1923.2); and Ashley Thorndike had traced the tendency of her artistry away from "the thrilling and passionate" and toward "the realistic and domestic," away from wit and humor, and toward intrigue, farce, and sentiment (B.1929.2). The major work of the 1960s and 1970s has helped us to see Mrs. Behn's dramatic achievement in larger contexts. Link began the consolidating effort with his Twayne volume (B.1968.1), where he presents her as an artist of incident, complication, and social issue, one who used artistic conventions to criticize political deviance and to define "what a love relationship . . . ought to be." Donald Bruce (B.1974.2) helped us to perceive her preference for honor over fashion and to catch the chilly undertone of her bitter melancholy. After Robert Hume (B.1972.2; B.1976.1) reminded us of her artistic diversity, Laura Brown (B.1981.2) articulated the very provocative generalization, gathering together much that was only hinted at before, that her critique of the "very society whose standards constitute the terms" of her dramatic action "leads her to ideological contradiction and formal satire."

In the criticism covered by this bibliography, five of Mrs. Behn's plays stand out as her major works. Twenty of the twenty-eight critics who indulged in ranking placed The Rover at the top, and its reputation has remained consistently high for three centuries. The play next most frequently praised (fifteen "votes") is The City-Heiress, though it did not begin to rise in esteem until the later nineteenth century. The Feign'd Curtizans, next in line with eleven high rankings, has relied for its reputation almost entirely on the eighteenth and twentieth centuries. Two other plays fairly frequently mentioned among the best, Sir Patient Fancy and The Town-Fopp, are later twentieth-century "discoveries."

Of these five only The City-Heiress has been neglected by analysts. Usually bracketed with The Roundheads as a political play (see B.1884.1; B.1921.1; B.1930.3), it has been closely examined only by Kronenberger (B.1952.1) who sees it as Whig satire modulating into a moral debate about sex. Until 1974, The Feign'd Curtizans also seemed to be slighted, but Donald Bruce's discussion of its debate about constant and inconstant love (B.1974.2), together with Ludwig's critical edition (B.1976.2), presage more probing and thorough treatments. Such treatments are beginning to be accorded The Town-Fopp, again heralded by Bruce's perceptive treatment, which presents the play as a dramatic condemnation of purely sensual love and of the beau monde. Novak follows up this observation (B.1977.5), and Staves (B.1979.6) places the play within generic, conceptual, and technical trends of its day. Sir Patient Fancy has had a muted following among those who, since the Temple Bar article (B.1884.1), have been able to appreciate its cleverness in spite of its bawdy, but earnest analysis did not begin until the 1940s with Southerne's investigation of the staging techniques (B.1941.2) and Mignon's observations about the satirical proviso scene (B.1947.1). Bruce again gave impetus to further analysis when he noticed that Sir Patient symbolizes the downfall of Cromwell's England while the play chronicles the relinquishing of reason to uxorious passion. Duffy picks up this thread (B.1977.1), and Robert Root discusses the play's treatment of marriage conventions (B.1977.6).

The earliest commentators on The Rover tended to condemn it for immorality (for example, B.1711.1). After Giles Jacob ranked it as one of Mrs. Behn's best works (B.1719.1), other critics divided into two camps: those who persisted in seeing only its lewdness (for example, B.1759.1) and those who were delighted by its vivacity (for example, B.1764.1). Nineteenth-century reviewers, biographers, and literary historians kept naming it as one of Mrs. Behn's most accomplished pieces, but they avoided close analysis. In the present century, a few early comments on sources and background were superceded by Woodcock's provocative examination (B.1948.8) of the play's intrigue form, reflections on libertine behavior, and autobiographical implications. Link then came forth (B.1967.2) with the first full examination of theme and form, and Loftis placed Mrs. Behn's technique in the light of Spanish influences (B.1973.3). Very recently, Musser (B.1979.4) and Brown (B.1981.2) have probed the play's structure in relation to the author's attitudes toward women and marriage.

Although none of Mrs. Behn's other plays has been so fully analyzed as these have, a few have been examined as special cases, and the rest receive some attention in general surveys like Woodcock's

(B.1948.8), Link's (B.1968.1), and Hume's (B.1976.1). The Second Part of the Rover is typically treated either as a lesser sequel to The Rover (for example, B.1832.1) or as an early instance of the use of harlequin figures in English drama (see B.1925.1; B.1926.1), but recently Maureen Duffy (B.1977.1) has argued that La Nuche is Mrs. Behn's finest comic creation and that the play masterfully rebuts the notion that women are to be treated as property. Even more interesting to critics for its use of harlequin figures, as well as for its farce and pantomime elements, has been Emperor of the Moon (see B.1764.1; B.1832.1; B.1926.1), especially after Gilder and Woodcock (B.1928.3; B.1948.8) ranked it very high as mixed-medium drama. Woodcock calls it a satire on human credulity; Hughes and Scouten view it in light of sources (B.1948.2); and Derek Cohen, comparing it with Rowe's The Biter (B.1979.1), finds it an effective farce-fantasy. Ever since The Retrospective Review (B.1852.1) noted Mrs. Behn's satire on colonial mismanagement, The Widdow Ranter has been noticed fairly frequently, though even its more recent analysts (B.1957.3; B.1971.5; B.1976.5) have allowed the historical and autobiographical background to inhibit critical response. Similarly, the crude political thrust of The Roundheads and its use of Tatham's The Rump have occupied commentators to the exclusion of disinterested criticism, although Upahdyaah's dissertation (B.1974.4) may have put these matters to rest and thus prepared the way for closer literary study. Critical opinion about Abdelazer has been wildly divergent and only sporadically expressed, some commentators seeing only the worst sort of gory melodrama, others finding the play operatic, lovely, even thought-provoking. Wilson (B.1965.2) thinks it is better than the average villain drama, and Staves (B.1979.6) is interested in what it reveals of Mrs. Behn's concept of "nature."

TRENDS IN LEE CRITICISM

Until the twentieth century, with its penchant for balanced, "scholarly" analysis, critical opinion about Nathaniel Lee has remained sharply divided. In most instances, the very qualities for which his art is damned by detractors are the qualities pointed to as his greatest strengths by proponents. What so many eighteenth- and nineteenth-century commentators saw as bombast and fustian (L.1680.2; L.1723.1; L.1783.1; L.1824.2; L.1864.1), many others defined as sublimity, elevation, or inspired poetry (L.1677.2; L.1721.1; L.1753.2; L.1873.1). Passions that seemed highly exaggerated to some (L.1695.1; L.1704.3; L.1824.2) struck others as well-drawn and moving (L.1677.2; L.1691.3; L.1747.4; L.1823.3; L.1856.2; L.1895.1). The well-documented madness for which Lee was confined to Bedlam gave negative critics a rationale for his extravagance (L.1688.2; L.1691.1; L.1735.4; L.1760.2; L.1820.2), and his defenders used it to help account for his highest flights in idea, imagery, and poetry (L.1775.2; L.1793.1; L.1838.1). Indeed, critics have differed interestingly about whether Lee's artistic efforts caused his madness or whether his madness caused the extravagance of his art (see

L.1700.1; L.1770.1). In 1823, Procter complained that Lee had no skill in characterization (L.1823.3) and this notion was later taken up by Garnett (L.1895.1), Sanders (L.1901.2), Bartholomew (L.1912.1), and Dobrée (L.1929.1), all of whom added that this exemplified Lee's general lack of intellectual and psychological subtlety. After Bartholomew pointed to Lee's apparent humorlessness, Dobrée went on to synthesize all these negative observations in the concept that Lee's dramatic world is driven by an artificial logic. The chief defenders of Lee's psychological and intellectual profundity have been Ham (L.1931.2), Knight (L.1962.2), Vieth (L.1975.2), and Armistead (L.1979.1), and the main proponent of his sense of humor (albeit a morbid sense and a black humor) has been Hume (L.1976.2-3).

On only one major subject has there been a marked shift in opinion: Lee's use of imagery and stage spectacle. Except for Dryden (L.1677.2), all the important critics of the Restoration and eighteenth century felt that Lee had gone too far with his grand word-pictures, scenic effects, and prodigies. In the nineteenth century, however, the continuation of this opinion was increasingly countered by critics who wished to commend him for skill in managing stage effects (see L.1834.1). In the twentieth century, a number of analysts, culminating in Philip Parsons (L.1901.2; L.1929.1; L.1931.3; L.1970.5; L.1971.3; L.1972.4), have felt that Lee's "operatic" management of imagery and stage resources earns him a place among the masters of "total theatre." Of course, the insistence on his extravagance, in its various forms, also continues to find its exponents (for example, L.1912.1; L.1948.2; L.1969.2).

A few qualities in Lee's work have been pointed to without much argument. Langbaine (L.1691.3) seems to have started over two centuries of praise for Lee's moving and tender love scenes (a subject that is rarely brought up in the twentieth century), and Saintsbury (L.1898.1) revived interest (after Dennis, L.1721.1, Scott, L.1808.4, and Hallam, L.1839.1) in his sonorous poetry, an interest that persists in our century (see L.1923.2; L.1976.5). Several writers have noted that Lee was responsible for the popular revival of blank-verse tragedy (Nettleton and Case, L.1939.1, express the general view), and increasing attention is being paid to his morbid cynicism (L.1923.2; L.1928.2; L.1939.1; L.1948.3; L.1965.4; L.1971.1) and his use of music (L.1928.1; L.1979.7). Additionally, commentators sporadically discuss influences on Lee by Seneca, Shakespeare, Webster, Ford, Milton, the French, and the Elizabethans generally, and note Lee's own influence on such writers and movements as Dryden, Congreve, Gildon, sentimental comedy, and she-tragedy. Other topics of potentially great critical interest have been raised but thus far left undeveloped: his obsession with father-son rivalries (see L.1908.1; L.1975.2), his skillful use of the occult (see L.1962.2; L.1979.2), and his lyricism (see L.1971.3; L.1979.1).

The attempt to move beyond praise and blame, and beyond discussion of sources and "characteristics," began with Philip Neve

(L.1789.1), who stressed Lee's purposeful use of history, his sublimity, and his uniqueness. The latter point was clarified by Harvey-Jellie (L.1906.2) and Singh (L.1963.2). Our present conception of Lee's overall artistic development seems to derive from William Bohn's notion that he moved from extravagant incoherence to restrained unity (L.1901.1). Subsequent analysis revealed that Lee also moved from heroics and platonic gallantry to impassioned, humanized tragedy (L.1928.2; L.1931.2-3; L.1979.8); from rhyme to blank verse (L.1939.1; L.1976.5); from favoring male to favoring female protagonists (L.1908.1; L.1976.5); from studying heroic behavior to dealing with contemporary problems (L.1969.1); and from Whig to Tory or republican to royalist (L.1963.1; L.1979.8). For a balanced view of Lee's attitudes toward sovereignty, see Barbour (L.1940.1); for the most perceptive and complete discussion of his move to affective tragedy, see Rothstein (L.1967.3); and for an attempt to find a more comprehensive pattern in his artistic development, involving his temperament, ideas, and style, see Armistead (L.1979.1).

Of the fifty-seven critics who ranked Lee's plays in terms of general excellence, thirty-six placed The Rival Queens at or near the top, and it consistently held this position until the 1970s. The reputation of Lucius Junius Brutus, listed in the highest group twenty-eight times, has been somewhat more sporadic. In the second quarter of the eighteenth century, the first of the nineteenth, and the first of the twentieth, it was rarely mentioned; but since World War II it has more frequently been named as Lee's best play than any other, including The Rival Queens. The reverse is true of Theodosius, next in line with twenty-three high rankings, for after being mentioned steadily once or twice each twenty years, it began to drop out of the listings increasingly after the 1860s, and except for a handful of notices, vanishes altogether after 1912. Mithridates, on the other hand, has continued to be mentioned about once every twenty years as one of Lee's best pieces, James Sutherland being the most recent proponent (L.1969.2). Only two other plays are named more than five times as among Lee's best: The Massacre of Paris experiences brief vogues in the last quarter of the nineteenth century and the second quarter of the twentieth (but see L.1801.1; L.1979.1), and Oedipus appears on the lists from the second quarter of the eighteenth century to the second quarter of the nineteenth, with Richard Garnett becoming its only important proponent thereafter (L.1895.1).

The "best" plays are not always the ones most often analyzed. The Princess of Cleve and Sophonisba, neither mentioned more than once or twice among Lee's better works, have been more frequently examined than either Mithridates or The Massacre of Paris. After being virtually ignored by all commentators for more than a century, The Princess of Cleve emerged between the Biographia Britannica of 1812 and Nettleton's survey of 1914 as the one example of real obscenity in Lee. In the later nineteenth and first half of the twentieth centuries, it also gained a reputation for perverting or vulgarizing Madame de Lafayette's novel upon which it was partly based. The truly fruitful line of investigation, however, began when Genest (L.1832.1) drew attention to the "spirited" comic plot, the characterization of Nemours, and the allusion to Rochester. To these observations, Ristine added (L.1910.4) that the tragic plot conveyed true pathos, a point that Nicoll (L.1923.2) and Stroup (L.1935.4) modified in identifying the play as a forerunner of sentimental drama. The prevailing view of the play, owing its currency to the contributions of Ham (L.1931.2), Summers (L.1935.3), Hume (L.1976.3), and Armistead (L.1979.1), is that it is a cynical black comedy, which uses a split-plot form to attack both romantic-heroic and libertine modes of behavior and which applies this satire to the contemporary political scene through allusions to the French religious wars. Sophonisba has never been actually ignored, but until the 1960s, its critical reputation was inconsistent and spotty. Although some disliked its seeming vulgarization of the characters of Hannibal and Scipio (L.1680.2; L.1732.1), its extravagant spectacle and language (L.1747.5; L.1901.2), or its unnatural versification (L.1750.2), others, in increasing numbers after 1900, praised its love scenes, fluent and affecting verse, and well-controlled plot (for example, L.1909.1; L.1923.2; L.1931.1; L.1933.6). Then, after almost thirty years of silence, G. Wilson Knight noticed its antiheroic implications (L.1962.2), Arthur Kirsch felt that it had strongly influenced Dryden's All for Love (L.1965.2), and Eric Rothstein observed how it split heroism into three resonating parts and explored subjective responses to the incompatibility of public and private values (L.1967.3). This vein of investigation was pursued further by Armistead (L.1978.1) in a reading that stressed the play's commentary on alternative forms of heroism in a changing society.

That Mithridates and The Massacre of Paris have been relatively neglected by critics is perhaps not surprising, considering that the former elaborates themes and techniques better employed in The Rival Queens, and the latter has tended to be mentioned as an afterthought in discussions of The Duke of Guise or of Lee's political ideas. Although neither play has received a full critical analysis, except by Armistead (L.1979.1), the extant criticism of each has been dominated by the same few themes throughout the three centuries. Dryden's praise for the affecting love scenes in Mithridates (L.1678.1) led through similar comments in the next two centuries (L.1719.1; L.1875.1) to the twentieth-century stress on the play's contribution to pathetic and sentimental drama (L.1909.1; L.1914.2; L.1933.6; L.1979.8). Almost every commentator has accepted Saintsbury's assertion that the play contains some of Lee's best poetry (L.1898.1), and after almost two centuries, the Dramatic Historiographer's observation (L.1735.1) that Mithridates succumbs to rebellion within his own psyche has been further explored by Bernbaum (L.1915.1), Knight (L.1962.2), and Armistead (L.1979.1). The latter has also analyzed the use of the supernatural in the play, and Arthur Scouten has named it as important in the move toward she-tragedy (L.1976.5).

Massacre has been commented upon for its simplicity of style (for example, L.1801.1; L.1963.1), influence on The Duke of Guise (L.1683.2, 4; L.1954.2), strong imagery (L.1733.1; L.1886.1), shocking horrors (L.1812.1; L.1963.1; L.1976.2), and political and religious ramifications (L.1690.1; L.1886.1; L.1973.5; L.1976.2; L.1977.10; L.1979.1, 8).

After The Rival Queens, the Dryden-Lee collaborations (Oedipus and The Duke of Guise) are the most often noticed plays in Lee's canon. Yet neither has been thoroughly analyzed in light of its sources, contexts, and themes. The Oedipus has of course been repeatedly compared with the versions by Sophocles, Seneca, and others. In general, however, there has been no agreement about whether the English Oedipus improves or ruins the ancient story, whether Lee's or Dryden's contributions are the more effective (though the more recent critics have favored Lee's: L.1928.2; L.1973.6; L.1978.4), and whether the spectacle and elevated language are sublimely moving or absurdly bombastic. The most promising line of discussion was initiated when Nettleton observed (L.1914.2) that in the English play the Elizabethan spirit overrules the classical. Later commentators, like Downer (L.1950.5), Kallich (L.1966.2), Hirt (L.1972.1), Myers (L.1973.4), and Brunkhorst (L.1976.1), agreeing that there is something peculiarly English about the play, have brought us to the point of recognizing that Dryden and Lee had their own artistic and thematic aims in view as they adapted the story, so that sexual love, Providence, and "concernment" loom much larger in their version than in previous ones. Like the Oedipus, The Duke of Guise has been much discussed but never fully examined. Especially during the Restoration and again since the mid-1950s, the play's political dimension has occupied critical attention almost to the exclusion of other considerations (see Loftis, L.1963.1, for context), the central issue being to identify precisely what were the author's satiric targets (see L.1683.1-4; L.1973.5). Several critics have asserted that Lee's part represents some of his best writing (L.1808.1; L.1820.1; L.1973.6), and others have noted the way in which the authors apply supernaturalism to political satire (L.1971.2; L.1979.5), but no one has followed up the implications of Genest's comment that the play shows a remarkably successful blend of styles (L.1832.1, and see L.1933.6) or Summers's assertion that it subordinates political aims to larger dramatic purposes.

The Rival Queens, Lucius Junius Brutus, and Theodosius, generally considered Lee's best plays, are also among the most closely analyzed. Only the latter received no full reading between Francis Gentleman's article (L.1770.1) and Armistead's chapter (L.1979.1). In a mixed review, Gentleman synthesized the three points that were consistently made about Theodosius during the eighteenth and nineteenth centuries: that it moves us with its tender love scenes and pathos (see L.1719.1; L.1791.2; L.1838.2; L.1901.2), that the pitiful Varanes is the most interesting character, and that Marcian and Pulcheria spoil the plot with their coarse, irrelevant, and inappropriate relationship (see L.1746.1; L.1764.2; L.1800.1; L.1938.2). Gentleman also seems to have started the trend of noting the unusual stylistic restraint that Lee exercised in this play (see L.1783.1; L.1819.1; L.1883.2). Starting with the Bell's edition of 1793, it became increasingly fashionable to regard Marcian and Pulcheria as interesting and structurally purposeful characterizations (see L.1823.1; L.1923.2; L.1928.2), and beginning in the later 1920s, the songs attracted increasing notice, all commentators until recently (see L.1979.1, 7) regarding them as almost irrelevant to the plot (see L.1928.1; L.1932.2; L.1961.2). Other critical points leading toward Armistead's recent reading include: Genest's comment that Lee happily mixes history and fiction in his plays (L.1832.1), Bohn's assertion that Theodosius humanizes love and honor (L.1909.1), Ham's perception that it was partly meant as a warning to Charles II (L.1931.2), Knight's delineation of the contrast between Christian lethargy and the old virilities (L.1962.2), and Rothstein's discussion of pastoralism (L.1967.3).

Often seen as Lee's "purest" and most carefully controlled tragedy, Lucius Junius Brutus has inspired continuing debate over its political stance. On the one hand, it was censured for supposedly antiroyalist expressions, and several important critics of this century, following the anonymous reviewer of 1830, have read it as a celebration of republican virtues and ideology (see L.1927.7; L.1963.1; L.1976.2; L.1977.9; L.1979.8). On the other hand, an equally convincing set of commentators has elaborated upon early observations (L.1703.3; L.1735.2; L.1901.2; L.1922.2) that Lee undercuts the play's republican triumph by making Brutus too severe, too calculating, and too despotic; by linking republican sentiments with the unworthy Vinditius and his mob of cits; and by showing the ill effects of legalism upon the attractively pathetic lovers Titus and Teraminta (see L.1931.5; L.1962.2; L.1967.3; L.1975.2; L.1976.5; L.1979.3). For an overview of the debate, as well as insights into the play's art and ideas, see especially Loftis (L.1967.1), Vieth (L.1975.2), Armistead (L.1979.3), and Brown (L.1981.1).

The Rival Queens has until very recently been considered Lee's best play, and it is still regularly listed among his best. The voices of opposition were strongest in the eighteenth century when it was fashionable to decry the play's extravagant language and imagery and to condemn it for presenting a less idealistically heroic Alexander than romance and even history had depicted (for example, see L.1710.2; L.1712.2; L.1735.4; L.1740.2). Late in the eighteenth century and throughout the next, however, many commentators felt that the play's passion and power redeemed its extravagance (Scott, L.1808.2, and Nettleton, L.1914.2, are typical). Since 1950, it has been usual to ignore such impressionism in favor of developing the notion perhaps first articulated by Cibber and Shiels (L.1753.2), but first explained by Bohn (L.1909.1), that the play somehow gains its structural unity, emotional power, and psychological penetration from the provocative depiction of Alexander's tortured personality (see L.1957.2; L.1962.2; L.1976.5; L.1978.5; L.1979.1). For still undeveloped observations about the play's baroque qualities, choric and scenic and operatic effects, supernaturalism, commentary on marriage, and contribution to affective tragedy, see L.1949.2; L.1962.1; L.1970.5; and L.1981.1.

The remaining four plays have suffered critical neglect primarily because they have not until very recently been thought worthy of analysis. To get beyond unsupported assertions about the extravagance and horrific anti-Romanism of Caesar Borgia, one must turn to Rangno (L.1973.5), Scouten (L.1976.5), Armistead (L.1977.1; L.1979.2) and Hagstrum (L.1980.2). To see Nero as more than an incoherent bloodbath, one must look into Nicoll (L.1919.3; L.1923.2), Knight (L.1962.2), Kastan (L.1977.7), and Armistead (L.1979.1-2). To arrive at a sympathetic view of Gloriana, one must consult The Retrospective Review (L.1821.3), which presents it as a blend of bombast and beauty; Malcolm Elwin (L.1928.2), who sees it as an almost perfect heroic tragedy; Louis Teeter (L.1936.2), who finds Gloriana herself innovative as a rebellious female; and Robert Hume (L.1976.2), who thinks the play well designed on the whole. Constantine has been fully analyzed by Armistead (L.1979.1), relying on the political studies by Cooke and Loftis (L.1950.4; L.1963.1), but no one to date has considered it a very well-wrought piece.

TRENDS IN OTWAY CRITICISM

In every decade since the 1680s, most criticism of Otway has been sympathetic, though there have been strong voices in the opposition (see OT.1680.2-3; OT.1682.2; OT.1770.1-3; OT.1820.3; OT.1923.1). On key issues, a small cluster of which has dominated attention, there has been strong disagreement until very recently. The one most frequently commented on is Otway's mastery of strong emotions, his ability to dramatize them and recreate them in the audience. Rather impressionistic praise for this ability began in the mid-eighteenth century to encounter opposition from those who observed that he could handle only a limited range of feelings (for example, OT.1747.2, 4), which he tended to overstrain and thus artificialize (for example, OT.1783.1), and that his pathos was achieved at the expense of intellectual subtlety and philosophical depth (for example, OT.1784.2; OT.1888.1; OT.1969.9). In the present century, his kind of affective art has been evaluated less often than it has been identified as his peculiar contribution to the development of English dramaturgy, especially the "sentimental" movement (for example, OT.1898.3; OT.1908.3; OT.1914.1; OT.1923.3; OT.1927.4; OT.1931.1-2; OT.1948.2-3; OT.1967.3; OT.1974.2; OT.1981.1).

Only two other aspects of Otway's art have almost as long a critical history as does his handling of passion and pathos: his depiction of the private relationships of less than royal personages and his penchant for writing from personal experience. The first of these, established as a major critical point by the editor of the 1712 Works, was most often noticed in the second half of the eighteenth century and during the period between Shaw's literary history (OT.1864.2) and Bredvold's (OT.1950.1). The second seems to have become a popular subject with Guthrie's Essay upon English Tragedy (OT.1747.4), and it has sporadically reappeared in critical commentaries up to Sherburn's survey of 1948. In the meantime, however, negative and unbiased analysts have suggested that because of his intense subjectivity, Otway allowed his own libertine and libertarian proclivities to inform his works (for example, OT.1759.3; OT.1791.1-2; OT.1838.1; OT.1870.1; OT.1928.7) and lacked emotional distance needed before he could endow his characters with their own distinctive complexities (OT.1820.1; OT.1929.1; OT.1931.2).

A few other topics have proved more transient and controversial. During the eighteenth century, for example, it was common to hear Otway spoken of as a dramatist who was guided by and who portrayed "nature," a point first made with influential force by Dryden (OT.1695.1) and repeated with varying emphases--and different assumptions about the definition of the term nature--by such worthies as Addison (OT.1711.1), Pope (OT.1739.2), Collins (OT.1747.3), Goldsmith (OT.1759.1), and Scott (OT.1811.2). In the nineteenth century, however, it was by no means clear that Otway was especially "natural" in any sense of the word, and beginning with the Temple Bar article of 1879, this particular observation came to be considered a relative matter: Otway was a good deal more "natural" than the writers of heroic drama. After the 1920s, the subject seems to have been dropped in favor of more precise or historically reliable approaches to his artistry. The early eighteenth-century notion that his poetic style is "natural" and "plain" and "flowing" (see OT.1718.1; OT.1719.1) began by mid-century to meet opposition from those who objected to what they regarded as inelegance and roughness of phrasing (for example, OT.1747.4; OT.1753.1), though these latter qualities were interpreted by more sympathetic analysts of the later eighteenth century as "vigour" and "energy" (OT.1764.1; OT.1779.1). After the first quarter of the nineteenth century, the issue became whether Otway's style was bombastic and turgid (for example, OT.1829.7; OT.1885.1) or whether one should call it rich and sensuous (OT.1829.4; OT.1834.1; OT.1848.2; OT.1920.2-3).

An even more embattled issue has been Otway's skill in characterization and plot design. Although most commentators since the 1712 Works have felt his characters are interesting and convincing, especially the depictions of females, an influential minority in each generation since the 1820s has argued that Otway lacks psychological insight and presents only a narrow range of types (OT.1823.1; OT.1885.1; OT.1909.1; OT.1914.1; OT.1932.2; OT.1955.3). As for his adeptness at plot construction, the early eighteenth-century critics saw this as a function of his adherence to or violation of the classical unities (see OT.1710.2-3; OT.1720.2; OT.1721.1; OT.1757.4). Then, after the middle of the century, a number of commentators began to note the apparent improbability or implausibility of his situations or actions (see OT.1753.1; OT.1764.1; OT.1770.1, 3; OT.1771.1; OT.1795.2), a trend that continued through the first third of the twentieth century (for example, OT.1903.3; OT.1932.3) but has been increasingly checked since 1888 when Noel pointed to Otway's classical tightness of structure and intensity of focus (see OT.1908.3; OT.1914.3; OT.1958.2).

The modern attempt to relate Otway's personality to his artistry developed out of two separate perceptions: that he wrote from personal experience, which was Guthrie's point in 1747, and that his techniques changed radically as he matured. An anonymous reviewer in the Royal Magazine (OT.1763.1) may have been the first to stress the gloomy outlook that Otway's autobiographical dramaturgy conveys, but the point was more influentially made by Shaw in 1864. Mosen (OT.1875.1) and Gosse (OT.1877.1) then blended it with the observation (earlier made by Neve, OT.1789.1) that in Don Carlos Otway invented his two favorite character types: vulnerable, vacillating males who reflected his own melancholy and cynicism, and innocent, distressed females who embodied his neurotically idealized vision of Mrs. Barry. The second perception leading to modern analysis emerged in 1784 when Davies argued that Otway moves from heroic artifice to a more "natural" mode. Thornton (OT.1813.3) named The Orphan as the key to this transition, and William Bohn (OT.1909.2) explained that the change was mediated by Otway's experimentation with fresh dramatic models from abroad. Hagemann (OT.1917.1) stressed the importance of the Shakespearean model. In 1931, Roswell Gray Ham pulled these two strands of investigation together into the first comprehensive description of Otway's artistic development: he moves from heroic drama, through efforts to express personal dilemmas in imitated structures, to a mature blend of heroic agony, personal disillusion, Elizabethan gloom, satire, and Racinian pathos--his favorite theme being the despair of separated lovers like himself and Mrs. Barry.

Since Ham's book was published, few commentators have been content merely to define Otway's artistic development, though some have discussed his role in the larger changes taking place in seventeenth- and eighteenth-century drama. Tatlock, for instance (OT.1916.1), notes that he links the tradition of Ford and Fletcher with that of Steele and Cumberland, and Praz (OT.1933.3) describes the same junction as one between Webster and Romanticism. Thinking along similar lines, Nicoll (OT.1923.3), Gosse (OT.1927.4), and Deane (OT.1931.1) asserted that Otway pioneered the school of pathos, and Nettleton (OT.1939.3), followed by Peake and others (OT.1941.2, and see OT.1970.3), added that he also initiated the trend toward feminized tragedy. A more fruitful approach has been to study more closely the intellectual and psychological dimensions of the plays. In the first half of the century, such analysis was dominated by the views of Dobrée (OT.1927.3) and Prior (OT.1947.2) that once Otway had moved from heroics to his own personal mode, he was inhibited from full artistic and intellectual maturity by a kind of maudlin self-indulgence. The most enlightening results of this attitude have been the increasingly sophisticated arguments of Leech (OT.1950.3), Wilson (OT.1965.4), Rothstein (OT.1967.3), and Brown (OT.1981.1) that, deliberately or not, he was aiming at an affective mode of tragedy. Through this mode the whole body of dramatic conventions is orchestrated to project psychological contours that evoke feelings in the spectator.

But even as Dobrée's followers were emphasizing Otway's emotionalism, others were beginning to credit him with more intellectual rigor and psychological insight than previously had been acknowledged. A glimmer of this new enthusiasm is to be seen in Fausset's 1932 review of Ghosh, where an interest in Otway's lyrical emotionalism produces the assertion that he wrote "dramas of enslavement, of a longing without limit caught in a net of circumstances." Stressing the psychological implications of this kind of perception, Aline Mackenzie-Taylor defined the major tragedies as dramas of self-contradiction (OT.1950.4). But the real breakthrough came in 1967, when Anne Righter and Thomas B. Stroup independently explained that in both comedies and tragedies Otway is bitterly pessimistic; he envisions a world whose degenerate social structures fail to embody moral values, protect virtue, or fulfill the deepest human needs. Hilary Spurling reaffirmed this view the following year, and since then it has informed all the major revaluations of Otway's contribution to larger shifts in dramatic genre and philosophical attitude. Both Staves and Brown, for example (OT.1979.4; OT.1981.1), associate Otway's pessimism with his contemporaries' growing awareness that the aristocratic myth of morally interdependent levels in society had given way to a pluralistic world view, one that presumes that neither individual values nor individual feelings readily find expression in general orders of belief and conduct.

Throughout the history of critical response to Otway, Venice Preserv'd consistently has been considered his best work, Alcibiades his worst, and the two "translations" (Titus and Berenice and The Cheats of Scapin) too insignificant for close study (but see OT.1956.5 and OT.1968.1). About the other plays, however, opinions have changed interestingly. Between the later eighteenth and mid-twentieth centuries, for instance, Caius Marius was thought to be only slightly better than Otway's worst piece (see OT.1791.3; OT.1838.1; OT.1875.2; OT.1932.1, 3). Yet since about 1745, respect has been mounting not only for its blend of Shakespeare and classical history, but also for its original qualities (for example, OT.1745.1; OT.1780.1; OT.1813.3; OT.1873.2; OT.1920.5; OT.1928.2; OT.1931.2). In 1953, Lucyle Hook argued that Otway's fusion of Shakespeare with Plutarch was guided by a desire to comment on current politics and to exploit the potential for a "new Heroine" created by the introduction of actresses on the Restoration stage. Hazel Batzer and Edward Langhans have recently elaborated upon Hook's views (OT.1969.1; OT.1980.3). Don Carlos has enjoyed a similar elevation in critical estimation, though, unlike Caius Marius, it has rarely been ranked near the bottom of Otway's dramas. A handful of commentators in the eighteenth and early nineteenth centuries found the play powerful (see OT.1732.1; OT.1838.1), but it was Gosse, the Temple Bar critic, and Noel who in the later Victorian era (OT.1877.1; OT.1879.1; OT.1888.1) balanced comments about its heroic artifice against the observation that it is among the most moving of all plays in the heroic mode. Although in the present century this positive approach has been widely accepted (see OT.1908.1; OT.1928.2), a full critical reading of the play has yet to appear. Some commentators regard it as a transitional piece in which Otway humanizes heroics by showing a more vulnerable hero, one whose personality is informed by the author's own feelings (OT.1905.1; OT.1923.3; OT.1963.2). Ghosh thinks it is a tragedy of old age (OT.1932.3), Praz equates its theme with that of Venice Preserv'd (OT.1933.3), and Hagstrum calls it an oedipal reading of Hamlet in which an "unconventional and obsessive" love "attacks the very roots of social and political stability" (OT.1980.2).

A far more radical shift in opinion shows up in comments on the comedies. Until the 1920s, their coarse bawdiness turned even the most sympathetic critics away from extended analysis. Genest's recommendation (OT.1832.1) that they deserve serious re-examination was ignored, as was Taine's perception (OT.1871.1) that they dramatize a moral critique of society. But after Summers insisted that they are brilliant, harsh, well-controlled satires (OT.1926.2), Ham studied them more closely (OT.1931.2) and found Friendship in Fashion a busy, biting satire, The Souldiers Fortune a penetrating assessment of the sex game, and The Atheist a nauseating revelation of what happens to ex-rakes and doting old lovers. Singh developed these ideas in 1963 by arguing that the comedies are problem plays in which the values of real life shatter the artificialities of fashion and expose the repulsive underside of sexual intrigue. In the late 1960s, Hilary Spurling and James Sutherland applied this kind of analysis to The Souldiers Fortune and The Atheist, respectively (OT.1968.4; OT.1969.9), and in 1973, Kerstin Warner expanded it to include political satire: the comedies ridicule Whig values. The latest, and at the moment the definitive, treatment is Robert Hume's presentation of Friendship as an ugly picture of broken relationships, The Souldiers Fortune as a five-stage satirical comedy, and The Atheist as a somewhat incoherent effort to demolish romance norms. Together, in Hume's view, the comedies depict a world whose conventions of behavior have been corrupted by self-seeking and animalism (OT.1976.3).

Despite such advances in our understanding of Otway's early works and of his "comic muse," he remains for most students of literary history the author of The Orphan and Venice Preserv'd, his two most frequently analyzed plays. The earliest critics of The Orphan concerned themselves with characterization, morality, and "probability," and all three issues continued to dominate critical thought until the twentieth century. The editor of the 1712 Works affirmed the tragic status of the play's less-than-illustrious main characters, and Addison (OT.1711.4) fueled the growing obsession with Monimia's conjugal tenderness. Her distresses moved successive generations of commentators, though Lamb thought she whined too much (OT.1801.1) and some sensed that she shared in the play's indecency (for example, OT.1822.2). The mid-eighteenth-century feeling that Acasto was unpatriotic spawned among more sympathetic critics the notion that perhaps he was meant to represent James, Duke of Ormonde, whose retirement from court chicanery many regarded as a noble gesture (see OT.1784.2; OT.1831.1; OT.1945.2). Others concentrated on the incongruous mixture of satire and sincerity in Acasto's advice to his children (for example, OT.1822.2). Whether Polydore is a villain and whether Castalio should be considered a victim or a cause of the tragedy were also favorite issues, especially in the eighteenth century (OT.1735.5; OT.1759.5; OT.1764.1; OT.1813.1).

Focusing on the subject of morality in The Orphan, Dennis (OT.1713.1) and Crusius (OT.1732.2) tried to counter Collier's objections to its coarseness and lack of poetic justice (OT.1698.2; OT.1700.2), but by mid-century Collier's position had triumphed. In 1748, Hawkins attacked the play not only for its supposedly low morality but also for technical flaws such as the awkward and absurd opening exposition (earlier noticed by Gildon, OT.1721.1) and the seeming inconsistency in Polydore's character. Among its moral deficiencies, he cited Acasto's lack of patriotism, Polydore's hedonism, Monimia's indelicacy, and a general hostility toward marriage, religion, and business. Cibber and Shiels reaffirmed several of these points and added that the whole situation upon which the tragedy rests is highly implausible (OT.1753.1). Thus, "immoral, improbable, poorly constructed, yet moving" seems to have been the consensus from about 1750 to about 1879 (when the Temple Bar critic argued for the first time since Thornton in 1813 that the play was, in fact, skillfully designed). Crusius had a handful of followers who thought they perceived Otway giving moral instruction about the importance of mistakes (OT.1757.1) or the consequences of lawless passion (OT.1813.1), and a few commentators pursued serious interest in sources (for example, OT.1763.1; OT.1765.1; OT.1821.2; OT.1910.1; OT.1915.1), topical references (OT.1893.1), and the play's innovatively low social level (OT.1866.1; OT.1878.2). To most, however, The Orphan remained either too indecent or too impious in its fatalism for sympathetic study.

The twentieth-century reputation of The Orphan reflects an increasing unwillingness to evaluate accompanied by an increasing desire to analyze. Nicoll sets the modern tone (OT.1923.3); he sees the play as combining high and domestic tragedy, and as introducing pathetic drama by transforming the ancient tragic hero, with his fatal lack of knowledge, into the modern antihero foiled by human weakness. Aline Mackenzie-Taylor (OT.1950.4) concentrates on the self-contradictions that trap both protagonists, and Geoffrey Marshall

(OT.1969.4) perceives a tragedy of verbal disorder caused by violation of Acasto's norm of plain speaking. When modern critics do evaluate the play, they tend to repeat Hazlitt's minority opinion of 1820: in overall effect, The Orphan is marred by "voluptuous effeminacy of sentiment and mawkish distress" (for example, OT.1904.2; OT.1925.2; OT.1957.1; OT.1963.1; OT.1965.4). Eric Rothstein, however, has tried to show that such emotionalism need not be regarded as inartistic (OT.1967.3). In his reading, the play shows how romantic love and passionate hedonism can be rendered destructive by failures of trust; thus, it reveals the disjunction of hero and society, and criticizes heroic drama and Restoration comedy. A variation on Rothstein's ideas has recently been rung by Laura Brown (OT.1981.1); Jean Hagstrum (OT.1980.2) has reinterpreted John M. Wallace's notion (OT.1969.10) that The Orphan should be read as a parable about the destruction of an English Eden through repeated original sins. Hagstrum's Eden is the familial state of nature, wherein primitive psychology has replaced Christian norms and human beings unwittingly commit tragic errors.

In some respects, criticism on Venice Preserv'd has followed a course parallel to that of criticism on The Orphan. In both cases, characterization has been the reigning obsession until after the first quarter of the present century, and in both cases, the earliest critics wrote a great deal about moral quality and the heroine's pathetic distresses. From the mid-eighteenth century to about 1830, several commentators on Venice Preserv'd, like those concerned with The Orphan, objected to instances of improbability in its plot, and the twentieth-century trend in reading both plays has been to analyze rather than to assess. Otherwise, Venice Preserv'd has fared rather better than its predecessor. The skillful control of its plot has never come into serious question, and its bawdy comic episodes, strong political references, sharp character contrasts, and blending of public with private interests have provided points of departure for many perceptive critics.

During the eighteenth and nineteenth centuries, when the subject of characterization dominated discussion, each of the main three figures underwent personality changes in the minds of the critics. To Restoration and eighteenth-century critics, for example, Belvidera admirably embodied distressed virtue and conjugal love (OT.1698.3-4; OT.1699.1; OT.1720.1; OT.1748.1-4; OT.1804.2; OT.1808.3), yet to some commentators of the Romantic period, such as Lamb and Byron (OT.1801.1; OT.1817.2; OT.1828.1), she seemed absurdly sentimental and mawkish. Meanwhile, others questioned whether she was not more sensuous than tender (see OT.1807.1; OT.1824.2; OT.1830.3). By the mid-nineteenth century, however, she had regained her place as an original creation depicting distressed virtue, and in the first quarter of the present century, she became for many the most important character (OT.1908.1; OT.1914.3; OT.1923.5). Until the second quarter of the eighteenth century, Jaffeir struck most observers as a weak but well-intentioned victim and as a loving husband (OT.1712.3), but then disagreement arose over whether he was meant to be a vacillating coward or a man of gloomy courage (OT.1731.1; OT.1747.6; OT.1748.2; OT.1759.5). From the later eighteenth to the mid-nineteenth century, he was usually regarded as a contemptibly weak and self-indulgent scoundrel (OT.1791.2; OT.1817.1; OT.1823.5; OT.1824.3; OT.1830.2; OT.1836.1; OT.1846.1), but he subsequently regained his original status as vulnerable but amiable victim of forces beyond his control.

Two aspects of Pierre's character have especially engaged commentators: his motives and his political status. If the introduction to the 1712 Works is representative of the early eighteenth-century view, he was then seen as a flawed but pathetic man of action. By mid-century, though, he seems to have been regarded as a bold adventurer (OT.1747.2), and critics of the later eighteenth and early nineteenth centuries intensely disagreed about whether he is a coldly scheming villain or a man of feeling driven to revenge by unjust treatment (see OT.1790.1; OT.1791.2; OT.1817.1, 3; OT.1820.1; OT.1823.5, 9; OT.1824.3; OT.1829.4; OT.1836.1). Early discussions of Pierre's political status tended to center on Otway's ability to create audience sympathy for a traitor (for example, OT.1711.1; OT.1712.1; OT.1752.1; OT.1753.1; OT.1767.1; OT.1791.2). In 1813, however, Thornton argued that to sympathize with any of the rebels is to gain moral insight, for they are all, including Pierre, instructively human in their weaknesses. On the other hand, an anonymous reviewer of 1829 saw Pierre as, in fact, a true patriot (OT.1829.4), and Campbell held in 1834 that any adaptation that stresses Pierre's patriotic qualities would be an improvement. Campbell seems to have been the last important critic to worry about this particular issue.

As in criticism of Pierre, reactions to Antonio, Aquilina, and Renault tended to cluster around two issues, moral value and political implication, which eventually converged. The first was usually raised in connection with the so-called Nicky-Nacky episodes, bizarre scenes of sexual perversion involving Antonio and Aquilina. These scenes began to generate revulsion in about 1700, as illustrated in Cobb's poem of that year, and until the 1920s, they continued to be considered both lewd and irrelevant. Only a few critics along the way ventured less prudish assessments. Not surprisingly, Aphra Behn was one of the first to see Antonio as a caricature of bad politicians (OT.1684.1), and in 1714, Steele felt that the Nicky-Nacky scenes demonstrate the fate of those who try to become what nature does not intend them to be. Davies (OT.1784.2) and Thornton (OT.1813.3) argued that these episodes were indispensable to the play's tragic rhythm, and in 1869, Robinson reported that Goethe saw them as illustrations of the kind of moral and political corruption against which Otway's rebels were conspiring. Early twentieth-century critics added that Antonio exemplifies the reasons for Otway's bitter pessimism (OT.1927.2), that the Nicky-Nacky scenes provide needed comic relief (OT.1928.1), and that the animalistic relationship between Antonio and Aquilina contrasts with the marital love of Jaffeir and Belvidera (OT.1931.2).

The identification of Antonio with the Earl of Shaftesbury seems to have been accepted, at least implicitly, since Mrs. Behn's song in 1684. Perhaps it was not clear to everyone, though, for Oldmixon seems vague when he guesses (OT.1695.5) Antonio must represent "some body" at court. That the somebody is Shaftesbury was reaffirmed by Davies (OT.1784.2) and Scott (OT.1808.4), and that Renault also represents Shaftesbury was first clearly articulated in literary criticism by Genest (OT.1832.1). Genest's opinion has prevailed in the twentieth century, though it has been attacked by Wright (OT.1916.2), Whiting (OT.1930.3), and Wilson (OT.1965.4). At first, twentieth-century critics failed to link the contradiction implicit in identifying both characters with Shaftesbury to the one implicit in statements that Venice Preserv'd is a Tory play which denounces the political leadership (see OT.1908.1; OT.1920.2; OT.1928.4). Then, drawing upon the work of Whiting and Ghosh (OT.1932.3), Zera Fink (OT.1945.1) resolved both contradictions by maintaining that Otway condemns not only the Whig conspirators but also the Whig-controlled legislative body. Antonio and Renault could thus be seen as complementary facets of Shaftesbury's political and personal behavior.

Such merging of character studies with related interests typifies the modern effort to achieve a "holistic" reading of Venice Preserv'd that synthesizes elements treated separately in the past: comic episodes, political meanings, and the relation between public and private concerns. The last of these had been highlighted in the introduction to the 1712 Works, in the Cibber-Shiels Lives (OT.1753.1), by Anderson (OT.1795.1), and by Thornton (OT.1813.3); but not really until the 1940s and 1950s did it become, through the efforts of Aline Mackenzie-Taylor, the central issue. Before then, the few critics who attempted comprehensive readings emphasized the structure of interpersonal relationships. In 1715, for instance, one writer said the play was about a woman causing chaos through the tragic exercise of virtue; later critics saw it as a study of passion influencing behavior (OT.1791.2) or of the conflict between duties and passions (OT.1820.1). Parsons (OT.1909.4) and Praz (OT.1933.3) argued that Otway was dramatizing the way in which uxoriousness can ruin a noble nature. By 1949, Mackenzie-Taylor could draw upon many of the strands of critical interest we have been discussing to argue that Otway was in full control of both public and private worlds, manipulating our responses to each so that the shifting of our ill wishes on the public level colors our feelings about the private distresses.

In 1958, Burton refined this to mean that the play shows private lives being destroyed by public conflicts, and in the same year, Hughes brought observations on Otway's "bitter pessimism" into a reading that presents Venice Preserv'd as a depiction of innocence isolated in a corrupt society. This reading has been further developed by McBurney (OT.1959.1), Van Voris (OT.1964.7), Bradbrook (OT.1965.1), Berman (OT.1969.2), and Spurling (OT.1969.8), all of whom stress that as Otway's main characters confront the bleak realities of history, their only consolation becomes a retreat inward.

The motif of retreat enters crucially into all the important interpretations of the 1970s, even Durant's (OT.1974.1), which focuses on the abandonment of familial covenants. It clearly informs Vieth's observation (OT.1975.5) that Jaffeir and Pierre existentially defy society in favor of arbitrarily chosen codes of honor, and it is embodied in Wikander's argument (OT.1977.7) that a turn to self becomes the main characters' alternative to choosing between two equally ignominious political orders, both meant to represent Whig realities of the Restoration. Recently, Gerald Parker (OT.1981.2) has tried to locate the retreat motif within the play's general rhythm, which he describes as a complex shift in perspective, from specific, personal, practical, and temporal, to general, public, and metaphysical.

Now that much of the groundwork has been laid, the prospect for future criticism about these four dramatists seems bright. We have just begun to agree that all four were capable of complex artistry and could explore contemporary issues well beyond their merely topical importance. The previous era of literary history, formalist analysis, and generalized investigations of contemporary milieux have put us into a position to undertake better documented studies of texts-in-context and texts-in-performance. Just how much potential such studies might realize is suggested by the recent work of Susan Staves, Peter Holland, Curtis Price, and Robert Hume. Compared to our predecessors, we have splendid research tools--not only reliable histories, source studies, editions, and biographies (the latter rather sketchy still), but new and remarkably useful records of primary information about the Restoration theater world: for example, _The London Stage, 1660-1800_ (1960-70), Leacroft's _The Development of the English Playhouse_ (1973), Langhans's _Restoration Promptbooks_ (1981), and the first volumes of _A Biographical Dictionary of Actors, Actresses, Musicians, Dancers, Managers, and Other Stage Personnel in London, 1660-1800_ (1973-). Such resources, together with respect for the achievements of earlier scholars and commentators, should enable late-twentieth-century drama critics to re-create something of the Restoration's own rich understanding of stage fictions by its favorite professional playwrights.

Abbreviations

Nineteenth- and twentieth-century serials are abbreviated using the acronyms established by the "Master List of Periodicals," which prefaces annual volumes of the *MLA International Bibliography of Books and Articles on Modern Languages and Literatures*. Additionally, the following abbreviations have been employed:

Link	Frederick M. Link. *English Drama, 1660-1800: A Guide to Information Sources*. Detroit: Gale Research, 1976.
McNamee	Lawrence F. McNamee. *Dissertations in English and American Literature, 1865-1964* and Supplements I (1964-68) and II (1969-73). New York: R.R. Bowker, 1968, 1969, 1974.
Stratman	Carl J. Stratman, David G. Spencer, and Mary Elizabeth Devine. *Restoration and Eighteenth Century Theatre Research: A Bibliographical Guide, 1900-1968*. Carbondale and Edwardsville: Southern Illinois University Press; London and Amsterdam: Feffer & Simons, 1971.

The Dramatic Works of Thomas Shadwell

Sullen Lovers; or, The Impertinents. A Comedy	1668
The Hypocrit	1669*
The Royal Shepherdess: A Tragi-Comedy	1669
The Humorists: A Comedy	1671
The Miser: A Comedy	1672
Epsom-Wells: A Comedy	1673
The Tempest; or, The Enchanted Island. A Comedy	1674
Psyche: A Tragedy	1675
The Libertine: A Tragedy	1676
The Virtuoso: A Comedy	1676
The History of Timon of Athens, the Man-hater	1678
The Woman-Captain: A Comedy	1680
The Lancashire-Witches, and Tegue O Divelly the Irish-Priest: A Comedy	1682
The Squire of Alsatia: A Comedy	1688
Bury-Fair: A Comedy	1689
A True Widow: A Comedy	1689

---

*A lost play. See S.1977.5.

The Amorous Bigotte, with the Second Part of Tegue O Divelly: A Comedy	1690
The Scowrers: A Comedy	1691
The Volunteers; or, The Stock-Jobbers: A Comedy	1693

Writings about Thomas Shadwell, 1668-1980

1668

1 PEPYS, SAMUEL. Entries for 2, 4, 5, and 6 May and 24 June. In *The Diary of Samuel Pepys*. Transcribed and edited by Robert Latham, William Matthews, et al. Vol. 9. Berkeley and Los Angeles: University of California Press, 1976, pp. 183-87, 249.

Sees the *Sullen Lovers* three times, at first finding it "tedious" and ill designed, "a very contemptible play," but gradually learning to like it better as the audiences begin to respond more favorably and as the personal satire becomes clearer (Sir Positive At-all represents Sir Robert Howard, and Mr. Woodcock stands for "my Lord St. Johns"). Pepys especially enjoys Shadwell's "many good humours" and "many little witty expressions," and he raves about "a little boy" who, "for a farce, doth dance Polichinelli." By 24 June, he regards the play as "pretty good." These entries were first published in two editions of the *Diary* by Richard, Lord Braybrooke: *Memoirs of Samuel Pepys, Esq. F.R.S.* (London: Henry Colburn, 1825), 2:225; and *Diary and Correspondence of Samuel Pepys, F.R.S.* (London: Henry Colburn, 1849), 4:431-32, 479.

2 SHADWELL, THOMAS. Preface to *Sullen Lovers; or, The Impertinents. A Comedy*. The Savoy: for Henry Herringman, n. pag.

Admits that he used Molière's *Les Fâcheux*, but says that he conceived the main characters before reading the French play. Unlike fashionable heroic plays, with their "wilde Romantick Tales" and artificial conflicts between love and honor, and unlike modern wit comedy, with its swearing and lewdness, this play subordinates overall design to the depiction of humors characters from whom the audience can gain practical instruction.

1669

1 PEPYS, SAMUEL. Entry for 14 April. In *The Diary of Samuel Pepys*. Transcribed and edited by Robert Latham, William

Matthews, et al. Vol. 9. Berkeley and Los Angeles: University of California Press, 1976, p. 519.

Finds, after at least four performances, that the Sullen Lovers "pleases me well still." This entry was first published in the edition of 1825 by Richard, Lord Braybrooke: Memoirs of Samuel Pepys, Esq. F.R.S. (London: Henry Colburn), 2:330.

1671

1 SHADWELL, THOMAS. Preface to The Humorists: A Comedy. London: for Henry Herringman, n. pag.

Asserts that in creating his humors characters he has been original, has observed decorum, and has kept in mind the following definition of "humour": "the Biasse of the Mind, / By which, with violence, 'tis one way inclin'd: / It makes our actions lean on one side still; / And, in all Changes, that way bends the Will."

1673

1 ANON. Remarks upon Remarques; or, A Vindication of the Conversations of the Town. London: by A.C. for William Hensman, pp. 99-102.

Recommends Epsom-Wells as "a thing of great ingenuity" that portrays a "Country Hero" (Clodpate) and satirizes "some absurdities of the Town" even as it renders "Town-haters ridiculous."

1674

1 [SETTLE, ELKANAH.] Notes and Observations on the Empress of Morocco Revised. London: for William Cademan, Preface and p. 69.

Alludes scathingly to Psyche and to the masque at the end of The Tempest (1674); remarks that Shadwell has wit "if he can keep it."

1675

1 DUFFETT, THOMAS. The Mock-Tempest; or, The Enchanted Castle. London: for William Cademan, 59 pp.

A full-scale, scene-by-scene parody in which, for example, the storm at sea becomes a raid on a whorehouse, Prospero is the keeper of Bridewell, and Ferdinand is a canting religious hypocrite.

2 HOOKE, ROBERT. Entry for 25 June. In The Diary of Robert Hooke 1672-1680. Edited by Henry W. Robinson and Walter Adams. London: Taylor & Francis, 1935, p. 166.
Calls The Libertine an "atheistical wicked play."

3 LOCK, MATTHEW. Preface to The English Opera; or, The Vocal Musick in Psyche, with the Instrumental Therein Intermix'd. To which is Adjoyned The Instrumental Musick in the Tempest. London: by T. Ratcliff & N. Thompson for the author and John Carr, n. pag.
Considers these two works "proportionable" to what Italians mean by the term opera: a "Grand Design" that is illustrated by "splendid Scenes and Machines" and that conveys its subject through appropriate "kinds of Musick." In Psyche and The Tempest, the music is "soft, easie, and . . . agreeable to the design of the Author," although "all the Tragedy be not in Musick: for the Author prudently consider'd" that the English "Genius" is more conducive than the Italian to a mixture of music and "interlocutions."

4 PHILLIPS, EDWARD. "Eminent Poets Among the Moderns." In Theatrum Poetarum; or, A Compleat Collection of the Poets. London: for Charles Smith, p. 183.
Names Sullen Lovers, The Humorists, and Epsom-Wells as "witty and ingenious Comedies," and calls Psyche a "Tragical Opera" that can vie "with the Opera's of Italy; in the pomp of Scenes, Machinery and Musical performance."

5 [ROCHESTER, JOHN WILMOT, EARL OF.] "An Allusion to Horace. The 10th Satyr of the 1st Book." In Poems on Several Occasions By the Right Honourable, the E. of R---. Antwerp: n.p., p. 42.
"Hasty Shadwel" and Wycherley are the only recent "Wits" who have "toucht, upon true Comedy." Shadwell's "unfinish'd works" are masterful in conveying the "force of Nature," but because of the author's carelessness, they have "bold strokes" instead of "Art."

6 _____. "Epilogue, As it was spoke by Mr. Haines." In Love in the Dark; or, The Man of Bus'ness. A Comedy, by Sir Francis Fane. London: by T.N. for Henry Herringman, n. pag.
Ridicules the charming nonsense of The Tempest and Psyche, in which "Players turn Puppets," poetry gives way to "Doggrel" and music and spectacle, and reconstituted plots and characters are sold to mindless citizens for novelties, as painted bawds pass "for maids twice o'er." Let "the graver Fops" attend such productions; true "Men of Wit" will "find one another" in the audience of Love in the Dark.

1676

1 HOOKE, ROBERT. Entries for 25 May, 1, 2, 3, and 25 June, 1 and 3 July. In The Diary of Robert Hooke 1672-1680. Edited by Henry W. Robinson and Walter Adams. London: Taylor & Francis, 1935, pp. 234-35, 238-40.

Hooke and his friends believe he is being personally satirized as Sir Nicholas Gimcrack in The Virtuoso: "People almost pointed."

1677

1 SETTLE, ELKANAH. "The Preface to the Reader." In Ibrahim The Illustrious Bassa: A Tragedy. London: by T.M. for W. Cademan, n. pag.

Shadwell is "a wretched Dabler in Verse," a "Comical Priest of Apollo" whose Humorists, Miser, and "Hypocrite" are "silly Plays," and whose Psyche is a shallow, senseless plagiarism that spoils the plot and morals of its sources. In The Virtuoso Longvil and Bruce are witless, and Sir Samuel Hearty is an outworn humors type.

1678

1 [DUFFET, THOMAS.] Psyche Debauch'd: A Comedy. London: for J. Smith, 87 pp.

Shadwell's spectacular, mythic world becomes a garish, absurd underworld of prostitutes and pimps.

1680

1 ANON. "A Session of the Poets." In Poems on Several Occasions By the Right Honourable, the E. of R---. Antwerp: n.p., p. 112.

Apollo tells wallowing Tom Shadwell that he should be happy if he had "half so much Wit, as he fancy'd he had." On the problem of attributing authorship of this poem, see David M. Vieth, Attribution in Restoration Poetry (New Haven and London: Yale University Press, 1963), pp. 296-321.

2 AUBREY, JOHN. "William Shakespeare (1564-1616)." In "Brief Lives," chiefly of Contemporaries, set down by John Aubrey. Edited by Andrew Clark. Vol. 2. Oxford: Clarendon Press, 1898, pp. 226-27.

Shadwell "is counted the best comoedian we have now." Clark dates most parts of the manuscript February 1680.

1681

1 D'URFEY, THOMAS. "Song." In Sir Barnaby Whigg; or, No Wit like a Womans. A Comedy. London: by A.G. & J.P. for Joseph Hindmarsh, act 3, scene 2, p. 28.

Shadwell is represented as lamenting the dwindling number of fashionable subjects to exploit, plays and poems to plagiarize; moreover, he finds that his "fancy's grown sleepy," that he has no "design or invention," and that his "Fidling and Drinking" has cost him "the Bays." He remembers old times when he delighted in science, "rifled" Molière, "rail'd" like a Fury, and wrote "like a Satyr." Though he falls "a damn'd Poet," he vows to "mount a Musician."

2 _____. "To the Right Honourable George Earl of Berkeley." In Sir Barnaby Whigg; or, No Wit like a Womans. A Comedy. London: by A.G. & J.P. for Joseph Hindmarsh, n. pag.

In an implied allusion to The Lancashire-Witches, D'Urfey derides plays that gain fame not because they are well wrought or instructive but because they entertain a "Faction" with "a Priest" and "a Witch, a Devil, or a Broomstick."

1682

1 [DRYDEN, JOHN.] Mac Flecknoe; or, A Satyr upon the True-Blew-Protestant Poet, T.S. London: for D. Green, 14 pp.

Shadwell writes witless nonsense in the florid, pedantic style of his own Sir Formal Trifle. On a par with Heywood, Shirley, and Ogleby, he is a dullard who "never deviates into Sence"; his efforts in tragedy make us smile, whereas his comedies put us to sleep. Among his achievements in dullness are Psyche, The Humorists, The Miser, The Hypocrite, and The Virtuoso.

2 [DRYDEN, JOHN, and NAHUM TATE.] The Second Part of Absalom and Achitophel: A Poem. London: for Jacob Tonson, pp. 15-16.

Og (Shadwell) is that "Monstrous mass of foul corrupted matter" regurgitated by "Devils" so that he can "in Clumsy verse, unlickt, unpointed" write treason against "the Lord's Anointed." When he was born, "The Midwife laid her hand on his Thick Skull, / With this Prophetick blessing--Be thou Dull."

3 [SHADWELL, THOMAS.] The Tory-Poets: A Satyr. London: for R. Johnson, p. 5.

Ironically damns himself for failing to write bawdy prologues, false wit, and nonsense, as Dryden does.

1683

1 DRYDEN, JOHN. The Vindication; or, The Parallel of the French Holy-League, and the English League and Covenant, Turn'd into a Seditious Libell. London: for Jacob Tonson, pp. 25-26.
Og should recognize that he was born to drink, not to dabble in poetry and prose, though "his Writings will never do the Government so much harm, as his Drinking does it good."

2 DUKE, RICHARD. "To Mr. Creech on his Translation of Lucretius." In Titus Lucretius Carus His Six Books of Epicurean Philosophy. Translated by Thomas Creech. London: for Thomas Sawbridge & Anthony Stephens, n. pag.
Shadwell and Settle are "dull Clods" who write "in despight / Of Art and Nature."

1685

1 [GOULD, ROBERT.] The Laurel: A Poem on the Poet-Laureat. London: for Benj. Tooke, pp. 20-21, 33.
Drunken, fat, and brainless, Shadwell typifies those who write "drowsie Verse" and butcher religion and art. He could pass for the "shapless Lump" of a bear at Smithfield Fair.

2 SAINT-EVRÉMOND, CHARLES de MARGUETEL de SAINT-DENIS, SEIGNEUR de. "Of the English Comedy." In Mixt Essays. London: for Timothy Goodwin, p. 17.
Like Jonson's Bartholomew Fair, Shadwell's Epsom-Wells focuses not on a central rogue but on several cheats as they operate "in publick places."

1687

1 ETHEREGE, GEORGE. "A Letter From Sir George Etherege, to his Grace the Duke of Buckingham." In Miscellaneous Works, Written by His Grace, George, Late Duke of Buckingham. 2d ed. London: for S. Briscoe & J. Nutt, 1704, pp. 139-40.
The Squire of Alsatia compensates for D'Urfey's wretched Fool's Preferment. The letter is conjecturally dated by Frederick Bracher in his edition of Letters of Sir George Etherege (Berkeley, Los Angeles, and London: University of California Press, 1974), pp. 92-97.

2 WINSTANLEY, WILLIAM. The Lives of the Most Famous English Poets. London: by H. Clark for Samuel Manship, p. 216.
Commends Shadwell for the "sweet Language and Contrivance" of his plays, and quotes (without acknowledgment) Phillips on the achievement of Psyche (S.1675.4).

1688

1 ETHEREGE, GEORGE. Letter to William Jephson, 8 March. In *The Letterbook of Sir George Etherege*. Edited by Sybil Rosenfeld. Oxford: Oxford University Press; London: Humphrey Milford, 1928, p. 338.

Asks to be sent Shadwell's new play (probably *The Squire of Alsatia*) "that I may know what follies are in fashion . . . he is likely to pick up the best collection of new ones."

2 _____. Letter to William Jephson, 24 May. In *Letters of Sir George Etherege*. Edited by Frederick Bracher. Berkeley, Los Angeles, and London: University of California Press, 1974, pp. 200-201.

In his latest play (*The Squire of Alsatia*), Shadwell "lays on heavyly. His fools want mettle, and his witty men will scarce pass muster among the last recruits our General made for the Dog and Partridge." Before Bracher's edition, this letter existed only in manuscript.

1689

1 GOULD, ROBERT. "The Play-House: A Satyr." In *Poems Chiefly Consisting of Satyrs and Satyrical Epistles*. London: n.p., pp. 173, 175.

The Squire of Alsatia is damned through being praised by a false critic, and Shadwell and Settle are said to "have abus'd, unpardonable things, / The best of *Governments* and best of *Kings*."

2 _____. "To Julian Secretary to the Muses, A Consolatory Epistle in his Confinement." In *Poems, Chiefly Consisting of Satyrs and Satyrical Epistles*. London: n.p., p. 280.

Shadwell and Settle "pretend to Reason, / Though paid so well for scribling *Dogrel Treason*."

1690

1 [BROWN, THOMAS.] "The Fable of the Bat and the Birds." In *The Late Converts Exposed; or, The Reasons of Mr. Bays's Changing his Religion . . . Part the Second*. London: for Thomas Bennet, p. 59.

Shadwell is represented as a "Buzzard."

1691

1 [AMES, RICHARD.] *A Search after Wit; or, A Visitation of the Authors*. London: for E. Hawkins, p. 8.

Shadwell is deceiving the town "with Poetical Titles," for "Since he left honest Prose, the old Stroke he ne'er hit, / And is equally admir'd for his Shape and his Wit." The Scowrers falls below his previous comedies in quality.

2 [DUNTON, JOHN.] Answer to "Quest. 1. Whom do you think the best Dramatick Professor in this Age?" Athenian Gazette: or Casuistical Mercury 5, no. 2 (5 December), n. pag.

Although Dryden excels in his range of poetic talents and in serious drama, Shadwell writes "true Comedy, and perhaps the best that comes on our Stage," though he could improve his plays by creating more virtuous characters than he usually does.

3 LANGBAINE, GERARD. An Account of the English Dramatick Poets. Oxford: by L.L. for G. West & H. Clements, pp. 442-53 and Appendix.

Counsels the reader not to judge Shadwell on the basis of Dryden's damning portrait in MacFlecknoe. Because of their great variety of characters "drawn from the Life" rather than from "other Mens Ideas," Shadwell's "Excellent Comedies" are superior to Dryden's, although Shadwell should have avoided making light of the Church of England, especially in The Lancashire-Witches. When he borrows from others, he usually acknowledges it and often improves on the original, as in Bury-Fair, The Miser, and The Lancashire-Witches, the latter being almost unique in its kind, except for Ben Jonson's Masque of Queens. If The Libertine, Psyche, The Squire of Alsatia, and Sullen Lovers are "diverting" plays, Epsom-Wells, A True Widow, and The Virtuoso are among the best comedies of this age. Shadwell is an outstanding creator of humors characters, indeed of characters in general. In the Appendix (n. pag.), Langbaine notes that The Scowrers, which is "wholly free from Plagiary," is one of Shadwell's better comedies.

1692

1 [MOTTEUX, PETER ANTHONY.] Notes. Gentleman's Journal; or, The Monthly Miscellany (May):26; (November):21.

Looks forward, in May, to the next comedy by Shadwell (The Volunteers), "whose Genius for that sort of Poetry, is sufficiently known to the Ingenious," but in November, after Shadwell's death, praises his overall comic achievement: his plays entertain and instruct by imaging human nature in all its contemporary shapes and colors; through his masterful "draughts of humours and characters . . . what store of fools and madmen did he not reform?"

1693

1 ANON. Epilogue to The Volunteers; or, The Stock-Jobbers. A Comedy . . . Being his last Play. London: for James Knapton, n. pag.

Eulogizes Shadwell as "the great Support oth' Comick Stage" with his union of "Mirth" and "Instruction," his "large Idea's," "flowing Pen," and skill at drawing characters "from Nature." He never fawned or took bribes, and "never sunk in Prose . . . so low as Farce" or "soar'd in Verse / So high as Bombast."

2 D'URFEY, THOMAS. Prologue to The Volunteers; or, The Stock-Jobbers. A Comedy . . . Being his last Play. London: for James Knapton, n. pag.

Refers to Shadwell's "Genius," "good Satyr," and "Wit."

3 RYMER, THOMAS. A Short View of Tragedy; It's Original, Excellency, and Corruption. London: by and for Richard Baldwin, p. 24.

Shadwell's The Virtuoso, like Jonson's Alchymist, reminds one of Aristophanes' Clouds.

4 TATE, NAHUM. Preface to A Duke and no Duke. London: for Henry Bonwicke, n. pag.

Compares the characters and comic devices in The Virtuoso to those in Aristophanes's plays: both authors deal in humor and farce.

1694

1 [WRIGHT, JAMES.] "Of the Modern Comedies." In Country Conversations: Being an Account of some Discourses that Happen'd in a Visit to the Country last Summer. London: for Henry Bonwicke, p. 6.

Condemns Epsom-Wells, The Virtuoso, and The Scowrers for their stock characters and formulaic intrigues.

1697

1 ANON. "To T____ W_____, Esq; May the 19th, 93." In Familiar Letters: Vol. II. Containing Thirty Six Letters, By the Right Honourable, John, late Earl of Rochester. London: for Sam. Briscoe, p. 176.

"Oily Shadwel," who was not below teaching "Sage Terence" the "brisk gay Nonsense of the Town," could effortlessly concoct plays out of his stock ingredients of "a Bully, / A Wench, a Usurer, a Cully."

1698

1 ANON. A Vindication of the Stage, with the Usefulness and Advantages of Dramatick Representations. London: for Joseph Wild, p. 26.

The Libertine is as effective as the pulpit in reforming the "most hardened and profligate Atheist," and The Squire of Alsatia teaches country gentry how to avoid "the Town Sharpers."

2 DENNIS, JOHN. The Usefulness of the Stage, To the Happiness of Mankind. To Government, and Religion. Occasion'd by a late Book, written by Jeremy Collier, MA. London: for R. Parker, p. 117.

In Shadwell's plays the moral aim is clear: "Thus Don John is destroyed for his libertinism and his impiety; Timon for his profusion and his intemperance."

3 [SETTLE, ELKANAH.] A Defence of Dramatick Poetry: Being a Review of Mr. Collier's View of the Immorality and Profaneness of the Stage. London: for Eliz. Whitlock, p. 73.

We remember Timon and Evandra, of The History of Timon of Athens, not because of their moral frailties but because each ultimately rejects the world of double-dealing for love, poverty, and death.

4 _____. A Farther Defence of Dramatick Poetry. London: for Eliz. Whitlock, pp. 23, 32, 41, 59.

Praises The Virtuoso as an "excellent" comedy owing much of its merit to exaggeration of character traits, and cautions against identifying Shadwell's own views with Don John's "Levity, Loosness or Atheism" in The Libertine.

1699

1 BROWN, THOMAS. "An Impromptu to Shadwell's Memory, by Dr. B---." In A Collection of Miscellany Poems, Letters, &c. London: for John Sparks, p. 29.

Asks heaven to take Shadwell's "loyal heart," but "As for the rest sweet Devil fetch a Cart."

2 _____. "In obitum Tho. Shadwell pinguis memoria. 1693." In A Collection of Miscellany Poems, Letters, &c. London: for John Sparks, p. 29.

After six Latin couplets degrading Shadwell as "Bavius," the final stanza comes forth in English: "Tom writ, but the Reader still slept o're his Book, / For he carefully writ the same Opium he took."

3 [GILDON, CHARLES,] and GERARD LANGBAINE. The Lives and Characters of the English Dramatick Poets. London: for W. Turner, pp. 124-26.

Shadwell seemed able to create almost every conceivable humors character, but he could not make "a Man of Wit." Although Epsom-Wells is perhaps not as good a play as Langbaine and Saint-Evrémond think it is (see S.1691.3 and S.1685.2), The Humorists is well designed, The Libertine "diverting," and The Scowrers, with its "noisy Humour," is "not unpleasant."

4 OLDMIXON, JOHN. Reflections on the Stage, and Mr. Collyer's Defence of the Short View. In Four Dialogues. London: for R. Parker & P. Buck, pp. 83, 97.

Although Shadwell's plays are now headed toward "oblivion," his The Scowrers is certainly amusing.

1702

1 ANON. A Comparison between the Two Stages. London: n.p., pp. 33, 104.

Shadwell's comedies "are true Copies of Nature, but generally low and aukward; his Tragedies are a mixture of Mirth and Melancholy, and those of his own making good for little." Although The Libertine was written in only twenty-one days, it is better than The Way of the World, which took two years.

1704

1 ANON. The Stage-Beaux toss'd in a Blanket; or, Hypocrisie Alamode; Expos'd in a True Picture of Jerry --- . . . A Comedy. London: by J. Nutt, pp. 39-40.

Hotspur wishes that Collier had seen something of himself in Sir Formal Trifle of The Virtuoso, for both men use false rhetoric and sophistry to "obscure the Truth, and . . . confound the Common Reader."

2 [BROWN, THOMAS.] Memoirs Relating to the late Famous Mr. Tho. Brown. With a Catalogue of his Library. London: by B. Brag, p. 17.

Considers Shadwell's plays "dull."

3 [DENNIS, JOHN.] The Person of Quality's Answer to Mr. Collier's Letter, Being a Disswasive from the Play-House. London: n.p., p. 8.

Satirically conjectures that Collier as a young man must have attended a performance of Epsom-Wells and "endur'd" its "Filth" before his "Prophetick Mission" was revealed to him.

1705

1 ANON. "A Congratulatory Poem to the Right Honourable Sir E. C. &c." In A New Collection of Poems Relating to State Affairs. London: n.p., p. 538.

Shadwell is seen as "the Muses Sport," a drudge from the stage who became a "drudge at Court." His verse merits the Laureateship, because it is better than Sternhold's or Hopkins's.

2 ANON. "Shadwell (Thomas)." In A Continuation of Mr. Collier's Supplement to the Great Historical Dictionary, &c. From 1688, to the Present Time. London: for H. Rhodes & T. Newborough, n. pag.

Shadwell is "a great Proficient in the Art of Poetry" whose comedies "shew him to understand Humour." Except for his not being able to draw "the Character of a Man of Wit, as well as that of a Coxcomb," there is "nothing wanting to the Perfection of his Dramatick Fables."

3 BEDFORD, ARTHUR. Serious Reflections on the Scandalous abuse and Effects of the Stage. Bristol: by W. Bonny, pp. 17-18.

The author of the Tempest (probably Shadwell's version) tries to imitate God's "Judgments in . . . Thunder, Lightning, Rain, Wind, Storms, and Shipwrecks"; he even brings Devils on the stage.

1707

1 ANON. "The Stage Vindicated: A Satyr. By I. H. Esq." Muses Mercury; or, Monthly Miscellany 1 (July):159-60.

Indirectly commends the satirical effectiveness of Clodpate (Epsom-Wells) and approves the moral instruction in Timon and The Libertine.

2 FILMER, EDWARD. A Defence of Plays; or, The Stage Vindicated from Several Passages in Mr. Collier's Short View, &c. London: for Jacob Tonson, pp. 43-44.

Indeed, The Libertine abounds in "Smut, Prophaness, Blasphemy, and Atheism," but its ending is exemplary when Hell "receives the trembling Atheist into her gaping, flaming Bowels."

1708

1 COLLIER, JEREMY. A Farther Vindication of the Short View of the Profaneness and Immorality of the English Stage. London: for R. Sare & G. Strahan, pp. 23-24.

The Libertine "has gone to the extent of an Atheistick Character. The strokes are gross, and daub'd all over the Piece."

1709

1 [STEELE, RICHARD.] Tatler, no. 7 (23-26 April), n. pag.

Epsom-Wells is "very just, and the Low Part of Humane Life represented with much Humour and Wit."

1710

1 GILDON, CHARLES. The Life of Mr. Thomas Betterton, the late Eminent Tragedian . . . To Which is added The Amorous Widow, or the Wanton Wife. London: R. Gosling, pp. 173-74.

After Shakespeare and Jonson, the first-rank writers of comedy are Etherege, Wycherley, Shadwell, Crowne, Congreve, and Vanbrugh.

2 [GILDON, CHARLES.] "Remarks on the Plays of Shakespeare." In The Works of Mr. William Shakespeare. [Edited by Nicholas Rowe.] Vol. 7. London: for E. Curll & E. Sanger, pp. 373-74.

In Timon, Shadwell corrupts Shakespeare and offends both religion and morals, because he makes Timon "a very scoundrel" and invents Melissa and Evandra, the one a noble lady who behaves like a whore, the other a whore who has a heart of gold.

1711

1 [ADDISON, JOSEPH.] Spectator, no. 35 (10 April), n. pag.

Shadwell "had . . . a great deal of Talent" for writing humors.

2 [HUGHES, JOHN.] Letter. Spectator, no. 141 (11 August), n. pag.

The Lancashire Witches is marred by on-stage displays of the supernatural which, unlike Shakespeare's, are neither solemn nor suitable for "the Affair of Comedy." Moreover, Shadwell inserts many indecent passages and excuses the patently immoral behavior of the two ladies (who selfishly marry without their parents' consent) by attributing its necessity to fate.

1713

1 [REYNARDSON, FRANCIS.] The Stage: A Poem. London: for E. Curll, pp. 6, 10.

Even though "blund'ring Shadwell now and then can please," unlike Jonson he writes shallow plays, and when, in The Lancashire Witches, he "gives his Ideot Clown [Young Hartfort] a Miss, / Gorg'd with the nauseous Ass true Criticks hiss."

1717

1 DENNIS, JOHN. Remarks upon Mr. Pope's Translation of Homer. London: for E. Curll, p. 4.

Ranks Shadwell as one of eight Restoration dramatists who wrote "good and diverting Comedies."

2 DUKE, RICHARD. "Answer to the Foregoing Epistle" [from Otway]. In Poems by the Earl of Roscommon . . . Together with Poems by Mr. Richard Duke. London: for J. Tonson, p. 515.
Comments on the dullness of Shadwell's "Men of Wit."

1719

1 ANON. Critical Remarks On the Four Taking Plays of this Season. London: for James Bettenham, p. 50.
In Charles Johnson's Masquerade, there is nothing of the "Comic Genius" and "Humour" which distinguishes "Ben Johnson, Shadwell, Wycherley, Congreve . . . from all those who have writ Comedy in any other Nation."

2 BEDFORD, ARTHUR. A Serious Remonstrance In Behalf of the Christian Religion. London: John Darby for Henry Hammond, Richard Gravett, and Anth. Piesley, pp. 187-88, 215-16.
The Squire of Alsatia encourages vice not only because Belfond Jr. and Trueman are debauchees but also because Sir Edward condones their behavior.

3 JACOB, GILES. The Poetical Register; or, the Lives and Characters of the English Dramatick Poets. With an Account of their Writings. London: E. Curll, pp. 222-26.
Although Shadwell could compose amusing comedies of humor and could depict "a Coxcomb in perfection," he "seem'd to be deficient in perfecting the Character of a fine Gentleman." The Virtuoso is notable for its "great variety of Humour," The Scowrers for its "great deal of low Humour." Epsom-Wells and The Lancashire Witches are "very entertaining," and The Libertine is considered one of his best plays. The Royal Shepherdess, The Woman-Captain, and The Squire of Alsatia were very successful in their own time.

1720

1 ANON. "Some Account of the Author and his Writings." In The Dramatick Works of Thomas Shadwell, Esq; In Four Volumes. Vol. 1. London: for J. Knapton & J. Tonson, 9 pp., n. pag.
Depicts Shadwell as a nonplagiarist who, with "that easie Turn of Conception and Language," "excell'd in Humour" and "drew . . . from Nature" and "from the World." This critique may have been written by John Shadwell, the author's son, who signed the dedication.

2 DENNIS, JOHN. The Characters and Conduct of Sir John Edgar, . . . In a Third and Fourth Letter to the Knight. London: by J. Roberts, p. 3.
Notes that Shadwell excelled Dryden in comedy.

1721

1 DENNIS, JOHN. "A Defence of Mr. Wycherley's Characters in the Plain-dealer. To William Congreve, Esq." In Proposals for Printing by Subscription . . . miscellaneous tracts, written by Mr. John Dennis. [London]: n.p., p. 26.

Shadwell "could not but have a true taste of Comedy, since he was so just a Writer of it."

1722

1 PARNELL, THOMAS. "The Book-Worm." In Poems on Several Occasions. London: for B. Lintot, p. 139.

The speaker "never miss'd" Shadwell's works until now, when he needs "the Leaves to wipe the Shrine" (that is, worm's guts).

1723

1 DENNIS, JOHN. Remarks on a Play, call'd The Conscious Lovers: A Comedy. London: for T. Warner, p. 11.

The Squire of Alsatia is "a very good and very entertaining Comedy," largely because Shadwell "took particular Care to supply from his own Invention the Ridicule that was wanting" in his source, the Adelphi.

1724

1 ANON. The Dancing Devils; or, The Roaring Dragon. A Dumb Farce. London: A. Bettesworth, J. Bately, & J. Brotherton, p. 8.

Approves of The Libertine because it shows "in Don John . . . the fate / Of Princely Rakes, who sin in state, / And prove as Wicked as they're Great."

1725

1 [MURALT, BÉAT LOUIS de.] Lettres sur les Anglois et les Francois: Et sur les Voiages. Cologne: n.p., pp. 26-32. Cologne: n.p., pp. 26-32.

Ridicules Shadwell's translation of Molière's The Miser.

1726

1 ANON. "Remarks on the Letters, concerning the English and French." In Letters Describing the Character and Customs of the English and French Nations. Anonymously translated from

Béat Louis de Muralt's Lettres (1725). 2d ed. London: by Tho. Edlin & N. Prevost, p. 18.

Dismisses Shadwell as "the most contemptible of all the English poets."

2 SWIFT, JONATHAN. "A History of Poetry, In a Letter to a Friend." In The Prose Works of Jonathan Swift. Edited by Herbert Davis. Oxford: Basil Blackwell, 1957, p. 274.

Wycherley had "a dull Co-temporary, who some times shew'd Humour, but his colouring was bad, and he could not SHADE-WELL." I was unable to see the original half-sheet of this work, printed by Waters, which is preserved in the National Library, Dublin.

1728

1 POPE, ALEXANDER. Comment. In Joseph Spence's Observations, Anecdotes and Characters of Books and Men, Collected from Conversation. Edited by James M. Osborne. Vol. 1. Oxford: Clarendon Press, 1966, item 480, pp. 205-6.

Shadwell's "general fault," as exhibited in The Virtuoso, is his failure to sustain the strength of his characterization throughout a play. "Wycherley used to say . . . that 'he knew how to start a fool very well, but that he was never able to run him down.'" This anecdote seems to have been first published in Edmond Malone's edition of Spence (London: John Murray, 1820), p. 115.

2 [RALPH, JAMES.] The Touch-stone; or, Historical, Critical, Political, Philosophical, and Theological Essays on the reigning Diversions of the Town. London: n.p., p. 157.

If Restoration playwrights were recalled from the grave, our modern audiences would no doubt neglect the best of them--Otway, Lee, and Dryden--in favor of Italian singers, French dancers, and the unworthy Settle and Shadwell.

1729

1 [POPE, ALEXANDER.] The Dunciad, Variorum. With the Prolegomena of Scriblerus. London: for A. Dod, p. 48.

"And Shadwell nods the poppy on his brows."

1730

1 [COOKE, THOMAS.] "On Comedy: A Criticism on The Squire of Alsatia." British Journal; or, The Traveller, no. 156 (26 December), n. pag.

Recommends Squire as a source of pleasurable instruction in the education and behavior of young people. This critique is published as Cooke's in Chapter 3 of "Considerations on the Stage," appended to The Triumphs of Love and Honour: A Play (London: for J. Roberts, 1731), pp. 58-63.

1732

1 CRUSIUS, LEWIS. The Lives of the Roman Poets. Vol. 2. London: for W. Innys, J. Clarke, B. Motte, & J. Nurse, p. 362.

As a comic writer, Shadwell is ranked below Congreve and Cibber and on a par with Wycherley, Farquhar, and Vanbrugh.

1735

1 ANON. The Dramatic Historiographer; or, the British Theatre Delineated. London: for F. Cogan & J. Nourse, pp. 278-86.

Shadwell's Timon "contains many useful and instructive morals," in that it shows the senators being "justly punished" and demonstrates to "the softer Sex . . . that Virtue has many branches, and, that Chastity, tho' a material one, is not of it self sufficient."

1738

1 ANON. "The Apotheosis of Milton: A Vision." Gentleman's Magazine 8:235.

Shadwell is represented as being "bloated," "forced, unnatural, and ungraceful," with his "ridiculous gestures" and "French Grimace."

1739

1 BERNARD, JOHN PETER, THOMAS BIRCH, JOHN LOCKMAN, et al. A General Dictionary, Historical and Critical. Vol. 9. London: G. Strahan, pp. 176-79.

Quotes Langbaine (S.1691.3) and Shadwell's own prefaces, and asserts that Shadwell has a true "relish and genius" for writing.

2 VOLTAIRE, FRANÇOIS MARIE AROUET. "Vie de Molière, avec de petits sommaires de ses pieces." In Oeuvres complètes de Voltaire. Vol. 47. [Paris]: La Société Litteraire-Typographique, 1784, p. 161.

Condemns Shadwell for his vanity and presumption in adapting L'Avare as The Miser: "La piece de Shadwell est généralement mésprisée." I was not able to see what appears to be the first edition of this work, Vie de Molière, avec des jugemens sur ses ouvrages (Paris: Chez Prault Fils, 1739).

1740

1 CIBBER, COLLEY. An Apology for the Life of Mr. Colley Cibber, Comedian. London: by John Watts for the author, pp. 88-89.

In Sir William Belfond, of The Squire of Alsatia, Shadwell "had . . . exactly chalk'd . . . the Out-lines of Nature."

1743

1 POPE, ALEXANDER. The Dunciad, in Four Books. London: for M. Cooper, p. 66.

Equated with Abraham, Shadwell is made the forefather of Cibber's race of dullards.

1747

1 ANON. A Companion to the Theatre; or, A View of our Most Celebrated Dramatic Pieces. Vol. 2. London: for J. Nourse, pp. 307-19.

Even though Shadwell was not trying to offer "Examples of a shining virtue" in The Squire of Alsatia, thinking it "sufficient to paint Nature as she is," the play nevertheless is to be commended for teaching the "Youth of both Sexes" how to avoid snares and how not to depend too much on oneself.

2 LeBLANC, JEAN BERNARD. "The Supplement of Genius; or, the art of composing dramatic poems, as it has been practised by many celebrated authors of the English theatre." In Letters on the English and French Nations. Vol. 2. London: for J. Brindley, R. Francklin, C. Davies, & J. Hodges, pp. 268-69, 276.

Considers Shadwell "an indifferent writer" whose Miser was "imitated from Molière" and whose Epsom-Wells displays lewd excesses.

1753

1 CIBBER, THEOPHILUS, [and ROBERT SHIELS]. The Lives of the Poets of Great Britain and Ireland. Compiled from . . . the MS. Notes of the late ingenious Mr. Coxeter and others. Vol. 3. London: R. Griffiths, pp. 48-54.

Mac Flecknoe misrepresents Shadwell, for he wrote comedies with "fine strokes of humour" and, in general, excellent characterization. Cibber and Shiels depend heavily on Langbaine (S.1691.3) and probably also on Jacob (S.1719.3).

1758

1 ANON. "The Poetical Scale." *Literary Magazine* 3 (January):7.
"As to *Shadwell* . . . he is below all criticism."

1762

1 ANON. *A New and General Biographical Dictionary*. Vol. 10. London: for T. Osborne et al., pp. 336-38.

Even in his poetry, notwithstanding Dryden's opinion, Shadwell "did not write nonsense," and his comedies are often "very good" with their "fine strokes of humor" and "original characters, strongly marked and well sustained." This article is repeated, with only minor variations, in at least the first six editions of the *Encyclopaedia Britannica*.

1763

1 ANON. *Biographia Britannica*. Vol. 6, Pt. 1. London: J. Walthoe et al., pp. 3624-27.

Paraphrases Cibber and Shiels (S.1753.1).

1764

1 [BAKER, DAVID ERSKINE.] *The Companion to the Play-house*. Vols. 1 and 2. London: T. Becket & P.A. Dehondt, C. Henderson, T. Davies, n. pag.

Although Shadwell "fell vastly short of Ben Jonson" and, in *The Tempest* and *Timon*, could not improve on Shakespeare, his comedies abound in original, well-drawn, well-sustained characters, especially humors characters. *Epsom-Wells* has "much of the true *Vis comica*," and *The Scowrers*, *The Woman-Captain*, and most notably *The Virtuoso* please us with their variety of character types and "multiplicity of . . . incidents." *The Virtuoso*, additionally, is very original, and the *Sullen Lovers* is "extremely regular." On the other hand, *The Libertine* is too irregular in design, offensively impious in sentiments, improbable in the depiction of Don John, and too horrid in the final scenes for stage representation.

1767

1 GOLDSMITH, OLIVER. Remarks on *Mac Flecknoe*. In *The Beauties of English Poesy. Selected by Oliver Goldsmith*. Vol. 1. London: for William Griffin, p. 167.

Today, we think Shadwell is below sustained criticism, "that Dryden's descending to such game was like an eagle's stooping to catch flies."

1770

1 [TOWERS, JOSEPH.] "The Life of Andrew Marvell." In British Biography. Vol. 6. London: for R. Goadby, pp. 292-94.

Quotes Baker (S.1764.1) and asserts that Shadwell "possessed real abilities," though he was not Dryden's equal.

1774

1 ANON. "The Fable of the New Comedy called, The Choleric Man." Universal Magazine 55 (December):316-17.

Though Cumberland fails to acknowledge it, he is probably more deeply indebted to Shadwell than to Terence.

2 ANON. "The Theatre: Drury Lane Theatre--Choleric Man." St. James's Chronicle; Or, British Evening-Post no. 2161 (20-22 December), n. pag.

Contains separate remarks on Terence, Molière, Shadwell, and Cumberland, presenting Shadwell as a "rough" and "manly" specialist in comic portraits of lower-class types. His Squire of Alsatia succeeds in its "honest design" to expose "petty Villains lurking in a privileged Place."

1776

1 MORTIMER, THOMAS. "The Life of John Dryden." In The British Plutarch. Rev. ed. Vol. 5. London: for E. & C. Diley, p. 205.

Calls Shadwell "a very indifferent poet." I find no evidence of an earlier edition of Mortimer's work.

1780

1 DAVIES, THOMAS. Memoirs of the Life of David Garrick, Esq. "New Edition." Vol. 2. London: for the author, p. 221.

Shadwell's Timon is better than Cumberland's, but both alterers were unequal to their task.

1791

1 [GARDENSTONE, FRANCIS GARDEN, LORD.] "Remarks on the Present State of the English Drama." In Miscellanies in Prose and Verse. Edinburgh: J. Robertson, pp. 145-46.

Despite incoherent sequences of scenes, improper characters, and slight plot, A True Widow has "easy and natural" language, "true unaffected wit." The Squire of Alsatia, however, "falls off remarkably, after the first act, which is a piece of true comedy"; yet its various episodes are amusing, its characters "natural" and "just" (especially Sir Edward), and its moral "liberal and good." On page 149, Gardenstone discusses what may be Shadwell's version of The Miser, saying that it is executed in good taste but that its chambermaid and footman have been Anglicized beyond the "simplicity" of the other characters.

1792

1 ANON. A New Theatrical Dictionary. London: S. Bladon, pp. 78, 143, 270, 292, 296, 310, 324.
Borrows practically every word on each of the plays from Baker's Companion (S.1764.1).

1800

1 DIBDIN, CHARLES. A Complete History of the Stage. Vol. 4. London: C. Dibdin, pp. 181-83, 245-46.
Regards Shadwell as a considerably better writer than Dryden presents us in Mac Flecknoe. The Sullen Lovers and The Scowrers are indifferent works. The Squire of Alsatia has "too much of the low and the vulgar," and Timon is no improvement on Shakespeare. Epsom-Wells, however, has "great merit"; The Miser is "very good" (though inferior to Fielding's version); The Libertine succeeds in evoking terror; and The Virtuoso, A True Widow, and The Woman-Captain are delightfully full of strong characters, lively satire, and "whimsical incidents."

2 WATKINS, JOHN. An Universal Biographical and Historical Dictionary. London: T. Davison & T. Gillet, n. pag.
Many of Shadwell's comedies "possess great merit."

1806

1 CUMBERLAND, RICHARD. Memoirs of Richard Cumberland. Written by Himself. New York: Brisban & Brannan, p. 135.
"Shadwell's comedy is little better than a brothel."

1807

1 SOUTHEY, ROBERT, ed. "Thomas Shadwell." In Specimens of the Later English Poets. Vol. 1. London: Longman, pp. 62-63.
Shadwell's comedies are full of indecencies, absurdities, and gross caricatures; he was a true Mac Flecknoe.

1808

1 SCOTT, WALTER, ed. Commentary on _Mac Flecknoe_. In _The Works of John Dryden_. Vol. 10. London: William Miller; Edinburgh: James Ballantyne, p. 430.

Agrees with Dryden that Shadwell had real faults: ineptness "at lyrical composition" in _Psyche_, "clumsy and coarse limning of . . . fine gentlemen in his comedies," and "his presumptuous imitation of Jonson." But Dryden ignores Shadwell's considerable assets: "insights into human life," knowledge of "the foibles and absurdities displayed in individual pursuits," and "bold though coarse delineation of character."

2 _____. "The Life of John Dryden." In _The Works of John Dryden_. Vol. 1. London: William Miller; Edinburgh: James Ballantyne, pp. 260, 263, 265, 274, 279.

Although Shadwell was "a worse poet than Settle" and was "deficient in that liveliness of fancy which is necessary to produce vivacity of dialogue," he was a perceptive observer of nature and "excelled even Dryden in the lower walks of comedy." He wrote _The Lancashire-Witches_ "to expose to hatred and ridicule the religion of the successor to the crown."

1811

1 [SCOTT, WALTER.] "Remarks on English Comedy." In _The Modern British Drama_. Vol. 3. London: William Miller; Edinburgh: James Ballantyne, p. iii.

"The heavy and forgotten Shadwell" vainly imitated "the style of Ben Jonson, and affected to draw characters of humour."

1814

1 AIKIN, JOHN. "Shadwell, Thomas." In _General Biography; or, Lives, Critical and Historical_. Compiled by Aikin and William Johnston. Vol. 9. London: for John Stockdale et al., p. 121.

Shadwell has not left a high reputation, "and his works have disappeared from the stage." He was thought to have mastered the delineation of humors characters, but most of those he created were "rather from his own conception, than from real nature."

1816

1 CHALMERS, ALEXANDER. _The General Biographical Dictionary_. Vol. 27. London: J. Nichols & Son, pp. 368-69.

Specializing in "original characters, strongly marked and well sustained," Shadwell was the best comic writer of his age and the best reflector of contemporary social life.

1817

1 COLERIDGE, SAMUEL TAYLOR. Chapter 23 in Biographia Literaria; or, Biographical Sketches of My Literary Life and Opinions. Vol. 2. London: Rest Fenner, pp. 260-72.

Finds The Libertine a convincingly imaginative work, its characters being, like Milton's Satan or Shakespeare's Caliban, "impersonated abstractions" that are wholly intelligible within the world of the play. That "happy balance of the generic with the individual" is achieved in Don John, who shows us that the highest personal attributes--intellectual superiority, self-reliance, gentlemanly charm and courage, and even honor--need not be accompanied by virtue. If not properly subordinated to conscience and the sense of a superior being, these traits may become means to "entire wickedness," to "ends . . . unhuman."

1819

1 HAZLITT, WILLIAM. Lectures on the English Comic Writers. Delivered at the Surry Institution. London: Taylor & Hessey, p. 103.

The Libertine "is full of spirit; but it is the spirit of licentiousness and impiety."

1821

1 ANON. "On the Alleged Decline of Dramatic Writing." Blackwood's Edinburgh Magazine 9, no. 51 (June):280-82.

Although Shadwell may be called the best tragedian after Dryden, Lee, and Otway, all his works are dull, "vulgar," "uncouth," and "destitute of wit." He has, nevertheless, left us some original characters, and his Libertine is an exciting, if dissolute, play, which would have been better without its comic scenes.

1828

1 ANON. "The Dramatic Works of Thomas Shadwell, Esq. in four Volumes." Retrospective Review, n.s. 2:55-96.

Pleads for a more sympathetic reading of Shadwell who, despite the lewdness of his comedies, was "a man of sense and information," an "accomplished observer of human nature" endowed with a "ready power of seizing the ridiculous" and a "considerable fund of humour." Through their amusing characterizations, their energy, and their vivid pictures of contemporary manners, plays like Epsom-Wells, The Squire of Alsatia, Bury-Fair, and The Volunteers compensate for moral indecencies. Sullen Lovers, A True Widow, and The Miser will also be found to be well worth reading. But Shadwell should more often have emulated his success in The Woman-Captain, which is not only one of his best, in terms of characters and effective scenes, but also "the least licentious." A few of his works fail because of some major deficiency--The Humorists because of a poor plot, The Virtuoso because it discourages scientific study, The Lancashire-Witches because Tegue is a "monstrous character" and the occult episodes are extravagant and unconvincing. The Amorous Bigotte and The Scowrers are indifferent productions, and Psyche is "destitute of merit."

2 LAMB, CHARLES. "Shakespeare's Improvers." In The Works of Charles and Mary Lamb. Edited by E.V. Lucas. Vol. 1. London: Methuen, 1903, p. 322.

Partly to satisfy his audience's demand for intrigue and amorous "drivel," Shadwell gives his Timon a loving female, Evandra, and gives her a rival, "thus making the moral of the piece in showing--not the hollowness of friendship conciliated by a mere undistinguishing prodigality, but--the superiority of woman's love to the friendship of men." I was unable to see the first edition of this essay in the London Spectator of 1828.

3 [SCOTT, WALTER.] "Molière." Foreign Quarterly Review 2:315.

Bury-Fair shows that Shadwell was a lesser Ben Jonson, an effective painter of humorous characters and manners; "his works ought not to be lost sight of by the English antiquary." This piece is included in The Prose Works of Sir Walter Scott, Bart., vol. 17 (Edinburgh: A. & C. Black, 1861), the cited passage appearing on pp. 152-53.

1832

1 [GENEST, JOHN.] Some Account of the English Stage, from the Restoration in 1660 to 1830. Bath: H.E. Carrington; London: Thomas Rodd, 1:86, 97-98, 110, 119, 137, 163-67, 186-89, 247-51, 265, 282-83, 314-17, 398, 459-60, 472-73, 476; 2:8-9, 28-29, 40-44.

Briefly summarizes plots and notes sources and casts for most of the plays, often adding evaluative comments. Shadwell's worst work appears in Psyche (a "dull" spectacle using Molière and failing to match Heywood) and Timon (the additional females and the character of Flavius spoil the original), and his best plays are Epsom-Wells and The Squire of Alsatia (which Genest briefly compares with Terence). Designated as "very good" are The Woman-Captain and The Scowrers, and the "good" include The Humorists (which says more about venereal disease than any other play), A True Widow, The Lancashire-Witches (though marred by presenting the witches as real; "by no means a political play," it was unjustly censured), and The Amorous Bigotte (though its satire on Roman Catholicism is out of place). The Miser, The Libertine (with its "highly finished character" of Don John), and The Virtuoso (despite some "heavy" scenes) are "pretty good." Only "tolerable," however, are The Sullen Lovers ("sadly deficient in plot and incident," "very happy" in its humors characters), The Royal Shepherdess (with its "unnatural plot" and indifferent serious scenes), Bury-Fair, and The Volunteers. Shadwell is remarkable for his lack of bawdy and profaneness (except in Epsom-Wells and The Virtuoso).

1833

1 HUNT, LEIGH. "A Walk to Chelsea." In Leigh Hunt's Political and Occasional Essays. Edited by Laurence Huston Houtchens and Carolyn Washburn Houtchens. New York and London: Columbia University Press, 1962, p. 333.

Shadwell was "under-rated by Dryden, and more over-rated by his party." I was unable to see the first edition of this essay in the London Weekly True Sun for 8 December 1833.

1836

1 SOUTHEY, ROBERT. "Life of Cowper." In The Works of William Cowper, Esq. Vol. 2. London: Baldwin & Cradock, p. 112.

As demonstrated by his despicable adaptation of Timon of Athens, Shadwell is unworthy even of negative criticism. He was a worse poet laureate than Tate, and his "bust in Westminster Abbey ought to have been cast in either lead or in brass, or in an emblematic amalgam of the two metals."

1838

1 CUNNINGHAM, GEORGE GODFREY. "Thomas Shadwell." In Lives of Eminent and Illustrious Englishmen. Vol. 4. Glasgow: A. Fullarton, pp. 297-98.

Shadwell's plays are too often licentious, his Psyche is "utterly contemptible," he has "mangled" Molière, and his treatment of Shakespeare shows "besotted tastelessness."

2 DUNHAM, SAMUEL ASTLEY. "Thomas Shadwell." In Lives of the Most Eminent Literary and Scientific Men of Great Britain. Lardner's Cabinet Cyclopaedia, vol. 3. London: Longman et al., pp. 155-64.

Although Psyche degraded the theater to a place of mere entertainment, and Timon is a "profanation" of Shakespeare, Shadwell usually wrote good plays, if inferior to those of Dryden or Jonson. Even The Libertine, despite its "over-drawn" villain, has an impressive catastrophe. Epsom-Wells, A True Widow, and The Woman-Captain are genuine comedies, "rich in humour, and diversified and well sustained in character," and many of his other comedies are most agreeable: Sullen Lovers, The Humorists (contains "well-pointed satire"), The Miser (better than other versions), and The Volunteers ("unabated" power of characterization). The Virtuoso, also a good play, "did not satirize the pursuit of knowledge, but the bye-roads men took to find it, and the trifling objects which they seized by the way."

1839

1 HALLAM, HENRY. Introduction to the Literature of Europe, in the 15th, 16th, and 17th Centuries. Vol. 4. Paris: A. & W. Galignani, p. 281.

Shadwell, Etherege, and Behn "have endeavoured to make the stage as immoral as their talents permitted," but at least Shadwell and Etherege were "not destitute of humour."

1843

1 CHAMBERS, ROBERT. Cyclopaedia of English Literature. Vol. 1. Edinburgh: William & Robert Chambers, p. 392.

Shadwell "possessed no inconsiderable comic power. His pictures of society are . . . coarse . . . but . . . often true and well-drawn."

1845

1 CRAIK, GEORGE L. Sketches of the History of Literature and Learning in England. Vol. 4. London: Charles Knight, p. 139.

Shadwell's works are "hardly worth while to mention."

1849

1 TICKNOR, GEORGE. History of Spanish Literature. Vol. 2. London: John Murray, p. 288, n.4.

The Libertine is "too gross to be tolerated anywhere now-a-days, and besides has no literary merit."

1851

1 MILLS, ABRAHAM. The Literature and the Literary Men of Great Britain and Ireland. Vol. 2. New York: Harper & Bros., pp. 73-74.

Quotes Chambers (S.1843.1) without acknowledgement.

1853

1 AUSTIN, WILTSHIRE STANTON, and JOHN RALPH. "Thomas Shadwell." In The Lives of the Poets-Laureate. London: Richard Bentley, pp. 183-95.

Shadwell's plays are neither profound nor subtle, but they can still amuse us with their perception of human foibles and accurate pictures of contemporary life.

2 SPALDING, WILLIAM. The History of English Literature. Edinburgh: Oliver & Boyd, p. 297.

Superior to Dryden in comedy, Shadwell wrote plays characterized by "a great deal of clumsy painting that looks very like real low-life."

1854

1 BELL, ROBERT. "Thomas Shadwell. 1640-1692." In The Annotated Edition of the English Poets. London: John W. Parker & Son, p. 248.

"His comedies, admirable as pictures of contemporary manners, supplied an appropriate setting for his coarse and reckless verses."

1855

1 MACAULAY, THOMAS BABINGTON. The History of England from the Accession of James the Second. Vol. 4. London: Longman, Brown, Green, & Longmans, pp. 65-66, 323.

The Volunteers amused the town with "the character of a courageous but prodigal and effeminate coxcomb"; its "best scene is that in which four or five stern Nonconformists . . . examine the question whether the godly may lawfully hold stock in a Company for bringing over Chinese ropedancers."

1857

1 KNIGHT, CHARLES. The English Cyclopaedia: Biography. Vol. 5. London: Bradbury & Evans, p. 434.

"A man of much tact, observation, and liveliness," Shadwell was a much better writer than Dryden makes him out to be, though his comedies are marred by his "extreme negligence and haste in writing."

1860

1 HALLIWELL, JAMES O. A Dictionary of Old English Plays. London: John Russell Smith, pp. 15, 171, 221.

The Amorous Bigotte is inferior to The Lancashire-Witches; The Miser is considerably changed by additions to the original; and The Scowrers "contains a great deal of low humour."

1861

1 ANON. "Choice Notes by William Oldys, Norroy King-at-arms." N&Q 23:182.

In learning, plotting, characterization, and morals, Shadwell was no match for Jonson. Captain Hackum in The Squire of Alsatia was "drawn . . . to expose Bully Dawson."

1864

1 DORAN, JOHN. "Their Majesties' Servants." Annals of the English Stage, from Thomas Betterton to Edmund Kean. Vol. 1. London: William H. Allen, pp. 205, 211-13.

Shadwell wrote "brisk" comedies full of "well conceived, and strongly marked" characters, his best works being The Squire of Alsatia, Bury-Fair, and Epsom-Wells.

1870

1 ALLIBONE, S. AUSTIN. A Critical Dictionary of English Literature. Vol. 2. London: Trübner; Philadelphia: J.B. Lippincott, pp. 2004-5.

Considers Shadwell an "indecent playwright."

1873

1 ANON. "Thomas Shadwell." New Monthly Magazine, n.s. 3:292-97, 353-61.

Dryden's attack on Shadwell was unfair, for Shadwell "possessed a fancy as bright, an imagination as lofty, and a humour as subtle, as any dramatist of his time. His style, if less polished than that of Congreve, is more vigorous. His dialogue, if less laden with wit, is more natural. In humour he approaches Farquhar, the best of the Restoration writers of comedy," and if he is indecent, he is less so than his contemporaries. In The Lancashire-Witches, with its straightforward action, natural characters, and unstudied dialogue, the supernatural scenes are made integral to the main plot. When seen by dupes with overactive imaginations, the witches are represented as horridly real, but when perceived through the lenses of common sense, they become old hags affecting witchery to make a living.

2 MORLEY, HENRY. A First Sketch of English Literature. London, Paris, and New York: Cassell, Petter, & Galpin, p. 678.
Shadwell's comedies, such as Epsom-Wells, Bury-Fair, and The Scowrers, clearly reflect the surfaces "of certain forms" of Restoration life. The Lancashire-Witches ridicules both Roman Catholic and Anglican clergymen, and offers "one of the earliest specimens of the stage Irishman."

1875

1 WARD, ADOLPHUS WILLIAM. A History of English Dramatic Literature to the Death of Queen Anne. Vol. 2. London: Macmillan, pp. 572-77.
Briefly notices sources, contemporary contexts, and influences of major plays, stressing the debt to Jonson and the gross indecency of Epsom-Wells and The Volunteers. The Virtuoso is given attention for its characterizations, The Squire of Alsatia for its social critique, and The Volunteers for its approximation to genuine "comedy of character." However deficient in artistry and moral texture, Shadwell's comedies are remarkable for their original characters and moral purpose. The author's hatred of "political shams and social abuses," indeed of "much that was really inimical to the national future, contributed to arrest the decay to which English comedy was hastening."

1878

1 MORLEY, HENRY. English Plays. Cassell's Library of English Literature, vol. 3. London, Paris, and New York: Cassell, Petter, & Galpin, p. 355.
Lacking first-rate poetic or dramatic powers, Shadwell "painted, like Etherege, the body of life, with conventional opinions of his day to stand for its spiritual truths."

1879

1 HAMILTON, WALTER. The Poets Laureate of England. London: Elliot Stock, pp. 112-23.
Shadwell's plays "have . . . passed into unmerited oblivion." The Virtuoso exemplifies both the "coarseness of . . . language" and the excellence in humors characterization, social observation, and wit, which are found in his better works.

1881

1 CUMMINGS, WILLIAM H. Henry Purcell 1658-1695. London: Sampson Low, Marston, pp. 26, 28.

With its "very bold" music, The Libertine merits a revival. Timon of Athens, however, is a "mutilation" of Shakespeare.

2 SAINTSBURY, GEORGE EDWARD BATEMAN. Dryden. New York: Harper & Bros., pp. 79, 86-87.

Sullen Lovers is "a much more genuinely amusing play than any of Dryden's," and The Squire of Alsatia, Bury-Fair, Epsom-Wells, and The Virtuoso are all important as social documents. Except for exploiting his talent for "detecting or imagining" human oddities, however, Shadwell misused his genius; and he possessed no critical faculties, for with the comic he indiscriminately mixes some of the dullest, coarsest matter to be found in English letters.

1883

1 DENNIS, JOHN. Heroes of Literature. English Poets. London: SPCK; New York: E. & J.B. Young, pp. 163, 175.

Sees Shadwell as a coarse and clever playwright but a dull poet.

1886

1 ANON. "Shadwell, Thomas." In Encyclopaedia Britannica. 9th ed. Vol. 21. New York: Charles Scribner's Sons, p. 727.

Using Jonson as his model, but drawing his materials from daily life, Shadwell wrote comedies that show "considerable cleverness in caricaturing the oddities of the time."

1888

1 GOSSE, EDMUND. Life of William Congreve. London: Walter Scott; New York: Thomas Whittaker; Toronto: W.J. Gage, p. 41.

Shadwell "preserved the old coarse tradition of Restoration comedy, with its violent demarcation of character, its fantastic jargon, and its vulgarly emphatic incident."

1889

1 BAKER, HENRY BARTON. The London Stage: Its History and Traditions from 1576 to 1888. Vol. 1. London: W.H. Allen, p. 47.

"An inferior Ben Jonson," Shadwell was "rather coarse than licentious."

2 BULLEN, A.H., ed. Preface to Musa Proterva: Love-Poems of the Restoration. London: Privately printed, p. vi.

"Shadwell is thoroughly representative of his age; he was . . . Jonson stripped of his graces." Though his plays "are well worth reading," they entirely lack "higher poetry."

1891

1 GISSING, GEORGE. New Grub Street: A Novel. Vol. 1. London: Smith, Elder, p. 64.

Notwithstanding Dryden's unfair satire, says Alfred Yule, "I put Shadwell very high among the dramatists of his time," for he "has distinct vigour of dramatic conception."

1895

1 COLLINS, JOHN CHURTON. "John Dryden." In Essays and Studies. London and New York: Macmillan, pp. 45-46.

Shadwell merits "some distinction" for his "rich vein of comic humour, keen power of observation, and . . . real dramatic power both in vivid portraiture and in the presentation of incidents." The Virtuoso is "truly amusing," and Epsom-Wells and The Squire of Alsatia are graphic social documents.

2 FURNESS, HORACE HOWARD, ed. Preface to A New Variorum Edition of Shakespeare, Vol. 9: The Tempest. Philadelphia and London: Lippincott, pp. viii-ix.

The 1674 Tempest is a "monstrosity,--to be fully hated it must be fully seen." It is the fruit of its times.

3 GARNETT, RICHARD. The Age of Dryden. London: George Bell & Sons, pp. 116-18.

Shadwell's characters are Dickensian, and "his coarsely indecent, but humorous comedies" instructively reflect "the manners of the time," as best illustrated by Epsom-Wells, The Squire of Alsatia, and The Volunteers.

4 HOWLAND, FRANCES LOUISE MORSE. The Laureates of England from Ben Jonson to Alfred Tennyson. New York and London: Frederick A. Stokes, pp. 52-55.

In depicting humors and manners, Shadwell "showed far more insight and real power than Dryden," but he had neither the intellect for probing beneath the surfaces nor the moral commitment needed for reforming or preaching. He could create original characters but could not develop them; his plots are interesting but irregular; and most of his works are sadly "disfigured" by "rank impurity."

1896

1 WRIGHT, J.C. *The Poets Laureate from the Earliest Times to the Present*. London: Jarrold, pp. 23-24.

Generally accepts Dryden's devaluation and wonders how Dryden could ever have considered Shadwell a serious rival.

1897

1 AITKIN, GEORGE ATHERTON. "Shadwell, Thomas." In *Dictionary of National Biography*. Edited by Sidney Lee. Vol. 51. London: Smith, Elder, pp. 340-43.

Inventive, acutely observant, but lacking wit, Shadwell "vainly tried to imitate" Jonson and "was grossly indecent without designing to be corrupt." His best comedies--*Epsom-Wells*, *The Scowrers*, and *The Squire of Alsatia*--succeed in spite of their coarseness.

2 BEBER, OSCAR. *Thom. Shadwell's Bearbeitung des Shakespeare'schen 'Timon of Athens.'* Rostock: Carl Hinstorffs Buchdruckerei, 55 pp.

Compares Shakespeare's *Timon* with Shadwell's adaptation, act by act, with emphasis on plot, dramatic composition, style, language, and metrics. Shadwell's version lacks artistry but interestingly mirrors his times. Its sources are the Shakespeare play and the *Ur*-Timon.

1898

1 SAINTSBURY, GEORGE E.B. *A Short History of English Literature*. New York: Macmillan, pp. 487-88.

Shadwell could not handle witty dialogue or poetic language, and he was imitative (mainly of Jonson) and coarse, yet if he "imagined little, he heard and saw much and he enables us to see and hear" what he did. *Sullen Lovers* presages all his future plays in terms of style, and *The Squire of Alsatia* influenced Scott and Macaulay.

1899

1 CRULL, FRANZ. *Thomas Shadwell's (John Ozell's) und Henry Fielding's Comoedien 'The Miser' in ihrem Verhältnis unter einander und zu ihrer gemeinsamen Quelle*. Rostock: Privately printed, 72 pp.

In extended comparisons, finds that Shadwell's *The Miser* (1672) is less convincing than Molière's *L'Avare* (1668) and that it had little influence on Fielding's *The Miser* (1733). Ozell's version (1732) is not discussed because it was unavailable in Germany.

1900

1 SAMTER, FRIEDA. Studien zu Ben Jonson mit Berücksichtigung von Shadwells Dramen. [Bern: n.p.], 70 pp.

On pages vii and 41-60, Shadwell is discussed as an admirer of Ben Jonson and the "humours" method of characterization. In comparisons of The Humorists with Jonson's Every Man in His Humour and Every Man out of His Humour, and of Epsom-Wells with Jonson's Bartholomew Fair, the resemblance between the latter two plays is shown to be not very strong. Bury-Fair, furthermore, is seen to reflect both Jonson's Epicoene and Molière's Précieuses ridicules.

1901

1 HASTINGS, CHARLES. The Theatre, Its Development in France and England. Translated by Frances A. Welby. London: Duckworth, p. 333.

Shadwell's "comedies of manners" are "amusing, though coarse-grained"; Sullen Lovers is one of his best.

2 LOUNSBURY, THOMAS R. Shakespeare as a Dramatic Artist. New York: Scribner's; London: Edward Arnold, pp. 310-11.

Discusses Shadwell's adaptation of Shakespeare's Timon.

3 THOMPSON, A. HAMILTON. A History of English Literature. London: John Murray, p. 358.

Epsom-Wells ranks "far above the average minor pieces of the time."

1903

1 BATES, ALFRED, ed. The Drama, Its History, Literature and Influence on Civilization. Vol. 14, British Drama. London and New York: Smart & Stanley, pp. 94-96.

Although Shadwell showed "considerable cleverness in caricaturing the oddities of the time," Dryden's depiction of him as dull was substantially accurate.

2 GOSSE, EDMUND. English Literature: An Illustrated Record. Vol. 3, From Milton to Johnson. New York and London: Macmillan, pp. 109-10.

Shadwell was by no means dull. As exemplified by The Virtuoso, most of his comedies of "manners" are both humorous and inventive.

3 SAINTSBURY, GEORGE, ed. Introduction and prefaces to the individual plays. In Thomas Shadwell. Mermaid Series. London: T. Fisher & Unwin; New York: Charles Scribner's Sons, pp. xi-xxviii, 3, 121, 232, 349.

Shadwell "has a much greater command of comic incident and situation, and a much sharper eye for a play, than Dryden himself." His lack of Wycherley's wit and imagination, and of Etherege's refinement and critical powers, contributes to making him Farquhar's equal as a faithful observer of life. He may write flat, long-winded dialogue and foul language, but he knows what will work on the stage. The Lancashire-Witches suffers from the burden of those explanatory notes that the author appended, and The Libertine is a "jumble of crimes that are merely farcical, and horrors which make one yawn." Epsom-Wells, however, is notably true to life, and Sullen Lovers is filled with amusing characters, "bustle and 'go.'" In A True Widow the characters are also excellent, especially Lady Busy, while "the playhouse scenes are curiously fresh and vivid." Shadwell's best comedies of "manners" are The Squire of Alsatia and Bury-Fair, though the former is almost spoiled by its uninteresting female characters and its overworking of the Terentian theme. Bury-Fair is his best, liveliest, least coarse comedy; its fair scenes and wit combats are convincing; its females are better drawn than usual; and its humors, such as Trim and Sir Humphrey Noddy, are clever samplings from human quirks.

1904

1 BAYLEY, A.R. "Shadwell's 'Bury Fair.'" N&Q 109:221-22.
Traces several allusions, notably one to "the 'wench' who . . . was associated with . . . Beaumont and Fletcher."

2 LAWRENCE, W.J. "Did Thomas Shadwell Write an Opera on 'The Tempest'?" Anglia 27:205-17.
Discusses the special frontispiece as evidence that the play was considered an opera, and notes Shadwell's distinctive "masque of Neptune at the close."

3 _____. "Plays within Plays." Englische Studien 33:401.
"A theatre within a theatre was first shown in England in" A True Widow, where Shadwell used it for "blunt satire on contemporary manners."

4 REIHMANN, OSKAR. Thomas Shadwells Tragödie 'The Libertine' und ihr Verhältnis zu den vorausgehenden Bearbeitungen der Don Juan-Sage. Leipzig: Heinrich John, 69 pp.
Discusses the plot, genesis, and early reception of The Libertine, a play that suited the lascivious taste of the Restoration audiences. Its major source was Rosimond's Nouveau Festin de Pierre ou l'Athée foudroyé (1669), and its minor sources were de Villiers' Les Festin de Pierre ou le fils criminel (1659) and Tirso de Molina's Burlador de Sevilla y Convidado de piedra (1630)

5 SEILER, OTTO. The Sources of Thomas Shadwell's Comedy "Bury Fair." Basel: Friedrich Reinhardt, 63 pp.

Sketches Shadwell's life, offers bibliographies of material related to this and his other plays, and summarizes the plots of Bury-Fair, Newcastle's Triumphant Widow, and Behn's False Count, the latter two plays having contributed characters to Shadwell's work. In Bury-Fair, he is also indebted to Jonson and Molière.

6 STEIGER, AUGUST. Thomas Shadwell's 'Libertine,' a Complementary Study to the Don Juan-Literature. Berne: Büchler, 74 pp.

Scarcely worth comparing with Tirso, Molière, or Mozart, Shadwell is the grossest and bloodiest "of all the Don Juan-dramatists," yet The Libertine is the most important of the English variations on the theme, and underneath the author's pandering to corrupt taste, the play has "a moral tendency." Basing his work on Rosimond's Nouveau festin de Pierre, Shadwell suppressed the reflective part and increased the action; though he tried to make his hero "a philosophical libertine," he created an impossible character, "a beast." He succeeds better with the minor characters.

1905

1 AMMAN, ERNST. Analysis of Thomas Shadwell's Lancashire Witches and Tegue O'Divelly the Irish Priest. Berne: Buchdruckerei Gustav Grunau, 60 pp.

Intersperses commentary with plot summary, identifying the target of each humors character and arguing for Shadwell's patriotism, morality, and deliberately ambiguous presentation of the occult (that is, to fascinate the ignorant and to show the enlightened that such superstition can be rationally explained). Shadwell's life and critical reception are surveyed, as are the backgrounds of his humors method and uses of the supernatural (witchcraft in England, magic and charms in Middleton and Shakespeare, documents of witch lore, Heywood's Late Lancashire Witches). His originality, piety (he had no intention of attacking the Anglican church), and social satire are stressed.

1906

1 CHARLANNE, LOUIS. L'Influence Francaise en Angleterre aux XVIIe Siècle. Paris: Société Francaise d'Imprimerie et de Librairie, 634 pp.

Chapter 9, section 2 discusses Molière and Shadwell.

2 CLARKE, ERNEST. "The 'Tempest' as an Opera." Athenaeum, no. 4113 (25 August), pp. 222-23.

Offers evidence for attributing the 1674 Tempest to Shadwell. See Lawrence (S.1906.6).

3 ERICHSEN, ASMUS. Thomas Shadwell's Komödie 'The Sullen Lovers' in ihrem Verhältnis zu Molière's Komödien 'Le Misanthrope' und 'Les Fâcheux'. Flensburg: J.B. Meyer, 50 pp.

Summarizes the plot of Shadwell's play and shows that both plot and main characters were influenced by Molière's Le Misanthrope, whereas the "situations" can be traced back to Les Fâcheux.

4 HARVEY-JELLIE, W. Les Sources du Thêatre Anglais a l'époque de la Restauration. Paris: Librairie Générale de Droit et de Jurisprudence, pp. 109-10.

Sees Shadwell as an imitator of the French, as one who failed to appreciate Shakespeare's genius, and as a disciple of Jonson who, nevertheless, could write humors as well as Molière. His plays, such as The Royal Shepherdess, Sullen Lovers, The Libertine, Psyche, Bury-Fair, and Timon, are not without "a certain merit."

5 KILBOURNE, FREDERICK W. Alterations and Adaptations of Shakespeare. Boston: Poet Lore, pp. 34, 133-37.

Mentions the revision of The Tempest, but says it has not survived, and asserts that Shadwell's Timon does not improve on Shakespeare, though the new scenes "in which the women appear . . . are not wholly without power, for Shadwell was a better dramatist than Dryden's . . . satire would lead us to think."

6 LAWRENCE, W.J. "Shadwell's Opera of 'The Tempest.'" Anglia 29:539-41.

Insinuates that Clarke (S.1906.2) is a plagiarist (see S.1904.2).

7 RICHARDS, ALFRED E. "A Literary Link between Thomas Shadwell and Christian Felix Weisse." PMLA 21:808-30.

Argues that Shadwell, not his brother-in-law Thomas Jevon, wrote most of The Devil of a Wife (1686), and traces adaptations of this play through The Devil to Pay (a musical of 1731) and Felix Weisse's Die verwandelten Weiber oder der Teufel is Los (published in 1768 but first performed in 1752).

1907

1 HEINEMANN, GEORG. Shadwell-Studien. Kiel: Privately printed, 105 pp.

Summarizes the plots of three Shadwell plays and compares each with its sources: The Squire of Alsatia with Terence's Adelphi, Psyche with Molière's Psyché, Bury-Fair with Molière's Précieuses ridicules and Les Femmes Savantes and with Newcastle's Triumphant Widow.

2 KERBY, W. MOSELEY. Molière and the Restoration Comedy in England. Rennes: n.p., pp. 30-38.

At least five of Shadwell's plays are indebted to Molière. Sullen Lovers is "regular and natural" but lacks the spirit of Les Fâcheux. The Squire of Alsatia is effective social satire but has "a coarseness and a vulgarity" not found in Molière's École des maris. Bury-Fair is "very poor" in comparison with Les Précieuses ridicules, and The Miser successfully adapts L'Avare because Shadwell retains "everything" from his source. Psyche is strongly indebted to Psyché, and The Libertine owes a great deal to Don Juan, ou le Festin de Pierre (even though their plots do not match).

3 VICKERY, WILLIS, ed. Introduction to The Life of Timon of Athens (The Text of the Folio of 1623, with That as Made into a Play by Thomas Shadwell in 1678). New York: Shakespeare Society of New York, pp. ix-xvii.

As illustrated by the effective scenes involving Evandra and Melissa, Shadwell was a better dramatist than Dryden would have us believe. Nevertheless, his Timon does not succeed as a revision of Shakespeare, especially considering that Shadwell ruined the dramatic excellence of Shakespeare's Flavius and Apemantus.

1908

1 MARKS, JEANNETTE. English Pastoral Drama . . . (1660-1798). London: Methuen, pp. 54-57, 128.

The Royal Shepherdess exhibits some "excellent blank verse," memorable aphoristic remarks, striking spectacle, and at least one scene (between Cleantha and Endymion in Act 3) that is "poetic," "dramatic," and psychologically perceptive. Despite the author's disclaimers, however, it also displays "the extreme licentious element common to most pastoral dramas." Unlike such predecessors as Aminta and The Faithful Shepherdess, which give the impression of innocence and simplicity of life, Shadwell's play is heroic and courtly.

1910

*1 MARTI, PAUL. Fletcher's Play: The Night-Walker and Shadwell's Comedy The Woman Captain. Dissertation, Berne, 75 pp.

Source: Stratman, p. 623.

2 MILES, DUDLEY HOWE. The Influence of Molière on Restoration Comedy. New York: Columbia University Press, pp. 32, 76, 116, 133-35, 194.

In Sullen Lovers, Shadwell "galvanizes" Jonson's humors technique "into strange contortions" while imitating the design of Le Misanthrope; the result fails to achieve unity. The Miser shows the ascendancy of Molière's manners over Jonson's style, and Bury-Fair draws both its design and main characters from Les Précieuses ridicules, though Shadwell achieves some success in Anglicizing what he borrows. Although The Squire of Alsatia is "well-nigh worthless" as literature, lacking both the wit of Etherege or Congreve and the "finish of Dryden or Crowne," it remains interesting as a social document.

3 PABISCH, MARIE. Picaresque Dramas of the 17th and 18th Centuries. Berlin: Mayer & Müller, pp. 26-92.

Uniting Molière and Jonson, but slavishly imitating neither, Shadwell tends to contrast roguery and stupidity in bawdy but morally purposeful plays like Sullen Lovers, The Squire of Alsatia (which has four rogues and which influenced Scott), and The Volunteers. "Shadwell has the knack of catching the fugitive expression of roguery more than any other playwright of his day." Even his courtesans are rogues. Although The Libertine is too coarse and horrible to be effective, The Virtuoso and The Scowrers are fun but indecent, and Epsom-Wells offers vivid portraits of men and manners. Shadwell aims at a wide range of satiric targets as he exploits his special talent for dramatizing human relationships.

4 RISTINE, FRANK HUMPHREY. English Tragicomedy, Its Origin and History. New York: Columbia University Press, pp. 159-60.

Regards The Royal Shepherdess as "only a conglomerate of old tragicomic motives and situations, linked to pastoral chiefly in the figure of the heroine."

1911

1 ANON. "Shadwell, Thomas." In Encyclopaedia Britannica. 11th ed. Vol. 24. New York: Encyclopaedia Britannica, p. 759.

The comedies that Shadwell wrote during the first fourteen years of his career "display a genuine hatred of shams, and a rough but honest moral purpose. They are disfigured by indecencies, but present a vivid picture of contemporary manners." His two best plays are Epsom-Wells and The Squire of Alsatia.

2 LAWRENCE, W.J. "Irish Types in Old-Time English Drama." Anglia 35:350-51.

Shadwell draws "vile caricatures" of the Irish in The Lancashire-Witches and The Amorous Bigotte, "which . . . merely derogate from the fame of the writer."

3 NOTESTEIN, WALLACE. A History of Witchcraft in England from 1588 to 1718. Washington, D.C.: American Historical Association, pp. 306-7.

In *The Lancashire-Witches*, Shadwell shows that he is "not interested in any side of the subject save in its use as literary material."

1912

1 GOSSE, EDMUND, ed. Introduction to *Restoration Plays from Dryden to Farquhar*. London and Toronto: Dent; New York: Dutton, p. xv.

Shadwell's "bustling" comedies, which graft Molière onto Jonson, may have less art and be less modern than Wycherley's, but they "have excellent qualities of humour."

2 SCHELLING, FELIX E. "The Restoration Drama I." In *The Cambridge History of English Literature*. Edited by A.W. Ward and A.R. Waller. Vol. 8. Cambridge: Cambridge University Press, pp. 120, n.2, 134.

Briefly discusses Shadwell's debts to Shakespeare and Molière.

3 WARD, A.W. "Dryden." In *The Cambridge History of English Literature*. Edited by A.W. Ward and A.R. Waller. Vol. 8. Cambridge: Cambridge University Press, p. 31.

Notes Shadwell's contributions to *The Tempest*.

4 WHIBLEY, CHARLES. "The Restoration Drama II." In *The Cambridge History of English Literature*. Edited by A.W. Ward and A.R. Waller. Vol. 8. Cambridge: Cambridge University Press, pp. 173-74.

Lacking "the sense of style, the mastery of language," Shadwell imitated Jonson's method of characterization and borrowed much of his action from Molière. His best play is *Bury-Fair*. In *The Miser*, he perverts Molière's *L'Avare*, and in *Timon*, he mangles Shakespeare. Among the "many faults" of *The Squire of Alsatia* are its "incredible" story and tactlessly handled dialect.

1913

1 BROWNE, WILLIAM HAND. "Thomas Shadwell." *SR* 21:257-76.

Despite his grossness and imitativeness, Shadwell wrote a number of very good "low" comedies with "more ease and lightness than Dryden." *Epsom-Wells* and *The Woman-Captain* are two of the best, both busy and full of intrigue. *The Virtuoso* is driven by "a new motive for comic action," and *A True Widow* presents in Lady Cheatly "a quite new character," together with vivacious dialogue and a great variety of other characters. Vivid pictures of the "under-side of London life" are shown in *The Squire of Alsatia* and *The Scowrers*; but *Bury-Fair* ("rather a farce than a comedy"), *The Amorous Bigotte*, and *The Volunteers* are indifferent productions. Sullen Lovers is lively but not witty, Psyche is spectacular but not tragic, and the "satanic grandeur" of Don John in The Libertine is degraded "by crude monstrosities," just as "the witchcraft business" detracts from the rest of The Lancashire-Witches. In the latter play, "we have . . . the first professed witch-finder in the English drama." Shadwell gives us amusing "oddities and perversities" but often carries "realism" too far in the direction of coarseness.

2 DUNCAN, CARSON S. The New Science and English Literature in the Classical Period. Menasha, Wis.: George Banta, pp. 67, 72-81, 101-8.

Sir Nicholas Gimcrack of The Virtuoso is the first and "most complete comic conception of the new philosopher," but in depicting his inventions, laboratory apparatus, experiments, and extravagant claims of achievement, Shadwell is not attacking "the true-blue Greshamites" but rather is exposing pretense and useless knowledge to ridicule. In doing so, he draws upon actual experiments and reports of the Royal Society, and exaggerates the language actually found in the works of Sprat, Boyle, Hooke, and others. Unfortunately, Sir Nicholas's "scientific humor" is "not an essential part either of him or of the plot," for when he is not in the laboratory, he becomes "a man about town, engaging in base intrigues." Other Shadwell plays that comment indirectly on the New Science or its implications are The Lancashire-Witches, The Squire of Alsatia, and Sullen Lovers.

3 GILLET, J.E. Molière en Angleterre 1660-1670. Brussels: Académie Impériale et Royale, pp. 52, 111.

Betterton's Amorous Widow draws upon The Libertine, and this play, Bury-Fair, and Newcastle's Triumphant Widow all borrow from Molière.

4 PALMER, JOHN. The Comedy of Manners. London: G. Bell & Sons, p. 2.

The comedy of manners would have developed without any contribution from Shadwell.

1914

1 ANON. "Shadwell's 'Bury Fair.'" Unidentified clipping, dated 20 March, in the Harvard Theatre Collection.

Reviews a production of Bury-Fair, finding that it is "almost a social comedy, in the modern sense," that it depends less on style than on high spirits, and that its dialogue is interesting, its satire still amusing.

2 GRAY, W. FORBES. The Poets Laureate of England: Their History and Their Odes. London, Bath, New York, and Melbourne: Sir Isaac Pitman & Sons, pp. 79-96.

A slavish imitator of Jonson and Molière and, in Timon and The Tempest, a corruptor of Shakespeare, Shadwell possessed "a sordid imagination, an uncouth expression, and a dull, heavy manner." Despite their energy, amusing caricatures, and funny situations, his "dramatic works are so much literary lumber." The Squire of Alsatia, a "picaresque" work, is his best play, and Psyche reveals his interest and skill in music. The originality and skillful characterizations in Epsom-Wells, however, are spoiled by indelicacies, and sordidness makes it impossible to appreciate the provocative anticlericism and depiction of occult beliefs in The Lancashire-Witches. The Amorous Bigotte, Bury-Fair, and The Scowrers can be ignored. Shadwell had "the unimaginative, if practical, mind of a politician rather than the soul of a poet."

3 NETTLETON, GEORGE HENRY. English Drama of the Restoration and Eighteenth Century (1642-1780). New York: Macmillan, pp. 41, 44, 56, 84-86, 105.

Presents Shadwell as a lesser dramatist who imitated Jonson and Molière, took part in scenic and operatic experimentation, and reproduced "details of fashionable Restoration life." Epsom-Wells is briefly discussed, Bury-Fair is called his best work, and a number of his other pieces are mentioned.

4 SCHELLING, FELIX E. English Drama. London: J.M. Dent; New York: E.P. Dutton, pp. 261-62.

Considers Shadwell imitative but inventive and endowed with "a broad rough humour" and "an honest sense of right which was blind . . . to generosity and delicacy alike." His pictures of London low life are as realistic as "the tediously reiterated gallantries of the school of Etherege and Sedley."

1915

1 BERNBAUM, ERNEST. The Drama of Sensibility . . . 1696-1780. Boston and London: Ginn, pp. 26, 67-69.

Unlike later adaptations of Plautus and Terence (for example, The Conscious Lovers), The Squire of Alsatia uses Roman comedy without losing its flexibility of method to the control of sentimental elements. Sir Edward verges on the sentimental, but he is neither saint nor sage, and his nephew, who has been willfully wicked throughout most of the play, reforms at the end, indeed, but for the wrong reasons.

2 WHITMORE, CHARLES EDWARD. The Supernatural in Tragedy. Cambridge, Mass.: Harvard University Press; London: Humphrey Milford, pp. 297-98.

The Lancashire-Witches is "not significant," and The Libertine, although it is "ambitious" in its use of the supernatural, lacks "poetry and illusion" and is marred by farce.

1916

1 DUNCAN, C.S. "The Scientist as a Comic Type." MP 14:284-88.
Reiterates the points made in The New Science and English Literature (S.1913.2), with perhaps a closer analysis of the originality and satiric import of Sir Nicholas.

2 WRIGHT, ROSE ABEL. The Political Play of the Restoration. Montesano, Wash.: A.E. Veatch, pp. 94-95, 150-57.
The satiric aim of The Volunteers is not really political, for although it exposes "the empty, fashionable life of the capital city," it commends both the "sturdy prowess of the Puritans" and the "rollicking good-fellowship of the Cavaliers." Wright analyzes the expunged portions of The Lancashire-Witches for their political implications and notes that The Amorous Bigotte, though not so anti-Roman Catholic as the former play, is just as low in moral content.

1918

1 PERRY, HENRY TEN EYCK. The First Duchess of Newcastle and Her Husband as Figures in Literary History. Boston and London: Ginn, pp. 156-59.
Parts of Bury-Fair come from Newcastle's Triumphant Widow, which Shadwell helped to write.

1919

*1 BORGMAN, ALBERT STEPHENS. "The Dramatic Works of Thomas Shadwell." Ph.D. dissertation, Harvard University, 392 pp.
Source: Stratman, pp. 623-24. Revised for publication: (S.1928.1).

1920

1 EDMUNDS, E.W. An Historical Summary of English Literature. London, New York, Toronto, and Melbourne: Cassell, p. 126.
Shadwell wrote plays that were "humorous but obscene," plays like Epsom-Wells, "a mirror of his age."

2 ODELL, GEORGE C.D. Shakespeare from Betterton to Irving. Vol. 1. New York: Scribner's, pp. 33-36, 46-48.
Discusses Shadwell's authorship of the 1674 Tempest and analyzes his Timon in comparison to Shakespeare's. Except for making Flavius a sneaky rascal and inserting "a genuine Restoration flirt" (Melissa), Shadwell did not so much pervert Shakespeare as adapt his play into an "excellent acting medium" for the later seventeenth-century stage.

3 REYNOLDS, MYRA. The Learned Lady in England 1650-1760. Boston and New York: Houghton Mifflin, pp. 380-82.

Mentions Lady Vaine in Sullen Lovers as a "Virtuosa" and examines Lady Fantast and her daughter in Bury-Fair as satiric caricatures of learned women.

4 WILLIAMS, STANLEY T. "Some Versions of Timon of Athens on the Stage." MP 18:270.

Briefly mentions Shadwell's innovations.

1921

1 BROADUS, EDMUND KEMPER. The Laureateship: A Study of the Office of Poet Laureate in England. Oxford: Clarendon Press, pp. 74-88.

Mentions that Shadwell wrote good plays but concentrates on his life and on the ineptitude of his poetry.

2 NICOLL, ALLARDYCE. "Political Plays of the Restoration." MLR 16:233.

In writing The Lancashire-Witches, Shadwell seems to have found he could not "sensibly" confine his satire to the subject of Roman Catholicism. The play has some interesting witch scenes.

3 SQUIRE, WILLIAM BARCLAY. "The Music of Shadwell's 'Tempest.'" Musical Quarterly 7:565-78.

Traces the evolution of The Tempest in the Restoration, tries to reconstruct successive musical contributions to the play after 1674 (in light of the recently discovered "Vocal Musick in the Tempest by Mr. Pelh. Humfrey"), and reprints Humphrey's music for the song, "My Lord, great Neptune, for my sake."

1922

1 JONES, VIRGIL L. "Methods of Satire in the Political Drama of the Restoration." JEGP 21:667.

Although Shadwell "never ceased to satirize the Puritans," he could also ridicule Jacobites and High Churchmen. The Volunteers, The Squire of Alsatia, and The Lancashire-Witches are cited.

1923

1 ARCHER, WILLIAM. The Old Drama and the New: An Essay in Re-valuation. Boston: Small, Maynard, pp. 176-77, 199.

By no means a gifted dramatist, Shadwell showed an early awareness, long before Collier, of the indecency of Restoration comedy. The "undercurrent of political allusion" in some of his own works provides some relief from the prevailing lewdness of the era.

2 NICOLL, ALLARDYCE. A History of Restoration Drama 1660-1700. Cambridge: Cambridge University Press, pp. 20, 62-63, 75, 81, 125, 173-76, 183, 186, 188-98, 203, 226, 230, 252-53, 260.

Ranks Shadwell just below Etherege, Wycherley, and Congreve, but on a par with Dryden, in comedy, and finds his works significant for their social realism, for their part in driving "pure tragedy from the stage," for giving impetus to manners comedy and later to sentimental comedy, and for their curiously independent use of sources and fashionable conventions.

In Psyche, Shadwell created "the first real non-Shakespearean opera," though it lacks interest today. He condemns manners comedy in Sullen Lovers yet practices it in A True Widow, writes obscenely in The Squire of Alsatia but with notable modesty in Bury-Fair. Unlike Wycherley, he seems not to have known how to use filth for larger dramatic purposes. He imitated Jonson but preserved his own integrity. Sullen Lovers and The Lancashire-Witches are interesting for their satire, socially oriented in the former, politically and religiously aimed in the latter, and the use of witchcraft in the latter is provocative. Contemporary satire of a more general nature characterizes The Humorists, a comedy of humours in which Shadwell contrasts a gay couple with "pure" lovers. In The Virtuoso, he draws too sharp a line between the pure lovers and the more debased figures, but the satire in this play is more subtle than usual.

The coarse, antiheroic Epsom-Wells and the modest and farcical Bury-Fair are two of his best plays, and The Miser is a fair adaptation of Molière in which Shadwell first shows his inclination toward manners comedy. A True Widow is a confused, indecent humors piece; The Woman-Captain, a worse play, albeit less Jonsonian, comments interestingly on women's problems; and The Squire of Alsatia fascinates with its "perverted morals," relating of art to life, and gross realism, though it lacks moral and intellectual control. Despite its originality and moral purpose, The Scowrers does not succeed well, and The Volunteers, possibly a relic of Shadwell's youth, is a somewhat clumsy mix of "undigested satire" and intrigue.

Shadwell was influenced by Shakespeare, Jonson, Molière, and in Bury-Fair, Newcastle (The Triumphant Widow). He in turn seems to have influenced Wycherley, Congreve, and George Powell, and his interest in the moral and sentimental generally contributed to later drama.

3 _____. An Introduction to Dramatic Theory. New York: Brentano's, pp. 132, 135-36, 158, 185, 189.

Notes the skepticism about the supernatural in The Lancashire-Witches, and contrasts the "vulgar" Squire of Alsatia with the "comparatively modest" Bury-Fair (which seems to have been influenced by Etherege's work). Shadwell was an inferior genius not because he lacked artistry, for he wrote and constructed well, but because he reproduced the surfaces rather than the "manners" of his age.

4 STEVENS, DAVID HARRISON, ed. "Notes: Bury Fair." In Types of English Drama 1660-1780. Boston, New York, and London: Ginn, pp. 885-87.

Observes analogues between some of Shadwell's characters and some of Newcastle's in The Triumphant Widow and of Behn's in The False Count; commends Bury-Fair and The Squire of Alsatia for carefully developed situations and realistic, well-defined character types. Combining Molière's urbanity and instinct for comic situations with Jonson's ruder realism, Shadwell studied the principles of contemporary behavior, like Jonson, and made his plays "critical commentaries on his environment."

1924

1 DOBRÉE, BONAMY. Restoration Comedy 1660-1720. London: Oxford University Press, pp. 33, 50, 116-20.

Shadwell had "great talent, but no literary sense," no "flashes of revelation," and "no knowledge of the human heart." His writing is often "prolix and prosy, clumsy and flabby." The derivative and obvious Bury-Fair and Sullen Lovers, "a travesty of Les Fâcheux," are pleasant enough, and The Squire of Alsatia is "a broad Middletonian bustle." A True Widow may be his best work. He reflects the influence of Jonson and Molière.

2 KRUTCH, JOSEPH WOOD. Comedy and Conscience after the Restoration. New York: Columbia University Press, pp. 5, 20-22, 41, 77.

Jonson was Shadwell's god, "his witty contemporaries his aversion"; he satirized moral vice with more "scrupulous realism" than they did, though he wrote coarsely and sometimes pandered to the fashionable interest in bawdy manners. He was usually honest about his intentions, and he gave the impression of having documented his plays in the way he did most clearly in The Lancashire-Witches. Sullen Lovers and The Humorists are dull pieces, but The Squire of Alsatia, Epsom-Wells, and Bury-Fair are excellent, mainly because they catch "the essence of the life" in a particular locale.

1925

1 DISHER, M. WILLSON. Clowns and Pantomimes. London: Constable, p. 74.

Points to an early imitation of commedia dell' arte in The Virtuoso, where Sir Formal attends a masquerade "'in Scaramouche's Habit' and there is a dance by a Scaramouche and six clowns."

2 NICOLL, ALLARDYCE. British Drama: An Historical Survey from the Beginnings to the Present Time. New York: Crowell, pp. 243-45.

Stylistically crude, vulgar, outspoken, but never really obscene, Shadwell possessed a strong sense of theater, great skill in creating humors characters, and unexcelled sensitivity to contemporary social realities. In his best plays--Sullen Lovers, Humorists, Epsom-Wells, Virtuoso, Squire of Alsatia, and Bury-Fair--he contributed significantly both to comedy of manners and to sentimental comedy. A too slavish imitation of Jonson was his main flaw.

1926

1 KIES, PAUL P. "The Sources and Basic Model of Lessing's Miss Sara Sampson." MP 24:66-67, 69-73.

Lessing was "well read in Shadwell," whose Squire of Alsatia provided the "general outline of the plot, the principal characters, and many of the details of Miss Sara Sampson."

2 LYNCH, KATHLEEN M. The Social Mode of Restoration Comedy. New York and London: Macmillan, pp. 55, 56, 159-60, 162-64, 176-77, 181-82, 187-92, 197-99, 201, 208-11.

Argues that although Shadwell clearly owed debts to Molière and Jonson, he was perhaps even more heavily influenced by the fashionable Restoration standards of gallantry and coquetry, the "précieuse dialogue," the intrigues and "licentious detail," which he found most effectively used in Etherege. In moving from Sullen Lovers, through The Miser and Epsom-Wells, to The Virtuoso, Shadwell moved ever closer to "genuine comedy of manners." In his "laboured" works, "Shadwell sturdily repeated the pattern of She Would if She Could, with a realistic emphasis on contemporary manners which, to some extent, redeems his dulness." Taking his art seriously, he nevertheless wrote "confused and inartistic" plays, yet he seems to have become a strong influence on Congreve.

3 SUMMERS, MONTAGUE. The History of Witchcraft and Demonology. London: Kegan Paul, Trench, Trubner; New York: Alfred A. Knopf, pp. 75, 296-99, 303.

In The Lancashire-Witches, Shadwell shows he "took Witchcraft seriously" and reflects the influence of Jonson's Masque of Queens, Heywood and Brome's Late Lancashire Witches, and at least two actual witch trials. The play owed its success entirely to spectacle, for the satire is muddy and lewd, Tegue is disgustingly depicted, and the witch scenes are "intolerably clumsy."

Though he lacked poetry and discrimination, Shadwell is usually a vigorously realistic writer.

1927

1 ARUNDELL, DENNIS. Henry Purcell. London: Oxford University Press and Humphrey Milford, pp. 90-91.

Discusses the fine musical dimension of the 1674 Tempest and observes that in the "strange" and melodramatic Libertine there is a pastoral scene with music that represents Purcell at his very best.

2 CAZAMIAN, LOUIS. A History of English Literature, Vol. 2: Modern Times (1660-1914). New York: Macmillan, p. 46.

Shadwell is not a first-rate dramatist, but Epsom-Wells, The Squire of Alsatia, and Bury-Fair, despite being "heavily written" and "clumsily constructed," provide interesting pictures of Restoration life.

3 CROSSE, GORDON. "Shakespeare Allusions in Shadwell." TLS, 16 June, p. 424.

Notes allusions in Squire of Alsatia, Bury-Fair, and Sullen Lovers.

4 RYE, WALTER. "The Poet Shadwell." In Some Historical Essays Chiefly Relating to Norfolk. Pt. 4. Norwich: H.W. Hunt, pp. 287-92.

Concentrates on the biography but calls Shadwell "the only Poet Laureate produced by Norfolk--and a poor one at that."

5 SPENCER, HAZELTON. Shakespeare Improved: The Restoration Versions in Quarto and on the Stage. Cambridge, Mass.: Harvard University Press, pp. 97, 114, 204-10, 181-87.

Calls The Squire of Alsatia "excellent," describes the 1674 Tempest at some length (noting Shadwell's masque, new song, musical sense, and elaborated staging), and concludes Shadwell's Timon the best of all Restoration "tamperings" with Shakespeare. Shakespeare's ending is strengthened, the added love story makes the original more unified and interesting, and when Shadwell interpolates his own language, it is usually appropriately, if rudely, vigorous. Melissa is not convincing, however, and Demetrius is changed for the worse. In the Restoration Timon, tragedy and comedy are not distinct from each other, there is no poetic justice, and the unities are violated.

6 SUMMERS, MONTAGUE, ed. Prefatory Note and Introduction to The Complete Works of Thomas Shadwell. Vol. 1. London: Fortune Press, pp. ix-ccli.

Sees Shadwell as a somewhat coarse and careless, yet energetic and realistic, writer who equaled any of his contemporaries in "vitality and humour." Reprehensible in his religious and political views, he was a powerful and dogmatic controversialist, "a leviathan of literature."

He imitated Jonson but created many memorable characters of his own: Sir Positive (Sullen Lovers), Crazy (Humorists), Clodpate (Epsom-Wells), Sir Samuel, Sir Nicholas, Sir Formal, and Snarl (Virtuoso), and Old Gripe (Woman-Captain). His best plays are Sullen Lovers, Epsom-Wells, The Libertine ("powerful" and "most edifying"), The Virtuoso (stereotyped lovers but excellent humors and a fine acting play), The Squire of Alsatia ("brilliant" but blotted by the character of Belfond Jr.), and Bury-Fair (sentimental in places, like Squire). Except for The Humorists, which was mutilated by censors and which overstresses character and topicality, and The Lancashire-Witches, a shadowy, gross, Whiggish play with a bad moral and clumsy occultism, all the rest of Shadwell's dramatic works are meritorious. Even Psyche, with its elegant dialogue, is pleasing, and Timon becomes, under Shadwell's hand, a "first-rate acting play."

His last works, often seen as showing a decline in powers, remain amusing, lively, and realistic, though The Amorous Bigotte is a bit grotesque and The Scowrers rough and boisterous. Summers surrounds his treatment of each play with a wealth of information about sources, literary traditions, staging, historical backgrounds, social and biographical contexts. For instance, he discusses "the pox" in literature and history when he comes to the character of Crazy in The Humorists, the Don Juan legend in relation to The Libertine, demonology in connection with The Lancashire-Witches. Later in this and the other four volumes, he provides rich prefaces and explanatory notes for each play.

1928

1 BORGMAN, ALBERT S. Thomas Shadwell: His Life and Comedies. New York: New York University Press, 279 pp.

Revision of S.1919.1. Six chapters on Shadwell's life, stage success, and reputation are followed by chapters devoted to each of the thirteen comedies. Ranked with Etherege and Wycherley, Shadwell is said to lack their polish, to equal them in contemporary satire, and to excel them in range of characters and novelty of settings.

His best plays, Epsom-Wells, The Squire of Alsatia, and Bury-Fair (with A True Widow running a close fourth), reveal him as a "grandson of Ben," a moralist who drew excellent characters. He was less influenced by Molière than has been thought. The Sullen Lovers, an above-average play and the first English comedy to ridicule heroic drama, applies Jonsonian methods of characterization to an idea suggested by Molière's Les Fâcheux (it owes nothing to Le Misanthrope). It benefits from Shadwell's instinct for good theater and from his deftness at satire, especially through the handling of Sir Positive At-all, a caricature of Sir Robert Howard.

Characterization again dominates The Humorists as Shadwell learns to depict low life, though the play contains more action and less satire than the previous one. Albeit based on Molière, The Miser is almost as much about the cheats and fools of the subplot as about the miser and his family; and influences from Molière and Jonson are slight in the largely original, Etheregean Epsom-Wells, one of the early Restoration's best plays.

Jonson's, but not Molière's, impression emerges again in The Virtuoso, a play in which a love story is made to carry perhaps too much satiric freight, though the satiric distortion of material from actual scientific writings, and the portrait of Sir Nicholas (the first fully drawn pseudoscientist in the drama), are delightful. Sir Formal, however, is the best character, for Sir Nicholas is inconsistent and Sir Samuel becomes "tiresome."

Drawing perhaps on the plot of Jonson's Alchymist and upon earlier Shadwell characters, A True Widow amusingly satirizes farce and freshly depicts a typical Restoration theater audience. The Woman-Captain is "comedy of intrigue" in Aphra Behn's manner, and it recalls "numerous Elizabethan and Restoration dramatists." Despite its novel use of rural gentry, and its operatic features, The Lancashire-Witches is an inferior work in which Shadwell vainly uses witch scenes to frustrate charges of atheism (though he clearly sides with the commonsensical Sir Edward) and irrelevantly attacks aspects of religion through Smerk and Tegue (who can be equated with Dominick Kelly, one of Godfrey's supposed murderers).

The influences of Molière and others again appear in The Squire of Alsatia, a free adaptation of Terence that promotes "soft" methods of education in what amounts to the earliest full dramatization of Alsatia and the canting dialect of Whitefriars; Lucia is a notable female character. Setting is only incidental in Bury-Fair, a morally serious comedy showing the influences of Molière and Shakespeare and containing effective satire against two types of wit. Though this is not Shadwell's best play, it contains his best scene, the one where the two Fantasts are made ridiculous by the barber-count.

Borrowing slightly from Molière, The Amorous Bigotte assembles some of Shadwell's previously used devices in an intrigue comedy whose characters are mere sketches. The Scowrers anticipates sentimental comedy, recalls aspects of The Squire of Alsatia, offers effective satire, and presents, in Sir Humphrey Maggot and the Jacobite alderman, Shadwell's most original characters. Strongly reminiscent of his earlier works, The Volunteers is a humors comedy that satirizes stock-jobbing for the first time in English drama, but it avoids didacticism and seems intended purely for entertainment.

2 DENT, EDWARD J. Foundations of English Opera: A Study of Musical Drama in England during the Seventeenth Century. Cambridge: Cambridge University Press, pp. 98-99, 105, 107-8, 110-24, 137-44, 147-48.

Focuses on Psyche but mentions the references to amateur composition and to instruments in Sullen Lovers and Humorists, discusses Shadwell's additions to The Tempest, and characterizes The Lancashire-Witches as "a strange experiment" anticipating "that mixed comic and fantastic opera" of the German romantic movement of the nineteenth century."

Unlike Molière, who treats play, machines, and music as separate matters, Shadwell in his Psyche works to unite the three parts to produce a single dramatic effect. The first to do so in a systematic way, he was endowed with "a good deal of musical understanding, and . . . a proper appreciation of his collaborator's abilities."

Beginning by visualizing the stage picture, he proceeded to "elaborate it with a very strong sense of musical effect." He "had the makings of a really good librettist." The play begins with much originality but the last two acts borrow heavily from Molière and seem "scrappy and disconnected." Psyche became the model for Congreve's Semele. Dent discusses Lock's and Draghi's music in relation to Shadwell's scenes.

3 ELWIN, MALCOLM. The Playgoer's Handbook to Restoration Drama. New York: Macmillan, pp. 44, 103-8.

Shadwell "had all the pomposity of the academicians" and was too obsessed with Jonson's method of characterization. His only good plays are The Libertine, Bury-Fair (though somewhat crude and farcical), and The Virtuoso (poorly constructed but cleverly satiric with excellent characters). The Sullen Lovers has some good characters, The Miser is a competent adaptation, and The Squire of Alsatia depicts the underworld interestingly. But each of these has serious flaws, and The Lancashire-Witches (crudely melodramatic), The Amorous Bigotte (no better), The Royal Shepherdess ("clap-trap"), Psyche ("stilted and stuffy"), Timon, and The Woman-Captain are all negligible.

4 SUMMERS, MONTAGUE, ed. "Explanatory Notes." In Roscius Anglicanus, by John Downes. London: Fortune Press, pp. 197, 228, 240, 247.

A True Widow is a "good" comedy, and Sullen Lovers, The Squire of Alsatia, Bury-Fair, and The Virtuoso ("a satire upon scientific pedantry") are all "excellent."

5 WALMSLEY, D.M. "The Influence of Foreign Opera on English Operatic Plays of the Restoration Period." Anglia 52:39-41, 43, 45-48.

"Apart from some spectacular devices and the French dancing, Psyche may be said to represent a natural development of the native masque-like play" (such as Peele's Araygnement of Paris and Heywood's Love's Mistress). The Tempest (1674) is mentioned, and The Royal Shepherdess is related to pastoral drama and masque.

6 WILSON, JOHN HAROLD. The Influence of Beaumont and Fletcher on Restoration Drama. Columbus: Ohio State University Press, pp. 35-38, 67, 72-73.

Shadwell's one original tragedy, The Libertine, is "formless and episodic." The Royal Shepherdess is a love-and-honor tragicomedy, romantic, erotic, Fletcherian, containing many reminiscences of Beaumont-Fletcher plays. But "the dramatic operas are in an entirely new method and show only contemporary influences." His comedies, after the Jonsonian Sullen Lovers, Humorists, and even Miser, renounce his earlier ideals and become vulgarly witty and obscene, with witty couples abounding. Epsom-Wells, the best of these, has possibly three humors, no Jonsonian ideas, and much indecency and cynicism along with realistic satire. Sir Timothy Kastril in The Volunteers imitates not his namesake in Jonson's Alchymist but La-writ in Beaumont and Fletcher's Little French Lawyer. In The Lancashire-Witches, Shadwell borrows a situation from Beaumont and Fletcher's Wit at Several Weapons.

1929

1 KIES, PAUL P. "Lessing's Early Study of English Drama." JEGP 28:19-22.

Offers evidence that Lessing studied and was influenced by Bury-Fair, The Volunteers, The Virtuoso, and The Squire of Alsatia.

2 LLOYD, CLAUDE. "Shadwell and the Virtuosi." PMLA 44:472-94.

Argues that The Virtuoso does ridicule both the aims and some of the practitioners (Sprat, Glanvill, More, and others) of the New Science, even though Shadwell may have intended to confine his attack to scientific pedantry.

3 MONTGOMERY, GUY. "The Challenge of Restoration Comedy." EIC 1:139.

In The Virtuoso, Shadwell is "much more severe upon the lack of knowledge on the part of the beaux and the wits than upon the misdirected enthusiasm of the Virtuoso himself," and maybe Shadwell "had a lurking suspicion that there was more in these curiosities of Gresham College than his age realized."

1930

1 BULL, A.J. "Thomas Shadwell's Satire on Edward Howard." RES 6:312-15.

In the course of discussing an unattributed satire, notes the portrait of Edward Howard as Poet Ninny and of Sir Robert Howard as Sir Positive At-all, both in Sullen Lovers.

2 WALMSLEY, D.M., ed. Introduction to "Epsom Wells" and "The Volunteers or The Stock-Jobbers" by Thomas Shadwell. Belles Lettres Series. Boston and London: D.C. Heath, pp. xviii-lxi.

Appropriating Jonson's humors method, Shadwell invented his own more natural and humane brand of character types, endowed them with fluent dialogue, and placed them in realistic settings. But he also experimented with dialects (in Squire of Alsatia), helped found the comedy of manners, contributed to the growth of English opera (in The Royal Shepherdess, The Tempest, and Psyche) and of sentimental comedy, and in The Libertine, created possibly the earliest, certainly the best, English version of the Don Juan legend. In The Woman-Captain and Amorous Bigotte, he shows he could write essentially romantic comedies, whereas in The Lancashire-Witches, he rather unsuccessfully attempts a curious mix of wit, humors, satire, and spectacular occultism.

Some of his best plays, such as The Virtuoso and The Squire of Alsatia, employ Jonsonian humors within larger contexts of meaning: satire on science in the one instance, commentary on education in the other. In Sullen Lovers, humors are contrasted to more "normal" types, and in Epsom-Wells they are contrasted with wit characters (albeit vaguely etched ones) in a moralized manners comedy. Strong foreshadowings of sentimental drama are found in A True Widow, Bury-Fair (almost a fully fledged manners comedy), and The Volunteers. This last play reveals a masterful Shadwell, skillfully blending wit, humors, and sentiment, convincingly staging a realistic environment, and aiming at social reform.

3 WHITING, GEORGE W. "Political Satire in London Stage Plays, 1680-83." MP 28:39.

Mentions Lancashire-Witches as the only Whig play allowed on stage in 1681 (but only after severe pruning).

1931

1 MacMILLAN, DOUGALD, and HOWARD MUMFORD JONES, eds. Headnote to The Squire of Alsatia. In Plays of the Restoration and Eighteenth Century. New York: Henry Holt, pp. 257-58.

Shadwell's better plays--Sullen Lovers, Virtuoso, Squire of Alsatia, Bury-Fair--are all Jonsonian in their use of humors, low-life realism, and topicality. The Squire of Alsatia is more representative, though less brilliant, than Bury-Fair; its theme is "the training of youth" for contemporary living.

2 SUMMERS, MONTAGUE. "A Note upon Shadwell." N&Q 161:279.

Finds in Sullen Lovers an allusion to Dr. Salvator Winter, compounder of "the True Elixir Vitae."

3 WHITE, ARTHUR F. "The Office of Revels and Dramatic Censorship during the Restoration Period." Western Reserve University Bulletin, n.s. 34, no. 13:32-35.

The best example of "Charles Killigrew at work" as Master of Revels is The Lancashire-Witches, from which all the long excisions have to do with the character of Smerk.

4 WOOD, FREDERICK T. "The Beginnings and Significance of Sentimental Comedy." Anglia 55:379.

Sees an "undercurrent of sentimentalism" in The Royal Shepherdess.

1932

1 HOLLAND, A.K. Henry Purcell: The English Musical Tradition. London: G. Bell, pp. 150-51, 199, 223-26.

In the 1674 Tempest, music begins to be conceived as a more significant part of the play; "the musicians for the first time, apparently, leave the obscurity of the stage-gallery and come out into the open as an orchestra." Purcell's contribution to The Tempest is discussed, and Shadwell is said to have, "in some respects," a greater "dramatic sense" than Dryden.

2 YOUNG, R. FITZGIBBON. "Premonitions of the Industrial Revolution." TLS, 14 January, p. 28.

Notes that the passages in The Virtuoso regarding the ribbon weavers' protest anticipate postindustrial violence against mechanization.

1933

1 ELLEHAUGE, MARTIN. English Restoration Drama: Its Relation to Past English and Past and Contemporary French Drama from Jonson via Molière to Congreve. Copenhagen: Levin & Munksgaard, pp. 192-93, 271-74, 297-302, 304-7.

Shadwell continues "the Jonsonian tradition" and writes plays that have strong moral points. Timon "shatters the illusions of the protagonist about friendship and love." The Virtuoso satirizes impractical knowledge. The Squire of Alsatia promotes "educational liberalism." The Lancashire-Witches ridicules Anglican and Roman Catholic ecclesiastical morals. In this play, Shadwell "was forced by censuring authorities to make the witches real" because the church preached faith in witchcraft.

2 SAINTSBURY, GEORGE E.B. Prefaces and Essays by the Late George Saintsbury. London: Macmillan, p. 96.

Asserts that Shadwell "in a somewhat mistaken sense" borrowed the humors method from Jonson and passed it along to Smollett.

3 WHITEHALL, HAROLD. "Thomas Shadwell and the Lancashire Dialect." In Essays and Studies in English and Comparative Literature. University of Michigan Publications in Language and Literature. vol. 10. Ann Arbor: University of Michigan Press, pp. 261-78.

"Quite alone among the dramatists of his day, Shadwell brought back to the playhouse the fully developed dialect rôle" and seems to have sensed "the intrinsic importance of dialect." In The Squire of Alsatia, Lolpoop speaks a Lancashire dialect. So do characters in The Lancashire-Witches; in fact, they use the same one employed by Otway in The Cheats of Scapin (which is different from that used by Heywood and Brome in Late Lancashire Witches). But Shadwell borrowed little of his language from these other writers; indeed, he may have had "spoken authority" for his Lancashire dialects, so that he "accidentally comes close to being one of the fathers of modern dialectology." Since he also knew dialects other than those of Lancashire, he should be more carefully studied in this light.

1934

1 MAYO, THOMAS FRANKLIN. Epicurus in England (1650-1725). Dallas: Southwest Press, pp. 147-54.

With their admiration of Lucretius, Bruce and Longvil in The Virtuoso "embody . . . the ideal personality implicit in a great part" of Restoration comedy, a personality that combines sanity, philosophical indifference to "the general fate of mankind," individualism, hatred of reformers, and irreverence toward "the crude romanticisms" of the New Science, especially its tendency to divorce knowledge from daily life. After 1688, however, Shadwell's Epicureanism began to disappear and he became the "official literary champion of the new synthesis of aristocratic and middle class ideals." In The Volunteers, he celebrates "the reconciliation of the landlord and the merchant classes," his morality having become stricter and his tastes more rural and sentimental.

1935

1 CROISSANT, De WITT C. "Early Sentimental Comedy." In The Parrott Presentation Volume. Edited by Hardin Craig. Princeton: Princeton University Press, pp. 59-60, 65-66, 68-69.

Finds "certain indirect sentimental qualities" in Sullen Lovers, Humorists, and Squire of Alsatia. The Royal Shepherdess mixes "comedy of manners characters, sentimental comedy moral tone, and romantic setting and plot" in what really amounts to "true sentimental drama, with virtue rewarded." A True Widow presents sentimental love between Bellamour and Isabella, and The Lancashire-Witches conveys a sentimental interest in women choosing their own mates.

2 MORGAN, A.E., ed. Headnote to Bury-Fair. In English Plays 1660-1820. New York and London: Harper & Bros., p. 290.

Presents Shadwell as a coarse but competent dramatist who "was scourging . . . with the lash of a satirist" while writers of manners comedy were "depicting society without moral concern." Consistently realistic, in his later works he "almost slips into sentimentalism." His best qualities show up unpleasantly in The Squire of Alsatia, but they delight us in Bury-Fair, a sprightly, farcical, and moral work containing "traces of sentimentalism."

3 SUMMERS, MONTAGUE. The Playhouse of Pepys. New York: Macmillan, p. 180.

Notices the satiric picture of Edward Howard as Poet Ninny in Sullen Lovers.

4 WILSON, F.P. "English Letters and the Royal Society in the Seventeenth Century." Mathematical Gazette 19:348.

Places The Virtuoso in the context of other responses to the Royal Society and notes that Shadwell "took some of his dialogue from Glanvill."

1936

1 HARBAGE, ALFRED. Cavalier Drama. New York: Modern Language Association; London: Oxford University Press, pp. 75, 246.

Implies that Shadwell's "cruel caricature" of Sir Robert Howard in Sullen Lovers was a way of returning Howard's condescension toward professional dramatists in general. Newcastle's Triumphant Widow and Humorous Lovers are said to owe whatever merit they have to Shadwell's collaboration.

2 PERKINSON, RICHARD H. "Topographical Comedy in the Seventeenth Century." ELH 3:271, 280, 284, 288-89.

In Epsom-Wells and The Squire of Alsatia, Shadwell plausibly re-creates particular locations with indigenous characters, and integrates both setting and characters with actions that contrast country and city ways. Epsom-Wells, "the first topographical play to utilize a fashionable spa for comedy of manners," may depend to some extent on Chappuzeau's Eaux de Pirmont, and The Squire of Alsatia may owe something to Barrey's Ram Alley. In Squire, Alsatia is pitted against "the country booby, . . . the country gentleman, . . . and society itself."

3 SMITH, DANE FARNSWORTH. Plays about the Theatre in England from 'The Rehearsal' in 1671 to the Licensing Act in 1737. London and New York: Oxford University Press, pp. 44, 52-56.

Discusses the "photographic reproduction" of a Restoration audience in Act 4 of A True Widow and asserts that the 1674 Tempest so exaggerates the original that it "ceases to set forth the impossible in the probable."

1937

1 DUGGAN, G.C. The Stage Irishman: A History of the Irish Play and Stage Characters from the Earliest Times. London and New York: Longmans, Green, pp. 174, 234-39.

In The Lancashire-Witches, the part of Tegue was probably played by a genuine Irishman, but Tegue's activities are not well integrated with either the main or the secondary plot. If in this play Tegue is a rogue, "foul-mouthed" and immoral, in The Amorous Bigotte he becomes "a prurient sinner." The latter play contains a direct allusion to Sir John Oldcastle. Shadwell seems to have spent only four months of his life in Ireland.

2 IACUZZI, ALFRED. "The Naïve Theme in The Tempest as a Link between Thomas Shadwell and Ramón de la Cruz." MLN 52:252-56.

Ramón de la Cruz based his Juanito y Juanita (1778) on Harni de Guerville's Georget et Georgette (1761) which, in turn, drew from Shadwell's version of The Tempest (1674).

3 WESTRUP, J.A. Purcell. London: J.M. Dent, pp. 76, 82, 84, 93, 112, 140, 145-49, 160, 248.

Calls Psyche "the first of the original semi-operas," briefly discusses songs in The Libertine and The Tempest, and says that for the latter play Purcell did his "most mature work for the theatre," fully absorbing "the Italian style."

1938

1 N.B.J.H. "Thomas Shadwell: A Biography." Caian (Gonville and Caius College, Cambridge) 46:93-99.

Shadwell's history is that "of the worst kind of mediocrity and scurrility," but had he "possessed even Settle's ability to write," his plays might have been less coarse and tedious, for he created "several well-constructed, humorous comedies of manners." With the Sullen Lovers, he became the leading comic writer of the day and the first to write "comedy of manners, rather than of wit." The 1674 Tempest is romance turned spectacular "pantomime"; Timon is drama turned "spectacle"; The Libertine is tragedy turned "farce"; and Psyche is simply "monumentally execrable." In The Lancashire-Witches Shadwell satirizes the Duke of York's religion, in The Virtuoso he pokes fun at the Royal Society, and in Epsom-Wells he tries to combine social satire with moral instruction but undercuts his purpose by using uncouth language and a lewd plot. The Squire of Alsatia is equally "repellent" in these respects. From Molière, he drew the inspiration for his two best plays, Sullen Lovers and Bury-Fair, both of which "show keen observation of human nature and a firm if ponderous delineation of character."

2 NETHERCOT, ARTHUR H. Sir William D'Avenant: Poet Laureate and Playwright-Manager. Chicago: University of Chicago Press, pp. 402-3.

In Shadwell's Tempest, spectacle and show submerged Shakespeare's poetry in an operatic exhibition.

3 STROUP, THOMAS B. "Shadwell's Use of Hobbes." SP 35:405-32.

Finds significant uses of Hobbes's thought--especially his ideas about free will, politics, and human nature--in The Royal Shepherdess, The Tempest, Psyche, The Libertine, Timon, The Woman-Captain, The Lancashire-Witches, and the dedication of Bury-Fair.

4 WILCOX, JOHN. The Relation of Molière to Restoration Comedy. New York: Columbia University Press, pp. 21-23, 65-67, 117-26, 185.

Shadwell became influential by combining "pre-Restoration dramatic modes with post-Restoration social attitudes." His allegiance to Ben Jonson, together with his own literary and political impulses, pulled him "toward the common-sense standards of the middle class and away from the immoralities of the court of Charles," so that Molière's "decency and sobriety" appealed to him. "After Wycherley, he was the only Restoration playwright to be seriously touched by ideas from the Continent." Sullen Lovers amplifies, complicates, and vulgarizes the plot and general satiric thrust of Les Fâcheux, yet fills it with good humors. The Miser fails to naturalize L'Avare as it lowers the social and moral tone and shifts the interest from the miser himself to his shrewd son and daughter. Molière reinforces Shadwell's turn away from Restoration bawdy in Bury-Fair, which draws upon Les Précieuses ridicules and Les Femmes savantes. The Squire of Alsatia shares the same source with Molière's L'École des maris but otherwise remains original and carefully realistic in developing its theme that well-guided urban experience conduces more to maturity than does country boorishness. Molière's influence is minor or nonexistent in The Humorists (indebted to Newcastle and Jonson), The Libertine (perhaps owing nothing to Le Festin de Pierre), Psyche, The Amorous Bigotte (a "potboiler"), and Epsom-Wells (where Shadwell shifts from humors and decency to manners and bawdy).

1939

1 BALL, ROBERT HAMILTON. The Amazing Career of Sir Giles Overreach. Princeton: Princeton University Press; London: Oxford University Press, p. 27.

A True Widow may be slightly indebted to A New Way to Pay Old Debts.

2 GRAHAM, C.B. "Jonson Allusions in Restoration Comedy." RES 15:200-201, 203.

Sullen Lovers and A True Widow have allusions not mentioned in The Jonson Allusion Book.

3 PERRY, HENRY TEN EYCK. Masters of Dramatic Comedy and Their Social Themes. Cambridge, Mass.: Harvard University Press, pp. 285, 291.

Bury-Fair, "one of the earliest comedies in English to display genuinely sentimental tendencies," gave Lessing material for The Would-be Wits; and Lessing's Miss Sara Sampson draws upon The Squire of Alsatia.

1940

1 EVANS, G. BLAKEMORE. "The Source of Shadwell's Character of Sir Formal Trifle in 'The Virtuoso.'" MLR 35:211-14.

D'Avenant's Sir Solemn Trifle in News from Plymouth seems to be a forerunner not only of Sir Formal Trifle but also of Sir Positive At-all (Sullen Lovers) and Sir Humphrey Maggot (The Scowrers).

2 HUGHES, LEO. "Attitudes of Some Restoration Dramatists toward Farce." PQ 19:273-77.

Although Shadwell himself had said that overdrawn characters are the central ingredients of farce, the play-within-a-play in A True Widow, which is "a burlesque farce," shows that "extravagant situation" and horseplay are the central ingredients.

1941

1 FREEDLEY, GEORGE, and JOHN A. REEVES. A History of the Theatre. New York: Crown, p. 166.

Shadwell was a mediocre realist among whose seventeen plays only Sullen Lovers is notable.

*2 SMITH, RUSSELL JACK. "Dryden and Shadwell: A Study in Literary Controversy." Ph.D. dissertation, Cornell University, 360 pp.

Source: CDI (1861-1972), 37:205.

1942

1 ALLEMAN, GELLERT SPENCER. Matrimonial Law and the Materials of Restoration Comedy. Wallingford, Pa.: n.p., pp. 12-13, 17, 21-24, 41-43, 45-47, 55, 63-64, 67-69, 71-72, 74, 76-77, 84-105, 108-10, 116-17, 138-39.

In eleven of Shadwell's plays, finds instances of such legal or quasi-legal matters as the rituals of spousal and preparations for marriage; unwelcome or faked contracts; mock, clandestine, tricked, and drunken marriages; criminal or false priests; and various forms of separation and their comic implications. Alleman provides additional evidence of Shadwell's status as social observer.

2 BARTLEY, J.O. "The Development of a Stock Character: I. The Stage Irishman to 1800." MLR 37:444.
"The misuse of after was first given to a stage Irishman by Shadwell in The Amorous Bigot."

3 GREENE, GRAHAM. British Dramatists. London: William Collins, pp. 27, 30.
Epsom-Wells is more gracefully written but narrower in scope than Jonson's Bartholomew Fair, for Shadwell "was fashioning an amusing bijou for the drawing room--a witty and scandalous joke against an unpopular and rather stupid neighbour." Greene's remarks are reprinted in "British Dramatists" in Romance of English Literature, ed. Kate O'Brien and W.J. Turner (New York: Hastings House, 1944), pp. 124, 126, 128.

*4 KELLY, MILDRED. "The Plays of Thomas Shadwell and the Courtesy Books of the Seventeenth Century." Ph.D. dissertation, Louisiana State University, 421 pp.
Source: CDI (1861-1972), 35:365.

1943

1 HOOKER, HELENE MAXWELL. "Dryden's and Shadwell's Tempest." HLQ 6:224-28.
By comparing the published version of Dryden's "Prologue Spoken at the Opening of the Theatre Royal, March 26, 1674" with a manuscript version of the prologue, Hooker reinforces Scott's notion that in the final couplet Dryden is sneering at Shadwell's rendering of The Tempest.

2 MONTAGU, M.F. ASHLEY. Edward Tyson, M.D., F.R.S. 1650-1708. Philadelphia: American Philosophical Society, p. 320.
Robert Hooke was "probably" the "principal butt" of Shadwell's satire in The Virtuoso.

1944

1 De BEER, E.S. "The Dramatist Sons of Thomas, Earl of Berkshire." N&Q 187:214-15.
That Lady Vaine in Sullen Lovers represents "Mary Uphill, whom Howard subsequently married, is extremely unlikely."

2 SCOTT, FLORENCE R. "'News from Plymouth' and Sir Positive At-all." MLR 39:183-85.

Rejects Evans's suggestion (S.1940.1) that Sir Positive derives partly from Sir Solemn Trifle in D'Avenant's play.

1945

1 SYMONS, JULIAN. "Restoration Comedy (Reconsiderations II)." KR 7:187.
Regards Shadwell as a "transitional dramatist; a good hand at a plot, but a clumsy and imperceptive writer, who failed to reconcile the comedy of humors that he wished to write and the comedy of manners towards which he laboriously but naturally moved."

1946

1 MANDACH, ANDRÉ de. Molière et la comédie de moeurs en angleterre (1660-68). Neuchatel: a la Baconnière, pp. 84-85, 100-101.
Reasserts that Sullen Lovers borrows heavily from Les Fâcheux.

1947

1 MIGNON, ELISABETH. Crabbed Age and Youth: The Old Men and Women in the Restoration Comedy of Manners. Durham, N.C.: Duke University Press, pp. 73-82.
Focusing on eight of Shadwell's plays, examines his dramatization of "tyrannous fathers," "lovers of the past," "amorous over-ripe ladies," "senile governesses," "amorous old male fops," and so on. The song in Psyche (IV.ii.318) sums up his attitude toward old age.

2 MILTON, WILLIAM M. "Tempest in a Teapot." ELH 14:207-18.
Reviews the evidence, citing practically all previous articles on the subject (some of which are not listed in this bibliography), and ends by supporting W.J. Lawrence's original (S.1904.2) attribution of the 1674, operatic Tempest to Shadwell.

1948

1 McKILLOP, ALAN DUGALD. English Literature from Dryden to Burns. New York and London: Appleton-Century-Crofts, pp. 73, 82.
Shadwell is best at combining humors with "bustle" and "farce" in roughly vigorous, realistic comedies such as Sullen Lovers, The Humorists, Epsom-Wells, The Virtuoso, The Squire of Alsatia, and Bury-Fair.

2 NICOLSON, MARJORIE HOPE. Voyages to the Moon. New York: Macmillan, p. 124.

Relates Sir Nicholas Gimcrack's enthusiasm for the moon in The Virtuoso to writings and experiments by Glanvill, Hooke, Wren, and Wilkins.

3 SHERBURN, GEORGE. The Restoration and Eighteenth Century (1660-1789). Vol. 3 of A Literary History of England. Edited by Albert C. Baugh. New York: Appleton-Century-Crofts, pp. 769-70.

In his best plays--Sullen Lovers, Epsom-Wells, The Virtuoso, The Lancashire-Witches, The Amorous Bigotte, The Squire of Alsatia, and Bury-Fair--Shadwell "pictures the bourgeoisie vividly and amusingly," though coarsely. And he tends to use country scenes more than his contemporaries do.

4 SMITH, JOHN HARRINGTON. "French Sources for Six English Comedies, 1660-1750." JEGP 47:390.

In The Woman-Captain, "the motif in which a woman impersonates a captain-brother" is borrowed from Montfleury's La Fille Capitaine (1672), but Shadwell adds extra violence and accentuates the husband's jealousy; the result is a "swashbuckling" play.

5 _____. The Gay Couple in Restoration Comedy. Cambridge, Mass.: Harvard University Press, pp. 32, 38-39, 61, 83-84, 120-30, 142, 202, 230.

"In determining the course which comedy would subsequently take," Shadwell "is the most important figure of his century." Except in Epsom-Wells, The Virtuoso, and parts of A True Widow, he favorably depicts "men and women of sense" and honest lovers in contrast with gay couples, fops, and silly, frivolous coquettes, much to the detriment of the latter. "Steele is Shadwell's prophecy brought to accomplishment."

In Sullen Lovers, despite some concessions to popular trends, he makes his hero an honest lover; in The Humorists an honest lover is shown to be a man of sense; and in The Miser the modest and sincere are approved, the cynics ridiculed or made unattractive. Woman gains the ascendancy in A True Widow as rake becomes honest suitor after being repulsed by virtuous female. The "most puerile" of Shadwell's plays, The Lancashire-Witches vainly tries to combine gaiety and sincerity, wit and virtue; but "a new era" becomes "imminent" with The Squire of Alsatia, which establishes the pattern of rake-hero restrained by serious heroine. A "spirit of reform" permeates Bury-Fair, where a man of reason and woman of sense rebuke the faults of a libertine couple. The Scowrers "repeats the formula" of Squire, and The Volunteers "so abounds in the spirit of reform as to resemble a tract."

6 _____. "Shadwell, the Ladies, and the Change in Comedy." MP 46:22-33.

Although he experimented with love games and cynical satire in *Epsom-Wells* and *The Virtuoso*, Shadwell joined "the ladies" in the 1680s to establish exemplary comedy as a formidable rival to witty sex comedy. *The Squire of Alsatia* (1688) and *Bury-Fair* (1689) fully responded to Shadwell's earlier objections to non-exemplary modes and satisfied the female audience's desire for kinds of comedy that would support constancy in love and show optimism about human nature. Other supposed causes of "the new comic method" (reforming pamphlets, middle-class tastes, the court of William and Mary, benevolism) either came too late or prove to be irrelevant to what happened in the 1680s. Smith bases his argument on prologues, prefaces, and passages in the plays.

1950

1 BREDVOLD, LOUIS I. "The Literature of the Restoration and the Eighteenth Century 1660-1798." In *A History of English Literature*. Edited by Hardin Craig. New York: Oxford University Press, p. 356.

"The most interesting" of the minor Restoration comic dramatists, Shadwell had a "heavy" wit but showed, especially in *Epsom-Wells* and *The Squire of Alsatia*, that he shared Jonson's "sturdy moral judgment and vigorous realism."

2 DOWNER, ALAN S. *The British Drama: A Handbook and Brief Chronicle*. New York: Appleton-Century-Crofts, pp. 193-94, 210-11.

Shadwell professed to write Jonsonian humors, love intrigue, and satire, but he sometimes slipped into obscene manners comedy. *Bury-Fair* implies criticism of the gay couple as it combines humors and manners, but it tends to display social attitudes without satire and it fails to integrate plot and setting. *A True Widow* is notable for its depiction of a Restoration theater audience, and there is also some reference to audience and performance in *The Virtuoso*. Some of Shadwell's later plays "are openly sentimental."

3 FREEHAFER, JOHN. "The Emergence of Sentimental Comedy, 1660-1707." Ph.D. dissertation, University of Pennsylvania, pp. 204-12.

Sees *Squire* as "the first true sentimental comedy" and one that "avoided the excesses of later sentimental comedy." With "something for every taste," it is "far more moralistic and didactic than its source," and its great importance lies in its "combination of realism with a presentation of . . . social problems." Belfond Jr. shows "the actions and many of the thoughts of a man of sense."

4 HUMBERT, BEATE. Die Lustspiele Wycherleys und Shadwells in ihrer Beziehung zu den Komödien Molières. Hamburg: n.p., 102 pp.

Critics have exaggerated Molière's influence on Shadwell. Only Sullen Lovers, The Miser, and Bury-Fair show more than slight indebtedness to the work of the Frenchman.

5 LEECH, CLIFFORD. "Restoration Tragedy: A Reconsideration." DUJ 42:107-8, 113.

Regards The Lancashire-Witches as a "piece of brutal horse-play," and asserts that in Timon, Shadwell invents a faithful mistress for the central character partly to "imply that his treatment of her made his ending just."

1951

*1 FELTHAM, FREDERICK G. "The Quality of the Wit in Comedies of Etherege, Wycherley, Congreve, and Shadwell." Ph.D. dissertation, University of Chicago, 242 pp.

Source: CDI (1861-1972), 34:386.

2 JONES, EVERETT L. "Robert Hooke and The Virtuoso." MLN 66: 180-82.

Judging from his diary entries (see S.1675.2; S.1676.1), Hooke regarded The Virtuoso "as a personal attack" (see S.1943.2).

3 WHITE, ERIC WALTER. The Rise of English Opera. London: John Lehmann, pp. 36-37.

Psyche is better than "the original of Corneille and Molière," because Shadwell was more sensitive "to the cues for music implicit in the action" and "took special care to make his words 'proper for Musick.'"

1952

1 BERKELEY, DAVID S. "The Penitent Rake in Restoration Comedy." MP 49:228, 231.

The Scowrers exhibits belief in the notion that a virtuous woman's charming eyes can convert a rake to commendable behavior.

2 CLINTON-BADDELEY, V.C. The Burlesque Tradition in the English Theatre after 1660. London: Methuen, p. 41.

Psyche is a "prodigiously foolish piece, an elaborate solemnity full of processions and sacrifices and priests chanting litanies."

3 HOGAN, CHARLES BEECHER. Shakespeare in the Theatre 1701-1800: A Record of Performances in London 1701-1750. Oxford: Clarendon Press, pp. 422-36, 437-48.

Analyzes Shadwell's changes in The Tempest and Timon, and lists performances, with casts, of both plays.

4 KRONENBERGER, LOUIS. The Thread of Laughter: Chapters on English Stage Comedy from Jonson to Maugham. New York: Alfred A. Knopf, pp. 93-104.

Considers Shadwell a hack with no "real social or intellectual or moral convictions," and "no sense of how . . . life might be heightened, or intensified, or metamorphosed into art." Because of its "rough and ready elegance," its convincing picture of Lady Busy, and its alarming exposure of the sin of keeping, A True Widow is his best play, though it is too long, too conventional, and lacks lightness of touch. The Squire of Alsatia is a well-contrived but overly complicated farce, realistic and funny, but neither brisk nor witty. Too stagey and "reportorial," it has "no creative quality of realism," no imaginative criticism. And Bury-Fair, an "inferior" play, is merely an inoffensive, rather dull and long-winded affair, full of obvious satire and juvenile pranks.

5 KUNITZ, STANLEY J., and HOWARD HAYCRAFT. British Authors before 1800: A Biographical Dictionary. New York: H.W. Wilson, pp. 457-58.

As in Sullen Lovers, Epsom-Wells, Squire of Alsatia, and Lancashire-Witches, "all that is best in Shadwell's works . . . comes from Jonson. He lacked . . . wit, polish and skill in construction . . . but his comedies contain a rich variety of eccentric characters, each carefully drawn from the life."

1953

1 HOOK, LUCYLE. "Shakespeare Improv'd, or A Case for the Affirmative." SQ 4:294.

In Timon, the new roles of Evandra and Melissa were supplied "for Mistress Betterton and Mistress Shadwell where no roles for women had existed before."

2 LYNCH, JAMES J. Box, Pit, and Gallery: Stage and Society in Johnson's London. Berkeley and Los Angeles: University of California Press, p. 80.

With his innovations, Shadwell transformed Timon into "the story of faithful and faithless love," interpreted through balance and counterbalance.

3 McMANAWAY, J.G. Introduction to "Songs and Masques in The Tempest." In Theatre Miscellany: Six Pieces Connected with the Seventeenth-Century Stage. Luttrell Society Reprints, no. 14. Oxford: Basil Blackwell, pp. 71, 79-83.

With new evidence in hand, concludes that Shadwell may be said to have participated in, but not authored, the 1674 redactio of The Tempest, which was probably performed more than once by 26 March. The dating of "The Ariels Songs" is also discussed.

1954

1 BARTLEY, J.O. Teague, Shenkin and Sawney, Being an Historical Study of the Earliest Irish, Welsh and Scottish Characters in English Plays. Cork: Cork University Press, pp. 105-6.

Shadwell possessed "genuine capability as a comic writer." His Tegue in The Lancashire-Witches, an anti-Irish and anti-Roman Catholic play, is given "casuistic immorality" and is ridiculed more for his religion than for his nationality. In The Amorous Bigotte, Tegue is taken off to Spain, again ridiculed for his religion, and made "more knavish and possibly less stupid."

2 BONNARD, GEORGES A. "Note sur les Sources de Timon of Athens." EA 7:66.

Compares Shadwell's Timon with an anonymous manuscript play.

3 GAGEN, JEAN ELISABETH. The New Woman: Her Emergence in English Drama 1600-1730. New York: Twayne, pp. 48-50, 99-100, 144-45, 149-50.

In Bury-Fair, Gertrude is the normative foil to the intellectually pretentious, foppish Fantasts, and in Sullen Lovers, Emilia, with her obsessive reading habits, is ridiculed by Carolina. Lucia and Carolina, of Epsom-Wells, use overt cynicism about love and marriage as a device to capture mates. The proviso drawn up by Stanford and Emilia, in Sullen Lovers, emphasizes equality between the sexes.

4 HOPKINS, KENNETH. The Poets Laureate. London: Bodley Head, pp. 32-43.

Although Shadwell "has little tragic power" and less poetry, his best comedies--Epsom-Wells, The Squire of Alsatia, Bury-Fair--show vigor, intelligence, acute observation, and an adeptness in depicting contemporary manners that equals Jonson's. The Squire of Alsatia should be revived.

1955

1 BERKELEY, DAVID S. "Preciosité and the Restoration Comedy of Manners." HLQ 18:118-19.

As exemplified by Bury-Fair, Shadwell was "as apt at anti-précieuse satire as the manners writers, and certainly more persistent than any save Congreve and Farquhar." In The Scowrers, however, he "succumbed" to the belief held by précieux and précieuses that virtuous and beautiful women can reform through irresistible charm.

2 _____. "Some Notes on Probability in Restoration Drama." N&Q 200:237, 239.

Notes that Sir William Rant, of The Scowrers, "speaks in prose when he is a common bully and in blank verse when he repents before his father."

3 SPEAIGHT, GEORGE. The History of the English Puppet Theatre. London, Toronto, Wellington, and Sydney: George C. Harrap, p. 84.

The influence of the puppet theater is reflected in Sullen Lovers when a boy dressed as Pulcinella enters the stage, sits on a chair, and dances a jig in imitation of a marionette.

1956

1 HUGHES, LEO. A Century of English Farce. Princeton: Princeton University Press, pp. 8-9, 32, 238, n.4., 276.

Notes the pantomime dance by the boy dressed as "Pugenello" in Sullen Lovers, condemns the dulling repetition and exaggeration in The Virtuoso, and maintains that the "burlesqued farce" in A True Widow is "aimed at just the sort of noisy slapstick Durfey and Mrs. Behn were turning out."

2 MANIFOLD, J.S. The Music in English Drama from Shakespeare to Purcell. London: Rockliff, pp. 119, 121, 126, 129-30, 132-33, 135, 152.

Comments on the use of, or allusion to, musicians and musical instruments (for example, "the new French hautboy") in Sullen Lovers, The Libertine, Bury-Fair, and Squire of Alsatia.

1957

1 ARUNDELL, DENNIS. The Critic at the Opera. London: Ernest Benn, pp. 101-3, 114-28.

Discusses changes in the 1674 Tempest and praises Shadwell's fusion of play, music, and staging in Psyche.

2 COLLINS, P.A.W. "Restoration Comedy." In From Dryden to Johnson. The Pelican Guide to English Literature, vol. 4. Harmondsworth, Eng.: Penguin, p. 165.

Shadwell's "admiration for Jonson led him to explore social classes which his contemporaries ignored," but his work is uneven "gaily bawdy in Epsom-Wells" and "virtually didactic in Bury Fair A True Widow "has some amusing satire," and The Squire of Alsatia vividly evokes the London underworld as background for "well-meant discussions on the theory of education." Contrary to Dryden's portrait of him, Shadwell was often as good a writer as his greater contemporaries.

3 HALLIDAY, F.E. The Cult of Shakespeare. London: Gerald Duckworth, pp. 24-29.

Although Shadwell competently adapted Timon, his Tempest "is one of the most unpleasant of the adaptations; all innocence is lost, and the delicate fantasy debased to a salacious musical comedy," while the poetry is "sacrificed to pantomime spectacle."

4 HOGAN, CHARLES BEECHER. Shakespeare in the Theatre 1701-1800: A Record of Performances in London 1751-1800. Oxford: Clarendon Press, pp. 639-54.

Lists performances and casts of Shadwell's version of The Tempest.

5 HUMPHREYS, A.R. "The Literary Scene." In From Dryden to Johnson. The Pelican Guide to English Literature, vol. 4. Harmondsworth, Eng.: Penguin, p. 91.

In Sullen Lovers, Epsom-Wells, Squire of Alsatia, and Bury-Fair, Shadwell ranges from "cheerful farce to coarse verisimilitude," but with his "strong and picturesque" language, his "prosaic but vigorous mind," he "plants the reader in Restoration life." He was the best "humorist" of his time.

1958

1 WILSON, JOHN HAROLD. All the King's Ladies: Actresses of the Restoration. Chicago: University of Chicago Press, p. 102.

Some of the changes in Timon were motivated by Shadwell's desire to give more roles to actresses.

1959

1 BYRNE, M. St. CLARE. "The Shakespeare Season at The Old Vic, 1958-59 and Stratford-upon-Avon, 1959." SQ 10:549-50.

Despite the unnecessary omissions from the 1674 text, a performance of Shadwell's Tempest was "ingeniously mounted and very handsomely costumed," giving us a "good glimpse of Restoration 'theatre' in action."

2 MERCHANT, W. MOELWYN. Shakespeare and the Artist. London, New York, and Toronto: Oxford University Press, pp. 27-33.

"So far as our imagination can re-create them, Shadwell's Tempest and Gildon's Measure for Measure alone had the true substance of baroque opera." Psyche could not match these in close integration of spectacle and plot.

3 PETERSON, WILLIAM M., and RICHARD MORTON. "Guns on the Restoration Stage." N&Q 204:270, 308-10.

Briefly notes the use of guns, and of the ideas associated with them, in The Squire of Alsatia, The Woman-Captain, The Libertine, and The Virtuoso.

1960

1 BARISH, JONAS A. Ben Jonson and the Language of Prose Comedy. Cambridge, Mass.: Harvard University Press, pp. 288-89.

Notes the lack of self-recognition exhibited by the humors characters in Sullen Lovers and asserts that in The Squire of Alsatia satire gives way to homiletic, sentimental "melodrama."

2 BROWN, JOHN RUSSELL. "Three Adaptations." ShS 13:138-39.

As performed at the Old Vic, the 1674 Tempest, "this lively play-with-music-and-dance," turns out to be "scarcely a satisfactory whole." The concluding masque, in particular, is not integral to the main action.

3 REDDING, DAVID C. "A Note on Jonson Attributions." N&Q 205: 52-53.

In the opening scene of Bury-Fair, Oldwit alludes to a familiar poem that probably dates from the early seventeenth century.

1961

1 HENIGEN, ROBERT H. "English Dramma per Musica: A Study of Musical Drama in England from The Siege of Rhodes to the Opening of the Haymarket Theater." Ph.D. dissertation, University of Missouri, pp. 226-29, 253-63.

The 1674 Tempest is not really a musical drama; it is an "opera" of the Restoration sort that influenced musical drama. But Psyche (1675) is "the finest English dramma per musica to date," for, despite an overly complicated plot and episodic construction, it exhibits an aesthetic unity of music, action, and spectacle.

2 MOORE, ROBERT ETHERIDGE. Henry Purcell and the Restoration Theatre. Cambridge, Mass.: Harvard University Press, pp. 29-31, 178-203.

Discusses the sources and art forms composing Psyche, which is "at once more unified and far less stylized than the French." In The Tempest of 1674, "the most popular play of the Restoration Shadwell's "ruling desire was to make as much as possible of the fine machinery and 'effects' of Dorset Garden." The masque in Timon is charming but less rewarding than the Neptune masque in the Tempest; Purcell's music for Timon "clearly lightened the drabness of what Shadwell offered as ancient Greece."

1962

1 CAMDEN, CARROLL. "*Songs and Chorusses in The Tempest*." *PQ* 41:117-18.

The song "for the Chorus of Spirits" may have been "inspired by the Devil's song, written by Shadwell, in the . . . opera" (II.iii).

2 KNIGHT, G. WILSON. *The Golden Labyrinth: A Study of British Drama*. London: Phoenix House, pp. 131, 141.

Citing *Sullen Lovers*, *A True Widow*, *Bury-Fair*, and *The Squire of Alsatia*, Knight comments on Shadwell's "good sense and comprehensive humanity" and his "clear-headed and sane handling of a varied material." *Squire* is called "a strong study in moral concern and educational psychology."

3 VERNON, P.F. "Marriage of Convenience and the Moral Code of Restoration Comedy." *EIC* 12:375.

By adding two female roles to *Timon*, Shadwell gave the play a "new function": "to contrast the dignity of disinterested free-love with the sordidness of 'mercenary, base . . . Marriage Love' (I, i)."

1963

1 LOFTIS, JOHN. *The Politics of Drama in Augustan England*. Oxford: Clarendon Press, pp. 24-25.

Consistently a Whig, Shadwell inserted some incidental political thrusts into *Bury-Fair* and *The Amorous Bigotte*, and made *The Scowrers* an anti-Jacobite satire.

2 MANDELL, OSCAR, ed. "Rosimond and Shadwell." In *The Theatre of Don Juan: A Collection of Plays and Views, 1630-1963*. Lincoln: University of Nebraska Press, pp. 164-69.

Sees Shadwell as "one of the sounder playwrights of the Restoration" and *The Libertine* as "one of the most impressive plays of its epoch." Far superior to Rosimond's *Le nouveau Festin de Pierre*, *The Libertine* shows "the vision of Atheism" and "the metaphysics of universal inanity" unleashing "the brute passions of man." Mandell compares the play to *Crime and Punishment* and to *The Stranger*.

3 PEARSALL, RONALD. "The Case for Shadwell." *Month* 216:364-67.

Shadwell begins with slick, Jonsonian plays like *Sullen Lovers*, but his later works lean toward "the comedy of manners." He writes with a realism and "raciness almost unique in the drama of the time," and he excels Dryden as a playwright.

4 SINGH, SARUP. *The Theory of Drama in the Restoration Period*. Bombay, Calcutta, Madras, and New Delhi: Orient Longmans, pp. 44, 193, 208, 223-27, 242-45, 250, 270.

Although in theory Shadwell consistently opposed any contemporary form of writing that tended to undermine "the old English dramatic tradition" of vigorous realism, in practice he sometimes made awkward attempts to dramatize "the social affectations and follies of fashionable men and women," using the "values . . . of the Comedy of Manners." Lacking the stylistic refinement and aristocratic breeding to succeed in this mode, however, he did his best work in plays that were founded on his own coarsely energetic language and on his own "earnest, practical, moral" attitudes. Epsom-Wells is his best manners comedy. In The Humorists, he shifts from "Jonsonian 'natural' humours to the Restoration social affectations."

5 TIEDJE, EGON. Die Tradition Ben Jonsons in der Restaurationskömodie. Hamburg: Cram, de Gruyter, 168 pp., passim.

Deals with the tradition (not just the influence) of Ben Jonson in the comedy of the Restoration. Shadwell is described as a passionate Jonsonian who frequently uses "humours."

6 TOWERS, TOM H. "The Lineage of Shadwell: An Approach to Mac Flecknoe." SEL 3:323-34.

Places Shadwell within the tradition of scenic display established by Heywood, Dekker, Shirley, and Ogilby in "the Beeston-Davenant theater."

7 VERNON, P.F. "Social Satire in Shadwell's Timon." SN 35: 221-26.

We should take more seriously Shadwell's insistence that he made Timon into a play, for his version is better constructed, presents more varied actions, and is more concerned with Timon as victim of social corruption than Shakespeare's is. Evandra is used to show that permanent, genuine ties between men and women need not depend on marriage; and the sympathy accorded her, despite her engaging in premarital sex, is unusual in Restoration drama. Though Shadwell deserves credit for introducing comic values into tragedy, he weakens the play somewhat by slipping into sentimentality toward the end. Vernon glances at two eighteenth-century adaptations of Timon, then concludes that Shadwell's version is "an intelligent attempt to adapt the social criticism of Shakespeare's play to the problems facing the theatre audience of his own day."

1964

1 FAIRCLOUGH, G. THOMAS. "Hazlitt, Shadwell and a Figure of Speech." N&Q 209:24.

In "On People with One Idea" (Table-Talk), Hazlitt may be alluding to Sir Positive At-all of Sullen Lovers.

2 KORNINGER, SIEGFRIED. The Restoration Period and the Eighteenth Century 1660-1780. English Literature and Its Background. Vienna and Munich: Österreichischer Bundesverlag, p. 57.

Writing in the Jonsonian tradition, Shadwell portrays neglected aspects of Restoration society in plays that are "rough in language, vulgar and outspoken, yet neither cynical nor frivolous."

3 McDONALD, CHARLES O. "Restoration Comedy as Drama of Satire: An Investigation into Seventeenth Century Aesthetics." SP 61:526, 534.

Shadwell is "naïvely moralistic" in insisting on instruction through positive example, and his "morally reformed heroes are far more 'fancied,' unrealistic, than any figures presented by the major playwrights, as well as less satirized and comic."

4 SORELIUS, GUNNAR. "Shadwell Deviating into Sense: Timon of Athens and the Duke of Buckingham." SN 36:232-44.

Timon may have been strongly influenced by Buckingham: by the aesthetics implied in The Rehearsal, by the political ideas of the country party, by Buckingham's distrust of marriage (as exhibited in The Chances and in his life), and by several traits that seem to be gathered up and embodied in Alcibiades.

5 WILKINSON, D.R.M. The Comedy of Habit: An Essay on the Use of Courtesy Literature in a Study of Restoration Comic Drama. Leiden: Universitaire Pers, pp. 87-88, 95, 98, 149-50.

Briefly notes parallels between ideas expressed in courtesy literature and passages in Shadwell's plays.

1965

1 HARRIS, BERNARD. "The Dialect of Those Fanatic Times." In Restoration Theatre. Edited by John Russell Brown and Bernard Harris. New York: St. Martin's Press, pp. 28-29.

Shadwell prefers "a simple debating manner" to witty repartee, and uses "his arts of language to preserve a traditional morality." Unlike Etherege, who employs similitudes to embody relationships between natural and human life, Shadwell presupposes a distinction between "the artificial and the natural," and he musters "a prodigious array of prose styles" to keep this distinction clear as he discusses "natural and unnatural breeding." His plays have been unfairly neglected.

2 MELLERS, WILFRID. Harmonious Meeting: A Study of the Relationship between English Music, Poetry and Theatre, c. 1600-1900. London: Dennis Dobson, pp. 220, 223-24.

Whereas Shadwell continued the process (begun by Dryden and Davenant) of reducing Shakespeare's range in The Tempest,

Purcell used the masque of Neptune, which he found to be free of limiting ties to the overall play, to restore some of the original depth and variety of feeling.

3 MERCHANT, W. MOELWYN. "Shakespeare 'Made Fit.'" In Restoration Theatre. Edited by John Russell Brown and Bernard Harris. New York: St. Martin's Press, pp. 214-16.

Shadwell's masque at Timon's feast is a classically structured set piece, which is less organic to the main plot than was Shakespeare's original "Masque of the Senses." In the 1674 Tempest, Shadwell surpasses Dryden and Davenant in integrating "scenic elaboration with the fundamental structure of Shakespeare's play," though Shadwell does have "moments of banality."

4 SPENCER, CHRISTOPHER, ed. Introduction to Five Restoration Adaptations of Shakespeare. Urbana: University of Illinois Press, pp. 9, 14, 18-19.

Reaffirms Shadwell's authorship of the 1674 Tempest, compares this version to that of Dryden and Davenant, and argues that although Shadwell cheapened the play by adding more women's parts (a sign of the times), on the whole it remains an enjoyable work.

5 WILSON, JOHN HAROLD. A Preface to Restoration Drama. Boston: Houghton Mifflin Co., pp. 23, 139, 150-54.

Presents Shadwell as a competent but "doctrinaire writer, cramped by the rigidity of his formula." He was "narrowly moralistic," tended to create loose plots and two-dimensional characters, and failed to transmute his acutely perceived social details into a "rounded interpretation of human experience." Sullen Lovers is "long on 'humors' and short on humor" (and on plot), while The Tempest is a "pleasant musical comedy" and The Squire of Alsatia is interestingly journalistic, though not realistic. In Sir Positive At-all (Sullen Lovers) and Sir Nicholas Gimcrack (The Virtuoso), Shadwell offers amusing portraits of contemporaries (Sir Robert Howard and Robert Hooke, respectively).

1966

1 CUNNINGHAM, JOHN E. Restoration Drama. London: Evans Brothers, pp. 151-52.

Albeit The Squire of Alsatia is impressively realistic, Shadwell generally was a "second-rate Jonson" who wrote "lumbering stuff."

2 DEARMIN, MICHAEL GEORGE. "Thomas Shadwell: Playwright." Ph.D. dissertation, University of Wisconsin, 235 pp.

Studies the plays in light of Shadwell's dramatic theories. In The Virtuoso "Shadwell, for the first time, uses social and moral criticism as unifying elements." A True Widow is his best "comedy of humours in the Jonsonian manner," but The Squire of Alsatia and Bury-Fair are, on the whole, "his two finest plays." Sullen Lovers and Epsom-Wells are also discussed at some length. See Dissertation Abstracts International 28 (1967):623A.

3 NICOLSON, MARJORIE, and DAVID STUART RODES, eds. Introduction to The Virtuoso. Regents Restoration Drama Series. Lincoln: University of Nebraska Press, pp. xi-xxvi.

A discussion of texts, theater history, and influences of the play precedes coverage of the backgrounds to its satire on science: origins of the Royal Society, seventeenth-century meanings of virtuoso and gimcrack, implications of references to Lucretian atomism, and sources for references to the moon, flight, microscopes, the weighing of air, transfusions, mechanized looms, and so on. No aesthetic criticism is attempted.

4 MILBURN, D. JUDSON. The Age of Wit 1650-1750. New York: Macmillan Co.; London: Collier-Macmillan, p. 72.

Refers to Shadwell as a "dully moralistic dramatist." His theories on dramatic art and wit are cited throughout the book.

5 ROGERS, KATHARINE M. The Troublesome Helpmate: A History of Misogyny in Literature. Seattle and London: University of Washington Press, pp. 181-82.

Gertrude in Bury-Fair offers "the correct view of woman's function."

6 SCOUTEN, A.H. "Notes toward a History of Restoration Comedy." PQ 45:65.

Sees Shadwell as moving from early, Jonsonian plays to post-Revolution works, such as The Squire of Alsatia, "which connected him with . . . sentimental comedy."

7 SORELIUS, GUNNAR. 'The Giant Race Before the Flood': Pre-Restoration Drama on the Stage and in the Criticism of the Restoration. Uppsala: Almqvist & Wiksells, pp. 106, 159, 187-89.

Defines The Sullen Lovers as a mixture of humors and wit, and notes its topical satire, aristocratic characters, and fashionable hostility to marriage. Sorelius believes that the most important changes in the 1674 Tempest involve stage directions and that Timon of Athens initiated "the vogue for adaptations of Shakespeare's classical and historical plays." In Timon Shadwell effectively combines the story of its titular character with the adventures of Alcibiades, the latter containing political comments on Buckingham's campaign to dissolve the House of Commons.

8 TRAUGOTT, JOHN. "The Rake's Progress from Court to Comedy: A Study in Comic Form." SEL 6:384-85.

"Shadwell's Don John in his Libertine, a perfectly insane product of that undeviatingly senseless mind," is "a morality play figure, a mindlessly malicious rapist, an absurd puppet calling down God's vengeance."

1967

1 ALSSID, MICHAEL W. "Shadwell's MacFlecknoe." SEL 7:387-402.
Analyzes dimensions of Dryden's criticism, refusing to accept easy interpretations of allusions that may be read several ways. To create the poem, Dryden "subverted Shadwell's critical ideas and dramatic practice," transforming him "into a humors character to show us a fool who, like the humors of his plays, persistently incriminates himself." The poem shows that Dryden was aware of Shadwell's incipient Whiggism.

2 _____. Thomas Shadwell. New York: Twayne, 191 pp.
Examines Shadwell's artistry in context to show that he was less a journalist than a satirist, and that his satire differs from that of Etherege, Wycherley, or Congreve, in that it is bolder, less sophisticated, and harsher. Shadwell employs humors characters to ridicule "man's deflection from wisdom and morality," his "incapacity to master his will and his existence," and his self-deceptive pride. Though the playwright never inquires into the reasons for man's self-enslavement, he shows society to be both the source and the setting for man's folly.

Sullen Lovers is a psychological comedy about misanthropy and how to deal with a selfish society. With its more subtle symbolism, The Humorists reveals that society caters to the sicknesses that humors express; and The Miser, the most original of all adaptations of L'Avare, indicates that young lovers must be devious to achieve their ends in a greedy world.

After these three apprentice plays, Shadwell writes more mature works, showing growing command over technique and theme. In Epsom-Wells, his only attempt at wit comedy, the setting symbolizes any place where people unmask and truths are revealed, where heroism and marriage are diseases and hedonism is health. But the "Lucretian-Epicurean ideal of wit and wisdom" is degraded in The Virtuoso, which blends wit and satire against man's futile efforts to understand nature.

The next three plays show woman as triumphant. A True Widow is about the arts of cheating and of creating illusions, and about making distinctions between conscious and unconscious pretension. The Woman-Captain is a farce concerning personal heroics in antiheroic London, with themes of education, social leveling, and the degeneration of males and of the older aristocracy. Female "witchcraft"--as true sorcery or as feminine mischief--dominates The Lancashire-Witches. Anticipating this motif of triumphant woman, The Royal Shepherdess contrasts pastoral, heroic, and comic modes and attitudes, softening a nearly sardonic tone with traces of sentimental pathos.

Shadwell's contribution to *The Tempest* is to underscore Dryden and Davenant's critical treatment of Shakespeare's romanticism; and in *Psyche* he successfully blends music, words, and spectacle. He presents Don John in *The Libertine* as a tragic rake who fails to discover a role. Evandra's role in *Timon* is also ambiguous, and as she and Timon belatedly learn about the world's infidelity and meanness, they demonstrate that strict deception and strict candor in the use of language are equally inept. In *The Squire of Alsatia* education is tested by action, and Alsatia symbolizes rebellion against established social patterns. *Bury-Fair* studies the extent to which a wit can control his own humor and his environment, the fair itself being a ritual site for human interaction, where kinds of education and approaches to the environment are tried. The nature and uses of language are important in this and the previous play.

The Amorous Bigotte shows that youth must learn and survive through naive dissembling, since the world offers no true educators; and *The Scowrers* suggests that the repressing of destructive lusts, together with the acceptance of love and wisdom, can be subtle ways of "scowring." Finally, *The Volunteers* stresses the notion that lovers, like warriors, must serve larger, less personal, more powerful entities in order to gain fulfillment. Shadwell thus ends his career with an implicit tribute to William and Mary, and with some anti-Puritan satire.

3 EDMUNDS, JOHN. "Shadwell and the Anonymous 'Timon.'" *N&Q* 212:218-21.

Offers evidence to suggest that Shadwell used the anonymous manuscript "Timon" as a direct source for his adaptation of Shakespeare.

4 LOVE, H.H.R. Review of the Regents Restoration Drama Series. *AUMLA* 27:107-8.

The Sydrophel episode in *Hudibras* anticipated *The Virtuoso*, in which Hooke was "Shadwell's principal target." *The Virtuoso*, however, is "neither as distinguished in purely comic terms as its author's early, neo-Aristotelian *The Sullen Lovers*, nor nearly as valuable as social comment as *A True Widow*."

5 SILVETTE, HERBERT. *The Doctor on the Stage: Medicine and Medical Men in Seventeenth-Century England*. Edited by Francelia Butler. Knoxville: University of Tennessee Press, pp. 42-43, 50, 57, 72, 81-83, 88, 90, 92, 102-3, 109, 145-46, 155-81, 183-91, 200, 211-12, 225-26, 231, 263.

Treats Shadwell as a journalistic dramatist and makes amusing observations about medical topics in twelve of his plays: for example, castration in *The Libertine*; bleeding, *album graecum*, asafetida, and quackery in *Sullen Lovers*; opium in *The Woman-Captain*; hartshorn in *The Volunteers*; venereal disease in *The Humorists*; and, of course, satire on science in *The Virtuoso* (adding nothing new).

6 TAYLOR, ALINE MACKENZIE. "Dryden's 'Enchanted Isle' and Shadwell's 'Dominion.'" In Essays in English Literature of the Classical Period. Edited by Daniel W. Patterson and Albrecht B. Strauss. SP, Extra Series, no. 4, pp. 39-53.

"The 'dominion' with which Father Flecknoe endows his 'son' glances at Shadwell's unabashedly triumphant 'improvements' on Dryden's adaptation of Shakespeare's play, the operatic and spectacular Tempest of 1674." By deliberately omitting his own name and including Dryden's original preface and prologue, Shadwell pre-empted overt complaints from the poet laureate. In MacFlecknoe Dryden got his own back, very subtly.

7 ZIMMERMAN, FRANKLIN B. Henry Purcell 1659-1695: His Life and Times. London, Melbourne, and Toronto: Macmillan; New York: St. Martin's, p. 219.

The Libertine (with Purcell's music) derives from Dorimon's Le Festin de Pierre, not from Molière's L'Athée foudroyé, as has been supposed.

1968

1 AUDUBERT, MICHELE. "Quatre adaptations de Molière sur la scène Anglaise a l'Époque de la Restauration: Thomas Shadwell, The Miser (1672)." In Dramaturgie et Société. Edited by Jean Jacquot et al. Vol. 1. Paris: Éditions du Centre Nationale de la Recherche Scientifique, pp. 343-52.

In The Miser Shadwell follows Molière's main plot and in the first two acts remains faithful to his source in other respects as well. Overall, however, he skillfully transforms Molière's play into a busier, more fun-loving drama in the English spirit. He exaggerates the traits of the main character, adds a secondary plot with its own characters and links it (albeit artificially) to the main action, obscures Molière's focus on the family, and substitutes an overt moral aim for Moliere's underlying seriousness. By using the secondary action to bring the Restoration English milieu to bear on Molière's story, Shadwell manages to inform even the setting with his own idiom. If Molière's play seems classical, Shadwell's comes across as typically English in its variety and vivacity.

2 FLETCHER, MARY CATHERINE. "Thomas Shadwell as Social Historian." Ph.D. dissertation, University of Mississippi, 454 pp.

Demonstrates that Shadwell's plays are "authentic source material" for "a consideration of the social history of Restoration England": "the gay and dissolute spirit of the age, contemporary science and superstition, habit and pastime, life in the city and the country, romance and family living, wit and wits, government, and religion." See Dissertation Abstracts International 29 (1969):3609A.

3 KUNZ, DON RICHARD, Jr. "From Satire to Sentiment: Thomas Shadwell's Dramatic Theory and Practice." Ph.D. dissertation, University of Washington, 312 pp.
Published: S.1972.5. See Dissertation Abstracts International 29 (1969):2217A-18A.

4 MATHIEU-ARTH, FRANÇOISE. "La 'Psyché' de Thomas Shadwell d'après Molière." In Dramaturgie et Société. Edited by Jean Jacquot et al. Vol. 1. Paris: Éditions du Centre Nationale de la Recherche Scientifique, pp. 373-93.
Traces the history of spectacular and musical drama in England and in France during the English Interregnum, stressing the influence of French theater on the English, especially through Davenant and Betterton. Endeavoring to compete with the rival company, Betterton persuaded Shadwell, fresh from his success with The Tempest, to create in Psyche an extravaganza of sights, sounds, and action. Although Shadwell's drama borrows heavily from the French source and seems hastily composed, it succeeds in its own way. Where the French version is carefully wrought so that the scenes lock together in a logical sequence, and so that the characters become moving symbols, the English Psyche is less rigidly coherent in action and dialogue, and its characters are psychologically more real and passionate. Above all, Shadwell's work is more sensuous and more complex in its theatrical offerings. With his own musical training to draw upon, Shadwell not only wrote the plot and dialogue but also instructed his musical collaborators, Lock and Draghi, in what sorts of songs and instruments to use. The result is an impressive blend of action, spectacle, dance, song, and dialogue, truly the first English opera.

5 NOVAK, MAXIMILLIAN. "Elkanah Settle's Attacks on Thomas Shadwell and the Authorship of the 'Operatic Tempest.'" N&Q 213:263-65.
Shows that Settle identified and attacked Shadwell's masque in the 1674 Tempest, and lends support to the view that the 1674 venture was a joint effort by Shadwell and others.

6 WAITH, EUGENE, ed. Introduction to Restoration Drama. New York: Bantam, p. xxii.
"The apostle of Jonsonian comedy, Thomas Shadwell, was markedly inferior" to Dryden, Etherege, Wycherley, Congreve, Vanbrugh, and Farquhar.

1969

*1 EDMUNDS, J.D. "Shadwell's Timon of Athens." Ph.D. dissertation, University of Birmingham, England.
Source: McNamee (1969-73), p. 291.

2 _____. "'Timon of Athens' Blended with 'Le Misanthrope': Shadwell's Recipe for Satirical Tragedy." MLR 64:500-7.

Indebted to Le Misanthrope rather than to The Plain-Dealer, Shadwell's Timon juxtaposes comic and tragic modes and motifs in order to make the audience reject "Hobbesian principles of conduct." Molière influenced Shadwell's rebellion against "the theatrical mood of his day," a rebellion that foreshadowed "the evolution of a healthier moral climate." As early as Sullen Lovers, a "fast-moving farce of a trivial, if dramatically effective, nature," Shadwell borrowed from Le Misanthrope.

3 GUFFEY, GEORGE ROBERT. Introduction to After the Tempest. Los Angeles: Clark Library, pp. i-xxiv.

Reviews the staging, publication, alterations, and problems of authorship of the Dryden-Davenant Tempest (1670), the Shadwell (et al.) version (1674), Duffet's Mock-Tempest (1675), and Garrick's operatic version (1756).

4 HUME, ROBERT D. "Formal Intention in The Brothers and The Squire of Alsatia." ELN 6:176-84.

Shadwell departs from Terence's conclusions but fails to create "a consistent or convincing alternative." He seems to affirm a town education yet satirizes Belfond Jr., who exemplifies the effects of such an education. Moreover, the reformation of Belfond Jr. "has no convincing basis." Thus, the play lacks control and is "artistically defective."

5 SUTHERLAND, JAMES. English Literature of the Late Seventeenth Century. New York and Oxford: Oxford University Press, pp. 43, 82, 88, 120-25, 151, 188, 377.

Although Shadwell inherits Jonson's awareness of human folly and his ability to blend "the fantastic and the nationalistic" in strong characters and downright language, he departs from Jonson by depicting gay couples and sexual intrigues, and he is generally kinder to his victims than Jonson was. Lacking easy wit, tending to belabor the obvious or the absurd, Shadwell nevertheless can recreate "the ebb and flow of contemporary conversation," can exploit the comic potential found in the "turns and twists of his dramatic action," and can effectively employ repetition, horseplay, and practical jokes. He is usually "critical of folly and affectation, rather than of loose living and vice," and his humor is "sardonic and disenchanted."

Like The Humorists, Epsom-Wells is rather a coarse play, and it contains an "unpalatable mixture" of humors and bawdy intrigue. A True Widow and The Squire of Alsatia, on the other hand, take strong moral stances and verge on sentimentalism. The Virtuoso satirizes pedantic collecting and experimentation, not the serious effort to establish scientific principles; Timon, "a tragic satire of genuine merit," attacks mercenary marriages and glorifies "the kept mistress." Sutherland also cites Sullen Lovers and Bury-Fair.

1970

1 GILDE, JOSEPH M. "Shadwell and the Royal Society: Satire in The Virtuoso." SEL 10:469-90.

Argues that "the Royal Society, far from being the object of the play's satire, provides a standard for judging the follies of the two principal fools" (Sir Nicholas Gimcrack and Sir Formal Trifle).

2 MUIR, KENNETH. The Comedy of Manners. London: Hutchinson, pp. 54-63.

Shadwell lacks polish, wit, and "a gift of style," but he is good at creating Jonsonian humors, at contriving farce, and at reflecting contemporary social life and conversation. His best plays are Sullen Lovers, a "satire of English manners" with a slight plot and amusing humors; The Humorists; Epsom-Wells; The Virtuoso, an enjoyably farcical, if dated, attack on the New Science, with rather uninteresting young lovers; A True Widow, The Squire of Alsatia, a swift-moving, spirited examination of con men and educational theories, with a "perfunctory" love-intrigue; and Bury-Fair, a "lively satirical picture of a provincial town," embodying an amusing wit plot, an indifferent romance plot, and some pre-sentimental moralizing. In this play, the fair itself is not really probed, but Shadwell's writing and characterizations are at their best.

3 SHAFER, YVONNE BONSALL. "The Proviso Scene in Restoration Comedy." RECTR 9, no. 1:4-5.

Compares the agreement between Courtine and Sylvia in Otway's Souldiers Fortune with the "inversion of the straight proviso scene . . . in Epsom Wells."

1971

1 BARNARD, JOHN. "Drama from the Restoration till 1710." In English Drama to 1710. Edited by Christopher Ricks. London: Sphere Books, p. 393.

Shadwell borrows from Jonson and Molière, and aptly dramatizes low life, in "vigorous but clumsy comedies of humours."

2 BERKOWITZ, GERALD M. "A Source for Shadwell's Amorous Bigotte." AN&Q 10:35.

Cites parallels that "might seem to establish" Corneille's Le Menteur (1642) "as the primary source for the plot of The Amorous Bigotte."

3 COLEMAN, ANTONY. "Shadwell's 'Country Hero.'" N&Q 216:459-60.

By reference to Remarks upon Remarques (see S.1673.1), argues that Epsom-Wells contributed "to a controversy between Town and Country which was then being conducted."

90

4 DONALDSON, IAN. "Ben Jonson." In English Drama to 1710. Edited by Christopher Ricks. London: Sphere Books, p. 279.

Shadwell "followed Jonson's manner competently, though with a faintly ridiculous spirit of devotion."

5 FORRESTER, KENT ALLEN. "Supernaturalism in Restoration Drama." Ph.D. dissertation, University of Utah, 191 pp.

By catering to the audience's love of spectacle and farce, the 1674 Tempest undermines "the significance of Shakespeare's original supernatural characters." Whereas The Lancashire-Witches seems uncertain about the audience's attitude toward the non-Christian supernatural, The Libertine has a hero who mocks "supernatural creatures in a manner that must have pleased many Restoration intellectuals." See Dissertation Abstracts International 32:1469A.

6 HAUN, EUGENE. But Hark! More Harmony: The Libretti of Restoration Opera in English. Ypsilanti: Western Michigan University Press, pp. 106-8, 118.

In discussing the 1674 Tempest, stressing its separation of singers and actors and its terminal masque, argues that Shadwell's changes so shift "the emphasis that the whole artistic involvement is recast."

7 KUNZ, DON R., Jr. "Shadwell's A True Widow: 'Promis'd a Play and Dwindled to a Farce'?" RECTR 10, no. 1:43-54.

"Shadwell tried revitalizing wit comedy by redefining it." This article becomes, with few changes, Chapter 4, section 1, of S.1972.5.

8 LOVE, HAROLD. "The Wives' Excuse and Restoration Comedy." KOMOS (Monash University, Australia) 2, no. 4:151.

Notes how at one point in A True Widow--Shadwell's "most interesting play"--a fool defeats a wit.

9 SCHNEIDER, BEN ROSS, Jr. The Ethos of Restoration Comedy. Urbana, Chicago, and London: University of Illinois Press, pp. 54, 64, 77, 109-10, 115, 158.

Briefly discusses dueling in Epsom-Wells; and preciosité prudish hypocrisy, and cast-off mistresses in The Squire of Alsatia. This latter play is "a labored argument against a tyrannous father," and Belfond Jr. is "the most virtuous libertine in Restoration comedy."

1972

1 BERMAN, RONALD. "The Values of Shadwell's Squire of Alsatia." ELH 39:375-86.

In Squire, Shadwell writes a cruder, more complicated play than the Roman original and is unable to emulate Terence in keeping role and value distinct. Shadwell's characters are "aggregates" of ideas which are moved about to realize three concepts: "the city is more civilized than the country; the man of the city, . . . a Whig, is superior to the insular and rustic Tory; the benevolent laws of Nature require only that we assent to their operation." Attempting to "justify both pleasure and order," the play depicts country life as unnatural because it is dull and undignified, and it dramatizes Locke's notion "that patriarchal authority leads to the anarchy of taste and morals." As prudence reconciles the brothers and saves the estate (thus making the city symbolic of salvation), the audience is asked to understand that youth must be allowed its license in order for it to grow into "mature conscience."

2 HUME, ROBERT D. "Diversity and Development in Restoration Comedy 1660-1679." ECS 5:380, 381, 391, 394-95.

A "vein of personal reference" makes Sullen Lovers and The Humorists "atypical both of Shadwell and contemporary comedy." Epsom-Wells, with its four plot strands, and The Virtuoso, with its balancing of serious romance and satire, have elements of manners comedy qualified by a broader social focus, more satire, and more romantic intrigue. Just as in these plays Shadwell employs comic methods he had earlier condemned, so in The Woman-Captain he gives us the "straight farce" that he had denounced in the preface to A True Widow and had delightfully burlesqued in Act 4 of the same play. A True Widow "minimizes the romantic plot to concentrate on the rogueries."

3 JORDAN, ROBERT. "The Extravagant Rake in Restoration Comedy." In Restoration Literature: Critical Approaches. Edited by Harold Love. London: Methuen, pp. 83-84.

Wildish of Bury-Fair and Longvil and Bruce of The Virtuoso are not extravagant rakes. "In them is made explicit what is largely implicit in the case of the Dorimants and the Horners--a concern with 'sense,' with 'understanding,' with intellectual awareness, and a cool sophistication even in their pleasures."

4 KROPF, C.R. "Educational Theory in 'The Squire of Alsatia.'" SAB 38, no. 2 (May):16-22.

In contrasting the miseducation of Tim with the ideal education of Ned, Shadwell draws on contemporary tracts and deals with more specific issues than heretofore noticed, issues such as the "usefulness of classical studies," "public versus private education, the relation of education to human nature, and the proper use of corporal punishment."

5 KUNZ, DON R. The Drama of Thomas Shadwell. Salzburg Studies in English Literature. Salzburg, Austria: Institut für Englische Sprache und Literature, 413 pp.

Revision of S.1968.3. Counters MacFlecknoe by studying Shadwell's artistic development in light of his theories and of social and aesthetic trends in his day. Shadwell is seen progressing from pessimistic satire to melioristic comedy, from aristocratic rationalism to middle-class fusion of sense and sensibility--all the while helping to re-establish, in place of repartee, rant, and intrigue, a traditionally English comedy of character, ideas, and theater.

His early plays reveal a search for a more instructive satiric comedy. Loosely plotted and depending mainly on negative examples, Sullen Lovers portrays humors and manners figures striving for tolerance and liberty in a pseudo-Hobbesian world. The Royal Shepherdess, a spectacular pastoral intrigue, opposes comedy of wit by offering positive examples of moral behavior; but negative examples again dominate The Humorists, though common sense norms are strongly implied as false wits and rakes are satirized in a manners structure peopled by post-Jonsonian humors (exhibiting willful affectation instead of temperamental deficiency). The Miser appeals to tender hearts, ridicules miserliness, cynicism, and promiscuity, and shows that the honest love of witty couples can institute a new society.

Contrary to prevailing critical opinion, Epsom-Wells is not a wit comedy; it uses the style and structure of wit comedy to undermine it. Through skillful management of diverse media in The Tempest and Psyche, Shadwell tries to reform the taste for showiness. If Psyche is a Restoration morality play, The Libertine, with its incongruent mingling of revenge tragedy, farce, heroics, masque, and pastoral, becomes a kind of mock-epic against libertinism.

Spectacle is used for political, moral, and aesthetic instruction in Timon, a play counseling reform of libertines and the re-establishment of democracy. The Virtuoso examines relations between reason and wisdom, rhetoric and ethics, and recommends utilitarian education as it satirizes abuses of science. After A True Widow ridicules farce and reargues the case for true wit using exemplary characters, The Woman-Captain bows to popular demand for buffoonery while it disparages marriages of convenienc and the sin of keeping; in the process, it "outlines a rational spectrum of sexual relations."

Shadwell intended to show, in The Lancashire-Witches, that good sense and patriotism, exemplified in Sir Edward (who blends Renaissance, Restoration, and Augustan ideals of manhood), can restore order amidst chaos; but under pressure from censors, the play became a spectacular, farcical piece of Whig propaganda, a critique of belief in natural causes, and an attack on false wit.

As the Williamite era was established, Shadwell found himself in a climate more conducive to his natural bent toward exemplary comedy. The Squire of Alsatia, an exploration of educational theories, shows him as a realist ill at ease with idealized notions of natural benevolence; and Bury-Fair argues rationally for good nature, based on responsible citizenship, as depicts a rake's reform by his peers and contrasts urban and pastoral. Distrust of emotion, and an effort to preserve laughte and wit without cruelty, inform The Amorous Bigotte, a farcical portrayal of false education by women and priests. In The Scowrers, social reform is achieved through appeals to both reason and emotion, and in The Volunteers, self-interested materialism is contrasted with good-natured humanitarianism, as knaves and fools from a neutered Hobbesian world become merely farcical; the good-natured man of feeling triumphs and laughter is integrated with exemplary comedy.

6 LEVISON, WILLIAM SAMUEL. "Restoration Adaptations of Shakespeare as Baroque Literature." Ph.D. dissertation, University of Illinois--Urbana/Champaign, 154 pp.

Timon is used to illustrate some characteristics of baroque style. See Dissertation Abstracts International 34 (1973):730A.

7 LOFTIS, JOHN. "The Limits of Historical Veracity in Neoclassical Drama." In England in the Restoration and Early Eighteenth Century: Essays on Culture and Society. Edited by H.T. Swedenberg, Jr. Berkeley, Los Angeles, and London: University of California Press, pp. 38-40.

Though Shadwell was the only dramatist of his day "whose vision transcended the prejudices of the court circle," even his plays are not so tolerant as they are comprehensive. Through Don John in The Libertine, the "first important rendering of the Don Juan legend in English," Shadwell seems to be commenting on the extreme of courtly libertinism and religious freethinking.

8 PERKIN, RICHARD. "Shadwell's Poet Ninny: Additional Material in a Manuscript of The Sullen Lovers." Library, 5th ser. 27: 244-51.

Considering newly discovered manuscript pages for the end of Act 3, "it seems likely . . . that the Huffe-Ninny incident was added to the text soon after the publication of the first edition . . . in September 1668 and that Ninny is indeed Edward Howard."

9 SEWARD, PATRICIA M. "Was the English Restoration Theatre Significantly Influenced by Spanish Drama?" RLC 46:120, 124.

The Amorous Bigotte depends to some extent on Spanish comedia de capa y espada, and The Libertine, of course, is "based on the Don Juan story."

10 VROONLAND, JAMES ALLEN. "The Dryden-Shadwell Controversy: A Preface to MacFlecknoe." Ph.D. dissertation, Kansas State University, 208 pp.

After Chapter 3 "documents the triumph of Shadwell in the theater and elsewhere," Chapter 4 interprets Timon of Athens as an attack on Dryden. See Dissertation Abstracts International 33:2399A.

1973

1 FISKE, ROGER. English Theatre Music in the Eighteenth Century. London, New York, and Toronto: Oxford University Press, pp. 29-30.

Traces the history of musical contributions to The Tempest.

2 JOSEPH, BERTRAM LEON. "Shadwell, Thomas." In Encyclopaedia Britannica. 14th ed. Vol. 20. Chicago and London: Encyclopaedia Britannica, pp. 309-10.

Presents Shadwell as a writer of realistic and "broad comedies of manners" which are notable for their "often brilliant" creations of character, skillfully controlled plots, lively prose dialogue, and vivid depictions of the "Restoration scene."

3 KUNZ, DON R. "Shadwell and His Critics: The Misuse of Dryden's MacFlecknoe." RECTR 12, no. 1:14-27.

Surveys the history of critical attitudes toward Shadwell, implies that Dryden is less vitriolic than usually thought, and maintains that we have tended to identify Shadwell too closely with the "fictional playwright" that Dryden invents in MacFlecknoe.

4 LEWIS, MINEKO S. "Humor Characterization in Restoration Comedy, 1660-1700." Ph.D. dissertation, University of Tennessee, 217 pp.

Places Shadwell's humors methods, not only in relation to Jonson's and the traditions he relied upon, but also in relation to the broader traditions of characterization being developed by Dryden, Wycherley, Etherege, Congreve, Vanbrugh, and Farquhar. See Dissertation Abstracts International 34:1247A.

5 LOFTIS, JOHN. The Spanish Plays of Neoclassical England. New Haven and London: Yale University Press, pp. 91, 131, 172-77, 251.

Drawing upon Tirso's El Burlador de Sevilla through French intermediaries, The Libertine is the first important version of the Don Juan story in English. It uses cape and sword conventions but its "emotional structure is different both from that of neoclassical tragedy and that of the other Spanish plots." It has a "gracioso" who maintains an "evaluating and contrasting relationship to his master," and its Don John, influenced by Milton, Marlowe, and Lucretius, is evil on principle. Becoming almost a burlesque figure through the "multiplicity and gravity" of his sins, Don John caricatures the amorality of libertines in Restoration society and comedy. In commenting on the moral consequences of "calculated philosophical atheism," The Libertine is "unique among the Restoration Spanish plots." Loftis also notes that in Tarugo's Wiles "Sydserfe anticipates by nearly a decade Shadwell's dramatic satire on the new science" in The Virtuoso.

6 ROBINSON, K.E. "Rochester and Shadwell." N&Q 218:177.
Discusses implications of an allusion in Timon to Rochester's "Satyr against Reason and Mankind."

7 ROSENFELD, SYBIL. A Short History of Scene Design in Great Britain. Totowa, N.J.: Rowman & Littlefield, pp. 45, 48, 51-53.
Discusses scenery in the 1674 Tempest and in Psyche, where the spectacle "for the first time" rivaled that of the court masque.

8 ROSS, J.C. "An Attack on Thomas Shadwell in Otway's The Atheist." PQ 52:753-60.
Argues that the presentation of Daredevil "involves a satirical assault upon Thomas Shadwell" and that "the plot-element built around this character is based on the Tory version of an incident in real life." Ross cites contemporary pamphlet accounts of an altercation between Shadwell and Nat Thompson, and he suggests both personal and political reasons for the breach between Shadwell and Otway.

1974

1 BLACK, JAMES. "Dryden on Shadwell's Theatre of Violence." DR 54:298-311.
While discussing MacFlecknoe as Dryden's version of The Rehearsal, Black asserts that the prevalent violence in Shadwell's comedies makes him "something of a Tobias Smollet of the stage." Sometimes the roughness becomes cruel and mean (in Sullen Lovers and The Virtuoso), and often it is linked to sex (in Epsom-Wells, The Humorists, and The Virtuoso).

2 BRUCE, DONALD. Topics of Restoration Comedy. New York: St. Martin's, pp. 19-20, 31-33, 62, 65-67, 70-71, 74, 76-77, 85, 97-99, 105-6, 126, 138-39.
Shadwell is "a prosaic and unflowing writer, but sharp-eyed and full of homely rationality and humour." Over the course of his twenty-five-year career, his comedies change in several respects: "knockabout content" gives way to enlarged discussions of social issues, hero portrayed as "man of mode" becomes hero portrayed as "man of honour," satiric effects give place to exemplary effects, anticipating Addison and Richardson as the courtly ideas in Shadwell's early plays shift to the religiously based ideals of the eighteenth century. Throughout the period, however, his comedies are Aristophanic, "in the sense that they are essentially conservative."

They usually favor urban over rural civilization; old-fashioned courtship, restraint, and self-sacrifice over fashionable licentiousness; intuition and instinctive benevolence over "schemes of the mind anxious for gain." Furthermore, A True

Widow shows that Shadwell is anti-Hobbesian, and The Virtuoso reveals that he is anti-Epicurean. Although he "sees that his characters receive what they deserve by letting them establish for themselves the conventions by which they are treated by other people," he considers mankind to be "inherently virtuous but vitiated by society. . . . All the heroes and heroines of [his] plays seek to escape from society into a life defined by themselves." Bruce also refers to The Royal Shepherdess, Epsom-Wells, Bury-Fair, Sullen Lovers, and The Squire of Alsatia.

3 FISHER, ALAN S. "The Significance of Thomas Shadwell." SP 71:225-46.

Argues that Shadwell is the "Laureate of Whiggery--Whiggery in all forms, political, cultural, ethical, aesthetic, and metaphysical." This means that for Shadwell good sense is a high value; that ideas and motives must be explained, distinguished, and expressed plainly and explicitly; that intense mystery must give way to crude psychology and melodrama; and that heroes must be defined as generous, pragmatic rakes (like Alcibiades/Buckingham in Timon) who gain the love of loyal women who like spirit, breeding, and constancy. Even though a few plays show less sympathy for such rakes (A True Widow, The Woman-Captain, Lancashire-Witches, the overarching attitude is reaffirmed in The Squire of Alsatia and The Scowrers. Additionally, some plays have Prospero-figures, again of a peculiarly Whig cast, who resolve contradictions and capture "the transcendant ideal in the amber of pragmatic give and take." Fisher ranges widely in Shadwell's works and in the cultural context.

4 JEFFARES, A. NORMAN, ed. General Introduction and Introduction to The Squire of Alsatia. In Restoration Comedy. London: Folio; Totowa, N.J.: Rowman & Littlefield. 1:xi; 3:107-8.

Shadwell combines Restoration comic conventions with Jonson's "capacity for ridiculing folly and yet propounding a serious view of life." He has "a flair for dramatic situations," "an ear for good dialogue," "a nice sense of humour," and "a solid commonsensical approach to life." The sources, influences, "cant," and central theme (a contrast of educational systems) of The Squire of Alsatia are briefly discussed.

5 RESER, LOREN D. "Elkanah Settle's The World in the Moon: A Critical Edition." Ph.D. dissertation, University of Missouri-Columbia, 381 pp.

In Chapter 4, Shadwell's Psyche is discussed as a prototypical dramatic opera. See Dissertation Abstracts International 36 (1975):283A-84A.

1975

1 BLOCH, ADÈLE. "Dom Juan and Don Giovanni." In Molière and the Commonwealth of Letters: Patrimony and Posterity. Edited by Roger Johnson, Jr., Editha S. Neumann, and Guy T. Trail. Jackson: University Press of Mississippi, p. 291.

The despicable hero of The Libertine "acquired some features from English Restoration lords like Rochester."

2 KEARFUL, FRANK J. "Molière among the English 1660-1737." In Molière and the Commonwealth of Letters: Patrimony and Posterity. Edited by Roger Johnson, Jr., Editha S. Neumann, and Guy T. Trail. Jackson: University Press of Mississippi, pp. 213-14.

"The key figure in the early development of Restoration sentimental drama is Thomas Shadwell." Among his earlier works, Sullen Lovers, The Miser, Psyche, and The Libertine show Molière's influence, an influence that seems to have encouraged Shadwell's movement "away from the comedy of manners emphasis on wit, libertinism, skepticism, and hard-edged satire toward a more 'decent,' civilized, good-natured, didactic, humane comedy." Bury-Fair and The Squire of Alsatia are landmarks along the course of this shift.

3 PERKIN, RICHARD, ed. Introduction to The Humorists by Thomas Shadwell. Dublin: Laurel House Press, pp. 1-6.

Compares the 1671 published version with a manuscript text, offers evidence that Shadwell intended to satirize Lady Castlemaine, and undertakes an act-by-act analysis of themes, tone, characterization, structure, and techniques. On the whole well controlled, if not ingenious in plot, the play is "a mordant black comedy about a fairly dingy society and with a very serious comment to make about it."

4 PERSSON, AGNES V. Comic Character in Restoration Drama. The Hague and Paris: Mouton, pp. 47, 51-52, 75-76, 83, 93-100, 105-8, 113-15, 128, 140.

Discusses Shadwell's humors characters, with emphasis on his "rather delightful plays," Sullen Lovers and The Squire of Alsatia. The former is seen as satire against the unexamined life. Persson points out the "rigidity and fantastic ignorance" of Shadwell's "wanton women," would-be wits, fops, and greedy old hypocrites, referring to The Humorists as well as to the plays mentioned above.

5 ROSS, JOHN. "Addenda to Shadwell's 'Complete Works': A Checklist." N&Q 220:256-59.

Adds three plays partly written by Shadwell, seven poems, five pamphlets, one letter, and a collection of receipts.

*6 ROSS, J.C. "Critical Editions of Two Plays by Thomas Shadwell: The Squire of Alsatia and Bury-Fair." Ph.D. dissertation, University of London (Birkbeck College).

Source: Index to Theses Accepted for Higher Degrees by the Universities of Great Britain and Ireland and the Council for National Academic Awards, ed. Geoffrey M. Paterson and Joan E. Hardy, vol. 25, pt. 1 (London: Aslib, 1976), p. 5.

1976

1 HUME, ROBERT D. The Development of English Drama in the Late Seventeenth Century. Oxford: Clarendon Press, pp. 9, 21, 37, 55, 61, 78-86, 141-42, 207-8, 214, 258-59, 262, 278, 294-96, 306-7, 312, 327-28, 332-33, 336-38, 357-58, 377-78, 390-91, 393, 492.

In the process of giving capsule critiques of each play, Hume defends Shadwell's integrity as a comic artist, stresses his reliance on characterization for his best effects (though he is said to improve in construction as he matures), argues that he has more in common with Etherege than has been thought, and presents him as, in a sense, the founder of "soft Augustan comedy."

Sullen Lovers and The Humorists, really the only comedies in which Shadwell puts his theories into practice, are both loosely plotted comedies of humor, the former somewhat redeemed by its portraits of contemporaries. A piece of competent hackwork, The Miser translates Molière into the popular mode of London low comedy. Epsom-Wells, purveying the sort of witty sex intrigues the author had been denouncing, shows that he could handle multiple plots and sustain a lively love chase, and The Tempest and Psyche show that he could orchestrate diverse theatrical media as well. The Virtuoso is a brilliant satire on impractical science and a good-natured critique of romantic love; The Libertine is a "highly diverting," sober-faced "burlesque" on the values of libertine comedy and the devices of tragedy. A tragic structure is used in another attack on "Carolean comedy's moral code" in Timon of Athens, a genuine play of ideas that embodies veiled political support for Buckingham, satire of the money-ethic, and provocative contrasts between exemplary and sex-comedy worlds. A True Widow is a complex, experimental, "beautiful" play, which employs a "representative cross-section" of character types and a "brilliant" travesty of D'Urfey's A Fond Husband. The Woman-Captain, on the other hand, is "straight farce."

An almost operatic Whig play with a double romance plot and satire on priests, The Lancashire-Witches confusingly juxtaposes Sir Edward's exemplary rationalism to real witches. The Squire of Alsatia is also confusing, in that its idealization of a liberal town education seems at odds with Belfond Jr.'s weaknesses, but it offers vivid pictures of London life, a busily interesting plot, a strong moral-didactic thrust, and almost no bawdy. It is crucial to an understanding of late-century generic developments, anticipating the sort of exemplary comedy that Shadwell himself came closer to perfecting in Bury-Fair, a well-controlled, bustling satire. The Scowrers is less effective because of its exaggerated reformation theme, but it exhibits some vivid social realism, and The Volunteers is too preachy to succeed with its topical satire and "rigorously schematic contrast of positive and negative examples." The Amorous Bigotte is "lively but mechanical" and has little subtlety or didactic zeal.

2 LOFTIS, JOHN. "The Social and Literary Context." In The Revels History of Drama in English, Vol. V: 1660-1750. Edited by Loftis, Richard Southern, Marion Jones, and A.H. Scouten. London: Methuen, p. 38.

Considers Shadwell the only Restoration dramatist who tries to broaden the social range of comedy, "providing engaging portraits of men outside fashionable society" and criticizing them for more than social affectation.

3 McBRIDE, M.F. "A Topical Index of Major References to Social History in the Plays of Thomas Shadwell." BB 33:226-29.

Indexes "references to various facets of life as Shadwell saw it about him." Sample topics: "Debauchery," "Divorce," "Medical Practices," and "Witches."

4 McDONALD, MARGARET LAMB. The Independent Woman in the Restoration Comedy of Manners. Salzburg, Austria: Institut für Englische Sprache und Literatur, pp. 60-63, 102.

When Shadwell tries in The Virtuoso to depict a witty young heroine, he ends up creating two, nonindividualized females who possess no polish or urbanity. He is "always more farcical than witty." But in Squire of Alsatia and Bury-Fair, he initiates the vogue for "a sensible young couple" that dominated eighteenth-century "sentimental comedy."

5 OLSON, ROBERT C. "Shadwell's Irish Pen." Expl 35, no. 1: 14-15.

Despite the fact that Shadwell could write lively comedies of humor, he was dull enough not to understand Dryden's use of "Irish" to describe Shadwellian style.

6 PYREK, STEVEN JOSEPH. "Thomas Shadwell's Comedies: The Evolution of Conscious Artistry." Ph.D. dissertation, University of Tennessee, 245 pp.

Presents Shadwell not only as the champion of humors but also as an experimenter in many other types of comic technique, including witty intrigue and sentimentalism. Stressing theme and structure, Pyrek examines the plays in three phases: apprenticeship (Sullen Lovers, Humorists, Miser, Epsom-Wells); the dark phase (Virtuoso, True Widow, Woman-Captain, Lancashire-Witches); and a final phase in which Shadwell uses profound irony, complex themes, and simpler structures (Amorous Bigotte, Squire of Alsatia, Bury-Fair, Scowrers, and Volunteers). The last two plays reveal a sentimental tendency held in check by irony.

7 ROOT, ROBERT L., Jr. "Rochester's Debt to Shadwell in 'Tunbridge Wells.'" N&Q 221:242-43.

The action in Epsom-Wells involving "foolish husbands, wanton wives, and predatory gallants forms the basis for Rochester's treatment of one segment of society at Tunbridge Wells."

8 SCOUTEN, A.H. "Plays and Playwrights." In The Revels History of Drama in English, Vol. V: 1660-1750. Edited by John Loftis, Richard Southern, Marion Jones, and A.H. Scouten. London: Methuen, pp. 188-93, 200, 223.

Although Shadwell skillfully portrayed individual eccentricities, wrote with energy and coarse realism, and contributed significantly to sentimental and exemplary drama, he lacked the abilities to develop dramatic conflicts, to interpret life, and to control his diverse artistry. Sullen Lovers is somewhat successful with its personal satire and contrasts between a serious and a gay couple, and Epsom-Wells is notable for its curious use of sex-comedy conventions that Shadwell had recently denounced. But his best play is The Virtuoso, because its dialogue is more fluent than usual, and its fine satire on sexual irregularity and hypocrisy muffles what might have become simplistic didacticism. In A True Widow the didacticism, if not simplistic, is poorly integrated with gay wit, though the play has a "lively play within a play" in Act 4; and the various elements of farce, moralizing, and melodrama never really jell in The Scowrers and The Volunteers.

After the "Whig propaganda" of The Lancashire-Witches, Shadwell approaches exemplary comedy in The Squire of Alsatia and Bury-Fair, the former lacking a consistent point of view, though it interestingly employs local dialects and contrasts educational theories. The farcical Woman-Captain, "unlike anything else being currently done," takes up lesbianism, parodies the proviso scene, and provides "chorus-like explanations."

1977

1 COX, STEPHEN D. "Public Virtue and Private Vitality in Shadwell's Comedies." RECTR 16, no. 1:11-22.

Argues that although Shadwell often makes his comic heroes into rakes, wits, and cynical hedonists, he nevertheless uses them to promote a civilized order, where both drudgery and criminal violence are eliminated. On the other hand, he never writes comedy primarily to instigate social reform, though this tendency grows as he moves toward The Volunteers. One of his best comic creations is Lady Cheatly of A True Widow.

2 HUME, ROBERT D. "The Myth of the Rake in 'Restoration' Comedy." SLitI 10, no. 1:35-37, 49-50, 54.

Bruce and Longvil in The Virtuoso are "genuine libertines, not merely convenient dramatic devices." Belfond Jr., in The Squire of Alsatia, is meant to depict "the maturation process of a virtuous and honourable young man." His womanizing is presented not as vicious, but rather as natural, and his "reform" is treated with a seriousness novel in its day. In The Scowrers, it is a "rakish gentleman," not a vicious rake, who is reformed; and the whole libertine philosophy is savagely attacked in The Libertine, a "sardonic mock-tragedy" that pushes materialistic ideas to an extreme.

3 LUCKETT, RICHARD. "Exotick but Rational Entertainments: The English Dramatick Operas." In English Drama: Forms and Development. Edited by Marie Axton and Raymond Williams. Cambridge, London, New York, and Melbourne: Cambridge University Press, pp. 132-33.

Psyche (and the 1674 Tempest) is "not masque, not play with music, but . . . a play conditioned by music and conditioned on music."

4 MAYNARD, OLGA. "Don Juan and His Artistic Metamorphosis." Dance Magazine 51, no. 1:51-65.

Contains no criticism of The Libertine but instructively places it in the context of dance: for example, ballets by Angiolini, Fokine, Ashton, and so on.

5 MILHOUS, JUDITH, and ROBERT D. HUME. "Lost English Plays, 1660-1700." HLB 25:16.

Shadwell's The Hypocrite (1669) is listed.

6 NOVAK, MAXIMILLIAN E. "Margery Pinchwife's 'London Disease': Restoration Comedy and the Libertine Offensive of the 1670's." SLitI 10, no. 1:13-15, 22-23.

In many of his plays, Shadwell's views on rakish behavior are ambiguous. Wits and fools are not well distinguished in Epsom-Wells, and Clodpate's ideas on rural virtue are not entirely negated by Bevil and Rains. Snarl's penetrating criticism of modern behavior in The Virtuoso is undermined by his own perversion, and Don John of The Libertine reveals little about Shadwell's attitude toward contemporary libertinism because he is "a protagonist in the Caligula tradition rather than the Don Juan tradition." A True Widow also leaves us uncertain about the author's position regarding fashionable morality. In The Squire of Alsatia and Bury-Fair, country and city ways are contrasted "in terms of Stoicism versus Libertinism and the contemplation of nature versus the active enjoyment of nature," and here Shadwell begins to adopt "a middle position in which the rake might benefit from his experience and yet be capable of true love for a worthy woman and of proper duty to his family."

7 ODEN, RICHARD L. Introduction to Dryden and Shadwell: The Literary Controversy and MacFlecknoe (1668-1679). Delmar, N.Y.: Scholar's Facsimiles and Reprints, pp. v-xxii.

In the course of surveying the quarrel, mentions Shadwell's satire on Dryden (as Drybob) in The Humorists and identifies The Virtuoso as the most immediate occasion for MacFlecknoe.

8 WILLSON, ROBERT F., Jr. "Sh------ and Shakespeare in Dryden's MacFlecknoe." Names 25:155-57.

"Sh------" signifies several things: Shadwell's name, the windy inspirations that inform his plays, excrement, and "an ironic comparison" with Shakespeare.

1978

1 ALBURY, W.R. "Halley's Ode on the Principia of Newton and the Epicurean Revival in England." JHI 39:33-34.

Like Sir William Temple, who condemned idle natural philosophy in "Upon the Gardens of Epicurus," Longvil and Bruce (The Virtuoso) are sensible, "aristocratic Epicureans" whose attitudes are contrasted with "the seemingly ridiculous pretensions of the natural philosopher."

2 BLACKALL, ERIC A. "Don Juan and Faust." Seminar: A Journal of Germanic Studies 14:75.

In The Libertine, Shadwell presents "a reasoning Don Juan who is quite different from the unreasoning hero of Tirso" but who resembles Molière's protagonist. Like Molière, but again unlike Tirso, Shadwell gives his Don an unrequited lover.

3 De LEÓN y MANALAYSAY, EDELMA PACITA. "The Restoration World Picture: Thomas Shadwell's Comic Vision." Ph.D. dissertation, University of Southwestern Louisiana, 229 pp.

Shadwell was an artistic dramatist executing a maturing comic theory incorporating "both instruction and amusement." He moved from integration of wit and humors, through bitter dramatic attacks on audience taste, to Squire of Alsatia and Bury-Fair, his best plays, which introduce exemplary characters and reformation of rakes by virtuous women. See Dissertation Abstracts International 39 (1979):4266A-67A.

4 MAREK, GEORGE R. "Twist to an Old Legend: Mozart and Da Ponte's Don Giovanni owes much to Molière." Opera News 42, no. 18 (18 March):12-15, 55-57.

Places The Libertine in the context of operatic versions of the Don Juan legend.

5 PARNELL, PAUL E. "The Etiquette of the Sentimental Repentance Scene, 1688-96." PLL 14:207-10.

Argues that in The Squire of Alsatia Belfond Jr.'s reform is basically self-interested and practical, involving "very little moral fervor." In The Scowrers, "the element of punishment is removed from consideration" as Shadwell relies "on the emotional aspects of repentance, particularly those benevolent emotions stemming from parental and filial love."

6 PELLEGRIN, HELEN TAYLOR. "A Critical Edition of The Libertine by Thomas Shadwell." Ph.D. dissertation, Stanford University, 299 pp.

The introduction and notes relate the play to earlier versions of the Don Juan legend and show what Shadwell contributed to the "Don Juan" personality. Expressing ideas "central to English libertine thought," The Libertine is a "satirical tragedy that mocks the conventions of tragic drama while simultaneously parodying what Shadwell perceived as the harmful aspects of English libertinism." See Dissertation Abstracts International 39:3603A.

1979

1 ARMISTEAD, J.M. "Occultism in Restoration Drama: Motives for Revaluation." MLS 9, no. 3:60-62, 66.

Studies The Lancashire-Witches against the background of occultism in English life and letters. "The confining rituals and habits of thought practiced by Sir Edward and the witches make them comically predictable and inflexible, while the two girls' openness to both natural and supernatural mysteries, their resiliency and inventiveness, enable them to cooperate with the full complexity of life and endow them with genuine powers in their world." Thus, "Shadwell seems to have been sure that there was more to life than meets the empirical eye. But he was equally sure . . . that the best mental disposition for limited, fallen beings was empirical and pragmatic."

2 HOLLAND, PETER. The Ornament of Action: Text and Performance in Restoration Comedy. Cambridge, London, New York, and Melbourne: Cambridge University Press, pp. 20, 152-53, 164-65.

The scenery in The Squire of Alsatia becomes "a visible structure for the play's argument for a morality of restraint." In The Volunteers, Shadwell "redefines our stock responses" to the actors and their roles "according to a scheme that emphasizes the good implicit in those roles, a scheme that is beyond the bounds of the traditional comedy within which it appears to operate." The two houses in The Volunteers embody the play's argument, and in the end, "the good controls the bad by absorbing the evil characters into itself." Moreover, "Blunt's house is as exemplary as the analysis of Hackwell's world is satiric."

3 PRICE, CURTIS A. Music in the Restoration Theatre. [Ann Arbor]: UMI Research Press, pp. 23-24, 31, 33, 35, 39-40, 74-75, 78, 82, 85, 105-6, 256 n.66, 271 n.31.

Although Shadwell often gives music "a dramatic, even a dynamic role," he nevertheless usually subordinates it to dialogue and action. In his later plays, he sometimes omits the actual music and words from the printed text, suggesting to future directors that any music might serve the purpose. This "music-hall approach" to theater is evident in The Woman-Captain. Price also discusses fiddlers in The Miser and Epsom-Wells, masques in Shadwell's drama, and the relation of music to theme, spectacle, and action in Psyche, A True Widow, and The Volunteers. Shadwell's own musical talents, the "Pugenello" dance in Sullen Lovers, and the orchestra in The Tempest are briefly commented upon. Other plays are cited in the rich footnotes, and the music in Shadwell's plays is cataloged.

4 SOELLNER, ROLF. Timon of Athens: Shakespeare's Pessimistic Tragedy. Columbus: Ohio State University Press, pp. 5-6, 58.

In his effort to make Timon more cheerful and noble, Shadwell spoiled the ethos and argument of the original, but he was right to give Apemantus a part in the conclusion.

5 STAVES, SUSAN. Players' Scepters: Fictions of Authority in the Restoration. Lincoln and London: University of Nebraska Press, pp. 135, 151-52, 168-70, 298, 307-13.

Discusses Shadwell's interest in the status of women, as illustrated by Epsom-Wells (involving a separation agreement between the Woodlys), The Woman-Captain (a play "about liberty cast in domestic terms" and showing a new interest in heroines), and The Scowrers (where Eugenia, like many of Shadwell's other female characters, is "particularly self-conscious about the political analogies" suggested by her attitudes). Shadwell's plays also illustrate a shift "from the libertine rake to the good-natured hero," though his later heroes, like Sir William Rant in The Scowrers, are reformed "not for religious reasons, but for hedonistic, pragmatic, and social ones." Don John, of The Libertine, falls "somewhere between a Herculean hero and a rake," and Epsom-Wells affirms the libertine ethos. The Lancashire-Witches, however, stops just short of attacking fashionable morality through Sir Edward, a good-natured rationalist, and in The Squire of Alsatia and Bury-Fair, the rakes give way to men of sense and benevolence. The Volunteers goes beyond conversion and presents two "good-natured, virtuous heroes" and a virtuous heroine.

6 VIETH, DAVID M. "The Discovery of the Date of MacFlecknoe." In Evidence in Literary Scholarship: Essays in Memory of James Marshall Osborn. Edited by René Wellek and Alvaro Ribeiro. Oxford: Clarendon Press, pp. 71-86.

Sorts out the actual from the supposed allusions to Shadwell's plays in MacFlecknoe, arguing that Dryden makes satirical references to The Hypocrite, The Humorists, The Miser, Epsom-Wells, The Tempest, Psyche, and The Virtuoso.

1980

1 LANGHANS, EDWARD A. Introduction to Five Restoration Theatrical Adaptations. New York and London: Garland, pp. vi-viii.

Based on the French version of Molière, Corneille, and Quinault, Shadwell's Psyche was "one of the first successful English attempts to make the music and dance sequences an integral part of the play, helping to forward it." Shadwell thus improved on the French and "established a pattern for English operas." Unfortunately, Psyche becomes a bit "ragged in the last acts."

2 LOFTIS, JOHN. "Political and Social Thought in the Drama." In The London Theatre World, 1660-1800. Edited by Robert D. Hume. Carbondale and Edwardsville: Southern Illinois University Press; London and Amsterdam: Feffer & Simons, p. 264.

After Shadwell returns to the theater in the later 1680s, his plays become progressively more political in orientation, from the almost apolitical Squire of Alsatia to the "vehemently political" Scowrers.

3 SCOUTEN, ARTHUR H., and ROBERT D. HUME. "'Restoration Comedy' and Its Audiences, 1660-1776." YES 10:53-54, 56-57.

During the "Watershed Years, 1678-1688," Shadwell first shifts from cuckolding comedy (Epsom-Wells, The Virtuoso) to "safer and more romantic play-types" (The Woman-Captain, The Lancashire-Witches); then, signaling "the rise of the 'new' style in comedy," he writes The Squire of Alsatia, which has "the rudiments of the 'reform' pattern common after 1700." Yet in this "avowedly moral" play, he is "not exerting pressure on the audience; rather, he is responding to a changing climate of opinion."

1981

1 BROWN, LAURA. English Dramatic Form, 1660-1760: An Essay in Generic History. New Haven and London: Yale University Press, pp. 105-9.

While Shadwell's plays illustrate the shift from satiric to moral drama, Shadwell himself becomes the spokesperson for the bourgeois form that finally triumphs over libertine intrigue comedy. Paralleling his endorsement of Jonsonian form as more instructive and less profane than comedy of wit or repartee, Shadwell's early works, like Sullen Lovers or The Virtuoso, substitute local ridicule of humors characters for the sex-chase common in major social satire. The Libertine is a dramatized attack on the amoral conventions of such witty sex comedy. The relatively weak and chaste action in these early works is readily transformed, beginning in The Lancashire-Witches, into moralized drama. Whereas in that play the local device of flying witches generates the exemplary Whig morality of the admirable characters, in The Squire of Alsatia morality becomes a formal end in itself. Here the ideology of the 1688 Revolution informs a strong plot in which the ultimately exemplary Belfond Jr. becomes a standard of Lockean values and is eventually rewarded for his virtue. In The Volunteers, this pattern of moral form and direct ideological assertion is repeated, with even greater emphasis on the exemplary virtue of its protagonists.

The Dramatic Works of Aphra Behn

The Forc'd Marriage; or, The Jealous Bridegroom: A Tragi-comedy 1671

The Amorous Prince; or, The Curious Husband: A Comedy 1671

The Dutch Lover: A Comedy 1673

Abdelazar; or, The Moor's Revenge: A Tragedy 1677

The Town-Fopp; or, Sir Timothy Tawdrey: A Comedy 1677

The Debauchee; or, The Credulous Cuckold: A Comedy 1677*

The Rover; or, The Banish't Cavaliers 1677

The Counterfeit Bridegroom; or, The Defeated Widow: A Comedy 1677*

Sir Patient Fancy: A Comedy 1678

The Feign'd Curtizans; or, A Nights Intrigue: A Comedy 1679

The Revenge; or, A Match in Newgate: A Comedy 1680*

The Second Part of the Rover 1681

The False Count; or, A New Way to Play an Old Game 1682

The Roundheads; or, The Good Old Cause: A Comedy 1682

The City-Heiress; or, Sir Timothy Treat-all: A Comedy 1682

Like Father, Like Son 1682*

The Young King; or, The Mistake 1683

The Luckey Chance; or, An Alderman's Bargain: A Comedy	1687
Emperor of the Moon: A Farce	1687
The Widow Ranter; or, The History of Bacon in Virginia: A Tragi-Comedy	1690
The Younger Brother; or, The Amorous Jilt: A Comedy	1696

---

*The Debauchee, The Counterfeit Bridegroom, and The Revenge are attributed to Mrs. Behn on doubtful authority. Like Father, Like Son is a lost play (see B.1977.4).

Writings about Aphra Behn, 1675-1980

1675

1 PHILLIPS, EDWARD. "Women Among the Moderns Eminent for Poetry." In Theatrum Poetarum, or a Compleat Collection of the Poets. London: for Charles Smith, p. 255.

Names "Astrea Behn" as "a Dramatic writer, so much the more considerable as being a Woman."

1681

1 DRYDEN, JOHN. Epilogue to Tamerlane the Great: A Tragedy, by Charles Saunders. London: for Richard Bentley & M. Magnes, n. pag.

Refers to Aphra as a "Woman Wit" who "has often grac'd the Stage."

1686

1 COTTON, CHARLES. "To the Admir'd Astrea." Prefixed to La Montre: or the Lover's Watch. London: R.H. for W. Canning, n. pag.

Aphra can handle the whole range of "Theams" in tragedy and comedy "with equal Skill and Grace," but she is especially effective when writing "of Love."

1688

1 PRIOR, MATTHEW. "A Session of the Poets (imperfect)." In Dialogues of the Dead and Other Works in Prose and Verse. Edited by A.R. Waller. Cambridge: Cambridge University Press, 1907, p. 300.

Considers Aphra a verbose writer. A.R. Waller was the first to publish this manuscript poem.

1689

1 ANON. "An Elegy upon The Death of Mrs. A. Behn; The Incomparable Astrea. By a Young Lady of Quality." In _A Little Ark Containing Sundry Pieces of Seventeenth-Century Verse_. Edited by G. Thorn-Drury. London: P.J. & A.E. Dobell, 1921, pp. 53-56.

Mrs. Behn's "ever-loyal Muse" was "of the bolder Sex," and now that her fluent "numbers," "heavenly Wit," and "moving natural Eloquence" are gone, no other woman will be able to overcome "Impotence or Fear" to compete with men so successfully. I was unable to see the original broadside containing this poem.

2 DRYDEN, JOHN. _The Prologue and Epilogue to the History of Bacon in Virginia_. London: for Jacob Tonson, 4 pp.

The prologue asserts that this is a witty drama ("or should at least, be"), that it will probably generate more laughter than better plays do, and that it is based on recent history. In the epilogue, it is called a "Farce of Government" written by one who was adept at painting love's passion. Like a bee, Aphra has left us this "Hive" of sweets.

3 GOULD, ROBERT. "The Play-House: A Satyr." In _Poems Chiefly Consisting of Satyrs and Satyrical Epistles_. London: n.p., p. 173.

Emperor of the Moon and _The City-Heiress_ are damned through praise by false critics.

1690

1 ANON. "To the much Honoured Madam Welldon." Prefixed to _The Widdow Ranter; or, The History of Bacon in Virginia: A Tragi-Comedy_. London: for James Knapton, n. pag.

The "true Comedy" in this witty play is necessarily "low," since most of the characters are to be understood as transported criminals and the like.

1691

1 [DUNTON, JOHN.] Answer to "Quest.1. Whom do you think the best Dramatick Professor in this Age?" _Athenian Gazette: or Casuistical Mercury_ 5, no. 2 (5 December), n. pag.

Speaks of "Mrs. _Behns_, whose _Rovers_ are pretty natural things."

2 LANGBAINE, GERARD. _An Account of the English Dramatick Poets_. Oxford: by L.L. for G. West & H. Clements, pp. 17-24.

Almost as "Eminent" as "Madam Katharine Phillips," Mrs. Behn is the author of sixteen plays, most of which are acknowled adaptations that considerably improve on their originals. Abdelazer, The Amorous Prince, and The Feign'd Curtizans illustrate this; but The Rover (both parts) owes more to its source than Mrs. Behn admits, and the source itself is a better piece than she allows.

3 LANSDOWNE, GEORGE GRANVILLE, BARON. "To Mrs. B---. By Mr. Granville." In The History of Adolphus, Prince of Russia . . . With a Collection of Songs and Love-Verses, By several Hands. London: by R.T., p. 54.

Because Aphra triumphs with both her eyes and her "Quill," her symbols of power should be "Hearts bleeding by the Dart, and Pen."

1696

1 ANON. "An Account of the Life of the Incomparable Mrs. Behn." Affixed to The Younger Brother; or, The Amorous Jilt: A Comedy. London: for J. Harris & R. Baldwin, n. pag.

Considers Mrs. Behn a born poet who developed wit and good judgment and, as a woman writer, combined "all the softness of her Sex, and all the fire of ours." Charles Gildon, whose dedicatory epistle precedes this, may have written the "Account."

2 ANON. "Memoirs on the Life of Mrs. Behn. Written by a Gentlewoman of her Acquaintance." In The Histories and Novels of the Late Ingenious Mrs. Behn: In One Volume. London: S. Briscoe, n. pag.

Even as a girl Aphra could compose "the prettiest, soft-engaging Verses," and since then "Nature" has shown itself "without . . . Art in e'ry thing she has Writ."

3 ANON. Prologue to The Younger Brother; or, The Amorous Jilt: A Comedy. London: for J. Harris & R. Baldwin, n. pag.

The author, like this play, could move the "softer Passions" and was "The Life of Humour, and the Soul of Love, / Wits Eldest Sister."

4 GILDON, CHARLES. "The Epistle Dedicatory. To Collonel Codrington." Prefixed to The Younger Brother; or, The Amorous Jilt: A Comedy. London: for J. Harris & R. Baldwin, n. pag.

The "Accomplish'd" Mrs. Behn has written a play with "intrinsic Merit . . . full of Humour, Wit, and Variety; the Conversation Gay and Genteel, the Love, Soft and Pathetic, the incidents Natural, and Easy, and the Conduct of the Plot very Justifiable." Gildon adds that he altered Act 2, scene 2.

1697

1 [PRIOR, MATTHEW.] "A Satyr on the modern Translators." In Poems on Affairs of State: From the Time of Oliver Cromwell, to the Abdication of K. James the Second. n.p., p. 196.

Since her contribution to the English Ovid shows she is inept at paraphrasing verse, even when she uses an English version instead of the Latin one, Mrs. Behn might as well return to writing plays from experience: "let her from the next inconstant Lover, / Take a new Copy for a second Rover," and, imitating her own "ill Arts," let her "describe the cunning of a jilting Whore." The poem is attributed to Prior by H. Bunker Wright and Monroe K. Spears, in The Literary Works of Matthew Prior, 2d ed., vol. 1. (Oxford: Clarendon Press, 1971), the quoted passage on p. 21.

1698

1 ANON. "By [sic] Madam Behn." In The Poetical Remaines of the Duke of Buckingham, Sir George Etheridge, Mr. Milton, Mr. Andre[w] Marvell, Madam Behn, Lord Rochester, Sir John Denham, Mr. Walle[r,] Mr. Shadwel, Madam Philips. London: by and for Thomas Minton, pp. 30-31.

Celebrates the "charming Musick" of Aphra's poetry. This poem is entitled "On Madam Behn" in Poems on Affairs of State (1703), II, the quoted passage on p. 263.

2 GILDON, CHARLES. "The Epistle Dedicatory, to Simon Scroop, Esq; of Danby, in Yorkshire." In All the Histories and Novels Written by the Late Ingenious Mrs. Behn, Entire in One Volume. 3d ed. London: for Samuel Briscoe, n. pag.

"Mrs. Behn, whose Genius was of that force like Homer's, to maintain its Gayety in the midst of Disappointments . . . she had a great Strength of Mind, and Command of Thought, being able to write in the midst of Company, and yet have her share of the Conversation."

1699

1 DRYDEN, JOHN. "Familiar Letters to Corinna." Letter II, in Miscellanea. In Two Volumes. Vol. 1. London: n.p., 1727, p. 151.

Mrs. Behn's loose writing gave "some Scandal to the Modesty of her Sex." First published in this collection, Dryden's letter is conjecturally dated by Charles E. Ward in his editon of The Letters of John Dryden (Durham, N.C.: Duke University Press, 1942), the quoted passage on p. 127.

2 [GILDON, CHARLES,] and GERARD LANGBAINE. The Lives and Characters of the English Dramatick Poets. London: for W. Turner, pp. 8-10.

"Aphara, not Astrea," endowed all her writings with "much of Nature." Except for some tedious blank-verse scenes, the factually based Younger Brother has "a great deal of Wit."

1700

1 [DEFOE, DANIEL.] The Pacificator. A Poem. London: by and for J. Nutt, p. 5.

Mrs. Behn, Cowley, Milton, and others are ranked as "Giants . . . of Wit and Sense." The poem is attributed to Defoe by Frank H. Ellis in Poems on Affairs of State, 6 (New Haven and London: Yale University Press, 1970), the cited passage on p. 166.

1702

1 ANON. Preface to Plays Written by the Late Ingenious Mrs. Behn. Vol. 1. London: Jacob Tonson, n. pag.

As a playwright Aphra excels "any of the Poets of this Age, Sir William Davenant and Mr. Dryden excepted," and "she never borrowes without improving for the better."

1703

1 ANON. "The Female Laureat." In Poems on Affairs of State, From The Reign of K. James the First, To this Present Year 1703. Vol. 2. n.p., "Printed in the Year 1703," pp. 146-48.

Savagely attacks Mrs. Behn for bringing on stage irrational, bombastic, impertinent, lewd, and profane men; virtuous women who hate virtue and chaste virgins who curse chastity; and a "vicious Widow . . ./Just reaking from a Stallion's rank Embrace." Maureen Duffy, in The Passionate Shepherdess (see B.1977.1), p. 219, believes Robert Gould wrote this poem.

1707

1 ANON. "The Grove: Or, the Rival Muses, 1701." In Poems on Affairs of State, from 1620, to this Present Year 1707. Vol. 4. London: n.p., p. 360.

With "all her softest Art," Aphra "could talk of Love, or touch the Heart."

1708

1 BROWN, THOMAS. "From worthy Mrs. Behn the Poetess, to the famous Virgin Actress." In The Second Volume of the Works of

Mr. Tho. Brown, Containing Letters from the Dead to the Living, and from the Living to the Dead. Pt. 2. London: for S.B. and B. Bragg, pp. 519-24.

Advises Mrs. Bracegirdle how to be promiscuous while seeming full of virtue.

2 _____. "The Virgin's Answer to Mrs. Behn." In The Second Volume of the Works of Mr. Tho. Brown, Containing Letters from the Dead to the Living, and from the Living to the Dead. Pt. 2. London: for S.B. & B. Bragg, pp. 524-28.

Despite Mrs. Behn's attempts to please the powers that be with "amorous Intrigues" and "Romantick Wit," her reputation remained that of "a Bawdy Poetess."

3 DOWNES, JOHN. Roscius Anglicanus, or an Historical Review of the Stage. London: by H. Playford, p. 34.

Mentions that The Forc'd Marriage was "a good Play and lasted six Days."

1711

1 [STEELE, RICHARD.] Spectator, no. 51 (28 April), n. pag.

The Rover illustrates that "the Writers of least Learning are best skill'd in the luscious Way," for the play shows near nudity and implicit sexual intercourse.

1719

1 JACOB, GILES. The Poetical Register: or, the Lives and Characters of the English Dramatick Poets. With an Account of their Writings. London: E. Curll, pp. 14-17.

Possessing "a strong Natural Genius," Mrs. Behn wrote better than all other women, and many men, of her day. The Feign'd Curtizans is one of her best plays, and The Younger Brother and both parts of The Rover "have a great deal of Wit."

1721

1 KENRICK, DANIEL. "To Mrs. Behn, on her Poems." In The Grove; or, A Collection of Original Poems, Translations, etc. London: for W. Mears, pp. 349-52.

Focuses on her talents as a poetess but implies praise for her literary achievements in general.

1735

1 [OLDYS, WILLIAM.] "Behn, (Aphara)." In A General Dictionary, Historical and Critical. Compiled by John Peter Bernard, Thomas Birch, John Lockman, et al. Vol. 3. London: by J. Bettenham, pp. 140-48.

Hints that Gildon's positive judgment (see B.1696.4; B.1698.2; and B.1699.2) was influenced by his personal intimacy with Aphra who, though she was a third-rate genius (inventive but careless) and could masterfully paint the passions, tended toward lewdness and immorality in her comedies. The Rover is in places "very shocking." Oldys takes credit for this biographical sketch in his Adversaria (see N&Q 23 [1861]:201).

1737

1 POPE, ALEXANDER. The First Epistle of the Second Book of Horace, Imitated. London: for T. Cooper, p. 17.

"The stage how loosely does Astraea tread,/ Who fairly puts all Characters to bed."

1738

1 ANON. "The Apotheosis of Milton: A Vision." Gentleman's Magazine 8:469.

Indignant that no woman should be allowed in this assembly of bards, Aphra appears loosely dressed in a robe de chambre, bare-breasted, fiery-eyed, self-assured.

1740

1 CIBBER, COLLEY. An Apology for the Life of Mr. Colley Cibber, Comedian. London: by John Watts for the author, p. 77.

Because of its lewdness, The Rover is "a Reproach to the Poet."

1747

1 ANON. A Companion to the Theatre: or, A View of our most Celebrated Dramatic Pieces. Vol. 2. London: for J. Nourse, pp. 244-58.

In The Rover (pt. 1), which will endure because of its "Wit," "Spirit," and "Variety of Incidents," Mrs. Behn chooses a carnival setting "to give more Latitude to the Behaviour of the Characters."

2 [BROUGHTON, THOMAS.] "Behn (Aphara)." In Biographia Britannica. Vol. 1. London: for W. Innys et al., pp. 665-69.

Aphra's comedies, "though not without wit and humour, are full of the most indecent scenes and expressions." In his Adversaria, William Oldys attributes this biographical entry to "Parson Broughton" (see N&Q 23 [1861]:201), whom the DNB identifies as Thomas Broughton, Prebendary of Salisbury, editor of Dryden, and author of Hercules. A musical Drama (1745).

3 [JOHNSON, SAMUEL.] "Prologue Spoken by Mr. Garrick." In Prologue and Epilogue, Spoken at the Opening of the Theatre in Drury Lane 1747. London: by E. Cave for M. Cooper & R. Dodsley, pp. 4-5.

Refers to Mrs. Behn as a prime example of those Carolean wits who wrote "as they felt": "Intrigue was Plot, Obscenity was Wit. / Vice always found a sympathetic Friend; / They pleas'd their Age, and did not aim to mend."

4 LeBLANC, JEAN BERNARD. "The Supplement of Genius: or, the art of Composing dramatic poems, as it has been practised by many celebrated authors of the English theatre." In Letters on the English and French Nations. Vol. 2. London: for J. Brindley, R. Francklin, C. Davies, and J. Hodges, p. 283.

Ridicules the practice, in comedies like The Rover, of shifting to verse in order to make tender scenes "more . . . pathetic."

1753

1 CIBBER, THEOPHILUS, [and ROBERT SHIELS.] The Lives of the Poets of Great Britain and Ireland. Compiled from . . . the MS. Notes of the late ingenious Mr. Coxeter and others. Vol. 3. London: R. Griffiths, pp. 17-32.

Quotes and paraphrases Langbaine (B.1691.2), Gildon (attributes to him the "Account" of 1696, above), Jacob (B.1719.1 and Biographia Britannica (B.1747.2), and maintains that Aphra's unjustified reputation for indecency, both in her life and in her works, arises from her incongruous participation in the male literary world, as well as from her naturally passionate nature and her catering to the tastes of the times. In fact, she was a true wit who gained the respect of Dryden and Southerne.

1757

1 ANON. Review of The Rover at Covent-Garden. London Chronicle 1, no. 24 (22-24 February):192.

Narrates amusing audience responses to the bawdy scenes, reminding the reader that the play "was written in the dissolute Days of Charles the Second."

1759

1 WILKES, [THOMAS.] A General View of the Stage. London: for J. Coote & W. Whetstone, pp. 16, 59, 79-80.

Calls The Rover "one continued tale of bawdery" and notes that Congreve was influenced by Emperor of the Moon, "a very ridiculous piece" that features "a speaking Harlequin."

1764

1 [BAKER, DAVID ERSKINE.] The Companion to the Play-house. Vols. 1 and 2. London: T. Becket & P. A. Dehondt; C. Henderson; T. Davies, n. pag.

Intricately plotted, "interlarded with trivial circumstances," and ending too bloodily, Abdelazer shows that Mrs. Behn was chiefly a comic writer. In comedy she exhibits witty dialogue, busy and ingenious plots, and all the "marks of Genius and understanding." Her "lively and amorous turn" leads to indecency only in compliance with "the corrupt Taste of the Times." When she borrows, as in The Amorous Prince or The Roundheads, she tends to improve her source, and some of her comedies are very entertaining indeed: The Feign'd Curtizans, her best, with its "great Variety"; The Rover, both parts full of "sprightliness"; and Emperor of the Moon which, "however absurd," is "many degrees more rational than the dumb shew of Pantomimes." The False Count is marred by the "low and farcical" character of the chimney sweep, The Luckey Chance is too bawdy for the modern stage, and The Younger Brother, despite some "very lively and pleasing wit," labors under some "heavy scenes in blank verse."

1769

1 GRANGER, JAMES. A Biographical History of England. Vol. 2. London: for T. Davies, pp. 347-48.

Depicts Mrs. Behn as an indelicate dramatist catering to corrupt tastes by writing obscene plays in which, had it not been for "the laws of the drama," she would have put her characters to bed "before the spectators."

1770

1 [TOWERS, JOSEPH.] "The Life of Aphara Behn." In British Biography. Vol. 6. London: for R. Goadby, pp. 325-30.

Despite their "wit and ingenuity," Mrs. Behn's plays are too lewd, immoral, and sacrilegious for public performance.

1778

1 ANON. "Behn (Aphara)." In Encyclopaedia Britannica. 2d. ed. Vol. 2. Edinburgh: for J. Balfour et al., p. 1088.

Mrs. Behn's works all "have a lively and amorous turn," and although they are ingeniously plotted and full of sparkling dialogue, they are marred by the indecent scenes and indelicate expressions that she put in to suit the corrupt tastes of her audiences.

1780

1 ANON. Biographia Britannica. 2d ed. Revised by Andrew Kippis et al. Vol. 2. London: for C. Bathurst et al., pp. 141-46.

To the 1747 entry on Mrs. Behn (B.1747.2) this edition adds a passage stressing her "natural talents," "wit," and indecency. The passage is signed "K" (for Kippis?).

1786

1 WALPOLE, HORACE. Letter to Lady Ossory, 12 December. In Letters Addressed to the Countess of Ossory, from the Year 1769 to 1797. By Horace Walpole, Lord Orford. Edited by R. Vernon Smith. Vol. 2. London: Richard Bentley, 1848, p. 283.

Refers ironically to Mrs. Behn's "Spartan delicacy."

1792

1 ANON. A New Theatrical Dictionary. London: S. Bladon, pp. 88, 159, 258, 338-39.

Quotes and paraphrases Baker's Companion (B.1764.1).

1800

1 DIBDIN, CHARLES. A Complete History of the Stage. Vol. 4. London: C. Dibdin, pp. 198-203, 251-52.

"What an excellent knack had this warm writer in heightening voluptuousness." The Amorous Prince is "a hash," The Young King and The Widdow Ranter are "incongruous" tragicomedies, and the other plays mentioned (Rover, Sir Patient Fancy, False Count, and Younger Brother) are too "low," too "gross," or too indecent for refined audiences.

1801

1 AIKIN, JOHN. "Behn, Aphara." In General Biography; or, Lives, Critical and Historical. Compiled by Aikin, "Mr. Nicholson," et al. Vol. 2. London: for J. Johnson et al., pp. 80-81.

Mrs. Behn's "merits do not go beyond a fluent easiness of style, rising to the warm and passionate when love is the topic," along with "sprightliness of thought and facility of common invention." Her works are remarkable for "gross indecency of plot and language."

1803

1 HAYS, MARY. "Aphara Behn." In Female Biography; or, Memoirs of Illustrious and Celebrated Women. Vol. 1. London: by Thomas Davison for Richard Phillips, pp. 273-90.

"Celebrated for her wit and dramatic powers," Aphra was "a plagiarist, rather from haste than sterility of imagination," and her notorious indelicacy was partly owing to the corrupt taste of her times.

1807

1 SOUTHEY, ROBERT, ed. "Aphra Behn." In Specimens of the Later English Poets. Vol. 1. London: Longman, p. 48.

Defends her as "a woman of rare talents" who has been "too severely condemned for the immorality of her writings, which should be considered as more characteristic of her age than their author."

1812

1 BAKER, DAVID ERSKINE, ISAAC REED, and STEPHEN JONES. Biographia Dramatica; or, A Companion to the Playhouse. Newly revised by Jones. Vol. 2. London: Longman, p. 122.

Adds one phrase to Baker's assessment of The Feign'd Curtizans (B.1764.1), a play with "great variety, whatever may be thought of its delicacy."

2 CHALMERS, ALEXANDER. The General Biographical Dictionary. Vol. 4. London: J. Nichols & Son, pp. 358-60.

Emphasizes the "obscenity" of her plays.

1821

1 FREEMAN, R. "Aphra Behn." In Kentish Poets. A Series of Writers in English Poetry. Vol. 2. Canterbury: G. Wood for Longman, Hurst, pp. 91-109.

Concentrates on the poetry but sees Mrs. Behn's art in general as a reflection of "corrupt manners" and "vicious example."

1825

1 DYCE, ALEXANDER. Specimens of British Poetesses. London: T. Rodd, pp. 111-12.

Despite their "many humourous scenes," Mrs. Behn's plays offend us with their grossness, which "does not consist of occasional blots . . . on the surface, but forms an essential and inseparable portion of the composition."

1828

1 HUNT, LEIGH. "Poetry of British Ladies." The Companion, no. 19 (14 May), in The Companion. London: Hunt and Clarke, pp. 268.

Aphra's comedies "indeed are alarming, . . . though it is probable, that a thoughtless good-humour made her pen run over, more than real licentiousness."

1832

1 [GENEST, JOHN.] Some Account of the English Stage, from the Restoration in 1660 to 1830. Bath: H.E. Carrington; London: Thomas Rodd, 1:120, 145, 154, 192-93, 206-8, 209-10, 212-13, 214-17, 242-44, 269-73, 286-89, 309-10, 317-19, 357, 359-63, 428, 455-57, 484-87; 2:78-79.

The best of all the female playwrights in English, Mrs. Behn "deserves a very high rank" among dramatists in general; "all her comic scenes are good, and many of them excellent." For most of the plays Genest gives a source or two, lists the original cast, sketches out the plot, and makes a brief, relative judgment of value. The Rover, The Feign'd Curtizans, and The Luckey Chance are "excellent" comedies, though the latter is "unusually indecent." In the first of these, Mrs. Behn has improved everything about her source except for the character of the Rover himself, and in the second Tickletext is a "very good character."

The "very good" plays are Abdelazer, Sir Patient Fancy, The City-Heiress, Emperor of the Moon, and The Younger Brother. The first (named with All for Love and The Orphan) is one of the few "rational Tragedies since the Restoration," and its characterizations of Abdelazer and Zanga are admirable; it is a "very loyal" piece. Sir Patient and City-Heiress are notably indecent, and Emperor is a farce with good stage effects. Listed as "good" dramas are The Debauchee, The Counterfeit Bridegroom, The Revenge (the best version of Marston's Dutch Courtesan), The Second Part of the Rover ("too farcical" and "considerably inferiour to the first part"), The False Count ("laughable farce"), The Roundheads ("extraordinary" in its depiction of recent public figures), and The Widdow Ranter (historically based and with "considerable merit"). The Amorous Prince and The Dutch Lover are "pretty good," the latter having better comic than serious scenes; and The Forc'd Marriage is "indifferent," The Town-Fopp an improvement on its source but marred by "dull scenes in blank verse," and The Young King "contemptible" in plot yet so busy as to be "never dull."

1838

1 DUNHAM, SAMUEL ASTLEY. "Aphara Behn." In Lives of the Most Eminent Literary and Scientific Men of Great Britain. Lardner's Cabinet Cyclopaedia, vol. 3. London: Longman, Orme, et al., pp. 146-54.

Sees Mrs. Behn as prostituting genuine talent for descriptive prose to the corrupt theatrical tastes of her day. Despite her facile, energetic, and sometime truly passionate writing, her comedies are among "the most licentious . . . that ever disgraced the stage."

1839

1 HALLAM, HENRY. Introduction to the Literature of Europe, in the 15th, 16th, and 17th Centuries. Vol. 4. Paris: A. & W. Galignani, p. 281.

Mrs. Behn and Shadwell "have endeavoured to make the stage as grossly immoral as their talents permitted."

1843

1 CHAMBERS, ROBERT. Cyclopaedia of English Literature. Vol. 1. Edinburgh: William & Robert Chambers, p. 393.

Considers Mrs. Behn "a female Wycherley" whose comedies "are grossly indelicate."

1845

1 CRAIK, GEORGE L. Sketches of the History of Literature and Learning in England. Vol. 4. London: Charles Knight, p. 140.

Aphra's novels and tales are more ingenious and amusing than her plays.

1848

1 ROWTON, FREDERIC. The Female Poets of Great Britain. London: Longman, Brown, Green, & Longmans, pp. 78-79.

"To a fine and subtle humour" Mrs. Behn "joins great grossness of thought; and to a lively and laughing imagination she unites an essential coarseness of passion." Thus, many of her plays "are amongst the grossest productions ever given to the world."

1850

1 [PARLBY, BROOKE BRIDGES.] Desultory Thoughts on the National Drama, Past and Present. London: by Onwhyn, pp. 8-9.

A wanton female who tried to compete with men in depicting "unrestrained indulgence," Mrs. Behn wrote plays in which "the sensual" triumphs over "all the finer qualities of the heart and mind."

1851

1 MILLS, ABRAHAM. The Literature and the Literary Men of Great Britain and Ireland. Vol. 2. New York: Harper & Bros., pp. 74-75.

Stresses the gross indelicacy of Mrs. Behn's comedies.

1852

1 ANON. "Mrs. Behn's Dramatic Writings." Retrospective Review, n.s. 1 (November):1-18.

Mrs. Behn wrote "the most perfect models of the drama of the latter half of the seventeenth century," exhibiting "both its merits and its defects." The merits include "brilliance of conversation," skillfully managed plots (complex on the surface, simple at bottom), and vivid realism in the depiction of Restoration society. The chief defect is looseness of language and sentiment. The Rover and Sir Patient Fancy are typical. The Roundheads is an "absurd libel on history"; The Widdow Ranter, a witty "satire on the mismanagement of our colonies," misrepresents the colonists; and The Luckey Chance and The City-Heiress expose the peculiarities of citizens. Mrs. Behn's often severe attitude toward the female sex--she represents them as vain, selfish, scheming, and unchaste--is well illustrated in The Town-Fopp.

1856

1 ANON. "Mrs. Behn." Dublin University Magazine 47:536-49.
Albeit she fought courageously for female equality in the literary world, Mrs. Behn merely imitated the male dramatists when she wrote her gross and "stupid" plays. The article in Littel's Living Age 49:800-11, is a reprint of this one.

2 KNIGHT, CHARLES. The English Cyclopaedia: Biography. Vol. 1. London: Bradbury & Evans, pp. 618-19.
Characterized by a "lively mediocrity," Aphra composed plays that are "astounding for their licentiousness."

1858

1 JEAFFRESON, J. CORDY. "Mrs. Behn." In Novels and Novelists, from Elizabeth to Victoria. Vol. 1. London: Hurst & Blackett, pp. 45-64.
Either reprints or plagiarizes from the piece in Dublin University Magazine (B.1856.1).

1860

1 HALLIWELL, JAMES O. A Dictionary of Old English Plays. London: John Russell Smith, pp. 16, 83, 96, 215.
Quotes and paraphrases (without acknowledgement) the Baker-Reed-Jones Biographia Dramatica (B.1812.1).

1861

1 ANON. "Choice Notes by William Oldys, Norroy King-at-Arms." N&Q 23:201-2.
"Superior to every other poetess of the age, and many of the poets too," Aphra possessed "command of pertinent expressions," "pregnant and fluent" fancy, and "warmth, especially in amorous subjects." Oldys sketches the background of The Widdow Ranter.

2 WILLIAMS, JANE. The Literary Women of England. London: Saunders, Otley, pp. 127-28.
Sees Aphra Behn as "the first English authoress upon record whose life was openly wrong, and whose writings were obscene." She created heroes who are "attractively displayed as triumphant libertines."

1862

1 KAVANAGH, JULIA. "Aphra Behn." In English Women of Letters: Biographical Sketches. Leipzig: Bernhard Tauchnitz, pp. 1-14
"With an independence worthy of a better cause," Mrs. Behn persisted in sullying her witty and boisterous plays with a grossness that "sank woman to the level of man's coarseness."

1863

1 ANON. "England's First Lady Novelist." St. James's Magazine 7:351-58.
Admits that her plays are licentious but emphasizes that they have "ingenious" plots and "brilliant" wit.

1864

1 DORAN, JOHN. "Their Majesties' Servants." Annals of the English Stage, from Thomas Betterton to Edmund Kean. Vol. 1. London: William H. Allen, pp. 221-22.
No one "save Ravenscroft and Wycherley" equals Aphra "in downright nastiness." At least Wycherley is inventive and can write graceful prose. Mrs. Behn adapts "skilfully," but "all her vivacity is wasted on filth."

2 SHAW, THOMAS B., and WILLIAM SMITH. A History of English Literature. London: John Murray, p. 264.
At best, Aphra's immoral comedies, half literary and half political, show "the state of literary and social feeling that prevailed at that agitated epoch."

1871

1 FORSYTH, WILLIAM. The Novels and Novelists of the Eighteenth Century. London: John Murray, pp. 174-95.
Notes the indecency of her plays.

1872

1 ANON. "Aphra Behn." Examiner, no. 3338 (20 January):74-75.
Reviews John Pearson's 1871 reprint, The Plays, Histories, and Novels of the Ingenious Mrs. Aphra Behn. On the whole, Mrs. Behn's writings may be read with amusement and profit. Her plays have "abundance of originality, and . . . wit," "smart writing," and "racy plotting," but they do reflect the coarse manners and thoughts of the Restoration, even though in general quality they rank between the plays of Etherege and Wycherley. Her best piece

The Rover, is humorous and saucy, but in The Feign'd Curtizans, equally effective as comedy, the indecency becomes excessive, and The City-Heiress is "the most indecent of all." Her first play, The Amorous Prince, is also her poorest.

2 ANON. "Literary Garbage." Saturday Review of Politics, Literature, Science, and Art 33, no. 848 (27 January):109-10.

Argues that Aphra's works are too licentious to have been reprinted by Pearson (see B.1872.7)--even in a limited edition, for it will lead to cheap editions that might corrupt the masses.

3 ANON. "Literary Garbage." American Bibliopolist 4, no. 42: 303-5.

Juxtaposes the generally favorable article in Retrospective Review (B.1852.1) to the negative one in Saturday Review (B.1872.3), implicitly affirming the former.

4 ANON. Remarks on Aphra Behn's writings. Bookseller, no. 171 (2 March):217.

Although her plays may be "dull and unreadable," surely they are no more indecent than more famous works by Swift, Fielding, or Smollett, and they do form a "valuable link in our literary history."

5 ANON. Remarks on Pearson's reprint of the Plays, Histories, and Novels. Athenaeum, no. 2315 (9 March):301-3.

Far from being a victim of Restoration taste, Mrs. Behn, with her "audacious licentiousness," was "one of the original corrupters and polluters of the stage." Moreover, her dull and plagiarized plays are full of "low brutalizing prose" and "impossible absurdities."

6 ANON. Two Centuries of Testimony in Favour of Mrs. Aphra Behn. London: John Pearson, 24 pp.

Probably compiled by Pearson himself, this booklet reprints nineteen earlier essays (including some of those annotated in this bibliography) in praise of Mrs. Behn's novels, poems, and plays.

7 PEARSON, JOHN. "Aphra Behn and 'Literary Garbage.'" Examiner, no. 3341 (10 February):151.

"Her coarseness is quite incidental, certainly not more frequent than that of Congreve or Wycherley, and often consists in a double entendre, only intelligible to those who already know more than the book could teach them."

1873

1 MORLEY, HENRY. A First Sketch of English Literature. London, Paris, and New York: Cassell, Petter, & Galpin, p. 683.

Mrs. Behn's plays "reflected the gross manners of the court" and occasionally satirized the Puritans.

1875

1 WARD, ADOLPHUS WILLIAM. A History of Dramatic Literature to the Death of Queen Anne. Vol. 2. London: Macmillan, p. 571.

Considers Mrs. Behn "the type of the worst profligacy of the Restoration drama," though she exhibited "great ingenuity in the contrivance of stage-situations."

1878

1 ANON. "Behn, Aphra." In Encyclopaedia Britannica. 9th ed. Vol. 3. New York: Samuel L. Hall, p. 509.

Lively, "amatory," well constructed, Mrs. Behn's works "are among the worst specimens of the later Stuart literature."

1880

1 GOSSE, EDMUND W. "Mrs. Behn." In The English Poets: Selections with Critical Introductions. Edited by Thomas Humphry Ward. Vol. 2. New York: Macmillan, pp. 419-20.

Despite her coarseness (she "wrote like a man" in a "debased age) and the irregularity of her "untutored" style, Mrs. Behn's wit and genius entitle her to "the first rank of English female writers." Indeed, "in power of sustained production she surpassed all her contemporaries except Dryden."

1882

1 FITZGERALD, PERCY. A New History of the English Stage. Vol. 1. London: Tinsley Brothers, pp. 188-90.

From 1671 to the end of the century, the "unsavoury, unfeminine" Aphra diligently poured "dramatic sewage . . . across the stage."

1883

1 ROBERTSON, ERIC S. English Poetesses: A Series of Critical Biographies. London, Paris, & New York: Cassell, pp. 9-13.

As illustrated by her best play, The Rover, Mrs. Behn was not only an "unsexed" writer of "corrupt plays" but also a genuine wit, ingenious at plotting and in control of "pert and amusing" dialogue.

1884

1 ANON. "Mrs. Aphra Behn." Temple Bar 71:388-402.

Like all women, Mrs. Behn was subjective, imitative, and conventional; thus, she tended to reflect the grossness of her age. Yet with her vivacity, humor, social realism, and control of "rapid series of striking events and situations," she was better, in purely literary terms, than all her contemporaries except Dryden and Wycherley. The Young King is an "excellent" romantic play, though it is stagy and melodramatic, and The Widdow Ranter is interesting as social history. Abdelazer, however, becomes turgid and bombastic in the altered parts, albeit Mrs. Behn has preserved some of the "true power" in borrowed scenes. Belmour of The Town-Fopp is one of the only virtuous characters in Mrs. Behn's comedies, some of which, like The Roundheads, are thoroughly gross and unscrupulous. The Luckey Chance is notable for its anti-Puritan satire and The City-Heiress, her "wittiest" play, for its satire against Shaftesbury. Sir Patient Fancy is "one of the cleverest although one of the most immoral of her comedies." This article is reprinted with the same title in Eclectic Magazine, n.s. 40, no. 3 (September):400-409.

1885

1 GOSSE, EDMUND. "Behn, Afra, Aphra, Aphara, or Ayfara." In Dictionary of National Biography. Edited by Leslie Stephen. Vol. 4. London: Smith, Elder, pp. 129-31.

"Gifted," "witty," vivacious, Mrs. Behn wrote plays that "are very coarse, but very lively and humorous." The Debauchee is her worst original drama, and The Amorous Prince and The Town-Fopp are notably coarse, the latter an attempt to write in the Jonsonian manner. In that, she attempted to write as the men of her time did; she was "the George Sand of the Restoration."

2 SAINTSBURY, GEORGE, ed. "Aphra Behn." In Specimens of English Prose Style from Malory to Macaulay. London: Kegan Paul, Trench, p. 117.

"Her plays have . . . a rather unfair reputation for license, but are of small literary worth."

3 SANBORN, KATHERINE ABBOTT [Kate Sanborn]. The Wit of Women. New York and London: Funk & Wagnalls, p. 195.

Because she was "so wicked and coarse," Mrs. Behn "forfeited all right to fame," though she was "an undoubted wit."

1889

1 BAKER, HENRY BARTON. The London Stage: Its History and Traditions from 1576 to 1888. Vol. 1. London: W.H. Allen, p. 47.

Mrs. Behn's comedies are licentious but "possess great merit," having "ingenious" and busy plots, "verve and vigour in the incidents and dialogue." Her characters, however, are "nearly all . . . drawn upon the same lines, the silly senile citizen, with a young and amorous wife, the daring gallant, the intriguing chambermaid, all modelled upon the Spanish comedy."

1895

1 GARNETT, RICHARD. The Age of Dryden. London: George Bell & Sons, p. 147.

Aphra's plays have "sufficient merit" to be mentioned and "sufficient indelicacy to be unreadable."

2 ROBINS, EDWARD, Jr. Echoes of the Playhouse: Reminiscences of Some Past Glories of the English Stage. New York and London: G.P. Putnam's Sons, pp. 74, 102.

Fortunately, Mrs. Behn's "discreditable career" ended ages ago, so that she can "no longer . . . invent filthy plays" like The Rover.

1897

1 HUDSON, WILLIAM HENRY. "Two Novelists of the English Restoration." In Idle Hours in a Library. San Francisco: William Doxey, pp. 154-69.

Focuses on Mrs. Behn's prose fiction but perpetuates the notion that she wrote licentious plays not worth seriously criticizing.

1898

1 HAMILTON, C.J. "The First Lady Novelist." Cornhill Magazine, n.s. 5:522-29.

Frank, sentimental, obsessed with the subject of love, totally lacking in ideals, Mrs. Behn wrote lewd plays for a corrupt age. She had "little sense of true comedy" and no talent "for inventing amusing situations"; her dialogue "sometimes drags" and her characters are confined to a narrow range: "either licentious rakes or pompous fools." A few of her works, such as The Forc'd Marriage and Abdelazer (one of her best), are not very objectionable; others, like The Rover ("dull reading"), The Dutch Lover ("elaborately feeble"), and Sir Patient Fancy, are "coarse without being amusing." Some of her scenes "were too revolting to be acted" even in the Restoration.

2 SAINTSBURY, GEORGE E.B. A Short History of English Literature. New York: Macmillan, pp. 480-81, 489, 517.

Mrs. Behn's plays are "far from despicable." The Rover and The City-Heiress are rather good, and The Town-Fopp, The Luckey Chance, The Widdow Ranter, and Sir Patient Fancy are worth looking into.

1901

1 ANDREWS, GERTRUDE. "Early Women Dramatists: Aphra Behn." New York Dramatic Mirror, 24 August, unpaginated clipping in the Harvard Theatre Collection.

Treats Aphra as a pioneer woman writer whose plays are not more bawdy than others of her day. The Forc'd Marriage, The Rover, The Roundheads, and The City-Heiress are cited.

2 THOMPSON, A. HAMILTON. A History of English Literature. London: John Murray, pp. 358-59.

Though her plays are "all of a second-rate type," The Rover is her best.

1902

3 ENGEL, EDUARD. A History of English Literature (600-1900). Translated by "several hands" and revised by Hamley Bent. London: Methuen, p. 265.

Aphra wrote "wearisome and disgusting" plays.

4 SIEGEL, P. "Aphra Behns Gedichte und Prosawerke." Anglia 25: 86-128, 329-85.

Briefly introduces her plays but concentrates on the poetry and prose fiction, treating them as important links between seventeenth- and eighteenth-century modes.

1904

1 HUGHES, S.C. The Pre-Victorian Drama in Dublin. Dublin: Hodges, Figgis, p. 114.

Since Mrs. Behn's plays are usually "of the filthiest Restoration type," we are fortunate to "have this farce," Emperor of the Moon, "tolerably clean."

1905

1 ANON. "The Early Novel." Living Age 247:125-27.
"The Comedy of the Restoration was a bad school for women, and Mrs. Behn was too apt a pupil in it." This article reviews Baker's Novels (B.1905.3).

2 ANON. Review of The Novels of Mrs. Aphra Behn. Athenaeum, no. 4061 (26 August):262-63.
Her licentious but spirited plays "constitute her chief claim to literary rank."

3 BAKER, ERNEST A., ed. Introduction to The Novels of Mrs. Aphra Behn. London: Routledge; New York: Dutton, pp. vii-xxvii.
The Amorous Prince is "very gross and immoral," Aldelazer is "merely rant and melodrama, masquerading as tragedy," and The Roundheads is "a cowardly attack on the fallen." But some of her other comedies, despite their revolting grossness, have redeeming features: The Dutch Lover is lively, witty, and well constructed; The Rover is full of "highly diverting scenes"; and The City-Heiress is witty and lightly satiric. One of Mrs. Behn's "most vivacious" plays, Sir Patient Fancy, is also "the most completely devoid of moral feeling," all its characters being "entirely absorbed in self," especially Lady Fancy, one of Aphra's most "shameless and . . . unscrupulous women." Lady Knowell is "a Mrs. Malaprop in Latin." Sir Patient's seven-year-old daughter is made, repulsively, the "confidante of her elder sister's highly improper love affairs."

1906

1 CHARLANNE, LOUIS. L'Influence francaise en angleterre aux XVIIe siècle. Paris: Société Francaise d'Imprimerie et de Librairie, 634 pp.
Chapter 9, section 2, discusses Molière and Mrs. Behn.

1907

1 KERBY, W. MOSELEY. Molière and the Restoration Comedy in England. Rennes: n.p., p. 40.
A "great genius," Mrs. Behn wrote socially realistic comedies in which "the dialogue is brilliant, the plots are skilfully arranged, and striking situations are produced." Sir Patient Fancy derives its plot from Le Malade imaginaire and some of its ideas from M. de Pourceaugnac; The False Count draws one minor feature from Les Précieuses ridicules.

1908

1 TUTIN, J.R. "Aphra Behn." In Four Early English Poetesses: Selected Poetry. Hull, Eng.: J.R. Tutin, p. 16.
Regards Mrs. Behn as "a woman who disgraced herself, in her Plays especially," but wrote fine lyrics.

1909

1 ALDEN, RAYMOND MACDONALD. "The Development of the Use of Prose in the English Drama: 1660-1800." MP 7:3.
The Dutch Lover, a play that for many reasons deserves oblivion, shows how prose became habitually employed even in passages where the tone did not demand it.

2 JUSSERAND, J.J. A Literary History of the English People. Vol. 3, pt. 2, From the Renaissance to the Civil War. New York and London: G.P. Putnam's Sons, p. 454 n.1.
The trap-door scene in The Rover, Act III, is taken from Middleton's Blurt, Master-Constable (1602), IV.ii.

3 MANTZIUS, KARL. A History of Theatrical Art in Ancient and Modern Times. Translated by Louise von Cossel. Vol. 5. London: Duckworth, p. 314.
Mrs. Behn, who gave us "eighteen witty and very immoral comedies," was "a showy adventuress, half courtesan, half political agent, as light in her morals as free with her tongue and with her pen."

1910

1 ANON. "Behn, Aphra." In Encyclopaedia Britannica. 11th ed. Vol. 3. New York: Encyclopaedia Britannica, p. 657.
Mrs. Behn was witty, vivacious, ingenious, very skillful in using the resources of the stage. Her "coarseness," which certainly "disfigures her plays," was "the fault of her time."

2 MILES, DUDLEY HOWE. The Influence of Molière on Restoration Comedy. New York: Columbia University Press, p. 108.
In using Le Malade imaginaire while writing Sir Patient Fancy, Mrs. Behn created a "confusing set of stratagems and dramatis personae."

3 RISTINE, FRANK HUMPHREY. English Tragicomedy, Its Origin and History. New York: Columbia University Press, p. 178.
Notes the "spectacular" denouement of The Forc'd Marriage, where "the supposedly murdered heroine" personates "first her own ghost and then her angel." In the "commonplace" play, The Young King, the characters are "decidedly those of French romance"

and the two subplots are "cleverly organized with the main theme." The Widdow Ranter is "a deliberate mixture of comedy and tragedy."

1911

1 HILL, HERBERT WYNFORD. "La Calprenède's Romances and the Restoration Drama." University of Nevada Studies 3, no. 2: 131-35.

The main plot of The Young King is closely modeled on the story of Alcamenes and Menalippa in La Calprenède's Cleopatra.

1912

1 SCHELLING, FELIX E. "The Restoration Drama I." In The Cambridge History of English Literature. Edited by A.W. Ward and A.R. Waller. Vol. 8. Cambridge: Cambridge University Press, pp. 122, 131, 140-42.

Although Mrs. Behn was "inventive in situations if not in whole plots" and could keep up a flow of "incessant action" and "vivacious dialogue," she was "predatory" in her borrowing and more "daring and risqué than any of her male competitors." Schelling notes the sources of The Dutch Lover, The Rover, The Debauchee, The Town-Fopp, The City-Heiress, and The Roundheads.

2 SMITH, GEORGE JAY. "A Long-Forgotten 'Hit.'" North American Review 96:264-77.

Discusses Aphra's life in relation to her Oroonoko, and argues that "the morality of her plays" is no worse than that of popular plays by her contemporaries.

1913

1 ANON. "Aphra Behn's Comedies." N&Q 128:469.

Asks help in identifying allusions in The City-Heiress and The Feign'd Curtizans. The "M.S." who wrote this note was probably Montague Summers.

2 DUNCAN, CARSON S. The New Science and English Literature in the Classical Period. Menasha, Wis.: George Banta, pp. 81-82.

Possessing only a vague idea of the New Science, Mrs. Behn created for Emperor of the Moon one Doctor Baliardo--an "old-time astrologer with new scientific apparatus"--whose "brain has been cracked by the perusal of extravagant fiction . . . respecting the moon."

3 PALMER, JOHN. The Comedy of Manners. London: G. Bell & Sons, p. 2.

The comedy of manners would have emerged without any contribution from Mrs. Behn.

1914

1 ANON. "Mrs. Behn's 'Emperor of the Moon.'" N&Q 129:231, 394.
Asks for information about the Patagonian Theatre, where Emperor of the Moon was acted in 1777, and both requests and provides information about the sources of this play. The "M.S." who wrote these notes was probably Montague Summers.

2 MATTHEWS, ALBERT. "Aphra Behn's Comedies." N&Q 129:116.
In reply to B.1913.1, Matthews suggests that the "Cartwright" alluded to in The Feign'd Curtizans is John Cartwright, author of The Preacher's Travels (1611).

3 NETTLETON, GEORGE HENRY. English Drama of the Restoration and Eighteenth Century (1642-1780). New York: Macmillan, pp. 46, 109, 114-15.
An unscrupulous plagiarist, but abler than Ravenscroft, Mrs. Behn wrote vivacious, ingenious, grossly humorous plays that were no more indecent than those of her contemporaries. The Dutch Lover and The Rover reflect Spanish influences, and the latter, plus The Roundheads and The City-Heiress, are her best dramas.

4 NORMAN, WILLIAM, and WILLIAM DOUGLAS. "Mrs. Behn's 'Emperor of the Moon.'" N&Q 129:275.
In reply to B.1914.1, provides details about the Patagonian Theatre.

5 SCHELLING, FELIX E. English Drama. London: J.M. Dent & Sons; New York: E.P. Dutton, p. 261.
Sees Mrs. Behn as "a clever and gifted woman" who was forced to cater to corrupt tastes, a formula writer of plays that are bustling and inventive but foul in dialogue and situation.

1915

1 ANON. "Astraea." TLS, 22 July, p. 245.
Reviews Summers's edition of The Works (B.1915.3), naming The Rover, The Roundheads, The Young King, The City-Heiress, and The Feign'd Curtizans as Mrs. Behn's best plays, notable for their skillfully handled plots and characters, wit, fancy, and "mastering reality." Mrs. Behn knows how to keep up the pace of action and how to make fresh whatever she borrows. Sometimes she seems "a combination of Congreve and Farquhar, though the equal of neither."

2 BERNBAUM, ERNEST. The Drama of Sensibility . . . 1696-1780. Boston and London: Ginn, pp. 50-52.

211

In showing the immorality of enforced marriage by evoking "pity for its innocent victims," The Town-Fopp derives its sentimentality from its Elizabethan source, though Mrs. Behn omits some of the pathos as she broadens the comic parts.

3 SUMMERS, MONTAGUE, ed. "Memoir of Mrs. Behn" and introductions to separate plays." In The Works of Aphra Behn. London: William Heinemann. 1:xv-lxi; 2:4, 103, 198, 304; 4:5-6, 218, 314.

The "Memoir" briefly covers the plays in context, and the introductions survey stage history and sources, often including critical comments on the use of sources. Each volume ends with explanatory notes that are full, curious, and sometimes extravagant, though almost always illuminating. Summers ranks as the best plays The Rover (showing "rare skill"), The Feign'd Curtizans, The City-Heiress (its witty caricatures of Shaftesbury and the cits never coarsening into mere invective), and The Luckey Chance. Somewhat less impressive, but still "capital," are Abdelazer (a "magnificent tapestry" aptly absorbing its source), The Young King ("a first-rate specimen of the romance drama" albeit lacking Calderon's "melody" and "deep philosophy"), Sir Patient Fancy (even though too hurried), The Roundheads ("a masterly pasquinade" showing the Puritans "in their most odious and veritable colours"), The False Count, Emperor of the Moon, and The Widdow Ranter ("vivid comedy . . . photographic in its realism").

Among the plays about which Summers lacks high enthusiasm are The Amorous Prince, The Counterfeit Bridegroom (yet "smart and spirited"), and The Second Part of the Rover ("surprisingly good"). Only The Forc'd Marriage ("a good tragi-comedy of the bastard Fletcherian Davenant type" yet not in her best vein), The Debauchee ("superficial though clever"), and The Younger Brother (less spirited than D'Urfey's Royalist) come in for anything like negative assessment. As a borrower from Molière, Mrs. Behn is "infinitely the best" English dramatist, and as a dramatic artist "she is worthy to be ranked with the greatest . . of her day, with Vanbrugh and Etherege; not so strong as Wycherle less polished than Congreve." As for her notorious indecency, she was not exceptional in her time.

1916

1 MORE, PAUL E. "A Bluestocking of the Restoration." Nation 103:299-302, 322-23.

In reviewing Summers's Works (B.1915.3), More argues that Summers glosses over Mrs. Behn's pronounced indecency and overpraises her artistry. In fact, she not only possessed cleverness without real genius and audacity without creativity, but also wrote plays that sanctioned the kind of female behavior and status that she herself rejected in practice (and sometimes in her prose). Clearly, she wrote plays without moral aims, purely for their value as entertainment. Granted, she had some fine moments, as in The Feign'd Curtizans, IV.i.; yet many of her dramas are not as worthy as Summers makes them out to be. For example, Abdelazer "exhibits the worst faults of the genre"; it is "a turmoil of gross passions set free from the laws of character." The Young King may be romantic, decent, and even well constructed, but it lacks Beaumont's morbidezza.

2 WRIGHT, ROSE ABEL. The Political Play of the Restoration. Montesano, Wash.: A.E. Veatch, pp. 76, 109-12.

Condemns The Roundheads, The False Count, and The City-Heiress for their vile immorality; briefly notes their political implications.

1917

1 BLASHFIELD, EVANGELINE WILBOUR. "Aphra Behn." In Portraits and Backgrounds. New York: Scribner's, pp. 115-283.

Given the dearth of biographical evidence, this "portrait" is placed in a richly painted "background" of social, political, and theatrical history. Mrs. Behn joined her contemporaries in plagiarism, bawdry, and spirited writing. Taking as her models Dryden and Etherege, she always avoided dullness and excelled in constructing complicated intrigues on the Spanish model. Abdelazer, with Purcell's songs and musical interludes, is operatic and often "lovely." The Rover is "a rollicking dare-devil comedy," and The Second Part retains all the "dash and spirit" of the first. The City-Heiress and The Roundheads are both anti-Puritan satires.

1918

1 WANN, LOUIS. "The Oriental in Restoration Drama." University of Wisconsin Studies in Language and Literature, 2:182-83.

The False Count and Abdelazer exhibit "a fair knowledge of the people and their customs." Ismael in The False Count is "a miniature Iago, whereas Abdelazer . . . reminds one of Othello."

1920

1 EDMUNDS, E.W. An Historical Summary of English Literature. London, New York, Toronto, and Melbourne: Cassell, p. 128.

Aphra is mentioned as "a woman of experience and wit" who wrote "eighteen lively but often offensive comedies."

2 REYNOLDS, MYRA. The Learned Lady in England 1650-1760. Boston and New York: Houghton Mifflin Co., pp. 128-30, 378-79.

Mistress of "rapid, bustling plots," "varied characters," facile dialogue, and cleverly managed intrigues, Mrs. Behn liked to emphasize "the vicious elements of the life about her." Nevertheless, she was "the most important" woman playwright of the later seventeenth century. Her Lady Knowell, in Sir Patient Fancy, is "a caricature of a learned lady" and a precursor of Mrs. Malaprop.

1921

1 NICOLL, ALLARDYCE. "Political Plays of the Restoration." MLR 16:233-34.

The City-Heiress loyally ridicules Commonwealthmen and radical protestants; its plot is "not . . . particularly brilliant or moral," and Tom Wilding is too unprincipled for modern tastes. The Roundheads is more an adaptation than an individual production.

1922

1 JONES, VIRGIL L. "Methods of Satire in the Political Drama of the Restoration." JEGP 21:667.

In The Roundheads, Mrs. Behn shows that she is a "specialist" in intrigue comedy, invents "conventional 'humour' characters," and treats Lady Cromwell more respectfully than Tatham did in The Rump.

1923

1 ARCHER, WILLIAM. The Old Drama and the New: An Essay in Re-valuation. Boston: Small, Maynard, pp. 174, 200, 207.

By and large, Mrs. Behn's plays are lewd, cynical, worthless "stuff." She influenced Farquhar, however.

2 NICOLL, ALLARDYCE. A History of Restoration Drama 1660-1700. Cambridge: Cambridge University Press, pp. 11, 24-25, 110, 130, 173, 176, 183, 208-12, 249-50, 254-57.

To stress the modish licentiousness of Mrs. Behn's comedies is to overlook more important points: she was "the first in this age to raise her voice against the fashionable vices of the time, to preach a return to more natural modes of life, and to present a genuine problem in her comedies." Moreover, as the first English female to earn a living by her pen, she was responsible for establishing a position for women in professional dramaturgy. She became the chief Restoration practitioner of intrigue comedy, as Shadwell was the principal writer of humors comedy.

Spanish intrigue informs The Dutch Lover, an overly complex tragicomedy, and other intrigue plays include The Amorous

Prince (pastoral, romantic, sentimental, but with "no dramatic or literary value"), The Rover and The Second Part (inferior but interesting for its use of a Harlequin figure), Sir Patient Fancy (an indecent intrigue), The Town-Fopp and The Widdow Ranter (a poor intrigue farce). In The Luckey Chance, Mrs. Behn combines manners, humors, and intrigue, while in Abdelazer she merges Elizabethan romantic tragedy and Restoration heroics. Her first piece, The Forc'd Marriage, paves the way for several romantic dramas about real problems or, at least, about serious issues. The Amorous Prince, The Young King, The Widdow Ranter (all urging the sinless delights of nature), The Town-Fopp, The Luckey Chance, and The Younger Brother (despite its poor artistry), all fit to some extent in this category.

Of the rest, The Debauchee is an adaptation, The Feign'd Curtizans a farcical, "poor and dull" affair, The False Count a flimsy farce, and The City-Heiress and The Roundheads protestant plays. Emperor of the Moon is notable only for its experimentation with Italian commedia dell' arte. Nicoll also deals briefly with Molière's influence on Mrs. Behn and with her influence on sentimental drama.

3 _____. An Introduction to Dramatic Theory. New York: Brentano's, p. 194.

Like Fletcher and Mrs. Centlivre, Mrs. Behn specialized in skillfully manipulating delicately conceived situations "leading to innumerable mistakes and amusing dénouements." She possessed "little wit," "practically no humour, and not a scrap of satire"--only "genuine comedy of situation."

1924

1 KRUTCH, JOSEPH WOOD. Comedy and Conscience after the Restoration. New York: Columbia University Press, pp. 22, 45-46, 196, 200-201, 226.

Not recognizing "the ugliness of vice," Mrs. Behn pandered shamefully to her audiences' lust with such plays as "the lascivious" Rover and the elaborately luscious Luckey Chance. Emperor of the Moon is a "wretched farce" hardly worth mentioning. She loved "to devise . . . amorous intrigues."

1925

1 DISHER, M. WILLSON. Clowns and Pantomimes. London: Constable, pp. 76-79.

Briefly discusses the use of Harlequin and Scaramouche in The Second Part of the Rover and calls Emperor of the Moon "an artless imitation of a witty original" in which Mrs. Behn has failed to integrate her buffoonery with the main action.

2 NICOLL, ALLARDYCE. British Drama: An Historical Survey from the Beginnings to the Present Time. New York: Crowell, pp. 248, 281.

Mrs. Behn's best plays--Rover, Dutch Lover, Town-Fopp, Sir Patient Fancy, and City-Heiress--demonstrate that she was mistress of ingenious intrigue and skillful portraiture, and that she had little wit but much vivacity. She is also memorable for her early explorations of social problems through the drama, especially those problems arising "out of social conventions."

1926

1 BEAUMONT, CYRIL W. The History of Harlequin. London: C.W. Beaumont, pp. 87, 100.

Discusses Aphra's early employment (earlier than any English dramatist except Ravenscroft) of Harlequin in The Second Part of the Rover and Emperor of the Moon, focusing on the acting of Jevon and Penkethman.

2 COX, JAMES E. The Rise of Sentimental Comedy. Olney, Ill.: by the author, pp. 42-43.

In The Forc'd Marriage and The Town-Fopp, Mrs. Behn "makes a greater approach toward sentimental comedy than any other writer of her day." The former play has a "sentimental hero and heroine, although its overall effect is prevented from becoming sentimental by the bawdy intrigue and lack of poetic justice. In The Town Fopp, an attack on the practice of dueling and the sentimental tendencies of Trusty the servant anticipate Steele.

3 LYNCH, KATHLEEN M. The Social Mode of Restoration Comedy. New York and London: Macmillan, p. 160.

The Amorous Prince and The Dutch Lover are Spanish-style intrigue comedies which "possess briskness of action, flavored at times with Restoration libertinism."

4 SPRAGUE, ARTHUR COLBY. Beaumont and Fletcher on the Restoration Stage. Cambridge, Mass.: Harvard University Press, pp. 44, 51, 166-67, 173, 239.

Demonstrates that Mrs. Behn recognized the pervasive influence of Beaumont and Fletcher on the drama of her time.

5 SUMMERS, MONTAGUE. The History of Witchcraft and Demonology. London: Kegan Paul, Trench, Trübner; New York: Alfred A. Knopf, p. 303.

Notes that The Luckey Chance is farcical in its treatment of the devil.

1927

1 BENNETT, R.E. "A Bibliographical Correction." RES 3:450-51.
As background to Emperor of the Moon, notes that Mrs. Behn cited Wilkins's The Discovery of a World in the Moone and "was the second English translator of Fontenelle's Entretiens sur la pluralité des mondes."

2 CAZAMIAN, LOUIS. A History of English Literature, Vol. 2: Modern Times (1660-1914). New York: Macmillan, p. 46.
Cites "The Rover . . . by Mrs. Behn, who by her varied production, her coloured descriptions, her lively dialogue, her adumbration of feminism, her relative decency of bearing, is an original figure in the literature of the time."

3 SUMMERS, MONTAGUE, ed. Introduction to The Complete Works of Thomas Shadwell. Edited by Summers. Vol. 1. London: Fortune Press, pp. clxvii, ccv.
Considers The City-Heiress a "delightful comedy" satirizing Shaftesbury, and maintains that The Town-Fopp and The Luckey Chance have "scenes of sensibility that rival Richardson."

1928

1 BORGMAN, ALBERT S. Thomas Shadwell: His Life and Comedies. New York: New York University Press, p. 210.
Angelica Bianca (The Rover) seems to have influenced Shadwell's portrayal of Termagant in The Squire of Alsatia.

2 ELWIN, MALCOLM. The Playgoer's Handbook to Restoration Drama. New York: Macmillan, pp. 50, 116-18, 120.
"The first of the emasculated male women, the pioneer of female emancipation," Mrs. Behn imitated the intrigue drama popularized by Tuke and linked it to sentimental comedy, as in her best plays, The Rover (which shows Dryden's influence), The Dutch Lover, Sir Patient Fancy ("good comedy cankered by coarseness"), and The Town-Fopp (a well-designed play). Abdelazer is Drydenesque, The Luckey Chance is Wycherleyan with earnest sentiment substituted for cynical satire, and Emperor of the Moon is notable for showing the early stages of pantomime. Of the other plays worth mentioning, The Forc'd Marriage has no outstanding merits, and The Feign'd Curtizans, The False Count, and The Second Part of the Rover are all frail, patchy farces.

3 GILDER, ROSAMOND. "Aphra Behn." Theatre Arts Monthly 12: 397-409.
Mrs. Behn was "an admirable and engaging human being" whose best plays, less original than ingenious, are distinguished by intrigue plots and racy dialogue. She was no bawdier than others of her day; in fact, in some of her scenes "a fine frenzy of

feeling" almost "shivers the brittle artificiality" of the mannered surface. In *The Dutch Lover* and *The Rover*, she found her best vein of romantic intrigue and rollicking wit, and in *The Town-Fopp*, a comedy of manners, she created "a vivid and speaking likeness of the times." *The Young King*, *The Amorous Prince*, and *Abdelazer*, however, are "sentimental and grandiose" serio-dramas, and *The Forc'd Marriage* is a weak production. In *Emperor of the Moon* she may have achieved "the best pantomime farce ever written."

4 SACKVILLE-WEST, V. *Aphra Behn: The Incomparable Astrea.* New York: Viking, 177 pp.

Regrettably, Mrs. Behn failed to explore through drama either her own sensibility or her rich experiences in literary-theatrical London. Neither did she create any memorably three-dimensional characters "in the broad ribald tradition of Juliet's nurse." Instead, she skillfully and energetically mixed stock ingredients in intricately plotted, sexy, entertaining (never really instructive) plays which illustrate "the peculiarly Caroline faculty of marrying the romantic to the everyday." Though "their indelicacy forbids" modern production, her best pieces are *The City-Heiress*, *The Rover*, *The Feign'd Curtizans*, and *The Dutch Lover*, with *The Luckey Chance* and *The Widdow Ranter* coming in a close second. The "Aphra Behn" section of *Six Brilliant Women* (London: Gerald Howe, 1930), pp. 9-93, reprints essentially all of this book.

5 SUMMERS, MONTAGUE, ed. "Explanatory Notes." In *Roscius Anglicanus*, by John Downes. London: Fortune Press, p. 227.

Highly praises *The Feign'd Curtizans* and *The City-Heiress*.

6 WILSON, JOHN HAROLD. *The Influence of Beaumont and Fletcher on Restoration Drama*. Columbus: Ohio State University Press, pp. 22, 30, 96, 98-101, 110, 114.

Although sophisticated "sex intrigue is her chief theme," Aphra could write romantically, farcically, satirically, and realistically. Her use "of English methods" of plotting and characterization against the backdrop of "some artificially romantic Spanish scene" probably shows the influence of Beaumont and Fletcher. Her most memorable characters are Sir Timothy Tawdry, a humors type in *The Town-Fopp*; Willmore, the "thoroughly unprincipled rake" of *The Rover*; Sir Signal Buffoon, a typical wild gallant in *The Feign'd Curtizans*; his counterpart, Freeman, in *The Roundheads*; Lady Fancy, a fine-mannered, emancipated woman in *Sir Patient Fancy*; and Olinda, the wanton maid of *The Dutch Lover*.

1929

1 JERROLD, WALTER, and CLARE. "Aphra Behn." In Five Queer Women. New York, London, and Paris: Brentano's, pp. 1-82.

Offers concise evaluations of those plays that, collectively, place Mrs. Behn "in the front rank" of Restoration dramatists: The Forc'd Marriage ("pure romance"), The Amorous Prince ("coarse" but theatrically skillful intrigue), The Dutch Lover, Abdelazer (containing some soft, melodious verse), The Town-Fopp ("lively but unlovely"), The Rover, Sir Patient Fancy (brisk and farcical), The Young King, The Feign'd Curtizans (with its original, ingenious situations), The Second Part of the Rover, The City-Heiress ("largely inspired by contemporary politics"), The Luckey Chance ("ingeniously contrived"), and Emperor of the Moon (an excellent farce worthy of revival).

2 THORNDIKE, ASHLEY H. English Comedy. New York: Macmillan, pp. 308-14.

In her early works, such as The Forc'd Marriage and The Amorous Prince, Mrs. Behn descends "down the Fletcherian scale from the thrilling and passionate to the realistic and domestic." Later, in such pieces as The Rover and The City-Heiress, The False Count and The Luckey Chance, she contributes distinctively to the later seventeenth-century move toward intrigue, farce, and sentiment. Sir Patient Fancy is more in the fashionable manners mode, though it has plenty of intrigue and some farcical mistakes in the darkness, and Emperor of the Moon helped popularize commedia dell'arte in England. The Roundheads is a "rude" satire. Not very inventive, but clever at manipulating her borrowings, Mrs. Behn dramatized the code "of the tender passion."

1930

1 HENDERSON, PHILIP, ed. Introduction to Shorter Novels: Jacobean and Restoration. Vol. 2. London: Dent; New York: Dutton, p. xiii.

Oroonoko shows the influence of Mrs. Behn's earlier dramatic experience.

2 SUMMERS, MONTAGUE. "A Note on Mrs. Behn and a Dickens Parallel." N&Q 159:274-75.

Identifies a proverbial expression perverted by Lady Knowell in Sir Patient Fancy and maintains that the main intrigue of The False Count is taken "wholesale" from Montfleury's L'Ecole des jaloux (1664).

3 WHITING, GEORGE W. "Political Satire in London Stage Plays, 1680-83." MP 28:37, 40-41.

By adding to her source the roles of Ananias Goggle (Titus Oates) and three cavaliers, Mrs. Behn ridicules the dissenters in The Roundheads and "effectively dramatizes the theme that the Whigs intended through civil war to restore the commonwealth." In The City-Heiress, Sir Timothy Treat-all is meant to caricature Shaftesbury.

1931

1 GILDER, ROSAMOND. "Aphra Behn: England's First Professional Woman Playwright." In Enter the Actress: The First Women in the Theatre. London, Bombay, and Sydney: George C. Harrap, pp. 173-201.

Reprints, with the following additional remarks, the article in Theatre Arts Monthly (B.1928.3). The Forc'd Marriage has "the seeds of . . . drama with a purpose" and begins a series of plays examining morality in marriage. The Amorous Prince reveals Shakespearean influences. In The Town-Fopp, Mrs. Behn lacks ironic detachment as she engages in pointed satire. Sir Patient Fancy is the "best" of her manners comedies; The Feign'd Curtizans offers clever intrigue; The Roundheads and The City-Heiress are political dramas; and The Luckey Chance is "spirited" but "wanton." Gilder generally praises The Widdow Ranter and The Younger Brother.

2 WATSON, HAROLD FRANCIS. The Sailor in English Fiction and Drama 1550-1800. New York: Columbia University Press, pp. 141, 144-45, 155, 189.

Willmore in The Rover "has little sea flavor . . . and is inferior to the other cavaliers chiefly in his lack of delicacy . . . and the swashbuckling manners which sometimes embarrass the rest of the party." The Rover seems to have influenced Ravenscroft's Canterbury Guests, a play called The Bravo Turn'd Bully (1740), and Griffith's School for Rakes (1769).

3 WOOD, FREDERICK T. "The Beginnings and Significance of Sentimental Comedy." Anglia 55:379-80.

While The Forc'd Marriage has a "genuine sentimental strain," The Town-Fopp and The Luckey Chance combine "sentiment, intrigue, and farce."

1932

1 ANON. "Behn, Aphra." In Encyclopaedia Britannica. 14th ed. 2d printing. Vol. 3. London and New York: Encyclopaedia Britannica, p. 331.

Names The Rover as an "excellent" example of her witty and lively comedies; notes her great "versatility" and briefly comments on The City-Heiress, The Roundheads, and The Widdow Ranter At some point between 1940 and 1973, this article, essentially unchanged, began to be signed by Victoria Mary Sackville-West.

I have been unable to see all the printings between these two dates to establish precisely when the contributor's initials first appeared.

2 HECHT, ILSE. Der heroische Frauentyp im Restaurationsdrama. Leipzig: Alexander Edelmann, pp. 110-11, 115-16.

Deals with types of "heroic" woman in Restoration drama. Urania (The Young King) is classified as an example of the woman longing for an Arcadian life, and Cleomana (same play) exemplifies the absolute sovereign.

3 POLE, EVELYN. "Aphra Behn: Colonist, Spy, Playwright and Wit." Bookman 82:242-43.

Mrs. Behn's wit and genius were always inferior to her "courage." In a long series of plays, with some scenes original and some shamelessly plagiarized, she wrote fluently to suit the taste of her audiences. The Young King is an "historical tragedy," and The Forc'd Marriage exhibits wit, "complex situations," and "a suspicion of purpose."

1933

1 ELLEHAUGE, MARTIN. English Restoration Drama: Its Relation to Past English and Past and Contemporary French Drama from Jonson via Molière to Congreve. Copenhagen: Levin & Munksgaard, pp. 195, 302-3.

Mentions The City-Heiress as an important anti-Puritan satire and asserts that Mrs. Behn considered playwriting "mere child's-play."

2 Van LENNEP, WILLIAM. "The Life and Works of Nathaniel Lee, Dramatist (1648?-1692): A Study of Sources." Ph.D. dissertation, Harvard University, p. 188 n.2.

"Mrs. Behn's Abdelazer . . . was the first blank verse tragedy by a Restoration dramatist."

1934

1 McMANAWAY, JAMES G. "Philip Massinger and the Restoration Drama." ELH 1:299-300.

In her adaptations (The City-Heiress is emphasized), Mrs. Behn "stimulates the senses in a way that would have shocked the moralist in Massinger and the realist in Middleton."

2 PLATT, HARRISON GRAY, Jr. "Astrea and Celadon: An Untouched Portrait of Aphra Behn." PMLA 49:544-59.

Chiefly biographical but helps answer a question relevant to the drama: "Why did Aphra Behn, a good Tory playwright, pick as the brutal villain of Oroonoko a reputable and violently Tory colonial governor?"

3 WAGENKNECHT, EDWARD. "In Praise of Mrs. Behn." Colophon, Pt. 18, 16 pp.

Although Aphra created one tragedy (Abdelazer), one play containing touches of heroic romance (The Young King), and one excursion into the fantastic (Emperor of the Moon), her "main stock in trade" was the complexly devised, sometimes realistic, amorous intrigue. Even in politically charged plays, "the serious business of life is breaking maidenheads," and her "obscenities are the more offensive . . . . because the author seems to have . . . no consistent standard of judgment with regard to them." Her only consistent moral stand is visible when she deals with forced marriage. Still and all, she comes across as a courageous, tolerant, flexible, and skillful dramatist.

1935

1 CROISSANT, De WITT C. "Early Sentimental Comedy." In The Parrott Presentation Volume. Edited by Hardin Craig. Princeton: Princeton University Press, pp. 47-71.

Finds sentimental elements in a number of Aphra's plays: The Feign'd Curtizans, The Amorous Prince, The Dutch Lover, The Town-Fopp, Sir Patient Fancy, and The Luckey Chance. All of these present noble and virtuous characters, and most employ moral lovers. The Luckey Chance is, on the whole, "a sentimental reformation play." The False Count is noted for its attack on marriage conventions.

2 SUMMERS, MONTAGUE. The Playhouse of Pepys. New York: Macmillan, pp. 79, 293.

Notes homosexuality in The Amorous Prince and calls The Rover a lively and first-rate adaptation.

1936

1 HARBAGE, ALFRED. Cavalier Drama. New York: Modern Language Association; London: Oxford University Press, p. 188.

In The Rover and The Roundheads, Mrs. Behn improved what she borrowed.

1937

1 WESTRUP, J.A. Purcell. London: J.M. Dent, pp. 95, 152, 154

Comments on an Italian song in The Feign'd Curtizans and on the music in Abdelazer.

1938

1 GRAHAM, C.B. "An Echo of Jonson in Aphra Behn's *Sir Patient Fancy*." *MLN* 53:278-79.

To heighten Wittmore's "discomfiture at sight of Sir Credulous" in *Sir Patient Fancy*, V.i, Mrs. Behn inserts almost verbatim the opening three lines of *Volpone*.

2 NOYES, ROBERT GALE. "Conventions of Song in Restoration Tragedy." *PMLA* 53:165, 172.

Abdelazer opens with a "functional" song and has "the earliest dinner music in Restoration tragedy."

3 WILCOX, JOHN. *The Relation of Molière to Restoration Comedy*. New York: Columbia University Press, pp. 130, 146-50.

Stripping Molière's *Le Malade imaginaire* of its "satiric import," Mrs. Behn transformed its skeleton into *Sir Patient Fancy*, "an English farce of gay cuckoldry and amorous intrigue." *The False Count* is indebted in a minor way to *Les Précieuses ridicules*. "None" of Mrs. Behn's many comedies "has any distinction," and "none contributed anything to the development of the Restoration comedy of manners."

1939

1 BALL, ROBERT HAMILTON. *The Amazing Career of Sir Giles Overreach*. Princeton: Princeton University Press; London: Oxford University Press, pp. 27-28.

Doubts that the "very bawdy" and complicated *City-Heiress* owes anything to *A New Way to Pay Old Debts*.

2 MATHEWS, ERNST G. "Montfleury's *Ecole des jaloux* and Aphra Behn's *The False Count*." *MLN* 54:438-39.

The Carlos-Julia plot of *The False Count* comes mainly from Montfleury's *comédia*, which, in turn, is indebted to Castillo Solórzano's *El Celoso hasta la muerte*. Mrs. Behn renders the piece less regular and more complex in plot, more licentious in language, and more farcical in action and tone.

3 Van LENNEP, WILLIAM. "Two Restoration Comedies." *TLS*, 28 January, pp. 57-58.

Cites Narcissus Luttrell's authority for dating the performance of *The False Count* late November-early December, 1681, and for attributing *The Revenge* (1680) to Mrs. Behn.

1940

1 HUGHES, LEO. "Attitudes of Some Restoration Dramatists toward Farce." *PQ* 19:284.

Considers *Emperor of the Moon* "out-and-out farce."

1941

1 FREEDLEY, GEORGE, and JOHN A. REEVES. A History of the Theatre. New York: Crown, p. 173.

Even her best plays--The Dutch Lover, both parts of The Rover, The Feign'd Curtizans, and The City-Heiress--"are of no great importance in the long view."

2 SOUTHERN, RICHARD. "Aphra Draws off a Scene." Life and Letters To-Day 31:106-14.

Demonstrates that Mrs. Behn "had a deep enough knowledge of theatrical technique for us to ascribe her stage directions largely to herself." Sir Patient Fancy is analyzed to show both Aphra's adeptness in using the theater and the innovations in stage scenery that distinguish the Restoration from previous periods of theater art.

3 SUMMERS, MONTAGUE. "Aphra Behn and Montfleury." MLN 56:562.

Responding to Mathews's note in B.1939.2, Summers reminds us that he had preceded Mathews in treating Mrs. Behn's debt to Montfleury (see B.1930.2).

1942

1 ALLEMAN, GELLERT SPENCER. Matrimonial Law and the Materials of Restoration Comedy. Wallingford, Pa.: n.p., pp. 6-7, 12-18, 20, 24-26, 28, 40-42, 52, 55-58, 64, 67-70, 72-73, 84-105, 111, 126-27, 134.

In eleven of Mrs. Behn's plays finds instances of such legal or quasi-legal matters as contracts for spousal (of several sorts), annulment, canonical hours, stealing of an heiress, mock or tricked or clandestine marriages, separation, and consanguinity.

2 BAKER, HERSCHEL. John Philip Kemble: The Actor in his Theatre. Cambridge, Mass.: Harvard University Press, pp. 164-65.

Kemble's Love in Many Masks omits the bawdy but fails to improve Mrs. Behn's The Rover.

3 _____. "Mrs. Behn Forgets." TSLL 22:121-23.

Alterations to the postscript of later copies of The Rover suggest that Mrs. Behn was working to block readers' bias against female authorship.

1943

*1 SUMMERS, MONTAGUE. "Bonny Mrs. Behn." Everybody's Weekly, 17 July, p. 11.

Cited by Timothy d'Arch Smith in A Bibliography of the Works of Montague Summers (New Hyde Park, N.Y.: University Books, 1964), p. 120.

1944

1 MacCARTHY, B.G. Women Writers: Their Contribution to the English Novel 1621-1744. Cork: Cork University Press; Oxford: B.H. Blackwell, pp. 25, 148-213.

While concentrating on the life and prose, MacCarthy argues that Mrs. Behn was as "brilliant" and decent as any dramatist of her generation.

2 STEARNS, BERTHA MONICA. "The Literary Treatment of Bacon's Rebellion in Virginia." Virginia Magazine of History and Biography 52:165-67.

The "earliest treatment of the Bacon story," The Widdow Ranter romanticizes Bacon but does not condone the rebellion.

1946

1 BOGORAD, SAMUEL NATHANIEL. "The English History Play in Restoration Drama." Ph.D. dissertation, Northwestern University, pp. 243-44.

Showing strong influences from Elizabethan staging methods, The Widdow Ranter "has no contemporary significance, either as a parallel with contemporary political events or as an interpretation of any aspect of history." Its historical materials are "not integral to the development of the plot."

2 HOBMAN, D.L. "A Restoration Petticoat." Life and Letters and the London Mercury 51:137-45.

Sees Mrs. Behn as a strong feminist, not unusually loose by the moral standards of her day, who "never thought of plays as anything other than light entertainment."

1947

1 MIGNON, ELISABETH. Crabbed Age and Youth: The Old Men and Women in the Restoration Comedy of Manners. Durham, N.C.: Duke University Press, pp. 82-93.

As a lesser dramatist who "reduced the material of the comedy of manners to the level of intrigue and farce," Mrs. Behn accepted the contemporary fashion of depicting youthful characters who ridicule, triumph over, and rue the coming of old age. Motteux's song in The Younger Brother, I.ii.331-32, epitomizes her attitude, and it is symbolized by the perverted proviso scene between Lady Knowell and Leander in Sir Patient Fancy, where, in essence, "old age is . . . enslaved to youth." Other plays in which old age is made repulsive are *The Feign'd Curtizans* *The Town-Fopp*, and *The Roundheads*.

1948

1 EVANS, B. IFOR. *A Short History of English Drama*. Harmondsworth, Eng.: Penguin, p. 126.

Mrs. Behn's lively plays "are neither as interesting nor as vivacious as her own life."

2 HUGHES, LEO, and A.H. SCOUTEN. Introduction to *Emperor of the Moon*. In *Ten English Farces*. Austin: University of Texas Press, pp. 39-45.

While most of Mrs. Behn's plays are sexually frank "comedies of intrigue with a generous mixture of farce," *Emperor of the Moon*, in which the romantic plot nearly vanishes behind the spectacle, dance, music, and buffoonery, is "the very essence of farce, rapid, clever, ludicrous in the extreme." Much of the play is independent of its source, *Arlequin empereur dans la lune* (1684), which Mrs. Behn probably saw rather than read.

3 JOHN, K. "Aphra Behn." *New Statesman and Nation*, n.s. 36: 507-8.

Argues that Woodcock overstates the case for Aphra (see B.1948.8): "the age . . . was really too brutal for her. . . . She is a casualty of letters; she had great talent, but in a vicious style it ran to waste." Her plays, which rarely "touch real life," are now "barely readable."

4 McKILLOP, ALAN DUGALD. *English Literature from Dryden to Burns*. New York and London: Appleton-Century-Crofts, p. 73.

Considers Aphra "one of the most competent writers of comedy of intrigue," citing *The Rover* as an example.

5 NICOLSON, MARJORIE HOPE. *Voyages to the Moon*. New York: Macmillan, pp. 89-93, 121.

Asserts and suggests, but does not analyze, links between *Emperor of the Moon*, Godwin's *Man in the Moone*, the popular *Arlequin empereur dans la lune*, Butler's "The Elephant in the Moon," and Wilkins's *Discovery of a New World*, as well as "other moon voyages." That Mrs. Behn succeeds in integrating the moon theme and the love chase is implied but not stated or developed.

6 SHERBURN, GEORGE. *The Restoration and Eighteenth Century (1660-1789)*. Vol. 3. of *A Literary History of England*. Edited by Albert C. Baugh. New York: Appleton-Century-Crofts, p. 770.

Influenced by "Spanish novels," Mrs. Behn "simply tried to write like the men, whom she in no way surpassed." *The Dutch*

Lover, The Rover, and The City-Heiress are cited as representative of her drama.

7 SMITH, JOHN HARRINGTON. The Gay Couple in Restoration Comedy. Cambridge, Mass.: Harvard University Press, pp. 83-84, 94-95, 97-98, 102-3, 110, 113, 119, 130, 167.

The Dutch Lover and The Amorous Prince have reformed rakes, and The Debauchee romanticizes its source, providing a virtuous wife and depicting human nature in a positive light. The Rover, however, shows "cynical sex-intrigue" replacing the "love game" that used to involve evenly matched partners. In The Feign'd Curtizans, Cornelia is more aggressive than Dryden's early females, and The Second Part of the Rover, The False Count, and The City-Heiress are genuinely cynical comedies, though in The False Count the honorable Antonio competes with Carlos for our attention. As a belated attempt to stage a cuckolding comedy, The Younger Brother was a failure.

8 WOODCOCK, GEORGE. The Incomparable Aphra. London and New York: T.V. Boardman, 248 pp.

Presents Aphra the dramatist as a pioneer in women's emancipation, an advocate of love and free choice in marriage, and a believer in the essential goodness of man. Her plays show "the first signs of transition from the Restoration comedy of manners to the drama of sensibility."

Each play is lucidly discussed, in terms of theme, form, sources, and artistry--from the first and "weakest," The Forc'd Marriage (which nevertheless reveals her adeptness at staging, sentimental inclinations, and penchant for social criticism), to the "really outstanding" pieces: The Rover, a masterful intrigue comedy reflecting not only the actual libertinism of Commonwealth cavaliers and of Restoration gallants, but perhaps also Mrs. Behn's personal experience as unrequited lover; Sir Patient Fancy, an outspoken, sexy comedy of manners, the best "derivation" from Molière to date; The City-Heiress, combining "a genuine satirical theme with all the elegance of true comedy of manners"; The Luckey Chance, another excellent manners comedy promoting marriage based on love and offering realistic pictures of slum life that may be autobiographical; Emperor of the Moon, "the best farce of its age," mixing commedia dell'arte, British pantomime, and comic opera in a lively satire on human credulity (with a strand of bitterness); and The Widdow Ranter, a farcical tragicomedy that skillfully blends satire on corrupt government with a delicately handled love tragedy, all set against an historical backdrop of colonial life.

Mrs. Behn wrote three other competent intrigue comedies: The Dutch Lover, her first in this mode, with an ingenious plot, effective stage wit, farcical satire, and a well-managed incest theme; The False Count, a hastily composed critique of forced marriage, containing some effective farce; and The Younger Brother, an indifferently successful mixture of intrigue and social criticism with strong moral implications. One other effort in the manners mode, *The Town-Fopp*, her "first play actually to deal with contemporary London life," protests against loveless marriage and has sentimental tendencies; and as her most original work, *The Feign'd Curtizans* remains an interesting "roccoco play" of bustling slapstick and music.

The Amorous Prince and *The Young King* are both romantic tragicomedies, the former contrasting urban and rural virtues (seemingly favoring the first) in a well-devised plot and a "neo-Elizabethan" style, the latter a politically suggestive but "immature" piece that continues Mrs. Behn's "vein of naturalistic thought." Her lesser plays are *Abdelazer*, which lacks "tragic spirit"; *The Second Part of the Rover*, interesting only for its praise of spontaneous love and use of Harlequin and Scaramouche; and *The Roundheads*, a crude piece of political propaganda in "brutal bad taste."

1950

1 HAHN, EMILY. *Purple Passage: A Novel about a Lady both Famous and Fantastic*. Garden City, N.Y.: Doubleday, 267 pp.

Covers Aphra's early career and provocatively re-creates the background of travel, theaters, taverns, and such persons as Ravenscroft and Tom Killigrew. Dramatic criticism is incidental and mainly implicit. The novel was reprinted in 1951 as *Aphra Behn* (London: Jonathan Cape).

2 PHELPS, ROBERT, ed. Introduction to *Selected Writings of the Ingenious Mrs. Aphra Behn*. New York: Grove Press, pp. 1-17.

Sympathetically surveys the life and works, affirming the critical attitudes of Summers (B.1915.3) and Sackville-West (B.1928.4). Additionally, *The Dutch Lover* is said to be a sexy social comedy using stock situations, "but Aphra brings it off, crisply, neatly, easily . . . [with] never a dull moment." Her plays demonstrate that "her beliefs had very little to do with the deeper intellectual movements of her time."

1951

1 LEECH, CLIFFORD. "Restoration Comedy: The Earlier Phase." *EIC* 1:165, 168-69.

Mrs. Behn wrote comedies with "no purpose beyond the provision of an evening's entertainment." *The Dutch Lover* is a goo example; its four plots, which do not unite in any "total effect are there merely to broaden the range of appeal.

1952

1 KRONENBERGER, LOUIS. The Thread of Laughter: Chapters on English Stage Comedy from Jonson to Maugham. New York: Alfred A. Knopf, pp. 105-15.

Amidst all the cold-hearted purveyors of sex comedy in the Restoration, "Mrs. Behn perhaps provided the one real shock--which was to make sex seem like sex." Yet her "great fault was not that she was morally but that she was artistically too easy-going." She lacked artistic purposefulness and tended to use "formulas and recipes" instead of exploiting her own very decided abilities.

The Town-Fopp is a formula play, pointlessly mixing cynicism and sentimentality, Spanish intrigue and Restoration realism, but conveying no "settled view of human nature," no real convictions about forced marriage, and no unified effect. The vivacious and farcical Luckey Chance offers a more plausible critique of forced marriage, but its exuberant sexuality serves no thematic or artistic purpose; the play gives us a sense of the author but not of the artist. In this respect, The City-Heiress is one of her better plays, for here sex is employed to arouse real issues; in a sense, the comedy as a whole rises from anti-Whig satire to "a moral debate about sex."

2 KUNITZ, STANLEY J., and HOWARD HAYCRAFT. British Authors before 1800: A Biographical Dictionary. New York: H.W. Wilson, pp. 35-37.

Depicts Aphra as "a pioneer of feminism" and as a hack writer of "risqué comedies packed full of action," "racy, vivid dialogue, and a fine, free, rapid style." Although she borrowed a great deal, she could also invent dramatically effective situations.

3 SOUTHERN, RICHARD. Changeable Scenery: Its Origin and Development in the British Theatre. London: Faber & Faber, pp. 144, 146-53.

Notes the scenic implications of Sir Signal Buffoon's "'Peeping out of the Chimney'" in The Feign'd Curtizans and reiterates the analysis, first published in Life and Letters (B.1941.2), of Sir Patient Fancy, Act 3, this time in broader context.

1953

1 STEVENSON, FLORENCE. "Loose Lady of the Couplets." Theatre Arts 37, no. 7:60-62.

Mrs. Behn's best plays are The Forc'd Marriage, "unique" in criticizing forced marriage and in presaging sentimental comedy; The Town-Fopp, "her first play to deal with contemporary London life"; The Rover, her very best; The City-Heiress, "a fine cynical satire"; The Luckey Chance with its vivid pictures of slum life; and Emperor of the Moon, which anticipates modern science fiction and is the first to use commedia dell'arte figures. The Amorous Prince and The Dutch Lover are "indifferent" pieces, while The Roundheads has "a scurrilous script of little merit."

1954

1 BARTLEY, J.O. Teague, Shenkin and Sawney, Being an Historical Study of the Earliest Irish, Welsh and Scottish Characters in English Plays. Cork: Cork University Press, pp. 151-52.

Notes the Highland dancing and bagpipes in The Widdow Ranter and finds that, while The Roundheads improves its source and tidies up its use of Scots dialect, some of the alterations "suggest" that Mrs. Behn's "direct knowledge of Scots was non-existent."

2 DUCLOS, PAUL-CHARLES. "Aphra Behn, la George Sand de la Restauration." RLV 20:439-51.

Makes fairly standard comments about Aphra's career and ends with an annotated list of her works, each annotation mentioning sources and attempting to characterize the work it concerns: for example, The Roundheads is "Satyre sur les derniers jours du Commonwealth puritain."

3 FLETCHER, IFAN KYRLE. "Italian Comedians in England in the 17th Century." TN 8:90.

The Second Part of the Rover had a "real Italian harlequin" who "spoke in Italian and probably extemporised his part." In 1687, "Hayns and Jevon," both familiar with Italian harlequin figures, "came together" in Emperor of the Moon, which was "the nearest approach to a Commedia dell'Arte performance given in England in the seventeenth century."

4 GAGEN, JEAN ELISABETH. The New Woman: Her Emergence in English Drama 1600-1730. New York: Twayne, pp. 44-45, 69-70, 112-14, 124-25, 178.

Accustomed to competing with men in the dramatic market, Mrs. Behn was able to create aggressive females in her plays: the titular character of The Widdow Ranter is "among the most blustering and unabashed of the mannish women of this period"; Olivia of The Younger Brother is a "rebellious" heroine determined to choose her own mate; even Lady Knowell, the "likeable old pedant" of Sir Patient Fancy, triumphs "over her traducers," earning our sympathy despite her faults.

1955

1 BERKELEY, DAVID S. "Some Notes on Probability in Restoration Drama." N&Q 200:343.

Notes that Prince Frederick of The Amorous Prince, though he is no paragon of virtue, is treated respectfully and in elevated language.

*2 HOGAN, FLORIANA T. "The Spanish Comedia and the English Comedy of Intrigue with Special Reference to Aphra Behn." Ph.D. dissertation, Boston University, 930 pp.

Source: CDI (1861-1972), 35:21.

3 WILSON, JOHN HAROLD. "Rant, Cant, and Tone on the Restoration Stage." SP 52:596.

The City-Heiress and The Luckey Chance contain satire on heroic "toning."

1956

1 HUGHES, LEO. A Century of English Farce. Princeton: Princeton University Press, pp. 26, 40-41, 49, 59, 95, 138-39, 237-40.

Discusses the farce elements in the Rover plays (which weld native and Continental influences), The Roundheads, The Revenge (significantly takes its farce from native sources), and, especially, Emperor of the Moon, treated as a "full-length borrowing from the Italian comedians."

2 NIKLAUS, THELMA. Harlequin Phoenix or The Rise and Fall of a Bergamask Rogue. London: Bodley Head, pp. 131-32.

Adds nothing new in a discussion of Emperor of the Moon, except perhaps to note that Mrs. Behn "drew upon Biancolelli's characteristic lazzi" (in the French version of the scenario).

1957

1 SHERBO, ARTHUR. English Sentimental Drama. East Lansing: Michigan State University Press, p. 98.

Critics who find sentimentalism in The Town-Fopp are ignoring the play's dominant note of bawdy humor.

2 STENTON, DORIS MARY. The English Woman in History. London: George Allen & Unwin; New York: Macmillan, pp. 198-202.

Defends the licentiousness of Aphra's plays on the grounds that current tastes required it.

3 WASHBURN, WILCOMB E. The Governor and the Rebel: A History of Bacon's Rebellion in Virginia. Chapel Hill: University of North Carolina Press, p. 3.

The Widdow Ranter, "based on little more than a newsletter account," is a "wildly imaginative creation" that contrasts "the cowardly Council and Deputy Governor and the dashing Bacon." Mrs. Behn may have been inspired by "the democratic ferment preceding the 'Glorious Revolution.'"

4 WERMUTH, PAUL C. "Bacon's Rebellion in the London Theater." Virginia Cavalcade 7, no. 1:38-39.

Based on Strange News from Virginia (1677), The Widdow Ranter shows Virginia's colonial administration as ludicrously incompetent, fairly accurately portrays Bacon, and amuses us with the "earthy" and lusty Widow. The main plot is more amusing, in fact, than the subplots.

1959

1 PETERSON, WILLIAM M., and RICHARD MORTON. "Guns on the Restoration Stage." N&Q 204:268, 270, 308, 310.

Notes the use of guns in The Amorous Prince, The Rover, Emperor of the Moon, The False Count, and The Luckey Chance--suggesting that in the latter two works old men are carrying arms as a substitute for impotency.

2 SHEFFEY, RUTHE TURNER. "The Literary Reputation of Aphra Behn." Ph.D. dissertation, University of Pennsylvania, 210 pp.

Mrs. Behn's reputation declined from 1690 to 1800 as critics increasingly attacked her for moral turpitude, but in the nineteenth century the moral disgust was somewhat counteracted by growing realization of her importance as novelist and songwriter. After about 1915, she began to gain a following among those who saw her as a satirist, humanitarian, and comic artist. This trend continues to date. See Dissertation Abstracts International 20:293.

1961

1 CAMERON, W.J. New Light on Aphra Behn. Auckland, New Zealand: University of Auckland, 106 pp.

A thorough review of available evidence "surrounding" Mrs. Behn's "journey to Surinam in 1663 and her activities as a spy in Flanders in 1666," Cameron's book contains no dramatic criticism but provides resources for future critics.

2 HARGREAVES, HENRY ALLEN. "The Life and Plays of Mrs. Aphra Behn." Ph.D. dissertation, Duke University, 308 pp.

Sees Aphra as typical of her time in the way she borrowed from previous drama, used stock characters and conventions, and ridiculed Whigs; but considers her unusual in several respects: (1) in writing a single play she sometimes blended elements from several sources; (2) she "made unusually skillful integrations of music, pageantry, and stage effects"; (3) she often mixed genres and comic techniques, combining wit and humor with manners, farce, and realism; and (4) she frequently treated comic characters seriously and interpolated essentially serious themes into generally comic works. See Dissertation Abstracts International 21:2274-75.

1962

1 LEJA, ALFRED ERIC. "Aphra Behn--Tory." Ph.D. dissertation, University of Texas, 216 pp.

Chapter 3, "Aphra, the Political Playwright," examines the Tory attitudes in The Dutch Lover, The Rover, Abdelazer, Sir Patient Fancy, The Young King, The Feign'd Curtizans, The Second Part of the Rover, The Roundheads, and The City-Heiress. Aphra was strongly loyal to the Stuarts. See Dissertation Abstracts International 23:1686-87.

2 SHEFFEY, RUTHE T. "Some Evidence for a New Source of Aphra Behn's Oroonoko." SP 49:52-63.

Chiefly dealing with Mrs. Behn's possible debts to the work of Thomas Tryon, Sheffey notes that in The Widdow Ranter, as in Oroonoko, Mrs. Behn "apparently saw no inconsistency in her strong antipathy to Royalists abroad and in the spirited Royalist partisanship apparent in her earlier works."

3 VERNON, P.F. "Marriage of Convenience and the Moral Code of Restoration Comedy." EIC 12:379.

Cites The Rover as a comedy in which forced or arranged marriage is condemned.

1963

1 SINGH, SARUP. The Theory of Drama in the Restoration Period. Bombay, Calcutta, Madras, and New Delhi: Orient Longmans, pp. 209, 230, 245, 275-76.

Mrs. Behn writes about the "'right-down honest Injoyment'" of love, not about the "intellectual companionship" or the "repartee between the lovers." Opting for farce and intrigue, she "rarely" deals in "the amoral comedy of brilliant wit" with its "delicate caricatures of contemporary high life." Her plays show her moving from the rejection to the employment of farce elements.

2 TIEDJE, EGON. Die Tradition Ben Jonsons in der Restaurationskomödie. Hamburg: Cram, de Gruyter, 168 pp., passim.

Discusses Mrs. Behn's use of "humours" and jargon, especially in her depiction of the Puritan "citizen."

1965

1 BARRETT, ALBERTA GREGG. "Plot, Characterization, and Theme in the Plays of Aphra Behn." Ph.D. dissertation, University of Pennsylvania, 229 pp.

Presents Aphra as an unsentimental, witty, satiric dramatist whose plays, which are both artistic and philosophically pointed, show her to be for the divine right of kings and against Puritans and Whigs, fops and fools, forced marraiges, and unjust treatment of women and younger brothers. See Dissertation Abstracts International 26 (1966):7294.

2 WILSON, JOHN HAROLD. A Preface to Restoration Drama. Boston: Houghton Mifflin Co., pp. 60-64, 106, 137, 142.

Considers Mrs. Behn a specialist in intrigue comedies with crudely simple characters and bustling, sensational action. The City-Heiress is cited for its satire on Shaftesbury, The False Count for its lively farce, Abdelazer as a "better than average villain play" which refined the original while adding "considerably" to its "sensuality and savagery."

1966

1 CUNNINGHAM, JOHN E. Restoration Drama. London: Evans Brothers, pp. 32, 153.

"The charming and versatile Mrs. Aphra Behn" wrote "very masculine" plays, mainly farcical intrigues like The Feign'd Curtizans, which "have more to them than mere naughtiness."

2 LANGHANS, EDWARD A. "Three Early Eighteenth Century Promptbooks." TN 20:142-50.

Contains details regarding a 1720's staging of The Rover.

3 SORELIUS, GUNNAR. 'The Giant Race Before the Flood': Pre-Restoration Drama on the Stage and in the Criticism of the Restoration. Uppsala: Almqvist & Wiksells, pp. 173-78.

Places four plays in the repertory of Restoration adaptations of earlier seventeenth-century drama. In comparing each play to its source, Sorelius calls The Rover an anti-Platonic fusion of heroic and gay-couple themes, with some romanticizing of the love element; notes that Behn avoids either romance or sentiment in The Debauchee; considers The Counterfeit Bridegroom a crudely constructed appeal to bourgeouis tastes; and points to a shift from satire and ethics to compassion and romance (but not sentimentalism) in The Revenge.

4 WEISE, GÜNTER. Epilogue and annotations to Oroonoko oder Die Geschichte des königlichen Sklaven. Translated by Christine Hoeppener, Insel-Bücherei, 596. Leipzig: Insel-Verlag, pp. 93-101, 103-6.

Sees Oroonoko as a work influenced by early Enlightenment thought; characterizes Mrs. Behn as a writer interested in the social and intellectual emancipation of women and as a novelist who departs from heroic tradition in search of more realistic modes of narration.

1967

1 HOGAN, FLORIANA T. "Notes on Thirty-one English Plays and Their Spanish Sources." RECTR 6, no. 1:57-58.

Lists The Dutch Lover, The Rover, and The Young King as embodying direct borrowings from Spanish plays; lists The Amorous Prince, Abdelazer, The Feign'd Curtizans, and The Luckey Chance as "showing Spanish influence in matter and form."

2 LINK, FREDERICK M., ed. Introduction to The Rover. Regents Restoration Drama Series. Lincoln: University of Nebraska Press, pp. ix-xvi.

After the "mediocre" Forc'd Marriage and Amorous Prince, Mrs. Behn shifts to intrigue and farce in The Dutch Lover but fails to achieve a really "fine comedy" until The Town-Fopp and The Rover. Although it does not fully succeed in integrating farce, intrigue, and wit, The Rover is a spectacular and entertaining comedy containing not only many delightful characters, effectively contrasted, but also one of Mrs. Behn's more carefully developed attacks on arranged marriage. Compared to its chaotic source, it is a well-wrought dramatic work. The free contract between the witty Hellena and the gallant and rakish Willmore is meaningfully juxtaposed to the more romantic relation between Belvile and Florinda and to the unacceptable attitudes toward love embodied in Blunt, Pedro, and Antonio. Blunt is revealed to be a fool who is both symbolically and literally rendered naked.

The play's weakest point is in the character of Angellica: her sense of rejection and serious grasp of her situation clash with the comic world of the play, and her shift from "a believable and individualized woman to an artificial and conventional type" is implausible. Link surveys texts and stage history at the start of his essay.

3 SILVETTE, HERBERT. The Doctor on the Stage: Medicine and Medical Men in Seventeenth-Century England. Edited by Francelia Butler. Knoxville: University of Tennessee Press, pp. 70-73, 90, 105, 107, 111, 150, 160, 198, 206-7, 218-19, 224, 232-33, 242, 248, 251-56.

Comments amusingly on such medical topics as quack doctors, alcoholism, "powder of sympathy," and the "pox" in relation to Mrs. Behn's plays. Eleven plays are cited.

1968

1 LINK, FREDERICK M. Aphra Behn. New York: Twayne, 183 pp.

Sketches the life in historical context, surveys the prose and poetry, includes a fairly full bibliography, and analyzes each of the plays, synthesizing previous critical views and source studies while adding fresh observations. Mrs. Behn's best comedies--The Town-Fopp, The Rover, and Sir Patient Fancy--are "as good as those of anyone in the period except Etherege, Congreve, and Wycherley." Highly conventional in many respects, often using plot suggestions and character outlines from several sources at once, usually strongly Tory in political bias, her plays are often technically skillful, witty, amusing, and--especially when she is dealing with her favorite topic of marriage--even philosophically interesting. She repeatedly points out that "the socio-economic factors in marriage are designed to counteract the power of love in the interests of a stable society" and that marriage is "merely a legalized convention made moral or immoral by the circumstances surrounding it."

Several of her plays dramatize what a love relationship ought to be like. In The Forc'd Marriage, a romantic tragicomedy a la Beaumont and Fletcher, treatment of this theme is marred by stilted language and superficial characters, though the plot is well constructed. A second such tragicomedy, The Amorous Prince, is more effectively theatrical, but its two actions are not well blended. With The Dutch Lover Mrs. Behn drops her reliance on Beaumont and Fletcher in favor of the kind of "Spanish" intrigue which, when mixed with farce and lively dialogue, became her specialty.

Abdelazer, a turgid romantic tragedy, demonstrates that she was "incapable of" writing "magnificent prosody" or of sustaining "organizing images," at least in tragedy; in The Town-Fopp, on the other hand, both diction and imagery are well controlled in a blend of intrigue and manners comedy that shows skillfully defined characters in a realistic setting. The Rover effectively integrates intrigue, wit, and low comedy, and resonantly contrasts characters (see B.1967.2), while in Sir Patient Fancy intrigue is ingeniously made to frame wit, social analysis, satire, farce, well-drawn characters, and impressively relevant spectacle. The Feign'd Curtizans, a farcical intrigue comedy with little wit, is poorly devised, and The Young King, a belated romantic tragicomedy clumsily depicting the happiness of rural life and the evil of forced marriage, is worse.

The Second Part of the Rover, however, employs a carefully wrought intrigue to contrast two value systems, though this central aim is almost obscured by farce and stage business. A breez and successful farce, The False Count, is followed by one of Mrs. Behn's worst plays, The Roundheads, in which farce is crudely turned to propaganda purposes, but in The City-Heiress she returns to well-constructed wit comedy and, in The Luckey Chance, to her favorite recipe of witty, farcical intrigue.

If Emperor of the Moon is an excellent combination of love intrigue, satire, commedia dell'arte, and operatic spectacle, The Widdow Ranter falls short of such integration when it tries to unify history, tragedy, heroic romance, intrigue, farce, and satire. The Younger Brother suffers from too much plot and too little focus. Among the plays doubtfully attributed to Mrs. Behn, Link rejects The Woman Turned Bully and accepts as hers The Debauchee, The Counterfeit Bridegroom (a good adaptation), and The Revenge (rather effective on the whole). Like Father, Like Son was never printed.

2 WITMER, ANNE, and JOHN FREEHAFER. "Aphra Behn's Strange News from Virginia." LC 34:7-23.

The Widdow Ranter is "the earliest extant English play to be based on a historical event in British America; it presents a more favorable and better informed picture of America than had appeared in any earlier English play." Probably written not long before Aphra's death, based on several sources, the play offers a fairly factual Bacon (whose flirtation with an Indian queen perhaps reflects Aphra's relation with William Scott) and a surprisingly realistic colonial Virginia (which may reflect what she knew of Surinam).

1969

1 STEPHENSON, PETER STANSFIELD. "Three Playwright-Novelists: The Contribution of Dramatic Technique to Restoration and Early Eighteenth-Century Prose Fiction." Ph.D. dissertation, University of California-Davis, 261 pp.

"Detailed analyses of the plays and novels of Mrs. Aphra Behn, William Congreve and Mrs. Mary Davys show how their experience with drama . . . led to improved characterization and increased realistic detail in their novels." See Dissertation Abstracts International 30 (1970):3920A.

2 SUTHERLAND, JAMES. English Literature of the Late Seventeenth Century. New York and Oxford: Oxford University Press, pp. 27, 120, 125, 132-37.

Less refined in style than her male contemporaries, given to "childish plotting," stock characters and situations, and borrowed materials, Mrs. Behn wrote plays in which "any criticism she had to offer tended to become obscured by her compliance with" modish attitudes and tastes in comedy. This tendency is exemplified in her intrigue comedies, like The Dutch Lover and The Rover, both highly conventional, the latter defeating "the ends of the comedy of intrigue by having too much of it." Willmore, however, is less boring than most of her "crude young men," and Hellena is "lively and attractive" with her blend of innocence and hedonism. The Luckey Chance, exhibiting craftsmanship and realism, is marred by "childish farce," and it lacks true wit. Of the plays dealing with the theme of forced marriage, The Forc'd Marriage itself is artificial, The Town-Fopp becomes a "grim comedy," and Sir Patient Fancy ends implausibly after failing to justify its young woman's dilemma (The False Count is mentioned as one of the plays in this group, too). Even when politically aimed, Mrs. Behn's plays tend to be formulaic, as are The Roundheads and The City-Heiress, neither of which has any "redeeming strokes."

1970

1 HARGREAVES, H.A. "New Evidence of the Realism of Mrs. Behn's Oroonoko." BNYPL 74:437.

"The compelling descriptions of colonial life" in The Widdow Ranter seem to reflect Aphra's experiences in Surinam.

2 MUIR, KENNETH. The Comedy of Manners. London: Hutchinson, p. 66.

"Superior to Otway" in comedy, Mrs. Behn "never produced a masterpiece" but "maintained a respectable level of professional skill."

1971

1 DUCHOVNAY, GERALD CHARLES. "Aphra Behn's Oroonoko: A Critical Edition." Ph.D. dissertation, Indiana University, 295 pp.

The second part of the introduction discusses Mrs. Behn's "background as a dramatist and its influence on her prose." See Dissertation Abstracts International 32 (1972):4559A-60A.

2 SCHNEIDER, BEN ROSS, Jr. The Ethos of Restoration Comedy. Urbana, Chicago, and London: University of Illinois Press, pp. 78-79, 156, 178, 180-81.

Notes the passive citizens in The False Count, the reform of Alonzo in The Dutch Lover, and the witty friendship of Hellena and Willmore in The Rover. Angelica Bianca, an "outrageous coquette-prude," shows that "Venus punishes all who defy her."

3 SIMPSON, JOAN MURRAY. "The Incomparable Aphra." Cornhill Magazine 178, no. 1067:368-71.

"She studied the market and wrote for her time, rowdy rumbustious plays full of bawdry and farce and bedroom tomfoolery."

4 WAITH, EUGENE M. Ideas of Greatness: Heroic Drama in England. New York: Barnes & Noble, p. 265.

In Abdelazer, Mrs. Behn altered her source very little and "revived the heroics of the Elizabethan period."

5 WARD, WILBER HENRY. "Bacon's Rebellion in Literature to 1861." Ph.D. dissertation, University of Tennessee, 235 pp.

In creating The Widdow Ranter, which depicts Bacon as "one consumed by personal ambition but still superior to the officers of the legal government," Mrs. Behn depended not primarily on London news pamphlets but rather on "the collection of government documents dealing with the insurrection." See Dissertation Abstracts International 32 (1972):4582A.

1972

1 ADBURGHAM, ALISON. Women in Print: Writing Women and Women's Magazines from the Restoration to the Accession of Victoria. London: George Allen & Unwin, pp. 19-20.

Possessing "tremendous talent," though "very much a creature of her time" in her "unashamed indecency," Mrs. Behn wrote "crisp and witty" intrigue comedies like The Rover, which "ingeniously counterpoints four contrasting pairs of lovers."

2 HUME, ROBERT D. "Diversity and Development in Restoration Comedy 1660-1679." ECS 5:390-92.

Briefly cites several plays to demonstrate that Mrs. Behn "in eight years . . . covers the full span from the pseudoheroic to the London farce, stopping along the way at various degenerate varieties of 'Spanish' romance."

3 JORDAN, ROBERT. "The Extravagant Rake in Restoration Comedy." In Restoration Literature: Critical Approaches. Edited by Harold Love. London: Methuen, pp. 70-73, 87.

In the freewheeling milieu of the carnival, Willmore of The Rover exhibits the extravagant rake's thorough frivolity of language and behavior. Alonzo of The Dutch Lover also displays the wildness of the type.

4 SCOTT, CLAYTON S., Jr. "Aphra Behn: A Study in Dramatic Continuity." Ph.D. dissertation, Texas Christian University, 260 pp.

Sees Mrs. Behn as an author of conventional, complex, nondidactic (except when she opposes forced marriage) intrigue plays that are not especially obscene. Only five of them are primarily original. The ones that are indebted to foreign sources evince radical departures from their originals as Mrs. Behn caters to current dramatic trends, but those based on earlier English works stick rather closely to their sources. Mrs. Behn's plays also show, particularly in their settings and methods of characterization, slight influences from Beaumont and Fletcher and from Jonson. See Dissertation Abstracts International 33:2344A.

5 SEWARD, PATRICIA M. "Caldéron and Aphra Behn: Spanish Borrowings in The Young King." BHS 49:149-64.

489

Except for The Feign'd Curtizans, which may turn out to have a Spanish source, none of the seven plays by Mrs. Behn that are said to rely on Spanish drama or prose actually shows any direct or specific Spanish influence, though some suggest that she was generally imitating the Spanish style. The Young King, however, was "mainly inspired by Caldéron's La Vida es sueño," though Mrs. Behn sacrifices Caldéron's philosophical point as she integrates her subplot into the main action. The play shows her interest in the civilizing power of woman.

6 _____. "Was the English Restoration Theatre Significantly Influenced by Spanish Drama?" RLC 46:102, 118-19.

The Dutch Lover, Sir Patient Fancy, and The Rover were probably not significantly influenced by specific Spanish plays, though they seem to imitate devices in Spanish drama. While The Feign'd Curtizans, The Second Part of the Rover, and The False Count show that Mrs. Behn knew the "form and content of the commedia de capa y espada," they do not depend on particular Spanish plays and exhibit no indebtedness to the serious type of comedia, such as Caldéron's La Vida es sueño, which influenced The Young King.

1973

1 FISKE, ROGER. English Theatre Music in the Eighteenth Century. London, New York, and Toronto: Oxford University Press, p. 69.

Discusses Emperor of the Moon: its use of Harlequin and Scaramouche, its horseplay and stage business.

2 KRAMER, RITA. "Aphra Behn: Novelist, Spy, Libertine." Ms 1, no. 8:16-18.

Perhaps Mrs. Behn "wrote and talked the language of her age," but she nevertheless spoke her own mind, making a plea for "the intellectual emancipation of women" from slavery of all kinds. Throughout The Rover, she attacks "arranged marriages for family prestige or economic power." Sir Patient Fancy is "her most sexually outspoken play."

3 LOFTIS, JOHN. The Spanish Plays of Neoclassical England. New Haven and London: Yale University Press, pp. 82-83, 131-50.

With its skillfully managed but complex plot, The Dutch Lover is probably based on Lord Bristol's English renderings of two plays by Caldéron. The Rover, Mrs. Behn's best play, uses Killigrew's Thomaso, the form of Dryden's Secret Love and An Evening's Love, and some hints from Bristol's translation of Caldéron's Mejor está que estaba; she creatively blends these into "a spirited rendering of the adventures of Cavaliers in exile." And in contrasting Spanish sensitivity to honor with the English Cavaliers' shift from melancholy wit to chivalric exuberance, she "gave expression to an aspect of the exile beyond the reach of those who had personally known it." Exaggerating the licentiousness of expatriate living, the "farcical" Second Part of the Rover shows much less Spanish influence. If, as seems likely, The False Count derives its narrative line from a Spanish novella, perhaps El Celoso hasta la muerte, the Spanish ingredients are thoroughly assimilated into English farce and intrigue. The Young King also assimilates its sources--Caldéron's La Vida es sueño, La Calprenède's Cleopatra, and the folk story of the sleeper awakened--into "a tale of exotic adventure." Caldéron contributes situations, the folk tale provides a key motif, and La Calprenède plus Restoration drama impart the tone. Mrs. Behn's plays seem lascivious and diversely busy compared to Caldéron's works, with their "chaste reticence and consistent moral structure."

4 METZGER, LORE, ed. Introduction to Oroonoko or The Royal Slave. New York: Norton, p. xv.

"In her greatest stage success, The Rover, she asserted her iconoclastic views of the woman's place in society."

5 RUBIN, BARBARA L. "'Anti-Husbandry' and Self-Creation: A Comparison of Restoration Rake and Baudelaire's Dandy." TSLL 14:588.

"Aphra Behn's plays move toward two pòles: dissolving of witty encounters into chase, chance, and vertigo actions, and serious critiques of the rake's character and his effect on women."

6 SUWANNABHA, SUMITRA. "The Feminine Eye: Augustan Society as Seen by Selected Women Dramatists of the Restoration and Early Eighteenth Century." Ph.D. dissertation, Indiana University, 173 pp.

In such plays as The Amorous Prince and The Luckey Chance, Mrs. Behn criticizes forced marriage and shows that women need both the security and the mutual affection ideally provided by wedlock. These views make her dramas different from those of contemporary male authors. See Dissertation Abstracts International 34 (1974):5932A-33A.

1974

1 BATTEN, CHARLES L., Jr. "The Source of Aphra Behn's The Widdow Ranter." RECTR 13, no. 1:12-18.

Engages in an act-by-act search for similarities between the play and the "Report of the King's Commission," concluding that this document, "or something closely derived from it," provided details that Mrs. Behn could not have found in Strange News from Virginia.

2 BRUCE, DONALD. Topics of Restoration Comedy. New York: St. Martin's, pp. 16, 22-23, 33-36, 61-62, 73-75, 85-87, 96-97, 102-3, 126, 127, 136-37, 148-52.

Though Mrs. Behn's comedies can be improbable, overly busy, and clumsily plotted, they are often ludicrously inventive, full of witty situations, and almost poetic in their gracefully cadenced expressions. Underneath, they might well be chilly, melancholy, "sour and watchful" with a "desperate glacial cynicism." Frequently commenting on forced, arranged, or January-May marriages, sometimes depicting "the downfall of a dissolute woman," they are "full-sailed, Baroque and gracious," yet "with what depths of bitterness under the timbers!" They probably reflect aspects of Aphra's own love life.

The Town-Fopp supports the strong family unit, criticizes male dominance and debauchery, condemns purely sensual love, and shows Mrs. Behn's bitterness toward the beau monde and its institutions. Sir Timothy's viciousness and Lord Plotwell's machinations to preserve his own order lead to disaster for the younger family members, who "betray their own hearts and suffer for it." In Sir Patient Fancy, which dramatizes the relinquishing of reason "to uxorious passion," Sir Patient's "fall from Presbyterian grace" re-enacts "the downfall of Cromwell's England." After making the hero of The Feign'd Curtizans "a Man of Honour," Mrs. Behn reverts to "the Man of Mode" in The City-Heiress; yet the latter play more powerfully promotes the honorable life, because "in it the disasters brought about by the Mode are allowed to speak for themselves." Mr. Galliard of Curtizans and Tom Wilding of Heiress are "defeated Epicureans, who in the end acquiesce in the commonplaces of impulsive humanity."

The Feign'd Curtizans is "the most sustained contribution to the debate between constant and inconstant love," the former winning only after Mrs. Behn injects some interesting farce and clever exploitation of the mask-versus-face motif. The dominating females in this play foreshadow the woman-centered comedy of the late seventeenth century and suggest that Mrs. Behn believed women must employ vice to get their way in a hostile, shackling world.

3 JEFFARES, A. NORMAN, ed. General Introduction and introductions to The Rover and The Luckey Chance. In Restoration Comedy. London: Folio; Totowa, N.J.: Rowman & Littlefield. 1:vii, xiv; 2:229-30; 3:3-4.

Stresses Mrs. Behn's delight in farce and sexual intrigue for their entertainment value alone. The only moral in The Rover is that "cuckolding" is not a "sufficient end in itself." Hellena and Willmore are interestingly contrasted to Florinda and Belvile, and Blunt is a well-drawn comic squire, but Angellica is not a consistent character. The play, which considerably improves on its main source, must be considered an "amoral romp." Nor should The Luckey Chance be "taken too seriously," even though it does voice opposition to forced marriage and evocatively contrasts youth and age. Act 4 drags a bit, and the end is a jumble, but on the whole the play is high-spirited, suspenseful, and full of delightful surprises--an ably contrived farce-melodrama.

4 UPADHYAY, LESLEY ANNE. "Two Political Comedies of the Restoration: An Annotated Old-spelling Edition, with Critical and Historical Introduction, of John Tatham's The Rump and Aphra Behn's Adaptation, The Roundheads." Ph.D. dissertation, University of London, 519 pp.

In the "General Introduction" (1-10), the "Introduction to The Roundheads (284-316), and the "Conclusion" (488-503), Upadhyay sketches Mrs. Behn's life, discusses her Toryism, and deals with the following aspects of The Roundheads: political background, stage history, verse forms, plot, and employment of dramatic conventions. "Less well conceived than her other adaptations," the play departs from its source chiefly by stressing the love interest and by changing some of the characters (for example, she makes Lambert more stupid and ridicules Fleetwood more for his hypocrisy than for his foolishness). Mrs. Behn is more fiercely anti-Puritan than Tatham. Although she does manage to tighten the play a little, she fails to blend politics and love, so that her comedy comes across as a clumsy "conglomerate of characters."

1975

1 GEWIRTZ, ARTHUR DAVID. "Restoration Adaptations of Early Seventeenth-Century Comedies." Ph.D. dissertation, Columbia University, 262 pp.

Sees The Rover as "a piece of trivia," which fails to unite attacks on marriage with the rake's final decision to marry. The Town-Fopp "illustrates an older response to traditional morality, and The Second Part of the Rover breaks new ground by moving into the area of romance." See Dissertation Abstracts International 36:2843A.

2 GUFFEY, GEORGE. "Aphra Behn's Oroonoko: Occasion and Accomplishment." In Two English Novelists: Aphra Behn and Anthony Trollope. Los Angeles: Clark Library, pp. 9-11.

Deals briefly with Aphra's strongly political plays: The Second Part of the Rover ("extremely Tory"), The City-Heiress ("biting satire . . . primarily directed at Shaftesbury"), and The Roundheads. The latter ridicules the avaricious, ambitious, and lustful behavior of Commonwealth figures who reflect actual men and women of Mrs. Behn's era. Interestingly, the females, who are less harshly treated than the males, are portrayed as being attracted to the Cavaliers.

1976

1 HUME, ROBERT D. The Development of English Drama in the Late Seventeenth Century. Oxford: Clarendon Press, pp. 56, 146, 201, 211, 214, 284-85, 303, 305, 308-9, 322, 328-29, 358-59, 369, 374-75, 397-98, 415.

Albeit the subject of forced marriage is often present in Mrs. Behn's plays, it is seldom the central concern, and they are noted for a variety of other strengths. They also make a good index to changing tastes in the period, especially in the 1670s (see B.1972.2). The Forc'd Marriage is a virtue-rewarded tragicomedy, The Amorous Prince a serious intrigue play, and The Dutch Lover another "mishmash of sword-play, love and honor, and mistaken identity" but this time "leavened" with buffoonery. In The Town-Fopp, with its well-integrated multiple plots, realism, and low scenes, we see Mrs. Behn "in midflight between the Italian intrigue romance and the London sex comedy."

The Rover, a delightful "action-centered" comedy displaying some acute psychology, is marred when the near-tragic Angelica is left dangling at the end. The Debauchee is a well-contrived, "fairly pure" intrigue drama with some moral implications, and Abdelazer is "a nonpolitical example of the blood and villainy mode." A belated "romantic intrigue tragicomedy," The Young King is "a tidy collection of love, politics, war, and disguise," while Sir Patient Fancy, one of Aphra's best, is a fast-paced, bawdy farce. In The Feign'd Curtizans she returns to "intricate, bustling intrigue." If The Roundheads is a disjointed affair, in The City-Heiress she deftly and inventively manipulates formulae while mixing in effective political satire. The Luckey Chance is a "cheerful city marriage farce," Emperor of the Moon a dazzlingly funny and unified blend of diverse elements, and The Widdow Ranter a rather too-subtle display of types of love, ironies, and counterironies. The Younger Brother is "complicated" and old-fashioned.

2 LUDWIG, JUDITH KARYN. "A Critical Edition of Aphra Behn's The Feign'd Courtesans (1679), with Introduction and Notes." Ph.D. dissertation, Yale University, 272 pp.

Covers the stage history, classifies the play as intrigue comedy presaging later seventeenth-century sentimentalism, and finds in it the key social issues of forced marriage, the nature of love, and personal autonomy. A section is devoted to discussing the influence of female actresses on Mrs. Behn's heroines. See Dissertation Abstracts International 38 (1977):284A.

3 MEREDITH, DAVID WILFRED. "Borrowing and Innovation in Five Plays by Aphra Behn." Ph.D. dissertation, Kent State University, 345 pp.

Mrs. Behn was no shallow entertainer. In adapting sources, she alters structure more than dialogue, omits irrelevant characters, enhances psychological credibility, formalizes action through symmetry and juxtaposition, and adds or intensifies social and moral themes: chiefly the problems of racial or political aliens, women, and dependent males. Of the five plays discussed, Abdelazer is the least changed; The Roundheads and The Town-Fopp are more radically modified; and The Rover and Second Part are altered beyond all recognition. See Dissertation Abstracts International 37 (1977):5145A.

4 SCOUTEN, A.H. "Plays and Playwrights." In The Revels History of Drama in English, Vol. V: 1660-1750. Edited by John Loftis, Richard Southern, Marion Jones, and A.H. Scouten. London: Methuen, pp. 202-4, 246.

Never very original, Mrs. Behn became adept at catering to changing tastes in plays (she preferred tragicomedy) that often deal with broken friendships and broken, loveless, or arranged marriages. In The Dutch Lover, she transforms Spanish intrigue into "a titillating sex chase," and she injects some psychological insight into The Town-Fopp, though it is an improbable and poorly executed piece, inconsistent in tone. Although The Rover, a lively and witty comedy, is better crafted, its sequel, The Second Part of the Rover, lacks structure and unity. Sir Patient Fancy shows skill in characterization, The City-Heiress is well constructed and displays good dialogue, and Emperor of the Moon, "taken entirely from the Italian improvised comedy," is spectacular and amusing.

5 WARD, WILBER HENRY. "Mrs. Behn's 'The Widow Ranter': Historical Sources." SAB 41, no. 4:94-98.

Discusses Mrs. Behn's departures from her main source, "A True Narrative of the Rise, Progresse, and Cessation of the Late Rebellion in Virginia" and describes her protagonist as a "Herculean," "pre-Byronic hero-villain." Her chief innovations were the substitution of a fictitious interim governor for the actual one (Sir William Berkeley) and the spreading out of blame among the colonists generally.

1977

1 DUFFY, MAUREEN. The Passionate Shepherdess: Aphra Behn 1640-89. London: Jonathan Cape, 324 pp.

Mainly biographical but comments on all the plays, in some cases making fresh observations. Abdelazer is said to resemble the work of Racine and Corneille more than that of Shakespeare, and The Town-Fopp (based less on The Miseries of Enforced Marriage than has been thought) is said to owe something to Twelfth Night and to Aphra's affair with John Hoyle. It draws a parallel between forced marriage and prostitution. In The Rover, which is really not superior to many of Mrs. Behn's other plays (including its sequel), Willmore is meant to suggest Rochester and Belvile to evoke Belville Grenville. Aphra herself identifies with Angelica Bianca. This is a light, elegant piece about various manifestations of sex that emerge as human beings search for mates.

Mrs. Behn's first politically loaded comedy, Sir Patient Fancy, effectively, complexly, and amusingly dramatizes the imaginary political sickness of the Whigs and suggests a cure. Lady Knowell reflects the Duchess of Newcastle and Sir Patient caricatures Sir Patience Ward. The Merchant of Venice and Volpone are pointedly quoted. The Duke of York is represented by Orsames in The Young King, a monarchist play that contrasts urban and rural values, employs some Hobbesian doctrines, and stresses the ability of women to match men without sacrificing feminine softness. In The Second Part of the Rover, Willmore again suggests Rochester and allows Mrs. Behn implicity to reject Rochester's deathbed repentance.

Elizabeth Barry plays herself in La Nuche, Aphra's "greatest dramatic creation, a complete rebuttal of Burnet's concept of women as property." Mrs. Behn's "clearest statement about both money and class" comes in The False Count, where she rejects the Whig confusion of property with liberty, and urges that the purpose of money is to ensure that everyone can realize his or her full potential. The Roundheads reminds us of a "terror-filled fairy tale." In The Luckey Chance Gayman is based on Otway, and in Emperor of the Moon, Dr. Balliardo echoes Prospero. The Widow Ranter is "the ultimate in Aphra Behn's pleas for equity."

2 HUME, ROBERT D. "The Myth of the Rake in 'Restoration' Comedy." SLitI 10, no. 1:50.

"An early experiment in the rake reforming to marry the girl he has seduced is Behn's (?) The Debauchee (1677)," though in this case the gallant is more a "rakish gentleman" than an extravagant or vicious blade.

3 LINDQUIST, CAROL A. "Aphra Behn and the First Epistolary Novel in English." PAPA 3, no. 2:29-33.

Mrs. Behn injects the "shape" and "power" of the Restoration comic stage into her Love Letters between a Nobleman and His Sister, reflecting the new materialism and the conflict between Hobbesian and Renaissance views of human nature.

4 MILHOUS, JUDITH, and ROBERT D. HUME. "Lost English Plays, 1660-1700." HLB 25:22.

Lists Like Father, Like Son (1682).

5 NOVAK, MAXIMILLIAN E. "Margery Pinchwife's 'London Disease': Restoration Comedy and the Libertine Offensive of the 1670s." SLitI 10, no. 1:20-21.

While ridiculing country squires, The Town-Fopp incongruously promotes in Bellmour a hero "who is completely disgusted with the very idea of sexual intercourse without love."

6 ROOT, ROBERT L., Jr. "Aphra Behn, Arranged Marriage, and Restoration Comedy." W&L 5, no. 1:3-14.

Places Mrs. Behn's preferred subject of arranged marriage in the context of earlier drama, conduct books, and other Restoration plays. Her handling of the theme is unique, in that she shows sympathy for wives and their lovers, awareness that adultery may grow out of sincere love, and sensitivity to the economic considerations of arranged wedlock. Only in Sir Patient Fancy, however, does she become so cynical as to make her lovers "deliberately set out to exploit the marital arrangements she found so corrupting." Although she was no social reformer, she often called attention to social issues as she manipulated "the stock situations of Restoration comedy." After briefly discussing The Forc'd Marriage, The Town-Fopp, The False Count, The Luckey Chance, and Sir Patient Fancy, Root asserts that Mrs. Behn's female successors in the 1690s turned from socially critical to exemplary comedy, thus helping along the demise of a type of Restoration comedy whose conventions depended on "implicit opposition to arranged marriage."

7 SAUL, SUZANNE MOSHER. "The Comic Art of Aphra Behn." Ph.D. dissertation, Howard University, 204 pp.

Examines Mrs. Behn's plays in relation to her fiction, arguing that she "differs markedly from her peers both in viewpoint and technique." Though she uses a single formula and repeatedly composes a tragicomic plot, she manages not only to take up topical issues but also to dramatize "the diversity of human perceptions and the perplexities these differences cause." Each play is a kind of "intellectual riddle," its language mirroring the complexity of its intrigue, its intrigue implying that appearances are unreliable bases for decision making and suggesting the difficulty of reconciling practical necessity with personal belief, social convention with moral choice. See Dissertation Abstracts International 38 (1978):6750A.

1978

1 CARVER, LARRY. "Aphra Behn: The Poet's Heart in a Woman's Body." PLL 14:414-24.

Mainly about the prose fiction but instructively defines the ironic voice of Mrs. Behn's prefaces to plays, a voice employed to outwit critics and sustain feminine integrity.

2 WOODCOCK, GEORGE. Review of Duffy's Passionate Shepherdess. Room of One's Own 3, no. 4:65-68.

Insists that Mrs. Behn be considered "an exceptional literary craftswoman" who "comes off well by comparison" with Shadwell, Etherege, Wycherley, "and even Dryden."

1979

1 COHEN, DEREK. "Nicholas Rowe, Aphra Behn, and the Farcical Muse." PLL 15:383-95.

Compares Emperor of the Moon to a less successful play which it influenced, Rowe's The Biter (1704). Unlike Rowe, Mrs. Behn writes (in this case) with no intention of examining social conventions; she wants chiefly to entertain and so "in her play creates her own conventions and standards of behavior." Emperor has the "mosaic effect" of farce and "relies heavily on extraneous actions for . . . effects," but its characters are well motivated and Harlequin and Scaramouch are delightful masters of verbal activity. In this play, the comedy "results from the audience's perception of the characters' knowledge of Baliardo's madness and the incongruity of their behavior from what it is normally to what it is in his presence." Mrs. Behn's characters "do not, like Rowe's protagonists, merely manipulate the action--they are involved in it."

2 HOLLAND, PETER. The Ornament of Action: Text and Performance in Restoration Comedy. Cambridge, London, and Melbourne: Cambridge University Press, pp. 41-42, 67-68.

Discusses Mrs. Behn's "obsessive" use of discoveries, often involving upstage acting and bedroom scenes. The two parts of The Rover show how she exploits repeat casting to reinforce the perception of alternative kinds of love relationships.

3 HUME, ROBERT D. "The Rover . . . University of Illinois at Chicago Circle, . . . March 2, 1979." Theatre Journal 31: 412-13.

To perform The Rover well, an acting company must realize that the play is "not pseudo-Congreve or even quasi-Wycherley . . . not comedy of 'wit' or 'manners'; rather, it is a raucous comedy of intrigue which relies heavily on sword-play and boisterous physical action." Hume offers his analysis of how Mrs. Behn's characters--which "may lack depth" yet "do make sense"--should be played: Willmore combines virility and a "voracious sexual appetite" with "the sensitivity to fall for Hellena"; Blunt is "gullible, but not just a buffoon"; Angelica is "strong-hearted" yet able to fall for Willmore "without becoming a kind of tragic heroine when he abandons her," and she "grows emotionally in the process."

4 MUSSER, JOSEPH F., Jr. "'Imposing Naught But Constancy in Love': Aphra Behn Snares The Rover." Restoration 3:17-25.

Though it is "not a consciously feminist play," The Rover is an early influence on the transition from lover to lady as center of attention in Restoration comedy. Angelica Bianca is the "key" to Mrs. Behn's effort to examine prospects for "social justice and sexual satisfaction" for women, "given the double standard." The play juxtaposes feminine and masculine definitions of love and contrasts various needs among lovers. Angelica makes her love worthless "by masculinizing it," but "Hellena . . . provides" Angelica's "revenge." Mrs. Behn "looks on marriage as the accommodating of male inconstancy to the natural feminine desire for stability," and "by joining the force of wit with the force of beauty," she (like Hellena) "suggests ways for women to 'maintain the Right they have in' men. She thus suggests a radical shift in power, and a concomitant alteration in the libertine society of the court of Charles II."

5 PRICE, CURTIS A. Music in the Restoration Theatre. [Ann Arbor]: UMI Research Press, pp. 4-5, 13, 37, 256, 267 n.36.

Catalogues the music in Mrs. Behn's plays, cites them extensively in the footnotes, and briefly discusses the melancholy opening songs in Abdelazer and The Young King, antic dancing and the harpsichord in Emperor of the Moon, and music in the wedding ceremony of The Forc'd Marriage. Mrs. Behn's use of the masque is tabulated.

6 STAVES, SUSAN. Players' Scepters: Fictions of Authority in the Restoration. Lincoln and London: University of Nebraska Press, pp. 41, 79, 131, 160, 168, 172-74, 186, 297-98.

Notes The Roundheads represents Royalists "uncritically" and that the lascivious queen in Abdelazer wishes to "exorcise" nature conceived as hierarchy and to realize a nature "of individual appetite." While Sir Patient Fancy is a farcical, meaninglessly bawdy and cynical comedy, The Town-Fopp becomes "a rough equivalent to the democratic romances" as it avoids the religious implications of adultery and joins the trends of beginning a comedy with the central characters already married, of treating marriage as problematic, and of shifting the burden of attention toward the female characters.

1980

1 BALCH, MARSTON STEVENS. "Mrs. Behn's (?) Counterfeit Bridegroom (1677)." In Thomas Middleton's "No Wit, No Help Like a Woman's" and "The Counterfeit Bridegroom" (1677) and Further Adaptations. Salzburg: Institut für Anglistik und Amerikanistik, pp. 9-58.

Closely compares Bridegroom and No Wit to show how the Restoration play prunes, simplifies, and speeds up the pace of Middleton's original, and subordinates the plot of della Porta to the wooing of the Widow. Balch does not investigate Behn's authorship of the Restoration version.

2 COTTON, NANCY. "Aphra Behn." In Women Playwrights in England, c. 1363-1750. Lewisburg: Bucknell University Press; London and Toronto: Associated University Presses, pp. 55-80.

Concisely synthesizes previous biographical and critical studies, presenting Aphra as an "independent, bawdy, witty, and tough" professional, who varied her formula of brisk dialogue, complex intrigue, farce, stage business, and spectacle to "suit the marketplace." "Her wit is more often in the plot than in the dialogue," and her distinctive theme is the misery and injustice of forced marriage. Through her three-dimensional portraits of courtesans, she urges that "the only difference between prostitution and marriage for money is that prostitution is the more candid, less hypocritical way for a woman to earn a living." And through portraits of amazonian women, she enlarges her analysis of "the battle of the sexes." The Rover, The Feign'd Curtizans, and Sir Patient Fancy are her best plays. Twelve of her other dramas are also discussed.

3 DAY, ROBERT ADAMS. "Muses in the Mud: The Female Wits Anthropologically Considered." WS 7, no. 3:61-74.

Speculates on why Mrs. Behn, Mrs. Pix, Mrs. Manley, and Mrs. Trotter were "taboo" in the late seventeenth century. Their fiction is emphasized, but drama is commented upon in a general way.

4 GARDINER, JUDITH KEGAN. "Aphra Behn: Sexuality and Self-respect." WS 7, nos. 1-2:67-78.

Stresses the poetry, but reaches some generalizations that might apply to the drama as well. For instance: Mrs. Behn identifies "with the exiled courtiers of Charles I who combined personal loyalty to a perfect political 'great Sufferer' . . . with a vigorous sexuality restrained only by . . . self-defined honor Esthetically and politically, she believes 'nobler Souls' . . . prove their superiority by their emotional sensitivity, that is, by being 'sensible of Love.'"

5 GOREAU, ANGELINE. Reconstructing Aphra: A Social Biography of Aphra Behn. New York: Dial Press, 346 pp.

This biography makes a well-informed guess at the dimensions of Aphra's personality by combining the scanty biographica evidence with reconstructions of relevant contexts, including th collective social experiences of seventeenth-century women in general. In the process, Goreau briefly criticizes the plays, though she adds only a few fresh remarks. The Forc'd Marriage, which dramatizes a "double perspective on the concept of honor,' presents a passive heroine whose dilemma regarding arranged marriage is resolved by the man. The Amorous Prince demonstrates the logic of Mrs. Behn's philosophy that virtue is what comes naturally. In The Young King, she juxtaposes love and war as feminine and masculine principles, with love defined as natural and war as a perversion.

6 HAGSTRUM, JEAN H. Sex and Sensibility: Ideal and Erotic Lo from Milton to Mozart. Chicago and London: University of Chicago Press, pp. 77-82.

The section entitled "Aphra Behn and Restoration 'Romanticism'" says nothing about the plays, but its insights regarding the prose fiction might usefully be employed in analyzing Aphra's dramatic art.

7 SCOUTEN, ARTHUR H., and ROBERT D. HUME. "'Restoration Comedy' and Its Audiences, 1660-1776." YES 10:55-56.

Treated under the heading "II The Watershed Years, 1678-1688," The Luckey Chance is said to be "no bawdier than a host of long-popular plays."

8 ZUTHER, SUSAN KELSO. "The World of Love and Its Ethic in Aphra Behn's Comedies." Ph.D. dissertation, University of Kansas, 189 pp.

Concluding that Mrs. Behn espouses "a compassionate system of justice and an ethic of love," Zuther highlights "humanizing innovations" in the comedies, which promote the notion that individual morality must be weighted "on love's scale." See Dissertation Abstracts International 41:2130A.

1981

1 BALCH, MARSTON STEVENS. Thomas Middleton's "A Trick to Catch the Old One," "A Mad World, My Masters" and Aphra Behn's "City Heiress." Salzburg: Institut für Anglistik und Amerikanistik, 84 pp.

Closely compares Behn's play to the two by Middleton, showing her indebtedness especially to A Trick, which has been somewhat neglected as a source for The City-Heiress. In addition to her borrowing of characters, events, and phrasing, she is said to have inherited something of Middleton's sensibility and artistry.

2 BROWN, LAURA. English Dramatic Form, 1660-1760: An Essay in Generic History. New Haven and London: Yale University Press, pp. 59-62.

Mrs. Behn's best play, The Rover, resembles the most sophisticated dramatic satires of its period in its "disjunction of social and moral values as well as in its problematic reconciliation of libertinism and royalism," though its unique power derives from the seriousness and sympathy with which it presents the contradictory position of women in a materialistic society. Angelica, the prostitute of The Rover, like analogous characters in The Second Part of the Rover and The City-Heiress, is caught between a pragmatic appreciation of the need for economic self-interest and the antimaterialist attractions of libertine free love. Although the play presumes that commercial exchange and mercenary marriage are inevitable facts, the free love offered to its female protagonist suggests an alternative to such commercial operations. Thus "the form implies a condemnation of that very society whose standards constitute the terms of its action."

But since Mrs. Behn envisions no real alternative to the status quo, her critique leads her to ideological contradiction and formal satire, albeit her very conservatism enables her to pose the contradiction inescapably for her prostitute-protagonists.

3 PAPETTI, VIOLA. Introduzione to Aphra Behn: Il Giramondo, commedia in cinque atti. Translated by Viola Papetti. Milan: La Tartaruga, pp 7-37.

Synthesizes the latest biographical information with some of the recent critical perspectives; concludes with a selective but useful bibliography.

The Dramatic Works of Nathaniel Lee

The Tragedy of Nero, Emperour of Rome 1675

Sophonisba; or, Hannibal's Overthrow: A Tragedy 1676

Gloriana; or, The Court of Augustus Caesar 1676

The Rival Queens; or, The Death of Alexander the Great 1677

Mithridates, King of Pontus: A Tragedy 1678

Oedipus: A Tragedy (co-authored by John Dryden) 1679

Caesar Borgia; Son of Pope Alexander the Sixth: A Tragedy 1680

Theodosius; or, The Force of Love: A Tragedy 1680

Lucius Junius Brutus; Father of His Country: A Tragedy 1681

The Duke of Guise: A Tragedy (co-authored by John Dryden) 1683

Constantine the Great: A Tragedy 1684

The Princess of Cleve 1689*

The Massacre of Paris: A Tragedy 1690*

Massacre seems to have been written in 1679, and *Cleve* was perhaps omposed in 1681. Discussions of the dates of composition and performance of these plays can be found in L.1954.1, L.1976.3, and .1979.1.

Writings about Nathaniel Lee, 1677-1980

1677

1 DRYDEN, JOHN. "The Authors Apology for Heroique Poetry; and Poetique Licence." Prefixed to The State of Innocence, and Fall of Man: an Opera. London: by T.N. for Henry Herringman, n. pag.

Lee's "Genius is able to make beautiful what he pleases."

2 _____. "To Mr. Lee, on his Alexander." Prefixed to The Rival Queens, or the Death of Alexander the Great. London: for James Magnes & Richard Bentley, n. pag.

Lee's play has "mighty Merit," because in it "Nature Triumphs over wretched Art," so that the feigned passions seem real and the "beauteous Images" are as convincing as those "of Titian, or of Angelo." Though Lee may seem to write with "too much vigour," he can stoop to a more "humble Stile" if he wishes.

1678

1 DRYDEN, JOHN. "Epilogue, by Mr. Dryden." In Mithridates King of Pontus, A Tragedy. London: by R.E. for James Magnes & Richard Bentley, n. pag.

Implies that the town will think Lee's powerful conception of heroic, faithful love "a meer Metaphor, a painted Fire," for sincere feelings have become unfashionable in the present cynical age.

1680

1 ANON. "A Session of the Poets." In Poems on Several Occasions By the Right Honourable, The E. of R---. Antwerp: n.p., p. 112.

Apollo recalled that Lee "had hit once in Thrice" (probably referring to Sophonisba, performed in 1675) and that, despite his occasional passages of bombast, he had "a Musical Note" and "as much Wit, as Wine cou'd supply." Thus, "owning he had Sense, t' encourage him for't, / He made him his Ovid in Augustus's Court." On the problem of attributing authorship of this poem, see David M. Vieth, Attribution in Restoration Poetry (New Haven and London: Yale University Press, 1963), pp. 296-321.

2 [ROCHESTER, JOHN WILMOT, EARL OF.] "An Allusion to Horace. The 10th Satyr of the 1st Book." In Poems on Several Occasions By the Right Honourable, the E. of R---. Antwerp: n.p., p. 42.

Calls Lee a "hot-brained Fustian Fool" who, in Sophonisba, "makes temp'rate Scipio, fret, and rave / And Hannibal, a whining Amorous Slave."

1681

1 ANON. "Utile Dulce." In Court Satires of the Restoration. Edited by John Harold Wilson. Columbus: Ohio State University Press, 1976, p. 51.

Lists Lee as one of the "bombast poets which infest the town." Wilson is the first to publish this manuscript, which he dates 1681.

1682

1 [DRYDEN, JOHN.] A Prologue spoken at Mithridates King of Pontus, the First Play Acted at the Theatre Royal this Year, 1681. London: for J. Sturton, n. pag.

The play is "as honest and as plain as an Addresse." This broadside was actually published in 1682, according to H.T. Swedenberg, Jr., and Vinton A. Dearing, eds., The Works of John Dryden (Berkeley, Los Angeles, and London: University of California Press, 1972), 2:185-86.

2 RADCLIFFE, ALEXANDER. "News from Hell." In The Ramble: an Anti-Heroick Poem. Together with Some Terrestrial Hymns and Carnal Ejaculations. London: for the author & Walter Davis, p. 6.

Lee's "lofty Fancy towers / 'Bove Fate, Eternity and Powers: / Rumbles i' th' Sky, and makes a bustle; / So Gods meet Gods i' th' dark and justle."

1683

1 ANON. The True History of the Duke of Guise. . . . Publishe for the undeceiving such as may perhaps be imposed upon by Mr. Dryden's late Tragedy. London: by and for R. Baldwin, 34 pp.

In "To the Reader" (n. pag), the author calls Guise a laughable, lamentable play which twists history in order to abuse both London's citizens and their sovereign. He then offers a kind of counterhistory to correct the balance.

2 DRYDEN, JOHN. The Vindication: or the Parallel of the French Holy-League, and the English League and Covenant, Turn'd into a Seditious Libell. London: for Jacob Tonson, pp. 1, 3, 7, 12, 41-42, 57.

Maintains that after Lee had collaborated on Oedipus (contributing Acts 2, 4, and 5), he had suggested a second joint effort in The Duke of Guise, for which he wrote parts of the first and last acts and all of the second and third. But whether, in the process, he cannibalized an earlier, unperformed play (The Massacre of Paris) Dryden professes not to know, though he has heard of such an earlier piece. The Duke of Guise, he says, was meant to compare the French Holy League with both the old Covenanters opposing Charles I and the new, radical Whigs ranged against Charles II. No personal satire was intended, and the supposed parallel between Charles II and Henry III of France is a malicious invention by those who wish to alter the English succession.

3 HUNT, THOMAS. A Defence of the Charter, and Municipal Rights of the City of London. London: by and for Richard Baldwin, pp. 24, 27-28, 30.

The Duke of Guise is an "inept" rhyming play, full of "atheism and Impiety," which is designed "to confound virtue and vice . . . and leave us without consciences." It specifically condemns London, its charter and magistrates, and depicts Monmouth as Guise, the Duke of York as Navarre.

4 [SHADWELL, THOMAS.] Some Reflections upon the Pretended Parallel in the Play called The Duke of Guise, In a Letter to a Friend. London: for Francis Smith, 25 pp.

"Deficient in Wit, good Characters, or Entertainment," The Duke of Guise not only abuses London, the magistrates, and the House of Commons, but also represents Monmouth as Guise and Charles II as the French Henry III; it even implies the judgment of God against the Duke of York and so, in spite of the author's seeming intentions, supports the exclusion. Lee had originally written a pious, sensible play (The Massacre of Paris), but Dryden tempted him to adapt it for the "diabolical" ends we see here: "the corruption of the Heads and Hearts . . . of so great a part of our young Gentry." Something is wrong with an age in which "Mercinary Poets . . . become Politicians."

1685

1 EVELYN, JOHN. "The Immortality of Poesie." In Poems by Several Hands, and on Several Occasions. Edited by Nahum Tate. London: for J. Hindmarsh, p. 92.

Lee's works will be remembered as long as Alexander the Great will be.

1688

1 PRIOR, MATTHEW. "Journey to Copt-Hall." In Dialogues of the Dead and Other Works in Prose and Verse. Edited by A.R. Waller. Cambridge: Cambridge University Press, 1907, p. 287.

Similes "are abus'd by frantic Lee." Circulated in manuscript, the poem was first published by Waller, its date authenticated by H. Bunker Wright and Monroe K. Spears in their second edition of The Literary Works of Matthew Prior (Cambridge: Cambridge University Press, 1971), 1:72-73.

2 _____. "A Session of the Poets (imperfect)." In Dialogues of the Dead and Other Works in Prose and Verse. Edited by A.R. Waller. Cambridge: Cambridge University Press, 1907, p. 299.

"Bloody hands, blazing Comets, Priests devils and Mummy": such "pritty tricks Lee in Bedlam can show." First published by Waller, this manuscript poem is dated, like the one above, by Wright and Spears (1971).

1689

1 GOULD, ROBERT. "The Play-House. A Satyr." In Poems Chiefly Consisting of Satyrs and Satyrical Epistles. London: n.p., p. 175.

Mithridates and The Rival Queens are achievements worthy of immortality, and in Lee's half of Oedipus his "Genius does with Lustre shine." Even his less judicious and moving works are "a'most worth all our Plays beside."

2 _____. "To Julian Secretary to the Muses, A Consolatory Epist in his Confinement." In Poems Chiefly Consisting of Satyrs and Satyrical Epistles. London : n.p., p. 280.

In Bedlam, Lee is better off "Than when applaus'd for writing Bombast Plays."

1690

1 [BROWN, THOMAS.] The Reasons of Mr. Joseph Hains the Player' Conversion and Re-conversion. Being the Third and Last Part to the Dialogues of Mr. Bays. London: for Richard Baldwin, p. 28.

Recalls the "weeping eyes . . . at the first acting of Mr. Lee's Protestant Play, The Massacre of Paris."

1691

1 [AMES, RICHARD.] A Search after Wit; or, A Visitation of the Authors. London: for E. Hawkins, p. 10.

"Poor Nat, thou has lost both thy Reason and Wit." Though now you try to write "a mad Play" upon a "mad Subject," once "the Theatre rung with thy brave Alexander."

2 [DUNTON, JOHN.] Answer to "Quest. 1. Whom do you think the best Dramatick Professor in this Age?" Athenian Gazette: or Casuistical Mercury 5, no. 2 (5 December), n. pag.

"Oedipus [by Dryden and Lee] . . . is indeed incomparable."

3 LANGBAINE, GERARD. An Account of the English Dramatick Poets. Oxford: by L.L. for G. West & H. Clements, pp. 320-27.

Lucius Junius Brutus, Mithridates, and The Rival Queens entitle Lee "to the First Rank of Poets," and Sophonisba and Theodosius exhibit well-drawn passions. Although the author could best create moving love scenes, he shows "Manly Spirit, Force and Vigour" in Brutus. In The Duke of Guise he used parts of both The Massacre of Paris and The Princess of Cleve.

1693

1 DENNIS, JOHN. The Impartial Critick: or, Some Observations Upon a Late Book, Entituled, A Short View of Tragedy, Written by Mr. Rymer. London: for R. Taylor, pp. 8-13.

Freeman and Beaumont disagree about the merits of the English Oedipus. The former thinks the play "would certainly have been much better, if Mr. Dryden had had the sole management of it," for in its present form, the protagonist is too innocent to satisfy Aristotle's dictum that a tragic hero should be admirable and yet flawed. Against the authority of Aristotle, Beaumont brings the data of experience: each time he has seen a performance, the Dryden-Lee Oedipus has made him feel "both Terrour and Pity."

2 D'URFEY, THOMAS. "Song, by way of Dialogue between a Mad-man and a Mad-woman. In Act II." Prefixed to The Richmond Heiress: or, a Woman Once in the Right. A Comedy, by Thomas D'Urfey. London: for Samuel Briscoe, n. pag.

Parodies Alexander's speech in the last scene of The Rival Queens (V.i.342-43).

1694

1 GILDON, CHARLES. "An Essay at a Vindication of Love in Tragedies, against Rapin and Mr. Rymer, Directed to Mr. Dennis." In Miscellaneous Letters and Essays, on Several

Subjects . . . in Prose and Verse . . . By Several Gentlemen and Ladies. London: for Benjamin Bragg, p. 170.

The love scenes in such tragedies as "Alexander and Others, of Mr. Lee's" have not prevented them from "e'ry day encreasing their Reputation."

1695

1 DRYDEN, JOHN. "Preface of the Translator, With a Parallel, Of Poetry and Painting." In De Arte Graphica. The Art of Painting, By C.A. Du Fresnoy. Translated by John Dryden. London: by J. Heptinstall for W. Rogers, pp. xxxix-xl.

Lee "had a great Genius for Tragedy" but, "following upon the fury of his natural temper, made every man and woman too in his Plays stark raging mad: there was not a sober person . . . . All was tempestuous and blustering; Heaven and Earth were coming together at every word; a meer Hurrican from the beginning to the end, and every Actour seem'd to be hastning on the Day of Judgment."

1698

1 ANON. A Vindication of the Stage, With the Usefulness and Advantages of Dramatick Representations. London: for Joseph Wild, p. 24.

The Dryden-Lee Oedipus outshines the version by Sophocles: its plot is "more surprising, . . . admirable, . . . and . . . probable"; its thoughts are more elegantly turned; its language is easier and more "Sublime"; and its characters, though "often Irregular," are "more Just, and Natural."

2 COLLIER, JEREMY. A Short View of the Immorality, and Profaneness of the English Stage. London: S. Keble, pp. 105-8, 171.

Lashes out at the "crude Fancies" in Lee's part of The Duke of Guise and at the bombast, anticlericism, and misogyny in Oedipus.

3 LANSDOWNE, GEORGE GRANVILLE, LORD. Preface to Heroick Love: A Tragedy, by George Granville, Lord Lansdowne. London: for F. Saunders, H. Playford, & B. Tooke, n. pag.

When audiences virtually ignore Dryden's part of Oedipus and applaud "the rants and the fustian of Mr. Lee, what can we say, but that madmen are only fit to write, when nothing is esteem'd Great and Heroick but what is un-intelligible."

4 [SETTLE, ELKANAH.] A Farther Defence of Dramatick Poetry. London: for Eliz. Whitlock, pp. 32, 59.

Despite Lee's bombast, The Rival Queens and Oedipus are among "our best English Tragedies," and along with Shakespeare's plays they exemplify how English variety surpasses French regularity.

1699

1 COLLIER, JEREMY. "To the Reader." In A Defence of the Short View of the Profaneness and Immorality of the English Stage. London: for S. Keble, R. Sare, & H. Hindmarsh, n. pag.

Caesar Borgia is full of smut and profanity.

2 [DRAKE, JAMES.] The Antient and Modern Stages Survey'd. London: A. Roper, pp. 132-33, 138, 147.

If the Dryden-Lee Oedipus seems amoral, perhaps even discouraging to those who believe in the rewards of virtue, it may be because the authors were less interested in modifying the ideas in Sophocles than in redesigning the plot. Certainly they achieved a more elegant play than Seneca did.

3 [GILDON, CHARLES], and GERARD LANGBAINE. The Lives and Characters of the English Dramatick Poets. London: for W. Turner, p. 85.

Lucius Junius Brutus is a masterpiece that has never been excelled.

4 OLDMIXON, JOHN. Reflections on the Stage, and Mr. Collyer's Defence of the Short View. In Four Dialogues. London: for R. Parker & P. Buck, pp. 176-77.

Cites Lucius Junius Brutus and Oedipus as evidence that the English dramatists, because of "the greatness of our Minds and excellence of our Reason," excel the French in evoking the pathetic, terrible, and sublime.

1700

1 [COBB, SAMUEL.] Poetae Britannici. A Poem, Satyrical and Panegyrical. London: for A. Roper, p. 18.

Though Lee failed to restrain "the Powerful heat, which o'er-inform'd his Soul" and thus "Nature's bounds surpast," he blazed away with truly tragic pity and terror, especially in Brutus. Regrettably, he sometimes prostituted his muse, fashioning fine trappings "for Amusement and surprise" without informing them with substance. This poem is the same as the one entitled "Of Poetry" and attributed to Cobb by Louis I. Bredvold in Series Two: Essays on Poetry and Language, No. 1 (Ann Arbor: Augustan Reprint Society, 1946).

2 GOULD, ROBERT. "On the Death of John Dryden, Esq." In Luctus Britannici: or the Tears of the British Muses; for the Death of John Dryden, Esq. London: for Henry Playford & Abel Roper, p. 38.

"Thy Faithful Lee--who never writ but pleas'd: / Tho' cooler Pens his Youthful Ardor blame, / Without his Fire, they'l never reach his Fame."

1702

1 ANON. A Comparison between the Two Stages. London: n.p., p. 101.

Notes Lee's "Vivacity . . . Spirit . . . Fire" and "Terror," ranking some of his plays with those of Shakespeare and Dryden. On the problem of attributing authorship of this work, see the edition by Staring B. Wells (Princeton: Princeton University Press, 1942).

1703

1 ANON. "Rochester's Ghost addressing it self to the Secretary of the Muses." In Poems on Affairs of State, from The Reign of K. James the First, To this Present Year 1703. Vol. 2. n.p., "Printed in the Year 1703," p. 131.

Suggests Lee may have joined Waller and Dryden in helping compose Mulgrave's "Essay upon Satire."

2 DENNIS, JOHN. Prologue to The Patriot, or the Italian Conspiracy, a Tragedy, by Charles Gildon. London: for William Davis & George Strahan, n. pag.

Calls Lucius Junius Brutus the "noblest Draught" by "fiery Lee," whose "Pegasus" sometimes "takes a wild ungovern'd Flight" and soars "too high for Mortal Eyes" or "lessens as He flies." Lee alternates between "well-proportion'd Raptures" and "false whining Passion."

3 [GILDON, CHARLES.] Preface to The Patriot, or the Italian Conspiracy, a Tragedy, by Charles Gildon. London: for William Davis & George Strahan, n. pag.

Of all Lee's plays, Lucius Junius Brutus has "the greatest Beauties, and . . . the greatest Faults." Its best scene is that between Brutus and Titus in Act 4. The descriptions of Lucrece's rape and death, however, are indecent, and the mob scenes make the Roman citizens seem unworthy of being rescued from tyranny. Moreover, Brutus' heroic appeal is lessened by irrelevantly introducing him as a buffoon and by giving him undignified or tediously long speeches. Too often, Lee's language is extravagant, even in the otherwise effective encounters between the lovers.

1704

1 ANON. "Dialogue III. Between Nat. Lee the Tragedian, and Colly Cibber the Plagiary." In Visits from the Shades: or, Dialogues Serious, Comical, and Political. London: n.p., p. 21.

Lee says that Cibber has ruined The Rival Queens by transforming the original heroes and heroines, who were "exact Patterns of Virtue and Honour" fleshed out from "Curtius and other Writers," into comic figures. This seems a reference to Cibber's burlesque The Rival Queans, not published until 1729 (see L.1729.1).

2 [BROWN, THOMAS.] Memoirs Relating to the late Famous Mr. Tho. Brown. With a Catalogue of his Library. London: by R. Brag, p. 18.

In "Elizium" Lee "may boast of his Bombast and Rapture."

3 WYCHERLEY, WILLIAM. "To Nath. Lee, in Bethlem." In Miscellany Poems. London: for C. Brome, J. Taylor, & B. Tooke, pp. 300-306.

Maintains that Lee is better off in Bedlam, because his "fustian Nonsense" and "High-flights" offended others, while his attempts to write and behave sensibly made him unhappy.

1708

1 BROWN, THOMAS. "From Bully Dawson to Bully W--." In The Second Volume of the Works of Mr. Tho. Brown, Containing Letters from the Dead to the Living, and from the Living to the Dead. Pt. 2. London: for S.B. & B. Bragg, p. 71.

Dryden calls red-faced Lee a madman who "never understood a Song in [his] life, nor any thing else, but jumbling the Gods about as if they were so many Tapsters in a Lumber-House."

1710

1 [GILDON, CHARLES.] "An Essay on the Art, Rise and Progress of the Stage in Greece, Rome and England." Prefixed to The Works of Mr. William Shakespeare. [Edited by Nicholas Rowe.] Vol. 7. London: for E. Curll & E. Sanger, p. xlvii.

Whereas Sophocles made Oedipus a mixture of virtue and vice, Dryden and Lee "have quite mistaken this Character; they have made him perfectly good."

2 [STEELE, RICHARD.] The Tatler, no. 191 (27-29 June), n. pag.

Chastises Lee for endowing both Alexander and Clytus (in The Rival Queens) with traits so inconsistent with their known characters. Ignoring Alexander's reputation for "generosity and chastity, in his treatment of the . . . family of Darius," Lee makes him "a monster of lust," "cruelty," and "bluster." Likewise, instead of investing Clytus with the "civility," "deference," and "sincerity of a bold artless soldier," the author depicts him as rough in mind and gesture, bombastic in language. "Such rude and undigested draughts of things are the proper objects" of Cibber's ridicule (presumably in his burlesque, first published in 1729: see L.1729.1).

1711

1 [ADDISON, JOSEPH.] *Spectator*, no. 39 (14 April), n. pag.
Of all modern English dramatists, Lee had the greatest talent for tragedy, but "the Impetuosity of his Genius" led to stylistic extravagance, preventing him from realizing his full potential except "in the Passionate Parts" where he kept "those Epithets and Metaphors" under control.

2 _____. *Spectator*, no. 40 (16 April), n. pag.
Of those plays that violate poetic justice by ending unhappily, *The Rival Queens* and *Theodosius* are among "the best." In *Oedipus* Lee tends to employ rant as a crowd-pleaser.

3 _____. *Spectator*, no. 92 (15 June), n. pag.
Sophonisba, *Mithridates*, and *The Rival Queens* have special appeal for the ladies, "but Theodosius . . . carries it from all the rest" (including *All for Love*, *Aureng-Zebe*, and *The Fatal Marriage*).

1712

1 [ADDISON, JOSEPH.] *Spectator*, no. 285 (26 January), n. pag.
Like Shakespeare, Lee sometimes writes the "false Sublime."

2 [STEELE, RICHARD.] *Spectator*, no. 438 (23 July), n. pag.
"If you would see Passion in its Purity, without Mixture of Reason, behold it represented in a mad Hero, drawn by a mad Poet" (Lee's Alexander in *The Rival Queens*).

1713

1 [ADDISON, JOSEPH.] *Guardian*, no. 110 (17 July), n. pag.
An example of how English tragic writers often give improper sentiments to their characters is seen when "*Leigh's Alcander* discovers himself to be a Cartesian in the first Page of Oedipus.--*The Sun's Sick too, / Shortly he'll be an Earth*--."

1717

1 ANON. "Dissertation sur la Poësie Angloise." Journal Literaire (the Hague) 9:199.

The best parts of the Dryden-Lee Oedipus were taken, sometimes word for word, from Corneille.

2 ANON. Essay recounting a dream about the choice of a Poet Laureate. The Censor, no. 41 (24 January), in The Censor. Vol. 2. London: for Jonas Brown, p. 74.

Dramatizes one of Lee's notorious fits, during which he demonstrates his friendship with Dryden and Otway, and his (presumed) anti-Puritan religious views.

3 DENNIS, JOHN. Remarks upon Mr. Pope's Translation of Homer. London: for E. Curll, pp. 8, 28.

Notes that Lee's "Fire and Enthusiasm" occasionally prevent him from expressing ideas clearly.

4 STEELE, RICHARD. Prologue to Lucius, the First Christian King of Britain, A Tragedy, by Delariviere Manley. London: for John Barber & Benjamin Tooke, Henry Clements & John Walthoe, n. pag.

Gives Lee's recipe for appealing to the various social classes in his audience (for example, "a Princess Young and Fair," a hero cutting down "Squadrons," "a Rape," "a Ghost," and so on). Calhoun Winton, in Sir Richard Steele, M.P. (Baltimore: Johns Hopkins University Press, 1970), p. 116, guesses that Steele was repeating Drury Lane gossip.

1719

1 JACOB, GILES. The Poetical Register: or, the Lives and Characters of the English Dramatick Poets. With an Account of their Writings. London: E. Curll, pp. 160-63.

Regards Lee as "an eminent Poet" who achieved "a Masterpiece in Lucius Junius Brutus" and some "extremely moving" love scenes in Mithridates and Theodosius. The Rival Queens also deserves "very great Applause."

1720

1 ANON. Miscellanea Aurea: or the Golden Medley. London: for A. Bettesworth & J. Pemberton, pp. 37-38.

In The Rival Queens, "the Passions were lively and strong."

1721

1 DENNIS, JOHN. "To Matthew Prior, Esq; upon the Roman Satirists." In Original Letters, Familiar, Moral and Critical. Vol. 2. London: for W. Mears, p. 433.

Places Lee and Etherege on a par as tragic and comic writers, respectively, and commends Lee's elevated thoughts, sonorous verse, and sublime language.

2 ____. "To Sir Richard Steele, Patentee of the Theatre in Drury-Lane." In Original Letters, Familiar, Moral and Critical. Vol. 1. London: for W. Mears, p. 111.

Why postpone Coriolanus "for that lamentable Tragick Farce Caesar Borgia"?

1722

1 ANON. "To the Author of the St. James's Journal." St. James's Journal, no. 33 (8 December):197.

"The Play of Alexander the Great is a better Burlesque upon Tragedy itself, than that which passes for a Burlesque upon Alexander, is upon that Play."

1723

1 JACOB, HILDEBRAND. Bedlam, A Poem. London: for W. Lewis & Tho. Edlin, pp. 6-7.

The section on "Damn'd Authors" includes quotations from Lee's plays and ridicules his bombast and extravagant imagery.

1725

1 [MURALT, BÉAT LOUIS de.] Lettres sur les Anglois et les Francois. Et sur les voiages. Cologne: n.p., p. 35.

Lee has genius but uses too much violent spectacle, expecially in Oedipus.

1726

1 ANON. "Remarks on the Letters, concerning the English and French." Prefixed to Letters Describing the Character and Customs of the English and French Nations. Anonymously translated from Béat Louis de Muralt's Lettres (1725). 2d ed. London: by Tho. Edlin & N. Prevost, pp. 19-20.

The spectacle in Oedipus is, indeed, excessive; it becomes laughable when the pasteboard king is thrown from a window onstage. Lee was obviously mad when he wrote his part of the play.

1727

1 [POPE, ALEXANDER.] "Peri Bathous: or, Martinus Scriblerus his Treatise of the Art of Sinking in Poetry." In Miscellanies. The Last Volume. London: for B. Motte, pp. 46-47, 50, 65-66.

Finds in Lee's plays some examples of "sinking" metaphors, "The Antithesis; or See-saw," and "The Alamode Stile, which is fine by being new, and . . . is as durable and extensive as the Poem itself."

1728

1 [RALPH, JAMES.] The Touch-stone: or, Historical, Critical, Political, Philosophical, and Theological Essays On the reigning Diversions of the Town. London: n.p., p. 157.

If Restoration dramatists were recalled from the grave, the depraved modern audiences would neglect the best of them, Lee, Otway, and Dryden, in favor of the Italian singers, the French dancers, the Settles, and the Shadwells.

1729

1 CIBBER, COLLEY. The Rival Queans, With the Humours of Alexander the Great. A Comical-Tragedy. Dublin: by Ja. Carson for Thomas Benson.

Thoroughly, if not subtly, burlesques The Rival Queens.

1731

1 FIELDING, HENRY. "H. Scriblerus Secundus; His Preface" to The Tragedy of Tragedies; or the Life and Death of Tom Thumb the Great. London: by J. Roberts, n. pag.

The Sophonisba of Lee and Mairet, unlike that of Corneille and Thomson, is made the "tender, passionate, amorous Mistress of Massinissa." The Tragedy of Tragedies (63 pp.) burlesques the works of many playwrights, including Lee's Nero, Sophonisba, Gloriana, Mithridates, Oedipus, Caesar Borgia, Lucius Junius Brutus, and The Duke of Guise.

1732

1 ANON. "Remarks on English Tragedy." Weekly Register: or, Universal Journal, no. 140 (16 December), n. pag.

Although in Sophonisba Hannibal and Scipio are not manly enough, in The Rival Queens Alexander is grand and the villains are magnificently wicked. This stately play shows that "Lee had a sublime Genius for Tragedy."

2 ANON. Remarks on Oedipus. Weekly Register: or, Universal Journal, no. 141 (23 December), n. pag.
Sees it as one of the most gripping of English plays and as an "admirable Piece of Poetry." Several passages are noted for their special beauty, but the author is full of praise for the work as a whole.

1733

1 ANON. "To Mr. Bavius, Secretary to the Society of Grub-street." Grub-street Journal, no. 167 (8 March), n. pag.
Commends The Massacre of Paris for its "strong" imagery, which makes such a "lasting impression in the mind."

1735

1 ANON. The Dramatic Historiographer: or, the British Theatre Delineated. London: for F. Cogan & J. Nourse, pp. 194-202, 212-20, 260-65.
Offers plot summaries of The Rival Queens, Oedipus, and Mithridates, approving of the poetically just and "livelily represented" deaths of Pharnaces and the titular character in the latter play. Mithridates fails not because Rome's army is superior to his and not because of traitors in his own ranks, but because he could not regulate his passions, those inner rebels.

2 DUNCOMBE, WILLIAM. Preface to Junius Brutus, A Tragedy. London: by J. Roberts, n. pag.
In Lee's ranting version of this story, "the Character of Brutus is . . . so shockingly Severe, without any Softnings of Tenderness and Humanity, that . . . it can scarce seem natural."

3 [POPPLE, WILLIAM.] Remarks on Lucius Junius Brutus. Prompter no. 29 (18 February), n. pag.
Neither Voltaire, in his cold imitation of Lee's Brutus, nor Duncombe, in his imitation of Voltaire, could approach the "true Roman Majesty" and deep pathos that Lee achieved.

4 _____. Remarks on The Rival Queens. Prompter, no. 105 (11 November), n. pag.
The "Fable is ill-chosen and worse conducted," for it represents Alexander in the grip of his worst traits (lust, effeminacy, drunkenness, choler, vanity) and yet has him assassinated not because of his wretched behavior but because "another envied his Greatness." This is "a Mad play, wrote by a Mad Poet, . . . revived by a Mad Manager, to introduce a Mad actor to a Mad town."

1738

1 BERNARD, JOHN PETER, THOMAS BIRCH, JOHN LOCKMAN, et al. A General Dictionary, Historical and Critical. Vol. 6. London: by J. Bettenham, p. 666.

Treats Lee as "an eminent English Poet" and cites Addison and Langbaine on his combination of tragic power and verbal excess.

1739

1 ANON. "The Apotheosis of Milton: A Vision." Gentleman's Magazine 9:20.

Lee, "whose Imagination got the Superiority of his Reason so far as to deprive him of his Senses," is represented with an awe-striking "Enthusiasm in his Eye," a whip in his hand "to discipline Dennis," and a frantic air. He wears torn garments that are three times too big for him.

1740

1 ANON. The Laureat: or, the Right Side of Colley Cibber, Esq. London: for J. Roberts, p. 32.

Agrees with Cibber (see L.1740.2) that many current tragedians developed their bombastic styles by copying Lee's practice, especially in The Rival Queens and Caesar Borgia.

2 CIBBER, COLLEY. An Apology for the Life of Mr. Colley Cibber, Comedian. London: by John Watts for the author, pp. 63-65, 68-69, 102.

The Rival Queens, which corrupted later tragic writers who imitated its ranting fustian, seems a great play only when there is a Betterton and a Mrs. Bracegirdle to embody and speak its "desperate Extravagance." The injudiciousness of its imagery is made plain when we realize that no painter could re-create Lee's images on canvas.

1741

1 CURLL, EDMUND, ed. The History of the English Stage, from the Restoration to the Present Time. London: for E. Curll, p. 19.

Without the fine acting of a Barry or a Bracegirdle, the characters of Roxana and Statira, in The Rival Queens, would be "a perfect burlesque on the Dignity of Majesty, and good Manners." Lee must have been "in a Rage the whole Time" he was composing the play, yet it does have some truly inspired poetry. On the problems associated with attributing authorship of this work, see Wilbur Samuel Howell, "Sources of the Elocutionary Movement in England: 1700-1748," QJS 45 (1959):12 and n. 64.

1742

1 FIELDING, HENRY. "A Discourse between the Poet and Player." In The History of the Adventures of Joseph Andrews, and of his Friend Mr. Abraham Adams. Vol. 2. London: for A. Millar, pp. 140, 143-44.

Quoting "thos harmonious Lines" from the second act of Theodosius, the "Player" laments the absence in modern drama of "your Shakespeares, Otways, and Lees."

1744

1 YOUNG, EDWARD. Letter to Samuel Richardson, 20 June. In The Correspondence of Edward Young. Edited by Henry Pettit. Oxford: Clarendon Press, 1971, p. 180.

Theodosius is one of "our three best plays" (along with Venice Preserv'd and The Orphan), partly because its ending leaves the heroine unhappy, despite the demand for poetic justice.

1745

1 ANON. "On the Poets and Actors in King Charles II's Reign." Gentleman's Magazine 15:99.

Considers Lee an "esteemed and beloved" author who possessed, "at intervals, inspiration itself."

2 WALPOLE, HORACE. Letter to Horace Mann, 29 March. In Letters of Horace Walpole Earl of Orford, to Sir Horace Mann, British Envoy at the Court of Tuscany. Edited by Lord Dover. Vol. 2. London: Richard Bentley, p. 85.

"I had rather have written the most absurd lines in Lee, than Leonidas or the Seasons."

1746

1 GARRICK, DAVID. Letter to John Hoadley, 19 August. In Some Unpublished Correspondence of David Garrick. Edited by George Pierce Baker. Boston: Houghton Mifflin Co., 1907, pp. 34-35.

"I am studying Veranes in Theodosius, there is something very moving in ye Character, but such a Mixture of Madness & Absurdity was never Serv'd up, upon ye Stage before, except by ye same incomprehensible Nat Lee."

1747

1 ANON. A Companion to the Theatre: or, A View of our Most Celebrated Dramatic Pieces. Vol. 2. London: J. Nourse, pp. 71-76, 329-35.

Redeemed only by Lee's "Diction," Caesar Borgia is a badly designed play consisting of a series of unprovoked murders; its moral is inappropriately delivered by Machiavel, one of its most wicked characters. The "many Beauties" of Theodosius, however, far outweigh its "few Faults," which clearly emerge from "the too great Warmth of the Author's Imagination." This play especially appeals to "the Ladies."

2 ANON. An Examen of the New Comedy call'd The Suspicious Husband. With Some Observations upon our Dramatick Poetry and Authors. London: for J. Roberts, pp. 42-43.
In The Rival Queens, Caesar Borgia, The Massacre of Paris, and Theodosius, Lee shows himself as a mad genius whose works are "the strongest Burlesque of Tragedy."

3 [FIELDING, SARAH.] "Letter XL. Valentine to David Simple." In Familiar Letters between the Principal Characters in David Simple. Vol. 2. London: by A. Millar, pp. 294-305.
Condemns "the Fustian of Lee and Rowe."

4 GUTHRIE, WILLIAM. An Essay upon English Tragedy, with Remarks upon the Abbe de Blanc's Observations on the English Stage. [London]: T. Waller, p. 16.
Because Lee had "dramatical fire" and "could both feel and describe distress," he was able to give more pleasure than could later tragedians who wrote more elegant and regular plays.

5 LeBLANC, JEAN BERNARD. "The Supplement of Genius: or, the art of composing dramatic poems, as it has been practised by many celebrated authors of the English theatre." In Letters on the English and French Nations. Vol. 2. London: for J. Brindley, R. Francklin, C. Davis, & J. Hodges, pp. 239, 255, 256-57, 260, 262.
Ridicules the use of songs in Nero and Theodosius, of prodigies and spectacles in Sophonisba and Oedipus, and of devils and diabolical pacts in Oedipus and The Duke of Guise.

6 WHINCOP, THOMAS. "A Compleat List of all the English Dramatic Poets." In Scanderberg: or, Love and Liberty. A Tragedy. London: W. Reeve, pp. 256-57.
Regards Lee as a "celebrated Poet" whose genius for sublime diction and tragic power was sometimes discounted by "bombast . . . which somewhat bordered upon . . . Madness."

1749

1 FIELDING, HENRY. The History of Tom Jones, A Foundling. Vol. 2. London: for A. Millar, p. 307.
Tom decides to write a farewell to Sophia, "being resolved . . . to pursue the Paths of this Giant Honour, as the gigantic Poet Lee calls it."

1750

1 [CHETWOOD, WILLIAM R.] The British Theatre. Containing the Lives of the English Dramatic Poets. Dublin: Peter Wilson, pp. 97-98.

Without acknowledgment, quotes Whincop's "Compleat List," for which, see L.1747.6.

2 [HILL, JOHN.] The Actor: A Treatise on the Art of Playing. London: for R. Griffiths, p. 191.

Sophonisba is difficult to act because of an "unnatural jingle" in the verse.

3 [JOHNSON, SAMUEL.] Rambler, no. 20 (26 May), in The Rambler. Vol. 1. London: by W. Suttaby, 1809, p. 118.

Recounts an anecdote and calls Lee "this great author."

1752

1 RACINE, LOUIS. Remarques sur les tragédies de Jean Racine; suivies d'un traité sur la poësie dramatique ancienne et moderne. Vol. 3. Amsterdam: Marc-Michel Rey; Paris: Desaint et Saillant, p. 227.

The Duke of Guise was written to ridicule religion and government; it is the sort of play that could have caused a revolution.

1753

1 ANON. The Present State of the Stage in Great-Britain and Ireland. London: P. Vaillant, p. 43.

No actor can make much of a figure playing Theodosius, because Varanes exhibits nearly the same passions and is a much more interesting character.

2 CIBBER, THEOPHILUS, [and ROBERT SHIELS.] The Lives of the Poets of Great Britain and Ireland. Compiled from . . . the MS. Notes of the late ingenious Mr. Coxeter and others. Vol. 2. London: R. Griffiths, pp. 227-32.

Shows the influence of Langbaine (L.1691.3), Addison (L.1711.1-3), Jacob (L.1719.1), and possibly A Companion to the Theatre (L.1747.1). Lee is a "great genius" whose plays are full of sublime and passionate passages, especially The Rival Queens (which delineates the "workings of the human soul"), Theodosius, and Lucius Junius Brutus ("one of the most moving plays in our language"). With his mastery of "the tender breathings of love," Lee was "born to write for the Ladies." His occasional lapses into bombast are negligible beside his many beautie

1754

1 ANON. An Essay on the Stage; or, the Art of Acting. A Poem. Edinburgh: John Yair & B. Bourn, p. 5.

"With caution soar with proud gigantic Lee, / From him learn grandeur, but from madness free."

1756

1 ANON. Theatrical Records: or, An Account of the English Dramatic Authors, and their Works. London: for R. & J. Dodsley, p. 71.

Paraphrases Whincop (L.1747.6) and Chetwood (L.1750.1).

2 [HAYWOOD, ELIZA.] The Husband. In Answer to the Wife. London: for T. Gardner, pp. 177-78.

Lee can write "extremely natural" descriptions of men who are superstitious, as exemplified in Oedipus, IV.i., where the protagonist is confronted by the ghost of Laius.

1758

1 ANON. "The Poetical Scale." Literary Magazine 3 (January):6.

Using the criteria of genius, judgment, learning, and versification, the author gives Lee a score of 51 out of 80, as compared, for example, with Shakespeare's 66, Jonson's 59, Congreve's 59, Southerne's 55, and Otway's 54.

1759

1 [GOLDSMITH, OLIVER "An Account of the Augustan Age of England." Bee, no. 8 (24 November):239.

"Lee had a great command of language, and vast force of expression."

2 WILKES, [THOMAS.] A General View of the Stage. London: for J. Coote & W. Whetstone, pp. 297-98.

Lee was a genius whose plays characteristically display tenderness and sensibility.

1760

1 ANON. Biographia Britannica. Vol. 5. London: for W. Meadows et al., pp. 2912-14.

Paraphrases the Cibber-Shiels Lives (see L.1753.2).

2 ANON. An Essay upon the Present State of the Theatre in France, England and Italy. London: for I. Pottinger, pp. 50, 58.

Unlike Varanes (of Theodosius), whom we can pity and love because we have formed no preconceptions about his historical character, Alexander is so well known to us as a great hero that we feel Lee has made him unnaturally vicious and extravagant. Moreover, by making Alexander "as mad as himself," Lee has violated the classical rule that tragic heroes should be virtuous (which involves sanity).

1762

1 ANON. The Life, Travels, and Adventures, of Christopher Wagstaff, Gentleman, Grandfather to Tristram Shandy. Vol. 2. London: for J. Hinman, p. 170.

Wishes that audiences would pay more attention to the written text of The Rival Queens, which "abounds with lessons of morality," instead of attending performances in order to enjoy the spectacle and rant.

2 ANON. A New and General Biographical Dictionary. Vol. 7. London: for T. Osborne et al., pp. 434-36.

Best at composing "passionate parts," especially those involving tender love expressed through restrained "epithets and metaphors," Lee too often allowed his powerful imagination "to break the bounds of sense." Some say his best play is Mithridates.

1763

1 ANON. "Remarks on the English Tragic Poets." Royal Magazine, or Gentleman's Monthly Companion 9 (July):41.

Ranks Lee "next to Otway."

1764

1 ANON. "Postscript. Intelligence Extraordinary." St. James's Chronicle; or, the British Evening-Post, no. 475 (20-22 March) n. pag.

Full of rant, bombast, and nonsense, The Rival Queens has "a mad Heroe drawn by a mad Poet."

2 [BAKER, DAVID ERSKINE.] The Companion to the Play-house. Vols. 1 and 2. London: T. Becket & P.A. Dehondt, C. Henderson, & T. Davies, n. pag.

Sees Lee as a great poetic dramatist who, in plays like The Rival Queens and Caesar Borgia, combined "beautiful flights of imagination and fancy" with "Rant, Bombast and Absurdity." Gloriana is his worst play, Oedipus and Lucius Junius Brutus are his finest (the former for sheer emotional power, the latter for manly vigor). Sophonisba and Theodosius are singled out for their excellence in presenting affecting love scenes, but the latter is considered less well managed because of the "trifling" and irrelevant episodes involving Marcian and Pulcheria. Parts of The Duke of Guise are described as "very fine."

1765

1 CHESTERFIELD, PHILIP DORMER STANHOPE, FOURTH EARL OF. Letter to his Godson. In The Letters of Philip Dormer Stanhope, 4th Earl of Chesterfield. Edited by Bonamy Dobrée. Vol. 6. London: Eyre & Spottiswoode, 1932, p. 2639.

Says that he is sending a copy of The Rival Queens, "another dish of blank verse and rhymes . . . to please your palate," recommending the play for its warning against selfish uses of sovereignty. Dobrée considers 1765 to be a conjectural date. I was unable to locate the first published version of this letter.

1767

1 ANON. The Rational Rosciad . . . In Two Parts. London: for C. Parker & J. Wilkie, pp. 7-8.

Lee unites great beauties with great faults, the most energetic raptures with the lowest absurdities, "Conceits the meanest, with sublimest thoughts."

1768

1 ANON. "The Life of Mr. Nathaniel Lee," prefixed to Theodosius. In The Theatre: or, Select Works of the British Dramatic Poets. Vol. 12. Edinburgh: for Martin & Wotherspoon, 2 pp., separately paginated.

Epitomizes Langbaine (L.1691.3), Addison (L.1711.1-3), Jacob (L.1719.1), and the Companion (L.1747.1), probably through Cibber and Shiels (L.1753.2). Lee was a "great genius."

2 WALPOLE, HORACE. Postscript to The Mysterious Mother. A Tragedy, by Horace Walpole. Strawberry-Hill: by and for the author, p. 10.

"Theatric genius . . . grew stark mad in Lee; whose cloak, a little the worse for wear, fell on Young; yet in both was still a poet's cloak."

1769

1 GRANGER, JAMES. A Biographical History of England. Vol. 2. London: for T. Davies, p. 336.

Lee's "rant" and Dryden's "pomp" are extremes between which Otway's art may be located.

1770

1 [GENTLEMAN, FRANCIS.] "Theodosius. A Tragedy: by Lee" and "A Summary View of the Most Known Dramatic Writers." In The Dramatic Censor; or, Critical Companion. Vol. 2. London: J. Bell; York: C. Etherington, pp. 190-205, 463.

Lee's frenzied extravagance is partly redeemed by Theodosius a play whose regularity, tenderness, interesting characters, and instructive sentiments (especially those on pastoral retreat and on kingship) are nevertheless undercut by tedious rhyming, breache of decorum (particularly in Marcian's speeches), improbabilities (Athenais' conversion, Theodosius' ignorance of Varanes's love sickness, Pulcheria's contradictory treatment of Marcian), and irrelevancies (mainly, the episodes with Marcian and Pulcheria). Theodosius is an "insipid" character, Leontine a strongly virtuous one, Varanes an interesting "medley of love and pride," and Athenais an even more interesting fusion of extreme self-denial and romantic self-indulgence. Her "abominable" suicide contributes to the amorality of a play which, because it does not observe poetic justice, might injure young minds by conveying "very extravagant notions of love."

2 [STEVENS, GEORGE ALEXANDER.] The Court of Alexander. An Opera, in Two Acts. London: for T. Waller, n. pag.

Comically alludes to The Rival Queens.

1771

1 ANON. "The British Theatre." London Magazine: or, Gentleman's Monthly Intelligencer 40 (May):264.

Condemns the "superstitious veneration" which ignores the fact that all of Lee's plays defy probability.

1772

1 ANON. Remarks on The Rival Queens. In The Theatrical Review; or, New Companion to the Play-House. Vol. 2. London: for S. Crowder, J. Wilkie, & J. Walter, p. 164.

Commonly regarded as "the best of this bombastic Writer's Tragedies," The Rival Queens is badly performed in a 7 April production.

1775

1 COOKE, WILLIAM. The Elements of Dramatic Criticism. London: G. Kearsly & G. Robinson, pp. 68, 75.

Though Lee is justly condemned for his rant, in The Rival Queens, he sometimes "sublimes" his ideas "to . . . the greatest beauties."

2 WALPOLE, HORACE. "Thoughts on Tragedy: in Three Letters to Robert Jephson, Esq.: Letter II." In The Works of Horatio Walpole, Earl of Orford. [Edited by Mary Berry.] Vol. 2. London: G.G. & J. Robinson & J. Edwards, 1798, p. 308.

Maintains that madness actually assisted Lee in achieving excellence. This letter is dated on the authority of Walpole's "Short Notes" in The Yale Edition of Horace Walpole's Correspondence, ed. W.S. Lewis, vol. 13 (New Haven: Yale University Press, 1948), p. 49 and n.

1776

1 MORTIMER, THOMAS. "The Life of John Dryden." In The British Plutarch. Rev. ed. Vol. 5. London: for E. & C. Dilly, p. 199.

Lee's tragedies, like those of Otway and Southerne, "are irresistibly moving" but not as "sublime" or "poetical" as Dryden's. I can find no evidence of an earlier edition of this work.

1779

1 JOHNSON, SAMUEL. "Dryden." In The Lives of the English Poets; and a Criticism on their Works. Vol. 1. Dublin: for Whitestone, Williams, et al., p. 276.

The Duke of Guise deserves notice "only for the offence which it gave to the remnant of the Covenanters."

1780

1 ANON. "Lee (Nathaniel)." In Encyclopaedia Britannica. 2d ed. Vol. 6. Edinburgh: for J. Balfour, W. Gordon, et al., p. 4164.

Lee is regarded as "a very eminent dramatic poet" whose eleven tragedies "contain a very great portion of true poetic enthusiasm." No dramatist before or since has "felt the passion of love more truly; nor could any ever describe it with more tenderness." Unfortunately, "this poet's imagination ran away with his reason."

1782

1 WALWYN, B. An Essay on Comedy. London: for M. Hookham, Miss Davis, & J. Fielding, pp. 16-17.

Lee's "partial" genius contains "more of madness than of reason." His Statira should be less fiery, so that her softness and simplicity would more strongly contrast with Roxana's volatile temperament.

1783

1 BLAIR, HUGH. Lectures on Rhetoric and Belles Lettres. London: for W. Strahan & T. Cadell; Edinburgh: for W. Creech. 1:78, 321; 2:525.

Lee is one of those "writers of genius" who sometimes become guilty of bombast or fustian, which means "forcing an ordinary or trivial object out of its rank, and endeavouring to raise it into the Sublime; or . . . attempting to exalt a Sublime object beyond all natural and reasonable bounds." In the romantic Theodosius, he usually avoids such extravagance, giving us, instead, "tenderness and warmth."

1784

1 DAVIES, THOMAS. "Dryden" and "Rival Queens, or Alexander the Great." In Dramatic Miscellanies. Vol. 3. London: For the author, pp. 174, 254-82.

Lee's best pieces are Mithridates, Theodosius, Lucius Junius Brutus, and The Rival Queens, the latter artfully weaving history and fiction. But in all of Lee's works, "blunder and beauty are blended," while in Sophonisba, there is obscenity and profaneness "fit only for a house of entertainment."

1785

1 ANON. Remarks on Lee. Lounger, no. 27 (6 August):105-8.

In Theodosius, a thin plot and tediously long speeches are obscured by hyperbolical expressions of amorous passions, so that the play could corrupt "the strength and purity of a young mind."

1789

1 [NEVE, PHILIP.] "Lee." In Cursory Remarks on Some of the Ancient English Poets, Particularly Milton. London: n.p., pp. 96-101.

Lee wrote histories, not tragedies; only Borgia and Massacre evoke pity and terror. Moreover, he often simply copies bold figures out of history, saving himself the trouble of inventing characters, and he tends to violate unity of action and time as he telescopes historical events. Furthermore, he has no sense of the domestic, writes rhyme awkwardly, and fills his dramas with verbiage and hyperbole. Nevertheless, he is "so distinguished, that there is no English author, to whom he can bear any degree of comparison. He is the most original dramatic writer since Shakespeare. His mind, sublime in its ideas, and extensive and powerful in its combinations, may be called, not great only, but majestic." This essay is reprinted as "Remarks on the English Poets: Lee," in Monthly Mirror 11 (1801):261-63.

1791

1 ANON. Remarks on Oedipus. In Bell's British Theatre. Vol. 8. London: J. Bell, 2 pp., separately paginated.

In terms of "sentiments and language," this play ranks "among the best productions of these authors," though we cannot approve the amorality of assigning responsibility for crime to fate instead of to human actions or intentions.

2 [GARDENSTONE, FRANCIS GARDEN, LORD.] "Remarks on the Present State of the English Drama." In Miscellanies in Prose and Verse. Edinburgh: J. Robertson, p. 162.

Theodosius is a "rapturous romantic play; it pleases men, women, and children, who have not formed their taste upon the sense and genius of Shakespeare, but on modern novels and plays."

1792

1 ANON. A New Theatrical Dictionary. London: S. Bladon, pp. 29, 100, 159, 207, 250, 287, 306-7.

Borrows practically every word from Baker's Companion to the Play-house (L.1764.2).

2 WALPOLE, HORACE. Letter to Thomas Walpole the Younger, 26 June. In Some Unpublished Letters of Horace Walpole. Edited by Sir Spencer Walpole. London, New York, and Bombay: Longmans, Green, p. 113.

Ridicules Lee's "mad rants . . ., when a Lover begs the Gods to annihilate time & space that he and his Mistress may meet incontinently, at the expense only of many years & miles."

1793

1 ANON. Remarks on The Rival Queens. In Bell's British Theatre. Vol. 16. London: J. Bell, 1 p.

This play is "a great and glorious flight of a bold, but frenzied imagination." It mixes sublimity and absurdity, passion and extravagance, and "the Poet, the genius, and the scholar, are every where visible."

2 ANON. Remarks on Theodosius. In Bell's British Theatre. Vol. 14. London: J. Bell, 2 pp., separately paginated.

Poetically powerful, luxuriantly fanciful, Theodosius exhibits some irregularities and straining. Although the underplot involving Marcian and Pulcheria serves as a foil to the loves of Varanes and Theodosius, Marcian "always sullies the splendor of the scene" with his "impure images" and "coarse" expressions.

1794

1 ALVES, ROBERT. Sketches of a History of Literature. Edinburgh: Alex. Chapman, p. 116.

Because Lee "soars too much in the regions of bombast," he cannot be considered as excellent a dramatist as Otway.

1796

1 [PENN, JOHN.] Letters on the Drama. London: for Elmsly, p. 40.

The songs in Theodosius are mediocre when compared with the choruses of Sophocles.

1797

1 WARTON, JOSEPH, ed. Note on line 87 of "The First Book of Statius's Thebais." In The Works of Alexander Pope, Esq. Vol. 2. London: for B. Law, J. Johnson, et al., p. 178.

Dryden and Lee "very unnaturally and injudiciously" introduce Oedipus "not only describing, but arguing on the dreadful crime he had committed."

1800

1 DIBDIN, CHARLES. A Complete History of the Stage. Vol. 4. London: C. Dibdin, pp. 170, 184-87, 247.

Regards Lee as "a writer of wonderful powers" and as "very forward among dramatic authors." Although Gloriana, Mithridates, Caesar Borgia, The Massacre of Paris, and The Princess of Cleve have too much declamation and frenzy mixed in with their fire and beauty, Oedipus, Sophonisba, Theodosius, The Rival Queens, and Lucius Junius Brutus are extremely effective plays. Oedipus is a great shocker; Sophonisba and Theodosius are memorable for tender distresses and exquisite language (though Marcian and Pulcheria almost spoil the latter play); The Rival Queens is a masterpiece of characterization and construction; and Brutus is manly and noble.

2 WATKINS, JOHN. An Universal Biographical and Historical Dictionary. London: T. Davison & T. Gillet for R. Phillips, n. pag.

Lee dominates our passions, but with language full of rant and bombast.

1801

1 LAMB, CHARLES. Letter to Robert Lloyd, 26 July. In Charles Lamb and the Lloyds. Edited by E.V. Lucas, London: Smith, Elder, 1898, p. 139.

Though "a fine play," Oedipus is less excellent than the "chastely" written Massacre of Paris and the exquisitely mad Rival Queens.

1802

1 ANON. "Biographical Sketch of Nathaniel Lee, the Poet." Monthly Mirror 13:75-78.

Quotes critical remarks by Cibber (L.1740.2), Addison (L.1711.1), and others.

1804

1 MALKIN, BENJAMIN HEATH. "To John Philip Kemble, Esquire." Prefixed to Almahide and Hamet, A Tragedy. London: Longman & Rees, p. 20.

Refers to "that extraordinary and spirited, though uncontroulable poet, Lee."

1807

1 AIKIN, JOHN. "Lee, Nathaniel." In General Biography; or, Lives, Critical and Historical. Compiled by Aikin, Thomas Morgan, and William Johnston. Vol. 6. London: for J. Johnson et al., p. 172.

Represents Lee as having mastered "high poetry" for the expression of passion, especially the passion of love "though [he is] always upon the verge of rant." Theodosius and The Rival Queens are mentioned as currently in the repertory.

1808

1 SCOTT, WALTER, ed. Commentary on The Duke of Guise. In The Works of John Dryden. Vol. 7. London: William Miller; Edinburgh: James Ballantyne, p. 10.

Lee's part is "very well written" and contains less rant than usual.

2 _____. Commentary on "Epistle the Fifth. To Mr. Lee, on his Tragedy of The Rival Queens, or Alexander the Great." In The Works of John Dryden. Vol. 11. London: William Miller; Edinburgh: James Ballantyne, p. 22.

In The Rival Queens, Lee's "most capital performance," nothing is merely satisfactory; "all is either exquisitely good, or extravagantly bombastic."

3 _____. Commentary on Oedipus, in The Works of John Dryden. Vol. 6. London: William Miller; Edinburgh: James Ballantyne pp. 117-22.

The rants in Lee's parts are excusable in light of his many "excellent passages." The play has a more mysterious conclusion than Sophocles' version, and though the underplot involving Adrastus and Eurydice is an ineffective addition, the Dryden-Lee characterization of Tiresias improves on the Greek original. Despite such achievements, however, the English Oedipus offends modern tastes with its gore, its theme of incest, and its obscure moral.

4 _____. "The Life of John Dryden." In The Works of John Dryden. Vol. 1. London: William Miller; Edinburgh: James Ballantyne, pp. 177, 183.

Regards Lee as "an excellent poet," and notes the pronounce "political character" of The Duke of Guise.

1811

1 [SCOTT, WALTER.] "Remarks on English Tragedy." In The Modern British Drama. Vol. 1. London: William Miller; Edinburgh: James Ballantyne, p. iv.

The only plays from Lee's "wild and ill-regulated genius" that are worthy of today's repertory are The Rival Queens, despite its "tumid language" and hyperbolical thoughts and passion and the "natural and affecting tragedy of Theodosius."

1812

1 BAKER, DAVID ERSKINE, ISAAC REED, and STEPHEN JONES. Biographia Dramatica; or, a Companion to the Playhouse. Newly revised by Jones. Vol. 3. London: Longman, pp. 29, 180, 211, 330.

To Baker's Companion (L.1764.2) adds that in The Rival Queens the characters are well contrasted. Theodosius is now termed "Lee's master-piece." The Massacre of Paris, lacking an "interesting private story," is "too shocking," and The Princess of Cleve is abominably obscene in parts.

2 BYRON, GEORGE GORDON, LORD. Letter to Lord Holland, 25 September. In Letters and Journals of Lord Byron: with Notices of his Life. Edited by Thomas Moore. Vol. 1. London: John Murray, 1830, p. 365.

Refers scathingly to "Lee's Bedlam metaphors." Although both Moore and Rowland E. Prothero, ed., The Works of Lord Byron: Letters and Journals, vol. 2 (1898-1901; rpt. New York: Octagon, 1966), p. 148, date this letter 25 September, it is dated 24 September by Leslie A. Marchand in "Famous in My Time": Byron's Letters and Journals, vol. 2 (Cambridge, Mass.: Harvard University Press, 1973), p. 207.

1815

1 CHALMERS, ALEXANDER. The General Biographical Dictionary. Vol. 20. London: for J. Nichols & Son, pp. 120-22.

Paraphrases Addison (L.1711.1), compares Lee to Ovid and Otway, and quotes the 1780 Encyclopaedia Britannica article (L.1780.1).

2 DIBDIN, THOMAS JOHN, ed. Remarks on The Rival Queens. In The London Theatre. Vol. 10. London: Whittingham & Arliss, p. 3.

Praises Lee's "glowing, though extravagant, fire of fancy" in this "strange melange of bombast and beautifully poetic imagery."

1817

1 BYRON, GEORGE GORDON, LORD. Letters to John Murray, 3 March and 14 June. In Letters and Journals of Lord Byron: With Notices of his Life. Edited by Thomas Moore. Vol. 2. London: John Murray, 1830, pp. 82, 125.

Manfred is "a drama as mad as Nat. Lee's Bedlam tragedy--which was in 25 acts and some odd scenes." Maturin's Manuel "seems to be declining into Nat. Lee."

1818

1 BYRON, GEORGE GORDON, LORD. Letter to John Murray, 11 April. In The Works of Lord Byron: Letters and Journals. Rev. ed. Edited by Rowland E. Prothero. Vol. 4. London: John Murray, 1899, p. 218.

Rather than become "wishy-washy," Byron would "rather be as bouncing as Nat. Lee." These remarks were left out of the letter in Moore's edition (above, L.1817.1) and in all others between 1830 and 1899.

2 OXBERRY, W., ed. Remarks on The Rival Queens. In The New English Drama. Vol. 3. London: W. Simkin & R. Marshall, pp. iii-vi.

Lee did not have "the madness of inspiration" in this play, with its poor phraseology, barren images, "indistinct" characters, undeveloped situations, and "one unvarying tune."

1819

1 CAMPBELL, THOMAS. "Nathaniel Lee." In Specimens of the British Poets; with Biographical and Critical Notices. Vol. 4 London: John Murray, pp. 332-34.

The pathetic Theodosius is an exception, because it exhibits little of Lee's proverbial "rant and turgidity."

1820

1 ANON. "The Dramatic Works of John Dryden." Retrospective Review 1:149-50, 152.

Many of the most beautiful lines in The Duke of Guise and Oedipus were written not by Dryden but by Lee, "a poet who has not had justice done him."

2 HAZLITT, WILLIAM. Lectures Chiefly on the Dramatic Literature of the Age of Elizabeth. Delivered at the Surry Institution. London: Stodart & Steuart; Edinburgh: Bell & Bradfute, p. 340.

Lee had "far more power and passion" than Dryden, but his constitutional morbidity made his work irregular and turbulent, and his genius was perverted "by carrying the vicious manner of his age to the greatest excess."

1821

1 ANON. "Nat Lee." Drama; or, Theatrical Pocket Magazine 1, no. 7 (November):341-44.

Urges a revival of interest in "this truly original . . . genius."

2 ANON. "On the Alleged Decline of Dramatic Writing." Blackwood's Edinburgh Magazine 9, no. 51 (June):280.

In general, Lee is better than Otway in tragedy, though not better than Dryden. His other works are "much inferior" to

The Rival Queens, despite its extravagance, and to Oedipus, the "most powerful tragedy . . . of that time."

3 ANON. "Plays, written by Mr. Nathaniel Lee." Retrospective Review 3:240-68.

While the fustian in Lee's plays is undeniable, his finest works, Lucius Junius Brutus, Mithridates, and Theodosius, exhibit "genuine passion," vivid imagery, and truly poetic frenzy. While Borgia and Constantine are worthless efforts, several of Lee's works--notably Nero, Gloriana, Sophonisba, and The Rival Queens--are blends of grossness or extravagance, on the one hand, and delicate or powerful beauty on the other. Both The Massacre of Paris and The Princess of Cleve "bear evident marks of a shattered mind." Brutus, Mithridates, and Theodosius are analyzed for particularly effective scenes, passages, and characters.

4 DALBY, J.W. "Memoir of Nathaniel Lee." Drama; or, Theatrical Pocket Magazine 2, no. 1 (December):29-31.

Of Lee's tragedies that are "remarkable for splendid metaphor, strong imagery, rant, and bombast," The Rival Queens is generally considered the best.

1822

1 ANON. "The Tragic Drama." European Magazine 82 (November): 411.

Amidst all the rant and bombast in Theodosius and The Rival Queens, there are "scenes which are true to nature, and bear the impress of the greatest talent."

2 [JEFFREY, FRANCIS.] "Lord Byron's Tragedies." Edinburgh Review 36:414.

The "disorderly scenes of Lee" exhibit "some strong and irregular flashes" of the "fires" of pre-Civil War drama.

1823

1 ANON. "An Essay on Dramatic Simplicity of Sentiment and Diction." Drama; or, Theatrical Pocket Magazine 5, no. 1 (1823):19.

Lee may have been mad, but his "amazing fancy" produced the convincingly mad hero of The Rival Queens, the amorous delicacy of Varanes and charming roughness of Marcian in Theodosius, and the generally fine writing of Lucius Junius Brutus. His plays often have "beautiful touches."

2 LACY, JOHN. "A Sixth Letter to the Dramatists of the Day." London Magazine 8 (December):647-48.

Lee writes an epic, rather than a tragic, style, and his "loud bombast" embodies little sense, passion, or fancy.

3 [PROCTER, B.W.] "English Tragedy." Edinburgh Review 38: 201-2.

Despite his fustian, Lee achieves beautiful tenderness in Theodosius and great power in The Rival Queens and The Massacre of Paris. In general, he possesses "more imagination and passion" but less skill in characterization (except in Massacre) than Otway.

1824

1 ANON. "Dramatic Poets Considered." Drama; or, Theatrical Pocket Magazine 7, no. 1 (October):17.

Lee was "nothing when not extravagant."

2 ANON. "Lee." Drama; or, Theatrical Pocket Magazine 7, no. 1 (March):23-25.

All "noise and nonsense," except for a few places in Theodosius, Lee gives us much spectacle and passion but no profundity or poetry. The Rival Queens, for instance, "contains neither character nor language." Alexander is a disgustingly vain talker, Clytus an unmannerly dog, Roxana and Statira "roaring termagents." At least in Theodosius, he tones down his bombast and draws in Varanes one convincing character.

3 SCOTT, WALTER. "Drama." In Supplement to the Fourth, Fifth, and Sixth Editions of the Encyclopaedia Britannica. Vol. 3. Edinburgh: Archibald Constable; London: Hurst, Robinson, p. 662.

Although he was bombastic, Lee "possessed considerable knowledge of dramatic art and of stage-effect."

1829

1 NEELE, HENRY. "Lectures on English Poetry." In The Literary Remains of the Late Henry Neele. London: Smith, Elder, pp. 141-42.

Some passages in Lee are "worthy of the brightest names in our dramatic annals," while too many others swell from strength and power to violence and extravagance. Occasionally he is movingly tender, often he is mad, but he is never merely dull or foolish. His best plays are The Rival Queens, Oedipus, and Theodosius.

1830

1 ANON. "Theatrical Journal--Drury Lane: Monday, January 11.-Brutus; Payne." Dramatic Magazine, 1 February, pp. 17-18.

With its "nervous and dignified language" and the noble, skillfully drawn motives of its protagonist, Lee's Brutus is superior to Payne's or Voltaire's, even though in the final scene he violates history. Unlike Voltaire's hero, Lee's "is not the cold stoic who sacrifices his son for the pure love of justice; he is actuated by a more powerful, and more excusable motive:--it is, that the lives of thousands might be saved."

1832

1 [GENEST, JOHN.] Some Account of the English Stage, from the Restoration in 1660 to 1830. Vol. 1. Bath: H.E. Carrington; London: Thomas Rodd, pp. 172-73, 182-85, 198-200, 226-29, 260-61, 277-78, 289, 310-11, 319-22, 393-98, 413-15, 475-76.

The plots and casts are given for some of the plays, the source(s) for most, and most are accorded a brief critical evaluation. Nero, Gloriana, and Oedipus are Lee's worst plays, the first two because they distort history and are full of bombast. In Oedipus, the scene involving the ghost of Laius is injudicious and that in which Oedipus throws himself from the window is a gross perversion of the original by Sophocles. Lee's part of the play abounds in fustian.

The moderately good plays are Sophonisba (which needs restraint), Mithridates, Lucius Junius Brutus (whose fine passages are discounted by botched love scenes, some indecency, unfortunate remarks about liberty, and a subject not well suited to stage presentation), The Princess of Cleve (with dull serious parts, "very good" comic parts, and a spirited portrayal of Nemours; the Rosidore passage alludes to Rochester), The Duke of Guise (having well-blended styles and interesting political implications but "sadly disgraced by a story similar to that of Dr. Faustus"), Constantine, and The Massacre of Paris (factual and refreshingly natural in style).

Genest seems to prefer Caesar Borgia, a "good play, with little bombast" and some historical grounding; Theodosius, a happy mix of history and fiction, better in some respects than Massinger's rendering of the story, though Pulcheria and Marcian's love affair travesties the truth and Lee's style is uneven; and The Rival Queens, "Lee's best," especially in the "banquet and mad scene," though the verse is irregular, the love plot indifferent, and some of the action a distortion of history.

1834

1 CAMPBELL, THOMAS. Life of Mrs. Siddons. Vol. 2. London: Effingham Wilson, p. 193.

Mrs. Siddons once told Hunt that Lee's poetry often had greater stage effect "than a mere reader would be apt to infer, from the superabundance of the poet's extravagance."

2 HUNT, LEIGH. "The Strand" and "Drury Lane, and the Two Theatres in Drury Lane and Covent Garden." Leigh Hunt's London Journal: Supplement to Part I, Supplements no. 3, p. xxiv, and no. 7, p. lv.

We pity Lee when we perceive madness transforming "true poetic fire" and "tenderness" into mere hyperbole. Despite its beauties, The Rival Queens contains much absurdity and lends an "improbable air . . . to a serious passion."

1838

1 CUNNINGHAM, GEORGE GODFREY. "Nathaniel Lee." In Lives of Eminent and Illustrious Englishmen. Vol. 3. Glasgow: A. Fullarton, pp. 348-50.

With his strong imagination and sense of elevation, Lee was occasionally able to achieve beautiful thoughts, but he lacked judgment, discipline, delicacy, subtlety, and the kind of well-stocked mind that could produce a variety of complex characters. His best play, The Rival Queens, shows that his wit was near to madness.

2 DUNHAM, SAMUEL ASTLEY. "Nathaniel Lee." In Lives of the Most Eminent Literary and Scientific Men of Great Britain. Lardner's Cabinet Cyclopaedia, vol. 3. London: Longman et al., pp. 134-45.

"His tragedies constitute a strange monument of genius and energy in excess." Such excess ruins Gloriana and (combined with obscenity) The Princess of Cleve, and it almost spoils the beauty and power of Sophonisba and Caesar Borgia. Nero displays an odd mingling of blank verse and rhyme, while in Mithridates historical accuracy is gained at the expense of "fire." The Rival Queens is poetically exciting and well conducted, but its wild flights would put modern audiences completely off, were it not for Lee's perennially appealing way with stage spectacle. His best plays are the "manly" Lucius Junius Brutus and the eloquently tender Theodosius, the latter being his "highest effort" despite "an unworthy episode in the under-plot of Marcian and Pulcheria."

1839

1 HALLAM, HENRY. Introduction to the Literature of Europe, in the 15th, 16th, and 17th Centuries. Vol. 4. Paris: A. & W. Galignani, p. 280.

"Lee . . . is, in spite of his proverbial extravagance, a man of poetical mind and some dramatic skill. But he has violated historical truth in Theodosius without gaining much by invention."

1840

1 HUNT, LEIGH, ed. "Biographical and Critical Notices." In The Dramatic Works of Wycherley, Congreve, Vanbrugh, and Farquhar. London: Edward Moxon, p. xxviii.

Only Mrs. Bracegirdle's rendering of Statira could have redeemed The Rival Queens from its "desperate extravagance."

1843

1 CHAMBERS, ROBERT. Cyclopaedia of English Literature. Vol. 1. Edinburgh: William & Robert Chambers, pp. 390-92.

"In tenderness and genuine passion," Lee excels Dryden, but his "tropical genius," nearly allied to madness, too often produced conceptual confusion and poetical exaggeration. His best works are The Rival Queens, Mithridates, Theodosius, and Lucius Junius Brutus.

1845

1 CRAIK, GEORGE L. Sketches of the History of Literature and Learning in England. Vol. 4. London: Charles Knight, p. 138.

Lee had almost as much tenderness and "much more fire and imagination than Otway," as best exemplified in The Rival Queens and Theodosius.

1848

1 CAMPBELL, THOMAS. An Essay on English Poetry; with Notices of the British Poets. London: John Murray, pp. 246-47.

Theodosius shows that Lee had real power and pathos, notwithstanding his reputation for "rant and turgidity." The 1819 edition of An Essay (Boston: Wells and Lilly) does not contain the remarks on specific poets.

1851

1 MILLS, ABRAHAM. The Literature and the Literary Men of Great Britain and Ireland. Vol. 2. New York: Harper & Bros., pp. 81-85.

Lee possessed genuine poetic gifts and could at times write gracefully or powerfully, as in The Rival Queens, Mithridates, Theodosius, and Lucius Junius Brutus. Usually, however, he lacked the sort of control fostered by "moral feelings or a sense of propriety," so that "extravagant frenzy" drove his plays into bombast and his mind into madness.

1853

1 SPALDING, WILLIAM. The History of English Literature. Edinburgh: Oliver & Boyd, pp. 297-98.

Lee is "nothing more than a poor likeness of Dryden."

1856

1 KNIGHT, CHARLES. The English Cyclopaedia: Biography. Vol. 3. London: Bradbury & Evans, p. 830.

Seldom gaining control of his muse, Lee typically gives us "impossible characters" using inflated language to utter commonplaces unredeemed by true feeling or tasteful phrasing.

2 MASSON, DAVID. "Dryden, and the Literature of the Restoration." In Essays, Biographical and Critical: Chiefly on English Poets. Cambridge: Macmillan, pp. 116, 121.

Neither Dryden nor Otway could match Lee in terms of his blend of tenderness and "a wild force of passion." This essay is erroneously said to be reprinted from The Quarterly Review of July 1854.

1860

1 HALLIWELL, JAMES O. A Dictionary of Old English Plays. London: John Russell Smith, pp. 109, 201.

The Princess of Cleve is a "curious drama," though it is both absurd and obscene.

1864

1 DORAN, JOHN. "Their Majesties' Servants." Annals of the English Stage, from Thomas Betterton to Edmund Kean. Vol. 1. London: William H. Allen, pp. 205, 215-16.

Lee can be "tender and impassioned" or "absurd and bombastic." He excels Otway in depicting "ardent love."

2 SHAW, THOMAS B., and WILLIAM SMITH. A History of English Literature. London: John Murray, pp. 261-62.

In dramatizing tenderness, Lee is superior to Dryden and Marlowe, and like the latter he could invoke "wild and exaggerated" images, "beautiful but feverish" declamation. He deserves a high reputation for The Rival Queens, Mithridates, Theodosius, and the "pathetic" Lucius Junius Brutus.

1870

1 ALLIBONE, S. AUSTIN. A Critical Dictionary of English Literature. Vol. 2. London: Trübner; Philadelphia: J.B. Lippincott, p. 1075.

As illustrated in The Rival Queens, Theodosius, Mithridates, and Lucius Junius Brutus, Lee was a "great genius" who mixed "crazy" rhapsodies with "true poetry."

2 THOMAS, J. Universal Pronouncing Dictionary of Biography and Mythology. Vol. 2. Philadelphia: J.B. Lippincott, p. 1392.

With his extravagant imagination Lee was "inclined to bombast."

1872

1 HETTNER, HERMANN. Geschichte der englischen Literatur von der Wiederherstellung des Königthums bis in die zweite Hälfte des achtzehnten Jahrhunderts, 1660-1770. 3d rev. ed. Braunschweig: Friedrich Vieweg und Sohn, pp. 99-101.

Sketches Lee's life and works, and compares him to the German playwright Grabbe.

1873

1 MORLEY, HENRY. A First Sketch of English Literature. London, Paris, and New York: Cassell, Petter, & Galpin, p. 680.

Into "the sound and fury of the heroic style," Lee brought wild imagination, elevated thoughts, "occasional pathos," impassioned love, and a "finer touch of nature than in any other of the dramatists of his time but Otway."

1875

1 WARD, ADOLPHUS WILLIAM. A History of English Dramatic Literature to the Death of Queen Anne. Vol. 2. London: Macmillan, pp. 516, 519, 543-47, 610.

Only in The Rival Queens and The Massacre of Paris does Lee's work deserve to be remembered. In the latter, the love plot happily remains secondary "and heightens, instead of absorbing, the effect of the whole." Lee's part of Oedipus is inferior to Dryden's, and his contributions to The Duke of Guise are mainly derivative. Nero is "an unhistorical medley of historical personages," Sophonisba an "unendurable" love-and-honor story, Mithridates a mere tale of love and lust with a "quasi-historical background," Caesar Borgia a crudely outrageous attempt to revive late-Elizabethan horror, Constantine a vulgar "drama of erotic passion," and The Princess of Cleve a "ribald comedy of almost unequalled grossness" (in which Rosidore is modeled on Rochester). Although Lee was too energetic to be merely an imitator, he spoiled his artistic originality with wanton imagery, hyperbolical diction, and political partisanship.

1878

1 MORLEY, HENRY. English Plays. Cassell's Library of English Literature, vol. 3. London, Paris, and New York: Cassell, Petter, & Galpin, pp. 355-56.

Commends the passion in The Rival Queens and the "sonorous tragic style" in all of Lee's better plays. "Lee had instincts of a poet."

1879

1 MOSEN, R. "Ueber Nathaniel Lee's leben und werke." Englische Studien 2:416-39.

Surveys the life and works, distinguishing three periods of Lee's artistry (which is characterized by excessive fancy): the beginnings (1675-76, including Nero, Sophonisba, and Gloriana), maturity and apogee (from The Rival Queens to Lucius Junius Brutus, 1677-81), descent and fall (from Constantine to The Massacre of Paris, 1684-90).

1881

1 SAINTSBURY, GEORGE EDWARD BATEMAN. Dryden. New York: Harper & Bros., pp. 59-60.

In the Oedipus, where both Dryden and Lee are "almost at their best," Lee mingles "his usual bombast with his usual splendid poetry."

1882

1 ANON. "Lee, Nathaniel." In Encyclopaedia Britannica. 9th ed. Vol. 14. New York: Charles Scribner's Sons, p. 399.

Lee's plays are artificial, extravagant, yet often poetically tender and graceful.

2 FITZGERALD, PERCY. A New History of the English Stage. Vol. 1. London: Tinsley Brothers, p. 220.

Notes Lee's inflated style but considers him "a leading contributor to the drama."

1883

1 [MARTIN, THEODORE.] "The English Stage." Quarterly Review (London) 155:197.

Garrick found Lee's "rant and fustian . . . odious," because he was "so deeply imbued with the spirit of Shakespeare." This essay is included in Martin's Essays on the Drama, 2d ser. (London: privately printed, 1889), the above passage on p. 257.

2 PERRY, THOMAS SERGEANT. English Literature in the Eighteenth Century. New York: Harper & Bros., pp. 90-91, 107, 109-11, 321.

Cites passages from Theodosius, Caesar Borgia, The Rival Queens, Mithridates, and Sophonisba to show that Lee could write "fine things amid his fustian," that, in fact, he surpassed Dryden "in certain kinds of tragedy." On the other hand, Lucius Junius Brutus shows the author's irrationality and the bad influence heroic drama had on him, while The Princess of Cleve basely travesties "a beautiful novel."

1886

1 WOTTON, MABEL E. "An Old-World Dramatist." Theatre. A Monthly Review of the Drama, Music, and the Fine Arts, n.s. 8: 76-86.

Unlike his contemporaries, Lee owed "little or nothing to France" but wrote plays that evinced strong Shakespearean influences and dealt "chiefly with the results of breaking the sixth and seventh commandments." His lightest play, The Princess of Cleve, shows him at his worst, his meanings clogged with inflated language, while in Mithridates this weakness is offset by great beauties. The Massacre of Paris excels the rest, though, with its grand imagery, fervent language, and well-drawn characters (especially Charles IX), it is well orchestrated to convey the evils of religious bigotry.

1888

1 GOSSE, EDMUND. Life of William Congreve. London: Walter Scott; New York: Thomas Whittaker; Toronto: W.J. Gage, p. 92.

Influenced by Milton's blank verse, Lee's poetic style strongly affected Congreve's in The Mourning Bride.

2 NOEL, RODEN, ed. "Thomas Otway." In Thomas Otway. The Mermaid Series. London: Vizetelly, pp. xi-xii, xvii, xxix.

Although he was generally inferior to Otway and was inferior to his predecessors in writing reflective soliloquies, Lee had "true dramatic genius"; his Rival Queens "is one of our excellent tragedies." He was also less frenchified than his contemporaries. The Dryden-Lee Oedipus, however, does not improve on Sophocles' original, and it is surpassed even by Crowne's Thyestes.

1889

1 BAKER, HENRY BARTON. The London Stage: Its History and Traditions from 1576 to 1888. Vol. 1. London: W.H. Allen, pp. 64-65.

Lee was a slightly mad genius who is remembered for The Rival Queens.

1892

1 LEE, SIDNEY, ed. "Lee, Nathaniel." In Dictionary of National Biography. Vol. 32. London: Smith, Elder, pp. 364-68.

In Lee's best works, "sparks of genius glimmer about the meaningless and indecent rhapsodies" that ruin Caesar Borgia and The Princess of Cleve. "Lee was a student of the Elizabethans."

1893

1 JEBB, R.C., ed. and trans. Introduction to Sophocles, The Plays and Fragments. Part I: The Oedipus Tyrannus. Cambridge: Cambridge University Press, pp. xxxviii-xxxix, xlv.

Influenced by Shakespeare and Corneille, the English Oedipus, unlike the one by Sophocles, divides our sympathies between Oedipus and Eurydice and creates in us not pity and fear but "loathing" and "disgust"; it "stupifies" our feelings. Moreover, by endowing Oedipus and Jocasta with a strange intuition of their true relationship, Dryden and Lee increase "the difficulty of explaining why the truth was not divined sooner" and lessen "the shock of discovery" when it is divined. Assisted "by an inferior hand" (Lee's), Dryden created an underplot that spoiled the main action and allowed his collaborator to compose "the worst rants of Acts IV and V."

1895

1 GARNETT, RICHARD. The Age of Dryden. London: George Bell & Sons, pp. 109-12.

Even Lee's best plays combine the most absurd rant and bombast with real poetic passion, as witness The Rival Queens, Mithridates, Oedipus, The Duke of Guise, Theodosius, and Lucius Junius Brutus. In overall construction, these plays have the economy of "French classical drama," but their characters, though bold and colorful, are either "transferred direct from history" or borrowed from the current stock of theatrical conventions.

1898

1 SAINTSBURY, GEORGE E.B. A Short History of English Literature. New York: Macmillan, pp. 502-4.

As a maker of plots, characters, and situations, Lee is less skillful than Otway, and his proverbial rants do interfere with the effectiveness of such plays as Theodosius and Caesar Borgia, Oedipus, and The Duke of Guise. But as a poet Lee has been underrated, for he can place words in rhythmical arrangements that are "perfect in sense and sound." Some of his best poetry appears in Mithridates.

1901

1 HASTINGS, CHARLES. The Theatre, Its Development in France and England. Translated by Frances A. Welby. London: Duckworth, p. 332.

Regards Lee and Otway as "the only serious disciples of Dryden" and briefly discusses the French sources of his two best plays, The Rival Queens and Lucius Junius Brutus.

2 SANDERS, H.M. "The Plays of Nat Lee, Gent." Temple Bar 124: 497-508.

Although Lee presents a limited range of characters, lacks artistic balance and intellectual subtlety, and fails to design whole plays as well as Otway, he exhibits a lively imagination, a "keen eye for tragic situations," a gift for portraying the "elemental passions," and a sure sense of stage effects. His worst plays are Nero (diffuse and extravagant), Borgia ("Elizabethan drama run mad"), and Cleve (ineffective tragicomedy). Gloriana and Constantine are somewhat better, though the former is marred by a pointless subplot. There is something of Otway and Ravenscroft in Constantine. Among his better plays, even if impaired by too much sound and fury, are Sophonisba, The Rival Queens, Mithridates, and Oedipus, and the very best are Theodosius, "a tragedy of pure pity" like Otway's Orphan and Ford's Broken Heart, and Lucius Junius Brutus, a noble tragedy that rises above petty political bias. Lee felt the influence not only of the Elizabethans but also of Milton, as in Cassander's allusive speech in IV.i.277-81 (which is rediscovered much later by Evans: see L.1949.2).

3 THOMPSON, A. HAMILTON. A History of English Literature. London: John Murray, pp. 355-56.

In "two remarkable plays," The Rival Queens and Mithridates, Lee demonstrates that he is a belated Elizabethan in the vein of Marlowe, and displays that "hyperbole of imagery and expression" that is both his chief strength and his basic fault.

1902

1 ENGEL, EDUARD. A History of English Literature (600-1900). Translated by "several hands" and revised by Hamley Bent. London: Methuen, p. 273.

The only dramatist of his day possessing a "truly poetical imagination" and one of the few who "renounced a comfortable income from indecent comedies," Lee was "a second Marlowe" whose works were handicapped by French influences and by his own lack of "a settled taste." Nevertheless, he was the only playwright of the Restoration "who was at all great."

2 LOUNSBURY, THOMAS R. Shakespeare and Voltaire. New York: Charles Scribner's Sons, pp. 76-77.

Defends Voltaire against charges that in his Brutus he plagiarized from Lee.

1903

1 CHASE, LEWIS NATHANIEL. The English Heroic Play. New York: Columbia University Press; London: Macmillan, p. 190.

Lee excelled in "plays which in form were not heroic."

2 COURTHOPE, W. J. A History of English Poetry. Vol. 4. London: Macmillan, pp. 422-25, 430-33.

Endowed with "great natural sensibility," Lee tended to write "operatic" plays with foppish, effeminate heroes and ranting love scenes. The Duke of Guise fails because its amorous episodes are stagy and its political plot "unintelligible." While Otway's art burned with a "steady flame," Lee thrived on "flashes of genius." Occasionally, though, he could achieve "genuine tenderness," as in Varanes of Theodosius.

3 DENCKER, HERMANN. Über die Quellen von Nathaniel Lee's Alexander the Great. Halle a.s.: C.A. Kaemmerer, 75 pp.

Examines Lee's use of sources, with emphasis on the debt to La Calprenède.

4 GOSSE, EDMUND. English Literature: An Illustrated Record. Vol. 3, From Milton to Johnson. New York and London: Macmillan, pp. 113-15.

Uses Theodosius and The Rival Queens to exemplify that Lee's bombastic tragedies are "singularly consistent and original in style."

1904

1 AUER, OTTO. Ueber einige Dramen Nathaniel Lee's mit besonderer Berücksichtigung seiner Beziehungen zum

französischen heroisch-galanten Roman. Berlin: E. Ebering, 103 pp.

Deals with Lee's dependence on the French novel and discusses the naturalness and simplicity of his plays by contrast to more typical heroic drama. Gloriana is based on La Calprenède's Cleopâtre, The Rival Queens relies on La Calprenède's Cassandre, Theodosius borrows from La Calprenède's Pharamond, Lucius Junius Brutus is indebted to Mlle. de Scudéry's Clélie, and The Princess of Cleve is based on Mme. de La Fayette's La Princesse de Clèves.

2 HUGHES, S.C. The Pre-Victorian Drama in Dublin. Dublin: Hodges, Figgis, p. 46.

Sees The Rival Queens as "a play of much beauty" that employs powerful contrasts between female characters.

3 RESA, FRITZ. Nathaniel Lees Trauerspiel Theodosius or The Force of Love. Literarhistorische Forschungen, 30. Berlin und Leipzig: Emil Felber, 219 pp.

Contains an introduction by Resa (pp. 1-110) and the text of the play (pp. 111-219) based on the 1680 quarto; gives the variants from the quartos of 1684, 1692, and 1708, and from the Dramatick Works of 1734 (London: W. Feales). The introduction surveys Lee's life and the textual history of Theodosius, summarizes the plot, discusses sources (especially La Calprenède's Faramond and Massinger's Emperor of the East), analyzes the play's structure (exposition, rising action, and so on), portrays the major characters, and briefly notes some early responses by critics such as Dryden, Addison, and Steele.

1906

1 CHARLANNE, LOUIS. L'Influence francaise en angleterre aux XVIIe siècle. Paris: Société Francaise d'Imprimerie et de Librairie, 634 pp.

Chapters 5 and 8 contain passages comparing Lee's work to that of Corneille and Racine.

2 HARVEY-JELLIE, W. Les Sources du théâtre anglais a l'époque de la Restauration. Paris: Librairie Générale de Droit et de Jurisprudence, p. 114.

Mentions The Rival Queens and Theodosius while arguing that Lee imitated the French less, and in heroic verse found his own voice more often, than did his contemporaries. His chief sources were French romances and classical history, and he was largely responsible for the revival of blank verse in Restoration drama.

1907

1 GEIERSBACH, WALTER. Nathaniel Lee's Zeittragödien und ihre Vorläufer im Drama Englands. Bernau: E. Gruner, 64 pp.

Includes part of the author's original dissertation. Aspects of the French civil wars are surveyed and some attention is given to Lee's Massacre of Paris and the Dryden-Lee Duke of Guise. The emphasis is on Marlowe's Massacre at Paris.

1908

1 THORNDIKE, ASHLEY H. Tragedy. Boston and New York: Houghton, Mifflin, pp. 261-62, 266-69, 290, 309.

Lee combines "the closeness of structure of French models" with rant, spectacle, and "Tourneurian . . . depravity and horror." He often uses supernatural elements and depicts a rivalry between father and son. With Otway, he started the trend toward using female protagonists. The "juvenile and worthless" Nero and the horrific Oedipus may be dismissed, while The Duke of Guise "deserves little consideration as satire or drama." But the other blank-verse plays are worthy efforts, especially Mithridates, which Lee seems to have written "without any knowledge" of Racine's play. In any case, Racine constructs plays on a simpler plan and provides more subtle psychological analyses than Lee.

1909

1 BOHN, WILLIAM E. "The Decline of the English Heroic Drama." MLN 24:51-52.

Shows Lee moving from incoherence in Nero through split-plot heroics in Gloriana and Sophonisba, both of which have the "sensuousness" of Beaumont and Fletcher, to the postheroic Rival Queens with its "genuinely human characters" and crude, tripartite plot tenuously held together by Alexander's personality. The achievement of artistic unity and restraint in Mithridates, a play exhibiting Fletcher's softness and Otway's pathos, is undercut by the "beastly, crude satire on the Catholics" in Caesar Borgia, but is restored by Theodosius, a play about love and honor on a human level, and Lucius Junius Brutus. Lee's turbulent imagination was "poetic rather than dramatic."

2 MANTZIUS, KARL. A History of Theatrical Art in Ancient and Modern Times. Translated by Louise von Cossel. Vol. 5. London: Duckworth, pp. 313, 326.

Though he produced no "mature masterpiece," Lee had "genuine poetic gifts"; he is "the poet of horrors, whose wild dramas point towards the past and turn our thoughts to Christopher Marlowe." The Oedipus, however, is "ghastly."

3 MEHR, OTTO. Neue Beiträge zur Leekunde und Kritik, insbesondere zum "Cäsar Borgia" und zur "Sophonisba." Berlin: Emil Felber, 154 pp.

Analyzes the plot, characters, and structure of Caesar Borgia, describing it as a mixture of "French-heroic" and "English-Elizabethan" elements. Identifies as probable or possible sources of Borgia: Tomasi's Vita del Duca Valentino, Guicciardini's Historia d'Italia, Dacres's translations of Machiavelli, Patrick's translation of Gentillet's Contre-Machiavel, Barnes's Devil's Charter, and Shakespeare's Othello. Sophonisba is seen as a pure heroic play, and its sources are discussed (Appian, Livy, Mairet's Sophonisbe, Marston's The Wonder of Women, Orrery's Parthenissa).

1910

1 BENTZIEN, WERNER. Studien zu Drydens "Oedipus." Rostock: Carl Boldt, 100 pp.

Compares the Dryden-Lee Oedipus, which is considered sensational and rather ornamental, to the previous versions of the story by Sophocles, Seneca, and Corneille, giving lengthy plot summaries of all four plays. Making only spare use of Seneca and Corneille, Dryden and Lee depend heavily on Sophocles. Like the Oedipus of Sophocles, that of Dryden and Lee is an agreeable character, though he is more "vehement" and less compliant than his counterpart in the Greek original.

2 HILL, HERBERT WYNFORD. "La Calprenède's Romances and the Restoration Drama." University of Nevada Studies 2, no. 3 (1910):1-56; 3, no. 2 (1911):57-158.

Recounts plots of the romances and analyzes their influence on Gloriana and The Rival Queens. While the former play owes some character traits and incidents to its source (Cleopatra), its overall plot and most of its phrasing are original. The Rival Queens, the period's best heroic play, takes hints for its main plot, the outline for its subplot, and some phrasing from Cassandra. But Lee adds emphasis to the female roles and controls his heroics better than he did in Gloriana.

3 MÜHLBACH, EGON. Die englischen Nerodramen des XVII. Jahrhunderts insonderheit Lees Nero. Weida in Thüringen: Thomas & Hubert, 105 pp.

Traces the tradition from 1603 to Lee's version, which is then discussed as an heroic play on pages 39-96. The dedication, prologue, epilogue, plot, and characters are examined, and Lee's departures from sources are discussed (for example, he intensifies the cruelty of Nero and the wantonness of Poppea). Influences are traced to Racine's Britannicus; Shakespeare's Troilus and Cressida, Julius Caesar, and Hamlet; Jonson's Catiline; May's Nero; and Dryden's Tyrannic Love.

4 RISTINE, FRANK HUMPHREY. English Tragicomedy, Its Origin and History. New York: Columbia University Press, p. 177.

In The Princess of Cleve, "the serious parts rise to real tragic pathos, while the comedy is disgustingly low."

1911

1 ANON. "Lee, Nathaniel." In Encyclopaedia Britannica. 11th ed. Vol. 16. New York: Encyclopaedia Britannica, pp. 361-62.

Sophonisba, Gloriana, and The Rival Queens are bombastic and extravagant, Borgia imitates "the worst blood and thunder Elizabethan tragedies," and Cleve is "a gross adaptation." Yet Lee's plays often contain "many passages of great beauty."

1912

1 BARTHOLOMEW, A.T. "The Restoration Drama II: Tragic Poets." In The Cambridge History of English Literature. Edited by A.W. Ward and A.R. Waller, Vol. 8. Cambridge: Cambridge University Press, pp. 179, 185-89.

Discusses Lee's sources and maintains that today his plays are "almost unendurable" because of their heavy-handedness in characterization and expression. At his best, in Theodosius for instance, he offers "a certain imposing picturesqueness and broad effectiveness" that faintly recalls the Elizabethans, though lacking their delicacy of perception and sense of humor. In his own time he succeeded because his works were fashionably heroic, sensuous, and pregnant with acting and staging possibilities.

2 LANG, ANDREW. History of English Literature from "Beowulf" to Swinburne. London, New York, Bombay, and Calcutta: Longmans, Green, pp. 371-73.

Characterized by "furious magnificence," Lee writes better blank verse than Otway but lacks Otway's "pathos, concentration, and construction." Nero, Mithridates, and The Rival Queens typify his passion and spectacle, and Oedipus, despite its gore and nonsense, is "worth reading as an example of the taste of the time."

3 MILLS, WEYMER. "Plumbagos." Connoisseur 34:6-7.

Through "the riotous language of his plays" there runs a "silver thread" that shows Lee "was always listening to some half divine air played on love's viol-da-gamba."

4 SAINTSBURY, GEORGE. "The Prosody of the Seventeenth Century." In The Cambridge History of English Literature. Edited by A.W. Ward and A.R. Waller. Vol. 8. Cambridge: Cambridge University Press, p. 235.

Sees Lee's prosody as "still more splendid but much rarer and briefer [in its] flashes" than Dryden's in All for Love.

5 WARD, A.W. "Dryden." In The Cambridge History of English Literature. Edited by Ward and A.W. Waller. Vol. 8. Cambridge: Cambridge University Press, pp. 16, 21, 30.

Lee's parts of Oedipus and The Duke of Guise are "unbalanced, but not wholly uninspired."

1913

1 HOLTHAUSEN, F., ed. Introduction to Nathaniel Lee's Sophonisba, or Hannibal's Overthrow. Nach der Quarto von 1681. Festschrift der Universität Kiel sur Feier des Geburtsfestes Seiner Majestät des Kaisers und Königs Wilhelm II. Kiel: Lipsius & Tischler, pp. i-v.

Very briefly comments on the play while comparing the 1681 quarto to the 1734 octavo.

2 SAINTSBURY, GEORGE. "Nathaniel Lee's Sophonisba. Herausgegeben von F. Holthausen. Kiel 1913." Englische Studien 47 (1913-14):96-97.

Though Lee is "inferior in facile and popular pathos to Otway," he is "a far greater poet" with "much wider range." The Rival Queens is "one . . . of his most remarkable works" and justifies "the famous saying as to the alliance of great wits and madness." No English dramatist "of anything like his merit has been so shamefully neglected."

1914

1 HORSTMANN, RICHARD. The Tragedy of Nero Emperour of Rome By Nathaniel Lee. Kieler Studien zur englischen Philologie, n.s. 6. Heidelberg: Carl Winters Universitätsbuchhandlung, 76 pp.

The introduction (pp. 1-6) surveys the textual history of Nero and characterizes the drama as a genuine "heroic" play. The text itself (pp. 7-69) follows the 1675 quarto and includes the poet's hand-written emendations in a copy of that quarto in the Bodleian Library; textual variants reflect the 1696 edition, the 1713 Works, and the 1734 Dramatic Works. In his annotations (pp. 70-76) the editor explains difficult words, topical references, and mythological allusions.

2 NETTLETON, GEORGE HENRY. English Drama of the Restoration and Eighteenth Century (1642-1780). New York: Macmillan, pp. 92, 95-99.

Ranks Lee as one of the best blank-verse tragedians, and as one of the few truly poetical dramatists, of the Restoration, even though "the impure element of insanity in his blood overran into his work." The Rival Queens is extravagant but moving, The Princess of Cleve coarse, Mithridates Racinian but sensational, and Caesar Borgia gory. In Oedipus the classical subject is overwhelmed by the Elizabethan style. Lee is capable of "real as well as 'false fire.'"

3 SCHELLING, FELIX E. English Drama. London: J.M. Dent; New York: E.P. Dutton, pp. 248-51.

Lee was "a man of unquestionable talent" who chose "ambitious subjects," employed splendid sets, and endowed "great historical persons" with "large heroic utterance." He could write beautiful, but too often bombastic, poetry. The Oedipus is a "nobler play" than The Duke of Guise, which panders to political prejudices.

4 SHERWOOD, MARGARET. Dryden's Dramatic Theory and Practice. New Haven: Yale University Press, pp. 93-97.

In Oedipus Dryden and Lee complicated, vulgarized, and sensationalized the classical original, dissipating its tragic effect and destroying its unity of action.

1915

1 BERNBAUM, ERNEST. The Drama of Sensibility . . . 1696-1780. Boston and London: Ginn, pp. 57-59, 94.

Lee's Mithridates differs artistically from Racine's play, but both dramatize the protagonist's defeat by his rebel passions, and Lee's Mithridates contrasts interestingly with Rowe's "faultless pacifist" in Tamerlane.

2 DUTTON, GEORGE B. "Theory and Practice in English Tragedy, 1650-1700." Englische Studien 49 (1915-16):203-4, 208-9.

Although Lee writes "blank verse dramas of rant and exaggeration approaching insanity," he does try to resist the lure of heroic drama by reviving "the older English models," as The Rival Queens, Mithridates, and The Duke of Guise illustrate.

3 WHITMORE, CHARLES EDWARD. The Supernatural in Tragedy. Cambridge, Mass.: Harvard University Press; London: Humphrey Milford, pp. 294-97.

Mentions the devil-motif in The Duke of Guise and lists the ghosts and portents in The Rival Queens, Mithridates, Caesar Borgia, and Constantine. Although the ghosts in Nero and Oedipus are not profoundly thematic, at least they do function in the action, unlike their purely decorative counterparts in the other plays.

1916

1 HAUPT, RICHARD WILHELM. Quellenstudien zu Lee's "Mithridates, King of Pontus." Kiel: Schmidt und Klaunig, 47 pp.

Lee did not know La Calprenède's La Mort de Mitridate (1637), and he is indebted to the historians Appianus Alexandrinus and Plutarch but not to Florus and Vellejus Paterculus. Lee's Semandra recalls Shakespeare's Lavinia (Titus Andronicus), Pelopidas is reminiscent of Iago (Othello), and Mithridates' dream recalls Clarence's (Richard III). Although Lee used Racine's Mithridate (1673), the end of the French play is more placatory than the cruel end of Lee's tragedy, and Lee's Monima is coarser than Racine's Monima. The reckless sensuousness of Mithridates is perhaps the major theme of Lee's drama.

2 WRIGHT, ROSE ABEL. The Political Play of the Restoration. Montesano, Wash.: A.E. Veatch, pp. 128-32.

Discusses The Duke of Guise as an anti-Whig play.

1919

1 BENSLEY, EDWARD. "'The Tragedy of Nero' and 'Piso's Conspiracy.'" N&Q 137:323.

Corrects Nicoll (L.1919.3) to the effect that Langbaine and others did not identify Piso's Conspiracy with Lee's Nero but rather with the 1624 Nero.

2 NEWELL, GEORGE. "'The Tragedy of Nero' and 'Piso's Conspiracy.'" N&Q 137:299-300.

Corrects Nicoll (L.1919.3) in the same manner as Bensley does (L.1919.1).

3 NICOLL, ALLARDYCE. "'The Tragedy of Nero' and 'Piso's Conspiracy.'" N&Q 137:254-57.

Details the differences between the two plays and calls Lee's Nero a darkly melancholy piece luridly brightened by flashes of genius. Its bombast and overstrained emotions soften occasionally "into pathetic little patches of pure poetry," and its protagonist is "a moon-struck villain" of Lee's own "diseased fancy." The author's "conception of royal excellence has marred what otherwise would have presented an ideal subject for Restoration blood-tragedy" in the tradition of Webster and Ford. Beneath Lee's excesses one finds beauty and sane humanity.

1920

1 EDMUNDS, E.W. An Historical Summary of English Literature. London, New York, Toronto, and Melbourne: Cassell, p. 126.

Lee's best plays, The Rival Queens and Mithridates, strangely mix passionate poetry and uncontrolled rant.

2 Van DOREN, MARK. The Poetry of John Dryden. New York: Harcourt, Brace & Howe, pp. 133-34.

The lines of Act 1 in Oedipus, where Tiresias comes on stage, could have been influenced by "the opening of Samson Agonistes" as well as by "at least five different scenes in classical tragedy."

1921

1 BRAWLEY, BENJAMIN. A Short History of the English Drama. New York: Harcourt, Brace, pp. 141-42.

Although Lee did not understand "the springs of simple emotion," he was a genuine poet who "could often thrill."

2 NICOLL, ALLARDYCE. "Political Plays of the Restoration." MLR 16:234.

As a royalist play, The Duke of Guise is "fairly good, although marred by the introduction of Melanax, a spirit, some devils, and Malicorne, a sorcerer."

1922

1 HAVENS, RAYMOND DEXTER. The Influence of Milton on English Poetry. Cambridge, Mass.: Harvard University Press, p. 14.

Near the end of the final scene in Caesar Borgia, Lee adapts Paradise Lost, iii, 487-96.

2 JONES, VIRGIL L. "Methods of Satire in the Political Drama of the Restoration." JEGP 21:663-64.

Notes that Lucius Junius Brutus is not so antimonarchical as it seems, for the worst ridicule of kings is put into the mouth of Vinditius, an unsympathetic character patterned after the tribunes in Coriolanus. The Duke of Guise seems to exhibit the four chief methods of satire used in the political drama of the time: parallels, typical characters, caricatures of individuals, and satiric remarks.

1923

1 ARCHER, WILLIAM. The Old Drama and the New: An Essay in Re-valuation. Boston: Small, Maynard, pp. 145, 151-59, 378-79.

Knowing nothing of craftsmanship or subtlety, Lee filled his plays with ranting declamation, inappropriate imagery, and melodious pathos. Theodosius and Constantine have some striking scenes but lack "sustained constructive power," while The Rival Queens suffers from irrelevancies (especially Clytus), disunity (caused by the disjunction between Alexander's problems and the conflict between his two wives), implausibility (especially that of Roxana), and "vulgarity of feeling."

2 NICOLL, ALLARDYCE. A History of Restoration Drama 1660-1700. Cambridge: Cambridge University Press, pp. 20, 86, 111-14, 118-19, 136, 260.

Lee was the best writer of "Drydenesque tragedy" and, next to Dryden himself, was possibly "the most influential man of his age." He was a true poet but had a "morbid" mind that liked to dwell on "odious" themes, as in Nero, a play whose tedious horrors and bombast are somewhat redeemed by the fine mad scenes. Sophonisba is a thrilling melodrama offering "the last of the madness of poetry," but the few effective scenes in Gloriana fail to compensate for its absurd rants, stock characters, and gratuitous gore. Our opinion of Lee's worth, however, is raised by his complex characterization of the protagonist in Caesar Borgia and of Pulcheria in Theodosius, and in Lucius Junius Brutus he achieves an excellent plot, finely developed emotional situations, and many passages of genuine poetry. The Princess of Cleve, on the other hand, is "worthless" except as a forerunner of the sentimental movement, and the "threadbare theme" of Constantine is poorly worked out.

1925

*1 BEERS, DOUGLAS STOWE. "The Life and Works of Nathaniel Lee." Ph.D. dissertation, Yale University.

Source: Stratman, p. 443.

2 NICOLL, ALLARDYCE. British Drama: An Historical Survey from the Beginnings to the Present Time. New York: Crowell, pp. 231-32.

Akin to Cowper, Smart, and Blake, Lee was "born with an undue share of enthusiasm and passion into a world of intellect and reason," so that he could find relief only in madness. Thus, his plays tend to be formless and roughly hewn, but beneath their absurdities one hears "the mighty voice of the Elizabethans." In Sophonisba, Gloriana, and Theodosius, there are many fine scenes.

3 WHITE, FELIX. "The Gordian Knot Untied." TLS, 11 June, p. 400.

Discusses marriage as Gordian Knot in Theodosius.

1926

1 SUMMERS, MONTAGUE. The History of Witchcraft and Demonology. London: Kegan Paul, Trench, Trübner; New York: Alfred A. Knopf, p. 301.

Remarks upon the presence of Tiresias and necromancy in Oedipus, Malicorne and Melanax in The Duke of Guise, and diabolical rites in Sophonisba.

1927

1 ARUNDELL, DENNIS. Henry Purcell. London: Oxford University Press and Humphrey Milford, pp. 63-64.

The opening ritual scene of Theodosius is vital musically, visually, and thematically, but the songs that punctuate the acts have no relation to the plot. On the whole, the play is a "popular drama of innocence and insipid heroics."

2 ASHBY, S.R. "The Treatment of the Themes of Classical Tragedy in English Tragedy between 1660 and 1738." Ph.D. dissertation, Harvard University, pp. 192-94.

Compares the Dryden-Lee Oedipus to Seneca's version, against the background of Sophocles and Greek tragedy, with special emphasis on the Englishmen's addition of supernatural elements.

3 BEATY, JOHN O. "The Drama of the Restoration." In An Introduction to Drama. Edited by Beaty and Jay B. Hubbell. New York: Macmillan, p. 321.

Even in his best plays, The Rival Queens, Mithridates, Borgia, and Massacre, vigorous declamation too often becomes mere rant.

4 CAZAMIAN, LOUIS. A History of English Literature, Vol. 2: Modern Times (1660-1914). New York: Macmillan, pp. 48-49.

Lee was an unbalanced "romanticist" whose plays, despite "flashes of intuitive art" that remind one of Marlowe or the later Elizabethans, are weakly constructed, intellectually barren, psychologically shallow, and swelling with forced frenzy and hyperbolical imagery. The Rival Queens, Mithridates, and Lucius Junius Brutus have some impressive passages, but The Princess of Cleve is a scandalous perversion of the French novel.

5 NEWTON, H. CHANCE. Crime and the Drama: or, Dark Deeds Dramatized. London: S. Paul, p. 56.

Classifies Caesar Borgia as one of the more "terrible" poison plays and says that is has "madness in its blank verse."

6 SUMMERS, MONTAGUE, ed. Introduction to The Complete Works of Thomas Shadwell. Vol. 1. London: Fortune Press, pp. clxvii, clxxxvi, clxxxvii-clxxxviii.

Shaftesbury is satirized as Ascanio in Caesar Borgia (an "effective melodrama") and as Arius in Constantine. The Massacre of Paris is a "fine drama," and The Duke of Guise is a "very great" tragedy in which "the political motives . . . are entirely subservient to the dramatic quality."

7 WHITING, GEORGE W. "The Condition of the London Theaters, 1679-83: A Reflection of the Political Situation." MP 25:200.
Maintains that Lucius Junius Brutus condemns the immorality of Charles II, vilifies the Anglican clergy, and champions "justice and the commonwealth."

1928

1 DENT, EDWARD J. Foundations of English Opera: A Study of Musical Drama in England during the Seventeenth Century. Cambridge: Cambridge University Press, pp. 149-53, 220.
Notes the scene in Oedipus where Tiresias invokes the ghost of Laius, which involves a recitative and chorus, "with a definite air . . . to charm the infernal powers." Purcell's first appearance as dramatic composer was in Theodosius; he wrote the "scenes of religious ceremony" and the songs between acts, these "having little or nothing to do with the drama." Though Purcell would become yet more skillful, the ritual scenes in Theodosius represent "a considerable advance on Locke's temple scene in Psyche."

2 ELWIN, MALCOLM. The Playgoer's Handbook to Restoration Drama. New York: Macmillan, pp. 86, 92, 94, 96, 101, 122-32.
Despite his "weakness for dead bodies and blood," Lee humanized heroics, combined "classical knowledge with the best privileges of the romanticists in . . . construction," and "attained the heights of tragedy." While Nero, The Massacre of Paris, and The Duke of Guise have no great merits, Sophonisba is poetically and emotionally appealing, and Gloriana is "one of the most perfect of purely heroic tragedies." Caesar Borgia is noteworthy for its distinctive theme and classical manner, Theodosius for the fine characterizations of Marcian and Pulcheria, and Oedipus, of which "the biggest and best part" is Lee's, for the impressive "machinery of visions and violence." But Lee's masterpieces are The Rival Queens, Mithridates, and Lucius Junius Brutus, each a well-designed, powerful tragedy, Mithridates surpassing anything of Dryden's, Brutus worthy of comparison with Shakespeare.

3 SUMMERS, MONTAGUE, ed. "Explanatory Notes." In Roscius Anglicanus, by John Downes. London: Fortune Press, pp. 135, 230, 237.
Gloriana is a "fine tragedy" and Mithridates an "excellent" one. In The Princess of Cleve "the serious scenes are pathetic and interesting; the comic episodes very good."

1929

1 DOBRÉE, BONAMY. Restoration Tragedy 1660-1720. Oxford: Clarendon Press, pp. 59, 61, 110-31.

There is much to admire in Lee, though he is by no means a great writer. He writes a fluid, "meaty" blank verse that is stronger, more disciplined than Otway's, and he has a good eye for dramatic situations. But while he can achieve emotional power, striking spectacle, and a kind of "operatic" quality, he lacks psychological insight, humor, precision of imagery and thought, and a steady awareness of the "checks of actual life." Consequently, his plays depend too heavily on the sheer force of words, on unrelieved anxiety, on music and theatricality designed for extraneous and isolated effects. His characters all seem obsessive, their worlds ordered by an artificial logic that seems unconnected with familiar values or behavioral patterns, though perhaps Lee meant them to symbolize the rituals of real life. If The Rival Queens is his best work, tumultuous yet dignified in its own way, his part of Oedipus, with its hyperbole and harshness, its "half-images" and "shadowy generalizations," contrasts sharply with Dryden's more judicious and mellow contribution.

2 KIES, PAUL P. "Lessing and Lee." JEGP 28:402-9.

Lessing knew Lee's work and based Das befreite Rom more on Lucius Junius Brutus than on Livy. Two of the actions in Brutus--the story of Lucretia and that of the banishment of Collatinus and election of Valerius--have no "integral connection" with the main plot ending with the execution of Brutus' two sons. Nevertheless, "Lee is one of the four chief tragedians of the same period, the other three being Dryden, Otway, and Southerne."

3 SAUPE, GERHARD. Die Sophonisbetragödien der englischen Literatur des 17. und 18. Jahrhunderts. Osterwieck am Harz: A.W. Zickfeldt, 78 pp.

Analyzes Marston's The Wonder of Women (1606), Thomas Nabbes's Hannibal and Scipio (1635), James Thomson's Sophonisba (1730), and Lee's Sophonisba (1676). For the latter, see especially pp. 15-19, 71-72. Lee's play is a heroic drama controlled by the heroic couplet and concentrating on the subject of love. Bombastic, operatic, tastelessly written, it is indebted to Dryden's essay "Of Heroic Plays," Mairet's La Sophonisbe, and Livy (particularly for historical and political material).

1930

1 WHITING, GEORGE W. "Political Satire in London Stage Plays, 1680-83." MP 28:33, 35, 43.

Regards Caesar Borgia as "a violent indictment of Romanism, Lucius Junius Brutus as a republican document that defends rebellion in a good cause, and The Duke of Guise as "a broadside fired at the whole Whig party."

1931

1 DEANE, CECIL V. Dramatic Theory and the Rhymed Heroic Play. London: Oxford University Press, pp. 84, 213-18.

Notable for individuality of style, striking situations, "an atmosphere of foreboding," and tragic endings, Lee's heroic plays amalgamate "the Drydenesque and the Fordian." While Sophonisba may lack the organic wholeness, "the pervading intensity and singleness of aim of tragedy," it is theatrically effective because its parallel love stories are clearly presented, its type characters well differentiated, its verse varied and fluent, and its individual scenes masterfully contrived.

2 HAM, ROSWELL GRAY. Otway and Lee: Biography from a Baroque Age. New Haven: Yale University Press, 260 pp.

Writing in "a fury of emotion trembling at times upon the brink of madness," Lee had more of "the heroic instinct" than Otway, and he broke away from "ranting heroism" more gradually, partly because he was "not so immediately influenced by the quieter, more natural acting style at Dorset Garden." Although he never created an "insufficient hero" of Otwavian dimensions, he anticipated Otway in imitating Elizabethan heroines and in appealing to the female sensibilities in his audience.

Nero, an implicit advisory to the crown, is Shakespearean, Jacobean, and Hobbist; Sophonisba exploits the "heroic formula"; and Gloriana, with its "florid word pictures," is a garishly dramatized romance, with "liberal drafts from history." While The Rival Queens is both "colossal" and "sentimental," and Mithridates employs ideas merely to decorate the passions, Caesar Borgia shows that Lee was basically more thoughtful, less sentimental than Otway. It also shows, with its Elizabethan atrocities and fierce anti-Catholicism, that Lee was "a Tory by policy . . . a Whig by blood." Again raising larger socio-political problems through the characters in Theodosius, he gains his independence from romance and, as in Nero, sermonizes Charles II regarding the fatal influence of women in politics. More political advice is given in the Whig play, Lucius Junius Brutus, which combines appropriate heroics with "Renaissance fancy."

Oedipus curiously blends classical, Latin, French, and Elizabethan background in a "scorching tragedy of somewhat Jacobean flavor," though it continues to use stock Restoration characters, actions, and complications. Like Borgia, The Massacre of Paris unites "papal intrigue and English terror," with possible contemporary references, and The Princess of Cleve is an "irreligious and cynical" drama comparable to Otway's Friendship in Fashion. If the ideas in The Duke of Guise show Lee reversing his political stance, the play's love scenes and prodigies reflect the author's growing madness. Constantine is "a flareback to his earlier heroic manner" and was probably based on the neglected manuscript of an earlier work.

3 MacMILLAN, DOUGALD, and HOWARD MUMFORD JONES, eds. Headnote to The Rival Queens. In Plays of the Restoration and Eighteenth Century. New York: Henry Holt, pp. 130-31.

Mentions The Massacre of Paris, "in which [Lee's] faults are less in evidence than in earlier dramas," and commends The Rival Queens for its use of history, its deeply flawed hero, and its "flashes of rhetorical splendor." For the Platonic gallantry of French heroic romances and of earlier heroic plays, Lee substituted "the hot speech of passion," thus making love, instead of love and honor, the central motive of action. This innovation, together with the injection of blank verse and liberal doses of spectacle, made Lee the founder of "the declamatory tragedy in which the eighteenth century was to delight."

4 SUMMERS, MONTAGUE, ed. Introduction to Dryden: The Dramatic Works. Vol. 1. London: Nonesuch Press, p. cix.

The Princess of Cleve is "somewhat chaotic," and The Massacre of Paris is primarily based on Gilbert Burnet's Relation of the Barbarous and Bloody Massacre (1678).

5 WHITE, ARTHUR F. "The Office of Revels and Dramatic Censorship during the Restoration Period." Western Reserve University Bulletin, n.s. 34, no. 13:30-31, 37-39.

"The first play affected by the political conditions of the time," Lucius Junius Brutus is nevertheless "unusually free from 'scandalous expressions.'" Its republican sentiments are channeled through Vinditius and the mob. One passage seems to reflect on Charles II's penchant for living among mistresses. The Duke of Guise must be regarded as a "political pamphlet" in which Guise is Monmouth, Marmontier is the Duchess of Monmouth, Henry of Navarre is the Duke of York, Blois is Oxford, and the lower house of the Estates is the House of Commons. The play clearly alludes to the Exclusion Crisis.

1932

1 HECHT, ILSE. Der heroische Frauentyp im Restaurationsdrama. Leipzig: Alexander Edelmann, pp. 30-43, 80-81, 85-88, 97, 99-101, 110-11, 117-19, 122-27, 132-33, 135.

Categorizes the "heroic" women in Lee's plays. Sophonisba, Bellamira (Caesar Borgia), Athenais (Theodosius), and the Princess of Cleve are "noble" heroines. Poppea (Nero) is the inwardly disruptive woman. Roxana (Rival Queens) is the wholly unscrupulous type. Bellamira (Caesar Borgia) and Athenais (Theodosius) are examples of the "daughter." Fausta (Constantine) and Narcissa (Gloriana) are women longing for an Arcadian life. Pulcheria (Theodosius) represents the absolute sovereign. Marmoutier (Guise) and Teraminta (Brutus) are women trying to influence politics through a certain man.

2 HOLLAND, A.K. Henry Purcell: The English Musical Tradition. London: G. Bell, pp. 178-80.

Speculates on French sources for the opening ritual scene in Theodosius and generally praises the fitness of syllables and phrasing to music throughout the play, despite the fact that the "lovely flowing" songs between scenes have only the most general relevance to the plot.

3 SUMMERS, MONTAGUE, ed. "Oedipus: Source." In Dryden: The Dramatic Works. Vol. 4. London: Nonesuch Press, pp. 345-46.

Avoids comparisons with Sophocles but maintains that "Seneca, . . . Corneille, and Voltaire . . . have been far surpassed by our English dramatists in power, in pathos, and in poetry." Creon, in the English version, is modeled on Shakespeare's Richard III.

1933

1 HÄFELE, WALTER, ed. Introduction to Nathaniel Lee. Constantine the Great. Heidelberg: Carl Winter, pp. 10-50.

Discusses the critics' neglect of the play, the possible historical sources (Zosimus, Zonares, Baronius, William Winstanley) and the more literary sources (Lyly's Alexander and Campaspe, Marlowe's Jew of Malta, Ravenscroft's Edgar and Alfreda, Otway's Orphan and Don Carlos, Racine's Mithridate), the authorship of the prologue (Otway or Lee) and of the epilogue (Dryden).

2 HARASZTI, ZOLTÁN. "Dryden's Adaptations and Operas." More Books: The Bulletin of the Boston Public Library 8:95.

Regards the English Oedipus as vastly inferior to that of Sophocles and considers Lee's contribution bombastic.

3 HOLLIS, CHRISTOPHER. Dryden. London: Duckworth, pp. 120-24.

Unlike Sophocles, Dryden and Lee in their Oedipus reject the classical practice of ascribing injustice to blind fate. Instead, they envision an ultimate justice beyond what man's limited mind can perceive. They also have the protagonist commit suicide, rather than showing him being banished. Hollis briefly discusses the political context of The Duke of Guise.

4 PRAZ, MARIO. "Restoration Drama." ES 15:9-10, 12.

Oedipus and Caesar Borgia illustrate that Lee was a precursor of "the worst excesses of the frénétique Romantics."

*5 STROUP, THOMAS BRADLEY. "Type-Characters in the Serious Drama of the Restoration with Special Attention to the Plays of Davenant, Dryden, Lee, and Otway." Ph.D. dissertation, University of North Carolina.

Source: Stratman, p. 545.

1933

6 Van LENNEP, WILLIAM. "The Life and Works of Nathaniel Lee, Dramatist (1648?-1692): A Study of Sources." Ph.D. dissertation, Harvard University, 711 pp.

Thoroughly discusses the sources, analogues, and historical context of each play, noting many allusions to, and apparent influences from, earlier literary works. Appendix III proves that Lee was not the author of the 1681 Lear, Appendix IV speculates that Fabritius in Brutus represents Etherege, and Appendix V links the "Curate of St. Eustace" in Guise with Edmund Hickeringill. Nero is monotonous but reflects Lee's potential power, which he begins to realize in the well-controlled Sophonisba. If Gloriana fails to capitalize on this developing artistry, The Rival Queens and Mithridates compensate by their effectiveness, though the latter is too sentimental. Oedipus is second-rate but forceful, Borgia too bloody but interestingly Websterian, The Princess of Cleve formally peculiar and forward-looking in its sentimentality, and Constantine without interest.

Of the top-flight works, The Massacre of Paris, with its simple, swift-moving plot, is Lee's "best acting play," while in Theodosius the characterization and well-modulated passions make up for a somewhat confusing structure. In The Duke of Guise, a surprisingly successful blend of the two collaborators' strengths results in a very effective drama. But Lee's true masterpiece is Lucius Junius Brutus, a noble tragedy worthy to rank with All for Love, Venice Preserv'd, and The Orphan.

7 WÜLKER, ANTON. Shakespeares Einfluss auf die dramatische Kunst von Nathaniel Lee. Emsdetten: Heinr. & J. Lechte, 64 pp.

Discusses Shakespeare's popularity on the Restoration stage and his general influence on all of Lee's plays, focusing on the specific debts of eight of Lee's works to such plays by Shakespeare as Julius Caesar, Othello, Macbeth, Hamlet, Lear, and Richard III. Lee owes a great deal not only to Shakespeare but to Elizabethan drama in general.

1934

1 BREDVOLD, LOUIS I. The Intellectual Milieu of John Dryden: Studies in Some Aspects of Seventeenth-Century Thought. Ann Arbor: University of Michigan Press, p. 140.

In a sense expanding the parallel drawn in lines 101-2 of Astraea Redux, Dryden and Lee created The Duke of Guise, an "indictment of Whiggism drawn in the form of a historical drama."

2 LEGOUIS, EMILE. A Short History of English Literature. Translated by V.F. Boyson and J. Coulson. Oxford: Clarendon Press, p. 188.

Even his best works--The Rival Queens, Theodosius, The Princess of Cleve, and The Massacre of Paris--do not match Otway's in quality, for Lee's "highly sensual imagination," capable of declamatory fire, tended to lose "itself in mere verbal fury."

3 McMANAWAY, JAMES G. "Philip Massinger and the Restoration Drama." ELH 1:297.
From Massinger's Emperour of the East, Lee takes only the notion of making Theodosius neglect public affairs to such an extent as to endow Pulcheria with power over his beloved Athenais, and although he took a good deal more from a translation of Pharamond, his Theodosius is conceived "in an entirely different spirit."

1935

1 GREENE, GRAHAM. "Rochester and Lee." TLS, 2 November, p. 697.
Supports Summers's identification of Nemours (in The Princess of Cleve) with Rochester (see L.1935.3) by noting that in I.ii. Nemours quotes Rochester's Valentinian.

2 LAWRENCE, W.J. "Rochester and Lee." TLS, 9 November, p. 722.
Replies to Greene (L.1935.1): although Lee may have lifted lines from Valentinian when he revised Cleve for the 1689 production, he probably did not see a manuscript of Rochester's play in 1681.

3 SUMMERS, MONTAGUE. The Playhouse of Pepys. New York: Macmillan, pp. 293, 301, 381.
Notes homosexuality in The Princess of Cleve and argues that the play twice refers to Rochester, through the allusion to "Count Rosidore" and in the portrait of Nemours. The Rival Queens, because of its "immense vogue," probably sparked dramatic interest in "the Alexander romance."

4 STROUP, THOMAS B. "The Princess of Cleve and Sentimental Comedy." RES 11:200-203.
Probably acted in 1681, well before the early sentimental comedies of Cibber and Southerne, Cleve combines heroic and sentimental elements and so should be considered a transitional piece.

1936

1 TEETER, LOUIS. "The Dramatic Uses of Hobbes's Political Ideas." ELH 3:155-56.
Notes Hobbesian implications of points made in The Duke of Guise, I.i.

2 _____. "Political Themes in Restoration Tragedy." Ph.D. dissertation, Johns Hopkins University, pp. 56-57, 63-64, 150 ff., 170 ff. 415-18.

In the course of reaching larger generalizations, makes acute observations about several of Lee's plays, noting, for example, the political ramifications of Nero's egotistical savagery, seeing some similarities between Machiavel (Caesar Borgia) and Scipio (Sophonisba), and describing Gloriana as "perhaps the only Restoration heroine who actually rebels in an attempt to right her wrongs." Unlike Dryden's earlier heroes, Lee's Mithridates succumbs to love and is "unfaithful to a superior demand." If Massinger's Theodosius is negligent, Lee's is hopelessly weak. In The Duke of Guise, the "expression of theory . . . is more extensive than in any other [play] of the time."

1937

*1 HASAN, M. "The Life and Works of Nathaniel Lee." Ph.D. dissertation, University of Oxford (St. John's College).

Source: Stratman, p. 445.

2 PITOU, SPIRE, Jr. "French and English Echoes of a Descriptive Passage in Tasso." MLN 52:265-66.

Theodosius borrows lines from La Calprenède's Faramond, which echo lines in Tasso's Gerusalemme liberata.

3 STROUP, THOMAS B. "Supernatural Beings in Restoration Drama." Anglia 61:188-89, 192.

Although Melanax, "the merry devil" of The Duke of Guise, merely adds to the spectacle and wit of the play, the ghosts in Nero, The Rival Queens, Mithridates, and Oedipus "perform definite dramatic functions."

4 WESTRUP, J.A. Purcell. London: J.M. Dent, pp. 37, 56, 67, 150.

Mentions the music in Theodosius and The Massacre of Paris and suggests that Purcell did not set the "Mad song" in Sophonisba.

1938

1 NOYES, ROBERT GALE. "Conventions of Song in Restoration Tragedy." PMLA 53:165-66, 169-70, 172, 179-80, 183, 185, 187

Lists, categorizes, and briefly comments on songs in Nero, Sophonisba, Gloriana, Mithridates, Oedipus, The Rival Queens, Caesar Borgia, Theodosius, The Princess of Cleve, and Constantin Cleve, for instance, has an opening song, a song to establish character type, one that parallels the dramatic situation, one designed to divert characters from important events, and a dirge

1939

1 NETTLETON, GEORGE H. "Blank-Verse Tragedy (1677-1700)." In British Dramatists from Dryden to Sheridan. Edited by Nettleton and Arthur E. Case. Boston, New York, Chicago, Dallas, Atlanta, and San Francisco: Houghton Mifflin, pp. 69-70.

Refers to "the nondescript Princess of Cleve" and briefly analyzes The Rival Queens to find Lee's usual ingredients: "impulsive action," "declamatory passion," "pictorial display and theatrical device," "compelling situations," the influences of French heroic romance and of classical history, blank verse, and an unhappy ending strung on the frame of rhymed heroic drama. Lee had "true poetic powers" but was irrational and morbid. He initiated the shift from rhyme to blank verse in Restoration serious drama. George Winchester Stone does not change this assessment in his 1969 revision of British Dramatists from Dryden to Sheridan (Boston: Houghton Mifflin).

1940

1 BARBOUR, FRANCES. "The Unconventional Heroic Plays of Nathaniel Lee." TSLL 20:109-16.

Except for one "negligible interlude," during which he wrote part of The Duke of Guise and all of Constantine, Lee always "preferred a virtuous illegitimate ruler to a legitimate tyrant" and felt that a people can rightfully depose an irresponsible, inefficient, or dishonest ruler. The post-1679 works differ from their predecessors only in that they begin to "furnish constructive solutions to problems raised in the earlier plays."

2 GASSNER, JOHN. Masters of the Drama. New York: Random House, p. 284.

"Frenzied plays like The Rival Queens and Mithridates," written "in the Elizabethan manner," "commend themselves to psychoanalysts rather than to the . . . public."

1941

1 FREEDLEY, GEORGE, and JOHN A. REEVES. A History of the Theatre. New York: Crown, p. 173.

Lee's most important works--Nero, Sophonisba, The Rival Queens, and The Duke of Guise--are "tumultuous and bombastic tragedies with passages of considerable poetic beauty."

1942

1 GREENE, GRAHAM. British Dramatists. London: William Collins, p. 30.

Speaks of Lee's "moral genius" and hears in The Princess of Cleve "a strange Jacobean echo." Greene's remarks are reprinted in "British Dramatists," in Romance of English Literature, ed. Kate O'Brien and W.J. Turner (New York: Hastings House, 1944), p. 125.

1945

1 SAINTSBURY, GEORGE. "John Dryden the Dramatist." In George Saintsbury: The Memorial Volume. London: Methuen, p. 74.

Unlike Dryden, who relied on admiration as his chief tragic effect, Lee followed Aristotle and Racine in stressing pathos.

1946

1 RUSSELL, TRUSTEN WHEELER. Voltaire, Dryden & Heroic Tragedy. New York: Columbia University Press, pp. 27, 30, 71, 84, 87.

Rehearses the early commentaries on Oedipus.

1947

1 PRIOR, MOODY E. The Language of Tragedy. New York: Columbia University Press, pp. 178-79.

With its "elegant violence," "nice dilemmas," and "exhibits of passion," The Rival Queens springs directly from the tradition of heroic drama.

1948

1 LEARY, LEWIS. "St. George Tucker Attends the Theater." WMQ 3d ser. 5:396-97.

Tucker was pleased by the scenery, but not the acting or costumes, when he attended an early production of The Rival Queens at the John Street Theatre in New York City.

2 McKILLOP, ALAN DUGALD. English Literature from Dryden to Burns. New York and London: Appleton-Century-Crofts, pp. 70-71.

As illustrated in The Rival Queens, Lee was an "undisciplined" writer whose "extravagant diction, rant, and spectacular effects" seem modeled on Elizabethan and Jacobean drama, especially Ford and Webster.

3 SHERBURN, GEORGE. The Restoration and Eighteenth Century (1660-1789). A Literary History of England. Edited by Albert C. Baugh. Vol. 3. New York: Appleton-Century-Crofts, pp. 757-58.

By fusing "the Elizabethan idiom with that of French tragedy and French heroic romance," Lee "recovered a sort of Jacobean decadence." Certainly he is bombastic, emotionally strained, sometimes vague and confusing, often unrealistic; but in words like Mithridates and Lucius Junius Brutus, he can thrill us with swift action, violent imagery, "gruesome tableaux," and crudely fascinating stories. He had the poetic gift and was capable of forward-looking sentimentality, but he lacked control.

1949

1 DARLINGTON, W.A. The Actor and His Audience. London: Phoenix House, pp. 40-41.

Perhaps The Rival Queens is "over-written and wild," but "Lee's whirling words" become "meaningless rant" only if the actor allows them to.

2 EVANS, G. BLAKEMORE. "Milton and Lee's The Rival Queens (1677)." MLN 64:527-28.

Cassander reflects the influence of "Milton's Satan (or Dryden's Lucifer)" and in IV.i.277-81 he echoes Satan (see L.1901.2).

1950

1 BOWERS, FREDSON. "Nathaniel Lee: Three Probable Seventeenth-Century Piracies." PBSA 44:62-66.

Argues that editions of The Rival Queens (1694), Nero (1696), and Sophonisba (1697), "each a careful . . . copy of an authorized edition," were piracies.

2 _____. "The Prologue to Nathaniel Lee's 'Mithridates,' 1678." PBSA 44:173-75.

Notes variations in a rare 1678 form of the prologue, suggesting that removal of Lee's name from the corrected state has no significance for assigning authorship.

3 BREDVOLD, LOUIS I. "The Literature of the Restoration and the Eighteenth Century 1660-1798." In A History of English Literature. Edited by Hardin Craig. New York: Oxford University Press, p. 359.

Lee is "theatrical and declamatory," and The Rival Queens is his best play.

4 COOKE, A.L., and THOMAS B. STROUP. "The Political Implications in Lee's Constantine the Great." JEGP 49:506-15.
In reflecting the Popish Plot and its sequels, Constantine makes its political commentary "more accurately and adequately than such plays as Venice Preserv'd."

5 DOWNER, ALAN S. The British Drama: A Handbook and Brief Chronicle. New York: Appleton-Century-Crofts, pp. 254-55, 360.
Lee wrote ranting, violent, verbosely passionate, and grandiose dramas about love, "honest or perverted," drawing subjects from the classics and a style from "the more extravagant of the Elizabethans." The Dryden-Lee Oedipus is more complex, ironic, and realistic than the original by Sophocles, and its emphasis has been shifted from fate to love.

6 LEECH, CLIFFORD. "Restoration Tragedy: A Reconsideration." DUJ 42:107, 110, 113.
Lee's chief aim was to present "distressed nobility." Theodosius, intended as a highly moral play, presents pardonably inept, though high-souled, characters; The Princess of Cleve corrupts the French novel by interlarding it "with scenes of the dullest lubricity."

1951

1 KIENDLER, GRETE. "Konvertierte Formen in den Dramen Otways und Lees. Ein Vergleich mit der Sprache Shakespeares." Ph.D. dissertation, University of Graz, 202 pp.
Catalogues the conversion of words (adjectives into nouns, adjectives into verbs, nouns into verbs, nouns into adjectives) in the dramas of Otway and Lee, with special reference to possible first uses of the converted forms in Shakespeare's works. For example, "to rumour" (meaning "to circulate by way of rumour") is a verbal form created from the noun, and it occurs in Richard III, IV.ii.51; in Otway's Venice Preserv'd; and in Theodosius.

2 LEECH, CLIFFORD. "Restoration Comedy: The Earlier Phase." EIC 1:165.
Unable to "recognize the character of the French original, Lee simply gave the audience what he thought they wanted in The Princess of Cleve, and the result is a hodgepodge of shrill heroics, noisy libertinism, and gross comedy, all remote from actuality.

1952

1 BERKELEY, DAVID S. "The Penitent Rake in Restoration Comedy." MP 49:229-30.

The relationship between Athenais and Pulcheria in _Theodosius_ repeats a common motif: through her divine charm, a woman of beauty and virtue converts an inferior female.

2 KUNITZ, STANLEY J., and HOWARD HAYCRAFT. _British Authors before 1800: A Biographical Dictionary_. New York: H.W. Wilson, pp. 315-16.

"Lee had no sense of measure, no true humor . . ., no ability in characterization, no delicacy, and his heroic tragedies . . . have no standing as poetry." Even his best plays are marred "by constant hysterical ranting and absurd confusion."

3 SOUTHERN, RICHARD. _Changeable Scenery: Its Origin and Development in the British Theatre_. London: Faber & Faber, p. 154.

Analyzes the stage directions for _Theodosius_, I.i.: "Here is an unexpected use of the wings, imaginative and decorative, instead of representative and subsidiary to the view."

1954

1 STROUP, THOMAS B. "The Authorship of the Prologue to Lee's 'Constantine the Great.'" _N&Q_ 199:387-88.

Ascribes it to Lee, not Otway.

2 STROUP, THOMAS B., and ARTHUR L. COOKE, eds. "General Introduction," "Life of Nathaniel Lee," introductions and notes to individual plays and to the poems. In _The Works of Nathaniel Lee_. New Brunswick, N.J.: Scarecrow Press. Vol. 1 (1954): 1-18, 21-23, 75-80, 147-49, 213-17, 287-90, 369-73, 451-84; Vol. 2 (1955):3-6, 67-70, 149-52, 231-35, 317-20, 389-93, 479-82, 549, 571-613.

Updates the biography, surveys major previous criticism, traces the stage history of each play, and makes conservative but fresh critical observations, in addition to establishing the texts. _Nero_, which shows the influence of Seneca and the heroic drama, is weak and ill-focused, while _Sophonisba_, just as poorly structured, is more restrained and uses spectacle and characters to better effect. Heroic and Jacobean elements define _Gloriana_. _The Rival Queens_ is saved from failure, despite inept construction and bombast, by its swift-moving action and rhetorical power, and in _Mithridates_ Lee finally combines careful design and poetic beauty, notwithstanding an uneven style and occasional plunges into bathos, in a drama with Fordesque tragic power. Similarly uneven but powerful is _Oedipus_, a blend of Sophocles, Seneca, and Corneille, with Jacobean and heroic elements.

The Massacre of Paris, an effective revenge tragedy, benefits from fast action and sharp dialogue, but _Caesar Borgia_ is simply too bloody to be appealing. There is something of Wycherley in the coarse satire of _The Princess of Cleve_, and it also contains some proto-sentimental ingredients. _Theodosius_ lacks strength but has a charming tenderness about it, and Lucius Junius Brutus, even with its patches of faulty motivation, awkwardness, and verbosity, is Lee's noblest, more virile drama, worthy to rank with All for Love and Venice Preserv'd. Although The Duke of Guise and Constantine have some felicities--some well-drawn characters and moving scenes--both are less than effective plays.

3 YOUNG, KENNETH. John Dryden: A Critical Biography. Longon: Sylvan Press, pp. 132-33.

While The Duke of Guise does equate Guise and Monmouth, it does not identify Henry III of France with Charles II of England.

1955

1 ADSHEAD, HAROLD. "The Mad Playwright of Hatfield." Hertfordshire Countryside 10, no. 37 (Summer):30-31.

Briefly surveys the life and offers derivative critical remarks.

1956

1 AXELRAD, A. JOSÉ. Le Thème de Sophonisbe dans les Principales Tragédies de la Littérature Occidentale (France, Angleterre, Allemagne). Lille: Bibliothèque Universitaire, pp. 54-58.

Discusses Lee's Sophonisba, mainly by summarizing the plot, in the course of surveying dramatic uses of the story from 1500 to 1913.

2 CROSS, GUSTAV. "Ovid Metamorphosed: Marston, Webster, and Nathaniel Lee." N&Q 201:244-45.

Finds an echo of Golding's translation of Ovid in the last act of Oedipus.

3 GRIFFITH, RICHARD RANDOLPH. "Science and Pseudo-Science in the Imagery of John Dryden." Ph.D. dissertation, Ohio State University, 178 pp.

Astrology in The Vindication of The Duke of Guise shows that Dryden and Lee deliberately used misstatement in the play to avoid "the implication" that they meant Henry III to represent Charles II. See Dissertation Abstracts International 17 (1957):1072-73.

4 MANIFOLD, J.S. The Music in English Drama from Shakespeare to Purcell. London: Rockliff, pp. 125, 129.

Theodosius, which contains Purcell's first work for the theater, is the exception among musical dramas, in that it does not employ "violins and continuo."

5 WRIGHT, H. BUNKER. "Prior and Gildon." N&Q 201:18-20.
Gildon's Titus and Teraminta is probably another adaptation of Lee's Lucius Junius Brutus.

1957

1 BARBOUR, FRANCES M. "William Gilmore Simms and the Brutus Legend." Midwest Folklore 7:160.
The Yemassee (1835) borrows an incident from Lee's Lucius Junius Brutus.

2 LEWIS, NANCY ELOISE. "Nathaniel Lee's The Rival Queens: A Study of Dramatic Taste and Technique in the Restoration." Ph.D. dissertation, Ohio State University, 162 pp.
In five chapters, introduces The Rival Queens as a representative Restoration tragedy, shows how it appealed to the audience's established interest in the "Alexander romance" and in the East, discusses its stage history and influence, and makes the following critical assessment after placing it in the contexts of contemporary and previous drama: using the fashionable formulas, Lee presents a tragic hero caught in the snare of his own passions, but because Lee was not able to penetrate below the surface and deal with more universal issues, the result is, at best, good theater, at worst shallow sensationalism.

3 MAGILL, LEWIS M. "Poetic Justice: The Dilemma of the Early Creators of Sentimental Tragedy." RS 25:30-32.
Compares Gildon's The Patriot (1701) with Lee's Lucius Junius Brutus, noting Gildon's simplifying and sentimentalizing of the relationship between Julio (Lee's Titus) and Teraminta.

4 SMITH, JOHN HARRINGTON. "Some Sources of Dryden's Toryism, 1682-1684." HLQ 20:236-42.
Discusses The Duke of Guise, tracing allusions to recent or contemporary political tracts.

1958

1 BURTON, K.M.P. Restoration Literature. London: Hutchinson, pp. 63-64, 86.
Notes Lee's tendency toward spectacle in The Rival Queens and Sophonisba, and cites Mithridates and Theodosius as "pathetic plays" that have dignity but "exploit suffering by dwelling on it." Lee also exploits "romantically pornographic descriptions of the heroine slumbering on a flowery bank in inadequate clothing."

2 NOYES, ROBERT GALE. The Neglected Muse: Restoration and Eighteenth-Century Tragedy in the Novel (1740-1780). Providence, R.I.: Brown University Press, pp. 28-29, 33-43.

Surveys criticism of The Rival Queens and Theodosius, and mentions that in Oedipus "the tones of mad Nat are paramount."

3 WILSON, JOHN HAROLD. All the King's Ladies: Actresses of the Restoration. Chicago: University of Chicago Press, p. 97.
Lee seems to have designed the paired female roles in Nero and The Rival Queens especially for Mistresses Marshall and Boutel.

1959

1 PARK, HUGH WINSTON. "Revenge in Restoration Tragedy." Ph.D. dissertation, University of Utah, 230 pp.
In the Restoration, with the exception of Lee's Caesar Borgia, "revenge as a theme was never permitted to supercede the 'heroic' aspects which made it escapist." See Dissertation Abstracts International 20:1097-98.

2 PETERSON, WILLIAM M. "Cibber's 'The Rival Queans.'" N&Q 204:164-65, 167.
Discusses ways in which Cibber uses "mock-heroic burlesque" to ridicule Lee's bombast.

3 SALMON, J.H.M. The French Religious Wars in English Political Thought. Oxford: Clarendon Press, pp. 140-42.
The Duke of Guise does draw a parallel between the English Exclusionists and the French Holy League, with the Duke of Guise reflecting either on Monmouth or on the late Earl of Shaftesbury. On the other hand, Dryden was right to deny any equation between Henry III of France and England's Charles II.

4 WILSON, JOHN HAROLD, ed. Introduction to Six Restoration Plays. Boston: Houghton Mifflin, p. xiii.
"'Mad' Nat Lee found a vein of emotional excitement in stories taken from classical antiquity, and captured the Town with his wild, ranting tragedy, The Rival Queens."

1960

1 DAICHES, DAVID. A Critical History of English Literature. Vol. 2. New York: Ronald Press, p. 551.
Lee writes undisciplined, verbose plays in which the "swirling images," unlike those in Elizabethan or Jacobean drama, "are not intended to build up a picture of a human situation or to explore human consciousness; they exist in their own right, to represent passion in a general sense."

2 DOBRÉE, BONAMY, ed. Introduction to Five Heroic Plays. London: Oxford University Press, pp. x, xii.

"Once, when a student complained to Quiller-Couch of the rant in Lee, Sir Arthur replied genially, 'Well, I like a good rant sometimes.'" Sophonisba, for instance, is rather a moving play, certainly "more respectable" than Settle's Empress of Morocco.

3 KNIGHT, G. WILSON. "The Plays of Nathaniel Lee." Venture 1:186-96.

Considers Lee psychologically astute and poetically skilled. Reprinted in L.1962.2.

4 McLEOD, A.L. "The Douai MS. of Lee's 'Mithridates.'" N&Q 205:69-70.

It is not a Lee holograph.

1961

1 BALL, ALBERT. "Charles II: Dryden's Christian Hero." MP 59:28-29.

Discusses The Duke of Guise in the context of Dryden's "sustained belief in the holy union of God and king." The play equates Holy League and Covenanters, Henry III and Charles II, the Duke of Guise and the Duke of Monmouth.

2 MOORE, ROBERT ETHERIDGE. Henry Purcell and the Restoration Theatre. Cambridge: Cambridge University Press, pp. 174-77.

Purcell's experience in writing sacred anthems prepared him well for his contributions to Theodosius: the "unadventurous" ritual scene and the songs between acts, the latter being unconnected with the play itself, their pastoralism jarring with its Byzantine atmosphere. The music in Oedipus is briefly discussed.

3 WARD, CHARLES E. The Life of John Dryden. Chapel Hill: University of North Carolina Press, pp. 133-34.

Prostituting their talents to fashionable tastes in spectacle, gore, and melodrama, Dryden and Lee made Oedipus "almost a travesty of Sophoclean tragedy."

1962

1 BIRLEY, ROBERT. "Nathaniel Lee: The Rival Queens." In Sunk without Trace: Some Forgotten Masterpieces Reconsidered. New York: Harcourt, Brace & World, pp. 40-75.

Places the play within several contexts: baroque art, Dryden's concept of characterization, earlier French and English drama, acting traditions, verse forms, and Lee's life and other plays (Brutus is "well worth reading," and Borgia offers a picture of insanity that could be written only by someone "who was on the verge of madness"). In the scene-by-scene analysis that follows, Birley notes a number of flaws: especially the failure to integrate Cassander's murder plot, his love for Roxana, and the rivalry between Lysimachus and Hephestion, into the main action. Other aspects of the play, though, are admirable: the use of Clytus as a kind of chorus, the scene in which Roxana murders Statira, and, in general, Lee's masterful handling of changes in fortune and passionate encounters. Lee understood theatrical effects, and he knew how to design a play on a grand scale.

2 KNIGHT, G. WILSON. The Golden Labyrinth: A Study of British Drama. London: Phoenix House, pp. 157-67.

Lee combines "the mordant judgements of Crowne" with "the dramatic fire of Settle" in plays that exhibit subtleties far "in advance of either": masterful versification, innuendo, evocative occultism, colloquial touches, and acute psychological insights. "His recurring theme is the instability, the wickedness yet pathos of tyranny."

Nero studies "the perverted logic" of self-centered despotism, and contrasts the angelic with the diabolical in human affairs. Sophonisba is a "nearly 'anti-heroic'" play, and The Rival Queens, a remarkable treatment of "the psychology of power," contains in IV.i. the best "scene of its kind in our drama: all humanity is in it." "Tyranny is countered by attempts at self-conquest" in Mithridates. In Theodosius, Lee "is at the heart of post-Christian history" with his contrast between "the old virilities" and "an enervate irresponsibility" allied with the new religion. He makes the point in Lucius Junius Brutus that "a republic is too logical to be safe," and in Constantine, he dramatizes the displacement of pagan virtues by "a new power."

3 PINTO, VIVIAN de SOLA. Enthusiast in Wit: A Portrait of John Wilmot Earl of Rochester 1647-1680. Lincoln: University of Nebraska Press, pp. 232-33.

The portrait of Count Rosidore in The Princess of Cleve involves references to Rochester's works and "is clearly the product of genuine affection and admiration."

4 WAITH, EUGENE M. The Herculean Hero in Marlowe, Chapman, Shakespeare and Dryden. New York: Columbia University Press; London: Chatto & Windus, p. 151.

Lee often depicted heroes being distracted from the pursuit of glory by "one or more enchantresses, and some of his most grandly heroic characters . . . are women: Sophonisba, Roxana, Statira."

1963

1 LOFTIS, JOHN. The Politics of Drama in Augustan England. Oxford: Clarendon Press, pp. 15-18, 23.

Argues that Lee's attitudes changed "from Whig to Tory, from anti-Catholicism to something very like republicanism to royalism." The Massacre of Paris is a "horror play" with tragic power uncommon in works exhibiting "the simplicity, directness, and emphasis of propaganda." Lucius Junius Brutus, a better tragedy than Addison's Cato, "celebrates the rule of law in a mixed government" and makes its hero "the type" of a "stern and selfless patriot." With its explicit parallels between Restoration England and sixteenth-century France, The Duke of Guise is "a blunt propaganda piece," "a dramatic gloss on Absalom and Achitophel." Constantine, too, is written to defend Charles II and the Duke of York.

2 SINGH, SARUP. The Theory of Drama in the Restoration Period. Bombay, Calcutta, Madras, and New Delhi: Orient Longmans, pp. 37, 46-47, 59-60, 85, 101, 229, 286-88.

Like Otway, Lee's personal vision obliterated external considerations such as the dicta of Horace and Aristotle, and the fashionable tastes for the heroic or the sentimental. He shared the morbid agony of Webster and Ford, and his innocent lovers, like Otway's, find themselves incapable of action in a world dominated by cruelty and evil. Sophonisba is marred by faulty motivation and gratuitous spectacle, while The Rival Queens has perhaps too much "of the Jacobean in it" to come across well as heroic tragedy. In The Massacre of Paris, domestic issues begin to weigh more heavily than in previous works, and in The Princess of Cleve, the beauty, artificiality, and cynical values of Restoration comedy succumb to chaos and brutality, to that "shadow" of impending disaster that hangs over Lee's world.

1964

1 KORNINGER, SIEGFRIED. The Restoration Period and the Eighteenth Century 1660-1780. English Literature and Its Background. Vienna and Munich: Österreichischer Bundesverlag, pp. 51-52.

Combining elements of Elizabethan, Jacobean, and heroic drama, Lee creates an unrealistic world of "feverish characters" who speak a declamatory language laced with confusing imagery.

1965

1 KING, BRUCE. "Anti-Whig Satire in The Duke of Guise." ELN 2:190-93.

Suggests the play drew Whig concepts from three possible sources.

2 KIRSCH, ARTHUR C. Dryden's Heroic Drama. Princeton: Princeton University Press, pp. 136-41.

Dryden was deeply influenced by the "anticipations of sentimental drama" in Lee's early works. Both Nero, which owes a great deal to Dryden's early heroic plays, and Gloriana, where "the court of Augustus is thoroughly domesticated," are sentimentally biased; and Sophonisba, its romantic intrigues posited on "the supposition that love is worth more than glory," influenced All for Love, as did The Rival Queens, which epitomizes the characters and themes of Lee's previous dramas.

3 PETERSON, WILLIAM M., ed. Introduction to The Rival Queans, With the Humours of Alexander the Great (1729), by Colley Cibber. Painesville, Ohio: Lake Erie College Press, pp. xii-xxii.

Usefully surveys the eighteenth-century reputation of Lee's The Rival Queens.

4 RIGHTER, ANNE. "Heroic Tragedy." In Restoration Theatre. Edited by John Russell Brown and Bernard Harris. New York: St. Martin's Press, pp. 144, 146.

Mentions whale imagery in Sophonisba and notes Lee's Websterian obsession with death.

5 ROPER, ALAN. Dryden's Poetic Kingdoms. London: Routlege & Kegan Paul, p. 29.

Observes the topicality of The Duke of Guise and its providential view of history.

6 THOMPSON, FRANCES DIANE. "Senecan Elements in the Plays of Nathaniel Lee." Master's thesis, University of Tennessee, 67 pp.

After a study of plots, stage devices, characters, and diction, concludes that from Seneca Lee derives the revenge motif, the habit of staging bloodshed and the supernatural, the stress on villain-heroes, and some of the set speeches in his plays. Special emphasis is given to Lee's part of Oedipus.

7 TUCKER, YVONNE YAW. "The Villains and Heroes of Nathaniel Lee: A Study in Dramatic Characterization." Ph.D. dissertation, Harvard University, 123 pp.

Categorizes the main characters (for example, "Vicious Villains," "Lustful Villains," "Ethical Heroes"), discusses theories of characterization, and critically analyzes each main character in the plays. Lee's villains become more plausible as his artistry matures, and he is unusual in showing sympathy for lustful villains and in accepting sex as a legitimate ingredient of love. Though his characters tend to be flat and mechanical, he did observe human nature honestly and, at times, he "can be a clever draftsman."

8 WILSON, JOHN HAROLD. A Preface to Restoration Drama. Boston: Houghton Mifflin, pp. 58, 64-65, 86-89.

Classifies Nero, Caesar Borgia, and The Massacre of Paris as "villain tragedies," adding very brief remarks about each. The Rival Queens is "an excellent blank verse tragedy" about Alexander's self-destruction, and it shows Lee at his typical best: his characters full of energy and emotional intensity; his imagery cosmic in scope, matching the largeness of his concepts; and his poetry rhapsodic. Lee had a "comprehensive soul."

9 ZEBOUNI, SELMA ASSIR. Dryden: A Study in Heroic Characterization. Baton Rouge: Louisiana State University Press, pp. 66-67.

Tiresias, of Oedipus, expresses the neoclassical interpretation of fate: the gods are indeed just, though they operate from a realm beyond our rational abilities to comprehend their justice.

1966

1 CUNNINGHAM, JOHN E. Restoration Drama. London: Evans Brothers, p. 152.

With his tormented rants, "horrific images," and fusion of late Jacobean tragedy with "gobbets of the classics," Lee wrote "strange stuff, easy to mock, difficult to read, impossible now to act."

2 KALLICH, MARTIN. "Oedipus: From Man to Archetype." CLS 3: 36-37.

Discusses the Dryden-Lee Oedipus in light of the versions by Sophocles, Voltaire, Gide, and Cocteau, finding that the Englishmen offer "an unusual sentimental reinterpretation of the classic myth." They make sexual love the central theme, which follows Dryden's latest theoretical defense of love as a tragic motif, and they promote Divine Right, enforce providential justice, and criticize the clergy. On the whole, however, the English Oedipus is noisy, sensational, and lacking in profundity.

3 KING, BRUCE. Dryden's Major Plays. New York: Barnes & Noble, p. 13.

Despite the "dry savage ironies" of its almost Jonsonian kind of humor, The Duke of Guise "is not of comparable quality to any of the heroic plays."

4 SORELIUS, GUNNAR. 'The Giant Race Before the Flood': Pre-Restoration Drama on the Stage and in the Criticism of the Restoration. Uppsala: Almqvist & Wiksells, pp. 123, 130.

Notes the influences of Seneca, Shakespeare, Corneille, and Rymer on Oedipus; of Shakespeare and Marston on Sophonisba; and of Shakespeare and Fletcher on Mithridates.

1967

1 LOFTIS, JOHN, ed. Introduction to Lucius Junius Brutus. Regents Restoration Drama Series. Lincoln: University of Nebraska Press, pp. xi-xxiv.

Covers the texts, stage history, sources and influences, and considers the play implicitly "a statement of the Whig constitutional position during the Exclusion controversy." With its emotional and intellectual range, structural coherence, and controlled style, Brutus is "one of the most satisfactory renderings of a Roman myth turned to English uses." Vinditius suggests Titus Oates; Brutus and the somewhat mawkish Titus divide between them the traditional traits of a tragic hero; and Brutus and Tiberius convey the play's anti-Catholic bias. In The Duke of Guise and Constantine, Lee reverses the political allegiance sustained in Brutus.

2 LOVE, H.H.R. Review of The Regents Restoration Drama Series. AUMLA 27:107.

Names The Massacre of Paris as one of the Restoration plays "which draw most rewardingly on the Jacobean and Caroline heritage."

3 ROTHSTEIN, ERIC. Restoration Tragedy: Form and the Process of Change. Madison, Milwaukee, and London: University of Wisconsin Press, pp. 79-88, 91-96, 109, 166.

In the "denatured rhymed" tragedies of Nero, Sophonisba, and Gloriana, Lee helped establish the pattern for unrhymed tragedies to come, and in Lucius Junius Brutus, he created one of the most interesting plays in this latter mode. To the heroic formula Nero adds the opposition between love and glory, but in Sophonisba love triumphs. Taking a hint from the unheroic Britannicus (Nero), Lee splits the hero of Sophonisba into three personalities, each mirroring the other two; one of these, Massinissa, who unites heroism with traits usually linked with the "friend" and who commits suicide at the end, is "totally novel in the heroic play." Heroic self-aggrandizement is depreciated in this work; public and private realms fail to harmonize; innocence and dream upstage prowess, empire, and fact; and language "begins to express, not a state of being, but a process of subjective perception."

In Lucius Junius Brutus, love, honor, and politics all seem external, while the emphasis falls on the pathos of characters' responses. "As the cause of the catastrophe, [Whiggery] is implicated along with all other political systems." Language now "clings to the connotative world in the minds of the audience rather than to the created world of the drama," and the verse is "highly patterned . . . controlled and metaphorical . . . its contrast and balance are verbal and syntactic, not prosodic."

4 ZIMMERMAN, FRANKLIN B. Henry Purcell 1659-1695: His Life and Times. London, Melbourne, and Toronto: Macmillan; New York: St. Martin's, pp. 73, 131, 219.

Mentions the music in Oedipus, suggests that the musical parts of Theodosius may not have been Purcell's first contributions to the theater, and notes that the "mad song" in Sophonisba, appearing in print "at a suspiciously late date," exhibits Purcell's mature style.

1968

1 HINNANT, CHARLES H. "The Background of the Early Version of Dryden's The Duke of Guise." ELN 6:102-06.

Finds "circumstantial evidence" to support Dryden's claim that he began Guise in 1660 with the intention of "identifying the nonconformists . . . with the Covenanters of 1641" and of "associating both with the Holy League in France," thereby discrediting all dissenters "as rebellious and fanatical." Astraea Redux shows that he perceived this parallel as early as 1660.

2 HUNEYCUTT, MELICENT. "The Changing Concept of the Ideal Statesman as Reflected in English Verse Drama during the Reign of Charles II: 1660-1685." Ph.D. dissertation, University of North Carolina.

In keeping with the gradual acceptance of Charles II by Englishmen, Sophonisba initiated the trend in drama of presenting statesmen as "cooler, more reasonable, and more responsible." The trend continued during the early eighties as a response to factionalism; Marcian, of Theodosius, combines "practicality with forthright integrity," and the titular hero of Lucius Junius Brutus shows a pragmatic interest in "balanced trade and . . . manufacturing." See Dissertation Abstracts International 30 (1969):685A-686A.

1969

1 HUNT, RUSSELL ARTHUR. "Nathaniel Lee: A Critical Study." Ph.D. dissertation, Northwestern University, 364 pp.

Stressing Lee's artistry, and distinguishing it from that of other dramatists of the day, discusses the plays within political and dramatic contexts. Lee moves from heroic drama to a drama more particularly focused on contemporary problems, and his best works are Mithridates, The Massacre of Paris, and Lucius Junius Brutus. See Dissertation Abstracts International 30 (1970):2970A-2971A.

2 SUTHERLAND, JAMES. English Literature of the Late Seventeenth Century. New York and Oxford: Oxford University Press, pp. 67-68, 71-75, 143-44.

Instead of letting "the situation tell on its own merits," Lee spoiled his plays with too much spectacle and rhetoric, especially Nero and Oedipus. Sophonisba and The Rival Queens, however, have "well-defined characters," "much fine rhetoric," powerful sensuousness, and effective mad scenes; and Caesar Borgia, despite its tedious horrors, presents an interestingly complex protagonist. If The Duke of Guise is shackled by its historical parallel, Lucius Junius Brutus succeeds in becoming a historical play with a "genuinely tragic argument," instructive contemporary relevance, and a "new weight of thought." Similarly thoughtful and rhetorically restrained, Theodosius is an emotional play with some Elizabethan echoes and "theatrical poetry." The Princess of Cleve is a cynical study of the "moral bankruptcy" of the times, as embodied in Nemours/Rochester. With his "natural extravagance," Lee could fly high, but he often descended disastrously.

1970

1 LOFTIS, JOHN. "Nathaniel Lee's 'Nit' and Mr. Vernier's 'Pick.'" N&Q 215:451-52.

Defends himself, as editor of Lucius Junius Brutus, along with John Harold Wilson, as editor of Crowne's City Politiques, and the Regents Restoration Drama Series generally, against Vernier's criticism (L.1970.3).

2 SKRINE, PETER N. "Blood, Bombast, and Deaf Gods: The Tragedies of Lee and Lohenstein." GL&L, n.s. 24:14-30.

More theatrical and less intellectual than Lohenstein, Lee wrote plays that were "devoid of all illusion" and seemed to reject divine intervention. Nero is a disjointed, hastily composed, hyperbolical "study of power and its effect on the individual"; like Caesar Borgia, it shows self-love leading to vice and contains a "veiled attack on contemporary society." Both Lee and Lohenstein created "highly-ornate baroque mirrors" of life, as in their different versions of the Sophonisba story. Unable to cope even imaginatively with the ambiguities of his world, Lee went insane.

3 VERNIER, C.P. "Footnotes to 'Lucius Junius Brutus' and 'City Politiques.'" N&Q 215:219-22.

Argues that the explanatory notes in the Regents editions by John Loftis (L.1967.1) and John Harold Wilson (City Politiques 1967) are sometimes "superfluous," "erroneous," or "inexplicable," and are "often entirely absent when they are most needed." See the reply by Loftis (L.1970.1).

4 _____. "Reply to Professor Loftis." N&Q 215:452-53.

Maintains his former position (L.1970.3).

5 VERNON, P.F., ed. Introduction to The Rival Queens. Regents Restoration Drama Series. Lincoln: University of Nebraska Press, pp. xiii-xxvii.

Discusses the texts, stage history, sources, influences, and reputation of the play, its initiation of the dramatic vogue for contrasting female characters, its contribution to the rise of pathetic drama, its contemporary relevance (a warning to Charles II and his mistresses, a commentary on marriage and domestic relations), and its artistic strengths and weaknesses. Although the episodes involving Parisatis and Lysimachus are weak, in general the play effectively explores "the limits of authority" through Alexander's megalomania and withdrawal from reality, and the visual dimension successfully reinforces a structure based on "four parallel forms of discontent." In most instances Lee's rant and extravagant imagery are meant to imply criticism of the speaker, but occasionally he seems to think (wrongly) that grand words will of themselves generate awe. His scenes of pathos have retained their appeal longer than have the more declamatory ones. No modern dramatic genre, except possibly opera, can recapture the "range of gestures and vocal inflexions, for which Lee's text provides."

1971

1 BARNARD, JOHN. "Drama from the Restoration till 1710." In English Drama to 1710. Edited by Christopher Ricks. London: Sphere Books, p. 378.

Full of "morbidity and disillusion," Lee's plays are "marked by a certain poetic ability, and an imagery which equals the violence of the action"; yet too often "intended sublimity" comes across "as turgid rant."

2 FORRESTER, KENT ALLEN. "Supernaturalism in Restoration Drama." Ph.D. dissertation, University of Utah, 191 pp.

Discusses the use of supernatural vehicles for political commentary in The Duke of Guise. See Dissertation Abstracts International 32:1469A.

3 WAITH, EUGENE M. Ideas of Greatness: Heroic Drama in England. New York: Barnes & Noble, pp. 236-42.

Lee's plays are "less schematic and less concerned with fine distinctions" than Dryden's; they are "lyrical" celebrations of extreme emotion, in which sound and spectacle often triumph over sense. In Nero the central character defines his own villainy through rant and immoral acts. The floridly staged Sophonisba evokes a mixture of pity and admiration through Lee's skillful blend into one character of the Sophonisbas portrayed by Marston, Mairet, and Corneille. The scenes of misunderstanding between Massinissa and Sophonisba are "more psychologically persuasive" than Dryden's equivalent scenes, and the closing episode recalls the double suicide of Antony and Cleopatra. The Hannibal-Rosalinda-Massina plot is "rousing." In The Rival Queens, Alexander's problems seem "tame" in comparison with the conflict between the two ladies; the play has several effective scenes.

1972

1 HIRT, A. "A Question of Excess: Neo-Classical Adaptations of Greek Tragedy." Costerus 3:56, 61-65, 67, 70.

Contrasts the Dryden-Lee Oedipus with other versions, especially those by Sophocles, Seneca, and Corneille. Though the English rendering observes the unities, it lacks classical conciseness. The addition of a subplot, the appearance of Laius' ghost, and the transformation of Creon into an Elizabethan villain--such innovations lessen the suspense, the sober tone, and the stark nature of Greek tragedy. The ghost of Hamlet's father is recalled in the Dryden-Lee ghost, which is less declamatory than Seneca's, more explicit than Corneille's; Lady Macbeth's sleepwalking seems to have suggested the infernal dream of Oedipus; and the closing admonition of Tiresias reminds one of Fortinbras at the end of Hamlet. Instead of a loyal chorus, as in Sophocles, Dryden and Lee use a hostile mob and symbolic prodigies; and, like Corneille, they do not have Oedipus blind himself with Jocasta's brooch, though the English version ends more bloodily and negatively than Corneille's. Significantly, Dryden and Lee dramatize the triumph of conjugal love over the repelling knowledge of incest.

2 JORDAN, ROBERT. "The Extravagant Rake in Restoration Comedy." In Restoration Literature: Critical Approaches. Edited by Harold Love. London: Methuen, p. 73.

The Princess of Cleve makes "the best generalized statement of the spirit in which" the extravagant rake's "life was pursued.

3 LOFTIS, JOHN. "The Limits of Historical Veracity in Neoclassical Drama." In England in the Restoration and Early Eighteenth Century: Essays on Culture and Society. Edited by H.T. Swedenberg, Jr. Berkeley, Los Angeles, and London: University of California Press, pp. 40-41.

Lucius Junius Brutus, one of the best Restoration tragedies, cautions against Tarquinian despotism and, in the titular character, celebrates "the rule of law." The play is a "Whig commentary" deriving its theme from the Popish Plot or its implications.

4 PARSONS, PHILIP. "Restoration Tragedy as Total Theatre." In Restoration Literature: Critical Approaches. Edited by Harold Love. London: Methuen, pp. 27-28, 32-33, 59-60.

"In his command of the full resources of the baroque Restoration stage, Lee is the outstanding creative figure." In Sophonisba, he uses scenic effects to presage Hannibal's overthrow and "interweaves several plots," keeping each fairly simple and presenting it "as a sequence of dramatic events" (unlike Dryden, who tends to narrate through the dialogue). The Rival Queens opens with a symbolic enactment of "the situation in both subplot and main plot" and shows the feast "as ironic backdrop for Alexander's petulance and vanity." In Mithridates, a false portent in I.i. suggests that "metaphysical and moral reality" may be "priestly hocus pocus" and foreshadows the king's discovery of his own moral nature. While the well-known opening scene in Theodosius actually is less emblematic of theme than it could have been, the three clusters of sacrificial imagery in Lucius Junius Brutus strikingly exemplify Lee's masterful blend of theater and poetry. The kissing of the bloody dagger is meaningfully juxtaposed to the diabolical blood ritual and to the final sacrifice of Brutus' sons. "Indeed, overtones of Christian blood sacrifice haunt the whole play."

5 SELDEN, R. "Rochester, Lee and Juvenal." N&Q 217:27.

"Rochester's comic wish to send Nathaniel Lee to Westminster School to have some ancient history beaten into him" alludes to "Juvenal's portrait of Hannibal in the tenth satire" and recognizes that "Lee's Hannibal is indebted to Juvenal's." Possibly knowing that Busby had expurgated Juvenal in his Juvenalis et Persit Satirae (1656), Rochester replaces "the sufferings . . . to be endured by Hannibal at the hands of future school boys with" Lee's chastisement by Busby.

6 VIETH, DAVID M. Introduction to All for Love. Regents Restoration Drama Series. Lincoln: University of Nebraska Press, pp. xxiii-xxv.

Argues that The Rival Queens "should be considered a further basis of 'imitation' in All for Love." Some actors and actresses "created corresponding roles in the two plays"; both plays present a "clash of cultures"; and both are structurally similar to Aureng-Zebe. Homosexuality is implied between Alexander and Hephestion as between Antony and Dolabella.

1973

1 BACHORIK, LAWRENCE L. "The Duke of Guise and Dryden's Vindication: A New Consideration." ELN 10:208-12.

Dryden's disclaimer in the Vindication is "less than sincere," for both he and Lee wrote politically sensitive plays just before collaborating on Guise, and "nearly every principal character" in the play corresponds to someone involved in the Exclusion Crisis. Thus, the play must have been intended "both to expose the factionalism of the Whigs and to defend the process of lawful succession."

2 FISKE, ROGER. English Theatre Music in the Eighteenth Century. London, New York, and Toronto: Oxford University Press, pp. 10, 321.

Mentions Purcell's music for The Rival Queens (1701?) and notes that J.A. Fisher's The Court of Alexander, with libretto by G.A. Stevens, is not a burlesque of Lee's play.

3 HINNANT, CHARLES H. "Comment and Controversy." ELN 10: 224-25.

Responds to Bachorik (L.1973.1) by making two points: (1) Hinnant's earlier ELN article (L.1968.1) "was concerned with the intellectual continuity of Dryden's political outlook," not with "the old charges of contemporary parallels in the text of The Duke of Guise." (2) By becoming too selective in the passages he cites, Bachorik misreads the Vindication.

4 MYERS, WILLIAM. Dryden. London: Hutchinson, pp. 17-18, 39-40, 100, 131.

Although the Vindication is rather effective, The Duke of Guise itself "is intellectually simplistic, psychologically crude, and metrically dead." Grillon resembles General Monck, whose simplicity made him, in Dryden's view, "the perfect instrument of Providence." Dryden and Lee's new "honesty" in juxtaposing faith in Providence with unjust events begins with Oedipus, a psychologically profound drama.

5 RANGNO, MELANIE COLLINS. "Nathaniel Lee's Plays of the Exclusion Crisis." Ph.D. dissertation, University of California at Los Angeles, 265 pp.

Shows how the political context from 1678 to 1683 is dealt with in The Massacre of Paris, Caesar Borgia, The Duke of Guise, and Constantine, with special attention to the uses of analogy, allusion, and politically charged history. An attempt is made to explain the "relative success" of Massacre and the "comparative failure" of Constantine.

6 VERDURMEN, JOHN PETER. "Lee, Dryden and the Restoration Tragedy of Concernment." Ph.D. dissertation, Stanford University, 320 pp.

Discusses the links between Dryden and Lee, showing that while Lee began by adapting Dryden's methods, he later influenced Dryden and became "instrumental in establishing the tragedy of concernment." Previous critics have misunderstood Lee's artistry his "scenic" plots, "cause-and-effect narrative" design, types of characters, and central themes. Lucius Junius Brutus, his best work, subtly probes the conflict between public and private life; and both Oedipus and The Duke of Guise are grounded in Lee's, not Dryden's, style. See Dissertation Abstracts International 33:6887A-6888A.

1975

1 MARSHALL, GEOFFREY. Restoration Serious Drama. Norman: University of Oklahoma Press, pp. 50, 53, 97-99, 101-2, 107, 124, 155-60, 163-70, 172-77, 217-18.

Lucius Junius Brutus epitomizes narrative techniques used in Restoration serious plays: the verbal representation of a scene already dramatized, the description of an imagined scene in order to move emotions, affective narration used as an alternative to verisimilar action, and self-conscious dialogue. Some of these elements are also found in Sophonisba and The Rival Queens. Sophonisba is diagrammed to show its "geometry," and its sentimental effects are analyzed.

Like most of his fellow dramatists, Lee rarely let actions speak for words, yet his diction is basically "substantive" and does not change as speakers or times or places change. His language communicates through its sensuousness and figurativeness, and he can sometimes effectively employ abstractions and grand generalizations, too. Often in his works, as in Lucius Junius Brutus, role becomes metaphor. In Oedipus, Creon's physical handicap mirrors his mind. In The Duke of Guise, outward appearance deceives, for the religious hypocrites are aided by the devil. Lee illustrates the conflict between inherited rhetoric and the lyric impulse in Restoration drama, where the characters tend to find analogues for their feelings instead of expressing them directly.

2 VIETH, DAVID M. "Psychological Myth as Tragedy: Nathaniel Lee's Lucius Junius Brutus." HLQ 39:57-76.

Among the very best Restoration tragedies, Lucius Junius Brutus defies Aristotelian theory, resists identification as a Whig manifesto, and succeeds despite its depiction of unmotivated actions. Its characters may be seen as "semi-symbolic projections of components in a unitary psychological situation" that emerges from "the basic myth" of the "son-father relationship . . . under the strain of rapid and . . . inevitable social change." Titus is "a kind of Jamesian 'center of consciousness.'" He and Tiberius, as masochist and sadist, represent opposite aspects of the generation gap. Because of his father's "overwhelming virtue," Titus feels unworthy to continue the generational cycle with Teraminta, who is "a projection" of his "superheated imagination." Their relationship is paralleled and illuminated by the rape and suicide of Lucrece. Brutus himself, meanwhile, must deal with "conflicting claims to absoluteness."

Like Shakespeare in Romeo and Juliet, Lee, who drew upon Otway's Caius Marius, is dramatizing the tragic reality that "any affirmation of static, permanent values is inseparably bound up with an experience of loss." Lucius Junius Brutus shows such loss "in the special context of the generational cycle." Vieth reinforces the analysis by exploring Lee's use of the imagery of body parts, physical mutilation, and water.

1976

1 BRUNKHORST, MARTIN. "Aspekte der 'Oedipus'-Adaption bei Dryden und Lee." GRM, n.s. 26:386-406.

Analyzes how Lee and Dryden blended their sources in order to make their version of the story appealing to Restoration audiences. In a richer and more dynamic plot than the one in Sophocles, Seneca, or Corneille, the English collaborators present Oedipus and Jocasta as passionate lovers, and glorify royal supremacy.

2 HUME, ROBERT D. The Development of English Drama in the Late Seventeenth Century. Oxford: Clarendon Press, pp. 198, 200-201, 204, 210, 221, 223-24, 289, 313-14, 316-17, 323-25, 344, 348-49, 355-57, 362, 401-2.

Lee combines spectacular staging with heroic elevation, intense emotion, exaggerated language, and abnormal psychology. His distinctive trait is "the centrality of violent emotion and its expression in streams of words forced past the limits of sense."

Nero is a villain-horror play, full of blood, supernaturalism, and madness, and it does not necessarily comment on Carolean courtly license. In Sophonisba, likewise, political implications are lost in "spectacle, fancy language, and overheated emotion"; artistically, it suffers from "slovenly construction and vague motivation." Although Gloriana is better designed, it is spoiled by rant and conventionality. The Rival Queens is Lee's first really successful application of heroics, spectacle, love, and honor to "a genuine tragedy of character," even though it lacks sustained focus. Capitalizing on the novel use of blank verse in The Rival Queens, Mithridates is impressive sounding and is well plotted, but it lacks artistic restraint. Once we move beyond classical expectations, Oedipus can be seen as interestingly plotted and gripping, a tragedy of concernment rather than one of pity and fear. The Massacre of Paris is a lurid, gory, and bathetic piece of "Popish Plot agit-prop," and Caesar Borgia, just as bloody, is a villain-horror play distinguished by complex characterization.

If the noble and pathetic Theodosius is only vaguely political, and nonpartisan, Lucius Junius Brutus is "a fiercely ideological play." It is a fine early example of the heroic-stoic mode, far superior to Addison's Cato. The Princess of Cleve, resembling Otway's bitter comedies, is "a great play" that savagely and sardonically attacks both romantic sentiment (especially as used in heroic drama) and nasty libertinism (especially as used in sex comedy), with a specific thrust at the Earl of Rochester. Lee ended his career with a "rather astonishing political about turn" in The Duke of Guise, "a Tory fable," and Constantine, which deserved extinction because of its sloppy construction and erratic motivation.

3 _____. "The Satiric Design of Nat. Lee's The Princess of Cleve." JEGP 75:117-38.

Suggests a date of "spring or summer . . . 1681" for the composition of Cleve and develops through analysis the points made about the play in The Development of English Drama in the Late Seventeenth Century (L.1976.2), pp. 355-57.

4 LOFTIS, JOHN. "The Social and Literary Context." In The Revels History of Drama in English, Vol. V: 1660-1750. Edited by Loftis, Richard Southern, Marion Jones, and A.H. Scouten. London: Methuen, pp. 39, 67.

Sees Lucius Junius Brutus as a Whig caution against royal tyranny and calls The Princess of Cleve, with its "broadening of the moral and emotional range," an early instance of sentimentalism.

5 SCOUTEN, A.H. "Plays and Playwrights." In The Revels History of Drama in English, Vol. V: 1660-1750. Edited by John Loftis, Richard Southern, Marion Jones, and A.H. Scouten. London: Methuen, pp. 269-72.

Although Lee did not learn to control levels of intensity in his tragedies until late in his career, he led the other dramatists in moving from rhyming couplets to blank verse, and in Theodosius he was one of the first to employ "weak, unstable and indecisive characters." Nero depends on Elizabethan models, and Sophonisba and Gloriana are notable for touches of pathos. The Rival Queens explores Alexander's personality, not his women or his death; it is about the conflicts caused by friction between his public and private affairs.

The part of Semandra in Mithridates shows Lee moving toward she-tragedy, as does the less pathetic role of Pulcheria in Theodosius. Caesar Borgia should be seen not as "crude, anti-Catholic propaganda" but as a "psychological examination of both Machiavel and Borgia," and Lucius Junius Brutus is less about politics than about passions overruling duty and obedience. It also reveals that Lee was learning to handle comic relief. To collaborate on The Duke of Guise, he had to abandon his own political views. Lee may have overdone his imagery at times, but he wrote masterful poetry in an impressive variety of styles and forms.

1977

1 ARMISTEAD, J.M. "Lee, Renaissance Conventions, and the Psychology of Providence: The Design of Caesar Borgia." ELWIU 4:159-73.

In this play, Lee "explores psychological relationships that are fundamentally relevant to the era of the Popish Plot and Exclusion Crisis. He shows the relationships and the actions they generate developing within an aesthetic environment of highly charged traditional symbols, symbols that connect psychology and behavior to political theory, morality, and religion." The result is "a symbolic paradigm showing how Providence unfolds implications inherent in the minds and hearts of the sorts which flourish in all eras of intense political intrigue."

2 _____. "Nathaniel Lee and Family: The Will of Richard Lee, D.D." N&Q 222:130-31.
The will identifies Nathaniel as the second, not the third, son, and it suggests that he was not out of favor at home, despite his having been committed to Bedlam for four years.

3 BROWN, CALVIN S. "Colonel Falkner as General Reader: The White Rose of Memphis." MissQ 30:587-88.
Notes a misquotation of The Rival Queens, IV.421, and a misattribution of the line to Byron.

4 CARVER, LARRY. "The Restoration Poets and Their Father King." HLQ 40:341.
By calling Brutus "the Father of His Country" in Lucius Junius Brutus, Lee was ironically showing that this title "connoted nothing of paternal, hereditary, or imperial government" but rather carried its original reference to "one who had freed his country from tyranny."

5 HUME, ROBERT D. "Marital Discord in English Comedy from Dryden to Fielding." MP 74:256.
In the "complex" Princess of Cleve, the Prince's death is ringed with "ironic juxtapositions which drastically undermine its heroic-romantic legitimacy."

6 _____. "The Myth of the Rake in 'Restoration' Comedy." SLitI 10, no. 1:37-38, 46-47.
The Princess of Cleve "travesties" its "précieuse source" and, through Nemours, a "genuine" libertine, systematically debunks "both Rochester in life and the libertine in comedy."

7 KASTAN, DAVID SCOTT. "Nero and the Politics of Nathaniel Lee." PLL 13:125-35.
Showing that Lee was politically sensitive before 1678, Nero is founded on "the controversies regarding sovereignty that the failure of the Restoration settlement had engendered." "Britannicus suffers, as Britain herself suffers in 1674," and the play ends pessimistically as a warning to Charles II. Lee is advancing "a limited and pragmatic conception" of monarchy.

8 PRICE, CURTIS A. "'. . . to make amends for One ill Dance': Conventions for Dancing in Restoration Plays." Dance Research Journal 10, no. 1 (1977-78):2.
Analyzes the shepherds' singing and dancing in Act V of The Duke of Guise, and notes how the play employs music "to signal death with powerful dramatic effect."

9 SUTHERLAND, JAMES, ed. General Introduction and headnote to Lucius Junius Brutus. In Restoration Tragedies. London, Oxford, and New York: Oxford University Press, pp. x-xi, 99-100.

Brutus is an "anti-monarchical" play that focuses on the inner strife of Titus. "In some ways Lee's finest work," it is a more disciplined and intellectually weighty composition than he usually managed.

10 WIKANDER, MATTHEW. "Thomas Otway's Venice Preserv'd as Tory Drama." Polit. A Journal for Literature and Politics 1, no. 1:78-79, 83, 85.

Treats the Lee of 1679-81 as a Whig whose plays reflect pressure from the Tory ascendancy. Thus, The Massacre of Paris substitutes "strident expressions of anti-Catholicism" for what might have become strong Whig sentiments, and although Lucius Junius Brutus "did endorse a change of government," its anti-monarchist ideas are softened by their association with "a benevolent despot without reference to notions of 'mixed government' so important to Whig thought." The epilogue to Caesar Borgia shows that Lee felt the Tories inhibited full success of the play in performance. In 1682 "Lee came to Toryism as one who had finally seen the light."

11 WYKES, DAVID. A Preface to Dryden. New York and London: Longman, pp. 170-73.

Sees Oedipus as "a bloody melodrama, very unclassical."

12 YOTS, MICHAEL. "Dryden's All for Love on the Restoration Stage." RECTR 16, no. 1:6.

Presents evidence to support the assertion that All for Love was directly influenced by The Rival Queens. The plays have similar plot structures, focus on the rivalry of two women, and use the same actors for equivalent roles.

1978

1 ARMISTEAD, J.M. "Hero as Endangered Species: Structure and Idea in Lee's Sophonisba." DUJ 71:35-43.

Lee "employs heroic conventions to study heroism itself in a context that is relevant to contemporary political life." The Hannibal-Rosalinda plot and the Massinissa-Sophonisba plot act out "the struggle of alternative kinds of heroism and love to survive" the development "of a new socio-political order," an order driven forward by Providence through the agency of Scipio, a new kind of hero.

2 LOVE, HAROLD, and ROSALEEN LOVE. "A Cartesian Allusion in Dryden and Lee's 'Oedipus.'" N&Q 223:35-37.

The opening lines seem derived from Descartes's cosmology as enunciated in the third and fourth books of Principia

Philosophiae (1644), in which case the allusion "supports Dryden's authorship of Act I."

3 LOVE, HAROLD. "Dryden's 'Unideal Vacancy.'" ECS 12:78-80, 89.
Analyzes a passage from Act I of Oedipus, showing how it develops Renaissance imagery and applying some of the implications to Lee. "Indeed, when Lee has his Nero sever the nexus of cause and effect with temporal succession by announcing 'I am a God; my self I Canonize,' he probably intended a burlesque of a vulgar Cartesianism which maintained that one had to think in order to be, without apparently recognizing a prior need to be in order to think."

4 McFADDEN, GEORGE. Dryden the Public Writer 1660-1685. Princeton: Princeton University Press, pp. 208-22.
Although the politically significant parts of Oedipus are Dryden's, the play's stage success was "probably owing to Lee in large measure."

5 VIETH, DAVID M. "Nathaniel Lee's The Rival Queens and the Psychology of Assassination." Restoration 2, no. 2:10-13.
Explores the "geometry of Lee's structure" which, under the influence of Dryden's Aureng-Zebe, "centers upon one overwhelming protagonist . . . to whom the lesser characters . . . relate more directly than they do to each other." This structure portrays "the social psychology of assassination" and involves providential implications.

6 WEINBROT, HOWARD D. Augustus Caesar in 'Augustan' England: The Decline of a Classical Norm. Princeton: Princeton University Press, pp. 72-73.
Gloriana, an "unintentionally comic masterpiece," melodramatically exploited "long-standing anger" at Augustus for his banishment of Ovid and his complicity in Cicero's death.

1979

1 ARMISTEAD, J.M. Nathaniel Lee. Twayne Series. Boston: G.K. Hall, 220 pp.
Updates the biography, surveys the Restoration milieu, analyzes each play in light of its sources and contemporary contexts, generalizes about Lee's artistry, closes with a genealogy chart and lengthy bibliography. Lee's plays are lyrical because their plots are emotionally, not intellectually, motivated, and because their figurative content expresses the author's, not his characters', personal explication of what is happening. While maintaining throughout his works essentially the same definition of effective sovereignty, Lee gradually develops a vision of cosmic order that modulates into confidence in providential design.

The plays fall into two cycles, each beginning with works in which conflicting forces are divided between two or more distinct personalities, each ending with works in which the discordant energies function as aspects of a single, tortured mind, while the other characters gain identity as correlatives to these mental conflicts. In moving from Nero to Mithridates, Lee explores increasingly sophisticated rhythms of psychological disintegration encouraged by demonic forces and exfoliating in social chaos and destruction; he grows in confidence that specific cases of such disorder and evil operate as aspects of a more general ecology of sociopolitical relations.

In the last six plays, constituting a formally and thematically more complex cycle, the religious scaffolding is overtly Christian (except for in Brutus), the infernal powers become more clearly defined, the hand of Providence comes into better focus, and the references to contemporary life become more specific. More and more the patterns of depravity and madness are seen as episodes in a providential history whose greater contours can only be pointed to by prodigies and the vocabulary of devil possession. But while this metaphysical confidence is conveyed through increasingly spectacular staging, accompanied by highly figurative, allusive language, Lee's characters continue to wrestle with basically the same egocentric lusts that plagued their counterparts in earlier works.

2 _____. "Occultism in Restoration Drama: Motives for Revaluation." MLS 9, no. 3:60-67.

Against an historical sketch of occultism in English life and letters, surveys the supernatural elements in The Princess of Cleve, Caesar Borgia, Nero, The Rival Queens, Mithridates, Lucius Junius Brutus, and Constantine. "Lee . . . saw and expressed the universe as a religious register, as responsive to God's influence and judgments, sometimes directly, more usually indirectly through the human psyche. . . . The occult . . . was a psycho-moral phenomenon to Lee, though its ramifications were still socio-political and, ultimately, metaphysical."

3 _____. "The Tragicomic Design of Lucius Junius Brutus: Madness as Providential Therapy." PLL 15:38-51.

Sees the play not as Whig propaganda but as a study of "republican hamartia" showing "the bittersweet victory of Brutus over Tarquin and Tiberius, superhuman law over savage prerogative," with the "desirable middle term, represented partially in the wedding of Titus and Teraminta, . . . lost in the tempestuous meeting of extremes." Sources, imagery, and dramatic structure are emphasized.

4 HOLLAND, PETER. The Ornament of Action: Text and Performance in Restoration Comedy. Cambridge, London, New York, and Melbourne: Cambridge University Press, pp. 146-47, 184.

"The pattern of aggressive rake and honourable wife naturally moved towards tragedy," as illustrated in Betterton's playing of Nemours (The Princess of Cleve) and Lovemore (Southerne's Wives Excuse) to Mrs. Barry's Princess of Cleve and Mrs. Friendall (Wives Excuse). Mrs. Barry's "nobility" as the Princess tended to stress "by contrast the uncontrolled sexuality of Nemours" as embodied by Betterton. Through their contrasting roles as Poppea and Cyara (Nero), Roxana and Statira (The Rival Queens), Mrs. Marshall and Mrs. Boutell came to symbolize "good and evil, light and dark--in hair as well as morality."

5 MILLER, RACHEL A. "Political Satire in the Malicorne-Melanax Scenes of The Duke of Guise." ELN 16:212-18.

Discusses the use of the supernatural for political satire in Restoration and pre-Restoration literature. To disparage Whig Exclusionists, Dryden and Lee equate them with Ligueurs involved in the sort of conjuring traditionally linked with the Jesuits. Shaftesbury, in particular, who is represented in the actions of both Melanax and Malicorne, becomes "both devilish leader of the mob and oracular inspirer of the aspirant to the throne."

6 OBER, KENNETH H., and WARREN U. OBER. "Percy's Nancy and Zhukovsky's Nina: A Translation Identified." SEER 57:398.

"Percy's song [O' Nancy, wilt thou go with me'] probably owes a considerable debt to a song in Nathaniel Lee's . . . Theodosius."

7 PRICE, CURTIS A. Music in the Restoration Theatre. [Ann Arbor]: UMI Research Press, pp. 4, 6-7, 11, 18, 34, 47, 61, 256.

Shows that Lee, "perhaps the greatest of the Restoration tragedians," used music in a variety of ways, usually with an eye to the ideas, situations, or tones he wished to reinforce. Illustrations are provided by Theodosius, Gloriana, Mithridates, The Rival Queens, The Duke of Guise, and Oedipus. Other plays are cited in Price's rich footnotes. He also notes the use of masques by Lee, and provides a catalogue of music in Lee's plays.

8 STAVES, SUSAN. Players' Scepters: Fictions of Authority in the Restoration. Lincoln and London: University of Nebraska Press, pp. 46, 78-79, 84, 86, 194, 234, 240-47, 297-99, 301, 303.

Reaffirms Lee's supposed political turnabout while offering fresh perspectives on several of his plays. In general, Lee moves from heroics to pathos, with Mithridates, a transitional piece, showing how conflicting loyalties, such as those informing most heroic drama, can become "destructive paradoxes." Caesar Borgia and The Massacre of Paris should be seen less as pro-Whig than as anti-Catholic. In Massacre, as well as in The Duke of Guise, recent European history gives protection against censorship and allows a more realistic handling of concrete political issues. In the latter play, Melanax can be understood as a bitter satire on the casuistry used during Commonwealth days for reconciling touchy consciences to the taking of contradictory oaths.

Lucius Junius Brutus, a "genuine Whig play" and one of the two greatest political tragedies of the time (the other being Venice Preserv'd), shows the dissolution of traditional "myths justifying constituted authority" and the continuing absence of "acceptable new myths" to fill the gap. Both Venice Preserv'd and Brutus feature "private men of feeling without any serious public ambition" who are destroyed by political forces with which they are unfit to cope. Both plays portray these anti-heroes as resisting the swearing of oaths, since they believe feelings to be more authentic than words, yet ultimately becoming sympathetic perjurers. In this respect, they are contrasted with cynical oath-takers who represent the unfeeling public world. The swearing is ritualized in both plays, and in both the heroines die while remaining faithful to their vows. If Brutus, unlike Otway's masterpiece, presents one public figure who keeps his promises (the titular character), he is not made a sympathetic personage, for Lee wishes us to perceive the republican-monarchist dichotomy as a complex one.

1980

1 BRAUER, GEORGE C., Jr. "Alexander in England: The Conqueror's Reputation in the Late Seventeenth and Eighteenth Centuries." CJ 76:36-38.

Discusses the "popular approach" used in The Rival Queens, where Lee "drew from La Calprenède the worst qualities of Alexander to exemplify what kingship should not be."

2 HAGSTRUM, JEAN H. Sex and Sensibility: Ideal and Erotic Love from Milton to Mozart. Chicago and London: University of Chicago Press, pp. 82-88, 189, 213.

Discusses five of the plays in terms of Lee's "obsessive theme of madness caused by love and crime." Nero crudely but powerfully portrays "two contrasting types of love mania" (as defined also by Armistead, pp. 40-41 of L.1979.1), while Caesar Borgia, an even bloodier and more Websterian depiction of erotic madness, savagely attacks the Restoration fop through the antics of Ascanio, revealing "the profound alienation of Lee's spirit from his age." The Restoration rake is similarly attacked in The Princess of Cleve (see L.1976.3). Swift's linking of "Christian enthusiasm and melancholy" is anticipated in Theodosius, which "raises vexing questions about the power and place of woman, the feminizing of life that is sometimes seen as a Christian phenomenon, and the dangers to civilized life when sexual distinction is blurred."

Lee's "finest play," Lucius Junius Brutus, is "a psychological family drama" (see L.1975.2) that pits "the archetypal father of the Western world" against "sentimental and sexual excess." Thus, "Lee has given us the exact antithesis of the close association between sexual love and revolutionary energy that we find in Blake, Shelley, and Marcuse." In the meantime, Lee strongly influenced Richardson.

3 PRICE, CURTIS A. "Music as Drama." In The London Theatre World, 1660-1800. Edited by Robert D. Hume. Carbondale and Edwardsville: Southern Illinois University Press; London and Amsterdam: Feffer & Simons, pp. 213-14.

Briefly discusses the successful weaving of "eerily effective music into the main subplot" of The Duke of Guise, especially in Acts 3 and 5.

4 SALGĀDO, GĀMINI. English Drama: A Critical Introduction. New York: St. Martin's Press, pp. 141-42.

Regards Lee as a purveyor of absurdly inflated notions of honor and an exploiter of theater as spectacle.

5 VISSER, COLIN. "Scenery and Technical Design." In The London Theatre World, 1660-1800. Edited by Robert D. Hume. Carbondale and Edwardsville: Southern Illinois University Press; London and Amsterdam: Feffer & Simons, p. 107.

Observes that scenes and machines from Oedipus linger "with the other machines in Hogarth's decrepit barn" in his engraving, "Strolling Actresses Dressing in a Barn."

1981

1 BROWN, LAURA. English Dramatic Form, 1660-1760: An Essay in Generic History. New Haven and London: Yale University Press, pp. 22-25, 71-81.

Though Lee's later plays, beginning with The Rival Queens, are best described as "affective tragedies," the early ones represent late, experimental versions of the "heroic action." For instance, Sophonisba shows heroic glory being transformed into irrationality, randomness, and gloom as Lee works toward a new standard of coherence: emotional response. The divided plot of the play embodies this formal indecision, and Sophonisba herself vacillates between defiant grandeur and innocent victimization. A parallel incoherence is visible in The Rival Queens, where Alexander is both vicious tyrant and suffering lover, but in this case the juxtaposition of pathos and anti-absolutist sentiment reveals the ideological basis of Lee's transition to affective tragedy.

In Lucius Junius Brutus, the combining of pathos and antimonarchism into a single, coherent action makes the unstated analogy in The Rival Queens explicit. The inconsistency in Alexander's character is resolved in the later play by dividing its two components, heroic virtue and suffering pathos, between

Brutus and Titus, respectively. The two components are integrated as both characters assume that tragic fragmentation of aristocratic standards that is the formal core of Lee's rejection of the heroic action. In this sense, *Lucius Junius Brutus* is the natural formal conclusion to Lee's growing ideological self-consciousness.

The Dramatic Works of Thomas Otway

Alcibiades: A Tragedy	1675
Don Carlos Prince of Spain: A Tragedy	1676
Titus and Berenice: A Tragedy . . . with a Farce called the Cheats of Scapin	1677
Friendship in Fashion: A Comedy	1678
The History and Fall of Caius Marius: A Tragedy	1680
The Orphan; or, The Unhappy-Marriage: A Tragedy	1680
The Souldiers Fortune: A Comedy	1681
Venice Preserv'd; or, A Plot Discover'd: A Tragedy	1682
The Atheist; or, The Second Part of the Souldiers Fortune	1684

Writings about Thomas Otway, 1680-1980

1680

1 ANON. "A Session of the Poets." In Poems on Several Occasions By the Right Honourable, the E. of R---. Antwerp: n.p., p. 113.

Calls Otway "the scum of a Play-House." On the problem of attributing authorship of this poem, see David M. Vieth, Attribution in Restoration Poetry (New Haven and London: Yale University Press, 1963), pp. 296-321.

2 [ROCHESTER, JOHN WILMOT, EARL OF.] "An Allusion to Horace. The 10th Satyr of the 1st Book." In Poems on Several Occasions By the Right Honourable, the E. of R---. Antwerp: n.p., p. 41.

Sneers that "puzling O----, labors . . . in vain" to please the rabble and court.

3 _____. "Epigram on Thomas Otway." In The Complete Poems of John Wilmot, Earl of Rochester. Edited by David M. Vieth. New Haven and London: Yale University Press, 1968, p. 148.

A "blustering bard" who falsifies Plutarch in "rough, unruly rhyme," Otway prefers "rapture before nature" and, having "himself turned his own imager," defaces God's image "in every character." Vieth dates the composition of this poem at 1680, but it was not published until 1953 in Poems by John Wilmot, Earl of Rochester (London: Routledge & Kegan Paul), p. 118.

1681

1 ANON. "An Essay of Scandal." In Court Satires of the Restoration. Edited by John Harold Wilson. Columbus: Ohio State University Press, 1976, p. 65.

Let Lord Beauclerc "remain in Otway's care / To make him (if that's possible to be) / A viler poet and more dull than he." The manuscript, dated 1681 by Wilson, has never previously been published.

2 ANON. "Utile Dulce." In Court Satires of the Restoration. Edited by John Harold Wilson. Columbus: Ohio State University Press, 1976, p. 51.

Otway is one of the "bombast poets which infest the town" (joining Settle, D'Urfey, Lee, and Crowne). Wilson, the first to publish this manuscript poem, dates it 1681.

1682

1 BEHN, APHRA. "Song sung by Lord Lambert." In The Roundheads or, The Good Old Cause, A Comedy. London: for D. Brown & H. Rhodes, IV.ii, pp. 38-39.

Has little direct bearing on Otway in this form; when given a new title in 1684, becomes a compliment on Venice Preserv'd. See OT.1684.1.

2 [SHADWELL, THOMAS.] The Tory-Poets: A Satyr. London: for R. Johnson, pp. 6-8.

Sees Otway as a dull, witless, bawdy, and "Beastly" dramatist who can write only when drunk.

1684

1 BEHN, APHRA. "The Cabal at Nickey Nackeys." In Poems upon Several Occasions: with a Voyage to the Island of Love. London: for R. Tonson & J. Tonson, pp. 125-26.

Implicitly compliments Venice Preserv'd by using Antonio to symbolize the "witty," malicious, plotting, masochistic "Statesman." See OT.1682.1.

2 DUKE, RICHARD. Epilogue to The Atheist. London: for R. Bentley & J. Tonson, n. pag.

Even when the Whig tide was at its height, Otway managed to sustain his principles. Now that the Tories have triumphed, confirming those principles, Otway's propensity to "lash the Follies of the Times" can be potently indulged. Those in our society who are likely targets of his satire should take heed.

1685

1 EVELYN, JOHN. "The Immortality of Poesie." In Poems by Several Hands, and on Several Occasions. Edited by Nahum Tate. London: for J. Hindmarsh, p. 92.

"When the aspiring Grecian in the East, / And haughty Philip is forgot in th' West, / Then Lee and Otways Works shall be suppress."

1689

1 GOULD, ROBERT. "The Play-House. A Satyr." In Poems Chiefly Consisting of Satyrs and Satyrical Epistles. London: n.p., pp. 173, 175.

The Cheats of Scapin is damned through praise by false critics, but The Orphan and Venice Preserv'd are said to deserve "lasting praise" and to merit attention as "long as the Sea defends our Land."

1691

1 LANGBAINE, GERARD. An Account of the English Dramatick Poets. Oxford: by L.L. for G. West and H. Clements, pp. 395-400.

Presents Otway as a steadily improving playwright who, while borrowing perhaps too much, wrote decorous tragedies and comedies that were a bit too libertine. Notes the elevation of the titular character in Alcibiades (over Plutarch's version). Describes Friendship in Fashion as "very diverting," and The Orphan as "very moving."

1694

1 GILDON, CHARLES. "An Essay at a Vindication of Love in Tragedies, against Rapin and Mr. Rymer, Directed to Mr. Dennis." In Miscellaneous Letters and Essays, on Several Subjects . . . in Prose and Verse . . . By Several Gentlemen and Ladies. London: for Benjamin Bragg, pp. 145-71, esp. pp. 169-70.

Venice Preserv'd and The Orphan are cited as finely passionate plays whose reputation endures despite their stress on the passion of love.

2 [PRIOR, MATTHEW.] "A Satyr against Poetry. In a Letter to the Lord D.---." In Chorus Poetarum: or, Poems on Several Occasions. By the Duke of Buckingham, the late Lord Rochester . . . and . . . other . . . Poets. London: for Benjamin Bragg, pp. 123-24.

Otway is "this great Poet" who "charm'd the Stage" with The Orphan, Venice Preserv'd, and The Souldiers Fortune. "Light'ning is less lively than his Wit." The version of this piece in Poems on Affairs of State (1703, Vol. 2, p. 142) shows a few minor variations but retains essentially the same critical stance.

1695

1 DRYDEN, JOHN, trans. "Preface of the Translator, With a Parallel, Of Poetry and Painting." In De Arte Graphica.

The Art of Painting, By C.A. Du Fresnoy. London: by J. Heptinstall for W. Rogers, p. xlv.

Otway mastered the expression of "the Passions and Motions of the Mind" as completely as "any of the Ancients or Moderns." Though Venice Preserv'd may be deficient in character motivation and "in the Height and Elegance of Expression," the "Passions are truly touch'd in it. . . . Nature is there, which is the greatest Beauty."

1698

1 ANON. A Letter to A.H. Esq.; Concerning the Stage. London: for A. Baldwin, p. 10.

Asks "who would reject the Orphan, because Mr. Collier objects against a loose Speech in it."

2 COLLIER, JEREMY. A Short View of the Immorality, and Profaneness of the English Stage. London: S. Keble, pp. 9, 62, 100, 101, 146.

Takes issue with Otway's use of "smutty" language, blaspheming, and anticlerical invective. Chamont, Castalio, Polydore and Monimia, of The Orphan, are singled out, especially the latter, whose lewd talk is said to show how, even in tragedy, a wicked playwright will make women speak dirt.

3 DENNIS, JOHN. The Usefulness of the Stage, To the Happiness of Mankind, To Government, and To Religion. Occasioned by a late Book, written by Jeremy Collier, MA. London: for R. Parker, p. 117.

That Otway means to instruct us morally is evident in The Orphan when Castalio is destroyed "for his falsehood to his Brother and friend," and in Venice Preserv'd when Jaffeir is punished "for his clandestine Marriage with the Daughter of his Benefactor; and Belvidera for her disobedience."

4 [SETTLE, ELKANAH.] A Defence of Dramatick Poetry: Being a Review of Mr. Collier's View of the Immorality and Profaneness of the Stage. London: for Eliz. Whitlock, p. 79.

Asserts that Otway teaches and reforms through the medium of emotion. In Venice Preserv'd and Caius Marius, "Virtuous Distress'd love" conveys instruction "by refining that Noble Passion . . . from Coldness and Libertinism, to Fidelity and Virtue."

1699

1 ANON. The Stage Acquitted. Being a Full Answer to Mr. Collier, and the other Enemies of the Drama. London: for J. Barnes & M. Gilliflower, p. 79.

Through Belvidera and Monimia, Otway instructs in how to be a good wife, for "they give so taking a Beauty to a Woman, that all the sensible Sex must be in Love with it." Thus, the playwright's powerful characterizations and mastery of the audience's feelings are morally benign.

2 COLLIER, JEREMY. A Defence of the Short View of the Profaneness and Immorality of the English Stage. London: for S. Keble, R. Sare, & H. Hindmarsh, "To the Reader" (n. pag.) and p. 19.

The Souldiers Fortune and other plays like it are "meer prodigies of Lewdness and Irreligion"; even its concluding lines "do more harm than good."

3 [DRAKE, JAMES.] The Antient and Modern Stages Survey'd or Mr. Collier's View of the Immorality and Profaness of the English Stage Set in a True Light. London: A. Roper, pp. 207-8.

Like "the Fable of the Oedipus," that of The Orphan moves "Terrour and Compassion"; but it excels the ancient play in terms of moral instruction. Polydore's "incontinence," bringing misery to himself and his family, "preaches Chastity to the Audience after the most effectual manner."

4 [GILDON, CHARLES], and GERARD LANGBAINE. The Lives and Characters of the English Dramatick Poets. London: for W. Turner, pp. 107-8.

"None equal'd" Otway in moving "Terror and Pity." Venice Preserv'd is "an incomparable play."

5 OLDMIXON, JOHN. Reflections on the Stage, and Mr. Collyer's Defence of the Short View. In Four Dialogues. London: for R. Parker & P. Buck, pp. 106, 177.

Antonio in Venice Preserv'd originally gave pleasure because he "was copy'd from some body that the Court design'd then to laugh at." This play and The Orphan demonstrate that the English can move pity and tenderness better than the French can.

1700

1 [COBB, SAMUEL.] Poetae Britannici. A Poem, Satyrical and Panegyrical. London: for A. Roper, p. 18.

Though Otway deserves praise for moving tragic pity and for the "genius" behind Jaffeir's characterization, "we mourn to see" him pandering to the audience's taste for the likes of Antonio and Aquilina, who "Ne're move the Head, though they divert the Eyes."

2 COLLIER, JEREMY. A Second Defence of the Short View of the Profaneness and Immorality of the English Stage. London: for S. Keble and G. Strahan, p. 77.

In The Orphan, a cruel fate descends, without distinction of merit, upon both virtuous and vicious.

3 GOULD, ROBERT. "On the Death of John Dryden, Esq." In Luctus Britannici: or the Tears of the British Muses; for the Death of John Dryden, Esq. London: for Henry Playford & Abel Roper, p. 38.

Remembers Otway as the darling of the stage; "charming were his Strains."

4 [KENRICK, DANIEL.] A New Session of the Poets, Occasion'd by the Death of Mr. Dryden. London: for A. Baldwin, p. 8.

Ranks Otway with Wycherley as poets who were guided by nature.

1701

1 [GILDON, CHARLES.] Preface to Love's Victim: or, The Queen of Wales. A Tragedy. London: by M. Bennet for Richard Parker & George Strahan, n. pag.

Sees Otway as the only English tragedian who mastered the whole spectrum of passions; commends him for using natural language consistently adjusted to the emotional state of the character who utters it.

2 ROWE, NICHOLAS. "To the Right Honourable the Earl of Jersey" and "The Prologue." Prefixed to The Ambitious Step-mother. A Tragedy. London: for Peter Buck, n. pag.

Otway's audiences, especially the ladies, "made poor Monimia's Grief their own" and, after seeing one of his plays, felt "a sort of regret proceeding from good nature."

1702

1 ANON. A Comparison between the Two Stages. London: n.p., pp. 33, 101.

While Otway succeeded in both comedy and tragedy, his comedies are marred by looseness and profanity, his tragedies by "humility and vulgarity of Expression." Nevertheless, his "Fables are well chosen, and his Passions are very moving." On the problem of attributing authorship of this work, see the edition by Staring B. Wells (Princeton: Princeton University Press, 1942).

1704

1 ANON. "Satyr." In Poems on Affairs of State, From 1640. to this present Year 1704. Vol. 3. n.p., "Printed in the Year 1704," pp. 123-24.

Ridicules the comic episodes of Venice Preserv'd but at the same time commends them as low buffoonery: "I heard an Ensign of the Guards declare, / . . . / He lik'd that Scene of Nicky Nacky more, / Than all that Shadwell ever writ before."

2 ANON. The Stage-Beaux toss'd in a Blanket: or, Hypocrisie Alamode; Expos'd in a True Picture of Jerry ----- . . . A Comedy. London: by J. Nutt, p. 29.

One "Dorimant" is made to say that The Souldiers Fortune, because it is so indecent, is "never frequented by the Boxes, or the better part of the Pit."

3 [DENNIS, JOHN.] The Person of Quality's Answer to Mr. Collier's Letter, Being a Disswasive from the Play-House. London: n.p., p. 8.

Implicitly appeals to human nature as an argument supporting the effectiveness of The Souldiers Fortune, supposing that as a young man Collier "endur'd" the "Bawdy" of this play before his "Prophetick Mission" was revealed.

1710

1 [ADDISON, JOSEPH.] Tatler, no. 133 (February 11-14). London: by John Morphew, n. pag.

Commends the last act of Venice Preserv'd, where Pierre, about to ask Jaffeir to spare him an ignominious death, bursts into tears. The "melancholy Silence" which follows "raises in the Spectators a Grief that is inexpressible, and an Idea of such a complicated Distress in the Actor as Words cannot utter."

2 [GILDON, CHARLES.] "An Essay on the Art, Rise and Progress of the Stage in Greece, Rome and England." Prefixed to The Works of Mr. William Shakespear. [Edited by Nicholas Rowe.] Vol. 7. London: for E. Curll & E. Sanger, pp. xl-xli.

Praises The Orphan as one of "few plays" in which "the Action is one, and every Episode, Part or under Action carries on, and contributes to the Main Action or Subject."

3 _____. "Remarks on the Plays of Shakespear." In The Works of Mr. William Shakespear. [Edited by Nicholas Rowe.] Vol. 7. London: for E. Curll & E. Sanger, pp. 273, 310, 440, 436.

Sees Otway as "the brightest and most Tragic Genius of our World," better than Dryden who lacked "a true Relish of Nature." After "three moderate Plays," Otway gave us The Orphan, which "still pleases and ever will," and Venice Preserv'd, which is especially uplifting when Jaffeir moralizes "on the frail and transitory State of Nature." Otway also gives aesthetic pleasure through his masterful plot construction, The Orphan being his best example of unified structure.

1711

1 [ADDISON, JOSEPH.] Spectator, no. 39 (April 14). London: for Sam. Buckley, A. Baldwin, & Charles Lillie, n. pag.
Otway "followed Nature in the Language of his Tragedy" and conveyed passion more forcefully "than any of our English Poets." Sometimes, however, he fails to raise the language to a level of dignity appropriate to the action or characters, and one wishes he had endowed the hero of Venice Preserv'd with "the same good Qualities in the Defence of his Country, that he showed for its Ruin and Subversion."

2 _____. Spectator, no. 40 (April 16). London: for Sam. Buckley, A. Baldwin, & Charles Lillie, n. pag.
Lists The Orphan and Venice Preserv'd, along with several other plays, as "the best Plays of this Kind": that is, the kind that end unhappily, supposedly violating the rule of poetic justice.

3 _____. Spectator, no. 44 (April 20). London: for Sam. Buckley, A. Baldwin, & Charles Lillie, n. pag.
Applauds the use in drama of ghosts, bells, and other such "Terrours" when they contribute to the overall design of a play. In Venice Preserv'd, for instance, the "sounding of the Clock . . . makes the Hearts of the whole Audience quake; and conveys a stronger Terrour to the Mind, than it is possible for Words to do."

4 _____. Spectator, no. 241 (December 6). London: for Sam. Buckley, A. Baldwin, & Charles Lillie, n. pag.
Cites the tenderness of Monimia's speech on the absence of her lover.

5 DENNIS, JOHN. Reflections Critical and Satyrical, upon a Late Rhapsody, call'd An Essay upon Criticism. London: for Bernard Lintott, p. 403.
Like Shakespeare, Otway was talented in both tragedy and comedy.

1712

1 ANON. "Some Account of the Life and Writings of Mr. Thomas Otway." In The Works of Mr. Thomas Otway. Vol. 1. London: for J. Tonson, 12 pp., n. pag.
"The faculty of mingling good and bad Characters, and involving their fortunes, seems to be the distinguishing excellence of this writer." He can be lively, gay, sometimes indecent, and always affecting when expressing passion. The characters in The Orphan are less than eminent in social status, but Otway's impassioned presentation of them "makes them great in effect."

In Venice Preserv'd, he alternates private and public calamities, controlling our response so forcefully and skilfully that "the Ruffian on the wheel is as much the object of pity, as if he had been brought to that unhappy fate for some brave action." Otway's plays show "the effect of Nature in a very good Genius."

2 [HUGHES, JOHN.] Spectator, no. 541 (November 20). London: for S. Buckley, J. Tonson, & A. Baldwin, n. pag.
Responds to Caius Marius, Act I, lines 305-7: "Pleasure dissolves into a luxurious, mild, tender and joyous Modulation."

3 [STEELE, RICHARD.] Spectator, no. 456 (August 13). London: for Sam. Buckley, A. Baldwin, & Charles Lillie, n. pag.
Praises Otway's spirited depiction of Jaffeir as a man made miserable by having his "effects" confiscated by law.

1713

1 DENNIS, JOHN. Remarks upon Cato, A Tragedy. London: for B. Lintott, pp. 12, 37-39.
Contrasts The Orphan, seen as powerfully moving, instructive, natural, and well constructed, to Addison's Cato, which copies key aspects of Otway's play but which is ruined by the display of "unseasonable" passions, improbabilities, and lack of structural unity.

2 [REYNARDSON, FRANCIS.] The Stage: A Poem. London: for E. Curll, p. 16.
Praises Otway's style, The Orphan in general, and the character of Pierre in Venice Preserv'd.

1714

1 [STEELE, RICHARD.] Lover, no. 12 (March 23). London: by Ferd. Burleigh, n. pag.
Discusses Antonio and Aquilina of Venice Preserv'd. She is an imperious "Wench," and he is a "silly disagreeable old Sinner," a "grim puzzled Leacher" whose every effort to please is rendered "offensive" by his ugly personality. He represents "the Fate of those who attempt to be what Nature never designed them, Wits, Politicians and Lovers."

1715

1 ANON. Discursive letter. In Town-Talk, in a Series of Letters to a Lady in the Country. [Edited by Richard Steele.] No. 1 (17 December), n. pag.

Condemns the taste of those who recently attended a production of Venice Preserv'd but paid greater attention to Belvidera's account of Renault's lust than to the play's truly fine features: "the distress of a couple undone by a generous passion, the misery of a whole nation shortly coming to pass, and a woman of honour involved in the ruin, though designing to serve her father and her country."

1717

1 DENNIS, JOHN. Remarks upon Mr. Pope's Translation of Homer. London: for E. Curll, pp. 4, 6.

Names Otway as one of "Eight Gentlemen alive at a Time, who have writ good and diverting Comedies." In his serious plays, Otway excels all but Euripides in touching "softer Passions."

1718

1 GILDON, CHARLES. The Complete Art of Poetry. Vol. 1. London: for Charles Rivington, pp. 237, 248, 258, 290.

The Orphan and Venice Preserv'd endure because they have no digressive actions and because Otway depended more on his own inventiveness than on his sources. His great success in touching the passions derived largely from his ability to imagine a character's gestures, facial expression, and voice modulation before he wrote the words. And he was best in using spare, brief expressions. "I remember Mrs. Barry has told me, that she never pronounced those three Words . . . Ah! poor Castalio, without Tears." A lesser tragedian would have used pompous, figured language.

1719

1 JACOB, GILES. The Poetical Register: or, the Lives and Characters of the English Dramatick Poets. With an Account of their Writings. London: for E. Curll, pp. 193-96.

In The Orphan and Venice Preserv'd, "two as fine and finished Tragedies as the English Theatre ever saw," the passions are touched with "masterly Strokes" and the style is "easy, flowing and natural." Other plays by Otway are mentioned without critical comment.

1720

1 ANON. Miscellanea Aurea: or the Golden Medley. London: for A. Bettesworth & J. Pemberton, pp. 25, 27, 96-97.

The Orphan and Venice Preserv'd violate unity of place, but Monimia is movingly pathetic, and nothing in French or English drama affects us so deeply as "all that passes between Jaffeir and Belvidera, Man and Wife." Especially artful and moving, too, is the opening exposition in Venice Preserv'd.

2 DENNIS, JOHN. "Letter II." In The Characters and Conduct of Sir John Edgar . . . . In Two Letters to Sir John Edgar. London: for M. Smith, p. 29.

"Heroick Love, and the Orphan, are certainly Two of the best of our Tragedies; and they are as certainly Two of the most regular."

1721

1 [GILDON, CHARLES.] The Laws of Poetry . . . Explain'd and Illustrated. London: W. Hinchliffe, pp. 34, 201-3, 205, 210-11.

One of the few gifted tragedians of the Restoration, Otway is "a true poet, nay a poet of the first magnitude," who draws the passions with masterful simplicity. He violates unity of time and place but sustains the more vital unity of action, and if in The Orphan, he presents the opening exposition awkwardly, in Venice Preserv'd, he handles the problem with subtle skill.

1723

1 STEELE, RICHARD. The Conscious Lovers. A Comedy. London: for J. Tonson, II.i, p. 34.

Indiana: "in my Thoughts, there's none of your Composers come up to Old Shakespear and Otway."

1725

1 ANON. A Letter to My Lord-------- on The Present Diversions of the Town. With the True Reason of the Decay of our Dramatic Entertainments. London: for J. Roberts, pp. 14, 17, 26.

Laments the absence on the contemporary stage of "Shakespeare, Otway, and Congreve," in whom we found "Nature in its greatest Beauties," especially "the Distresses of Othello and Jaffeir." Apollo is made to say near the end of the essay, "I gave my Otway ev'ry Charm / To raise Your Griefs, and then those Griefs disarm."

2 [MURALT, BÉAT LOUIS de.] Lettres sur les Anglois et les Francois. Et sur les voiages. Cologne: n.p., p. 35.

Although Otway is a true genius, he employs too much violent spectacle in Venice Preserv'd.

1726

1 ANON. "Remarks on the Letters, concerning the English and French." Prefixed to Letters Describing the Character and Customs of the English and French Nations. Anonymously translated from Béat Louis de Muralt's Lettres (1725). 2d ed. London: by Tho. Edlin & N. Prevost, p. 20.

Defends Otway against Muralt's charge that he used excessive violence on stage. This charge appears in the translation on p. 30 and has neither lost nor gained in the English version. See OT.1725.2.

2 SWIFT, JONATHAN. "A History of Poetry, In a Letter to a Friend." In The Prose Works of Jonathan Swift. Edited by Herbert Davis. Vol. 4. London: Basil Blackwell, 1957, p. 274.

". . . we were then famous for Tragedy and Comedy; the Author of Venice Preserv'd is seldom O'T AWAY." I was unable to see the original half-sheet on which this piece was first published by Waters of Dublin; it is preserved in the National Library, Dublin.

3 WELSTED, M. Prologue to Money the Mistress. A Play, by Thomas Southerne. London: for J. Tonson, n. pag.

Otway and Southerne are considered peers in dramatic genius, and both are ranked below Dryden.

1728

1 [RALPH, JAMES.] The Touch-stone: or, Historical, Critical, Political, Philosophical, and Theological Essays on the reigning Diversions of the Town. London: n.p., p. 157.

Modern tastes in drama are such that, if Restoration playwrights were recalled from the grave, Otway, Lee, and Dryden would be allowed to starve or go insane again, while the Italian singers and French dancers, the Settles and Shadwells, would be "caress'd."

1730

1 THOMSON, JAMES. "Winter." In The Seasons. London: n.p., p. 218, ll. 643-47.

"Dread o'er the scene . . . / . . . poor Monimia mourns; / And Belvidera pours her soul in love. / Assenting terror shakes; the silent tear / Steals o'er the cheek. . . ." These lines do not appear in the 1726 edition of "Winter."

1731

1 ANON. "To the Author of the Weekly Register." Weekly Register, nos. 86, 91, 92 (4 December 1731; 8, 15 January 1732), n. pag.

Purports to show how Venice Preserv'd illustrates a moral--"that Virtue attended by Vice loses its Value, and can receive Pity only in Lieu of Admiration"--but this immediately gives way to a fairly detailed critique which praises the opening passages, notes Jaffeir's "gloomy Bravery," counters Gay's burlesque (in The What d'ye Call It) of the scaffold scene, and marvels at how subtly the catastrophe arises out of "the Barbarity of Priuli . . . the Sufferings of Belvidera . . . and an Injury [to Pierre] from a Senator." Despite the gratuitous mad scene and the lewd revels of Antonio, Venice Preserv'd is "the finest Tragedy that ever was wrote": the most moving, the best "conducted," the "nearest to Nature," and the most entertaining.

2 FIELDING, HENRY. The Tragedy of Tragedies; or the Life and Death of Tom Thumb the Great. London: by J. Roberts, 63 pp.

Although Fielding is easier on Otway than on Banks and Lee, he does burlesque some scenes and passages in Otway's plays, especially Caius Marius, II.iii (on p. 21), and Don Carlos, II.viii (on p. 32).

3 VOLTAIRE, FRANÇOIS MARIE AROUET. "A Discourse on Tragedy." Prefixed to An Essay upon the Civil Wars of France. 4th ed. London: for N. Prevost, pp. 8-10, 23.

Superior to the Manlius of La Fosse, Otway's Venice Preserv'd does not tell the story of the Venetian conspiracy as well as Saint-Réal does in his history. And although Otway ably composes Renault's speech to the conspirators, in other regards the play is seriously flawed. For example, Renault's lust for Belvidera and her complaint about his advances are indecent and not necessary to the development of the plot. Earlier editions of Voltaire's Essay seem not to include the "Discourse on Tragedy."

1732

1 ANON. Memoirs of the Life of Robert Wilks, Esq. London: by W. Rayner, pp. 26-28.

"As Shakespear exceeded in Nobleness of Thought, so Otway, of all our Tragic Writers, moved the Passions with greatest Violence. . . . [He] tuned . . . the Musick of our Souls." While Alcibiades "abounds with wonderful Images, and easy Diction," Don Carlos "glows with the true Spirit of Dramatic Rage." Of Otway's two masterpieces, The Orphan and Venice Preserv'd, the latter combines the striking depiction of love, friendship, and hatred with the "artful Weaving" of "Incidents, Sentiments, and Language" to produce the "most tender, moving, exquisite Performance the English stage could ever boast."

2 CRUSIUS, LEWIS. The Lives of the Roman Poets. Vol. 2. London: for W. Innys, J. Clarke, B. Motte, & J. Nurse, p. 275.
Calls The Orphan a "great" tragedy which demonstrates how a "faithful picture of the Passions is of itself sufficient to make us fear them" and wish "to avoid them." The play's catastrophe is caused by the combination of Castalio's love and jealousy, and Polydore's "blind passion."

1735

1 ANON. The Dramatic Historiographer: or, the British Theatre Delineated. London: F. Cogan, pp. 220-25.
Summarizes the plot of The Orphan and describes it as an emotionally powerful play.

2 ANON. "To Henry Stonecastle, Esq.; Author of the Universal Spectator," and editor's reply. In Universal Spectator and Weekly Journal (22 February), n. pag.
Describes Otway, Southerne, and Dryden as "the greatest Masters at touching the Passions."

1737

1 POPE, ALEXANDER. The First Epistle of the Second Book of Horace, Imitated. London: for T. Cooper, p. 16.
"Not but the Tragic spirit was our own, / And full in Shakespear, fair in Otway shone: / But Otway fail'd to polish or refine."

1738

1 ANON. "The Apotheosis of Milton: A Vision." Gentleman's Magazine 8:235, 469.
Otway is seen affecting the same style as Shadwell but not instinctively. He wears an upper garment like Shadwell's; underneath, however, he has on a fine vest, and the sword on his belt seems "to have the same Virtue with the Cestus ascribed to the Goddess of Beauty." His buskins are "peculiar to himself, and different from [those] of the rest of the Company." His writings "are . . . the envy, delight, and admiration of Posterity," but if his genius was of the highest rank, "the Habits he contracted, threw him into the lowest."

1739

1 BERNARD, JOHN PETER, THOMAS BIRCH, JOHN LOCKMAN, et al. A General Dictionary, Historical and Critical. Vol. 8. London: G. Strahan, pp. 69-71.

Regards Otway as "an eminent tragick writer" and cites Langbaine, Gildon, and Dryden on his power to move passion and on the libertinism of his comedies.

2 POPE, ALEXANDER. Remark on Otway. In Observations, Anecdotes, and Characters of Books and Men. Collected from Conversation, by Joseph Spence. Edited by James M. Osborne. Vol. 1. Oxford: Clarendon Press, 1966, item 482, p. 206.

In Otway's two "pathetic" tragedies, "'Tis a talent of nature rather than an effect of judgement to write so movingly." This anecdote, dated by Osborne 1739, seems to have been first published in Edmond Malone's edition of Spence (London: John Murray, 1820), p. 100.

1741

1 ANON. "Memoirs of Mrs. Anne Oldfield." Bound (but separately paginated) with The History of the English Stage, from the Restoration to the Present Time. Edited by Edmund Curll. London: E. Curll, p. 70.

Virtually quotes Steele (OT.1712.3), without acknowledgement, regarding Otway's spirited depiction of misery in "a Man, whose Effects are in the Hands of the Law" (that is, Jaffeir).

1742

1 FIELDING, HENRY. "A Discourse between the Poet and Player." In The History of the Adventures of Joseph Andrews, and of his Friend Mr. Abraham Adams. Vol. 2. London: for A. Millar, pp. 140, 143-44.

The "Player" laments the absence in modern drama of "your Shakespeares, Otways, and Lees."

1744

1 YOUNG, EDWARD. Letter to Samuel Richardson, 20 June. In The Correspondence of Edward Young. Edited by Henry Pettit. Oxford: Clarendon Press, 1971, p. 180.

To have given the heroines of Venice Preserv'd, The Orphan, and Lee's Theodosius happy conclusions to their distresses "would have utterly ruined our three best plays."

1745

1 [HAYWOOD, ELIZA.] Response to "Distrario." In The Female Spectator. Vol. 2, Book 8. London: for A. Millar, W. Law, & R. Carter, pp. 77-78.

Shakespeare would have been "thankful" that in Caius Marius Otway "moderniz'd, and cleared . . . part of its [that is, Romeo and Juliet's] rubbish." One could wish he had lopped off even more than he did, especially the scenes involving the nurse and the whole part of Sulpitius. Nevertheless, "he has improved and heightened every beauty that could receive addition," and he has judiciously left alone those portions that were "above the reach of amendment."

2 THOMSON, JAMES. Prologue to Tancred and Sigismunda. A Tragedy. London: for A. Millar, n. pag.

Now that prodigies, rhyme, ranting, and overly ornamented language have been "tumbled" from the stage, I wish we could "awake soft Otway's tender Woe."

1747

1 ANON. A Companion to the Theatre: or, A View of our most Celebrated Dramatic Pieces. Vol. 2. London: for J. Nourse, pp. 62-66, 335-39.

Summarizes the plots of Caius Marius and Venice Preserv'd, noting the alterations from Shakespeare in the former and wishing Otway "had cleans'd it yet more from that Rubbish which frequently choaks up the Beauty of the Sentiment." Although Venice Preserv'd is flawed by the comic scenes, it remains "one of the best and most striking" English tragedies. These two critiques were not included in The Dramatic Historiographer (see OT.1735.1).

2 ANON. An Examen of the New Comedy call'd The Suspicious Husband, With Some Observations upon our Dramatick Poetry and Authors. London: for J. Roberts, p. 43.

While Otway is "certainly a Genius," he is no Shakespeare. "He wants Variety, and can touch none of the Passions masterly, but Love." Moreover, his poetry is "low and creeping" even though frequently "sweet and harmonious, and sometimes nervous and elated." Commends the "tenderness and fine distress" in Jaffeir and Belvidera, Castalio and Monimia, but terms Chamont's rage "unnatural" though his affection for his sister is "finely touched." Polydore has "great gallantry, spirit, and Nature," and Pierre has "a strong characteristic boldness."

3 COLLINS, WILLIAM. "Ode. to Pity." In Odes on Several Descriptive and Allegoric Subjects. London: for A. Millar, pp. 2-3, st. 3-4.

While still an infant, Otway was shown Pity's bower, where he "sung the Female Heart, / With Youth's soft Notes unspoil'd by Art." Although the title page is dated 1747, these odes were actually published in December 1746.

4 GUTHRIE, WILLIAM. An Essay upon English Tragedy, with Remarks upon the Abbe de Blanc's Observations on the English Stage. [London]: T. Waller, pp. 4, 15, 22-23, 27.

Shakespeare and Otway were the only two great geniuses in English tragedy, Otway the lesser of the two because his range of human understanding was narrower, focused as it was on "mankind in common life" and on his own heart. Though Otway lacked refinement, his work is much to be preferred over that of the typical modern tragedian, who writes "the language of poetry without passion." The modern dramatist analyzes and defines too much, makes his characters sound more like Virgil, Lucan, or Seneca than like themselves. He considers less "what a character would say were he in the poet's place" than "what he would say were he in the place of the character." The publication date of this work is not firm.

5 LeBLANC, JEAN BERNARD. "The Supplement of Genius: or, the art of composing dramatic poems, as it has been practised by many celebrated authors of the English theatre." In Letters on the English and French Nations. Vol. 2. London: for J. Brindley, R. Francklin, C. Davis, & J. Hodges, pp. 242, 258, 260-262.

Regards Otway and Southerne as "two of the greatest English tragic poets" and sees Venice Preserv'd as "one of the most tragic pieces on the English stage." Even so, LeBlanc ridicules Otway's intermixing of comedy with his serious action and scoffs at several aspects of the staging (the use of the bell, for example).

6 [WARTON, THOMAS.] The Pleasures of Melancholy. A Poem. London: for R. Dodsley & M. Cooper, pp. 17-18.

The speaker wishes to "cultivate" his mind with "the soft thrillings" of tragedy, as exemplified by The Orphan (Monimia's incestuous joys, "polluted love," and "streaming eyes") and Venice Preserv'd (Jaffeir kneeling "for one forgiving look").

7 WHINCOP, THOMAS. "A Compleat List of all the English Dramatic Poets." In Scanderberg: or, Love and Liberty. A Tragedy. London: W. Reeve, pp. 271-73.

"This celebrated Poet . . . was certainly a Man of Genius and excellent Parts, tho' he did not appear to great advantage in his first play; but rose upon the World in every Attempt, till he wrote in his Venice Preserved, a finished piece."

1748

1 ANON. An Essay on Wit. London: for T. Lownds, pp. 8-10.

Gives The Orphan as an example of "sublime and noble" writing.

2 ANON. "Remarks on Mr. Otway's Venice Preserv'd." Universal Magazine 2 (May):209-13 and continued in Supplement to vol. 2 on pp. 306-8.

If one overlooks the "loose religious principles" and indecent language that Otway occasionally gave to his characters "to please a dissolute court," then this play must be regarded as excellent in every respect. The plot is well controlled and focused, the characters interestingly developed, the sentiments and arguments forcefully and convincingly expressed, the diction in general pleasingly natural. Jaffeir should be regarded not as a mere whiner but as a man of courage caught in the most trying situation. In its pathos, this play equals the best of Shakespeare. In its "satirical sallies" and stage business, it is peculiarly Otway's.

3 [HAWKINS, JOHN.] "Remarks on the Tragedy of The Orphan." Gentleman's Magazine 18 (November-December):502-6, 551-53.

"Next to Shakespear, scarce any has been so much applauded as Otway," and yet in The Orphan he exhibits both low morals and mean abilities. Although the play is emotionally powerful and has one exemplary and convincing character in Chamont, it contains no useful lessons. Indeed, its ending conveys a "very immoral" and irrelevant maxim, and in several other respects, it provides vicious sentiments and illustrations: Acasto's lack of patriotism, Castalio's lust, Polydore's hedonism, Monimia's indelicacy, and a general atmosphere hostile to good breeding, religion, marriage, and business. A number of inconsistencies mar construction and character development, from the "grossly ridiculous" opening dialogue to the libertine Polydore's supposed feelings of guilt. "Virtue and Genius" are always "allied," and Otway's deficiency in the one respect reflects his failing in the other. For the attribution of this essay to Hawkins, see Bertram H. Davis, A Proof of Eminence (Bloomington: Indiana University Press, 1973), pp. 33-38.

4 RICHARDSON, SAMUEL. Clarissa; or, The History of a Young Lady. The Shakespeare Head Edition of the Novels of Samuel Richardson, vol. 8. Oxford: Basil Blackwell, 1930, pp. 152-56, 201.

Because Clarissa thinks Venice Preserv'd is a morally exemplary play, Lovelace will take her to a performance, hoping that she will become more receptive to him once she sees how trivial are her distresses by contrast to those of Belvidera and Jaffeir. Afterwards, she writes to Anna Howe that the play was "deep and affecting" and that, in fact, it seemed to soften Lovelace's hard heart.

1750

1 [CHETWOOD, WILLIAM R.] The British Theatre Containing the Lives of the English Dramatic Poets. Dublin: Peter Wilson, 1750, pp. 98-99.

Quotes Whincop's "Compleat List," for which, see OT.1747.7.

2 [HILL, JOHN.] The Actor: A Treatise on the Art of Playing. London: for R. Griffiths, pp. 19, 174, 183, 233, 256.

In The Orphan, there is "genius" in the creation of Monimia, but Castalio is unevenly realized. Venice Preserv'd is remarkable for its "masterly" presentation of conjugal love and for "the air of nature, of ease, and unaffected plainness" in "the relation Pierre gives to Jaffeir of the ruin of his affairs."

1752

1 DERRICK, SAMUEL. "Remarks upon the Tragedy of Venice Preserv'd." In The Dramatic Censor; being Remarks upon the Conduct, Characters, and Catastrophe of our Most Celebrated Plays. Vol. 1. London: for Richard Manby & H.S. Cox, 88 pp.

Attempts a balanced assessment. On the one hand, this play has many merits which make it second only to Shakespeare's best tragedies: it is imaginative, for the most part beautifully expressed and skillfully plotted, and emotionally powerful. Especially effective are Jaffeir's soliloquy on his and Belvidera's misery, Pierre's speech on his own villainy and his persuasion of Jaffeir to join the conspiracy, Belvidera's opposing persuasions and her mad scene, Priuli's speech upon relenting. Even Pierre's anticlerical remarks can be defended as being leveled at only the worst part of the priesthood.

On the other hand, the play has some serious flaws. Jaffeir is regrettably insensitive to Priuli's rights as a father, while Priuli deals too harshly with his daughter. Pierre, despite his courage, is an unpatriotic, personally vindictive assassin who often speaks and behaves coarsely. It is unlikely that Belvidera would have consented to appear in a prostitute's house, and the rendering her hostage to Renault and the others is highly improbable. All in all, this is a finely moving tragedy lamentably flawed by improbabilities, grossness, and lapses in characterization.

2 MASON, WILLIAM. "Letters concerning the Following Drama." Prefixed to Elfrida, A Dramatic Poem. London: J. & P. Knapton, pp. xii-xiii.

In order to give "a moral view" to the many vicious expressions and actions in Venice Preserv'd, a chorus should be added.

1753

1 CIBBER, THEOPHILUS, [and ROBERT SHIELS.] The Lives of the Poets of Great Britain and Ireland. Compiled from . . . the MS. Notes of the late ingenious Mr. Coxeter and others. Vol. 2. London: R. Griffiths, pp. 324-36.

Synthesizes many previous critiques, especially Addison's in Spectator, no. 39 (see OT.1711.1), the anonymous introduction to the 1712 Works (see OT.1712.1), and Hawkins's "Remarks" in Gentleman's Magazine (see OT.1748.3). Offensively libertine in his comedies, Otway is England's greatest genius "in the passionate parts" of tragedy. He excels in the natural, the familiar, and the domestic, sometimes failing to elevate his language in appropriate places. Despite its moral looseness, bombast, and difficulties in motivation, The Orphan is a powerfully moving play. Venice Preserv'd is a skillful blend of good and bad characters, private and public concerns. On the whole it excites pity and terror, though we cannot feel much admiration or sympathy for the rebels. In tragedy Otway is a greater dramatist than Dryden; he manipulates our passions, whereas Dryden only charms us. Otherwise, Dryden is the finer poet.

2 GARRICK, DAVID. "Advertisement." In Romeo and Juliet. By Shakespear. With Alterations, and an additional Scene. London: for J. & R. Tonson & S. Draper, n. pag.

Acknowledges that Otway was the first to show Juliet waking in the tomb before Romeo dies but wonders why "so great a dramatic Genius did not work up a Scene from it of more Nature, Terror and Distress." In correcting "the failure of so great a Master," Garrick hopes that he will not be considered an arrogant plagiarist. This caveat does not appear in the first edition of Garrick's alteration.

3 [HURD, RICHARD.] "Notes on the Art of Poetry." In Q. Horatii Flacci Ars Poetica, Epistola ad Pisones: With an English Commentary and Notes. Vol. 1. London: for W. Thurlbourne, R. Dodsley, J. Beacroft, & M. Cooper, p. 41.

Part of the commentary on line 19 of the Ars Poetica maintains that The Orphan, "notwithstanding its real beauties, could hardly have taken so prodigiously . . . if there were not somewhere a defect of good taste as well as of good morals." These "Notes" are attributed to Hurd in the Works, I (London: for T. Cadell & W. Davies, 1811), the quoted passage on p. 68.

4 [MORGAN, MACNAMARA.] A Letter to Miss Nossiter. Occasioned by Her first Appearanace on the Stage. London: for W. Owen & G. Woodfall, p. 50.

While discussing Miss Nossiter's playing of Juliet to Barry's Romeo, Morgan commends Otway, whom he ranks "next to Shakespeare's self," for altering the final scene of Shakespeare' play to allow Juliet (Lavinia in Caius Marius) to awaken before her lover dies.

5 RICHARDSON, SAMUEL. The History of Sir Charles Grandison. In a Series of Letters. Vol. 5. London: for S. Richardson, C. Hitch, L. Hawes, et al., p. 106.

Charlotte reflects: "What a fool has Otway made of Castalio, raving against the whole sex . . . when the fault . . . were owing to his own baseness of heart, in being ashamed to acquaint his brother, that he meant honourable Love. . . . I pitied the impetuous Polydore, more than I did the blubbering great boy Castalio; tho' I thought both brothers deserved to be hanged."

1754

1 ANON. An Essay on the Stage; or, the Art of Acting. A Poem. Edinburgh: John Yair & B. Bourn, p. 5.

Recommends speaking "Otway's sense, with nature, strength and ease."

1755

1 [PICKERING, ROGER.] Reflections upon Theatrical Expression in Tragedy. London: W. Johnston, pp. 3-6, 35-37, 54-56.

Gives detailed advice on how to impersonate Jaffeir and Pierre, especially the former's "conjugal tenderness" and the latter's gestures when he persuades the conspirators to believe in Jaffeir's fidelity to the cause. Venice Preserv'd, III.i., illustrates the dramatically effective use of silence.

1756

1 HAYWOOD, ELIZA. The Husband. In Answer to the Wife. London: for T. Gardner, pp. 246-48.

Daphne is moved by the parallel between her own distressful relationship with Corydon and Belvidera's relationship with Jaffeir in "Mr. Otway's excellent tragedy."

1757

*1 ANON. Memoirs of Sir Thomas Hughson and Mr. Joseph Williams, with the Remarkable History, Travels, and Distresses of Telemachus Lovet. Vol. 3. London: for the author, pp. 136-37.

Source: Robert Gale Noyes, The Neglected Muse: Restoration and Eighteenth-Century Tragedy in the Novel (1740-1780) (Providence, R.I.: Brown University Press, 1958), pp. 54-55. In discussing The Orphan, Periander and Luisa stress its value as moral instruction and note the significance of "mistakes and misrepresentations" in the plot.

2 ANON. Remarks on The Orphan. London Morning Chronicle (8-10 March), cited by Aline Mackenzie Taylor, in Next to Shakespeare: Otway's Venice Preserv'd and The Orphan and Their History on the London Stage. Durham, N.C.: Duke University Press, 1950, p. 115.

Even though the play offers "beautiful" scenes of love and distress "from Domestic Incidents," its catastrophe is built on "gross and shocking" circumstances, and the scene in which Polydore enters Monimia's bedroom is rather coarse, as is Polydore's subsequent behavior. I was unable to see this issue of the Morning Chronicle.

3 ANON. "Remarks on the Tragedy of Douglas." London Chronicle 1, no. 36 (22-24 March):286-87.

Compares Home to Otway for mastery of passionate language, "though perhaps the latter sometimes goes out of his Way for poetical Ornaments."

4 HUME, DAVID. The History of Great Britain, Vol. II: The Commonwealth and the Reigns of Charles II and James II. London: for A. Millar, p. 453.

"Otway had a genius finely turned to the pathetic; but he neither observes strictly the rules of the drama, nor the rules, still more essential, of propriety and decorum."

1758

1 ANON. "The Poetical Scale." Literary Magazine 3 (January):6.

On the bases of genius, judgment, learning, and versification, Otway makes a score of 54 (out of 80) as compared, for example, to Shakespeare's 66, Jonson's 59, Congreve's 59, Southerne's 55, and Lee's 51.

1759

1 [GOLDSMITH, OLIVER.] "An Account of the Augustan Age of England." Bee, no. 8 (24 November):238.

Without learning or "critical knowledge," Otway became excellent "in catching every emotion just as it rises from the soul, and in all the powers of the moving and pathetic." He was our greatest genius, "next to Shakespeare." Both painted directl from nature.

2 _____. "Art. IX. The Orphan of China, a Tragedy." Critical Review (May), p. 436.

"Shakespear, Otway, and Rowe, seemed to have been perfect oeconomists of their distress. . . . they were so sensible of a necessary gradation in this respect, that their characters frequently make their first appearance in circumstances of joy and triumph."

3 HUME, DAVID. "To the Reverend Mr. Hume, Author of Douglas, A Tragedy." In Four Dissertations. London: for A. Millar, pp. v-vi.

Maintains that Home possesses "the true theatric genius of . . . Otway, refined from the unhappy . . . licentiousness" of that author.

4 JOHNSON, SAMUEL. "The Idler, No. 61." Universal Chronicle, or Weekly Gazette, 2-9 June, p. 177.

Dick Minim, the pseudocritic, found in Otway "uncommon powers of moving the passions, but was disgusted by his general negligence, and blamed him for making a Conspirator his Hero. He never concluded his disquisition without remarking how happily the sound of the clock is made to alarm the audience."

5 WILKES, [THOMAS.] A General View of the Stage. London: for J. Coote & W. Whetstone, pp. 24, 26, 63, 241-47, 252-53, 270-71, 281.

If Shakespeare is sublime, Otway is tender and speaks "more immediately to the heart than any" of his successors except Rowe. His "choice of subject is always judicious . . . and his incidents striking." The Orphan calls upon us to pity the father and daughter, not Castalio or Polydore, the "one being a perfidious, equivocating friend; the other, a wild, intemperate villain." In Venice Preserv'd, our hearts are touched by the impassioned relationships between Jaffeir and Pierre, Jaffeir and Belvidera; "neither do I know any character where the miseries of a fond husband, a misguided friend, and a weak man are so strongly drawn as by Otway in this Play."

1760

1 ANON. "Essay upon the Merits of Racine and Otway." British Magazine 1:462-64.

Like Racine, Otway is pathetic, expert at "descriptive poetry," and inept in comedy. He is superior to Racine in that he "has touched all the passions in a very masterly manner."

2 ANON. An Essay upon the Present State of the Theatre in France, England and Italy. London: for I. Pottinger, pp. 7, 46-47, 61-62, 93-94.

Venice Preserv'd is better than The Orphan, because to the pathetic it joins the sublime. Surprisingly, Jaffeir affects us with a "pleasing melancholy" as we witness his inner conflicts, and Polydore and Pierre demonstrate how, despite their vices, independent and bold characters tend to interest us more than prudent ones do. Although Jaffeir's actions grow naturally from his personality, Renault's attempt on Belvidera's virtue ill suits his age and dominant passions. Otway probably inserted this scene under the influence of those libertine proclivities "so conspicuous in all his works."

3 ANON. "Parallele entre Otway & Racine; traduit littéralement de l'Anglois." Journal Encyclopédique 7, pt. 3 (1 November): 118-22.

Makes essentially the same points as those in OT.1760.1.

1761

1 [BOSWELL, JAMES.] An Ode to Tragedy. By a Gentleman of Scotland. Edinburgh: by A. Donaldson and J. Reid for Alex. Donaldson, p. 10.

Stanza 12 seems to praise The Orphan for its pathos.

1762

1 ANON. A New and General Biographical Dictionary. Vol. 9. London: for T. Osborne et al., pp. 78-79.

Considers Otway "a distinguished poet and playwright" who "excells in touching the tender passions in tragedy."

2 KAMES, HENRY HOME, LORD. Elements of Criticism. Edinburgh: for A. Kincaid & J. Bell; London: for A. Millar. 1:84-85, 179-80; 3:233-34.

Venice Preserv'd shows that Otway has "fine taste" in depicting the passion of friendship. In The Orphan, justice is ultimately served; when Polydore provokes Castalio to be his executioner, both brothers are punished, the former for his crime, the latter for his breach of faith. Otway fills the "chief place" in each of his two best plays "with an imperfect character, from which a moral can be drawn," but he also manages effectively to place "perfect" characters, Monimia and Belvidera, in the underplots.

3 VOLTAIRE, FRANÇOIS MARIE AROUET. "On the English Tragedy." In The Works of M. de Voltaire. Translated by Tobias Smollett T. Francklin, et al. Vol. 17. London: for J. Newberry, p. 135.

Notes the grossness of the scenes involving Antonio and Aquilina.

1763

1 ANON. "Remarks on the English Tragic Poets." Royal Magazine, or Gentleman's Monthly Companion 9 (July):40-41.

Refutes Voltaire's negative comments on Otway (see OT.1731. and OT.1762.3) by comparing Otway to Shakespeare, noting some borrowings in Venice Preserv'd and The Orphan. Chamont's descriptio of the witch is Shakespearean in spirit and quality, and Venice Preserv'd, its dark plot as effectively depicted as that of

Julius Caesar, "has retained all the terrible graces of Shakespear" and has "touched the passions" as skillfully as "that great genius himself could have done."

1764

1 [BAKER, DAVID ERSKINE.] The Companion to the Play-house. Vols. 1 and 2. London: T. Becket & P.A. Dehondt, C. Henderson, T. Davies, n. pag.

In the first volume, Friendship in Fashion, The Souldiers Fortune, and The Atheist are said to be witty, busy, and entertaining, yet too "loose in respect to sentiment and moral." The Orphan has "poetical, tender and sentimental" language, "affecting" circumstances, and a "distressful" catastrophe. The causes of this distress, however, are "improbable and bungling," and Polydore's libertinism early in the play unnecessarily prejudices us against him when, in fact, we should pity him instead of Castalio. In Venice Preserv'd, Belvidera is the only "truly valuable character." Volume 2 presents Otway as "too licentious" in comedy but as one of England's greatest tragedians, perhaps the greatest in "touching the passions, particularly the tender passion." His fables are usually "familiar and domestic," and his expression has "amazing energy."

1765

1 WALPOLE, HORACE. To the Rev. Thomas Percy, 5 February. In The Letters of Horace Walpole, Fourth Earl of Orford. Edited by Paget Toynbee. Vol. 6. Oxford: Clarendon Press, 1904, p. 183.

"The ditty of Glasgerion seems evidently to have given birth to the tragedy of The Orphan, in which Polidore profits of Monimia's intended favours to Castalio." This letter apparently remained in manuscript until Mrs. Toynbee included it in her edition.

1767

1 ANON. The Rational Rosciad . . . In Two Parts. London: for C. Parker & J. Wilkie, p. 8.

Praises Otway's tenderness--"His audience sympathetically feels, / What his own sensibility reveals"--but objects to his impiety and lack of correctness, especially in the case of Pierre, a traitor for whom we are made to feel compassion.

1768

1 ANON. "The British Theatre." London Magazine 37 (March):124.
In his versions of Venice Preserv'd and The Orphan, Garrick justly expunged some of Otway's grosser lines, but he did not go far enough; too much indecency remains.

2 ANON. "The Life of Mr. Thomas Otway." Prefixed to The Orphan in The Theatre: or, Select Works of the British Dramatic Poets. Vol. 7. Edinburgh: for Martin & Wotherspoon, 6 pp., separately paginated.
Reinforces previous critiques, borrowing heavily from Addison (OT.1711.1) and the "Life" prefixed to the 1712 Works (OT.1712.1). Otway is presented as a skillful artist and master of pathos who sometimes failed to observe decorum, moral decency, and patriotic duty (as a writer).

3 WALPOLE, HORACE. Postscript to The Mysterious Mother. A Tragedy. "Printed at Strawberry-Hill," p. 7.
Otway revived the theatrical genius that had been dead since Shakespeare. "Shakespeare wrote as a philosopher, Otway as a poet."

1769

1 GRANGER, JAMES. A Biographical History of England. Vol. 2. London: for T. Davies, p. 336.
Otway concentrates on "domestic life" and masters the passions both of his characters and of the audience. "His language is that of nature, and consequently the simplest imaginable. He has equally avoided the rant of Lee, and the pomp of Dryden."

1770

1 [GENTLEMAN, FRANCIS.] "The Orphan. A Tragedy by Otway." In The Dramatic Censor; or, Critical Companion. Vol. 2. London: J. Bell; York: C. Etherington, pp. 40-60.
A detailed analysis, mainly focusing on flaws, that concludes the play should be "banished . . . both from the closet and the stage." As always, Otway touches our hearts, but his improbable plot stems from "a most gross and offensive principle, repulses us with licentiousness, and employs characters who give an "unfavourable idea of human nature." Gentleman cites examples to support each of these negative assertions.

2 _____. "A Summary View of the Most Known Dramatic Writers." In The Dramatic Censor; or, Critical Companion. Vol. 2. London: J. Bell; York: C. Etherington, pp. 457-74.

Otway had "true Pathos," and "his versification is the most unaffected and natural for dialogue of any we know." Except for The Orphan and Venice Preserv'd, however, his serious plays are "meagre, and his comedies not only poor, but infamous." Through a "bewitching power," he "annexes pity to the distress of such characters as should rather fall under contempt."

3 _____. "Venice Preserved. A Tragedy by Mr. Otway." In The Dramatic Censor; or, Critical Companion. Vol. 1. London: J. Bell; York: C. Etherington, pp. 313-40.

Sees it as a moving play that is seriously marred by lewdness (Aquilina, Renault), improbabilities and absurdities (Jaffeir's offering his wife as a hostage, the Senate's promise of pardon, the ghosts, Belvidera's death through distraction), violence or descriptions of violence, and impiety (especially in Pierre). Rhyme makes some passages laughable. Bedamar should have been given a larger role, something equivalent to his historical importance. Otway should have given us at least one thoroughly exemplary character, and he should have made the rebels less obnoxious (after all, this is a free country). Otway "wrote to the heart without properly remembering the head."

4 HIFFERNAN, PAUL. Dramatic Genius. In Five Books. London: for the author, pp. 88, 91-94.

Ranks Otway next to Shakespeare and above Southerne and Lillo. Although Venice Preserv'd is better without the comic parts and the ghosts ("which are but the ideal progeny of Belvidera's disordered imagination"), it is a work of genius that exhibits the "four classes of tragic effect": the admirable, the pitiable, the terrible, and the horrible. Its "spirited opening is superior to that of all the tragedies I have read"; its first act provides the "Criteria of Dramatic Genius in Composition"; Jaffeir's giving of his wife as a pledge "is a master-stroke of art bearing in it the seeds of that change which was to be wrought in him afterwards." The final act, especially its last scenes, is powerfully moving.

1771

1 ANON. "The British Theatre." London Magazine: or, Gentleman's Monthly Intelligencer 40 (May):262-65.

Condemns the "superstitious veneration" for Otway's plays which, despite their emotional force, defy probability and clothe vice in an appealing public garb.

1772

1 [HEARD, WILLIAM.] "The Tryal of Dramatic Genius." In The Tryal of Dramatic Genius: A Poem. To which are added A

Collection of Miscellaneous Pieces. London: by W. Goldsmith & P. Shatwell, p. 2.

Apollo summons the "Spirits of Shakespear, Dryden, Otway, [and] Gay" to judge the dramatic excellence of many mid-eighteenth-century authors. The date of this work is based on a note in the Critical Review for December 1772.

2 [POTTER, JOHN.] Remarks on The Orphan. In The Theatrical Review; or, New Companion to the Play-House. London: S. Crowder. 1:70-80; 2:100-101.

Although the play has great emotional force and energetic language, it is full of coarseness, impiety, and improbabilities. Its confused plot comes across particularly badly in a recent performance. The remarks in the first volume of The Theatrical Review are attributed to Potter by Robert Gale Noyes in The Neglected Muse (Providence, R.I.: Brown University Press, 1958), p. 50.

3 [TOWERS, JOSEPH.] "The Life of Thomas Otway." In British Biography. Vol. 7. London: for R. Goadby, pp. 96-99.

A standard set of critical comments is included. Otway is the master of passion and of natural language. His comedies are entertaining but lewd; The Orphan is poetically tender and moving; Venice Preserv'd, with its interesting plot and affecting catastrophe, is "one of the most moving plays upon the English stage."

1774

1 LYTTLETON, GEORGE, LORD. "To a young Lady, with the Tragedy of Venice Preserv'd." In The Works of George Lord Lyttleton. London: for J. Dodsley, pp. 652-53.

In "tender Otway's moving scenes," Belvidera shows us how powerfully a woman's charms can work for virtue. Jaffeir illustrates "A mind, to Honour false, to Virtue true, / In the wild storm of struggling passions tost."

1775

1 [COLMAN, GEORGE, THE ELDER.] Review of Jephson's Braganza. Monthly Review; or, Literary Journal 52:248.

Speaks of "the free spirit, the magnificent simplicity, the familiar vigour of Shakespeare, Beaumont and Fletcher, Otway and Southerne."

2 COOKE, WILLIAM. The Elements of Dramatic Criticism. London: G. Kearsly & G. Robinson, pp. 52-53, 66, 73, 119.

Sees Otway as an "elegant painter of the human passions." In Venice Preserv'd, Jaffeir's change from tender, good-natured husband to potential rebel and murderer "is very reconcileable from the beginning; if we consider his distressed fortune, his resentment to his father-in-law . . . and his inviolable affection to Belvidera." Priuli's abrupt transformation in response to Belvidera's pleading is not convincing, but her language in this scene well exemplifies how the diction of anguish or distress, unlike that of more pleasant states of excitement, must not abound in imagery. The obscene comic scenes threaten to ruin this otherwise fine drama.

3 WALPOLE, HORACE. "Thoughts on Tragedy: in Three Letters to Robert Jephson, Esq.: Letter II." In <u>The Works of Horatio Walpole, Earl of Orford</u>. [Edited by Mary Berry.] Vol. 2. London: G.G. & J. Robinson & J. Edwards, 1798, p. 308.

"Otway, the next to Shakespeare in boldness, though only next but one [that is, Southerne] in strokes of nature . . ., as I prefer the tragic scenes in The Fatal Marriage and Oroonoko to Venice Preserved and The Orphan, has miscarried wofully in Don Carlos." This letter is dated on the authority of Walpole's "Short Notes" in <u>The Yale Edition of Horace Walpole's Correspondence</u>, edited by W.S. Lewis, vol. 13 (New Haven: Yale University Press, 1948), p. 49 and n.

1776

1 MORTIMER, THOMAS. "The Life of John Dryden." In <u>The British Plutarch</u>. Rev. ed. Vol. 5. London: for E. & C. Dilly, p. 199.

"The Tragedies of Otway, Lee, and Southern, are irresistibly moving" but not as "sublime" or "poetical" as Dryden's. I can find no evidence of an earlier edition of this work.

1777

1 WALKER (or HAMILTON), LADY MARY. <u>Memoirs of the Marchioness de Louvoi</u>. In Letters. Vol. 1. London: for Robson & Walter, p. 72.

Lady Susan Danvers notes that in <u>Venice Preserv'd</u> "the passions are finely touched . . ., though perhaps there is something to be desired both in the foundation of them, and in the height and elegance of expression . . . but nature is there."

1779

1 JOHNSON, SAMUEL. "Otway." In <u>The Lives of the English Poets; and a Criticism on their Works</u>. Vol. 1. Dublin: for Whitestone, Williams, et al., pp. 441-48.

Sees Otway as "one of the first names in the English drama," sharing "some" of Shakespeare's and Jonson's "excellencies." On

The Orphan: "Its whole power is upon the affections; for it is not written with much comprehension of thought, or elegance of expression." Venice Preserv'd is a great work, "notwithstanding the want of morality in the original design, and the despicable scenes of vile comedy." With stronger images and more energetic language than The Orphan, Venice Preserv'd is "the work of a man not attentive to decency, nor zealous for virtue; but of one who conceived forcibly, and drew originally, by consulting nature in his own breast." Johnson's biography is extensively quoted, without acknowledgment, in "Life of Thomas Otway," prefixed to Venice Preserv'd in The British Drama, vol. 4 (London: for C. Cooke, 1817), separately paginated iv-vii.

1780

1 DAVIES, THOMAS. Memoirs of the Life of David Garrick, Esq. "New Edition." Vol. 1. London: for the author, pp. 117-18.

Caius Marius, in which "the most affecting scenes are borrowed from Shakespeare," comments on the contemporary feuding of Whigs and Tories. Garrick "improved" Otway's modification of Shakespeare's ending.

2 HODSON, WILLIAM. "Postscript, containing Observations on Tragedy." Appended to Zoraida: A Tragedy. London: by W. Richardson for G. Kearsly, pp. 71, 81.

Like Euripides, Otway "is such a master of each avenue to the heart, that he . . . . strikes us blind to his imperfections." Sees the final act of The Orphan as "little more than an extended catastrophe."

1781

1 ANON. "Otway (Thomas)." In Encyclopaedia Britannica. 2d ed. Vol. 8. Edinburgh: J. Balfour et al., p. 5787.

Although Otway is "deemed too licentious" in comedy, in his tragedies, with their "familiar and domestic" stories and "amazing energy" of expression, he is unsurpassed in "touching the passions."

1782

1 ANON. "Remarkable Circumstances that occasioned the Deaths of Four English Poets." Scots Magazine 44:595.

"His feelings must be great, who could so nobly describe affection in his Venice Preserved."

2 BAKER, DAVID ERSKINE, [and ISAAC REED.] Biographica Dramatica or, A Companion to the Playhouse. "A New Edition." Vol. 2. London: Rivingtons, pp. 23, 267, 389-90.

In addition to what Baker said in The Companion to the Playhouse (see OT.1764.1), Reed quotes Samuel Johnson, without proper acknowledgment, on The Orphan and Venice Preserv'd (see OT.1779.1).

1783

1 BLAIR, HUGH. Lectures on Rhetoric and Belles Lettres. Vol. 2. London: for W. Strahan & T. Cadell; Edinburgh: for W. Creech, pp. 503, 505, 525.

Regards Otway, with reference to Venice Preserv'd and The Orphan, as a genius who too often mixes indecency with tragedy and puts too wearing a strain on the emotions. "He is the very opposite of French decorum." Monimia and Belvidera show that less than illustrious characters can deeply interest us. Jaffeir's case exemplifies how modern tragedy aims at a higher object than ancient tragedy did. Whereas the latter merely preached submission to destiny, Venice Preserv'd is "theatre of passion . . . showing the direful effects which . . . strong emotions, when misguided, or left unrestrained, produce."

1784

1 CARRÉ, JEROME. "Du Théatre Anglais." In Oeuvres complètes de Voltaire. Vol. 47. [Paris]: La Société Litteraire-Typographique, pp. 290, 305-11.

Speaks of "le tendre Otwai, tres-supérieur au tendre Racine." In a section headed "L'Orpheline, tragédie," Carré discusses The Orphan and compares Otway with Racine.

2 DAVIES, THOMAS. "Otway." In Dramatic Miscellanies. Vol. 3. London: For the author, pp. 176-253.

A fresh, full, and (for its time) penetrating assessment, which gives Otway credit for moving dramatic language away from heroic artifice and toward "its true and genuine tone." He lacked Dryden's "numbers," learning, and intellectual fitness, and he needed the inspiration of Shakespeare, but his language "cannot be mended or improved;--through [it] nature speaks." Alcibiades is his weakest work. In The Orphan, he shows himself our greatest master of pathos, though Polydore's "gross address and brutal courtship" must be softened for modern audiences and we must overlook the near-fatalistic final two lines. Acasto may be a portrait of James, Duke of Ormand.

Venice Preserv'd is "a grand historical painting," by no means inferior to St. Réal's narrative ("as Voltaire presumptuously asserts"). The plot is artfully conducted, the dialogues animated, the whole full of moving scenes. Pierre may seem an attractive villain, but he is punished. Elliot should never have been included: Otway has branded treason on a revered name. And perhaps Aquilina should have been used more as a foil to Belvidera.

Although we are justly offended by the disgusting scenes involving Antonio and Aquilina, they cannot be cut without ruining Otway's pacing, and they did once effectively satirize Shaftesbury. Still and all, these comic episodes, like the author's full-scale attempts at comedy, are unworthy of his powers.

1785

1 ANON. Remarks on Otway. Lounger, no. 28 (13 August):109-12.
The Orphan is "grossly immoral," and it "dignifies distresses." In Venice Preserv'd, "weaknesses are flattered," "passions [are] indulged," and the audience is wickedly made to condemn the constituted rulers of a state.

1788

1 ANON. "Reflections on the English Drama." European Magazine 13 (April):252.
Indiscriminately praises The Orphan and Venice Preserv'd as unexcelled masterpieces by a dramatist who is superior to Virgil, Shakespeare, and Racine, "and all the poets that ever existed" in his "mastery of the passions."

1789

1 [NEVE, PHILIP.] "Otway." In Cursory Remarks on Some of the Ancient English Poets, Particularly Milton. London: n.p., pp. 89-95.
Despite the unworthy Alcibiades and the badly designed, lewd comedies, Otway ranks with Shakespeare and Rowe in his abil ity to imitate nature and delineate passions. No other writer has borrowed more from Shakespeare, or more nearly approximated his style, than Otway. Whenever he wrote on a subject that "bor analogy to his own feelings," his genius gained extra enthusiasm from "a rooted, frantic passion" (his love for Mrs. Barry). In his letters, poems, and plays, Don Carlos, "the Lover, the Swain Polydore, Jaffier, and Otway" are all "the same person." Reprinted as "Remarks on the Dramatic Poets: Otway" in Monthly Mirror 12 (1801):46-48.

1790

1 STANLEY, EDWARD. "Thoughts on Tragedy." Appended to Elmira A Dramatick Poem. Norwich: Crouse & Stevenson, p. 139.
An interesting attempt to go beyond merely noting that Venice Preserv'd is emotionally effective. "The variety of passions displayed . . . form an elegant contrast to the

character of Pierre, and by exciting a previous sensibility, make his speeches more effectually strike the heart." Addison's Cato is a lesser play, primarily because its title character is too cool, declamatory, and condescending. In contrast, Pierre is an instinctive patriot, "a man of feeling," "one of the people."

1791

1 ANON. Remarks on The Orphan. In Bell's British Theatre. Vol. 4. London: J. Bell, 1 p., separately paginated.

Because he has the "powers of the true poet," Otway can take an improbable story such as this one, do a poor job of embodying it in a dramatic plot, and yet "erect a tragic structure which will please to the end of time." The "excellence" of his "sentiment and diction bears down everything," even his "coarse and impure" materials and the "tinge of licentiousness" that discolors all his works.

2 ANON. "Thomas Otway" and Remarks on Venice Preserv'd. In Bell's British Theatre. Vol. 2. London: J. Bell, 5 pp., separately paginated.

Otway is a "great author" who exemplifies "the sublime pre-eminence, and indiscreet abasement of Genius." Venice Preserv'd, a play about "the influence of passion on life," reflects the corruption of Otway's mind, for the tender and dutiful Belvidera is the only character whose distresses deserve our commiseration. Pierre "is sunken by cruel ambition," while Jaffeir, unmanly and contemptible, can consider destroying his country but cannot withstand "poverty, the importunities of a wife, or the reflections of treachery to a friend."

3 [GARDENSTONE, FRANCIS GARDEN, LORD.] "Remarks on the Present State of the English Drama." In Miscellanies in Prose and Verse. Edinburgh: J. Robertson, pp. 137-38.

Sees Caius Marius as tedious and second-hand.

4 JOHNSON, SAMUEL. Remark recorded in 1780. In The Life of Samuel Johnson, LL.D, by James Boswell. Vol. 2. London: by Henry Baldwin for Charles Dilly, pp. 339-40.

"'Sir, . . . if Otway had written this play [Dodsley's Cleone], no other of his pieces would have been remembered.' . . . it must be remembered, that Johnson always appeared not to be sufficiently sensible of the merit of Otway."

1792

1 ANON. A New Theatrical Dictionary. London: S. Bladon, pp. 6, 213, 286-87, 322.

Synthesizes previous criticism, adding nothing new. _Alcibiades_ is Otway's worst piece, _Venice Preserv'd_ his best, _The Orphan_ moving but improbable, the comedies entertaining but morally disgusting.

2 GARDENSTONE, FRANCIS GARDEN, LORD. "Horace, LIB. IV. ODE IX." In _Miscellanies in Prose and Verse_. 2d ed. Edinburgh: n.p., p. 217.

"And Otway woeful nonsense wrote, / But still Monimia melts the soul." This poem does not appear in the first edition of the _Miscellanies_ (see OT.1791.3).

1793

1 AIKIN, JOHN. "On the Impression of Reality Attending Dramatic Representations, Read October 7." In _Memoirs of the Literary and Philosophical Society of Manchester_. Vol. 4., pt. 1. Manchester, n.p., pp. 102-4.

When Mrs. Siddons plays Belvidera, "I sob, weep, am almost choaked with the mixed emotions of pity, terror, and apprehension and totally forget the theatre. . . . What I feel is _genuine sympathy_."

1794

1 ALVES, ROBERT. _Sketches of a History of Literature_. Edinburgh: Alex. Chapman & Co., pp. 116, 139-40, 230.

Ranks Otway just below Shakespeare, Jonson, Beaumont, and Fletcher. Otway's appeal to our sense of pity is contrasted with Dryden's appeal to the imagination rather than to the heart. Shakespeare's passion is more terrible than pathetic, but Otway's in _Venice Preserv'd_ and _The Orphan_ "has more of the soft and tender than of the sublime." No later dramatist, except possibly Southerne in _Oroonoko_, has equaled Otway in the generating of the pathetic.

1795

1 ANDERSON, ROBERT. "The Life of Otway." In _The Works of the British Poets. With Prefaces, Biographical and Critical_. Vol. 6. London: John & Arthur Arch; Edinburgh: Bell & Bradfute, & J. Mundell & Co., pp. 443-45.

Synthesizes previous criticism, making minor additions; grants, for instance, that _The Orphan_ has blemishes, but insists that "where the heart is interested, comprehension of thought or elegance of expression may be wanting, yet not missed." _Venice Preserv'd_ lacks virtuous characters, gives way too often to absurdly comic scenes, suffers from indelicacies, yet retains power over our feelings by virtue of its fully realized characters, blend of public and private distresses, and energetic language. The comedies are deservedly neglected for their licentiousness, but the tragedies continue to draw tears.

2 JACKSON, WILLIAM. "Letter XIV." In Thirty Letters on Various Subjects. 3d ed. "with considerable additions." London: for T. Cadell, p. 96.

Notes "a degree of improbability in the plot of our best tragedies" such as The Orphan and Venice Preserv'd.

1797

1 ANON. "Life of Otway." In The Poetical Works of Thomas Otway. Cooke's Pocket Edition. London: C. Cooke, pp. v-x.

The first real attempt to revise the criticism that appeared in the 1712 Works (see OT.1712.1), though there had been editions of the plays which were prefaced by critical biographies in 1736 and 1757. Nevertheless, the revisions amount to no more than interpolations from key critical comments made since 1712 by Baker, Johnson, and others. Before the milestone edition by Thornton (see OT.1813.3), there would be another biocritical sketch in the first volume of the 1812 Works, but it makes no advances.

2 CALSABIGI, RANIERI Di. A Translation of Ranieri Di Calsabigi's Letter to Count Alfieri, on Tragedy. With Notes . . . By J. Penn, Esq. London: for Elmsly, Faulder, Sewell, Owen, & White, p. 20.

Refers to "the warm but incoherent Otway."

1798

1 DRAKE, NATHAN. "On the Poetry of the Ages of Elizabeth and the Charleses, and of the Present Reign." In Literary Hours or Sketches Critical and Narrative. London: by J. Burkitt for T. Cadell, Jr., & W. Davies, p. 445.

"Not Shakespeare himself can vie with Otway in eliciting the tear of pity."

1799

1 SEWARD, ANNA. Letter to Thomas Whalley, 8 July. In Journals and Correspondence of Thomas Sedgewick Whalley, D.D. Edited by Hill Wickham. Vol. 2. London: Richard Bentley, 1863, p. 122.

Praises Otway for renouncing the unities. This appears to be the earliest printing of the letter.

1800

1 DIBDIN, CHARLES. A Complete History of the Stage. Vol. 4. London: C. Dibdin, pp. 96-108.

Regards Otway as "a great and extraordinary writer" who "melted the heart, and refined into nature what the mathematical poets had squared by rules of art." Alcibiades and Caius Marius lack artistry, and the comedies are entertaining but immoral. The Cheats of Scapin is "a very pleasant farce." The Orphan, which is not founded on improbabilities, is a strangely powerful blend of the revolting and the sweet, while Venice Preserv'd forcibly appeals both to the mind and to the heart. Pierre, especially, is well drawn and should always serve as a lesson for leaders in avoiding ingratitude and for private persons in avoiding rebellious actions.

2 [WALDRON, FRANCIS GODOLPHIN, et al.] A Compendious History of the English Stage. London: J.S. Jordon, p. 38.

A standard sketch, depicting Otway as the master of passions

3 WATKINS, JOHN. An Universal Biographical and Historical Dictionary. London: T. Davison & T. Gillet for R. Phillips, n. pag.

Another stock survey: "Otway excels in touching the tender passions in tragedy."

1801

1 LAMB, CHARLES. Letter to Robert Lloyd, 26 July. In Charles Lamb and the Lloyds. Edited by E.V. Lucas. London: Smith, Elder, & Co., 1898, p. 139.

"Pierre and Jaffeir are the best things in Otway. Belvider is a poor Creature, . . . Monimia is a little better, but she whines. I like Calista in the Fair Penitent better than either of Otway's women." This appears to be the first printing of this letter.

2 _____. Letter to Thomas Manning, April. In The Letters of Charles Lamb. Edited by Thomas Noon Talfourd. Vol. 1. London: Edward Moxon, 1837, p. 175.

First printed here, the letter speaks of "the interesting Otway."

3 MURPHY, ARTHUR. The Life of David Garrick, Esq. Dublin: by Brett Smith for Wogan, Burnet, et al., pp. 90-94, 99.

In Venice Preserv'd, Antonio and Aquilina are gross and irrelevant to the main design, but Pierre is strikingly depicted and Jaffeir as a role is "perhaps the fittest for the stage in t whole circle of drama." An epitome of the Aristotelian mixed hero, he possesses a virtuous disposition that is undercut by weakness, and his "several virtues . . . acting separately . . . lead him into error." Caius Marius is "a most unnatural mixture" in which Otway seems to forget "his power over the passions," especially in the catastrophe.

1802

1 ANON. "Drury-Lane Theatre, Friday, Jan. 15." Theatrical Repertory; or, Weekly Rosciad, no. 18 (18 January):281-82.
Recommends the "genuine tenderness and sensibility" in "Otway's exquisite tragedy of Venice Preserved."

2 WALKER, GEORGE. "On Tragedy and the Interest in Tragical Representations." In Memoirs of the Literary and Philosophical Society of Manchester. Vol. 5, Pt. 2. London: for Cadell & Davies, pp. 329-30.
"Otway, the eldest son of Shakespeare, has . . . greatly lessened the impression of his genius, by the immorality and profligacy of his principal characters." At least his Monimia and Belvidera are there to "relieve the horror of the villains with whom they are associated."

1804

1 MALKIN, BENJAMIN HEATH. "To John Philip Kemble, Esquire." Prefixed to Almahide and Hamet, A Tragedy. London: Longman & Rees, pp. 25-26.
Otway was a great dramatist, "yet so infected were his pieces with the reigning absurdities and improprieties of his age" that only The Orphan and Venice Preserv'd hold the stage. If it were not for their emotional power and natural characters, even these two would have gone the way of Otway's obscene comedies.

2 [SCOTT, WALTER.] "Preface of the Editor." In The British Drama: . . . Tragedies. Vol. 1, Pt. 1. London: William Miller, p. iv.
Praises the tender and affecting interview between Castalio and Monimia in the final act of The Orphan; recommends the picture "of conjugal affection, and persisting fidelity, in . . . Belvidera" of Venice Preserv'd; and sees Otway as a master at depicting love on the stage.

1805

1 HOLCROFT, THOMAS. "An Essay on Dramatic Composition." In The Theatrical Recorder. No. 2. London: C. Mercier & Co., pp. 140, 142.

Regards Venice Preserv'd as the first of a "few tragedies, besides those of Shakespeare," which show "knowledge of the human heart." Otway equals Shakespeare and Rowe in terms of the capacity to render "the frantic passions of the mind."

1807

1 HUNT, LEIGH. "Mrs. Henry Siddons" and "Miss Smith." In Critical Essays on the Performers of the London Theatres. London: John Hunt, pp. 206, 213.

On Belvidera: "There is a vigour about the glowing Venetian, an instant obedience to impulse, and I had almost said a prurient vehemence, which Otway was always too apt to mingle with his idea of youth: in an Italian female perhaps it is more natural than an actress with English feelings could represent." He gives Belvidera "a violence of passion that would render her masculine, did it arise from any thing but love."

2 SOUTHEY, ROBERT, ed. "Thomas Otway." In Specimens of the Later English Poets. Vol. 1. London: Longman, p. 1.

Otway's tragedies are "peculiarly tender, and forcible."

1808

1 AIKIN, JOHN. "Otway, Thomas." In General Biography; or, Lives, Critical and Historical. Compiled by Aikin, Thomas Morgan, and William Johnston. Vol. 7. London: for J. Johnson, pp. 547-48.

Synthesizes previous criticism, and notes, in addition, that Venice Preserv'd was thought too powerful to stage during times of political unrest.

2 GILLILAND, THOMAS. The Dramatic Mirror. Vol. 1. London: C. Chapple, pp. 488-90.

Standard stuff.

3 INCHBALD, ELIZABETH, ed. Remarks on The Orphan and Venice Preserv'd. In The British Theatre. Vol. 12. London: Longman, Hurst, Rees, & Orme, noncontinuous pag.

Although The Orphan deserves oblivion for its despicable characters and its ultimately horrifying effect, it does have power, and "that mistake of one brother for the other" is not so improbable as critics have maintained. Venice Preserv'd is better; "amongst a great deal of political declamation, anger, and fury, is" tenderly moving pathos, chiefly arising from the display of conjugal affection between Jaffeir and Belvidera. Otway's great emotional power derives from his endowing characters like Jaffeir with anguish reflecting his own personal experience.

4 SCOTT, WALTER, ed. "The Life of John Dryden." In The Works of John Dryden. Vol. 1. London: William Miller; Edinburgh: James Ballantyne, pp. 193, 280n.

Remarks that Otway was "a rival [to Dryden] more formidable . . . than either Settle or 'starch' Johnny Crowne," and notes that Antonio in Venice Preserv'd was "said to be meant for Shaftesbury."

1809

1 [BYRON, GEORGE GORDON, LORD.] English Bards and Scotch Reviewers. A Satire. London: for James Cawthorn, pp. 2, 35; ll. 13-16, 425.

Ranks Otway with Shakespeare, Massinger, and Congreve. His "scenes" could "melt" in those days when "nature . . . an English audience felt"; since his day, he has resigned his place "to feebler Bards."

1810

1 ANON. "Greek and English Tragedy." Reflector 1, no. 1 (1810-11):69, 71.

Otway's simple language and the effective opening exposition in Venice Preserv'd are to be commended. Moreover, like Euripides, Otway masterfully evokes "the pathetic." His depictions of love, however, were hardened and made more sensuous by the infection of Charles II's court.

1811

1 [LAMB, CHARLES.] "On the Genius and Character of Hogarth; with some Remarks on a Passage in the Writings of the late Mr. Barry." Reflector 2, no. 3 (March-December):68.

Unlike the gravedigger in Hamlet and the fool in Lear, the comic parts of Venice Preserv'd are "pure, irrelevant, impertinent discords." Attributed to Lamb on the authority of Joan Coldwell, ed., Charles Lamb on Shakespeare (New York: Barnes & Noble, 1978), p. 45.

2 [SCOTT, WALTER.] "Remarks on English Tragedy." In The Modern British Drama. Vol. 1. London: William Miller; Edinburgh: James Ballantyne, p. iv.

Notes that "the Orphan, and Venice Preserved, contain . . . exquisite touches of passionate and natural feeling."

1812

1 BAKER, DAVID ERSKINE, ISAAC REED, and STEPHEN JONES. Biographia Dramatica; or, A Companion to the Playhouse. Newly revised by Jones. London: Longman & Co., 2:252; 3:105-6, 377-

Slightly alters Baker's emphasis on a few points (see OT.1764.1). Friendship in Fashion is now seen to be a good deal less objectionable than the other comedies, perhaps because it is felt to be dramaturgically better than the rest. Jones deletes Reed's negative comments on the language and thoughts of Venice Preserv'd (see OT.1782.2) but adds references to Voltaire's opinions about the play (see OT.1731.3 and OT.1762.3). Moreover, he now maintains that Belvidera is not the only exemplary character, since Pierre also is "nobly drawn."

1813

1 ANON. Review of Thornton's edition of The Works of Thomas Otway. Anti-Jacobin Review, and True Churchman's Magazine 44, no. 179 (April):390-93.

Laments "violations of decency" in both comedies and tragedies, and opposes Thornton by maintaining that the moral of The Orphan is not the dangers of lying but rather "the fatal consequence of an unrestrained indulgence of lawless passion." Furthermore, Castalio's concealing of his marriage was no act of deception; he "was actuated rather by a prudent and natural reserve." Polydore is the true villain of the piece. The final lines do not, despite critical consensus to the contrary, dismiss human moral responsibility; they suggest humble resignation to divine providence.

2 BYRON, GEORGE GORDON, LORD. Letter to Annabella Milbanke, 6 September. In The Works of Lord Byron: Letters and Journals. Rev. ed. Edited by Rowland E. Prothero. Vol. 3. London: John Murray, 1899, pp. 399-400.

Asserts that Joanna Baillie "is our only dramatist since Otway and Southern; I don't except Home." This appears to be the first printing of this letter; it was not included in Prothero's 1892 Works.

3 THORNTON, THOMAS, ed. "The Life of Thomas Otway" and prefaces to individual works. In The Works of Thomas Otway. London: T. Turner. 1:vii-lx, 3-4, 77-80, 163-64, 205-6; 2:3-4, 109-10, 201-6, 291-92; 3:3-8, 99-100.

Definitive, both critically and textually, for its time, this critique presents Otway as a great creator of pathos and the familiar style. While his best work ranks "among the noblest efforts of dramatic genius," his comedies are inferior to those of Crowne and Shadwell.

Alcibiades is his worst play in all respects. Don Carlos, with its hyperbolic love scenes, did not merit the success it gained. In Titus and Berenice, Otway versifies better than Racine but retains essentials of the original even while reducing its scope. Friendship in Fashion would be entertaining in several respects if it were not so obscene. Notwithstanding some ludicrous scenes, Caius Marius improves Shakespeare's diction and shows Otway can borrow judiciously and can manage blank verse.

With The Orphan, Otway finds his own voice and style, leaving fashion and romance in favor of nature and truth. "Among the most admirable productions of the English drama," it benefits from a convincing, if somewhat improbable, plot; focused construction; skillfully drawn characters; ideas, passions, and language that are natural and familiar. Perhaps the closing lines are too fatalistic, the author's attitudes toward the two brothers more sharply distinguished than necessary, some of the language and action indecent, and Acasto's advice to his sons confusingly divided between satire and sincerity. The Souldiers Fortune is brisk and various but unfit, because of its licentiousness, for public performance.

Otway's masterpiece is Venice Preserv'd. It combines great events and domestic woe with admirable effectiveness. The characters are transformed by Otway's theatrical genius from historical personages to complex, interesting human beings. Otway may be justly condemned for creating those disgusting scenes with Antonio and Aquilina, but to omit them in modern productions is to spoil the rhythm of movement from scene to scene. And he should not be censured for generating compassion for his rebels; their dilemma is instructively human. The Atheist is an engaging play in terms of bustle and novelty, but it is artistically poor and morally repulsive. "It may here be urged, in mitigation of the censure which oppresses Otway's comedies, that their very grossness destroys, in a great measure, their pernicious influence."

1814

1 DIBDIN, THOMAS JOHN, ed. Remarks on Venice Preserv'd. In The London Theatre. Vol. 1. London: Whittingham & Arliss, p. 3.

Antonio is omitted because "the picture drawn of his disgusting follies was by no means calculated either to improve or amuse."

1815

1 ANON. "Theatre Royal, Covent Garden: Saturday, Dec. 2--Otway's Tragedy of The Orphan." Theatrical Inquisitor 7 (December):474-78.

Considers it a fine, powerful play, inoffensive to moral principles but offensive to "the eye of delicacy" when it shows "all but the very act of fornication."

2 CHALMERS, ALEXANDER. The General Biographical Dictionary. Vol. 23. London: J. Nichols & Son, pp. 419-25.
Synthesizes previous criticism.

3 SCHLEGEL, AUGUSTUS WILLIAM. A Course of Lectures on Dramatic Art and Literature. Translated by John Black. Vol. 2. London: Baldwin, Cradock, and Joy; Edinburgh: William Blackwood; Dublin: John Cumming, pp. 310-11.
That "incongruous" plagiarism from Shakespeare, Caius Marius, shows "how little Otway understood the true rules of composition." The Orphan and Venice Preserv'd are "far from being good; but there is matter in them, especially in the last; and amidst much empty declamation there are some truly pathetic passages."

1816

1 BYRON, GEORGE GORDON, LORD. Letter to Thomas Moore, 17 November. In Letters and Journals of Lord Byron: With Notices of his Life. Edited by Thomas Moore. Vol. 2. London: John Murray, 1830, p. 54.
The city of Venice "is a poetical place; and classical, to us, from Shakespeare and Otway."

2 DIBDIN, THOMAS JOHN, ed. Remarks on The Orphan. In The London Theatre. Vol. 18. London: Whittingham & Arliss, p. 3.
The play required careful revision because, "with numberless beauties, it exhibits as much inconsistency as if it were the wildest romance."

3 [HAZLITT, WILLIAM.] Review of Schlegel's Lectures on Dramatic Art and Literature. Edinburgh Review 26 (February):105.
Otway's plays are "only the ebullitions of a fine, enthusiastic, sanguine temperament: and his genius would no more have improved with age, than the beauty of his person."

4 JONES, CHARLES INIGO. Memoirs of Miss O'Neill; containing her Public Character, Private Life, and Dramatic Progress. London: for D. Cox, pp. 24-35, 73-82.
Considers The Orphan and Venice Preserv'd Otway's greatest works, though the former is too often indecent, presents "a crime too horrid for the feelings to dwell on," and allows our pity for the main characters to obscure their guilt. The Orphan contains some interesting parallels with Southerne's Fatal Marriage. Venice Preserv'd, with its masterful "concatenation of circumstances," is perhaps the best of all English plays in terms of stage effect. Emphasizing Miss O'Neill's acting, Jones discusses a number of scenes from the two plays.

1817

1 CUMBERLAND, RICHARD. "Critique on Venice Preserved." Prefixed to the play in The British Drama. A Collection of the Most Esteemed Dramatic Productions. Vol. 4. London: for C. Cooke, separately paginated, pp. viii-xv.

Presents a scene-by-scene plot summary and analysis. The play is "an altar to obscenity . . . . one of the most corrupt and vicious compositions in the language," albeit there are a few dramatically powerful parts in it. In making Pierre a mad pagan, a traitor, and a hypocrite who masks the desire for personal revenge with high-sounding political rhetoric, Otway abuses his own talent, just as he does in portraying Jaffeir as a "ruined spendthrift" and in making Belvidera a hostage to cutthroats in a prostitute's house. And as for the scenes involving Antonio and Aquilina, they are "the invention of hell-born wickedness."

2 BYRON, GEORGE GORDON, LORD. Letter to John Murray, 2 April. In Letters and Journals of Lord Byron: With Notices of his Life. Edited by Thomas Moore. Vol. 2. London: John Murray, p. 94.

"I . . . am a very great admirer of his [of Otway's],--all except of that maudlin b___h of chaste lewdness and blubbering curiosity, Belvidera, whom I utterly despise, abhor, and detest."

3 [HAZLITT, WILLIAM.] "Drury-Lane Theatre." Times (London), 10 October, n. pag.

Venice Preserv'd is a "noble tragedy." The character of Pierre is especially interesting: "not one of blunt energy, but of deep art. It is more sarcastic than fierce, and even the fierceness is more calculated to wound others than to shake or disturb himself. He is a master-mind, that plays with the foibles and passions of others, and wields their energies to his dangerous purposes with conscious careless indifference."

4 [HUNT, LEIGH.] "Theatrical Examiner. No. 301." Examiner, no. 511 (12 October):650.

"Belvidera is a heroine of strong passions, but they are founded on great tenderness." Attributed to Hunt in Leigh Hunt's Dramatic Criticism 1808-1831, ed. Lawrence Huston Houtchens and Carolyn Washburn Houtchens (New York: Columbia University Press, 1949).

1818

1 BYRON, GEORGE GORDON, LORD. Childe Harold's Pilgrimage. Canto the Fourth. London: John Murray, pp. 5, 12; stanzas iv, xviii.

"Shylock and the Moor, / And Pierre, can not be swept or worn away." Otway, Ratcliff, Schiller, Shakespeare's art, / Had stamp'd her [Venice's] image in me, even so."

2 OXBERRY, W., ed. Remarks on Venice Preserv'd. In The New English Drama. Vol. 4. London: W. Simkin & R. Marshall, pp. i-iv.

Feels that Otway is overrated. In Venice Preserv'd, "there is neither poetry of thought nor of expression; it is prose without the variety of prose." The play has indistinct, one-dimensional characters, and its pathos is not as powerful as Ford's, Webster's, or Shakespeare's. What pathos there is inheres in situation, for in Otway's language there is only "delirium."

1819

1 CAMPBELL, THOMAS. "An Essay on English Poetry." In Specimens of the British Poets; with Biographical and Critical Notices. Vol. 1. London: John Murray, p. 249.

The Orphan and Venice Preserv'd are "two beautiful plays" which form an exception to the "degeneracy" of ranting and rhyming. Campbell's An Essay on English Poetry (Boston: Wells & Lilly, 1819) is a separate printing of this same piece.

2 HAZLITT, WILLIAM. Lectures on the English Comic Writers. Delivered at the Surry Institution. London: Taylor & Hessey, p. 130.

In "Lecture III," asserts that "Otway's comedies do no sort of credit to him: on the contrary, they are as desperate as his fortunes."

1820

1 HAZLITT, WILLIAM. Lectures Chiefly on the Dramatic Literature of the Age of Elizabeth. Delivered at the Surry Institution. London: Stodart & Steuart; Edinburgh: Bell & Bradfute, pp. 335-37.

Sees Otway as the most recent creator of a "regular," "classic" tragedy "of indisputable excellence and lasting interest." Venice Preserv'd rivets the attention and touches the heart both on stage and in the closet. It exhibits "awful suspense," "touches of nature and pathos," "conflict of duties and passions," and a "solemn march of . . . tragical events to the fatal catastrophe." Jaffeir's "effeminacy [and] luxurious and cowardly indulgence" are interestingly juxtaposed to Pierre's "bold intrepid villainy and contemptuous irony." On the other hand, The Orphan is neither heroic nor pathetic; it is a display of "voluptuous effeminacy of sentiment and mawkish distress." Otway's main fault was that he "indulged his mere sensibility too much, yielding to the immediate impression or emotion excited in his own mind, and not placing himself enough in the minds and situations of others, or following the workings of nature sufficiently with keenness of eye and strength of will into its heights and depths, its strongholds as well as its weak sides."

2 MATTHEWS, HENRY. The Diary of an Invalid. London: John Murray, pp. 274-75.

In an interesting parallel to Byron's remarks in the 1816 letter to Moore and in Childe Harold (see OT.1816.1 and OT.1818.1), Matthews finds that Shakespeare and Otway--"Othello and Shylock," "Pierre and Jaffeir"--have provided him with a more vivid mental context for enjoying Venice than have historical accounts.

3 [TALFOURD, THOMAS NOON.] "Rymer on Tragedy." Retrospective Review 1:15.

"Venice Preserved is cast in the mould of dignity and of grandeur; but the characters want nobleness, the poetry coherence, and the sentiments truth." Attributed to Talfourd in his Critical and Miscellaneous Writings (Philadelphia: A. Hart, 1850), pp. 21-28.

1821

1 ANON. "On the Alleged Decline of Dramatic Writing." Blackwood's Edinburgh Magazine 9, no. 51 (June):280-81.

Regards Otway as the third best tragedian of the Restoration (after Dryden and Lee); takes exception to the comic scenes in Venice Preserv'd but feels that both it and The Orphan are first-rate.

2 ANON. "Otway's 'Orphan.'" Drama; or, Theatrical Pocket Magazine 1, no. 1 (May):21-23.

Discusses the play in relation to its presumed source, a pamphlet entitled English Adventures.

3 ANON. "Otway's 'Venice Preserved.'" Drama; or, Theatrical Pocket Magazine 1, no. 14 (August):167-69.

Finds the scenes involving Antonio satirically powerful in their "wantonness" but feels they have been "properly reprobated."

4 ANON. Remarks on The Orphan. In English Theatre: Tragedies. Vol. 1. London: for John Bumpus, n. pag.

The language is "poetical and tender, and the incidents affecting; but . . . there is great inconsistency."

1822

1 ANON. "The Tragic Drama." European Magazine 82 (November): 410.

Despite his tendency to exaggerate emotional effusions and to make his characters whine, Otway writes "condensed and powerful" plays, rich in poetry and pathos, comparable to Massinger and Ford. The Orphan and Venice Preserv'd are "marked by the finest genius."

2 ANON. "Dramatic Errors." Drama; or, Theatrical Pocket Magazine 2, no. 3 (January):132.

In The Orphan, Monimia's cool reply to Polydore's rudeness at the close of Act 1 is unnatural. Acasto's advice to his children incongruously mixes politics, irony, wit, and profligacy. The play also treats clergymen rather badly. In the middle of Act 4 of Venice Preserv'd, the dialogue between Jaffeir and Belvidera is poorly managed.

3 [JEFFREY, FRANCIS.] "Lord Byron's Tragedies." Edinburgh Review 36:414.

"Otway, with the sweet and mellow diction of the former age, had none of its force, variety, or invention." Ascribed to Jeffrey in his Contributions to the Edinburgh Review (London: Longman et al., 1844), II.

1823

1 ANON. "Cursory Remarks on the Relation between the Tragedy of Venice Preserved, by Otway, and The History of the Conspiracy on which that Drama is Founded." In The Conspiracy of the Spaniards against the Republic of Venice, by César Vichard, l'Abbé de Saint-Réal. Anonymously translated. London: J. Carpenter & Son, pp. 119-27.

While Venice Preserv'd is a moving play, "great" in its way it shows that Otway lacked the capacity to construct a complex plot or to develop multifaceted characters. He missed several opportunities to dramatize historically interesting incidents, and he should certainly have employed either Bedamar or the Duke of Ossuna instead of the repulsive Antonio. As an original creation, the relationship between Jaffeir and Belvidera is effective albeit marred by some inconsistencies and absurdities. Aquilina should have been more carefully contrasted with Belvidera; Priuli's absence on business at a crucial moment should have been exploited; more should have been made of the wedding of the Doge to the Adriatic; and so on.

2 ANON. "The Drama." London Magazine 8 (November):549-50.

Venice Preserv'd is dull to read, lively to see. Its "pathos and florid eloquence" give it a "second-rate superiority" akin to Massinger's.

3 ANON. "An Essay on Dramatic Simplicity of Sentiment and Diction." Drama; or, Theatrical Pocket Magazine 5, no. 1 (August):17-18.

Through the bewitching quality of his language, Otway transforms immoral or criminal characters into objects of our sympathy. If Otway is "the voice of nature" and of the pathetic, he is also the master of "verbal delusion."

4 ANON. "Lord J. Russell--Don Carlos, A Tragedy." Quarterly Review 29, no. 58 (July):372-73.

The rhyming verse in Otway's version of Don Carlos was "peculiarly ill adapted to his rough and vigorous mind."

5 ANON. "Theatre-Royal: Venice Preserv'd." Edinburgh Dramatic Review 5, no. 225 (12 August):97-99.

Otway has never been equaled in "grand simplicity" of style, and he is "almost" the only pathetic writer who combines "vigour with tenderness." In performing Venice Preserv'd, the part of Belvidera should be played not as cloyingly sweet or girlish but as dignified, even matronly, while Jaffeir should come across as "a very sorry scoundrel, upon whose sufferings we can bestow no sympathy," and Pierre should be portrayed as vengeful but not villainous.

6 BRUGIÈRE de BARANTE, AMABLE GUILLAUME PROSPER, BARON. "Sur Otway" and "Sur Venise sauvée." In Melanges historiques et littéraires. Vol. 3. Bruxelles: J.P. Meline, 1835, pp. 235-57.

A conventional piece of biocriticism, with some comparisons between Otway and French dramatists, and between Venice Preserv'd and the related works of Saint-Réal, le Cardinal de Retz, Sarrazin, Lafosse, and Laplace. While this section is dated 1823, the publication in which it originally appeared is not indicated.

7 [HAZLITT, WILLIAM.] Review of "The Periodical Press." Edinburgh Review 38 (May):352.

Depicts Otway as the last straggler from "the veteran corps of tragic writers" such as Shakespeare and Marlowe.

8 LACY, JOHN. "A Sixth Letter to the Dramatists of the Day." London Magazine 8 (December):647-48.

"Otway's hollow heroics" cannot be "defined mentally": they are mostly sound without sense. Venice Preserv'd is more epic than tragic.

9 [PROCTER, B.W.] Review of Knowles's Virginius and Beddoes' Bride's Tragedy." Edinburgh Review 38:202-3.

Venice Preserv'd gains its effectiveness from spirited dialogue, strong and simple diction, intensity of focus, and the character of Pierre, who is like "a pleasant discord in music." Without him the play would become tedious. Though Otway shows more dramatic power than Lee, he is not a great poet.

1824

1 ANON. "Dramatic Poets Considered." Drama; or, Theatrical Pocket Magazine 7, no. 1 (October):16.

As exemplified by The Orphan and Venice Preserv'd, Otway excelled Dryden in the dramatizing of pathos.

2 ANON. "Theatre-Royal: Venice Preserv'd." Edinburgh Dramatic Review 7, no. 333 (6 February):133.

Otway meant for Belvidera to be "surcharged with feminine affection" and to demonstrate "luscious fondness and devoted attachment."

3 ANON. "Theatre-Royal: Venice Preserv'd." Edinburgh Dramatic Review 8, nos. 369, 390 (19 March, 13 April):71-73, 155-57.

The role of Jaffeir challenges the best actors, for it blends melancholy and uxoriousness into selfishness. Pierre's part was not written to be represented as an Iago-like villain; when properly analyzed, he becomes "radically a man not only of ardent courage and impatience of wrong" but also of "the kindliest affection" that is "not the less strong" coming from one who "disavows all ordinary sensibility."

4 DIBDIN, THOMAS FROGNALL. The Library Companion; or, The Young Man's Guide, and The Old Man's Comfort in the Choice of a Library. London: Harding, Triphook, & Lepard, pp. 822-23.

Recommends Venice Preserv'd as "a legitimate English classic."

5 RAYNOUARD, M. "Review of Chefs-d'oeuvre des Théâtres Étrangers." Journal des Savans, December, pp. 729-36.

Discusses Don Carlos, The Orphan, and Venice Preserv'd.

6 SCOTT, WALTER. "Drama." In Supplement to the Fourth, Fifth, and Sixth Editions of the Encyclopaedia Britannica. Vol. 3. Edinburgh: Archibald Constable; London: Hurst, Robinson, p. 662.

"The talents of Otway, in his scenes of passionate affection, rival, at least, and sometimes excel, those of Shakspeare [sic]."

1828

1 ANON. "Covent Garden Theatre." Theatrical Observer, no. 192 (12 February), n. pag.

Venice Preserv'd has gained undeserved repute from the excellent performances of gifted actors and actresses. The text i typified by bombastic language, exaggerated sentiments, and the "absence of real passion in scenes where it is most required." Belvidera is monotonously sorrowful.

2 MACAULAY, THOMAS BABINGTON. Review of The Poetical Works of John Dryden. Edinburgh Review 47 (January):27.
"Otway pleased without rant; and so might Dryden have done, if he had possessed the power of Otway."

1829

1 ANON. "The Drama: Drury Lane." Athenaeum, no. 78 (22 April):253.
Calls Venice Preserv'd a "short" but "tiresome" play.

2 ANON. "Miscellanies: Otway's Venice Preserved." Dramatic Magazine, 1 May, pp. 88-89.
Explains the origins of the custom according to which the Doge of Venice must marry the sea.

3 ANON. "Miss Kemble." Athenaeum, no. 112 (16 December):781.
Otway may have been eloquent, but he was unable to create individualized characters: witness Pierre, Jaffeir, and Belvidera.

4 ANON. "Remarks: Venice Preserved." In Cumberland's British Theatre. Vol. 2. London: John Cumberland, pp. 5-8.
Standard remarks. Ranks Otway third as a dramatic writer, after Shakespeare and Massinger; defends Pierre's patriotism and Jaffeir's human weakness; sees Otway as pathetic, fashionably indelicate, eloquently simple in language, and especially gifted in drawing female characters.

5 FOOTE, HORACE. A Companion to the Theatres; and Manual of the British Drama. London: for Edward Philip Sanger, p. 98.
Ranks Otway "next to Massinger" (who on p. 96 is placed second to Shakespeare), naming Venice Preserv'd and The Orphan as his best plays.

6 LAWSON, JOHN PARKER. History of Remarkable Conspiracies Connected with European History During the Fifteenth, Sixteenth, and Seventeenth Centuries. Vol. 2. Edinburgh: Constable; London: Hurst, Chance, pp. 55-56.
Designates Venice Preserv'd "one of the finest . . . tragedies in our language" and notes the relation between Saint-Réal's work and the plots of Venice Preserv'd and Don Carlos.

7 NEELE, HENRY. "Lectures on English Poetry." In The Literary Remains of the Late Henry Neele. London: Smith, Elder, & Co., pp. 139-41.
Regards Otway as effective though licentious in comedy, bombastic and turgid in tragedy (yet always powerfully pathetic). He was not very skillful in plot construction or in the realistic portrayal of characters. The Orphan is clumsy and indelicate.

Venice Preserv'd is marred by improbabilities, and all its characters except Pierre are "but sketches." Jaffeir inspires only contempt. In some passages Otway's imagery is beautifully delicate, his descriptions often moving.

1830

1 ANON. "Theatrical Journal--Covent Garden: Wednesday, December 9.--Venice Preserved." Dramatic Magazine, 1 January, p. 331.

Even in the closet, the character of Belvidera excites deep emotion; on the stage, her character "is one of those in which the poet has done so much for the actress, that the actress has but little scope for illustrating the poet."

2 ANON. "Theatricals: Drury-Lane." Athenaeum, no. 161 (27 November):749.

Because Jaffeir is such a contemptible character, "the greater is the merit of him who acts it well."

3 ANON. "The Play-Goer. By the Original Theatrical Critic in the Examiner." Tatler 1, no. 29 (7 October):116.

Under the influence of his dissolute age, Otway "debauched his tragic muse." In Venice Preserv'd, that "beautiful, most painful, and in some respects disagreeable play," "sensuality takes the place of sentiment."

1831

1 ANON. Literary and Graphical Illustrations of Shakespeare and the British Drama. London: Hurst, Chance, pp. 78-81.

Notes sources and sketches stage histories of The Orphan and Venice Preserv'd, commenting that Acasto may be a portrait of James Butler, Duke of Ormonde, that the Nicky-Nacky scenes are disgusting, and that Otway's ghosts are ridiculous. Nevertheless, both plays are powerful.

1832

1 [GENEST, JOHN.] Some Account of the English Stage, from the Restoration in 1660 to 1830. Vol. 1. Bath: H.E. Carrington; London: Thomas Rodd, pp. 177-78, 190-91, 205-6, 244, 279, 283-86, 311-13, 352, 416, 428.

For most of the plays, casts, source(s), and plots are given, followed by very brief critical assessments. While Alcibiades, Titus and Berenice, and Caius Marius are considered poor or indifferent, the comic works are accorded unusually positive evaluations: The Cheats of Scapin is "an excellent Farce,"

Friendship in Fashion is "very good," and The Atheist is "not . . . bad." The Souldiers Fortune "is an excellent play, but very indecent." "Otway's merit as a Comic writer has not, of late years, been sufficiently attended to." Genest observes that Shaftesbury is represented by both Antonio and Renault, and that Otway intends his audience to understand that contemporary Whigs are "as unprincipled as the Conspirators in his Tragedy." Along with All for Love and others, The Orphan is one of "the first rational Tragedies written since the Restoration."

1834

1 CAMPBELL, THOMAS. Life of Mrs. Siddons. Vol. 1. London: Effingham Wilson, pp. 181-88.

By deleting Antonio and Aquilina and the ghosts, modern producers have made Venice Preserv'd pure and symmetrical, in the process transforming Pierre from "a miserable conspirator," driven by illicit love and jealousy, into a "mixture of patriotism and of excusable misanthropy." Thus "redeemed," the play never fails to command tears, and one comes away from each performance feeling that Belvidera "might rank among Shakespeare's creations."

2 HUNT, LEIGH. "Drury Lane, and the Two Theatres in Drury Lane and Covent Garden." Leigh Hunt's London Journal: Supplement to Part I, Supplement no. 7, p. lv.

"Even in Otway there is a hot bullying smack of the tavern, very different from the voluptuousness in Shakespeare."

1835

1 BALZAC, HONORÉ de. Le Père Goriot, Histoire Parisienne. Vol. 2. Paris: Librairie de Werdet, p. 63.

Vautrin is made to say, "Pierre et Jaffeir, voilà ma passion. Je sais Venise sauvée par coeur."

2 CHAMBERS, ROBERT. History of the English Language and Literature. Edinburgh: William & Robert Chambers; London: Orr & Smith, p. 88.

Venice Preserv'd "exhibits very successfully some of the darker and more violent passions of human nature, beautifully relieved and contrasted with the sorrows of an unoffending and virtuous female."

1836

1 ANON. "Music and the Drama." Athenaeum, no. 431 (30 January):92.

Sees Jaffeir as a "faulty character," "a snivelling, drivelling animal," and Pierre as a gory villain.

1838

1 CUNNINGHAM, GEORGE GODFREY. "Thomas Otway." In Lives of Eminent and Illustrious Englishmen. Vol. 3. Glasgow: A. Fullerton, pp. 344-46.

Otway's comedies are brutally obscene and intolerably stupid, and his tragedies are neither thoughtful nor very imaginative. Caius Marius is an "execrable travestie" of Shakespeare. Nevertheless, the concluding scene of Don Carlos, all of The Orphan, and parts of Venice Preserv'd show that the author, even while failing to instruct us or to make us admire his artistry, could put characters in interesting situations and could convey strong passions. This is a full critique, considering the type of publication in which it appears.

2 DUNHAM, SAMUEL ASTLEY. "Thomas Otway." In Lives of the most Eminent Literary and Scientific Men of Great Britain. Lardner's Cabinet Cyclopaedia, vol. 3. London: Longman et al., pp. 123-33.

Mostly derivative but covers all the plays and is freshly phrased. Dunham holds that Venice Preserv'd succeeds only because it provides roles that actors can shine in. "As a dramatist, Otway has been much over-rated. He displays skill in the management of his plots; but very little in the delineation of character. His lines are generally artificial and monotonous, . . . being for the most part deficient in simplicity. But a certain tenderness . . . supplies . . . the place of higher requisites."

1839

1 ANON. "Dramatic Vestiges and Fragments: Otway's Tragedy of the Orphan." Actors By Daylight, no. 48 (26 January):76.

Reprints the ballad "Glasgerion," from which "there is every reason to believe that the idea of this tragedy was taken." See OT.1765.1.

2 HALLAM, HENRY. Introduction to the Literature of Europe, in the 15th, 16th, and 17th Centuries. Vol. 4. Paris: A. & W. Galignani, p. 279.

Calls The Orphan and Venice Preserv'd the "best tragedies of this period," regarding both as moving and sometimes poetically eloquent; commends Venice Preserv'd with special attention to its "highly dramatic" plot and to the characterization of Pierre and of Belvidera.

1843

1 CHAMBERS, ROBERT. Cyclopaedia of English Literature. Vol. 1. Edinburgh: William & Robert Chambers, pp. 386-90.

Despite some "rugged" verse and "inflated" expressions, Venice Preserv'd nearly equals Shakespeare and far surpasses "the great master Dryden." It is especially effective in scenes of passion or distress and in the provocative unfolding of its plot. The Orphan, on the other hand, is better left in obscurity where its "indelicacy and painful associations" can offend no one.

1844

1 JEFFREY, FRANCIS. "Lord Byron's Tragedies." In Contributions to the Edinburgh Review. Vol. 2. London: Longman, Brown, Green, & Longmans, pp. 356-57.

In a section not included in the original article (see OT.1822.3), asserts that Marino Faliero is "merely another Venice Preserved . . . recalling, though certainly without eclipsing, the memory of the first." Jeffrey contrasts Byron's "sense and vigour" to Otway's "passion and pathos" and maintains that "though our new conspirators are better orators and reasoners than the gang of Pierre and Reynault, the tenderness of Belvidera is . . . more touching [and] . . . more natural than the stoical and self-satisfied decorum of Angiolina."

1845

1 CRAIK, GEORGE L. Sketches of the History of Literature and Learning in England. Vol. 4. London: Charles Knight, p. 138.

Although his comedies have been justly banished for their lewdness, The Orphan and Venice Preserv'd show Otway to be "the most pathetic and tear-drawing of all our dramatists."

1846

1 ANON. "The Acting Drama: Marylebone." Theatrical Times, no. 15 (19 September):118.

Venice Preserv'd "will always live on the stage, and be preferred to others intellectually greater," because "it appeals to the feelings powerfully, and affords scope for good acting. Pierre, we think, the best character in the tragedy--for we cannot help despising the vacillating Jaffeir."

2 ANON. "The Acting Drama: Sadler's Wells." Theatrical Times, no. 25 (28 November):213-14.

Venice Preserv'd and The Orphan are the only two Otway plays "of more than ordinary power," and the latter "contains passages even more replete with thrilling pathos than the former." Although Venice Preserv'd is not one of the greatest English tragedies, its characters are drawn with psychological subtlety; Belvidera, in particular, offers a challenging role for the actress sensitive to gradations of passion.

3 ANON. "The British Theatre . . . Part I." Dublin University Magazine 28, no. 167 (November):527.

Cites "the scaffold scene in Venice Preserved" as a rare instance of the effective use of stage spectacle.

4 SARGENT, EPES, ed. Editorial Introduction to Venice Preserv'd. In The Modern Standard Drama. Vol. 3., no. 20. New York: William Taylor, pp. iii-vi.

With only slight yet ingenious borrowing from Saint-Réal, Otway fashions in Venice Preserv'd "one of the noblest imaginative works of which literature can boast." It has, however, been improved by the omission of Antonio's indecent scenes, which, if left in, would have made the play almost as "distasteful" as The Orphan.

1847

1 ANON. "The Dramatic Literature of England." Theatrical Times, no. 69 (28 August):268.

Now that Venice Preserv'd is not so popular, we can see that its frequent recurrence in the repertory was owing more to its offering three major parts for good actors than to its intrinsic value as a literary work. In fact, "as a poetical conception, 'The Orphan' is superior to 'Venice Preserved,' but the nature of the plot will probably prevent its ever being acted again." Although we now rank Otway well below Shakespeare, he excels Marlowe in construction, if not in poetry.

1848

1 ANON. "Acting Drama: Sadler's Wells." Theatrical Times, no. 133 (18 November):442.

"The part of Jaffeir is weak, though amiable, . . . a puling saint." Pierre was "conceived in Otway's happiest manner."

2 ANON. "Sadler's Wells." Athenaeum, no. 1099 (18 November): 1155.

Much abused by recent critics, Otway "should be permitted to live, if only for the music of his verse and the pathos of his style."

1851

1 HUNT, LEIGH. "Otway." In Table-Talk. To which are added Imaginary Conversations of Pope and Swift. London: Smith, Elder, p. 151.

"Otway is the poet of sensual pathos. . . . His very friendship, though enthusiastic, is violent, and . . . he seems to dress up a beauty in tears, only for the purpose of stimulating her wrongers."

2 MILLS, ABRAHAM. The Literature and the Literary Men of Great Britain and Ireland. Vol. 2. New York: Harper & Bros., pp. 76-81.

Although The Orphan is too indelicate and "painful" for modern performance, Venice Preserv'd continues to move us with its deep, well-managed plot, its pathos, and its effective character contrasts. It is flawed by some rugged, inflated passages and by "occasional redundancies."

1853

1 SPALDING, WILLIAM. The History of English Literature. Edinburgh: Oliver & Boyd, p. 298.

In Venice Preserv'd and The Orphan, there is "something much nearer [than in Lee] to a revival of the ancient strength of feeling, though alloyed by false sentiment and poetic poverty."

1856

1 MASSON, DAVID. "Dryden, and the Literature of the Restoration." In Essays, Biographical and Critical: Chiefly on English Poets. Cambridge: Macmillan, pp. 116, 121.

Otway is still read for his "mastery of dramatic pathos." This essay is erroneously said to be reprinted from the Quarterly Review of July 1854.

2 RAPP, MORIZ. "Studien über das englische Theater. VII: Milton und Otway." Archiv 20:384-94.

Surveys the lives and dramatic works of Milton (pp. 385-87) and Otway (pp. 387-94), briefly introducing each of the plays except Titus and Berenice and Cheats of Scapin. Otway is seen as a talented (but immoral) playwright who was especially adept at creating stage effects.

1857

1 [HANNAY, JAMES.] "English Political Satires." Quarterly Review (London) 101:224.

Considers it "shocking to find so tender a spirit as Otway writing comedies which might appal an editor of Petronius." The piece is attributed to Hannay in his Essays from 'The Quarterly Review' (London: Hurst & Blackett, 1861), pp. 77-126.

2 KNIGHT, CHARLES. The English Cyclopaedia: Biography. Vol. 4. London: Bradbury & Evans, pp. 602-3.

A conventional depiction of Otway as a powerful but too often indecent dramatist.

1864

1 DORAN, JOHN. "Their Majesties' Servants." Annals of the English Stage, from Thomas Betterton to Edmund Kean. Vol. 1. London: William H. Allen, pp. 203, 214-16.

Denounces Otway for "ruthlessly" marring Shakespeare's Romeo and Juliet and for writing "detestable" comedies. In tragedy he does succeed in touching the heart, but he is inferior to Lee in expressing "ardent love."

2 SHAW, THOMAS B., and WILLIAM SMITH. A History of English Literature. London: John Murray, pp. 260-61.

Regards Otway as the best of the exclusively tragic writers in the Restoration, better than Dryden himself in generating pathos. Although his depiction of dark, fierce passions and hysterical distress compares favorably with the highest achievements of Ford, Beaumont, and Fletcher, his portrayal of madness is distinctly "second-rate," for it shows merely a "disordered fancy" rather than (as in Lear or Ophelia) "lurid flashes of reason and consciousness lighting up . . . the tossings of a mind agitated to its profoundest depths." Venice Preserv'd deserves our admiration for its "exciting and animated plot," "declamatory scenes," domestic details, and vigorous style, even though the Nicky-Nacky scenes are "too disgusting" to be staged.

1866

1 HANNAY, JAMES. A Course of English Literature. London: Tinsley Brothers, p. 137.

Sees Otway as the best Restoration dramatist and points to The Orphan as "the earliest of . . . domestic . . . familiar tragedies."

1868

1 FITZGERALD, PERCY. The Life of David Garrick. Vol. 2. London: Tinsley Brothers, pp. 81-83.

The character of Chamont, in The Orphan, offers a great actor some fine contrasts, "from rage to calmness, from roughness to tenderness . . . to jealousy." Although Venice Preserv'd suffered from the "absurdities" of eighteenth-century staging (such as the emphasizing of ghosts), it is an "enchanting" and "touching" play, "all tears and tenderness and passion, clothed in the richest and most melodious poetry."

2 GRISY, A. De. Etude sur Thomas Otway. Paris: Ernest Thorin, 216 pp.

1869

1 ROBINSON, HENRY CRABB. Diary, Reminiscences, and Correspondence of Henry Crabb Robinson. Edited by Thomas Sadler. Vol. 1. London: Macmillan, p. 187.

Recounts a discussion with Goethe in which the two men agree that the comic scenes in Venice Preserv'd are integral to the main plot. They show, observes Goethe, "how utterly unfit for government the Senate had become" and thus account for the conspiracy.

2 SMITH, WILLIAM, [and JAMES ROWLEY.] A Smaller History of English Literature. London: John Murray, p. 142.

With his Jacobean flavor and powerful emotional effects, Otway became the best tragic dramatist of the Restoration. His depiction of madness, however, leaves much to be desired.

1870

1 ALLIBONE, S. AUSTIN. A Critical Dictionary of English Literature. Vol. 2. London: Trübner; Philadelphia: J.B. Lippincott, p. 1468.

All of Otway's "eloquence, pathos, and beauty" cannot save even his best plays from being "disgraced by intolerable indecencies."

1871

1 TAINE, HIPPOLYTE ADOLPH. History of English Literature. Translated by H. Van Laun. Vol. 2. New York: Holt & Williams, pp. 18, 24-26.

For the most part Otway joins his contemporaries in writing dull, rhetorical plays, half English, half French; but in Venice Preserv'd, and to some extent in The Orphan, he sometimes approaches the living style of Shakespeare or the gloomy savagery of Webster and Ford. Antonio is "an obscene caricature" worthy of Shakespeare, while Belvidera is not unlike Imogen. In his comedies, despite their lewdness, Otway attempts a moral criticism of society. Generally speaking, his style is a caricature of Racine's.

1872

1 YONGE, CHARLES DUKE. Three Centuries of English Literature. London: Longmans, Green & Co., pp. 48-56.

Caius Marius is absurd, and Alcibiades, Don Carlos, and Titus and Berenice lack high merit. The Orphan and Venice Preserv'd, however, are fine plays, second only to Shakespeare's in their capacity for moving pathos. Because he did manage to avoid licentiousness in some of his plays, Otway is "the only dramatist of the Restoration period from whose works it is possible to produce extracts."

1873

1 ARNOLD, THOMAS. A Manual of English Literature, Historical and Critical. 3d rev. ed. London: Longmans, Green, p. 236.

While Otway's comedies are "of small account," his Caius Marius, Orphan, and Venice Preserv'd "rank high among English dramas." This assessment of Otway does not appear in the two earlier editions of the Manual (1862 and 1867).

2 MORLEY, HENRY. A First Sketch of English Literature. London, Paris, and New York: Cassell, Petter, & Galpin, pp. 680-82.

Discusses sources, especially French influences, and sees Caius Marius as an adaptation of Shakespeare to "the new sense of the polite literature." The Orphan is a carefully written domestic play, a "touching picture" of distressed innocence, with a plot perhaps too dependent on the motivation of "animal passion." More natural than the heroic plays, The Orphan and Venice Preserv'd are the best of "later Stuart drama." Otway's comedies reflect the "low morals of the court."

1874

1 MAIDMENT, JAMES, and W.H. LOGAN. Remarks on The Destruction of Jerusalem. In The Dramatic Works of John Crowne. Vol. 2. Edinburgh: W. Paterson, p. 221.

Calls Titus and Berenice "a poor abridgement."

1875

1 MOSEN, REINHARD. Über Thomas Otway's Leben und Werke, mit besonderer Berücksichtigung der 'tragedies'. Jena: Ratz, 47 pp.

Surveys the life and tragedies, indicating the improvement in Otway's artistry and ranking him second to Shakespeare. Finds two types of characters in the tragedies: the mild, innocent, and passive (figures of the light) and the gloomy and dark (figures of the night).

2 WARD, ADOLPHUS WILLIAM. A History of English Dramatic Literature to the Death of Queen Anne. Vol. 2. London: Macmillan, pp. 547-52.

Comments on sources as he assesses each of the plays. Though Alcibiades is clearly Otway's worst tragedy, it shows "a sure perception of stage-effect." Don Carlos pleases with its variety. Caius Marius draws upon the author's military experience but is a "monstrous plagiarism." In The Orphan, we find Otway mastering his distinctive expression of pathos. Venice Preserv'd is grossly blemished by the Antonio scenes, but these are more than compensated for by the tenderly powerful depiction of love between Jaffeir and Belvidera, which is "unparalleled . . . in our later drama."

1877

1 [GOSSE, EDMUND W.] "Thomas Otway." Cornhill Magazine 36:679-700.

Notwithstanding the "tiresome" Alcibiades and the "appalling" comedies, Otway is "the greatest tragic poet of the age," and Venice Preserv'd is "the greatest tragic drama between Shakespeare and Shelley." Even Don Carlos, despite its staginess, is better than Dryden's rhymed tragedies; it is well designed, and it introduces the two character types for which Otway would become famous (the soft, simple female; the feverish, irresolute male). Between Don Carlos and Venice Preserv'd in overall quality, The Orphan combines natural passions, bold versification, convincingly drawn characters, and overwhelming improbabilities with a powerful tenderness. In Venice Preserv'd, the poetic is subordinated to the dramatic, and neither those "nauseous" comic passages nor the weak motivation of Jaffeir's personal rebellion seriously mars this noble masterpiece or much detracts from the charming characterization of Belvidera. In his versification and command of the pathetic, Otway is the most French of the Restoration dramatists. This essay is attributed to Gosse in his Seventeenth-Century Studies (London: Kegan Paul, Trench & Co., 1883), pp. 269-305.

2 MOSEN, R. "Ueber Thomas Otway's Leben und Werke, mit besonderer Beruecksichtigung der 'Tragedies.'" Englische Studien 1:425-56.

A slightly more elaborate version of Mosen's published dissertation (OT.1875.1).

1878

1 KEMBLE, FRANCES ANN. Record of a Girlhood. Vol. 2. London: Richard Bentley, pp. 85-86.

"Belvidera seemed to me a sort of lay figure in a tragic attitude, a mere 'female in general.' . . . there was nothing in the part itself that affected my feelings or excited my imagination." Goes on to assert that Otway is much inferior to Shakespeare.

2 MORLEY, HENRY. English Plays. Cassell's Library of English Literature, vol. 3. London, Paris, and New York: Cassell, Petter, & Galpin, pp. 355, 368-69.

Strongly praises The Orphan and Venice Preserv'd, in both of which Otway expresses "the grace and tenderness of his own nature." Yet in The Orphan, the first tragedy to dispense with "the dignity of royal birth," Morley regretfully finds that "the love of the two brothers . . . is mainly animal."

1879

1 ANON. "Otway." Temple Bar, 57:95-113.

A standard evaluation, though up-to-date (quotes Gosse's Cornhill article at one point: see OT.1877.1). Alcibiades is both feeble and bombastic, Don Carlos artificial yet occasionally moving, the comedies coarsely licentious, Caius Marius a "monstrous" production. The Orphan, however, is moving and artistic, despite some prurience of thought, and Venice Preserv'd is the equal of any except the very best of Shakespeare: masculine, natural, masterfully designed, "terribly sublime."

1880

1 GOSSE, EDMUND W. "Thomas Otway." In The English Poets: Selections with Critical Introductions. Edited by Thomas Humphry Ward. Vol. 2. New York: Macmillan, p. 430.

Sees Otway as a tragic genius who failed in comedy and who "was absolutely unable to write even a fairly good song."

1881

1 HERFORD, C.H. A Sketch of the History of the English Drama in Its Social Aspects. Cambridge: E. Johnson, p. 73.

Otway had "crude tragic power" but had lost "the secret" of the Elizabethans' "instinctive felicity" of language. Belvidera's pathos moves us, but the representation of "Monimia's fraternal lovers" is "impure."

1882

1 SCHERR, JOHANNES. A History of English Literature. Translated by M.V. London: Sampson Low, Marston, Searle, & Rivington, pp. 123-24.

Easily the best play of the Restoration, Venice Preserv'd "will remain for ever one of the classical tragedies of English literature."

1883

1 [MARTIN, THEODORE.] "The English Stage." Quarterly Review (London) 155:195.

The disappearance from the stage of plays like Venice Preserv'd "is due not to their want of merit, but to the disappearance of the high order of tragic power which is demanded for the impersonation of their heroines." Attributed to Martin in his Essays on the Drama (2d ser., London: privately printed, 1889).

2 PERRY, THOMAS SERGEANT. English Literature in the Eighteenth Century. New York: Harper & Brothers, pp. 95, 107, 113-17.

Although in the Restoration "the stage was dying," as witness the need to copy greater drama of the past in plays such as Caius Marius, Otway did achieve genuine pathos and became the first prominent writer to focus a play on persons "outside of a royal family." The Orphan and Venice Preserv'd still have power.

1885

1 GARNETT, RICHARD. "Otway, Thomas." In Encyclopaedia Britannica. 9th ed. Vol. 18. New York: Charles Scribner's Sons, pp. 70-71.

"In everything but pathos Otway is mediocre," for he has very ordinary ideas, no psychological insight, and no stylistic eloquence. Except for the interestingly autobiographical military scenes in Souldiers Fortune, his comedies are indecent and "tiresome." Alcibiades is "poor," and Don Carlos is "puerile in conception," shows little "knowledge of human nature," but is "full of declamatory energy." Though the characters in The Orphan and Venice Preserv'd are not intrinsically interesting, they generate much pathos as they confront difficult situations in both plays. "The love scenes between Jaffeir and Belvidera cannot be surpassed; and no plot more skilfully calculated to move the emotions than that of Venice Preserv'd was ever contrived by dramatist." Belvidera's mad scene, however, is almost a burlesque on itself. As master of pathos, Otway is "the Euripides of the English stage."

2 STRONG, ROWLAND, ed. "Preface" and "Analysis." Prefixed to *Venice Preserv'd*. Exeter: William Pollard, n. pag.

Straightforward textual comments and plot summary.

1886

*1 LOEWENBERG, JAKOB. *Über Otway's und Schiller's Don Carlos*. Lippstadt: A. Staats, 123 pp.

Source: *National Union Catalogue Pre-1956 Imprints*, vol. 338:421.

1888

1 NOEL, RODEN, ed. "Thomas Otway" and prefaces to the individua plays. In *Thomas Otway*. The Mermaid Series. London: Vizetelly & Co., pp. vii-xlix, 2, 174, 288-89.

Distinguishes Otway's artistic traits, including a classica simplicity, a Greek sense of fatalism, and an unexcelled ability to concentrate on "one motive of action, involving the utmost intensity of feeling." He drives the plot forward with great rapic ity without sacrificing "the noble organic harmony and sanity of his whole creation." Because he focuses so intensely on a few characters in domestic dilemmas, and allows almost no real personality development, his plays need their occasional comic relief or bawdiness to add lyricism.

Previous critics have erroneously damned Otway for developing situations at the expense of characterization, or for presen ing only wicked characters: in fact, his characters are emotionally convincing and are no worse or better than ordinary human beings (except for his heroines). In respect to "sobriety and truth to nature," Otway's plays excel those "of his illustrious forerunners," and his language is more natural and more precise than that of most earlier dramatists. He is no match for the Elizabethans in "reflective soliloquy," his verse is inferior to Dryden's, his range of characters is narrow, and he has little command of theology or philosophy. He tends to embod his own feelings in his characters, which helps account for thei intensity, their quality of stifled love, and their lack of a sense of Christian hope. There is no local color in Otway--his "scenes might be in abstract space"--and he wrote no true comedies, only "some bustling, occasionally funny, dirty, rollicking farces."

While *Alcibiades* is poor but promising and *Caius Marius* has merit only in the original scenes, *Don Carlos* is "the best 'heroic' play of the time," though it lacks that political and historical sense which enriches the later serious plays. *The Souldiers Fortune* may be lewd, but it is swift-moving, funny, rather well designed, and interesting for its autobiographical suggestiveness. *Venice Preserv'd* deserves its reputation as a powerful and moving tragedy. Pierre is finely contrasted with the "luxuriously feminine" Jaffeir, and the comic scenes work in most respects, except that they fail to parody Shaftesbury's actual way of speaking. Roden interpolates comparisons between Otway's plays and those of Greek, German, French, and other English playwrights.

1889

1 ANON. "Books: Otway's Best Plays." Spectator 62:645-46.

Distinguishes Otway from the Jacobeans, he being "melting and feminine," they "severer and deeper." Though he wrote the best tragedy between Shakespeare and Shelley, he was no poet and no thinker. His strength lay in dramatic structure and focus. Don Carlos is diffuse in general style, and its "bustle and intrigue" is balanced, on the negative side, by "feminine voluptuousness." The Souldiers Fortune is "as tiresome and disgusting as any comedy of Wycherley's, and . . . wholly destitute of wit or humour." Only as author of Venice Preserv'd does Otway deserve a high reputation.

2 BAKER, HENRY BARTON. The London Stage: Its History and Traditions from 1576 to 1888. Vol. 1. London: W.H. Allen & Co., pp. 48, 220.

Otway was England's last genuine tragedian, and The Orphan and Venice Preserv'd are "the two noblest tragedies written from the time of Charles the First to the present day."

1890

1 MITCHELL, DONALD G. English Lands, Letters and Kings. Vol. 2, From Elizabeth to Anne. New York: Charles Scribner's Sons, p. 237.

"With much native refinement and extraordinary pathetic power," Otway wrote only two enduring plays, among many poor ones.

1891

1 SINGER, HANS WOLFGANG. Das bürgerliche Trauerspiel in England. Leipzig-Reudnitz: Oswald Schmidt, pp. 81-83.

Because its plot and way of thinking are not based on bourgeois life, The Orphan cannot be called a bourgeois tragedy.

1893

1 WHITEFORD, ROBERT N. The Drama of the Restoration Period: Thomas Otway. [Crawfordsville, Ind.]: Wabash College, 92 pp.

Places Otway's life and works within a context of theatrical and social history. Alcibiades and Don Carlos are seen as apprentice works. While Caius Marius is praised, Titus and Berenice is said to be "poor, as Racine is poor." The Orphan, however, is a great play that fictionalizes the interrelations between Otway himself (Castalio), Rochester (Polydore), and Mrs. Barry (Monimia). In The Souldiers Fortune, Otway becomes Beaugard ("he despised himself in this bawdy drama"). Venice Preserv'd shows the author at the summit of his powers, and The Atheist shows him in a precipitous decline. Otway lacked introspection, intellectual subtlety, and a sense of nature and of what transcends nature. His characters are plain and narrowly defined, and he tends toward coarseness in depicting them. Yet he excelled all his contemporaries and successors in creating theatrically effective pictures of love and human courage.

1894

1 KNIGHT, JOSEPH. David Garrick. London: Kegan Paul, Trench, Trübner, & Co., pp. 49, 116, 332-33.

Scoffs at Otway's modifications of Romeo and Juliet but commends the creator of Pierre and Jaffeir.

1895

1 ANON. "Old Authors: Thomas Otway." Citizen 1, no. 9:213-15.

As author of The Orphan, Venice Preserv'd, and Don Carlos, Otway is a master of classic structure and a "poet of blood and passion." He is weak in providing convincing tragic motives, in creating the illusion of reality, in keeping control of the expression of passions, and in writing comedy.

2 ANON. "Venice Preserved." Boston Evening Transcript, 6 December, n. pag.

Surveys the stage history of Venice Preserv'd in France, the history of French critical responses to the play, and the spectrum of French critiques of a production at the Théâtre de l'Oeuvre on 8 November 1895.

3 GARNETT, RICHARD. The Age of Dryden. London: George Bell & Sons, pp. 99, 102-5.

Sees Otway as "the only born dramatist" of his period. As author of The Orphan and Venice Preserv'd, he is deservedly name the "English Euripides," though Caius Marius is an "audacious plagiarism" and Don Carlos is "ever trembling on the brink of the ridiculous." While The Orphan is admirable for its poetry, plainness of language, and pathos, Venice Preserv'd excels it in subtlety of characterization, "tragic grandeur, . . . variety of action, and . . . intensity of interest." Belvidera, however, "interests only through her sorrows," and Antonio's scenes are "trash." Otway did have a true feeling for nature (cites the opening speech of The Orphan, IV.ii.).

4 LEE, SIDNEY, ed. "Otway, Thomas." In Dictionary of National Biography. Vol. 42. London: Smith, Elder, pp. 346-52.

Alcibiades and Don Carlos are bombastic and extravagant, while the comedies are contemptibly indecent. But The Orphan, notwithstanding its implausibility, is tender and beautiful, and Venice Preserv'd ranks just below Shakespeare in tragic power, interesting characterization, and imaginative use of history. Of course, those irrelevant scenes with Antonio and Aquilina are "a serious blot."

1898

1 GWYNN, STEPHEN. Memorials of an Eighteenth Century Painter (James Northcote). London: T. Fisher Unwin, pp. 97-98.

At dinner with Sir Joshua Reynolds, Samuel Johnson is overheard saying "that there was not forty good lines to be found" in Venice Preserv'd. Goldsmith asserts that Venice Preserv'd, of all tragedies, is "the one nearest equal to Shakespeare," and Northcote himself agrees.

2 HAGEN, PAUL, trans. "Vorwort." In Die Verschwörung gegen Venedig. Tragödie in 5 Akten von Thomas Otway. Leipzig: Eduard Avenarius, pp. iii-v.

Briefly surveys some German responses to Venice Preserv'd (Goethe's, Schiller's, Schreyvogel's, Grillparzer's) and offers the play as Otway's greatest tragedy.

3 HEATH, H. FRANK. "Restoration Drama: A Lecture Delivered at Toynbee Hall." Modern Quarterly of Language and Literature, no. 3 (November):186-87.

With his penchant for gloom and tender feelings, Otway was out of step with his contemporaries, who preferred rhetorical, intellectual, critical, and satiric writing. His relatively simple plots, middle-class protagonists, and sentimental interests made him a forerunner of Richardson.

4 SAINTSBURY, GEORGE E.B. A Short History of English Literature. New York: Macmillan, pp. 500-502.

Otway enjoys a higher reputation than he deserves. Even in the great Venice Preserv'd, he utterly lacks a feeling for poetic expression. His verse is unmusical, unsuggestive, and coarsely colloquial. Except for the worthless Nicky-Nacky scenes, though, the play is moving and well constructed for theatrical appeal. The Orphan is his next best play, Don Carlos has "some merit in its kind," but The Atheist (and, by implication, his other comedies) is poor indeed.

5 SCHRAMM, WILLY. Thomas Otway's 'The History and Fall of Gaius [sic] Marius' und Garrick's 'Romeo and Juliet' in ihrem Verhältnis zu Shakespeare's 'Romeo and Juliet' und den übrigen Quellen. Greifswald: Julius Abel, 76 pp.

Focusses on Otway in pages 5-44, discussing his indebtedness to North's translation of Plutarch (1579) and Shakespeare's Romeo and Juliet (the quartos of 1597 and 1637).

1899

1 CARO, JOSEF. "Lessing und die Engländer." Euphorion 6:465-90.

Discusses The Atheist as a source for Lessing's Der Freigeist, Venice Preserv'd as a source for Lessing's Henzi, and Alcibiades as a source for Lessing's Alcibiades.

2 SANDERS, H.M. "Thomas Otway." Temple Bar 118:372-86.

Although Alcibiades is "prodigiously uninteresting," Don Carlos meritorious only in isolated passages, and the comedies "neither . . . witty nor decently clean" (except for The Souldiers Fortune, which has wit), Otway achieved the highest success in two plays. The Orphan reminds one of Ford's The Broken Heart, though Monimia is more "loveable and lifelike" than Penthea and Otway's depiction of horror and gloom derives from a more personal source than Ford's does. This is "a tragedy of weakness and ill-fortune rather than of crime." Like The Orphan, Venice Preserv'd focuses on a small group of characters, a weak and impulsive hero (another Otway), and intense passions expressed through admirably simple diction. With its compelling plot stemming from the well-drawn character of Jaffeir, this "great" play, Elizabethan in some respects, is "one of the gems amongst English tragedies." Otway's reputation rests securely on his creation of "pity and passion," not "the terrible, the weird, or the grand."

1901

1 HASTINGS, CHARLES. The Theatre, Its Development in France and England. Translated by Frances A. Welby. London: Duckworth & Co., p. 332.

Otway "revived the spirit of Shakespearean Tragedy" and borrowed from Racine and Molière.

2 JOHNSON, ALFRED. Lafosse, Otway, Saint-Réal: Origines et Transformations d'une Thème Tragique. Paris: Librairie Hachette, 449 pp.

Surveys the extent of La Fosse's debt to Otway and of Otway's to Saint-Réal, proving that Otway used a translation. After giving plot summaries and analyses of Venice Preserv'd, Manlius Capitolinus, and La Conjuration des Espagnols, Johnson notes the "absence" of literary relations between France and England at the close of the seventeenth century. He then traces the evolution of the theme of Venice Preserv'd through other French works.

3 LOUNSBURY, THOMAS R. Shakespeare as a Dramatic Artist. New York: Scribner's; London: Edward Arnold, pp. 304-5, 324-25.

Sees Caius Marius as a "grotesque" mixture of "blood-letting and love-making" and ridicules Otway's adaptation of the balcony scene.

4 THOMPSON, A. HAMILTON. A History of English Literature. London: John Murray, pp. 353-55.

A fairly standard assessment, though less negative about the Nicky-Nacky scenes and more scathing about Belvidera's mad ravings.

1902

1 ENGEL, EDUARD. A History of English Literature (600-1900). Translated by "several hands" and revised by Hamley Bent. London: Methuen, pp. 271-73.

A strongly negative evaluation: sees Caius Marius as "valueless," the comedies as "devoid of humour" and filthy, Alcibiades as negligible except for a few passages, The Orphan as "disgusting and dull," Don Carlos as "a comic puppet-show." While Venice Preserv'd may contain some "highly dramatic scenes," it is "not a drama." In most of his plays, Otway "laid sacrilegious hands on Shakespeare."

2 LUICK, KARL. "Über Otway's 'Venice Preserved.'" Beiträge zur Neueren Philologie. Wien und Leipzig: Wilhelm Braumüller, pp. 146-80.

In using a 1675 translation of Saint-Réal's "Conjuration des Espagnols," Otway turns his Venice Preserv'd away from the conventions of heroic drama by emphasizing the theme of matrimonial love.

3 PEARCE, J.W. "Otway's Orphan: Smollett's Count Fathom." MLN 17:230.

Notes apparent borrowings from The Orphan.

1903

1 BATES, ALFRED, ed. The Drama, Its History, Literature and Influence on Civilization. Vol. 14, British Drama. London and New York: Smart & Stanley, pp. 96-101.

A derivative sketch of Otway as Dryden's peer and as master of naturally pathetic situations. The scenes involving Antonio and Aquilina are regarded as acceptable satire.

2 CHASE, LEWIS NATHANIEL. The English Heroic Play. New York: Columbia University Press; London: Macmillan, p. 190.

Briefly notes that Otway was best at plays that were not heroic in form.

3 COURTHOPE, W.J. A History of English Poetry. Vol. 4. London: Macmillan, pp. 425-30.

Locates Otway's excellence in his creation and skillful development of pathetic situations. In this respect, Otway is like Euripides. He did not, however, have Shakespeare's ability to "conceive his dramas organically" and to represent "the nature of man in society." Instead, he usually invents implausible "stage situations" and renders them effectively through a strong, simple style.

4 GEROULD, GORDON HALL. "The Sources of Venice Preserved." JEGP 5:58-61.

Lee's Caesar Borgia seems to have suggested several situations and character traits to Otway: Bellamira becomes Belvidera the giving of Seraphino as a hostage suggests Jaffeir's giving his wife as a hostage, and Ascanio's perverted droolings over Bellamira anticipate Antonio's Nicky-Nacky scenes.

5 GOSSE, EDMUND. English Literature: An Illustrated Record. Vol. 3, From Milton to Johnson. New York and London: Macmillan, pp. 111-13.

Names Venice Preserv'd as the best play of the Restoration, calls The Orphan "the very masterpiece of tragic pathos," and describes The Atheist as an "indifferent tragedy."

1904

1 ANON. "Drama: The Week." Athenaeum, 18 June, pp. 795-96.

Until the late eighteenth century, Venice Preserv'd was popular for its political satire and its tear-jerking characterization of Belvidera. Today, it "is found to make but moderate demands upon sensibility and no pretence to poetry. It may be seen once, if only for educational purposes."

2 ANON. "Royalty Theatre." Times (London), 14 June, p. 11.

While The Orphan is "too mawkish and unpleasant for production," and the comedies lack both wit and decency, Venice

Preserv'd remains a fast-moving stage play, though it borders always on hyperbole and contains little of intellectual interest.

3 CANFIELD, DOROTHEA FRANCES. Corneille and Racine in England. New York: Columbia University Press; London: Macmillan, pp. 92-101.

Sees Titus and Berenice as the most "satisfactory" and in some respects "the most interesting" of all English translations of Racine. It brilliantly transforms French "tristesse majestueuse" into English pathos, reproducing "the exact atmosphere of the original" and even excelling the original in some ways. By changing the ending, however, Otway shows his tendency toward the sentimental incapacity to follow a dilemma to its unhappy conclusion. Titus and Berenice was also influenced by Corneille.

1905

1 TUPPER, JAMES W. "The Relation of the Heroic Play to the Romances of Beaumont and Fletcher." PMLA 20:584-621.

Like The Conquest of Granada, Don Carlos and Alcibiades revolve around conflicts between idyllic and sensual love and between love and honor. Like Dryden, Otway in Don Carlos manages to combine individually effective scenes with overall unity of design. Otway's heroes, however, are "not fashioned on quite the same conventional pattern as Dryden's," and, unlike Dryden's, they are finally overwhelmed by adverse fate.

1906

1 CHARLANNE, LOUIS. L'Influence francaise en angleterre aux XVIIe siècle. Paris: Société Francais d'Imprimerie et de Librairie, 634 pp.

Chapters 4, 5, and 9 contain passages on Otway, mainly relating his work to that of Scarron, Racine, and Molière.

2 FALKE, JOHANNES. Die deutschen Bearbeitungen des 'geretteten Venedig' von Otway (1682). Ph.D. dissertation, University of Rostock, 62 pp.

Lists and describes seventeen German adaptations and translations of Venice Preserv'd, from the anonymous Die Verschworung wider Venedig of 1754 to Hugo von Hofmannsthal's Das gerettete Venedig of 1905.

3 HARVEY-JELLIE, W. Les Sources du théâtre anglais a l'epoque de la Restauration. Paris: Librairie Genérale de Droit et de Jurisprudence, pp. 113-14.

Considers Otway more original than many of his contemporaries in that what he borrowed was usually taken from sources other than French ones or other than those favored by the French. His one major adaptation of Racine, Titus and Berenice, lacks the French master's control and novelty but does not corrupt the original, as many English borrowings do. Caius Marius, on the other hand, does mangle Shakespeare, and The Cheats of Scapin is a vulgar and immoral rendering of Molière. The relations of Don Carlos and Venice Preserv'd to Saint-Réal's works is briefly discussed. Harvey-Jellie's Le Théâtre classique en angleterre (Montreal: Librairie Beauchemin Linitee, [1932?]) reprints this section virtually unchanged.

4 KILBOURNE, FREDERICK W. Alterations and Adaptations of Shakespeare. Boston: Poet Lore Co., pp. 129-31.

In Caius Marius a "contemptible piece of thieving" produces a "strange hodgepodge."

1907

1 KERBY, W. MOSELEY. Molière and the Restoration Comedy in England. Rennes: n.p., pp. 44-45.

The Cheats of Scapin is a "very clever representation of Molière's piece," but the wit "is much coarser in Otway."

1908

1 McCLUMPHA, CHARLES F., ed. "Life" of Otway and "Introduction." In The Orphan and Venice Preserved. The Belles-Lettres Series. Boston and London: D.C. Heath, pp. v-xxxix.

A comprehensive and sympathetic survey, drawing upon the important previous scholarship and criticism, and stressing links between the plays and Otway's life, especially his military experiences and his infatuation for Mrs. Barry. Otway is ranked among the very best translators from the French, and he is commended for the death scene in Alcibiades and the overall design of Don Carlos. Although improbable in plot and lacking historical sources, The Orphan is powerful and seems to have "an underlying symbolic reference to circumstances . . . at Court and problems of the day." Venice Preserv'd clearly symbolizes current political history from a Tory point of view. While the Antonio-Aquilina scenes are lewd and unnecessary, the creation of Belvidera is "a stroke of dramatic genius" that gives human depth to the story. She deserves a place beside the greatest heroines of English drama.

*2 SPERLIN, OTTIS BEDNEY. "The Relation of Otway's Tragedies to the Heroic Play." Ph.D. dissertation, University of Chicago.

Source: Stratman, p. 543.

3 THORNDIKE, ASHLEY H. Tragedy. Boston and New York: Houghton Mifflin & Co., pp. 269-72.

For his time Otway was unconventional in focusing on domestic dilemmas of less than noble persons. Venice Preserv'd, one of the best Restoration tragedies, is almost undone by "buffoonery and excess." It shares with The Orphan an Elizabethan sense of poetry, a French tightness of structure, and a capacity for generating pity through "situations rather than through the study of motives." Though still too obscene for modern tastes, Otway's plays influenced the sentimental and domestic trend of the eighteenth century, and Byron's "two Venetian plays . . . recall . . . 'Venice Preserved.'"

1909

1 ANON. "Drama: The Orphan and Venice Preserved." Athenaeum, 31 July, p. 136.

Although influenced by Shakespeare and Racine, Otway lacks the latter's psychological subtlety and the former's evocative language and "tumultuous imagination." With Racine, however, he does share classical dramatic form and "truth and intensity of emotion." Like all fine playwrights, he possesses "a wonderful feeling for dramatic situations." His most interesting protagonists, Don Carlos, Castalio, and Jaffeir, reflect his own character and "tragic passion for Mrs. Barry."

2 BOHN, WILLIAM E. "The Decline of the English Heroic Drama." MLN 24:49-54.

Already in Alcibiades and Don Carlos Otway was moving away from the heroic toward the pathetic and tragic. Then, after casting about for new models in the translations (Titus and Berenice and Caius Marius are both "sadly bungled"), he found his own style in The Orphan, a "noble tragedy of domestic life."

3 MANTZIUS, KARL. A History of Theatrical Art in Ancient and Modern Times. Translated by Louise von Cossel. Vol. 5. London: Duckworth, p. 313.

Although Otway never produced a "mature masterpiece," his Don Carlos and Venice Preserv'd "show him as an embryonic Schiller."

4 PARSONS, FLORENCE MARY (WILSON). The Incomparable Siddons. London: Methuen, pp. 82-83.

Venice Preserv'd is about "the shame and downfall brought upon an originally noble nature, by excessive uxoriousness--a unique theme . . . in acting drama." The Orphan is a "painful" play whose plot suffers from "inadequate causation."

1910

1 BAYNE, RONALD. "Lesser Jacobean and Caroline Dramatists." In The Cambridge History of English Literature. Edited by A.W. Ward and A.R. Waller. Vol. 6. Cambridge: Cambridge University Press, p. 219n2.

A romantic subplot in Robert Tailor's The Hog hath lost his Pearl deals with material similar to that in The Orphan.

2 MILES, DUDLEY HOWE. The Influence of Molière on Restoration Comedy. New York: Columbia University Press, p. 103.

Notes that The Cheats of Scapin is a rather faithful translation but generally dismisses Otway as a writer of comedy.

3 SCHIFF, HERMANN. Über Lord Byrons "Marino Faliero" und seine anderen geschichtlichen Dramen. Marburg: Robert Noske, pp. 1-30.

Byron's Marino Faliero is revolutionary, pessimistic, fairly subjective, and "heroic"; while Otway's Venice Preserv'd is antirevolutionary, relieved by comic elements, not so subjective, and "bourgeois." Byron's drama has more local color than Otway's.

1911

1 ANON. "Otway, Thomas." In Encyclopaedia Britannica. 11th ed. Vol. 20. New York: Encyclopaedia Britannica, pp. 376-77.

Alcibiades and The Atheist are weak, Friendship in Fashion is indecent, The Souldiers Fortune is "indifferent," and both The Orphan and Venice Preserv'd are masterpieces worthy of Shakespeare in their pathos. In Don Carlos are introduced the two character types that became Otway's trademark: "the impetuous, unstable youth, who seems to be drawn from Otway himself" and "the gentle pathetic character repeated in his more celebrated heroines, Monimia and Belvidera." The political meaning of Venice Preserv'd is briefly discussed.

1912

1 BARTHOLOMEW, A.T. "The Restoration Drama III: Tragic Poets." In The Cambridge History of English Literature. Edited by A.W. Ward and A.R. Waller. Vol. 8. Cambridge: Cambridge University Press, pp. 181-85.

Surveys the canon, noting sources and making standard critical comments. Titus and Berenice is "careful and scholarly," Alcibiades "dreary and stilted," Don Carlos vigorous and theatrically effective, and the comedies unsatisfactory. In The Orphan, Otway abandons the artificial and heroic in favor of the natural and ordinary, and although it becomes implausible and, in places, indecorous, the play has great tragic force. Venice Preserv'd, with its fine characterizations of Belvidera and Jaffeir, the "notable simplicity" of its style, and its display of "elemental emotions," ranks with the later masterpieces of the previous era.

2 GOSSE, EDMUND, ed. Introduction to Restoration Plays from Dryden to Farquhar. London and Toronto: Dent; New York: Dutton, p. xii.
Sees Otway's simple, tenderly domestic plays as "almost the solitary exception" to the "historical oratorio" of Restoration tragedy in general.

3 LANG, ANDREW. History of English Literature from "Beowulf" to Swinburne. London, New York, Bombay, and Calcutta: Longmans, Green, & Co., pp. 369-71.
Although Otway had "no real comic genius," allowed his characters to rant too much, and achieved no distinction in poetry, he could contrive ingenious, tightly knit plots, and The Orphan and Venice Preserv'd are both movingly pathetic.

4 PREVITÉ-ORTON, C.W. "Political and Ecclesiastical Satire." In The Cambridge History of English Literature. Edited by A.W. Ward and A.R. Waller. Vol. 8. Cambridge: Cambridge University Press, p. 94.
The Nicky-Nacky scenes in Venice Preserv'd show that Otway was inept at caricature.

1913

1 LEVI, EZIO. Il "Don Carlos" di Tommaso Otway. Pisa: F. Mariotti, 50 pp.

2 NETTLETON, GEORGE HENRY. "The Drama and the Stage." In The Cambridge History of English Literature. Edited by A.W. Ward and A.R. Waller. Vol. 10. Cambridge: Cambridge University Press, pp. 74, 86-87.
Discusses Otway's popularity in the eighteenth century and makes the following distinction: "Otway's Orphan, like most of the domestic tragedies that precede Lillo's, seems rather to neglect the aristocratic tone of tragedy than to magnify its democratic character."

1914

1 NETTLETON, GEORGE HENRY. English Drama of the Restoration and Eighteenth Century (1642-1780). New York: Macmillan, pp. 95, 99-103, 119, 155, 160, 202, 233, 264-65.

Commends Otway for his truth to nature, his terse and lucid phrasing, and his compelling plots, yet notes the narrowness of his character conceptions, the "poverty" of his comic powers, and his "lack of high lyrical poetry." While the comedies are dismissed, Don Carlos is regarded as promising, The Orphan as an early domestic tragedy, and Venice Preserv'd as one of the best modern tragedies. Otway's appeal to feminine sensitivities and his innovations in Caius Marius strongly influenced eighteenth-century drama. His simplicity looks even farther ahead, to Hawthorne.

2 SCHELLING, FELIX E. English Drama. London: J.M. Dent & Sons; London: E.P. Dutton, pp. 254-55, 272, 310.

In a shorter space, covers the same ground and arrives at the same conclusions as Nettleton does (see OT.1914.1) but gives Otway somewhat more credit for "a poet's command of imagery" and "an admirably smooth, yet varied blank verse."

3 TUPPER, FREDERICK, and JAMES W. TUPPER, eds. "Thomas Otway: Venice Preserved." In Representative English Dramas from Dryden to Sheridan. New York: Oxford University Press; London, Toronto, Melbourne, and Bombay: Humphrey Milford, pp. 77-81.

Listing as Otway's best quality his ability to achieve emotional intensity without sacrificing the overall harmony of dramatic design, the two Tuppers praise the "nervous strength," compact phrasing, and apt imagery in his language, though they find that his blank verse is negatively influenced by his earlier use of the heroic couplet. They see The Souldiers Fortune as "comedy of highly flavored personal reminiscence" and feel that the action of Venice Preserv'd ultimately derives from Belvidera's situation.

4 WINTHER, FRITZ. Das Gerettete Venedig: Eine vergleichende Studie. University of California Publications in Modern Philology, 3, no. 2. Berkeley: University of California Press, 160 pp.

Compares the dramatizations of friendship, marriage, and conscience, and the depictions of the Orient and the Renaissance, in La Fosse's Manlius Capitolinus, Otway's Venice Preserv'd, and Hugo von Hofmannsthal's Das gerettete Venedig. If the first of these represents French classicism, in the sense that reason dominates fantasy, Otway's play falls between the "impulsive" works of Shakespeare and rationalistic Restoration literature (though fantasy has the edge in Otway), and in Hofmannsthal's neoromantic drama fantasy and reason are combined.

1915

1 BERNBAUM, ERNEST. The Drama of Sensibility . . . 1696-1780. Boston and London: Ginn & Co., pp. 54, 57, 151.

Compares The Orphan to Tailor's The Hog hath lost his Pearl, noting that whereas Otway had "successfully created an imaginary world" for his pathetic characters, Tailor "had tried to represent them in the real one." Venice Preserv'd is less a drama of sensibility, because its characters are not idealized. Notes Otway's influence on Lillo.

2 DUTTON, GEORGE B. "Theory and Practice in English Tragedy, 1650-1700." Englische Studien 49 (1915-16):202, 209.

Venice Preserv'd and The Orphan are more neoclassical in design and more naturally emotional than Don Carlos.

1916

1 TATLOCK, JOHN S.P., and ROBERT G. MARTIN, eds. "Thomas Otway: Venice Preserved, or, A Plot Discovered." In Representative English Plays from the Middle Ages to the End of the Nineteenth Century. New York: Century, pp. 458-59.

Sees Otway as both more Elizabethan and more modern than his contemporaries. He recalls Ford and Fletcher, and looks ahead to Steele and Cumberland. Although he can create more convincing female characters than male characters, he never depicts romantic lovers, only the mercenary or married kind. Essentially better at designing situations than at drawing characters, he nevertheless excels at making us "feel deeply" for individuals with whom we cannot entirely sympathize. The Nicky-Nacky scenes are repulsive but integral to the action.

2 WRIGHT, ROSE ABEL. The Political Play of the Restoration. Montesano, Wash.: A.E. Veatch, pp. 113-17, 173.

Seriously doubts that Renault was intended to represent Shaftesbury. Antonio probably was supposed to be Shaftesbury, but "this political element mars what would otherwise be a very excellent play and serves only as a vile excrescence."

1917

1 HAGEMANN, GUSTAV. Shakespeare's Einfluss auf Otway's künstlerische Entwicklung. Münster: Westfälische Vereinsdruckerei, 70 pp.

Though some scenes, situations, and phrases in Alcibiades can be traced to Shakespeare, in Don Carlos, with its heavy indebtedness to Othello and echoes of Hamlet and Lear, Otway takes Shakespeare as his model and frees himself from the pompous verbosity and shallowness of heroic drama. Shakespeare taught Otway the essence of tragic literature.

1920

1 ANON. "Phoenix Society: Otway Preserved." Morning Post (London), 1 December, n. pag.

Venice Preserv'd is better than any Shakespearean play "in point of construction," but it lacks "soul" and "many melodramas have a stronger human appeal. As poetry it is infinitely inferior to Webster's 'Duchess of Malfi.'" It does "afford clear directions for the display of . . . tones, attitudes, and gestures."

2 ANON. "The Phoenix Society. 'Venice Preserved.'" Sunday Times (London), 5 December, n. pag.

With all the faults and excellences of youth, and "little of the judgment of age," Venice Preserv'd "exalts friendship . . . etherealises married love . . . denounces State tyranny" and "ridicules senatorial eloquence and senile goatishness." It is a "noble work" showing "a rich command of language."

3 ANON. "'Venice Preserv'd': Revived by Phoenix Society." Times (London), 2 December, p. 12.

Comments on the full, swelling language; cannot see the likeness between Antonio and Shaftesbury; and notes that the Nicky-Nacky scenes must have suggested "a certain episode in Zola's 'Nana.'" "Otway seems, like Shelley, to have had a grudge against old men."

4 EDMUNDS, E.W. An Historical Summary of English Literature. London, New York, Toronto, and Melbourne: Cassell & Co., pp. 125-26.

Although Don Carlos is ruined by rhyme and The Souldiers Fortune is Otway's only presentable comedy, The Orphan produces the classically required pity and terror, while even the grossly indecent comic scenes do not prevent Venice Preserv'd from being "the greatest tragedy of the time."

5 ODELL, GEORGE C.D. Shakespeare from Betterton to Irving. Vol. 1. New York: Scribner's, pp. 44, 51-53.

Counters the prevailing trend by praising Caius Marius as an "astounding" and ingenious fusion of Romeo and Juliet with the story of Marius and Sylla.

1921

1 ANON. "Thomas Otway." Christian Science Monitor, 8 January, p. 3.

Although Otway lacks "intellectual power . . . feeling for nature . . . humor . . . poetic expression" and "the rhythmical contemplation . . . of lyrical impulse," he "ranks high" for "gentleness . . . tenderness . . . pathos . . . naturalness . . . . rushing intensity" and "truth." His style is free of bombast and his characters are "sane and credible" if "not subtle."

2 BRAWLEY, BENJAMIN. A Short History of the English Drama. New York: Harcourt, Brace, & Co., pp. 142-44.
A compact but standard synthesis.

3 DULONG, GUSTAVE. L'Abbé de Saint-Réal. Vol. 2. Paris: Librairie Ancienne Honoré Champion, pp. 80-86.
Contains a section entitled "Les adaptations dramatique de Dom Carlos: II.--Otway."

4 NICOLL, ALLARDYCE. "Political Plays of the Restoration." MLR 16:236.
The Antonio sections are to be "deeply regretted," not because they are lewd but because they detract from the play's artistry.

1922

1 ECCLES, F.Y. Racine in England. Oxford: Clarendon Press, pp. 4-6.
Although Titus and Berenice does retain Racine's simplicity and union of "tenderness and devouring passion," it misses out "the logic of passion" because of Otway's "merciless excisions."

2 SUMMERS, MONTAGUE. Introduction to Shakespeare Adaptations. London: Jonathan Cape, p. lxxxvii.
Venice Preserv'd is "Otway's masterpiece."

1923

1 ARCHER, WILLIAM. The Old Drama and the New: An Essay in Re-valuation. Boston: Small, Maynard, pp. 142, 145, 156, 159, 160-65, 174, 177, 190, 379.
The strongest negative evaluation since Engel's (see OT.1902.1). The Cheats of Scapin and Caius Marius distort and vulgarize their originals, and the comedies are lewd and preposterous. The Orphan is almost as full of cant and nonsense as Alcibiades, while Venice Preserv'd anticipates "half the dead tragedies of the eighteenth century" with its coarse bombast, implausible actions and motives, and "impotent" ending.

2 BENHAM, ALLEN R. "Notes on Plays: 2." MLN 38:252.
Those who regard Jaffeir as primarily autobiographical overlook the character's debt to love-versus-honor conflicts in earlier heroic plays.

3 NICOLL, ALLARDYCE. A History of Restoration Drama 1660-1700. Cambridge: Cambridge University Press, pp. 20, 24, 89, 110-11, 152-55, 174, 176-77, 246.

Sympathetically surveys the canon, arguing that Otway was one of the few dramatists of his time who found his own mode of expression, instead of merely following fashion. Caius Marius defaces Shakespeare, Alcibiades is not wholly unworthy, and the comedies can be ignored (though Friendship and Souldiers are interesting). But Don Carlos is "truly a triumph of the heroic species "because of Otway's personal style, and The Orphan, which introduces "true pathos" into the English drama, would be "a masterpiece in any age." Despite the somewhat digressive Antonio scenes, Venice Preserv'd is "even finer," given the insightful rendering of Pierre and Jaffeir, the effective ending, and the universal interest of the theme.

4 _____. An Introduction to Dramatic Theory. New York: Brentano's, pp. 36, 49-50, 95-100, 106, 109.

Points out that The Orphan is both domestic and high tragedy and that it combines two conceptions, "the Greek idea being modified by the more modern element of direct human frailty, based not on a mere lack of knowledge." The Orphan and Venice Preserv'd exemplify tragedies in which the catastrophe grows from the clash between two heroes, tragedies that are both domestic and universal, and tragedies that are weakened by stress on the feminine. Nicoll comments on the use of comic relief in The Orphan.

5 STEVENS, DAVID HARRISON, ed. "Notes: Venice Preserved." In Types of English Drama 1660-1780. Boston, New York, and London: Ginn & Co., pp. 884-85.

Discusses sources and influences, commends Otway for creating convincingly human characters, and sees Belvidera as "the natural center of a well-devised tragic action."

1924

1 DOBRÉE, BONAMY. Restoration Comedy 1660-1720. London: Oxford University Press, p. 56.

Otway used "the natural English method" of writing tragedy.

2 SCHUMACHER, EDGAR. Thomas Otway. Bern: N. Durrenmattegger, 175 pp.

A sustained analysis of the life and works, stressing the shift from humanized heroics to pathetic tragedy. Special attention is given to the influences of Racine and Shakespeare, and separate chapters are devoted to Don Carlos and to Venice Preserv'd.

1925

1 ANON. "The Drama: The Orphan . . . The Aldwych Theatre." London Mercury 12:200-201.

Even though Otway knew how to write smooth, musical, colloquial verse, The Orphan turns out to be "heartless hack-work," "a cheap play in the tragic mode," "one of the worst ever written."

2 ANON. "Otway's 'The Orphan' Revived." Christian Science Monitor, 28 May, n. pag.
Regards the play as "tragically intense," Greek in its fatalism but not in its softness, and seriously marred by bombast, by poor motivation and characterization, and by lack of humor.

3 ANON. Review of the Phoenix Society revival of The Orphan. Referee, 1 May, n. pag.
If Venice Preserv'd is "intensely gripping," this play is "heart-rending" despite its "splodges of turgid bombast" and unpleasant comic relief.

*4 HAM, ROSWELL GRAY. "The Life and Works of Thomas Otway." Ph.D. dissertation, Yale University.
Source: CDI (1861-1972), 34:852. Revised for publication: OT.1931.2.

5 MacCARTHY, DESMOND. "Drama: The Orphan." New Statesman 25: 134-35.
Sees the play as hopelessly outdated by its inflated style.

6 NICOLL, ALLARDYCE. British Drama: An Historical Survey from the Beginnings to the Present Time. New York: Crowell, pp. 224, 232-34, 264, 267-68.
Epitomizes the survey in the History (see OT.1923.3), emphasizing Otway's influence on the future of pathetic drama and of farce.

7 ROYDE-SMITH, N.G. "The Drama: The Orphan . . . The Phoenix Society." Outlook (London) 55:329.
Its finer passages made it worthy of attention, though "we all giggled at its plot and chuckled over its rhetoric."

1926

1 COX, JAMES E. The Rise of Sentimental Comedy. Olney, Ill.: by the author, p. 55.
Notes that Monimia is the prototype for Steele's Indiana and thinks Otway meant us to understand that Polydore indirectly assumes blame for the sin of adultery on which the play focuses.

2 SUMMERS, MONTAGUE, ed. Introduction to The Complete Works of Thomas Otway. Vol. 1. London: Nonesuch Press, pp. xiii-civ.
Here and in the apparatus relating to each play as its text is given in subsequent volumes, Summers provides less critical

analysis than rich resources for future critics: details of staging and stage history, sources and backgrounds, influences, imitations and adaptations, and comparisons with other plays in world drama.

He sees Alcibiades as "a typical heroic tragedy," spirited but faulty; Don Carlos as second only to Dryden's rhymed tragedies; the French translations as effective; and Caius Marius as powerful and ingenious. He finds no improbabilities in The Orphan and regards it as both poignant and realistic. Venice Preserv'd is a masterpiece of design and psychological analysis, given "strange power and dark significance" by the Antonio scenes which, together with the character of Renault, do satirize aspects of Shaftesbury and are indispensable to the plot. Summers becomes the first to praise Otway as a comic genius: he considers Friendship in Fashion a brilliantly harsh social satire, The Souldiers Fortune a masterfully controlled comedy of wit and intrigue, and The Atheist a lively and topical commentary.

1927

1 BEATY, JOHN O. "The Drama of the Restoration." In An Introduction to Drama. Edited by Beaty and Jay B. Hubbell. New York: Macmillan, pp. 321-22.

"Though Venice Preserved has not the literary merit of All for Love, it is probably a better stage play," partly because, with its interweaving of family and political problems, it "seems much more modern than most Restoration plays." Otway "excelled in characterization and plot."

2 CAZAMIAN, LOUIS. A History of English Literature, Vol. 2: Modern Times (1660-1914). New York: Macmillan, pp. 32, 49-50.

In ascending order of merit, Don Carlos, The Orphan, and Venice Preserv'd are Otway's best works, the latter being "a last excrescence of the Elizabethan vein" and fusing "romanticism with something . . . of the classical spirit." Its pathos sometimes "goes beyond the limits of moral sensibility, and has recourse to wholly physical means," and its depictions of tender emotions appeal "less to the heart than to the nerves." The Antonio scenes, which have a Shakespearean appropriateness, highlight a "bitter pessimism" that darkens the whole play. Otway is more disciplined and better balanced than Lee, and his verse is "more flexible," his characters deeper than Lee's.

3 [DOBRÉE, BONAMY.] "Thomas Otway." TLS, 3 March, pp. 133-34.

An implicit corrective to Summers (see OT.1926.2): names as failures The Cheats of Scapin (because Otway tried to turn farce into comedy), Alcibiades (because of its absurdities), Friendship in Fashion (because it has "all the ill-nature of Restoration comedy without any of the fairy wit of Etherege or the mournful grace of Congreve"), and The Atheist (a "disordered attempt at fantasy" that fails to combine "grimness, romance, and laughter"). The Souldiers Fortune, however, succeeds as "a terrible comedy of disillusion," and if The Orphan is a good play, Venice Preserv'd is second only to All for Love in the Restoration. Otway's forward-looking obsession with emotional love, deriving from his unrequited passion for Mrs. Barry, provided him with a distinctive alternative to religion and to the more fashionable brand of witty love; but while such romantic feeling "made him the poet that he was," it probably stifled a greater poetic talent.

4 GOSSE, EDMUND. "Gentlest Otway." Sunday Times (London), 13 March, n. pag.

Seems to be reviewing Summers's edition (see OT.1926.2). Otway is considered "a pioneer in the new kind of elegiac tragedy" who wrote lewd, malignant comedies and, in Alcibiades, at least one "mawkish piece of rhyming rant." He was "the most Racinian of all our poets."

5 HERFORD, C.H. English Literature. London: Ernest Benn, p. 28.

Lacking "the high temper" of pre-Restoration tragedy, Venice Preserv'd relies for its effect on "an extraordinarily powerful plot."

6 SPENCER, HAZELTON. Shakespeare Improved: The Restoration Versions in Quarto and on the Stage. Cambridge: Harvard University Press, pp. 292-98.

Caius Marius grotesquely mixes Roman and Renaissance elements, with chaotic and dull results. Otway's "bold appropriation" is discussed in some detail.

7 SUMMERS, MONTAGUE, ed. Introduction to The Complete Works of Thomas Shadwell. Vol. 1. London: Fortune Press, pp. clxvi, ccxxvi.

Notes that the elder Marius in Caius Marius represents Shaftesbury. The Atheist is a "capital" play.

1928

1 DOBRÉE, BONAMY, ed. Introduction to Five Restoration Tragedies. Oxford: Oxford University Press; London: Humphrey Milford, pp. xii-xiii.

Venice Preserv'd is a "splendid, gloomy tragedy" that looks ahead to Rousseau with its "extreme abandonment to the emotions." Though the Nicky-Nacky scenes are revolting, they do relieve the sustained tension of pathos and heroics.

2 ELWIN, MALCOLM. The Playgoer's Handbook to Restoration Drama. New York: Macmillan, pp. 84, 96, 132-45.

Dismisses Alcibiades and Titus and Berenice but treats the other plays sympathetically. Elwin continues the trends of praising Caius Marius for its original merits, of regarding Don Carlos as the best of all heroic plays, of appreciating the briskness of Cheats, of perceiving effective satire and intrigue in the comedies (except for The Atheist), and of ranking Venice Preserv'd, "a scathing satire on human nature," higher than Dryden's best efforts in tragedy. Renault's lust and the comic perversions of Antonio and Aquilina are compatible with the rest of the play.

*3 GHOSH, J.C. "An Edition of the Works of Thomas Otway, with Biography and Commentary." Ph.D. dissertation, Oxford University.

Source: McNamee (1865-1964):515. Revised for publication OT.1932.3.

4 MOORE, JOHN ROBERT. "Contemporary Satire in Otway's Venice Preserved." PMLA 43:166-81.

Lists and briefly analyzes satirical allusions to the Popish Plot trials, the English Parliament, the general character of the Whig conspiracy, and the Earl of Shaftesbury (through both Antonio and Renault). Moore pioneers the study of how Otway's alterations of his source contribute to a larger design, and he recognizes, but does not elaborate on, the importance of swearing in the play.

5 SUMMERS, MONTAGUE, ed. "Explanatory Notes." In Roscius Anglicanus, by John Downes. London: Fortune Press, pp. 225, 229.

Sees The Souldiers Fortune and The Orphan as excellent plays.

6 VILLARD, LÉONIE. "Bérénice en angleterre." Revue de l'Universitée de Lyons 1 (January):106-11.

Discusses Titus and Berenice in relation to Racine and refers to Venice Preserv'd as "le plus beau drame romantique de la fin du XVIIe siècle."

7 WILSON, JOHN HAROLD. The Influence of Beaumont and Fletcher on Restoration Drama. Columbus: Ohio State University Press, pp. 33, 70-71, 77.

Sees Friendship in Fashion as a typical Restoration comedy of intrigue, wit, satire, and farce. Wilson notes that The Atheist draws upon The Custom of the Country but for no organic purpose, and he rejects Langbaine's (see OT.1691.1) connection of The Souldiers Fortune to Monsieur Thomas. Otway's "hard cynicism" is linked to "his utter moral depravity."

1929

1 DOBRÉE, BONAMY. Restoration Tragedy 1660-1720. Oxford: Clarendon Press, pp. 43, 59-61, 64, 96, 132-48.

Reiterates, in places word for word, the TLS article on Otway (see OT.1927.3), making a few additions and minor changes derived, mainly, from the introductory remarks in Five Restoration Tragedies (see OT.1928.1). Among the fresh comments: Otway lacks the strength of Lee and "the strict correspondence of word and image with emotion or thought" that characterizes the verse of Dryden and the best Elizabethans. In Venice Preserv'd the obsession with romantic love becomes incongruous with the other, more Elizabethan elements, and tends to undermine the play's "emotional structure." Otway usually had trouble concentrating his feeling, linking his ideas rapidly, and preparing the audience for the tersely phrased sentiments that could have become his most effective dramatic tool. His great potential was stifled by emotional self-indulgence, but he gives us interesting studies of man's "capacity for feeling, even for self-torture."

2 KIES, PAUL P. "Lessing's Early Study of English Drama." JEGP 28:18-19.

In his Alcibiades, Lessing twice refers to Otway's version of the same story.

3 MOSES, MONTROSE J., ed. "Thomas Otway: Venice Preserv'd; or, A Plot Discover'd." In British Plays from the Restoration to 1820. Vol. 1. Boston: Little, Brown, & Co., pp. 329-34.

A discriminating assessment, adding very little new criticism: sees Otway as a true poet whose comedies are harsh and indecent, whose Caius Marius comes off well if regarded as a careful adaptation, and whose tragedies "gave a new spirit to the declining tragic impulse . . . with a departure along the faint but . . . new lines of domestic tragedy and romantic passion." Venice Preserv'd is like a diluted Elizabethan play in many respects, lacking the humor, contrast, imagination, and power of its predecessors. It is intense and depressing.

1930

1 EATON, WALTER PRICHARD. The Drama in English. New York, Chicago, and Boston: Charles Scribner's Sons, pp. 171-75.

Too stagy and bombastic for modern audiences, Venice Preserv'd presents an interesting central problem, but the love scenes are "almost stifling in their insistence on the physical," while the confrontations between Jaffeir and Pierre are painfully sentimental.

2 LIEDER, FREDERICK W.C. "The Don Carlos Theme." Harvard Studies and Notes in Philology and Literature 12:14-15.

Of the 105 versions of the theme covered, Otway's is said to be "one of the most important," a "masterly" handling of Saint-Réal, influenced by Shakespeare and French classical drama, and influencing later writers.

3 WHITING, GEORGE W. "Political Satire in London Stage Plays, 1680-83." MP 28:34, 41.

In The Souldiers Fortune, political satire is not stressed, though Sir Davy clearly becomes a type of the city commonwealth's man. Most of the satire in Venice Preserv'd makes the general point that opposition to the court is unprincipled. "It is understood . . . that a part of Parliament is included in the opposition; and this accounts for Otway's satirical treatment of the Venetian senate." Antonio may be taken as a satirical portrait of Shaftesbury, but Renault probably was not intended as a reflection on the Whig leader.

1931

1 DEANE, CECIL V. Dramatic Theory and the Rhymed Heroic Play. London: Oxford University Press, pp. 18-19, 159.

Although Titus and Berenice was the first English adaptation to recreate some of Racine's "passion and pathos," it is marred by Otway's catering to the audience's demand for poetic justice and happy endings. The Orphan and Venice Preserv'd "established the school of pathos."

2 HAM, ROSWELL GRAY. Otway and Lee: Biography from a Baroque Age. New Haven: Yale University Press, 260 pp.

Revision of OT.1925.4. Still the best biography and, in its time, the best piece of literary criticism on the plays. Alcibiades combines Elizabethan and Restoration qualities, moving from "themes of 'will' and 'reputation' to those . . . of the Restoration mind, 'the futility of conscience' and 'ambition.'" In Don Carlos, Otway begins to write from the heart and learns from Saint-Réal and Racine to combine structure and passion. Titus and Berenice and Caius Marius show that Otway was "a talented adapter" who shaped his originals to new purposes and informed them with his own sensibility. Otway's comedies lack comic distance but have their own kind of integrity. Friendship in Fashion is a busy, biting satire; The Souldiers Fortune a serious look at "the game of sex"; The Atheist an intentionally nauseating critique on what becomes of doting lovers and old rakes. With The Orphan, Otway gains full control over passion but has yet to master thought. He becomes more intelligent and philosophical in Venice Preserv'd, successfully blending Elizabethan crowdedness, Racinian economy and unity, heroic agony, and a new mastery of emotional modulation. The characters, especially Belvidera, are more complexly and intensely realized than in The Orphan, and the Nicky-Nacky scenes effectively contrast with the love encounters between Jaffeir and his wife.

Otway tended to write plays about "two lovers in the perpetual attitude of separation and despair," about heroes who are "strong and weak in turns" and who cannot understand themselves, about heroes who reflected himself and heroines who were the "transfigured" images of Mrs. Barry. His "intuitive and highly emotional nature" perhaps prevented him from fully realizing his artistic potential as he outgrew the influence of his many predecessors and sources (special attention is given to Shakespeare, Racine, and Lee, though a number of others are pointed out and discussed).

3 MacMILLAN, DOUGALD, and HOWARD MUMFORD JONES, eds. Headnote to Venice Preserved. In Plays of the Restoration and Eighteenth Century. New York: Henry Holt & Co., pp. 213-14.

Dismisses the early plays, Caius Marius, and the comedies (except for The Souldiers Fortune, where Otway "turned his army experiences to good account"); calls The Orphan a "masterpiece," and ranks Venice Preserv'd as "his supreme achievement," with its beautiful verse, romantic passions, and mysterious political backdrop. Otway was "the Byron of the Restoration."

4 WATSON, HAROLD FRANCIS. The Sailor in English Fiction and Drama 1550-1800. New York: Columbia University Press, p. 142.

Briefly locates The Cheats of Scapin in the tradition.

1932

1 ERVINE, ST. JOHN. "At the Play: Otway." Unidentified clipping, dated 17 April, in the Harvard Theatre Collection.

His plays show that Otway was "a mixture of genius and humbug, charlatan and poet." Caius Marius is a carelessly contrived, impudent "atrocity," and Alcibiades is artless and clumsy. In The Souldiers Fortune, with its powerful bitterness, the author shows promise as a writer of dark comedies, but Friendship in Fashion turns out to be tedious, while The Atheist is "a poor, schemeless thing," demonstrating that Otway had really no sense of humor. Venice Preserv'd is a "ramshackle tragedy, in which the characters behave with . . . ineptitude"; "what a vaporous ass is Jaffeir"! Otway hated old men, and he seems to have had no originality.

2 FAUSSET, HUGH I'A. "Thomas Otway." Bookman 82:32-33.

Reviews Ghosh's edition (see OT.1932.3) and finds that Otway wrote only three plays worth reading, Don Carlos, The Orphan, and Venice Preserv'd, none of which is truly tragic. Lacking imaginative power, intellectual subtlety, and psychological insight, Otway achieved a musical mode of composition: actors and actresses, like language itself, became for him the media through which he could express emotional contours, blending "sensuousness, sentiment and idealism" into dramas "of a longing without limit caught in a net of circumstances." In some respects he anticipates the Romantic movement.

3 GHOSH, J.C., ed. Introduction to The Works of Thomas Otway. Vol. 1. Oxford: Clarendon Press, pp. 1-94.

Revision of OT.1928.3. Competently synthesizes previous criticism, commenting instructively on each play, occasionally adding to or differing with Ham's analyses (see OT.1931.2). Alcibiades is "a poor piece." Although The Souldiers Fortune has some diverting moments, in general Otway's comedies are "dull, featureless, purposeless," Friendship in Fashion being the "only one of them in which it is possible to read a satiric purpose." Don Carlos is a fine "tragedy of old age" in which Otway redeems heroic drama and discovers his special brand of characters. While Titus and Berenice and Cheats are good adaptations, Caius Marius is clumsy, crude, stiff, and disorderly. Despite its improbabilities and overdoses of pathos, The Orphan is a moving tragedy which, contrary to received opinion, does grow out of the characters of Castalio and Polydore. It anticipates Southerne and Rowe. Venice Preserv'd deserves its high reputation, though it is flawed by conflicting views of Shaftesbury and by the careless construction of Act 4. Deep ironies emerge when we realize that Renault embodies the very sort of corruption that Pierre and Jaffeir set out to destroy. Sources and the stage history of each play are discussed.

4 HECHT, ILSE. Der heroische Frauentyp im Restaurationsdrama. Leipzig: Alexander Edelmann, pp. 25-29, 81-83, 128-30, 132-33, 135.

Classifies Otway's "heroic" women. Elisabeth (Don Carlos) is the "noble" heroine, Deidamia (Alcibiades) the wholly unscrupulous type, Belvidera (Venice Preserv'd) the woman trying to influence politics through a certain man.

1933

1 ANON. "That Once Renowned Tragedy, Otway's 'Venice Preserved' Exhibited at Yale." Boston Evening Transcript, 19 December, n. pag.

Sketches Otway's life, traces the play's stage history, and surveys the history of critical responses to successive performances. Almost spoiled by artifice and fustian in the early acts, Venice Preserv'd grows into "a stark as well as a somber tragedy of friendship betrayed" which "holds us by a very personal emotion." Pierre's speeches of disillusionment, Jaffeir's remorse, and the Nicky-Nacky scenes are singled out for special praise. The confrontations between Jaffeir and Belvidera are felt to be too lengthy.

2 MOORE, CECIL A., ed. Introduction to Twelve Famous Plays of the Restoration and Eighteenth Century. New York: Modern Library, pp. ix-x.

Venice Preserv'd and The Orphan are the only two lastingly great tragedies composed during the century following the Restoration. They convey genuine feeling, and Belvidera and Monimia are justly ranked with Shakespeare's best female characterizations.

3 PRAZ, MARIO. "Restoration Drama." English Studies 15:5n, 8, 9.

Queen Deidamia in the "feeble Alcibiades" seems modeled on Racine's Phèdre, and Belvidera in Venice Preserv'd is paralleled by La Marmoutier in The Duke of Guise. The Nicky-Nacky scenes were suggested by Charles II, and they have "a companion" in Shadwell's Virtuoso. The "central theme" in both Don Carlos and Venice Preserv'd "is that of a man deliberately led to sacrifice by the woman he loves." Otway reflects Webster and anticipates "certain morbid aspects of Romanticism."

*4 STROUP, THOMAS BRADLEY. "Type-Characters in the Serious Drama of the Restoration with Special Attention to the Plays of Davenant, Dryden, Lee, and Otway." Ph.D. dissertation, University of North Carolina.

Source: Stratman, p. 545.

5 Van LENNEP, WILLIAM. "The Life and Works of Nathaniel Lee, Dramatist (1648?-1692): A Study of Sources." Ph.D. dissertation, Harvard University, pp. 477-88.

Shows that Caius Marius influenced Lee's Lucius Junius Brutus, which in turn influenced Otway's Venice Preserv'd.

6 WHITEHALL, HAROLD. "Thomas Shadwell and the Lancashire Dialect." Essays and Studies in English and Comparative Literature. University of Michigan Publications in Language and Literature, vol. 10. Ann Arbor: University of Michigan Press, pp. 266-75.

Comparing certain passages in The Cheats of Scapin to certain ones in Shadwell's The Lancashire-Witches and The Squire of Alsatia, concludes that the two writers used essentially the same South Lancashire dialect but that Shadwell did not borrow significantly from Otway.

1934

1 ANDERSON, PAUL BUNYAN. "English Drama Transferred to Prévost's Fiction." MLN 49:178-80.

Much of the plot from The Orphan is woven into M. de Sauveboeuf's story of his own life in Memoires et avantures d'un homme de qualité.

2 LEGOUIS, EMILE. A Short History of English Literature. Translated by V.F. Boyson and J. Coulson. Oxford: Clarendon Press, pp. 187-88.

A routine assessment with no fresh ideas. The Orphan is domestic, Elizabethan, and romantic; Venice Preserv'd intensely studies friendship versus love against a historical background.

3 MAZEL, HENRI. "Une source de 'Nana.'" Mercure de France 253: 223.

Zola's Nana borrows from the Antonio-Aquilina scenes in Venice Preserv'd.

1935

1 AURIANT. "'Venise sauvée' ou les débiteurs découverts." Mercure de France 258:297-308.

2 MORGAN, A.E., ed. Headnote to Venice Preserv'd. In English Plays 1660-1820. New York and London: Harper & Bros., pp. 237-38.

"He wrote orthodox heroic tragedy, unremarkable comedy, and two great tragedies. . . . Otway was not a master of plot construction, but he could depict with remarkable power individual scenes of passion and dramatic intensity." Belvidera has "rare beauty and pathos."

3 RIVA, SERAFINO, ed. and trans. Introduzione to Venezia Salvata ossia Una Conjiura Scoperta. Venezia: Gazzettino Illustrato, pp. 15-115.

4 SUMMERS, MONTAGUE. The Playhouse of Pepys. New York: Macmillan, pp. 293, 408.

Notes homosexuality in The Souldiers Fortune and points out that The Atheist is indebted to the ninth chapter of Scarron's Le Roman Comique.

1936

*1 RIVA, S. "Otway, Saint Real e la 'Venezia Salvata.'" Dante, Revue de Culture Latine, June, pp. 278-82.

Source: Stratman, pp. 545-46.

2 TEETER, LOUIS. "Political Themes in Restoration Tragedy." Ph.D. dissertation, Johns Hopkins University, pp. 93, 138 ff., 247 ff.

Discusses Machiavellian qualities in Alcibiades and Don Carlos, in one instance comparing the latter to Chapman's Bussy d'Ambois.

1937

1 DUGGAN, G.C. The Stage Irishman: A History of the Irish Play and Stage Characters from the Earliest Times. London: Longmans, Green, & Co., pp. 285-86.

The Cheats of Scapin has an example of how "in adaptations of Molière's comedies . . . the Irishman takes the place of some foreign character or of someone who in the original speaks in patois."

2 EICH, LOUIS M. "A Previous Adaptation of Romeo and Juliet." Quarterly Journal of Speech 23:589, 592-93.

In light of the recent Howard-Shearer movie, with its reverence for Shakespeare, Otway's Caius Marius seems an outright "manhandling" of Shakespeare's original. Briefly discusses the Restoration habit of "improving" Shakespeare.

3 FROHMAN, DANIEL. Encore. New York: Lee Furman, pp. 1-4.

One of the earliest American dramatic productions, The Orphan was acted in 1750 at a coffeehouse on King Street in Boston. Otway "wrote charmingly of love," but his plays were too topical to endure.

4 STROUP, THOMAS B. "Supernatural Beings in Restoration Drama." Anglia 61:188-89.

Notes the functional use of ghosts in Alcibiades and Venice Preserv'd.

1938

1 NOYES, ROBERT GALE. "Conventions of Song in Restoration Tragedy." PMLA 53:166, 171, 177-78, 182, 186.

Finds in The Orphan a typical song to intensify or allay grief, and in Alcibiades notes a seduction song, a wedding song, a song used as medicine to cure sorrow, and a song in the presence of death.

2 WILCOX, JOHN. The Relation of Molière to Restoration Comedy. New York: Columbia University Press, pp. 34, 144-46.

In comedy Otway ranks below Dryden and Shadwell, on a level with Aphra Behn. Although Cheats is creditably translated from an insignificant work by Molière, and there are slight debts to the Frenchman in The Souldiers Fortune and The Atheist, Otway's style was not compatible with Molière's, so that Otway did not become a channel for French influences on comedy.

1939

1 AURIANT. "'Venise sauvée' ou les débiteurs découverts." Mercure de France 289:760-76.

2 GRAHAM, C.B. "Jonson Allusions in Restoration Comedy." RES 15:202.

The Souldiers Fortune has an allusion not mentioned in The Jonson Allusion Book.

3 NETTLETON, GEORGE H. "Blank-Verse Tragedy (1677-1700)." In British Dramatists from Dryden to Sheridan. Edited by Nettleton and Arthur E. Case. Boston, New York, Chicago, Dallas, Atlanta, and San Francisco: Houghton Mifflin, pp. 71-72.

An even-handed but slightly stale commentary, reliably noting sources and backgrounds, and stressing Otway's leading move toward pathos, sentiment, and female distress. George Winchester Stone does not revise this section's approach to Otway in his 1969 revision of British Dramatists from Dryden to Sheridan (Boston: Houghton Mifflin).

1940

1 GASSNER, JOHN. Masters of the Drama. New York: Random House, pp. 284-85.

Second-rate but moving, The Orphan was "a finger exercise" for the "flawed but powerful Venice Preserved," which became the "best tragedy for the next century and more."

2 HUGHES, LEO. "Attitudes of Some Restoration Dramatists toward Farce." PQ 19:280.

Otway's comedies were mere hackwork.

3 WILEY, AUTREY NELL. Rare Prologues and Epilogues 1642-1700. London: George Allen & Unwin, pp. 57-58.

The prologue and epilogue to Venice Preserv'd are important early examples of the "newly conceived stage oration" which commented journalistically upon current events.

1941

1 FREEDLEY, GEORGE, and JOHN A. REEVES. A History of the Theatre. New York: Crown, pp. 166-67.

Regards Don Carlos as "declamatory" and Venice Preserv'd as "alive despite its bombast and some long, dull passages." Except for Jaffeir and Belvidera during their love scenes, Otway's characters were "like puppets who moved through intense human suffering."

2 PEAKE, CHARLES HOWARD. "Domestic Tragedy in Relation to Theology in the First Half of the Eighteenth Century." Ph.D. dissertation, University of Michigan, p. 143.

Cites The Orphan as the first sharp reaction, in tragedy, against the heroic play, and as the first important attempt to give a domestic cast to the action by centering it on the heroine.

3 SUMMERS, MONTAGUE. "Letters to the Editor: A Note on Otway." TLS, 7 June, p. 275.

Perhaps the relationship between Antonio and Aquilina (Venice Preserv'd) follows a hint in Saint-Réal, but could the name "Aquilina" allude to the famous Venetian courtesan addressed in two poems by the Florentine writer Grazzini (1508-83)? At any rate, Balzac was impressed by the Nicky-Nacky episodes. See OT.1835.1 and OT.1973.2.

1942

1 ALLEMAN, GELLERT SPENCER. Matrimonial Law and the Materials of Restoration Comedy. Wallingford, Pa.: n.p., pp. 82, 86, 116, 118, 122.

Finds that Otway is the only Restoration dramatist among those studied who avoided using the devices of trick or mock marriages, though in Cheats, Friendship in Fashion, and The Souldiers Fortune, there is plenty of material for the student of matrimonial law in Restoration comedy: clandestine marriage, efforts to discard wives, references to court proceedings, and so on.

2 GREENE, GRAHAM. British Dramatists. London: William Collins, p. 30.

Venice Preserv'd "hardly justifies its reputation. . . . Otway deserves to be remembered better for The Souldier's Fortune, a prose comedy which ranks only just below Wycherley." Reprinted in the section, "British Dramatists," in Romance of English Literature, ed. Kate O'Brien and W.J. Turner (New York: Hastings House, 1944), pp. 125-26.

1943

1 AGATE, JAMES. These Were Actors: Extracts from a Newspaper Cutting Book 1811-1833. London, New York, and Melbourne: Hutchinson, pp. 108-13.

Offers plot summaries; summarizes critiques by Roden, Archer, Gosse, and others; and calls Otway a writer of "patent absurdity" and "turgid nonsense."

*2 MACKENZIE, ALINE F. "Otway and the History of His Plays on the London Stage: A Study of Taste." Ph.D. dissertation, Bryn Mawr College.

Source: CDI (1861-1972), 35:834. Revised for publication: OT.1950.4.

1945

1 FINK, ZERA S. The Classical Republicans: An Essay in the Recovery of a Pattern of Thought in Seventeenth-Century England. Evanston, Ill.: Northwestern University Press, pp. 144-48.

Venice Preserv'd is too complex to be taken as an allegory of the Popish Plot. The Venice of the play is "not worth saving," for it is "a hostile, Tory representation, not of the England that the Whigs were accused of conspiring against, but of what is taken as the Whig ideal of a Venetian state." The Whigs are satirized not only for their conspiring but also for their "wishing to introduce a corrupt and vicious Venetian system into England." This makes sense of a story in which Renault/Shaftesbury tries to overthrow Antonio/Shaftesbury.

2 MACKENZIE, ALINE. "A Note on the Date of The Orphan." ELH 12:316-26.

Using stage history, biographical data, and internal evidence, argues that the play was composed in early summer 1678, that is, before Caius Marius. In proving this, Miss Mackenzie shows that Acasto should not be identified with the Duke of Ormonde, and she discusses influences on Otway by French writers, Elizabethan dramatists, and heroic drama.

3 SAINTSBURY, GEORGE. "John Dryden the Dramatist" and "The Two Tragedies." In George Saintsbury: The Memorial Volume. London: Methuen, pp. 74, 139-41.

Contrasts Otway's sense of pathos as the chief tragic emotion with Dryden's emphasis on admiration. Venice Preserv'd is more sentimental than tragic, because its catastrophe rests more on "causeless misery and inextricable victimizing" than on an "adequate, necessary, and just connection of cause and effect." Belvidera's marrying the "despicable and idiotic" Jaffeir does, in a sense, cause the catastrophe, but, as a cause, it has "neither the adequacy nor the necessity of tragedy." In creating Belvidera, Otway must have had Desdemona in mind, just as he must have been thinking of Brutus and Cassius as he created Jaffeir and Pierre.

1947

1 MACKENZIE, ALINE. "A Note on Pierre's White Hat." N&Q 192:90-93.

Argues that the wearing of white hats by actors playing Pierre from about 1707 to 1748 may have signified Jacobite sentiments.

2 PRIOR, MOODY E. The Language of Tragedy. New York: Columbia University Press, pp. 185-92.

Having moved tragedy away from heroic drama, with its "balancing of intellectually framed positions," geometric positioning of highly stylized characters, and artificial plot complications, Otway overstressed his emotional effects. In Venice Preserv'd the language, ordered to describe alternative states of "pity, misery, and melting love," weakens what might have been a swiftly moving, progressive plot. At its best, the language is free and easy, figuratively apt, and, in Pierre, ironically indirect, becoming "suggestive of a hidden sense of wrongs and a determination not to weaken under them." In general, though, the emotional effusions become detached from the elements that direct action, and the imagery is not fused "into any sort of coordinate relation with the play as a whole." "The final effect is one of overloaded feeling, almost of stasis."

1948

1 EVANS, B. IFOR. A Short History of English Drama. Harmondsworth, Eng.: Penguin, p. 124.

The Orphan is improbable but moving, and Venice Preserv'd, which focuses on Jaffeir's character, is theatrically effective melodrama.

2 McKILLOP, ALAN DUGALD. English Literature from Dryden to Burns. New York and London: Appleton-Century-Crofts, pp. 69-70.

Though Otway wrote "rather undistinguished comedies," Don Carlos is a "significant historical play" and The Orphan substitutes "a pathetic and domestic for a heroic theme," anticipating the sentimental movement. In Venice Preserv'd heroic love and honor achieve "a finer level of poetry and psychology" as "high Roman conceptions of political and personal loyalty" are blended with "softness and pathos."

3 SHERBURN, GEORGE. The Restoration and Eighteenth Century (1660-1789). Vol. 3 of A Literary History of England. Edited by Albert C. Baugh. New York: Appleton-Century-Crofts, pp. 758-60.

Traces Otway's transition from the heroics of Alcibiades through the humanized heroics of Don Carlos and the pathos of The Orphan to the "powerful emotional appeal" of Venice Preserv'd, with its effective combination of pathos, political satire, and comedy. Otway wrote from the heart.

4 SMITH, JOHN HARRINGTON. The Gay Couple in Restoration Comedy. Cambridge, Mass.: Harvard University Press, pp. 40, 97-98, 188n.

Friendship in Fashion and The Souldiers Fortune are dominated by gross cuckolding strategies, and in the former play Lady Squeamish is "perhaps as unmoral a predatory female" as any in Restoration drama. Smith notes that Friendship influenced Southerne's The Wives Excuse, and he calls The Atheist "an aggregate of cheap romance and cheap farce."

*5 SUMMERS, MONTAGUE. "Tender Thomas Otway." Everybody's Weekly 20 March, p. 12.
Source: Timothy d'Arch Smith, A Bibliography of the Works of Montague Summers (New Hyde Park, N.Y.: University Books, 1964), p. 126.

1949

1 MACKENZIE, ALINE. "Venice Preserv'd Reconsidered." Tulane Studies in English 1:81-118.
Argues that Otway began composing Venice Preserv'd amidst the Whig upsurge of 1679, put it aside when the censorship of Lee's Lucius Junius Brutus and Tate's Richard III showed the dangers of dramatizing Whig sentiments, and completed a revised version after the Tory triumph of March 1681, only then adding the Nicky-Nacky scenes inspired by contemporary satire on Shaftesbury. "The emotional structure of the main plot permitted the topical interest of the conspiracy to yield to the topical interest in Shaftesbury." The ultimate effect of the shifting of ill wishes from side to side is "to divorce all sympathy from the political conflict" and to concentrate it on the domestic issues. Praises Otway's craftsmanship in weaving together main action and subplot.

2 MAGILL, LEWIS MALCOLM. "Elements of Sentimentalism in English Tragedy, 1680-1704." Ph.D. Dissertation, University of Illinois.
Sees in Otway's plays a cult of sympathy for victimized protagonists. See Dissertation Abstracts (1950):89-90.

3 OLSON, ROBERT CHARLES. "Thomas Otway's Venice Preserved and the Critics." Master's thesis, University of Colorado, 139 p.
While the earliest critics reacted fairly consistently to "the nuances of rhetoric and gesture which governed each scene" and in combination produced the total effect, more recent critics clash in their opinions of the play's merits, since they seem not to share this sensitivity to rhetoric and gesture.

1950

1 BREDVOLD, LOUIS I. "The Literature of the Restoration and the Eighteenth Century 1660-1798." In A History of English

Literature. Edited by Hardin Craig. New York: Oxford University Press, p. 359.

A lucid but unoriginal overview of "the finest tragic genius of the period." With his "insight into the psychology of passion and suffering," his domestic focus, his sensitive portrayals of females, and his independent movement toward a simpler, less bombastic, and less pageant-like style than Lee and the others, Otway prepared "for the domestic tragedy of Southerne and Rowe and the later drama of sensibility."

2 DOWNER, ALAN S. The British Drama: A Handbook and Brief Chronicle. New York: Appleton-Century-Crofts, pp. 255-58.

Although Venice Preserv'd returns "to the panoramic tradition" of Shakespeare, it becomes "over-explicit and over-literal" in both imagery and emotion, so that its final effect "is neither truth nor tragedy, but pathos." It anticipates the eighteenth-century merging of serious and comic drama. Mentions The Orphan and Caius Marius.

3 LEECH, CLIFFORD. "Restoration Tragedy: A Reconsideration." DUJ 42:110, 112-13.

That both The Orphan and Venice Preserv'd contain many flaws in design and plausibility reinforces one's impression that "Otway was not concerned with a coherent dramatic structure, but aimed at a strenuous emotional exercise. The woes of Jaffeir and Belvidera are not derived from things as they are: they exist to furnish theatrical excitement."

4 TAYLOR, ALINE MACKENZIE. Next to Shakespeare: Otway's Venice Preserv'd and The Orphan and Their History on the London Stage. Durham, N.C.: Duke University Press, 338 pp.

Revision of OT.1943.2. In this indispensable "essay in the history of dramatic taste," the first two chapters seek the "enduring qualities" of each play. The unity and credibility of The Orphan depend on its audience's suspending disbelief as near-comic trickery modulates into horrible deeds and consequences. Within the context of Restoration beliefs, Polydore and Castalio can be seen as victims of self-contradiction. Suicide is Polydore's escape from his chaos of attitudes: libertinism, stoic pride, a sense of personal honor, and a sacramental view of marriage. Castalio's initial act of concealment is a way of handling the conflict between heroic conventions precluding marriage and the libertine code favoring extramarital affairs. Sources and influences are discussed, and the play's supposed reflection of Otway's personal life is dismissed for lack of evidence.

Full appreciation of Venice Preserv'd is shown to depend on an even more complex balancing of antitheses: love versus friendship, personal versus political motives, patriot versus malcontent, natural versus artificial language, the shifting of audiences' sympathies between conspirators and senate. The

Nicky-Nacky scenes are analyzed as in the Tulane Studies article (see OT.1949.1), and the dagger symbol is discussed. Chapters 3 and 4 show how successive stage productions differently interpreted each play's characters and structure.

The final chapter, in charting the course of Otway's reputation from the Restoration to 1898, tries to account for the high and low points. Late-Restoration praise for his depiction of women gave way to an Augustan objection to his nonclassical pathos, and his mid-eighteenth-century popularity among those caught up in the vogue for natural tenderness was quelled by later-century reactions against his supposed immorality and supposedly heroic style. Then a new, and final, era of ascendancy came with the Revolutionary fervor of the eighties and nineties, with the cult of feeling, and with the acting triumphs of Mrs. Siddons and Kemble. As the nineteenth century wore on, Otway's plays began to seem artificial and hyperbolical, and in the present century his fame "is purely academic." Argues in general that Otway's plays are best studied in terms of their stage performances. Extensive back matter includes performance lists as well as bibliography, index of actors and actresses, and general index.

1951

1 KIENDLER, GRETE. "Konvertierte Formen in den Dramen Otways und Lees. Ein Vergleich mit der Sprache Shakespeares." Ph.D. dissertation, University of Graz, 202 pp.

Catalogues the conversion of words (adjectives into nouns, adjectives into verbs, nouns into verbs, nouns into adjectives) in the plays of Otway and Lee, with special reference to possible first uses of the converted forms in Shakespeare. For example, "to rumour" (meaning "to circulate by way of rumour") is a verbal form created from the noun, and it occurs in Richard III, Otway's Venice Preserv'd, and Lee's Theodosius.

2 LEECH, CLIFFORD. "Restoration Comedy: The Earlier Phase." EIC 1:166-68.

Finds no real satiric thrust in The Atheist, only some inconsistent attitudes toward morality and institutions. The Souldiers Fortune shows similar inconsistencies, though it is a "vigorous . . . farce."

3 MEYERSTEIN, E.H.W. "The Dagger in 'Venice Preserv'd.'" TLS, 7 September, p. 565.

The "token" that Jaffeir sends to his wife in V, 474-77 must surely be the dagger that makes four other appearances in the play.

1952

1 CLARK, DONALD B. "An Eighteenth-Century Adaptation of Massinger." MLQ 13:243-45, 247, 250.

Rowe is deeply indebted to Otway. Lothario in The Fair Penitent reflects Otway's Don John (Don Carlos), whose philosophical and active libertinism becomes humanized by some "engaging traits" and by "Otway's pervasive sentimentalism." With his pathetic women and vacillating males, Otway reduced Elizabethan masculinity to the late-seventeenth-century effeminacy that Rowe took up.

2 HOGAN, CHARLES BEECHER. Shakespeare in the Theatre 1701-1800: A Record of Performances in London 1701-1750. Oxford: Clarendon Press, pp. 404-10.

Analyzes differences between Romeo and Juliet and Caius Marius, listing performances and (when available) casts of the latter.

3 KUNITZ, STANLEY J., and HOWARD HAYCRAFT. British Authors before 1800: A Biographical Dictionary. New York: H.W. Wilson, pp. 386-88.

Routinely identifies The Orphan and Venice Preserv'd as Otway's best plays; notes that his work is more Racinian than Shakespearean and that he is better at depicting females than at portraying males.

1953

1 ANON. "Lyric Theatre, Hammersmith: 'Venice Preserv'd' by Thomas Otway." Times (London), 16 May, p. 8.

Although Otway is excellent in treating psychological development and in eliciting "imaginative sympathy with the working of human passion," his Venice Preserv'd fails, as do all post-Elizabethan plays, to "make good its pretensions to tragic grandeur."

2 HOBSON, HAROLD. "Venice Preserv'd: Lyric, Hammersmith." Sunday Times (London), 24 May, p. 9.

Despite frigid and inflated verse, and Jaffeir's tedious moodiness, Venice Preserv'd remains a powerful and even timely play. If the Antonio scenes are outdated, the main plot is relevant to the McCarthy trials. Pierre is a revolutionary idealist, but Jaffeir acts from personal motives.

3 HOOK, LUCYLE. "Shakespeare Improv'd, or a Case for the Affirmative." SQ 4:295-97.

"A Restoration audience could not understand Juliet as Shakespeare had written her because she did not fit into a preconceived pattern." It took Otway's sense of "genuine feminine emotion," acted out against a potent political background by "an untyped actress," to bring "the new heroine" to post-Civil War drama. Thus began she-tragedy, "with the emphasis upon love for one woman and the absence of every other motive in life."

4 LYNCH, JAMES J. Box, Pit, and Gallery: Stage and Society in Johnson's London. Berkeley and Los Angeles: University of California Press, pp. 100-101, 296.

Discusses Caius Marius as an adaptation, ascribing key changes to the need for extra pathos. The treatment of incest in The Orphan--a very rare appearance of this subject on the mid-century stage--is "dignified and profound."

*5 SPRING, JOSEPH E. "Two Restoration Adaptations of Shakespeare' Plays--Sauny the Scot; or, The Taming of the Shrew by John Lacy and The History and Fall of Caius Marius, Thomas Otway's Appropriation of Romeo and Juliet." Ph.D. dissertation, University of Denver, 345 pp.

Source: CDI (1861-1972), 37:269.

6 TYNAN, KENNETH. "Venice Preserv'd by Thomas Otway, at the Lyric, Hammersmith." In Curtains: Selections from the Drama Criticism and Related Writings. New York: Athenaeum, pp. 50-51.

In this "last great verse play in the English language," Otway "writes grandly, with a sort of sad, nervous power, about a large subject--the ethics of betrayal." Driven by "private pique, masquerading as public spiritedness," Pierre the "cynic and man of action" conflicts with Jaffeir the "romantic and man of feeling." The reader of this play develops "the eerie sensation of being underground, trapped in a torch-lit vault."

1954

1 BARTLEY, J.O. Teague, Shenkin and Sawney, Being an Historical Study of the Earliest Irish, Welsh and Scottish Characters in English Plays. Cork: Cork University Press, pp. 119, 138.

In The Cheats of Scapin, "mimicry of an Irishman consists mainly in assuming an Irish accent and a ferocious manner." Briefly comments on the Welshman in Cheats.

2 GAGEN, JEAN ELISABETH. The New Woman: Her Emergence in English Drama 1600-1730. New York: Twayne, p. 150.

Notes the proviso drawn up between Sylvia and Courtine in The Souldiers Fortune, stressing Sylvia's determination not to suffer infidelity in silence.

1955

1 ANON. "Theatre: Otway Tragedy." New York Times, 14 December, n. pag.

A romantic tragedy exhibiting some bombast, Venice Preserved appeared eight years too late to be in step with the elegant, cynical plays of its time.

2 SPEAIGHT, GEORGE. The History of the English Puppet Theatre. London, Toronto, Wellington, and Sydney: George C. Harrap & Co., p. 86.

In discussing the influence of the puppet theater on commercial drama, notes that in Act 3 of Friendship in Fashion Malagene is told to "speak in Punchinello's voice."

3 SYPHER, WYLIE. Four Stages of Renaissance Style: Transformations in Art and Literature 1400-1700. Garden City, N.Y.: Doubleday, pp. 259, 263-64.

If Milton's language reflected "his vision and his will," Otway's "is an effort to expand a . . . formula" of love and honor. Thus Otway's characters "experience the will . . . as a need to comply" with this formula rather than as "a felt impulse," and their humanity suffers as their "declamation is substituted for tragic psychology."

1956

1 BATZER, HAZEL MARGARET. "Heroic and Sentimental Elements in Thomas Otway's Tragedies." Ph.D. dissertation, University of Michigan, 378 pp.

Deals with the plays as transitions from heroic drama to "so-called drama of sensibility." See Dissertation Abstracts 17 (1957):136-37. Revised for publication: OT.1974.2.

2 BIGGINS, D. "Source Notes for Dryden, Wycherley and Otway." N&Q 201:300.

Alcibiades owes debts to Dryden's Conquest of Granada, especially to the scene in which Zulema attempts to rape Almahide.

3 HUGHES, LEO. A Century of English Farce. Princeton: Princeton University Press, pp. 74-75, 144.

Because he felt that an English audience would find a single French tragedy "devoid of incident," Otway gave English drama its first double billing, Titus and Berenice and The Cheats of Scapin, the latter being the only early Restoration play in less than five acts. The Souldiers Fortune employs a scene borrowed from Sganarelle.

4 MANIFOLD, J.S. The Music in English Drama from Shakespeare to Purcell. London: Rockliff, pp. 114, 136.

"Otway is unusually short of musical S.D. and has not one for trumpets in any of his better known plays." Notes the inappropriateness of accompanying Belvidera's madness with soft music in Venice Preserv'd, V.iv.

5 WHEATLEY, KATHERINE E. "Thomas Otway's Titus and Berenice." In Racine and English Classicism. Austin: University of Texas Press, pp. 26-56.

By making Antiochus the stock "'mourant' of French précieux poetry" and Berenice the stock coquette, together with many "thoughtless excisions and incongruous interpolations," Otway obscures Racine's psychological subtlety. Otway does carry over more of Racine's classical simplicity of structure than other adapters do, but he damages the classical effect by using bombastic language.

1957

1 SHERBO, ARTHUR. English Sentimental Drama. East Lansing: Michigan State University Press, pp. 133-34, 139.

Notes the "revelling in emotion for its own sake" in The Orphan.

1958

1 BURTON, K.M.P. Restoration Literature. London: Hutchinson, pp. 86, 90-93.

Sees The Orphan as one of the "more dignified" examples of pathetic drama. Venice Preserv'd is almost unique for its age in dealing movingly with a real issue (the destruction of private relationships by "the corruption and violence of public life") without oversimplifying, becoming bombastic, or sacrificing the clear treatment of moral issues to pathetic effects. The play falls just short of being truly tragic.

2 HAUSER, DAVID R. "Otway Preserved: Theme and Form in Venice Preserv'd." SP 55:481-93.

Argues that the play, despite some "lumbering" and bathos, is artistically organic, socially and morally verisimilar. The characters exhibit realistically mixed qualities and live in a familiar world in which good and evil are not clearly distinct. The imagery works integrally with the action, symbolizing or reflecting the conflicting attitudes and helping to convey a pattern of sin-salvation in Jaffeir, Pierre, and Belvidera.

3 HUGHES, R.E. "'Comic Relief' in Otway's 'Venice Preserv'd.'" N&Q 203:65-66.

Sees the Antonio-Aquilina scenes not merely as satire against Shaftesbury, the senate, or moral perversion in general, but as a special form of comedy requiring the audience to do a "double-take" in perception that is equivalent to the play's theme: "the exile of innocence" as it sees the ugliness beneath the surface of public life. Thus the comedy functions "not simply as complement to the main action, but as corollary."

4 NOYES, ROBERT GALE. The Neglected Muse: Restoration and Eighteenth-Century Tragedy in the Novel (1740-1780). Providence, R.I.: Brown University Press, pp. 48-78, 84, 92.

Mentions Otway's influence on Rowe and surveys the many allusions (some critical) to The Orphan and Venice Preserv'd in novels of the period covered.

5 WILSON, JOHN HAROLD. All the King's Ladies: Actresses of the Restoration. Chicago: University of Chicago Press, pp. 96, 103-4.

Notes the tradition of regarding Monimia and Belvidera as passionate idealizations of Mrs. Barry, and suggests that it was for the benefit of Mrs. Barry that Otway made his Lavinia in Caius Marius more worldly and articulate than Shakespeare's Juliet.

1959

1 McBURNEY, WILLIAM H. "Otway's Tragic Muse Debauched: Sensuality in Venice Preserv'd." JEGP 58:380-99.

Sees the play not as a forerunner of eighteenth-century domestic tragedy but as a culmination of Restoration forms, "a dark satiric tragedy" that indicts the late Restoration world. Its central symbol--rape--unites a public action, in which political values are farcically debased in an atmosphere of fraud and exploitation, to a domestic action in which friendship and love are threatened by degenerate lust. The dagger, Pierre's stress on the seizing of the marriage bed, the invasion of the Adriatic by Spanish ships--all are symbolic variations on the rape motif. Passionately physical encounters punctuate the action on both levels, underlining the reduction of love, honor, and friendship. On the whole, the plot seriously parodies the basic Restoration comic plot and "approaches the farcical brutality of his own comedies." All the main characters exhibit traits borrowed from figures in Friendship in Fashion and The Souldiers Fortune and, in a sense, the background of Venice Preserv'd is the same as that of The Souldiers Fortune. Conventions of heroic drama are also perverted as part of the bitter satire.

2 WILSON, JOHN HAROLD, ed. Headnote to Venice Preserved. In Six Restoration Plays. Boston: Houghton Mifflin Co., pp. 246-47.

Considers it basically a domestic play involving the intensely emotional conflict between love or humanity and honor or friendship. Despite some bombast and flaws in plot and characterization, it is "excellent theatre."

1960

1 DAICHES, DAVID. A Critical History of English Literature. Vol. 2. New York: Ronald Press, pp. 551-52.

Describes Don Carlos as a "lively and craftsmanlike" heroic play, The Orphan as a pathetic drama in Fletcherian blank verse, and Venice Preserv'd as "a powerful and genuinely tragic work" that artfully informs the old love-and-honor conflict with moral and psychological complexities. "The blank verse is more rhetorical and less poetically complex than Shakespeare's, but more disciplined than Marlowe's, and wholly lacking in the haunting poetic morbidities of Webster."

2 LEFEVRE, ANDRÉ. "Racine en angleterre au XVIIe siècle: 'Titus and Berenice' de Thomas Otway." RLC 34:251-57.

1961

1 HOY, CYRUS. "The Effect of the Restoration on Drama." TSL 6:90.

"A tragic heroine such as Monimia in Otway's Orphan may have affinities with Aspatia in Beaumont and Fletcher's Maid's Tragedy, but in all important respects she belongs to the world of Clarissa Harlowe."

2 KOZIOL, HERBERT. "Zu Thomas Otways Venice Preserved und Hugo von Hofmannsthals Das gerettete Venedig." In Österreich und die angelsächsische Welt. Kulturbegegnungen und Vergleiche. Edited by Otto Hietsch. Wien und Stuttgart: Wilhelm Braumüller, pp. 418-31.

These two plays have only the subject matter in common. Their verse, imagery, dialogue, and stage directions reflect the literary and dramatic conventions typical of their respective eras (Otway's seventeenth century, Hofmannsthal's modern age).

1962

1 JEUNE, SIMON. "Hamlet d'Otway, Macbeth de Dryden: ou Shakespeare en France en 1714." RLC 36:560-64.

2 KNIGHT, G. WILSON. The Golden Labyrinth: A Study of British Drama. London: Phoenix House, p. 167.

Sees Otway as "a specialist, like Fletcher, in pathos and situation" who concentrates on individuals, sometimes at the expense of "general implication." In Alcibiades and Don Carlos, notes "intuitions of spirit life," "some poignant situations," and "a fine poetry of distraction." The Orphan is suspenseful and moving but fails to rise above the individual. While Venice Preserv'd does contain some "communal issues" and realistic agony, it has "little of Lee's nobility," its characters' suffering seems "purposeless," and its main action is spoiled by the comic subplot.

3 WAITH, EUGENE M. The Herculean Hero in Marlowe, Chapman, Shakespeare and Dryden. New York: Columbia University Press; London: Chatto & Windus, p. 151.

Otway did not create Herculean heroes, but rather exemplary ones, like "the fiery Don Carlos, who in a Herculean moment, contemplates rebellion against his unjust father, but comes finally to generous forgiveness."

1963

1 LOFTIS, JOHN. The Politics of Drama in Augustan England. Oxford: Clarendon Press, pp. 18-19.

Unlike The Orphan, where the pathos is "unrelieved by the play of ideas," Venice Preserv'd effectively fuses politics and pathos in what becomes "the finest political satire in dramatic form." The political conflict between two contemptible groups evokes intense emotions in the main characters, universalizing the issues at both public and private levels, and preventing the play from perishing in excessive topicality. Loftis sustains the traditional opinion that Shaftesbury is represented by both Antonio and Renault.

2 SINGH, SARUP. The Theory of Drama in the Restoration Period. Bombay, Calcutta, Madras, and New Delhi: Orient Longmans, pp. 16, 58, 60, 87, 90, 119, 228-29, 286, 289, 290-92.

Otway and Banks initiated the move to sentimentalism, the former's Don Carlos being the first pathetic tragedy. The Orphan, however, is domestic "only in an emotional sense," and Monimia's distresses fail to raise basic questions about life. As a comic writer, Otway refused to become fashionably cynical and amoral. His best comedies, Friendship in Fashion and The Souldiers Fortune, are problem plays in which the values of real life shatter the artificial world of the characters and make the sex game seem disgusting.

1964

1 ANON. "Otway Farce a Frisky but Minor Piece." Daily Telegraph (London), 21 July, n. pag.

Although it has an "outrageously ingenious" plot that is "refreshingly easy to follow," The Souldiers Fortune is merely a typical antimarital farce in which "the doings are those of all Restoration comedy and the vagaries are Thomas Otway's." It is less skillfully managed than other comedies of its day, and it is certainly not as witty as many of them.

2 ANON. "Stylish Restoration Comedy." Times (London), 21 July, n. pag.

The Souldiers Fortune is Restoration comedy with "a difference." Like the rest, it depends on adultery, disguise, and intrigue, but it has a distinctive realism and "an acid detachment, reminiscent of Ben Jonson." At the end, the author seems to depart not with the "sanctimonious shrug" of an Etherege, but with "a knowing grin" all his own.

3 COOKE, M.G. "The Restoration Ethos of Byron's Classical Plays." PMLA 79:576-77.

Pierre of Venice Preserv'd and Israel Bertuccio of Byron's Marino Faliero both compare themselves with ancient heroes as a means of establishing the grandeur of their pedigrees. In his play Byron creates "a more unadulterated heroic temper."

4 KORNINGER, SIEGFRIED. The Restoration Period and the Eighteenth Century 1660-1780. English Literature and Its Background. Vienna and Munich: Österreichischer Bundesverlag, pp. 52-55.

Ranks Otway above Dryden in tragedy, credits him with starting the pathetic and sentimental movement in English drama, and briefly describes as his best plays Alcibiades, Don Carlos, The Orphan, and Venice Preserv'd.

5 MARSHALL, GEOFFREY. "Themes and Structure in the Plays of Thomas Otway." Ph.D. dissertation, Rice University, 281 pp.

Analyzes Otway's artistry against literary backgrounds such as sentimentalism, rhetorical practices, psychological beliefs, genres, and conflicts of loyalty in characters. Some conclusions: Otway's plays are less partisan, less distinct from one another in genre, and more coherent thematically than previously thought. In The Orphan and Venice Preserv'd, Otway did explore "new areas of dramatic subject matter," but he did not fabricate a new dramatic genre. See Dissertation Abstracts International 25 (1964):1918-19.

6 VANHELLEPUTTE, MICHEL. "Hofmannsthal und Thomas Otway: Zur Struktur des Geretteten Venedig." RBPH 42:926-39.

By no means merely an adaptation of Otway's play, Das gerettete Venedig has its own plot and atmosphere; it also has more local color, sticks closer to historical fact, and attends more closely to geographical and historical details than Venice Preserv'd does.

7 Van VORIS, W. "Tragedy through Restoration Eyes: Venice Preserv'd in Its Own Theatre." Hermathena 99:55-65.

Tries to recreate the play as seen in a Restoration theater (where Otway knew how to make "tragic satire" work) by the likes of Charles II and John Dryden. Otway has composed a "tragedy of frustrated wills" in which the main characters vainly search for "some way in which their sense of right can be valid" until, as a last resort, they seek refuge in suicide or madness as all rational or ethical choices disintegrate into pathos. Emotion is held up as the only reliable guide in a corrupt urban world. Antonio is part Shaftesbury, part Charles II; Renault is "a synthesis of all plotters whether at home or abroad."

1965

1 BRADBROOK, M.C. English Dramatic Form: A History of Its Development. New York: Barnes & Noble, p. 117.

Cites Venice Preserv'd and All for Love as evidence that the natural alternative to heroic tragedy was the pathetic play in which a "delight in atrocity" is counterpointed with the assumption "that private virtue and domestic joys are the sole consolation for man in a rapacious and treacherous society."

2 FRIED, GISELA. Gestalt und Funktion der Bilder im Drama Thomas Otways. Göttingen: Vandenhoeck und Ruprecht, 154 pp.

Discusses the form and function of imagery in all the plays: for example, the "heroic" imagery and metaphors of poison in Don Carlos, the use of imagery in characterizing Caius Marius, the function of Arcadian imagery in The Orphan, and the changes in Otway's use of animal imagery.

3 RIGHTER, ANNE. "Heroic Tragedy." In Restoration Theatre. Edited by John Russell Brown and Bernard Harris. New York: St. Martin's Press, pp. 156-57.

Finds an interesting common denominator of "harshness and nihilism" at the heart of Otway's tragedies and comedies. The ugly hedonism of The Souldiers Fortune and The Atheist is not unlike the "pessimism and death-wish" of The Orphan and Venice Preserv'd. In the latter play, death becomes "the only positive value remaining in the world."

4 WILSON, JOHN HAROLD. A Preface to Restoration Drama. Boston: Houghton Mifflin Co., pp. 65, 95-112.

Otway was "fascinated by sensitive characters who were the victims of their own emotions and their too vivid imaginations," and he mastered a "fluid, emotional verse." Alcibiades is not mainly an heroic play, but rather is a villain tragedy. In Venice Preserv'd, politics are secondary to Otway's tragic vision of two lovers destroyed by the protagonist's own passions and by the conflict between "mercenary revolutionists" and a "cruel, oligarchic state." Pierre is closer to being a bloodthirsty, cynical villain than to being a patriotic hero. The play contains some improbabilities but also some realistic "studies of abnormal sex." Neither Renault nor Antonio seems directly satiric of Shaftesbury, the latter character more probably invented to provide a particularly suitable role for the actor Anthony Leigh. Together with Aquilina these characters act out the "background of lechery, depravity, and perversion" which discredits the senate and sets off the "frank, honest, conjugal love" of Jaffeir and Belvidera. The Orphan, with its poor motivation, weak characterization, amorality, and bombast, is a "tragedy of tears" carried entirely by Otway's emotion-freighted language.

1966

1 CUNNINGHAM, JOHN E. "Thomas Otway." In Restoration Drama. London: Evans Brothers, pp. 96-110.

Mixes stale generalizations with a few fresh remarks. Among the latter: Don Carlos is written poorly, with its awkward couplets, "forced metaphors," and "barren symbols." In general, however, "Otway's verse has more nervous vitality, and far less concern with the dogma of 'correctness' than that of any other dramatist of the time." Only in comedy was he "wholly himself." The Souldiers Fortune, in particular, benefits from shrewd, original observations of mankind and from the skillful characterizations of Sir Jolly Jumble and Sir Davy Dunce. In Venice Preserv'd love is given the power that fate, God, or statistics usually have in tragedy, and Belvidera's emotional effusions are given more attention than the play's design can easily carry.

2 GILLESPIE, GERALD. "The Rebel in Seventeenth-Century Tragedy." CL 18:334-36.

Sees Venice Preserv'd as an excellent treatment of the conflicts between "heart" and "reason," personal and political interests, nobility and corruption. Gillespie notices parallels between the tensions in individual characters and those in the state. He describes each character's mixed attitudes and motives, and points to a similarity between Pierre and Lohenstein's Epicharis (in the play of that title).

3 KEARFUL, FRANK J. "The Nature of Tragedy in Rowe's The Fair Penitent." PLL 2:357.

Unlike Rowe, Otway is less interested in "making his tragedy serve as a moral exemplum" than in evoking sympathy for his characters' distresses. The Orphan moralizes through dramatic implication, The Fair Penitent moralizes explicitly.

4 LANGHANS, EDWARD A. "Three Early Eighteenth Century Promptbooks." TN 20:142-50.

Gives details of a staging of The Cheats of Scapin, c. 1730

5 SORELIUS, GUNNAR. 'The Giant Race Before the Flood': Pre-Restoration Drama on the Stage and in the Criticism of the Restoration. Uppsala: Almqvist & Wiksells, p. 124.

Venice Preserv'd "comes perhaps closest of all Restoration tragedies to recapturing some of the external features of Shakespeare."

1967

1 BAUER, ROGER. "'A Souldier of Fortune'--Als Soldat und brav,'" in Festschrift für Richard Alewyn. Edited by Herbert Singer and Benno von Wiese. Cologne and Graz: Böhlau Verlag, pp. 230-41.

The scene "Nacht. Strasse for Gretchens Tur" in Goethe's Faust I was influenced by Otway's The Orphan.

2 KLIENEBERGER, H.R. "Otway's 'Venice Preserved' and Hofmannsthal's 'Das Gerettete Venedig.'" MLR 62:292-97.

Some of Hofmannsthal's changes were made simply to give the play a more modern and realistic appearance. Others, especially the idealizing of the friendship between Pierre and Jaffeir, reflect Hofmannsthal's relationship with Stefan George.

3 ROTHSTEIN, ERIC. Restoration Tragedy: Form and the Process of Change. Madison, Milwaukee, and London: University of Wisconsin Press, pp. 79, 86, 99-110, 134, 139, 161-62, 164.

Analyzes Otway's artistry and, in the process, develops key implications in previous criticism--especially that of Taylor (OT.1950.4), Hauser (OT.1958.2), Hughes (OT.1958.3), McBurney (OT.1959.1), and Righter (OT.1965.3). But Rothstein also makes strong original contributions. He shows that Otway surpasses Lee and Banks in "detailed intelligence of execution," in projecting psychology "into the world . . . through symbolism," and in creatively using comic techniques in serious plays.

Alcibiades and Don Carlos are "denatured rhymed" tragedies that helped set the pattern for unrhymed tragedies with suicidal, pathetic heroes. Unlike Lee's tragedies of choice or Banks's tragedies of oppression, The Orphan is a tragedy of imagination in which "nature becomes vicious because the characters, like those in Restoration comedy, assume that it was vicious to begin with." Thus, The Orphan "seems to rebuke the blending of naturalism and individual romance that makes up Restoration comedy, and in another way, the heroic play."

In Venice Preserv'd, "world and character seem to shape each other and generic patterns seem to have faded before more lifelike and less univocal kinds of order." The principle of form shifts from social or moral bases to the basis of audience empathy, which "makes public the hero's subjectivity" and elevates his consciousness into a formal force. The play successfully integrates comic and serious episodes, "equates the physically and politically unnatural," and helps redefine honor and duty as loyalty. By making the relationship between Jaffeir and Pierre the center of "language and complexity of feeling," Otway "maintained a spatial unity in his play, as he would in an oration, so that the relationships between the parts could be kept implicitly constant . . . balanced, despite the inordinate attention paid to whatever happened to be going on at the moment."

4 SILVETTE, HERBERT. The Doctor on the Stage: Medicine and Medical Men in Seventeenth-Century England. Edited by Francelia Butler. Knoxville: University of Tennessee Press, pp. 81, 98, 115, 210, 248, 265.

Amusing observations on asafetida in The Souldiers Fortune, amberbead against fits in Friendship in Fashion, "hair of the dog" treatment in Don Carlos, the "pox" in The Cheats of Scapin, and satire against doctors in The Souldiers Fortune and The Atheist.

5 SPURLING, HILARY. "What Is This Thing Called Froth?" Spectator 218:71-72.

Reflecting on a Royal Court production of The Souldiers Fortune, ranks this "bleak and bitter" comedy and Venice Preserv'd as "the two great works of Otway's maturity." The author's comic frankness "is saved from being brutal by his energy and courage, by the beauty of his language and the delicate relationships between his characters."

6 STROUP, THOMAS B. "Otway's Bitter Pessimism." In Essays in English Literature of the Classical Period. Edited by Daniel W. Patterson and Albrecht B. Strauss. SP, Extra series, no. 4, pp. 54-75.

Carefully develops the implications of Righter's observations (OT.1965.3), showing that Otway's tragedies as well as his comedies are satirically pessimistic: in their dialogue; in their use of curses, bitter oaths, mocking set speeches, "and other formalized action"; and in their avoidance of poetic justice, purgation, and morally satisfying conclusions. Thus, Otway anticipates "the drama of a meaningless, chaotic, unintelligible world in which only the individual has a place and the individual will, in which order and degree, system and law, ceremony and ritual are remembered only in ridicule."

*7 WALKER, JOHN D. "Moral Vision in the Drama of Thomas Otway." Ph.D. dissertation, University of Florida--Gainesville.

Source: McNamee, Supplement One (1964-68):205.

1968

1 MICHEL, JEAN-PAUL. "Quatre adaptations de Molière sur la scène anglaise a l'epoque de la Restauration: Thomas Otway,

The Cheats of Scapin (1676)." In Dramaturgie et Société. Edited by Jean Jacquot et al. Vol. 1. Paris: Éditions du Centre Nationale de la Recherche Scientifique, pp. 361-71.

Although in The Cheats of Scapin Otway takes over the outline of Molière's plot, he eliminates many lines; oversimplifies the characters (depriving them of psychological subtlety); ignores the pattern of motives which, in Molière, blends with the pattern of action; and, instead of using the love theme to deepen the human comedy, reduces love to a sex game. He fails, moreover, to duplicate Molière's lightness of movement or his symbolic employment of gestures. For the Frenchman's richly depicted stage world, Otway substitutes the artificial milieu of Restoration comedy, where women hold a lower status than in Molière and where topical allusions are obligatory. In general, Otway impoverishes his source, transforming its organic wholeness into a mere skeleton.

2 NICOLL, ALLARDYCE. English Drama: A Modern Viewpoint. New York: Barnes & Noble, p. 90.

Although The Orphan and Venice Preserv'd are the only two Restoration tragedies that might appeal to modern audiences, both plays owe "such quality as they possess" to Otway's variation on "earlier styles of dramatic writing."

3 ROSTON, MURRAY. Biblical Drama in England: From the Middle Ages to the Present Day. Evanston, Ill.: Northwestern University Press, p. 175.

Scoffs at Titus and Berenice.

4 SPURLING, HILARY. "Remembering Poor Otway." Spectator 221: 293-94.

Uses a review of the reprinted Works edited by Ghosh (see OT.1932.3) to celebrate "Otway's peculiar honesty," his fascination with the gap between illusion and reality that put him at odds with the dramatic conventions of his day. His early tragedies are undermined by cynical frivolity, and the heroes of The Orphan and Venice Preserv'd strikingly resemble "his comic heroes, but without their dangerous self-knowledge." In his finest comedy, The Souldiers Fortune, Belvidera and Pierre have matured into the sourly wise Sylvia and Beaugard, who embody the play's unique mood of bitterness "free from rancour." Here Otway faithfully reflects the real London of his day "in an unwavering, harsh, comic light which yet skims the depths and delicate nuances of tragedy." Neither Shakespeare nor Congreve attempted this, and no later dramatist has achieved it.

5 WAITH, EUGENE, ed. General Introduction and Introduction to Venice Preserv'd. In Restoration Drama. New York: Bantam, pp. xxi, 310-12.

Compactly synthesizes previous criticism, favoring the satiric identification of Shaftesbury with both Antonio and

Renault, praising Otway's preparation for the tragic dilemma and his contrasting of Belvidera with Pierre, and noting his "emphasis upon laceration" to reinforce and complicate pathos.

1969

1 BATZER, HAZEL M. "Shakespeare's Influence on Thomas Otway's Caius Marius." Revue de l'Université d'Ottawa 39:533-61.
Otway's sentimental tendencies guided his use of Shakespeare and of the classical material. The general situation in the play parallels that of England in the summer of 1679.

2 BERMAN, RONALD. "Nature in Venice Preserv'd." ELH 36:529-43.
Proceeding from a background of political and moral philosophy, argues that the play is "a rigorous and intelligent representation of the failure of freedom to acknowledge the limits of creation." Thus, it is "a secular equivalent to the Miltonic epic," another exploration of the notion "that Nature promises us a condition more authentic than that allowed by merely historical life." Pierre becomes, then, one of a group of European literary figures "whose business it is to query the relationship of social forms to the supposed truths underlying them."

3 KELSALL, MALCOLM, ed. Introduction to Venice Preserved. Regents Restoration Drama Series. Lincoln: University of Nebraska Press, pp. xi-xxii.
Well-rounded discussion, placing the play in literary and political contexts but offering few new observations. Kelsall analyzes the use of the dagger symbol and surveys perspectives on the main characters, noting that, like Shakespeare, Otway creates characters moved "by inner compulsions." Antonio, who seems intended as some sort of ironic comment on Jaffeir, embodies "all the evil and . . . stupidity in the action." Pierre is, in fact, a true idealist. The closest parallels to Otway's achievement in later drama are found in Byron, Ibsen, and Strindberg.

4 MARSHALL, GEOFFREY. "The Coherence of The Orphan." TSLL 11: 931-43.
"When viewed from the 'single point of view' provided by Acasto's ideal of plain-speaking, Castalio's concealment of his marriage and Polydore's libertinism and suicide must be seen as integral parts of the whole." To some degree each main character shares the guilt for precipitating the catastrophe because each helps weaken the binding force of communication by his irony, confused speech, riddling, or silence. Such verbal disorder becomes "a metaphor for potential universal disorder."

5 PASQUARELLI, ROBERT. "On the Nicky-Nacky Scenes in Venice Preserv'd." RECTR 8, no. 2:38-41.

Rejecting the exclusivity of previous interpretations, argues that these scenes serve several purposes in the play: deepen the contrast between the degenerate urban world and the "almost 'green' world" of Jaffeir and Belvidera, create the illusion of a time gap between scenes in the main plot, and offer comic relief from high emotional intensity.

6 POYET, ALBERT. "Un écho d'Absalom and Achitophel dans le prologue d'Otway a Venice Preserved." Caliban 6:27-28.

Because the prologue contains an apparent allusion to Dryden's description of Shaftesbury in Absalom and Achitophel, it reinforces the view that Renault was intended as a satiric portrait of the Whig leader.

7 RIVES, FRANÇOISE. "Un dramaturge à la croisée des chemins: Otway dans Venice Preserved: Essai d'interprétation du personnage de Jaffeir." Caliban 6:17-25.

8 SPURLING, HILARY. "Venice Well Preserved." Spectator 222:216.

Praises Otway's moving and bitterly honest juxtaposition of "the tragic and the squalid," "heroic bombast" and "the bleak, humorous truthfulness characteristic of Restoration comedy."

9 SUTHERLAND, JAMES. English Literature of the Late Seventeenth Century. New York and Oxford: Oxford University Press, pp. 78-81, 141-43.

A compact, sensibly conservative description and critique of the plays. Regards Alcibiades, Titus and Berenice, and Caius Marius as negligible. Don Carlos and The Orphan lack depth and probability, but the former is dignified, restrained, and Racinian in tone, while the latter has a "touching simplicity" and "a melodious hopelessness." With its credible dilemma, emotional integrity, and complexly personal focus, Venice Preserv'd is an "enduring" tragedy, though its comic scenes distract rather than relieve, and it has little intellectual range. The comedies are disturbingly powerful, especially The Souldiers Fortune, with Otway's personal experience supporting it and the memorable characterization of Sir Jolly Jumble giving it "infectious good humour" in spite of his perversion. The Atheist mixes "lewd comedy and satire" in a disconcerting look at the rake after marriage.

10 WALLACE, JOHN M. "Dryden and History: A Problem in Allegorical Reading." ELH 36:284-85.

Although in the context of its first performance The Orphan may have seemed a remote metaphor for the "inability of King and Parliament to understand one another better," in the long view it becomes a kind of parable about "the destruction of an English Eden through original sin."

1970

1 CROWHURST, G.W. "The Dramatic Opening--A Comparative Study of Otway and Hofmannsthal." Theoria (Natal) 35 (October): 51-58.

A sustained comparison, making some interesting points: Hofmannsthal makes greater dramatic use of Venice as a locality; while Otway puts key events on stage, Hofmannsthal conveys them through personal reflection, transforming a chain of actions into "a series of states"; in Hofmannsthal "it is not the individual figure which determines the course of the drama as with Otway, but the 'configuration.'"

2 EASSON, ANGUS. "Dr. Johnson and the Cucumber: The Question of Value." N&Q 215:300-302.

Both Johnson and Otway make use of the old tradition that cucumbers are without value. Cites Venice Preserv'd, V.i.132-40.

3 KLINGER, GEORGE CHARLES. "English She-Tragedy, 1680-1715; Its Characteristics and Its Relationship to the Sentimental Tradition." Ph.D. dissertation, Columbia University, 168 pp.

"The triumph of she-tragedy begins with Otway's The Orphan." See Dissertation Abstracts 31 (1971):4722A-23A.

4 MUIR, KENNETH. The Comedy of Manners. London: Hutchinson, pp. 63-66.

The most negative assessment since Archer's (OT.1923.1). Otway's comedies "have none of the talent displayed in his tragedies," and his tragedies have been overrated. Although his comic heroes are coarsely honest, they lack wit and behave farcically in plots that are "not funny enough to excuse their improbabilities, nor satirical enough to correct the manners of the age." Everything Otway does in comedy "has been bettered by another dramatist. Only in the bitter comic relief in Venice Preserved do we have something genuinely his own."

5 MYER, MICHAEL GROSVENOR. "Venice Preserved." Guardian, 19 November, n. pag.

The play clearly shows that "Otway is . . . no Shakespeare, nor even a Tourneur or Middleton."

6 PARSONS, PHILIP. "Restoration Melodrama and Its Actors." KOMOS (Monash University, Australia) 2:81-88.

Employs a reference to The Orphan and some scenes from Caius Marius to help demonstrate that Restoration "melodrama" aims not to represent life or to explore character, as in Shakespeare or Ibsen, but rather to make "a statement about life expressed in a pattern of emotional or moral postures," thus offering us "a significant ballet of figures larger, simpler more harmonious than life, having existence only in their own artificial world, yet relevant to our own."

7 SHAFER, IVONNE BONSALL. "The Proviso Scene in Restoration Comedy." RECTR 9, no. 1:4-5.

Notices the "inverted proviso" in The Souldiers Fortune and compares Sylvia and Courtine to Woodly and spouse in Shadwell's Epsom-Wells.

1971

1 BARNARD, JOHN. "Drama from the Restoration till 1710." In English Drama to 1710. Edited by Christopher Ricks. London: Sphere Books, p. 378.

Notes his "shift towards pathos" and his mingling of bawdy, morbidity, satire, disillusion, and pathos.

2 HUGHES, DEREK W. "A New Look at Venice Preserv'd. SEL 11: 437-57.

In Venice Preserv'd, a study in Hobbesian regression to animalism, Otway questions heroic ideals, explores the degeneration of language, parodies Christianity, and builds on images of sacrifice. The Nicky-Nacky scenes are central to the play's meaning. Hughes compares Otway to Jean Genet.

3 KLINGLER, HELMUT. Die Künstlerische Entwicklung in dem Tragödien Thomas Otways. Wien und Stuttgart: Wilhelm Braumüller, 251 pp.

Although Otway's plays never reach the extremes of "heroic" or "sentimental" tragedy, they do shift from imitative dramas of situation with an heroic flavor to unique dramas of character featuring weak heroes. The Orphan marks the turning point.

4 NABI, SAIYID ALE. "Thomas Otway and the Poetics of Late Seventeenth-Century Tragedy." Ph.D. dissertation, University of Colorado, 173 pp.

Examining the plays against a background of heroic and sentimental conventions, argues that, especially in The Orphan and Venice Preserv'd, Otway applied a "Racinian theory" of tragic composition. See Dissertation Abstracts International 32:3960A.

5 PROFFITT, BESSIE. "Religious Symbolism in Otway's Venice Preserv'd." PLL 7:26-37.

The play's many allusions to the Bible and biblical traditions show that Otway was exploring the inconstancy and imperfection of fallen human nature, a broader purpose than has been previously attributed to him.

6 WAITH, EUGENE M. Ideas of Greatness: Heroic Drama in England. New York: Barnes & Noble, pp. 192, 242-53.

Not until The Orphan does Otway definitely break with the heroic conventions. Don Carlos is interesting for its parallels and contrasts between characters, for the similarity of its queen to Dryden's Almahide, and for the "feeling of 'tristesse majestueuse'" with which it closes. In *Venice Preserv'd*, potentially heroic characters are prevented by circumstances from acting heroically. The play becomes a tragedy of conflicting loyalties, and the pervasive dagger image reinforces its unity and "provides a symbol for the theme of laceration which dominates" the action. Otway shared Lee's concern for the passions without Lee's spectacle, rant, elevation, or power. Otway's language lacks the rich suggestiveness of Shakespeare's and the "pointedness" of Dryden's, but it is admirably clear and fraught with emotional implication.

1972

1 JORDAN, ROBERT. "The Extravagant Rake in Restoration Comedy." In *Restoration Literature: Critical Approaches*. Edited by Harold Love. London: Methuen, p. 83.

Truman and Valentine in *Friendship in Fashion* represent "the more normal rakish gentleman," rather than the extravagant rake.

2 LOFTIS, JOHN. "The Limits of Historical Veracity in Neoclassical Drama." In *England in the Restoration and Early Eighteenth Century: Essays on Culture and Society*. Edited by H.T. Swedenberg, Jr. Berkeley, Los Angeles, and London: University of California Press, p. 41.

Sees *Venice Preserv'd* as a conservative Tory commentary on the constitutional issues posed by the Popish Plot, its theme being "the need for stability in government even at the cost of corruption and injustice." Its political meaning is "more subtly revealed than is that of *Lucius Junius Brutus*."

3 PARSONS, PHILIP. "Restoration Tragedy as Total Theatre." In *Restoration Literature: Critical Approaches*. Edited by Harold Love. London: Methuen, pp. 27, 41, 63.

On the one hand, Otway lacks "the Jacobean sense of realize personality," even though he helped return Restoration tragedy to a more familiarly human level. On the other, he is "still workin within the legacy of the masque." His "figures are assembled from a range of isolated, sharply defined, impersonal gestures no less than Dryden's or D'Avenant's before him." He is Dryden's superior, however, in terms of the "command of the theatrical medium," especially in his later works, with their "chastened visual and overwhelming situational appeal."

4 WAITH, EUGENE M. "Tears of Magnanimity in Otway and Racine." In *French and English Drama of the Seventeenth Century*. Introduced by Henry Goodman. Los Angeles: Clark Library, pp. 3-22.

Neither in Racine nor in Otway does the evoking of tears necessarily constitute a sharp break with heroic drama. Magnanimous tears of the sort we are called upon to shed as witnesses to Venice Preserv'd combine pity and admiration; they represent the continuity of the heroic tradition through the seventeenth century. In regard to this issue, Racine is to Corneille as Otway is to Dryden and Lee. Don Carlos also asks for generous weeping, but The Orphan allows little admiration to be mixed with the tears it generates.

1973

1 DURANT, JACK D. "The Relapse, Shakespeare's Romeo, and Otway's Marius." RECTR 7, no. 2:46-49.

Thoroughly surveys the apparent lines of influence from Caius Marius to The Relapse. Not only does Hoyden become "a kind of inverted" Juliet/Lavinia, but also Metellus suggests Sir Tunbelly Clumsey, Sylla suggests Lord Foppington, Marius suggests Young Fashion. The nurse's speeches in Vanbrugh parallel those in Otway, and the vows of constancy between Marius and Lavinia are reflected in those between Loveless and Amanda and, inversely, in those between Hoyden and Young Fashion. Notes that Otway's The Souldiers Fortune seems to have influenced both The Relapse and The Provoked Wife.

2 McVICKER, C.D. "Balzac and Otway." RomN 15:248-54.

Finds evidence of the influence of Venice Preserv'd on Cousin Pons, Illusions perdues, and Splendeurs et misères des courtisanes.

3 PINTO, VIVIAN de SOLA. "Otway, Thomas." In Encyclopaedia Britannica. 14th ed. Vol. 16. Chicago and London: Encyclopaedia Britannica, p. 1162A.

Calls Alcibiades "poor" and Caius Marius a "curious mixture," but finds Don Carlos a worthy heroic play, The Souldiers Fortune his "best comedy," and Venice Preserv'd a "masterpiece." In the latter play, Antonio is meant to suggest Shaftesbury (no mention is made of Renault in this connection).

4 ROSS, J.C. "An Attack on Thomas Shadwell in Otway's The Atheist." PQ 52:753-60.

Argues that the presentation of Daredevil "involves a satirical assault upon Thomas Shadwell" and that "the plot element built around this character" derives from contemporary pamphlet accounts of an altercation between Shadwell and Nat Thompson. Political and personal reasons are suggested for the break between Otway and Shadwell.

5 SHERWOOD, IRMA Z. "Vanbrugh's 'Romeo and Juliet': A Note on The Relapse." RECTR 7, no. 2:41-45.

Less thoroughly than Durant (see OT.1973.1), shows that Caius Marius gave Vanbrugh "a precedent for coarsening the Romeo and Juliet material and yoking it with alien elements." Vanbrugh's results were better than Otway's.

6 WARNER, KERSTIN SOFIA PEDERSON. "Thomas Otway's Strumpet Fortune." Ph.D. dissertation, University of Minnesota, 126 pp.

Otway's earlier works were rather "academic," but the later ones reflect his personal distresses and his growing concern over political and social problems. In the tragedies he conveys a "profound moral vision." In the comedies he exposes "the Whig values of piety, prudence with money, and ambition as the hypocrisy, meanness, and cruel self-serving that he believed them to be." See Dissertation Abstracts International 34:291A.

7 YARROW, DAVID ALEXANDER. "A Stage History of Shakespeare's Romeo and Juliet in London, 1597 to 1800." Ph.D. dissertation, University of New Brunswick (Canada).

Defends Caius Marius against charges that it is merely plagiarized and offers "political and theatrical reasons" for its stage success. See Dissertation Abstracts International 34 (1974):4475A.

1974

1 DURANT, JACK D. "'Honor's Toughest Task': Family and State in Venice Preserved." SP 71:484-503.

Reacting against recent critical stress on sexual perversion and psychological morbidity in the play, argues that Otway affirms marital and familial bonds by dramatizing how political and personal ruin follow "the abandonment of family covenants for the sake of appetites, petty sentiments, heroic posturings, and vain republican dreams."

2 POLLARD, HAZEL M. BATZER. From Heroics to Sentimentalism: A Study of Thomas Otway's Tragedies. Salzburg: Institut für Englische Sprache und Literatur, 305 pp.

Revision of OT.1956.1 Traces Otway's transition from heroic play to a "unique admixture [of] the psychology of the 'Man of Feeling,' or sensibility, and the philosophy of sentimentalism, or sensibility."

3 WHITWORTH, CHARLES W. "The Misfortunes of Romeo and Juliet: Richard Penn Smith's 'Revival' of Otway's Caius Marius." CahiersE 6:3-7.

Richard Penn Smith, a Philadelphia lawyer, wrote Caius Marius: A Tragedy (1831) "with Otway's play open before him."

1975

1 HOGG, JAMES, ed. "The 1953 Production of Venice Preserv'd." In Poetic Drama and Poetic Theory. Salzburg: Institut für Englishe Sprache und Literatur, pp. 2-11.

Gives some details about the production at the Lyric Theatre, Hammersmith, followed by quotations from the contemporary reviews.

2 MARSHALL, GEOFFREY. Restoration Serious Drama. Norman: University of Oklahoma Press, pp. 37, 55-56, 87-91, 100-103, 106, 110-11, 119, 125, 137-38, 196, 198, 203, 212-13, 218-19.

Subordinates readings of individual plays to more general concerns but contains interesting observations. Passages from Alcibiades, Don Carlos, and The Orphan are used to show how the language of status and role can convey "whole complexes of idea and emotion." A diagram of Alcibiades is drawn to reveal the play's "geometry." The Hobbesian, Satanic Don John of Don Carlos is distinguished from Dryden's Almanzor in terms of the two characters' understanding of natural freedom. Marshall sees the search for role as central to Caius Marius, and he discusses the use of sentimental vignette and imagined scene in that play. As in OT.1969.4, he regards The Orphan as a tragedy of false perception and false communication.

He considers Venice Preserv'd a monument to Jaffeir, who is a comic character caught in tragic circumstances. Jaffeir's inner complexity reflects the complexity of his world, a world whose ambiguities render Belvidera's effort to redeem him inadequate. The relationship between these two characters reverses the traditional process whereby a self-possessed but incorrigible hero is brought into line with social structures through the endeavors of his loved one. Marshall also discusses the dagger symbol, the use of status and role to evoke pity, and the technique of "doubling"--that is, presenting a scene once as action, then as narrative, to increase the effect. He points out, moreover, that key characters in Don Carlos, The Orphan, and Venice Preserv'd are destroyed partly because they fail to recognize that circumstances have deprived them of natural ways to advance socially or politically. To Marshall, Otway's plays suggest the need for broader use of the term sentimental.

3 MÜLLER, ROBERT. "Zur Rezeption von Otway's Venice Preserv'd in der Restaurationzeit." In Poetic Drama and Poetic Theory. Edited by James Hogg. Salzburg: Institut für Englische Sprache und Literatur, pp. 12-39.

Considered in terms of the monarchist thought presented in the writings of Sir Robert Filmer, Venice Preserv'd becomes, without incongruity, both political allegory and love-and-honor story.

4 RINTZ, DON. "Garrick's 'Protective Reaction' to a Charge of Plagiarism." RECTR 14, no. 1:31-35, 50.

Garrick was right to defend himself against charges that he plagiarized from Caius Marius when he altered Shakespeare's Romeo and Juliet, for he took only nine lines from Otway.

5 VIETH, DAVID M. "Psychological Myth as Tragedy: Nathaniel Lee's Lucius Junius Brutus." HLQ 39:61-62, 66, 75n.

Notes that Caius Marius influenced Lee and that the sadomasochistic split between Tiberius and Titus is similar to that between Renault and Antonio in Venice Preserv'd. Vieth contrasts the death of Titus, involving "a healing and a reintegration into the ongoing processes of society," to the death of Pierre and Jaffeir, which is "an existential defiance of society and universe through the affirmation of an arbitrarily chosen code of honor, closely resembling the death of the hero in a typical story by Ernest Hemingway."

1976

1 FRAJND, MARTA. "Prevod Otvejeve 'Spasene Venecije' u Srba u XIX veku." In Uporedna istraživanja. Edited by Nikša Stipčevíc. Vol. 1. Beograd: Inst. za knjizevnost i umetnost, pp. 307-15.

The English summary on p. 315 says that the essay compares Venice Preserv'd to a little-known Serbian translation (1840) of a German adaptation of Otway's play, providing some information on the nineteenth-century Serbian stage, and speculating that the translation was done by Jovan Klajic, "one of the outstanding Serbian romantic painters."

2 HUME, ROBERT D. The Development of English Drama in the Late Seventeenth Century. Oxford: Clarendon Press, pp. 200-201, 204-5, 218-19, 223, 310-11, 313, 315, 321-22, 331-32, 346-47, 350, 353-54, 368.

Places the plays within the context of current dramatic theories and changing tastes, offering compact plot summaries and brief critical evaluations. Alcibiades is seen as a competent horror play, Titus and Berenice as negligible except for the appended Cheats of Scapin (anticipating eighteenth-century afterpieces), and Don Carlos as bombastic, lusty, and bloody, but movingly centered on relatively complex characters whose problems convey a sense of the tragic. Caius Marius continues to seem strange and silly, despite its artistry, but The Orphan remains moving, a tragedy of corrupt nature and groundless mistrust, even though it lacks plausible motivation. Seen in context, it seems strikingly "domestic and personal." Venice Preserv'd is both "a brilliant anti-Whig fable"--with its great satire of Shaftesbury (through Antonio and Renault) and "potent political message"--and "a tragedy which transcends such particulars" in a vision of human inadequacy. The unjustly neglected comedies (see OT.1976.3) sardonically satirize not only contemporary behavior and institutions but also the dramatic modes of depicting contemporary life. The Atheist is less well controlled than Friendship in Fashion and The Souldiers Fortune, but all three are well worth attention.

3 _____. "Otway and the Comic Muse." SP 73:87-116.
Shows that the three comedies are "violent but curiously cold satires" whose "harsh, macabre gaiety" scarcely masks "the author's . . . disillusionment and despair." Friendship in Fashion drags a little but presents "a truly ugly picture of broken friendship" against a background of "an intolerably dirty and dishonest" world of fashionable behavior. The Souldiers Fortune is an effective "five-stage comedy," and The Atheist is an "impressive experiment" that is undercut by its own complexity. Otway shocks us and defeats our comic expectations by taking a "harsh view of romantic myths and upper-class civilities."

4 LOFTIS, JOHN. "The Social and Literary Context." In The Revels History of Drama in English, Vol. V: 1660-1750. Edited by Loftis, Richard Southern, Marion Jones, and A.H. Scouten. London: Methuen, p. 39.
Paraphrases the remarks on Venice Preserv'd in OT.1972.2.

5 SCOUTEN, A.H. "Plays and Playwrights." In The Revels History of Drama in English, Vol. V: 1660-1750. Edited by Scouten, John Loftis, Richard Southern, and Marion Jones. London: Methuen, pp. 201, 204-5, 272-76.
Concurs in Hume's positive analysis of the comedies (see OT.1976.3), adding instructive observations on the thematic link between The Souldiers Fortune and The Atheist. Scouten considers Otway's tragedies more important than Lee's and regards Alcibiades and Don Carlos, in terms of pathos, as artistically weak forerunners of The Orphan. The latter, no model of dramaturgy in itself, is seen as significant for its introduction of a moral weakling as a main character. Venice Preserv'd, the best Restoration tragedy, exhibits complex characters, meaningful use of comic episodes, and emotional power. The potentially tragic effect of Pierre's fate is eventually overwhelmed by the pathos generated from the distresses of Jaffeir and Belvidera. Scouten analyzes Otway's use of sources (for example, he splits Saint-Réal's "Antonio Priuli" into two characters) and joins J.H. Wilson (see OT.1965.4) in questioning the identification of Antonio with Shaftesbury.

6 TAYLOR, ALINE MACKENZIE, ed. Introduction to The Orphan. Regents Restoration Drama Series. Lincoln: University of Nebraska Press, pp. xiii-xxx.
Covers much the same scholarly and critical ground examined more closely in Next to Shakespeare (see OT.1950.4), perhaps

stressing more strongly Otway's juxtaposition of "court corruption" and "pastoral setting," the centrality of Acasto, and the employment of fashionable ideas and conventions in dramatic functions usually reserved for fate. Taylor rejects the labels of heroic tragedy, domestic tragedy, pathetic tragedy, and she-tragedy, favoring the term "tragedy of manners" for this play. Appendix A suggests that because of Otway's infatuation with Mrs. Barry, he invested his plays with more personal passion than Racine did. Appendix B contains advice on staging, given Otway's concept of the set. This book was also published in London by Edward Arnold in the same year.

1977

1 HUME, ROBERT D. "Marital Discord in English Comedy from Dryden to Fielding." MP 74:254-56.

Friendship in Fashion contains ugly satire of marriage and "a grating parody of the usual happy ending." The Souldiers Fortune criticizes enforced marriage but not marriage itself, and The Atheist demolishes "romance norms."

2 _____. "The Myth of the Rake in 'Restoration' Comedy." SLitI 10, no. 1:36.

Mentions the use of cuckolding as a form of revenge in The Souldiers Fortune.

3 JUMP, JOHN D. "A Comparison of 'Marino Faliero' with Otway's 'Venice Preserved.'" ByronJ 5:20-37.

After discussing Byron's attitude toward Otway and Byron's composition of his tragedy, focuses on several points of contrast between the two plays: in Venice Preserv'd the rebels are motivated chiefly by private grievances, in Marino Faliero by public ideals; while Venice Preserv'd is punctuated by theatrical personal clashes which modify the disputants' attitudes, Marino Faliero exhibits eloquent debates in which no one changes his mind; Venice Preserv'd comes across better in performance than Byron's play does, but as closet dramas the two tragedies are equally effective.

4 MATLACK, CYNTHIA S. "'Spectatress of the Mischief Which She Made': Tragic Woman Perceived and Perceiver." SECC 6:319-20, 324-25.

Otway's handling of his female characters falls somewhere between "the sensational posturings of women by earlier Restoration playwrights" and Rowe's "use of sensuality for didactic purposes." In The Orphan, Monimia understands "the nexus between chastity and cash" and perceives that "sexual violation or misconduct leads to total loss." In Venice Preserv'd, the sensuality of Aquilina, which promotes revolution, is contrasted with that of Belvidera, which helps pacify the "instinctive brutishnes of males." Otway's heroines can be instructively analyzed in the context of pathetic tragedies where the heroine's chastity is violated and her fate is "irrevocably determined by the betrayal of . . . paternal inheritance."

5 SUTHERLAND, JAMES, ed. General Introduction and headnote to Venice Preserv'd. In Restoration Tragedies. London, Oxford, and New York: Oxford University Press, pp. x-xi, 269-70.

Pierre is "the only character of complete integrity." Jaffeir is the unheroic hero--agonizing rather than acting, the victim rather than the manipulator of circumstances--which Otway had invented for Don Carlos and The Orphan. Otway sometimes sacrifices the credibility of his characters in order to gain audience "concernment," something he may have learned from Beaumont and Fletcher, or in order to convey a political message.

6 VARNEY, A.J. "Swift's Dismal and Otway's Antonio." N&Q 222: 224-25.

Antonio's inadvertently self-satiric oratory in Venice Preserv'd seems to have influenced Swift's "An Excellent New Song being the Intended Speech of a famous Orator against Peace," which was probably meant to ridicule the Earl of Nottingham.

7 WIKANDER, MATTHEW. "Thomas Otway's Venice Preserv'd as Tory Drama." Polit, a Journal for Literature and Politics 1, no. 1:77-89.

In light of both political and literary contexts, Wikander argues that Otway creates the tragedy by forcing his main characters "to choose between two equal ignominies" in a "Tory hell" where "Whigs govern corruptly even as other Whigs seek to overthrow their 'ideal' government." Thus, the play shows that "political instability begets moral chaos--a chaos which is reflected both in the state and in the rebels against it." Faced with their tragic choice, Jaffeir, Belvidera, and Pierre retreat into self or into a pastoral unreality which becomes "a dead end."

1978

1 DOWNIE, J.A. "Swift's Dismal." N&Q 223:43.

Argues that Varney (OT.1977.6) does not have enough evidence to make his point stick.

2 HARE, ARNOLD. "English Comedy." In Comic Drama: The European Heritage. Edited by W.D. Howarth. London: Methuen, pp. 135-36.

Names The Souldiers Fortune and The Atheist as "the last" of the Restoration comedies which give us pleasure through "the playwright's shaping craftsmanship." Although the later play is spoiled by its complex plot, Souldiers is redeemed "by the virility of . . . young soldiers on the loose, and the indefatigable pertinacity of . . . bawdy old men."

3 OGDEN, JAMES. "Literary Echoes in Otway's Comedies." N&Q 223:26.
The Souldiers Fortune and The Atheist contain echoes of Macbeth and Absalom and Achitophel, respectively.

4 SHAFER, RONALD G. "Thomas Otway's The Orphan, Ed. Aline MacKenzie Taylor." SCN 36:50-52.
Purports to notice "some of the play's interesting complexities which were largely untouched in the 'Introduction'"; adds nothing new.

1979

1 ATTRIDGE, DEREK. "Dryden's Dilemma, or, Racine Refurbished: The Problem of the English Dramatic Couplet." YES 9:58, 72.
In Titus and Berenice, Otway compresses the action and adds a little "spice," but through his simple style conveys "something of Racine's controlled intensity" in expressing "the heroine's dignified mastery of grief."

2 HOLLAND, PETER. The Ornament of Action: Text and Performance in Restoration Comedy. Cambridge, London, New York, and Melbourne: Cambridge University Press, pp. 38-39, 41, 64.
Cites Alcibiades to illustrate how tragedies tended to use discovery scenes "set and acted in the scenic area"; finds "specific parody of tragic style" in the staging of The Souldiers Fortune; and notes that in The Atheist "Beaugard's description of Porcia, though he 'never saw her in my Life,' is comic because it is an inaccurate description of Mrs. Barry--whom Otway knew particularly well."

3 PRICE, CURTIS A. Music in the Restoration Theatre. [Ann Arbor]: UMI Research Press, pp. 3-4, 16, 22, 99.
Briefly comments on the musical elements, in relation to themes or stage effects, in Caius Marius, Friendship in Fashion, The Orphan, and Venice Preserv'd. Other plays are cited in footnotes as illustrations of a variety of more general points about music in the drama of the day.

4 STAVES, SUSAN. Players' Scepters: Fictions of Authority in the Restoration. Lincoln and London: University of Nebraska Press, pp. 79, 85-88, 113, 160, 163-67, 175, 187, 234, 239-46, 303-4.
In the process of making more general points, places the major plays revealingly in social, legal, and philosophical contexts. Don Carlos exemplifies how the "paradoxes of conflicting loyalty" in heroic drama give way to more destructive paradoxes, and how a basically sympathetic character can be made to utter Machiavellian sentiments. The Orphan typifies serious plays of the 1680s in which sympathetic characters unwittingly commit crimes or are falsely accused of crime.

Venice Preserv'd is the greatest of those political tragedies that dramatize the "dissolution of the older myths justifying constituted authority and the absence of any . . . acceptable new myths." Like others of its genre, it revolves around a hero who has few ideas, little public ambition, and no control over the hostile forces in the larger society around him. Jaffeir's speech on the virtue-engendering charms of women sets the tone for later she-tragedies and sentimental drama and fiction. Like Lee's Lucius Junius Brutus, Venice Preserv'd deals with false vows, with cynical public figures who swear only out of self-interest, and with sensitive characters who are victimized partly because they find feelings more authentic than words. Jaffeir is like Titus in some respects, and Belvidera resembles Teraminta.

The Souldiers Fortune and The Atheist are among the best of the cynical comedies which expose the corruption of traditional hierarchies, of sex without love, and of marriages without meaning. The Atheist verges on being a problem play.

1980

1 AAGAARD, GAIL ELIZABETH. "A Critical Study of the Plays of Thomas Otway." Ph.D. dissertation, York University (Canada).

Otway's plays, both comic and serious, dramatize antitheses such as love versus freedom, innocence versus heroism, appearance versus reality. As his artistry matures, the treatment of these antitheses becomes increasingly complex as the characters confuse appearance and reality, misuse language, and pursue hollow visions of other-worldly innocence. The Atheist resolves most of the antitheses in the person of Beaugard, who is unique in his affirmation of a post-lapsarian world. See Dissertation Abstracts International 41 (1981):4401A.

2 HAGSTRUM, JEAN H. Sex and Sensibility: Ideal and Erotic Love from Milton to Mozart. Chicago and London: University of Chicago Press, pp. 90-98, 189, 217.

Informing the "elevated and mythic world" of Otway's tragedies there is the harsh pessimism that we find in his comedies. Don Carlos, the first part of which may be seen as an Oedipal reading of Hamlet, exhibits an "unconventional and obsessive love" attacking "the very roots of social and political stability." In their "world of primal psychology," their "familial state of nature" devoid of Christian norms, the characters of The Orphan "commit, with a kind of tragic and choiceless inevitability, the narcissistic sins against which Milton had warned."

The whole of Venice Preserv'd, like its own Nicky-Nacky scenes, is "instinct with morbid and regressive sexuality." Both love and friendship become forcefully erotic in response to frustration and ambiguity as the youthful, compassionate characters are "destroyed by their elders."

Although Otway's kind of drama influenced both Richardson and Rousseau, it tended to demonstrate not that feeling redeems but that sensibility leads to the grave. "It has not been sufficiently realized that the tears Otway shed and produced are as much the tears of morbidity as magnanimity."

3 LANGHANS, EDWARD A. Introduction to Five Restoration Theatrical Adaptations. New York and London: Garland, pp. ix-x.
Briefly traces the stage history of Romeo and Juliet to 1679, then notes Otway's subordination of Shakespeare to Plutarch (perhaps also to political aims) in Caius Marius.

4 LOFTIS, JOHN. "Political and Social Thought in the Drama." In The London Theatre World, 1660-1800. Edited by Robert D. Hume. Carbondale and Edwardsville: Southern Illinois University Press; London and Amsterdam: Feffer & Simons, pp. 261-63.
Maintains that, "for all the dramatic power of this, the best of Otway's tragedies" (Venice Preserv'd), it remains Royalist propaganda which employs a "satiric technique akin to that Gay used later in The Beggar's Opera: establishing briefly a parallel between a character and his satirical target, rapidly replacing that parallel with another." A case in point is the way in which Otway alternately identifies Antonio and Renault with Shaftesbury.

5 LUND-BAER, KERSTIN. "The Orphan": Tragic Form in Thomas Otway. Stockholm: Almqvist & Wiksell, 118 pp.
Centered on the theme of moral disorder, The Orphan depicts the breakdown of human relationships, both domestic and political through the exercise of deceit and disloyalty. By using sentimental language and techniques of characterization, Otway evokes empathy for his unfortunate protagonists.

6 SALGĀDO, GĀMINI. English Drama: A Critical Introduction. New York: St. Martin's Press, pp. 139-40.
In Venice Preserv'd, the bitter political satire is placed "in a context so inflated that it loses a lot of its power." The blank verse in Venice Preserv'd suffers from its Fletcherian tendency to attitudinize, "to make a 'scene' out of every speech, which results in "thinness of texture."

1981

1 BROWN, LAURA. English Dramatic Form, 1660-1760: An Essay in Generic History. New Haven and London: Yale University Press, pp. 86-95.
The Orphan and Venice Preserv'd clearly exemplify affective form, in which pathos, innocence, privatization, and depoliticization are central, interrelated characteristics. In The Orphan, the explicit rejection of public life signals the affective

premises of the play, where a domestic dilemma and a passive, innocent female protagonist generate despair, hysteria, and death. Otway tends to handle characters as means to pathos rather than as psychologically plausible individuals, so that the key figure in this play's dilemma, Polydore, comes across both as honorable youth and as malicious villain.

In Venice Preserv'd, Pierre is inconsistent for the same reason. As noble friend, he increases the pathos attendant upon Jaffeir's betrayal of him; as vengeful, diabolical villain, Pierre explains Jaffeir's political treason yet permits him to remain innocent and sympathetic. This ambiguity extends even to the play's political allusions: to the extent that the conspiracy is linked with Pierre, it is rendered meaningless. Otway breaks with the values embodied in heroic drama, neutralizing all possible evaluative standards in favor of the moving power of pathos. His "sense of the inefficacy of aristocratic and absolutist ideals constitutes a manifestation, in literary form, of the ideological turmoil attendant upon the last days of English absolutism."

2 MUNNS, JESSICA. "A Critical Study of Thomas Otway's Plays." Ph.D. dissertation, University of Warwick, England.

Analyzes all the known plays, showing that the comedies and tragedies share certain themes, plot structures, character types, and imagery. Otway depicts the erosion of man's rational faculties and the collapse, mockery, or misuse of the institutions and rituals that enshrine a common morality.

This annotation derives from an abstract sent to me by the author. The dissertation is listed in Index to Theses Accepted for Higher Degrees by the Universities of Great Britain and Ireland and the Council for National Academic Awards, ed. Geoffrey M. Paterson and Joan E. Hardy, vol. 31, pt. 1 (London: Aslib, 1982), p. 10. Neither source indicates the number of pages in the dissertation.

3 PARKER, GERALD D. "The Image of Rebellion in Thomas Otway's Venice Preserv'd and Edward Young's Busiris." SEL 21:389-407.

Perceives a movement, almost a rhythm, in the attitudes and perspectives dramatized in the play: from the specific, personal, practical, and temporal kinds of rebelliousness, to the general, public, and metaphysical "dimensions of rebellion." As "rebellion acquires a spirit and life of its own," the main characters seek release from a growing sense of the world's bondage by turning to "nature," self, or the Christian vision of a realm apart. On the surface of the play's structure, the characters seem to be dragged along by the hectic pace of revolutionary events, while underneath there is a recurrent apocalyptic tone. In the thick of the action, each of the central figures is tugged between the "'Yes' and 'No'" of tragedy.

Index

To save space and encourage cross-referencing, I have combined into one what might have been four separate indexes. Each citation is prefixed by a capital letter or letters indicating to which section of the bibliography it refers: S = Shadwell, B = Behn, L = Lee, and OT = Otway. Thus, L.1974.2 would guide the user to the second entry of 1974 in the bibliography of writings about Nathaniel Lee.